The Essential
Neoconservative Reader

The Essential Neoconservative Reader

Edited by Mark Gerson
Foreword by James Q. Wilson

Addison-Wesley Publishing Company, Inc.
Reading, Massachusetts • Menlo Park, California • New York
Don Mills, Ontario • Harlow, England • Amsterdam • Bonn
Sydney • Singapore • Tokyo • Madrid • San Juan
Paris • Seoul • Milan • Mexico City • Taipei

Many of the designations used by manufacturers and sellers to distinguish their products are claimed as trademarks. Where those designations appear in this book and Addison-Wesley was aware of a trademark claim, the designations have been printed in initial capital letters.

Library of Congress Cataloging-in-Publication Data

The essential neoconservative reader / edited by Mark Gerson ;
   foreword by James Q. Wilson.
            p.   cm.
       Includes bibliographical references and index.
       ISBN 0-201-47968-0
       ISBN 0-201-15488-9 (pbk)
       1. Conservatism—United States.   I. Gerson, Mark.
    JC573.2.U6E87   1996
    320.5′2′0973—dc20

                                                95-53007
                                                CIP

Cover design by Andrew Newman
Text design by Joyce Weston
Set in 10.5-point Sabon by Pagesetters, Inc.

1 2 3 4 5 6 7 8 9 10-MA-0100999897
First printing, May 1996
First paperback printing, May 1997

Addison-Wesley books are available at special discounts for bulk purchases by corporations, institutions, and other organizations. For more information, please contact the Corporate, Government, and Special Sales Department, Addison-Wesley Publishing Company, Reading, MA 01867, 1-800-238-9682.

CONTENTS

FOREWORD

James Q. Wilson

THE ESSAYS GATHERED by Mark Gerson in this volume capture the spirit of the neoconservative tendency in American political thought even though some writers included here may not think of themselves as neoconservatives, and some of those who do wish they weren't. That is one of the fascinating aspects of this intellectual impulse: Since it is neither an ideology nor a movement, and was given its name by its critics, there has never been a credo to endorse (or repudiate) or an organization to join (or attack). The neoconservative impulse has more significance in the eyes of the beholder than in the minds of its adherents.

An ideology is a systematic worldview that seeks to explain and evaluate the world. There is nothing systematic about neoconservatism, and, to the extent it exists at all, it has never claimed to explain very much. It is an intellectual orientation and has never had anything like a mass following, much less a slogan, banner, or meetinghouse. For some participants it may involve a lasting commitment (though exactly to what is not clear), but for many others it has been either a way station in the journey from liberalism to conservatism or a brief detour along a straight political path—a place to pause, so to speak, and take stock without really changing direction.

People arrived at this way station or detour by many different routes. It is usually said that neoconservatives are liberals who were mugged by reality or Marxists who came in from the cold. This may describe some adherents, but it does not fit me or several others I know. For me and for some others, what came to be called neoconservatism was a perspective that was in part substantive and in part procedural.

Let me start with the procedural. Neoconservatism is an awkward and not very accurate name for an attitude that holds social reality to be complex and change difficult. If there is any article of faith common to almost every adherent, it is the Law of Unintended Consequences. Things never work out quite as you hope; in particular, government programs often do not achieve their objectives or do achieve them but with high or unexpected costs. A true conservative may oppose change because it upsets the accumulated wisdom of tradition or the legacy of history; a neoconservative questions change because, though present circumstances are bad and something ought to be done, it is necessary to do that something cautiously, experimentally, and with a minimum of bureaucratic authority. Neoconservatives, accordingly, place a lot of stock in applied social science research, especially the sort that evaluates old programs and tests new ones.

Of course, many liberals like research, too, but they are more confident, I think, that if the data reveal a problem, the means can be found to solve it. At the risk of outraging some intelligent and public-spirited liberals, let me suggest that liberals are a bit more likely to let what they want to believe influence what the facts allow them to believe. Though this is, of course, an exaggeration, and a somewhat self-serving one at that, it helps us understand the difference in the reactions liberals and neoconservatives have to the facts about, for example, income distribution, educational achievement, and criminal rehabilitation. Liberals desire greater social equality, so they embrace any data that show that inequality is bad or getting worse; neoconservatives are not friends of inequality but find the reality underlying these data complex and often counterintuitive. Everyone values education, but liberals have customarily thought that more of it could be obtained by spending more money on it; neoconservatives think the data show that there is little or no relationship between spending and achievement. Liberals would like to reform criminals; neoconservatives keep throwing cold water on the studies that claim to find any rehabilitative effect.

A liberal can easily rejoin that neoconservatives are equally disposed to accept uncritically dubious or nonexistent data about the beneficent effects of capitalism, the great value of school choice, and the crime-reduction effects of punishment. My response is that when they do this they are not being good neoconservatives.

The fact that self-styled neoconservatives also ignore complex reality and the Law of Unintended Consequences shows that there is a substantive side to this disposition. Critics will say that this side is conservatism, pure and simple; neoconservatives are really hard-edged conservative wolves wearing fuzzy sheep's clothing. Well, in some cases, perhaps. I would put it rather differently, however. What I am most struck by among my friends who wear this clothing is that they have great sympathy for and often take their cues from the general and settled convictions of the average American. Not all these convictions, mind, but at least those that arise out of the better side of human nature. In particular: Americans love America and think it very much worth defending; so do neoconservatives. Americans (and people generally) think that families are vital, mediating institutions important, and public order desirable; so do neoconservatives. Americans believe—perhaps more deeply than people anywhere else—that rewards should be allocated on the basis of merit and individuals held responsible for their own actions; so do neoconservatives. And perhaps most important of all, neoconservatives embrace the American conviction that many of the central problems of our society arise out of a want of good character and human virtue.

Do not misunderstand me; I am not saying that liberals, libertarians, or the various sorts of traditional conservatives deny these things. I am only saying that, over the years, the neoconservative temperament has come to assign an increasingly high value to these beliefs and to interpret social problems and government policy in light of their implications. Neoconservatives look to markets and voluntary action more than liberals do, but unlike economic conservatives they think that markets must be judged by their effects on human character as well as by their capacity to generate prosperity. Neoconservatives never toyed with the idea that there were really any alternatives to the traditional two-parent family, though only of late have they given that institution the emphasis it now has. Neoconservatives have almost always been skeptical of affirmative action but never, I think, opposed to the enforcement of civil rights laws.

However one characterizes the neoconservative tendency, many of the people identified with it have changed. I recall when some endorsed the negative income tax as a solution to poverty; I doubt these writers today, focused as they are on the cultural roots of the underclass, would still do so. Neoconservatives were once distinguished from traditional (paleo?) conservatives by their acceptance of the broad outlines of the welfare state; now, in the midst of a new debate over the proper size of government, many of the former are indistinguishable from most of the latter. When neoconservatives first wrote, it was often in reaction against the less plausible ideas of the Great Society. Since then we have not had an activist government with the power and ambition of the Johnson administration, so there is somewhat less focus, and perhaps less agreement, among neoconservatives than once was the case. Intellectual tendencies, like broad social movements, are often made possible by the existence of a common enemy.

Let me end by noting what has been to me one of the most appealing and enduring features of the neoconservative impulse, especially worth remarking now that that outlook may be transforming itself into something else. We all liked one another, and still do. At the party celebrating Irving Kristol's seventy-fifth birthday, I was struck by the companionship and good cheer of people who, in some cases, had drifted apart politically or intellectually. This fact owes much to the sweet temper of the founders of the impulse, especially Kristol himself, and is clear evidence that neoconservatism was never an ideology or a movement and never will be either.

ACKNOWLEDGMENTS

THERE ARE MANY people to whom I am indebted for their great help in translating a vague idea into the reality that is this book. When I first conceived of this book in the spring of 1994, I consulted many friends and teachers who provided much encouragement and invaluable advice on what to include. Special thanks are due Matthew Berke, Don Carlson, Tucker Carlson, Kristin Daley, Jon Fielder, Gary Jacobsohn, Ben Kerschberg, Dan Mahoney, Adam Meyerson, Jorge Pedraza, Noah Pickus, Julie Ruder, Jay Webber, and Jeff Weintraub.

I am also deeply in debt to the contributors of this volume, many of whom offered valuable advice at every stage of preparing this book. They gave freely of their time and wise counsel, as early as 1993, when I was a college junior beginning an exploration of intellectual history. I will always greatly appreciate the generosity they have shown me, then and now.

I would like to offer many thanks to my marvelous agent, Chris Calhoun of Sterling Lord Literistic. Chris's constant determination, good humor and loyalty made him the perfect person with whom to work on this project, or any project for that matter. In the same vein, the terrific editorial staff at Addison-Wesley is due my warm gratitude. Henning Gutmann is a masterful editor and a pleasure to work with; it is no exaggeration to say that his broad-minded spirit and intellectual dedication made this book possible. It is no surprise that a man of Henning's talent would surround himself with excellence. The extraordinary meticulousness of Lynne Reed, the production supervisor, is greatly appreciated. Similarly, Henning's assistants, Jack Dew and Albert DePetrillo, ensured that the process of making this book was smooth and enjoyable for everyone involved.

Most of all, I would like to thank my parents, Susan and Michael Gerson, and my brother Rick for providing me with such a wonderful family and loving home.

INTRODUCTION

W HAT IS NEOCONSERVATISM? The label "neoconservative" in American political discourse evades simple characterization. The term applies broadly to a prominent group of intellectuals
who, once *considered* to be on the left, are now on the right. The central
figure in neoconservatism (often called the godfather) is Irving Kristol. He
is joined by a host of other intellectuals, with specialties in many disciplines: criminology, economics, history, foreign policy, sociology, theology
and more. Because the neoconservatives are a diverse group of independent
thinkers with a variety of expertise, many have had trouble locating a
unifying theoretical and ideological orientation. The distinguished political sociologist Seymour Martin Lipset has written,

> Neoconservatism, both as an ideological term and as a political
> grouping, is one of the most misunderstood concepts in the politi-
> cal lexicon. The reason is simple, the word has never referred to a
> set of doctrines to which a given group of adherents subscribed.
> Rather, it was invented as an invidious label to undermine political
> opponents, most of whom have been unhappy with being so de-
> scribed.

Though Lipset is one who speaks with unusual authority on these
matters, his statement is only partially correct. While it may not encapsu-
late a set of doctrines, the term "neoconservative" does in fact capture a
genuine political grouping with a coherent and distinctive ideological orientation. However, Lipset is correct in saying both that neoconservatism is
grossly misunderstood and that it was originally conceived as an insult; the
socialist Michael Harrington first used it in print as a criticism in a 1973
Dissent article. A lot of labels throughout history have originated in scorn.
The artistic category "impressionist" was coined by a disgruntled critic

who thought that the impressionists were undisciplined dilettantes. Irving Kristol did this with "neoconservative," writing, "I myself have accepted the term, perhaps because, having been named Irving, I am relatively indifferent to baptismal caprice." He later conceded, "The more I hear it, the more I like it." Yet, as Nathan Glazer notes, "There is hardly one of us who has written an article explaining what neoconservatism is."

At least partially for that reason, Lipset is also correct in stating that discussion of neoconservatism tends to be invidious as well as perplexed. The left considers neoconservatism with a curiosity that veers into animosity. Something about neoconservatism often drives otherwise level-headed liberals into a frenzy. The left perceives the neoconservatives as an undeniably intelligent and influential group of thinkers who speak their language, cite their sources—in short, understand them perfectly but almost always come down on the wrong side.

The right, too, traditionally has had difficulty with neoconservatism. While there is now a broad conservative consensus on most issues, the neoconservatives continue to accept the welfare state, though not in its present incarnation. This is troubling to many conservatives, who have long regarded the infringement of government into the economy as a negation of freedom and the first step in what Friedrich von Hayek called the road to serfdom. Nonetheless, most on the right have come to realize that the neoconservatives are especially effective in challenging the left and, at a minimum, have come to appreciate the power of neoconservative social science to illustrate the failure of sweeping government programs.

But neoconservatism is far more than just a method of critiquing the Great Society, a reaction to the counterculture, or a conservative defense of a limited welfare state. It is an intellectual persuasion, a comprehensive outlook on economics, politics, culture, and society linked by common principles and a distinctive vision. Though the neoconservatives are political intellectuals, their persuasion is a philosophical one that happens to have political relevance. They believe in the fragility of social institutions, that all human enterprises will have monumental unintended consequences, that man has a moral responsibility to forcibly confront evil, and most of all, that the world is governed, in the end, by ideas. Applying this persuasion to the full range of important issues of our time—issues ranging from Alger Hiss to radical students to judicial activism to environmentalism—the neoconservatives have created an intellectual force of great importance in American political thought.

In 1952, the sociologist Karl Mannheim wrote, "Conservatism arises as a counter-movement in conscious opposition to the highly organized, coherent and systematic 'progressive' movement." From Edmund Burke to the present, systematic conservative theory tends to find much of its motivating impulse in critique. True to Mannheim's characterization, neoconservatism, too, has formulated its political positions in response to ideas generated by the left. From the early 1950s to the present day, neoconservatives have castigated liberalism for ignorance of the complexity of social action and the embedded wisdom in human systems, a lack of resolve in confronting evil, a laissez-faire attitude toward human virtue, and an unwillingness to defend the critical ideas of American civilization from its discontents. Practically every neoconservative argument and position can be seen as a reaction to one of the central ideas of liberalism.

Anti-Communism? This is obvious; much of the nascent neoconservative animosity toward Communism took the form of bitter attacks against American intellectuals whom they considered insufficiently cognizant of the evils of totalitarianism. Defense of bourgeois institutions? This was launched in response to the student radicalism of the 1960s and the tepid response to it of the liberal faculty at elite universities. Capitalism? The neoconservatives noted that a non-Marxist anti-capitalism resembling that of the Old Right had become the fundamental fact of left-wing politics in the mid 1970s. They surmised that nothing the left hated as much as capitalism could be that bad, so they investigated it. Shortly after, they produced a unique, comprehensive, and sociologically significant moral defense of the free market. Mediating structures? The neoconservatives saw the crime of the welfare state to be its displacement of community organizations and local mores that nourished public life for vast numbers of people and provided essential assistance for the poor. So they developed a comprehensive and sociologically significant case for mediating structures. Religion? In the past several years, the neoconservatives have perceived a moral decline fueled by a militant secularism pervading the culture. Seeking to retrieve the notion of public virtue they deemed necessary for civilization, the neoconservatives turned to the source of those values, religion. Consequently, they developed a defense of religion in the public square that incorporates all who share the Judeo-Christian heritage.

Much of the success of the neoconservatives has been, perhaps paradoxically, due to the early attachment many of them had with the left. Writing of his experience and that of many of his friends as socialist college students, Irving Kristol explained in 1977, "Joining a radical movement when one is young is very much like falling in love when one is young. The girl may turn out to be rotten, but the experience of love so valuable that it can never be entirely undone by the ultimate disenchantment." The young neoconservatives were highly trained in Marx, which meant that they were imbued with a sociologically sophisticated way of looking at the way the world works. Educated to approach ideas as coherent systems rather than as conglomerations of isolated issues, the neoconservatives have naturally plunged beneath the surface of social questions, seeking to ascertain the internal logic (or lack of logic) of whatever situations or ideas they are addressing. Whether it is Norman Podhoretz writing in 1963 that civil rights laws, though just, are far too blunt to solve the deep problems of race relations; Irving Kristol stressing in 1971 that real prosperity has little to do with economics and a lot to do with virtue; James Q. Wilson and George Kelling writing in 1986 that the key to crime prevention is clean neighborhoods; or Daniel Patrick Moynihan attributing in 1993 many modern social problems to confusion over the ideas of normalcy and deviancy, the neoconservatives have been able to analyze society from a unique, forceful and persuasive perspective.

Neoconservatism is now coming to an end, as it becomes clear that only one generation of thinkers identifies themselves as such. As with the retirement of American nuclear bombers that hovered in striking range of the Soviet Union during the Cold War, the end of neoconservatism is the ultimate testimony to its success. The neoconservatives have so changed conservatism that what we now identify as conservatism is largely what was once neoconservatism. And in so doing, they have defined the way that vast numbers of Americans view their economy, their polity and their society. How is this possible—that ideas in primarily low-circulation journals have had such an impact on people who will never see an issue of *Commentary*? John Maynard Keynes, the author of the book that defined Western economics for half a century, *The General Theory of Employment and Money*, explained in that work,

> The ideas of economists and political philosophers, both when they are right and when they are wrong, are more powerful than is commonly understood. Indeed the world is ruled by little else. Practical men, who believe themselves to be quite exempt from any intellectual influences, are usually the slaves of some defunct econ-

omist. Madmen in authority, who hear voices in the air, are distilling their frenzy from some academic scribbler of a few years back. I am sure that the power of vested interests is vastly exaggerated compared with the gradual encroachment of ideas. . . . Soon or late, it is ideas, not vested interests, which are dangerous for good or evil.

Indeed, the career of neoconservatism was not only about the issues and ideas addressed by its various thinkers. It is an education about what Lionel Trilling called "the bloody crossroads"—where ideas and politics meet. And its lessons are universal; they can be absorbed, understood and utilized by any future generation of intellectuals who are concerned with the juxtaposition of ideas and politics. Indeed, perhaps the greatest contribution of neoconservatism will be proof that ideas do have consequences, and that well-articulated visions of man and his relationship with social institutions can have profound consequences, for good or evil.

The Essential
Neoconservative Reader

1. Liberalism Confronts Simplicity

*I*n the 1950s, the liberal anticommunists, later to be neoconservatives, were fierce opponents of Communism—which they be-
lieved to be a totalitarian evil, the irreconcilable enemy of any honest brand
of liberalism. As the liberal anticommunist editor Melvin Lasky wrote in
1952, "The historical uniqueness of Nazism should not blind us to the fact
that morally and politically it is identical with Stalinism." These thinkers
unleashed bitter condemnation of liberals whom they saw as blind to the
great power of Communism to destroy liberalism. Irving Kristol published
what is probably his most controversial essay, "Civil Liberties, 1952—A
Study in Confusion," assailing liberals for choking on their greatest
strength, tolerance, in approaching a dedicated adversary. He unleashed
something of a fury in the intellectual world with words that would spark
controversy for half a century: "For there is one thing that the American
people know about Senator McCarthy: he, like them, is unequivocally anti-
Communist. About the spokesmen for American liberalism, they feel they
know no such thing. And with some justification."

The liberal anticommunists had no faith that liberalism would take
the necessary steps to ensure its own survival. In a 1957 essay, Norman
Podhoretz accused liberalism of being unable to "take a sufficiently complicated view of reality," characterizing it as "a conglomeration of attitudes
suitable only to the naive, the callow, the rash: in short, the immature." The
liberal anti-communists considered the dominant branch of liberalism—

what they sometimes called "revisionary liberalism" or "Doughface Progressivism"—to be an undignified, indeed dangerous philosophy for the leading nation in the West to entertain. Unable to condemn enemies on its Left when that enemy was as forthright an opponent as Communism, what would liberalism do with more subtle adversaries, those that made an effort to co-opt it? This mistrust of liberalism is evoked in numerous early neoconservative writings, but two from the early period of neoconservatism stand out as especially telling.

The first is Norman Podhoretz's "My Negro Problem . . . and Ours," an essay inspired by a discussion with James Baldwin that sparked a literary firestorm when published in February 1963. Though a supporter of civil rights from the beginning, Podhoretz explains—by recounting and interpreting childhood experiences—how little a political movement can accomplish in the arena of race relations. This essay is followed by a 1993 postscript and is slightly revised for this volume.

In a very different mode, Daniel Patrick Moynihan comes to a similar conclusion in "The Negro Family: The Case for National Action" widely known as the "Moynihan Report," published in 1965. In this controversial government document, Moynihan, then an aide to President Johnson, speaks of the cultural pathologies—rather than the political deprivations—that lay at the root of many of the problems of black America.

"My Negro Problem . . . and Ours" and the Moynihan Report were both enormously controversial in their day, and became the center of racial discussion for some time after publication. Indeed, Podhoretz and Moynihan were the first "liberals" to be denounced as "racists" by leaders of mainstream civil rights organizations. Podhoretz was so taken aback by the attacks on him that he considered suing Stokely Carmichael, then the head of the Southern Nonviolent Coordinating Committee, for slander. Podhoretz's professional interest in weak libel and slander laws kept him from pursuing that idea. The Moynihan Report, originally intended as a government document for no more than one hundred readers, was leaked to the press and hailed as the Johnson administration's response to the

Watts riots. The response to the Moynihan report was such that most of Moynihan's liberal colleagues in academia did not defend him out of fear of being labeled "racist" for doing so. In this response, the neoconservatives first found common ground with the right. Moynihan commented later, "My God, I was not a racist, I was not a bigot, but all the good guys were calling me a racist, [while] here was this fellow [William] Buckley saying these thoughtful things. [Nathan] Glazer and I began to notice that we were getting treated in National Review *with a much higher level of intellectual honesty [than in liberal publications]."*

My Negro Problem—and Ours

Norman Podhoretz

If we—and . . . I mean the relatively conscious whites and the relatively conscious blacks, who must, like lovers, insist on, or create, the consciousness of the others—do not falter in our duty now, we may be able, handful that we are, to end the racial nightmare, and achieve our country, and change the history of the world.

—*James Baldwin*

TWO IDEAS PUZZLED me deeply as a child growing up in Brooklyn during the 1930s in what today would be called an integrated neighborhood. One of them was that all Jews were rich; the other was that all Negroes were persecuted. These ideas had appeared in print; therefore they must be true. My own experience and the evidence of my senses told me they were not true, but that only confirmed what a daydreaming boy in the provinces—for the lower-class neighborhoods of New York belong as surely to the provinces as any rural town in North Dakota—discovers very early: *his* experience is unreal and the evidence of his senses is not to be trusted. Yet even a boy with a head full of fantasies incongruously synthesized out of Hollywood movies and English novels cannot altogether deny the reality of his own experience—especially when there is so much deprivation in that experience. Nor can he altogether gainsay the evidence of his own senses—especially such evidence of the senses as comes from being repeatedly beaten up, robbed, and in general hated, terrorized, and humiliated.

Reprinted from Commentary *(February 1963).*

And so for a long time I puzzled to think that Jews were supposed to be rich when the only Jews I knew were poor, and that Negroes were supposed to be persecuted when it was the Negroes who were doing the only persecuting I knew about—and doing it, moreover, to *me*. During the early years of the war, when my older sister joined a left-wing youth organization, I remember my astonishment at hearing her passionately denounce my father for thinking that Jews were worse off than Negroes. To me, at the age of twelve, it seemed very clear that Negroes were better off than Jews—indeed, than *all* whites. A city boy's world is contained within three or four square blocks, and in my world it was the whites, the Italians and Jews, who feared the Negroes, not the other way around. The Negroes were tougher than we were, more ruthless, and on the whole they were better athletes. What could it mean, then, to say that they were badly off and that we were more fortunate? Yet my sister's opinions, like print, were sacred, and when she told me about exploitation and economic forces I believed her. I believed her, but I was still afraid of Negroes. And I still hated them with all my heart.

It had not always been so—that much I can recall from early childhood. When did it start, this fear and this hatred? There was a kindergarten in the local public school, and given the character of the neighborhood, at least half of the children in my class must have been Negroes. Yet I have no memory of being aware of color differences at that age, and I know from observing my own children that they attribute no significance to such differences even when they begin noticing them. I think there was a day—first grade? second grade?—when my best friend Carl hit me on the way home from school and announced that he wouldn't play with me any more because I had killed Jesus. When I ran home to my mother crying for an explanation, she told me not to pay any attention to such foolishness, and then in Yiddish she cursed the goyim and the *schwartzes*, the *schwartzes* and the goyim. Carl, it turned out, was a *schwartze*, and so was added a third to the categories into which people were mysteriously divided.

Sometimes I wonder whether this is a true memory at all. It is blazingly vivid, but perhaps it never happened: can anyone really remember back to the age of six? There is no uncertainty in my mind, however, about the years that followed. Carl and I hardly ever spoke, though we met in school every day up through the eighth or ninth grade. There would be embarrassed moments of catching his eye or of his catching mine—for whatever it was that had attracted us to one another as very small children remained alive in spite of the fantastic barrier of hostility that had grown up between us, suddenly and out of nowhere. Nevertheless, friendship would have been impossible, and even if it had been possible, it would have been unthinkable. About that, there was nothing anyone could do by the time we were eight years old.

Item: The orphanage across the street is torn down, a city housing project begins to rise in its place, and on the marvelous vacant lot next to the old orphanage they are building a playground. Much excitement and anticipation as opening day draws near. Mayor LaGuardia himself comes to dedicate this great gesture of public benevolence. He speaks of neighborliness and borrowing cups of sugar, and of the playground he says that children of all races, colors, and creeds will learn to live together in harmony. A week later, some of us are swatting flies on the playground's inadequate little ball field. A gang of Negro kids, pretty much our own age, enter from the other side and order us out of the park. We refuse, proudly and indignantly, with superb masculine fervor. There is a fight, they win, and we retreat, half whimpering, half with bravado. My first nauseating experience of cowardice. And my first appalled realization that there are people in the world who do not seem to be afraid of anything, who act as though they have nothing to lose. Thereafter the playground becomes a battleground, sometimes quiet, sometimes the scene of athletic competition between Them and Us. But rocks are thrown as often as baseballs. Gradually we abandon the place and use the streets instead. The streets are safer, though we do not admit this to ourselves. We are not, after all, sissies—that most dreaded epithet of an American boyhood.

Item: I am standing alone in front of the building in which I live. It is late afternoon and getting dark. That day in school the teacher had asked a surly Negro boy named Quentin a question he was unable to answer. As usual I had waved my hand eagerly ("Be a good boy, get good marks, be smart, go to college, become a doctor") and, the right answer bursting from my lips, I was held up lovingly by the teacher as an example to the class. I had seen Quentin's face—a very dark, very cruel, very Oriental-looking face—harden, and there had been enough threat in his eyes to make me run all the way home for fear that he might catch me outside.

Now, standing idly in front of my own house, I see him approaching from the project accompanied by his little brother who is carrying a baseball bat and wearing a grin of malicious anticipation. As in a nightmare, I am trapped. The surroundings are secure and familiar, but terror is suddenly present and there is no one around to help. I am locked to the spot. I will not cry out or run away like a sissy, and I stand there, my heart wild, my throat clogged. He walks up, hurls the familiar epithet ("Hey, mo'f——r"), and to my surprise only pushes me. It is a violent push, but not a punch. A push is not as serious as a punch. Maybe I can still back out without entirely losing my dignity. Maybe I can still say, "Hey, c'mon Quentin, whaddya wanna do *that* for? I dint do nothin' to *you*," and walk away, not too rapidly. Instead, before I can stop myself, I push him back—a token gesture—and I say, "Cut that out, I don't wanna fight, I ain't got nothin' to fight about." As I turn to walk back into the building, the corner of my eye catches the motion of the bat his little brother has handed him. I try to duck, but the bat crashes colored lights into my head.

The next thing I know, my mother and sister are standing over me, both of them hysterical. My sister—she who was later to join the "progressive" youth organization—is shouting for the police and screaming imprecations at those dirty little black bastards. They take me upstairs, the doctor comes, the police come. I tell them that the boy who did it was a stranger, that he had been trying to get money from me. They do not believe me, but I am too scared to give them Quentin's name. When I return to school a few days later, Quentin avoids my eyes. He knows that I have not squealed, and he is ashamed. I try to feel proud, but in my heart I know that it was fear of what his friends might do to me that had kept me silent, and not the code of the street.

Item: There is an athletic meet in which the whole of our junior high school is participating. I am in one of the seventh-grade rapid-advance classes, and "segregation" has now set in with a vengeance. In the last three or four years of the elementary school from which we have just graduated, each grade had been divided into three classes, according to "intelligence." (In the earlier grades the divisions had either been arbitrary or else unrecognized by us as having anything to do with brains.) These divisions by IQ, or however it was arranged, had resulted in a preponderance of Jews in the "1" classes and a corresponding preponderance of Negroes in the "3's," with the Italians split unevenly along the spectrum. At least a few Negroes had always made the "1's," just as there had always been a few Jewish kids among the "3's" and more among the "2's" (where Italians dominated). But the junior high's rapid-advance class of which I am now a member is overwhelmingly Jewish and entirely white—except for a shy lonely Negro girl with light skin and reddish hair.

The athletic meet takes place in a city-owned stadium far from the school. It is an important event to which a whole day is given over. The winners are to get those precious little medallions stamped with the New York City emblem that can be screwed into a belt and that prove the wearer to be a distinguished personage. I am a fast runner, and so I am assigned the position of anchor man on my class's team in the relay race. There are three other seventh-grade teams in the race, two of them all Negro, as ours is all white. One of the all-Negro teams is very tall—their anchor man waiting silently next to me on the line looks years older than I am, and I do not recognize him. He is the first to get the baton and crosses the finishing line in a walk. Our team comes in second, but a few minutes later we are declared the winners, for it has been discovered that the anchor man on the first-place team is not a member of the class. We are awarded the medallions, and the following day our home-room teacher makes a speech about how proud she is of us for being superior athletes as well as superior students. We want to believe we deserve the praise, but we know we could not have won even if the other class had not cheated.

That afternoon, walking home, I am waylaid and surrounded by five Negroes, among whom is the anchor man of the disqualified team. "Gimme my medal, mo'f——r," he grunts. I do not have it with me and I tell him so. "Anyway, it ain't yours," I say foolishly. He calls me a liar on both counts and pushes me up against the wall on which we sometimes play handball. "Gimme my mo'f——n' medal," he says again. I repeat that I have left it home. "Let's search the li'l mo'f——r," one of them suggests, "he prolly got it *hid* in his mo'f——n' *pants*." My panic is now unmanageable. (How many times had I been surrounded like this and asked in soft tones, "Len' me a nickel, boy." How many times had I been called a liar for pleading poverty and pushed around, or searched, or beaten up, unless there happened to be someone in the marauding gang like Carl who liked me across that enormous divide of hatred and who would therefore say, "Aaah, c'mon, le's git someone else, *this* boy ain't got no money on 'im.") I scream at them through tears of rage and self-contempt, "Keep your f——n' filthy lousy black hands offa me! I swear I'll get the cops." This is all they need to hear, and the five of them set upon me. They bang me around, mostly in the stomach and on the arms and shoulders, and when several adults loitering near the candy store down the block notice what is going on and begin to shout, they run off and away.

I do not tell my parents about the incident. My teammates, who have also been waylaid, each by a gang led by his opposite number from the disqualified team, have had their medallions taken from them, and they never squeal either. For days, I walk home in terror, expecting to be caught again, but nothing happens. The medallion is put away into a drawer, never to be worn by anyone.

Obviously experiences like these have always been a common feature of childhood life in working-class and immigrant neighborhoods, and Negroes do not necessarily figure in them. Wherever, and in whatever combination, they have lived together in the cities, kids of different groups have been at war, beating up and being beaten up: micks against kikes against wops against spicks against polacks. And even relatively homogeneous areas have not been spared the warring of the young: one block against another, one gang (called in my day, in a pathetic effort at gentility, an "SAC," or social-athletic club) against another. But the Negro-white conflict had—and no doubt still has—a special intensity and was conducted with a ferocity unmatched by intramural white battling.

In my own neighborhood, a good deal of animosity existed between the Italian kids (most of whose parents were immigrants from Sicily) and the Jewish kids (who came largely from East European immigrant families). Yet everyone had friends, sometimes close friends, in the other "camp," and we often visited one another's strange-smelling houses, if not for meals, then for glasses of milk, and occasionally for some special event like a wedding or a wake. If it happened that we divided into warring factions and did battle, it would invariably be halfhearted and soon patched up. Our parents, to be sure, had nothing to do with one another and were mutually suspicious and hostile. But we, the kids, who all spoke Yiddish or Italian at home, were Americans, or New Yorkers, or Brooklyn boys: we shared a culture, the culture of the street, and at least for a while this culture proved to be more powerful than the opposing cultures of the home.

Why, *why* should it have been so different as between the Negroes and us? How was it borne in upon us so early, white and black alike, that we were enemies beyond any possibility of reconciliation? Why did we hate one another so?

I suppose if I tried, I could answer those questions more or less adequately from the perspective of what I have since learned. I could draw upon James Baldwin—what better witness is there?—to describe the sense of entrapment that poisons the soul of the Negro with hatred for the white man whom he knows to be his jailer. On the other side, if I wanted to understand how the white man comes to hate the Negro, I could call upon the psychologists who have spoken of the guilt that white Americans feel toward Negroes and that turns into hatred for lack of acknowledging itself as guilt. These are plausible answers and certainly there is truth in them. Yet when I think back upon my own experience of the Negro and his of me, I find myself troubled and puzzled, much as I was as a child when I heard that all Jews were rich and all Negroes persecuted. How could the Negroes in my neighborhood have regarded the whites across the street and around the corner as jailers? On the whole, the whites were not so poor as the Negroes, but they were quite poor enough, and the years were years of Depression. As for white hatred of the Negro, how could guilt have had anything to do with it? What share had these Italian and Jewish immigrants in the enslavement of the Negro? What share had they—downtrodden people themselves breaking their own necks to eke out a living—in the exploitation of the Negro?

No, I cannot believe that we hated each other back there in Brooklyn because they thought of us as jailers and we felt guilty toward them. But does it matter, given the fact that we all went through an unrepresentative confrontation? I think it matters profoundly, for if we managed the job of hating each other so well without benefit of the aids to hatred that are supposedly at the root of this madness everywhere else, it must mean that the madness is not yet properly understood. I am far from pretending that I understand it, but I would insist that no view of the problem will begin to approach the truth unless it can account for a case like the one I have been trying to describe. Are the elements of any such view available to us?

At least two, I would say, are. One of them is a point we frequently come upon in the work of James Baldwin, and the other is a related point always stressed by psychologists who have studied the mechanisms of prejudice. Baldwin tells us that one of the reasons Negroes hate the white man is that the white man refuses to *look* at him: the Negro knows that in white eyes all Negroes are alike; they are faceless and therefore not altogether human. The psychologists, in their turn, tell us that the white man hates the Negro because he tends to project those wild impulses that he fears in himself onto an alien group which he then punishes with his contempt. What Baldwin does *not* tell us, however, is that the principle of facelessness is a two-way street and can operate in both directions with no difficulty at all. Thus, in my neighborhood in Brooklyn, *I* was as faceless to the Negroes as they were to me, and if they hated me because I never looked at them, I must also have hated them for never looking at *me*. To the Negroes, my white skin was enough to define me as the enemy, and in a war it is only the uniform that counts and not the person.

So with the mechanism of projection that the psychologists talk about: it too works in both directions at once. There is no question that the psychologists are right about what the Negro represents symbolically to the white man. For me as a child the life lived on the other side of the playground and down the block on Ralph Avenue seemed the very embodiment of the values of the street—free, independent, reckless, brave, masculine, erotic. I put the word *erotic* last, though it is usually stressed above all others, because in fact it came last, in consciousness as in importance. What mainly counted for me about Negro kids of my own age was that they were "bad boys." There were plenty of bad boys among the whites— this was, after all, a neighborhood with a long tradition of crime as a career open to aspiring talents—but the Negroes were *really* bad, bad in a way that beckoned to one, and made one feel inadequate. We all went home every day for a lunch of spinach-and-potatoes; *they* roamed around during lunch hour, munching on candy bars. In winter *we* had to wear itchy woolen hats and mittens and cumbersome galoshes; *they* were bareheaded and loose as they pleased. We rarely played hooky, or got into serious trouble in school, for all our street-corner bravado; *they* were defiant, forever staying out (to do what delicious things?), forever making disturbances in class and in the halls, forever being sent to the principal and returning uncowed. But most important of all, they were *tough*; beautifully, enviably tough, not giving a damn for anyone or anything. To hell with the teacher, the truant officer, the cop; to hell with the whole of the adult world that held *us* in its grip and that we never had the courage to rebel against except sporadically and in petty ways.

This is what I saw and envied and feared in the Negro: this is what finally made him faceless to me, though some of it, of course, was actually there. (The psychologists also tell us that the alien group which becomes the object of a projection will tend to respond by trying to live up to what is expected of them.) But what, on his side, did the Negro see in me that made me faceless to *him*? Did he envy me my lunches of spinach-and-potatoes and my itchy woolen caps and my prudent behavior in the face of authority, as I envied him his noontime candy bars and his bare head in winter and his magnificent rebelliousness? Did those lunches and caps spell for him the prospect of power and riches in the future? Did they mean that there were possibilities open to me that were denied to him? Very likely they did. But if so, one also supposes that he feared the impulses within himself toward submission to authority no less powerfully than I feared the impulses in myself toward defiance. If I represented the jailer to him, it was not because I was oppressing him or keeping him down: it was because I symbolized for him the dangerous and probably pointless temptation toward greater repression, just as he symbolized for me the equally perilous tug toward greater freedom. I personally was to be rewarded for this repression with a new and better life in the future, but how many of my friends paid an even higher price and were given only gall in return.

We have it on the authority of James Baldwin that all Negroes hate whites. I am trying to suggest that on their side all whites—all American whites, that is—are sick in their feelings about Negroes. There are Negroes, no doubt, who would say that Baldwin is wrong, but I suspect them of being less honest than he is, just as I suspect whites of self-deception who tell me they have no special feeling toward Negroes. Special feelings about color are a contagion to which white Americans seem susceptible even when there is nothing in their background to account for the susceptibility. Thus everywhere we look today in the North, we find the curious phenomenon of white middle-class liberals with no previous personal experience of Negroes—people to whom Negroes have always been faceless in virtue rather than faceless in vice—discovering that their abstract commitment to the cause of Negro rights will not stand the test of a direct confrontation. We find such people fleeing in droves to the suburbs as the Negro population in the inner city grows; and when they stay in the city we find them sending their children to private school rather than to the "integrated" public school in the neighborhood. We find them resisting the demand that gerrymandered school districts be rezoned for the purpose of overcoming de facto segregation; we find them judiciously considering whether the Negroes (for their own good, of course) are not perhaps pushing too hard; we find them clucking their tongues over Negro militancy; we find them speculating on the question of whether there may not, after all, be something in the theory that the races are biologically different; we find them saying that it will take a very long time for Negroes to achieve full equality, no matter what anyone does; we find them deploring the rise of black nationalism and expressing the solemn hope that the leaders of the Negro community will discover ways of containing the impatience and incipient violence within the Negro ghettos.

But that is by no means the whole story; there is also the phenomenon of what Kenneth Rexroth once called "crow-jimism." There are the broken-down white boys like Vivaldo Moore in Baldwin's *Another Country* who go to Harlem in search of sex or simply to brush up against something that looks like primitive vitality, and who are so often punished by the Negroes they meet for crimes that they would have been the last ever to commit and of which they themselves have been as sorry victims as any of the Negroes who take it out on them. There are the writers and intellectuals and artists who romanticize Negroes and pander to them, assuming a guilt that is not properly theirs. And there are all the white liberals who permit Negroes to blackmail them into adopting a double standard of moral judgment, and who lend themselves—again assuming the responsibility for crimes they never committed—to cunning and contemptuous exploitation by Negroes they employ or try to befriend.

And what about me? What kind of feelings do I have about Negroes today? What happened to me, from Brooklyn, who grew up fearing and envying and hating Negroes? Now that Brooklyn is behind me, do I fear them and envy them and hate them still? The answer is yes, but not in the same proportions and certainly not in the same way. I now live on the Upper West Side of Manhattan, where there are many Negroes and many Puerto Ricans, and there are nights when I experience the old apprehensiveness again, and there are streets that I avoid when I am walking in the dark, as there were streets that I avoided when I was a child. I find that I am not afraid of Puerto Ricans, but I cannot restrain my nervousness whenever I pass a group of Negroes standing in front of a bar or sauntering down the street. I know now, as I did not know when I was a child, that power is on my side, that the police are working for me and not for them. And knowing this I feel ashamed and guilty, like the good liberal I have grown up to be. Yet the twinges of fear and the resentment they bring and the self-contempt they arouse are not to be gainsaid.

But envy? Why envy? And hatred? Why hatred? Here again the

intensities have lessened and everything has been complicated and qualified by the guilts and the resulting overcompensations that are the heritage
of the enlightened middle-class world of which I am now a member. Yet
just as in childhood I envied Negroes for what seemed to me their superior
masculinity, so I envy them today for what seems to me their superior
physical grace and beauty. I have come to value physical grace very highly,
and I am now capable of aching with all my being when I watch a Negro
couple on the dance floor, or a Negro playing baseball or basketball. They
are on the kind of terms with their own bodies that I should like to be on
with mine, and for that precious quality they seem blessed to me.

The hatred I still feel for Negroes is the hardest of all the old feelings to
face or admit, and it is the most hidden and the most overlarded by the
conscious attitudes into which I have succeeded in willing myself. It no
longer has, as for me it once did, any cause or justification (except, perhaps,
that I am constantly being denied my right to an honest expression of the
things I earned the right as a child to feel). How, then, do I know that this
hatred has never entirely disappeared? I know it from the insane rage that
can stir in me at the thought of Negro anti-Semitism; I know it from the
disgusting prurience that can stir in me at the sight of a mixed couple; and I
know it from the violence that can stir in me whenever I encounter that
special brand of paranoid touchiness to which many Negroes are prone.

This, then, is where I am; it is not exactly where I think all other
white liberals are, but it cannot be so very far away either. And it is
because I am convinced that we white Americans are—for whatever
reason, it no longer matters—so twisted and sick in our feelings about
Negroes that I despair of the present push toward integration. If the pace
of progress were not a factor here, there would perhaps be no cause for
despair: time and the law and even the international political situation are
on the side of the Negroes, and ultimately, therefore, victory—of a sort,
anyway—must come. But from everything we have learned from observers who ought to know, pace has become as important to the Negroes
as substance. They want equality and they want it *now*, and the white
world is yielding to their demand only as much and as fast as it is
absolutely being compelled to do. The Negroes know this in the most
concrete terms imaginable, and it is thus becoming increasingly difficult
to buy them off with rhetoric and promises and pious assurances of

support. And so within the Negro community we find more and more people declaring—as Harold R. Isaacs recently put it*—that they want *out*: people who say that integration will never come, or that it will take a hndred or a thousand years to come, or that it will come at too high a price in suffering and struggle for the pallid and sodden life of the American middle class that at the very best it may bring.

The most numerous, influential, and dangerous movement that has grown out of Negro despair with the goal of integration is, of course, the Black Muslims. This movement, whatever else we may say about it, must be credited with one enduring achievement: it inspired James Baldwin to write an essay† which deserves to be placed among the classics of our language. Everything Baldwin has ever been trying to tell us is distilled here into a statement of overwhelming persuasiveness and prophetic magnificence. Baldwin's message is and always has been simple. It is this: "Color is not a human or personal reality; it is a political reality." And Baldwin's demand is correspondingly simple: color must be forgotten, lest we all be smited with a "vengeance that does not really depend on, and cannot really be executed by, any person or organization, and that cannot be prevented by any police force or army: historical vengeance, a cosmic vengeance based on the law that we recognize when we say, 'Whatever goes up must come down.' " The Black Muslims Baldwin portrays as a sign and a warning to the intransigent white world. They come to proclaim how deep is the Negro's disaffection with the white world and all its works, and Baldwin implies that no American Negro can fail to respond somewhere in his being to their message: that the white man is the devil, that Allah has doomed him to destruction, and that the black man is about to inherit the earth. Baldwin of course knows that this nightmare inversion of the racism from which the black man has suffered can neither win nor even point to the neighborhood in which victory might be located. For in his view the neighborhood of victory lies in exactly the opposite direction: the transcendence of color through love.

Yet the tragic fact is that love is not the answer to hate—not in the

---

* "Integration and the Negro Mood," *Commentary*, December 1962.

† Originally published in *The New Yorker* under the title "Letter from a Region in My Mind," subsequently published in book form (along with a new introduction) under the title *The Fire Next Time*.

world of politics, at any rate. Color is indeed a political rather than a human or a personal reality and if politics (which is to say power) has made it into a human and a personal reality, then only politics (which is to say power) can unmake it once again. But the way of politics is slow and bitter, and as impatience on the one side is matched by a setting of the jaw on the other, we move closer and closer to an explosion and blood may yet run in the streets.

Will this madness in which we are all caught never find a resting-place? Is there never to be an end to it? In thinking about the Jews I have often wondered whether their survival as a distinct group was worth one hair on the head of a single infant. Did the Jews have to survive so that six million innocent people should one day be burned in the ovens of Auschwitz? It is a terrible question and no one, not God himself, could ever answer it to my satisfaction. And when I think about the Negroes in America and about the image of integration as a state in which the Negroes would take their rightful place as another of the protected minorities in a pluralistic society, I wonder whether they really believe in their hearts that such a state can actually be attained, and if so *why* they should wish to survive as a distinct group. I think I know why the Jews once wished to survive (though I am less certain as to why we still do): they not only believed that God had given them no choice, but they were tied to a memory of past glory and a dream of imminent redemption. What does the American Negro have that might correspond to this? His past is a stigma, his color is a stigma, and his vision of the future is the hope of erasing the stigma by making color irrelevant, by making it disappear as a fact of consciousness.

I share this hope, but I cannot see how it will ever be realized unless color does *in fact* disappear: and that means not integration, it means assimilation, it means—let the brutal word come out—miscegenation. The Black Muslims, like their racist counterparts in the white world, accuse the "so-called Negro leaders" of secretly pursuing miscegenation as a goal. The racists are wrong, but I wish they were right, for I believe that the wholesale merging of the two races is the most desirable alternative for everyone concerned. I am not claiming that this alternative can be pursued programmatically or that it is immediately feasible as a solution; obviously there are even greater barriers to its achievement than to the achievement of integration. What I am saying, however, is that in my opinion the Negro problem can be solved in this country in no other way.

I have told the story of my own twisted feelings about Negroes here, and of how they conflict with the moral convictions I have since developed, in order to assert that such feelings must be acknowledged as honestly as possible so that they can be controlled and ultimately disregarded in favor of the convictions. It is *wrong* for a man to suffer because of the color of his skin. Beside that clichéd proposition of liberal thought, what argument can stand and be respected? If the arguments are the arguments of feeling, they must be made to yield; and one's own soul is not the worst place to begin working a huge social transformation. Not so long ago, it used to be asked of white liberals, "Would you like your sister to marry one?" When I was a boy and my sister was still unmarried, I would certainly have said no to that question. But now I am a man, my sister is already married, and I have daughters. If I were to be asked today whether I would like a daughter of mine "to marry one," I would have to answer: "No, I wouldn't *like* it at all. I would rail and rave and rant and tear my hair. And then I hope I would have the courage to curse myself for raving and ranting, and to give her my blessing. How dare I withhold it at the behest of the child I once was and against the man I now have a duty to be?"

Postscript (1993)

"My Negro Problem—and Ours" has often been treated as an event in the history of black-Jewish relations. Yet even though I spoke explicitly as a Jew throughout, and even though in the concluding section I drew a comparison between blacks and Jews, I was writing not as a Jew but as a white liberal (my conversion to neoconservatism, though perhaps fore-shadowed to some extent in the essay, was still years away); and it was as a statement about liberal feeling in general, rather than about Jewish feeling in particular, that the essay was generally read upon its original publication in 1963. In later years, with the spread of black anti-Semitism, "My Negro Problem" began being cited as evidence that "the Jews" were hypocritical in their professions of support of black aspirations and demands. This was in fact an egregious and slanderous misrepresentation of the American Jewish community, which (even in the face of the rising tide of black hostility to Jews) has to this day remained far more sympathetic to blacks than any other white ethnic group. It was also a distortion of what I was saying—though that distortion, and the political purposes it has served, may be one of the factors which has kept the essay alive.

Other factors which may have kept it alive have served other purposes. When "My Negro Problem" first came out, a critic said that there was something in it to offend everyone. He was right. Integrationists, white and black alike—who were the dominant force in the civil rights movement at the time—took offense at my prediction that integration was not going to work. Black nationalists—who were mounting an increasingly influential challenge to the integrationists—took offense at my slighting references to the history and culture of their people as nothing more than a "stigma." And Jews were offended by my willingness to entertain the possibility that the survival of the Jewish people might not have been worth the suffering it had entailed.

As the years wore on, however, a curious reversal occurred. Now it began to seem that "My Negro Problem" had something in it to please, if not everyone, then a growing body of sentiment both among blacks and whites. This something was the idea that all whites were incorrigibly racist. To be sure, I had not exactly endorsed that idea. What I had actually said was that all whites were sick and twisted in their feelings about blacks. But to most readers, it seems, this formulation was the functional equivalent of a charge of universal white racism. It thereby lent itself nicely to the view that *the* "Negro problem"—indeed the only Negro problem—was external oppression, and that nothing blacks themselves did or failed to do made, or could ever make, more than a trivial difference.

The almost complete abdication of black responsibility and the commensurately total dependence on government engendered by so obsessive and exclusive a fixation on white racism has been calamitous. It has undermined the very qualities that are essential to the achievement of independence and self-respect, and it has spawned policies that have had the perverse effect of further discouraging the growth of such qualities. It has thereby contributed mightily to the metastasis of the black underclass—a development which, in addition to destroying countless black lives, has subjected more and more whites to experiences like the ones I described going through as a child in "My Negro Problem."

In 1963 those descriptions were very shocking to most white liberals. In their eyes Negroes were all long-suffering and noble victims of the kind who had become familiar through the struggles of the civil rights movement in the South—the "heroic period" of the movement, as one of its most heroic leaders, Bayard Rustin, called it. While none of my white critics went so far as to deny the truthfulness of the stories I told, they themselves could hardly imagine being afraid of Negroes (how could they when the only Negroes most of them knew personally were maids and cleaning women?). In any case, they very much disliked the emphasis I placed on black thuggery and aggression.

Today, when black-on-white violence is much more common than it was then, many white readers could easily top those stories with worse. And yet even today few of them would be willing to speak truthfully in public about their entirely rational fear of black violence and black crime. Telling the truth about blacks remains dangerous to one's reputation: to use the now famous phrase I once appropriated from D. H. Lawrence in talking about ambition, the fear of blacks has become the dirty little secret of our political culture. And since a dirty little secret breeds hypocrisy and cant in those who harbor it, I suppose it can still be said that most whites are sick and twisted in their feelings about blacks, albeit in a very different sense from the way they were in 1963.

The opening section of "My Negro Problem," then, is perhaps even more relevant today than it was then. I cannot, however, say the same for other parts of the essay. Obviously I was for the most part right in predicting that integration as it was naively envisaged in those days (blacks, with discriminatory barriers lowered, more and more moving on their own individual merits into the middle class and working and living harmoniously together with whites in all areas of society) would not come about in even the remotely foreseeable future. The one and perhaps the only institution in which the old integrationist ideal has been fully realized is—to the surprise and chagrin of many liberals—the army. Almost everywhere else—to my own surprise and chagrin—a diseased mutation of integrationism, taking the form of a quota system and euphemistically known as affirmative action, went on to triumph in the end.

It has been a bitter triumph, attained at the cost of new poisons of white resentment and black self-doubt injected into the relations between the races. True, more blacks are economically better off today than they were in 1963, and the black community has more political power than it did then. But at the same time relations between whites and blacks have deteriorated. Gone on the whole are the interracial friendships and the interracial political alliances that were very widespread thirty years ago. In their place we have the nearly impassable gulfs of suspicion and hostility that are epitomized by the typical college dining hall of today where black students insist on sitting at tables of their own and whites either are happy to accept this segregated arrangement or feel hurt at being repulsed.

Then there is the other great cost—the damage done to the precious American principle (honored though it admittedly once was more in the breach than in the observance) of treating individuals as individuals rather than as members of a group. The systematic violation of that principle as applied to blacks has opened the way to its violation for the sake of other "disadvantaged minorities" (a category that now includes women, who are a majority, and is beginning to include homosexuals, who are as a group economically prosperous). And so the dangerous and destructive balkanization of our culture and our society proceeds.

With respect to blacks, this development grew out of the unexpected co-optation of black-nationalist passions by the ideology of reverse discrimination. The Black Muslims are still out there preaching separationism, but their old driving force—the call for "black power"—is now firmly harnessed to the integrationist mutation. This mutated integrationism, moreover, has gone beyond demanding that blacks be force-fed by government coercion into jobs and universities and professional schools in proportion to their numbers in the population. It now demands that districts be gerrymandered to ensure the election of black legislators; and if it ever gets its way, the next step will be government coercion to ensure that these black legislators will be "authentic" (i.e., committed to the endless extension of reverse discrimination). Like meritocratic standards, elections may soon be denounced as subtle instruments of "institutional racism."

Failing to anticipate these developments in "My Negro Problem," I found no escape from the trap I was describing except the wholesale merging of the two races. And because my objective in writing the essay was to speak the truth as I saw it and to go where it took me no matter what the consequences, it would have been a cowardly betrayal to shrink from the conclusion to which my analysis inexorably led. Yet if I did the right thing from the perspective of intellectual coherence and literary fitness, I was wrong to think that miscegenation could ever result in the elimination of color "as a fact of consciousness," if for no other reason than that (as Ralph Ellison bitingly remarked to me) the babies born of such marriages would still be considered black.

Why, then, have I permitted "My Negro Problem—and Ours" to be reprinted here, as I have dozens of times before, without revision? The answer, frankly, is that I have always been proud of it as a piece of writing (and I like to believe that its virtues as a literary essay have been another, and possibly even the main, factor in keeping it alive). It is in the nature of a successfully realized literary work that it achieves an existence independent of its author, and so it is with "My Negro Problem—and Ours." Long ago it ceased belonging to me, and for better or worse I feel that I have no right to tamper with it or to kill it off. I do, however, hope to write at length about all these issues again someday—if, that is, I can ever muster the kind of nerve that came very hard even to my much younger and more reckless self.

The Negro Family: The Case for National Action

Daniel Patrick Moynihan

T HE UNITED STATES is approaching a new crisis in race relations.

In the decade that began with the school desegregation decision of the Supreme Court, and ended with the passage of the Civil Rights Act of 1964, the demand of Negro Americans for full recognition of their civil rights was finally met.

The effort, no matter how savage and brutal, of some State and local governments to thwart the exercise of those rights is doomed. The nation will not put up with it—least of all the Negroes. The present moment will pass. In the meantime, a new period is beginning.

In this new period the expectations of the Negro Americans will go beyond civil rights. Being Americans, they will now expect that in the near future equal opportunities for them as a group will produce roughly equal results, as compared with other groups. This is not going to happen. Nor will it happen for generations to come unless a new and special effort is made.

There are two reasons. First, the racist virus in the American blood stream still afflicts us: Negroes will encounter serious personal prejudice for at least another generation. Second, three centuries of sometimes unimaginable mistreatment have taken their toll on the Negro people. The harsh fact is that as a group, at the present time, in terms of ability to win out in the competitions of American life, they are not equal to most of those groups with which they will be competing. Individually, Negro Americans reach the highest peaks of achievement. But collectively, in the spectrum of

Excerpts published by the Office of Policy Planning and Research. U.S. Department of Labor (March 1965).

American ethnic and religious and regional groups, where some get plenty and some get none, where some send eighty percent of their children to college and others pull them out of school at the eighth grade, Negroes are among the weakest.

The most difficult fact for white Americans to understand is that in these terms the circumstances of the Negro American community in recent years has probably been getting *worse, not better.*

Indices of dollars of income, standards of living, and years of education deceive. The gap between the Negro and most other groups in American society is widening.

The fundamental problem, in which this is most clearly the case, is that of family structure. The evidence—not final, but powerfully persuasive—is that the Negro family in the urban ghettos is crumbling. A middle-class group has managed to save itself, but for vast numbers of the unskilled, poorly educated city working class the fabric of conventional social relationships has all but disintegrated. There are indications that the situation may have been arrested in the past few years, but the general postwar trend is unmistakable. So long as this situation persists, the cycle of poverty and disadvantage will continue to repeat itself.

The thesis of this paper is that these events, in combination, confront the nation with a new kind of problem. Measures that have worked in the past, or would work for most groups in the present, will not work here. A national effort is required that will give a unity of purpose to the many activities of the Federal government in this area, directed to a new kind of national goal: the establishment of a stable Negro family structure.

This would be a new departure for Federal policy. And a difficult one. But it almost certainly offers the only possibility of resolving in our time what is, after all, the nation's oldest, and most intransigent, and now its most dangerous social problem. What Gunnar Myrdal said in *An American Dilemma* remains true today: "*America is free to choose whether the Negro shall remain her liability or become her opportunity.*"

The Negro American Revolution

The Negro American revolution is rightly regarded as the most important domestic event of the postwar period in the United States.

Nothing like it has occurred since the upheavals of the 1930s which led to the organization of the great industrial trade unions, and which in turn profoundly altered both the economy and the political scene. There have been few other events in our history—the American Revolution itself, the surge of Jacksonian Democracy in the 1830s, the Abolitionist movement and the Populist movement of the late nineteenth century—comparable to the current Negro movement.

There has been none more important. The Negro American revolution holds forth the prospect that the American Republic, which at birth was flawed by the institution of Negro slavery, and which throughout its history has been marred by the unequal treatment of Negro citizens, will at last redeem the full promise of the Declaration of Independence.

Although the Negro leadership has conducted itself with the strictest propriety, acting always and only as American citizens asserting their rights within the framework of the American political system, it is no less clear that the movement has profound international implications.

It was in no way a matter of chance that the nonviolent tactics and philosophy of the movement, as it began in the South, were consciously adapted from the techniques by which the Congress Party undertook to free the Indian nation from British colonial rule. It was not a matter of chance that the Negro movement caught fire in America at just that moment when the nations of Africa were gaining their freedom. Nor is it merely incidental that the world should have fastened its attention on events in the United States at a time when the possibility that the nations of the world will divide along color lines seems suddenly not only possible, but even imminent.

(Such racist views have made progress within the Negro American community itself—which can hardly be expected to be immune to a virus that is endemic in the white community. The Black Muslim doctrines, based on total alienation from the white world, exert a powerful influence. On the far Left, the attraction of Chinese Communism can no longer be ignored.)

It is clear that what happens in America is being taken as a sign of what can, or must, happen in the world at large. The course of world events will be profoundly affected by the success or failure of the Negro American revolution in seeking the peaceful assimilation of the races in the United States. The award of the Nobel Peace Prize to Dr. Martin Luther King was as much an expression of the hope for the future, as it was recognition for past achievement.

It is no less clear that carrying this revolution forward to a successful conclusion is a first priority confronting the Great Society.

The End of the Beginning

The major events of the onset of the Negro revolution are now behind us.

The *political events* were three: First, the Negroes themselves organized as a mass movement. Their organizations have been in some ways better disciplined and better led than any in our history. They have established an unprecedented alliance with religious groups throughout the nation and have maintained close ties with both political parties and with most segments of the trade union movement. Second, the Kennedy-Johnson administration committed the Federal government to the cause of Negro equality. This had never happened before. Third, the 1964 Presidential election was practically a referendum on this commitment: if these were terms made by the opposition, they were in effect accepted by the President.

The overwhelming victory of President Johnson must be taken as emphatic popular endorsement of the unmistakable, and openly avowed course which the Federal government has pursued under his leadership.

The *administrative events* were threefold as well: First, beginning with the establishment of the President's Committee on Equal Employment Opportunity and on to the enactment of the Manpower Development and Training Act of 1962, the Federal government has launched a major national effort to redress the profound imbalance between the economic position of the Negro citizens and the rest of the nation that derives primarily from their unequal position in the labor market. Second, the Economic Opportunity Act of 1964 began a major national effort to abolish poverty, a condition in which almost half of Negro families are living. Third, the Civil Rights Act of 1964 marked the end of the era of legal and formal discrimination against Negroes and created important new machinery for combating covert discrimination and unequal treatment. (The Act does not guarantee an end to harassment in matters such as voter registration, but does make it more or less incumbent upon government to take further steps to thwart such efforts when they do occur.)

The *legal events* were no less specific. Beginning with *Brown* v. *Board of Education* in 1954, through the decade that culminated in the recent decisions upholding Title II of the Civil Rights Act, the Federal judiciary, led by the Supreme Court, has used every opportunity to combat unequal treatment of Negro citizens. It may be put as a general proposition that the laws of the United States now look upon any such treatment as obnoxious, and that the courts will strike it down wherever it appears.

The Demand for Equality

With these events behind us, the nation now faces a different set of challenges, which may prove more difficult to meet, if only because they cannot be cast as concrete propositions of right and wrong.

The fundamental problem here is that the Negro revolution, like the industrial upheaval of the 1930s, is a movement for equality as well as for liberty.

Liberty and Equality are the twin ideals of American democracy. But they are not the same thing. Nor, most importantly, are they equally attractive to all groups at any given time; nor yet are they always compatible, one with the other.

Many persons who would gladly die for liberty are appalled by equality. Many who are devoted to equality are puzzled and even troubled by liberty. Much of the political history of the American nation can be seen as a competition between these two ideals, as for example, the unending troubles between capital and labor.

By and large, liberty has been the ideal with the higher social prestige in America. It has been the middle-class aspiration, par excellence. (Note the assertions of the conservative right that ours is a republic, not a democracy.) Equality, on the other hand, has enjoyed tolerance more than acceptance. Yet it has roots deep in Western civilization and "is at least coeval with, if not prior to, liberty in the history of Western political thought."[1]

American democracy has not always been successful in maintaining a balance between these two ideals, and notably so where the Negro American is concerned. "Lincoln freed the slaves," but they were given liberty, not equality. It was therefore possible in the century that followed to deprive their descendants of much of their liberty as well.

The ideal of equality does not ordain that all persons end up, as well as start out equal. In traditional terms, as put by Faulkner, "there is no such thing as equality *per se*, but only equality *to*: equal right and opportunity to make the best one can of one's life within one's capability, without fear of injustice or oppression or threat of violence."[2] But the evolution of American politics, with the distinct persistence of ethnic and religious groups, has added a profoundly significant new dimension to that egalitarian ideal. It is increasingly demanded that the distribution of success and failure within one group be roughly comparable to that within other groups. It is not enough that all individuals start out on even terms, if the members of one group almost invariably end up well to the fore, and those of another far to the rear. This is what ethnic politics are all about in America, and in the main the Negro American demands are being put forth in this now traditional and established framework.[3]

Here a point of semantics must be grasped. The demand for Equality of Opportunity has been generally perceived by white Americans as a demand for liberty, a demand not to be excluded from the competitions of life—at the polling place, in the scholarship examinations, at the personnel office, on the housing market. Liberty does, of course, demand that everyone be free to try his luck, or test his skill in such matters. But these opportunities do not necessarily produce equality: on the contrary, to the extent that winners imply losers, equality of opportunity almost insures inequality of results.

The point of semantics is that equality of opportunity now has a different meaning for Negroes than it has for whites. It is not (or at least no longer), a demand for liberty alone, but also for equality—in terms of group results. In Bayard Rustin's terms, "It is now concerned not merely with removing the barriers to full *opportunity* but with achieving the fact of *equality*.[4] By equality Rustin means a distribution of achievements among Negroes roughly comparable to that among whites.

As Nathan Glazer has put it, "The demand for economic equality is now not the demand for equal opportunities for the equally qualified: it is now the demand for equality of economic results. . . . The demand for equality education . . . has also become a demand for equality of results, of outcomes."[5]

Some aspects of the new laws do guarantee results, in the sense that upon enactment and enforcement they bring about an objective that is an end in itself, e.g., the public accommodations title of the Civil Rights Act.

Other provisions are at once terminal and intermediary. The portions of the Civil Rights Act dealing with voting rights will achieve an objective that is an end in itself but the exercise of those rights will no doubt lead to further enlargements of the freedom of the Negro American.

But by and large, the programs that have been enacted in the first phase of the Negro revolution—Manpower Retraining, the Job Corps, Community Action, et al.—only make opportunities available. They cannot insure the outcome.

The principal challenge of the next phase of the Negro revolution is to make certain that equality of results will now follow. If we do not, there will be no social peace in the United States for generations.

The Prospect for Equality

The time, therefore, is at hand for an unflinching look at the present potential of Negro Americans to move from where they now are to where they want, and ought to be.

There is no very satisfactory way, at present, to measure social health or social pathology within an ethnic, or religious, or geographical community. Data are few and uncertain, and conclusions drawn from them, including the conclusions that follow, are subject to the grossest error.* Nonetheless, the opportunities, no less than the dangers, of the present moment, demand that an assessment be made.

That being the case, it has to be said that there is a considerable body of evidence to support the conclusion that Negro social structure, in particular the Negro family, battered and harassed by discrimination, injustice, and uprooting, is in the deepest trouble. While many young Negroes are moving ahead to unprecedented levels of achievement, many more are falling further and further behind.

After an intensive study of the life of central Harlem, the board of directors of Harlem Youth Opportunities Unlimited, Inc. summed up their findings in one statement: "Massive deterioration of the fabric of society and its institutions . . ."[6]

It is the conclusion of this survey of the available national data, that what is true of central Harlem, can be said to be true of the Negro American world in general.

---

* As much as possible, the statistics used in this paper refer to Negroes. However, certain data series are available only in terms of the white and nonwhite population. Where this is the case, the nonwhite data have been used as if they referred only to Negroes. This necessarily introduces some inaccuracies, but it does not appear to produce any significant distortions. In 1960, Negroes were 92.1 percent of all nonwhites. The remaining 7.9 percent is made up largely of Indians, Japanese, and Chinese. The combined male unemployment rates of these groups is lower than that of Negroes. In matters relating to family stability, the smaller groups are probably more stable. Thus 21 percent of Negro women who have ever married are separated, divorced, or their husbands are absent for other reasons. The comparable figure for Indians is 14 percent; Japanese, 7 percent; Chinese 6 percent. Therefore, the statistics on nonwhites generally *understate* the degree of disorganization of the Negro family and underemployment of Negro men.

If this is so, it is the single most important social fact of the United States today.

The Negro American Family

At the heart of the deterioration of the fabric of Negro society is the deterioration of the Negro family.

It is the fundamental source of the weakness of the Negro community at the present time.

There is probably no single fact of Negro American life so little understood by whites. The Negro situation is commonly perceived by whites in terms of the visible manifestations of discrimination and poverty, in part because Negro protest is directed against such obstacles, and in part, no doubt, because these are facts which involve the actions and attitudes of the white community as well. It is more difficult, however, for whites to perceive the effect that three centuries of exploitation have had on the fabric of Negro society itself. Here the consequences of the historic injustices done to Negro Americans are silent and hidden from view. But here is where the true injury has occurred: unless this damage is repaired, all the effort to end discrimination and poverty and injustice will come to little.

The role of the family in shaping character and ability is so pervasive as to be easily overlooked. The family is the basic social unit of American life; it is the basic socializing unit. By and large, adult conduct in society is learned as a child.

A fundamental insight of psychoanalytic theory, for example, is that the child learns a way of looking at life in his early years through which all later experience is viewed and which profoundly shapes his adult conduct.

It may be hazarded that the reason family structure does not loom larger in public discussion of social issues is that people tend to assume that the nature of family life is about the same throughout American society. The mass media and the development of suburbia have created an image of the American family as a highly standardized phenomenon. It is therefore easy to assume that whatever it is that makes for differences among individuals or groups of individuals, it is not a different family structure.

There is much truth to this; as with any other nation, Americans are producing a recognizable family system. But that process is not completed by any means. There are still, for example, important differences in family patterns surviving from the age of the great European migration to the

United States, and these variations account for notable differences in the progress and assimilation of various ethnic and religious groups.[7] A number of immigrant groups were characterized by unusually strong family bonds; these groups have characteristically progressed more rapidly than others.

But there is one truly great discontinuity in family structure in the United States at the present time: that between the white world in general and that of the Negro American.

The white family has achieved a high degree of stability and is maintaining that stability.

By contrast, the family structure of lower class Negroes is highly unstable, and in many urban centers is approaching complete breakdown.

N.B. There is considerable evidence that the Negro community is in fact dividing between a stable middle-class group that is steadily growing stronger and more successful, and an increasingly disorganized and disadvantaged lower-class group. There are indications, for example, that the middle-class Negro family puts a higher premium on family stability and the conserving of family resources than does the white middle-class family.[8] The discussion of this paper is not, obviously, directed to the first group excepting as it is affected by the experiences of the second—an important exception. (See "The Tangle of Pathology.")

There are two points to be noted in this context.

First, the emergence and increasing visibility of a Negro middle-class may beguile the nation into supposing that the circumstances of the remainder of the Negro community are equally prosperous, whereas just the opposite is true at present, and is likely to continue so.

Second, the lumping of all Negroes together in one statistical measurement very probably conceals the extent of the disorganization among the lower-class group. If conditions are improving for one and deteriorating for the other, the resultant statistical averages might show no change. Further, the statistics on the Negro family and most other subjects treated in this paper refer only to a specific point in time. They are a vertical measure of the situation at a given moment. They do not measure the experience of individuals over time. Thus the average monthly unemployment rate for Negro males for 1964 is recorded as 9 percent. But *during* 1964, some 29 percent of Negro males were unemployed at one time or another. Similarly, for example, if 36 percent of Negro children are living in broken homes *at any specific moment*, it is likely that a far higher proportion of Negro children find themselves in that situation *at one time or another* in their lives.

The Tangle of Pathology

That the Negro American has survived at all is extraordinary—a lesser people might simply have died out, as indeed others have. That the Negro community has not only survived, but in this political generation has entered national affairs as a moderate, humane, and constructive national force is the highest testament to the healing powers of the democratic ideal and the creative vitality of the Negro people.

But it may not be supposed that the Negro American community has not paid a fearful price for the incredible mistreatment to which it has been subjected over the past three centuries.

In essence, the Negro community has been forced into a matriarchal structure which, because it is so out of line with the rest of the American society, seriously retards the progress of the group as a whole, and imposes a crushing burden on the Negro male and, in consequence, on a great many Negro women as well.

There is, presumably, no special reason why a society in which males are dominant in family relationships is to be preferred to a matriarchal arrangement. However, it is clearly a disadvantage for a minority group to

Percent Distribution of Ever-Married Females with Husbands Absent or Divorced, Rural-Urban, 1960

| | Urban | | Rural Nonfarm | | Rural Farm | |
	Nonwhite	White	Nonwhite	White	Nonwhite	White
Total, husbands absent or divorced	22.9	7.9	14.7	5.7	9.6	3.0
Total, husbands absent	17.3	3.9	12.6	3.6	8.6	2.0
Separated	12.7	1.8	7.8	1.2	5.6	0.5
Husbands absent for other reasons	4.6	2.1	4.8	2.4	3.0	1.5

Source: U.S. Census of population, 1960, Nonwhite population by Race, PC (2) 1c, table 9, pp. 9–10.

be operating on one principle, while the great majority of the population, and the one with the most advantages to begin with, is operating on another. This is the present situation of the Negro. Ours is a society which presumes male leadership in private and public affairs. The arrangements of society facilitate such leadership and reward it. A subculture, such as that of the Negro American, in which this is not the pattern, is placed at a distinct disadvantage.

Here an earlier word of caution should be repeated. There is much evidence that a considerable number of Negro families have managed to break out of the tangle of pathology and to establish themselves as stable, effective units, living according to patterns of American society in general. E. Franklin Frazier has suggested that the middle-class Negro American family is, if anything, more patriarchal and protective of its children than the general run of such families.[9] Given equal opportunities, the children of these families will perform as well or better than their white peers. They need no help from anyone, and ask none.

While this phenomenon is not easily measured, one index is that middle-class Negroes have even fewer children than middle-class whites, indicating a desire to conserve the advances they have made and to insure that their children do as well or better. Negro women who marry early to uneducated laborers have more children than white women in the same situation; Negro women who marry at the common age for the middle class to educated men doing technical or professional work have only four-fifths as many children as their white counterparts.

It might be estimated that as much as half of the Negro community falls into the middle class. However, the remaining half is in desperate and deteriorating circumstances. Moreover, because of housing segregation it is immensely difficult for the stable half to escape from the cultural influences of the unstable one. The children of middle-class Negroes often as not must grow up in, or next to the slums, an experience almost unknown to white middle-class children. They are therefore constantly exposed to the pathology of the disturbed group and constantly in danger of being drawn into it. It is for this reason that the propositions put forth in this study may be thought of as having a more or less general application.

In a word, most Negro youth are in *danger* of being caught up in the tangle of pathology that affects their world, and probably a majority are so entrapped. Many of those who escape do so for one generation only: as things now are, their children may have to run the gauntlet all over again.

Children Born per Woman Age 35 to 44: Wives of Uneducated Laborers who Married Young, Compared with Wives of Educated Professional Workers who Married After Age 21, White and Nonwhite, 1960*

	Children per Woman	
	White	Nonwhite
Wives married at age 14 to 21 to husbands who are laborers and did not go to high school	3.8	4.7
Wives married at age 22 or over to husbands who are professional or technical workers and have completed 1 year or more of college	2.4	1.9

*Wives married only once, with husbands present.
Source: 1960 Census, *Women by Number of Children ever Born*, PC (2) 3A, table 39 and 40, pp. 199–238.

That is not the least vicious aspect of the world that white America has made for the Negro.

Obviously, not every instance of social pathology afflicting the Negro community can be traced to the weakness of family structure. If, for example, organized crime in the Negro community were not largely controlled by whites, there would be more capital accumulation among Negroes, and therefore probably more Negro business enterprises. If it were not for the hostility and fear many whites exhibit toward Negroes, they in turn would be less afflicted by hostility and fear and so on. There is no one Negro community. There is no one Negro problem. There is no one solution. Nonetheless, at the center of the tangle of pathology is the weakness of the family structure. Once or twice removed, it will be found to be the principal source of most of the aberrant, inadequate, or antisocial behavior that did not establish, but now serves to perpetuate the cycle of poverty and deprivation.

It was by destroying the Negro family under slavery that white America broke the will of the Negro people. Although that will has reasserted itself in our time, it is a resurgence doomed to frustration unless the viability of the Negro family is restored.

The Case for National Action

The object of this study has been to define a problem, rather than propose solutions to it. We have kept within these confines for three reasons.

First, there are many persons, within and without the Government, who do not feel the problem exists, at least in any serious degree. These persons feel that, with the legal obstacles to assimilation out of the way, matters will take care of themselves in the normal course of events. This is a fundamental issue, and requires a decision within the Government.

Second, it is our view that the problem is so inter-related, one thing with another, that any list of program proposals would necessarily be incomplete, and would distract attention from the main point of inter-relatedness. We have shown a clear relation between male employment, for example, and the number of welfare dependent children. Employment in turn reflects educational achievement, which depends in large part on family stability, which reflects employment. Where we should break into this cycle, and how, are the most difficult domestic questions facing the United States. We must first reach agreement on what the problem is, then we will know what questions must be answered.

Third, it is necessary to acknowledge the view, held by a number of responsible persons, that this problem may in fact be out of control. This is a view with which we emphatically and totally disagree, but the view must be acknowledged. The persistent rise in Negro educational achievement is probably the main trend that belies this thesis. On the other hand our study has produced some clear indications that the situation may indeed have begun to feed on itself. It may be noted, for example, that for most of the postwar period male Negro unemployment and the number of new AFDC cases rose and fell together as if connected by a chain from 1948 to 1962. The correlation between the two series of data was an astonishing .91. (This would mean that 83 percent of the rise and fall in AFDC cases can be statistically ascribed to the rise and fall in the unemployment rate.) In 1960, however, for the first time, unemployment declined, but the number of new AFDC cases rose. In 1963 this happened a second time. In 1964 a third. The possible implications of these and other data are serious enough that they, too, should be understood before program proposals are made.

However, the argument of this paper does lead to one central conclusion: Whatever the specific elements of a national effort designed to resolve this problem, those elements must be coordinated in terms of one general strategy.

What then is that problem? We feel the answer is clear enough. Three centuries of injustice have brought about deep-seated structural distortions in the life of the Negro American. At this point, the present tangle of pathology is capable of perpetuating itself without assistance from the white world. The cycle can be broken only if these distortions are set right.

In a word, a national effort towards the problems of Negro Americans must be directed towards the question of family structure. The object should be to strengthen the Negro family so as to enable it to raise and support its members as do other families. After that, how this group of Americans chooses to run its affairs, take advantage of its opportunities, or fail to do so, is none of the nation's business.

The fundamental importance and urgency of restoring the Negro American Family structure has been evident for some time. E. Franklin Frazier put it most succinctly in 1950:

> As the result of family disorganization a large proportion of Negro children and youth have not undergone the socialization which only the family can provide. The disorganized families have failed to provide for their emotional needs and have not provided the discipline and habits which are necessary for personality development. Because the disorganized family has failed in its function as a socializing agency, it has handicapped the children in their relations to the institutions in the community. Moreover, family disorganization has been partially responsible for a large amount of juvenile delinquency and adult crime among Negroes. Since the widespread family disorganization among Negroes has resulted from the failure of the father to play the role in family life required by American society, the mitigation of this problem must await those changes in the Negro and American society which will enable the Negro father to play the role required of him.[10]

Nothing was done in response to Frazier's argument. Matters were left to take care of themselves, and as matters will, grew worse not better. The problem is now more serious, the obstacles greater. There is, however, a profound change for the better in one respect. The President has committed the nation to an all-out effort to eliminate poverty wherever it exists, among whites or Negroes, and a militant, organized, and responsible Negro movement exists to join in that effort.

Such a national effort could be stated thus:

The policy of the United States is to bring the Negro American to full and equal sharing in the responsibilities and rewards of citizenship. To this end, the programs of the Federal government bearing on this objective shall be designed to have the effect, directly or indirectly, of enhancing the stability and resources of the Negro American family.

NOTES

1. Robert Harris, *The Quest for Equality* (Baton Rouge, Louisiana State University Press, 1960), p. 4.

2. William Faulkner, in a speech before the Southern Historical Society in November 1955, quoted in *Mississippi: The Closed Society*, by James W. Silver (New York, Harcourt, Brace and World, Inc., 1964), p. xiii.

3. For a view that present Negro demands go beyond this traditional position, see Nathan Glazer, "Negroes and Jews: The Challenge to Pluralism," *Commentary*, December 1964, pp. 29–34.

4. Bayard Rustin, "From Protest to Politics. The Future of the Civil Rights Movement," *Commentary*, February 1965, p. 27.

5. Nathan Glazer, op. cit., p. 34.

6. *Youth in the Ghetto*, Harlem Youth Opportunities Unlimited, Inc., New York, 1964, p. xi.

7. Nathan Glazer and Daniel Patrick Moynihan, *Beyond the Melting Pot* (MIT Press and Harvard University Press, Cambridge, 1963), pp. 290–291.

8. E. Franklin Frazier, *Black Bourgeoisie* (New York, Collier Books, 1962).

9. E. Franklin Frazier, *Black Bourgeoisie* (New York, Collier Books, 1962).

10. E. Franklin Frazier, "Problems and Needs of Negro Children and Youth Resulting from Family Disorganization," *Journal of Negro Education*, Summer 1950, pp. 276–277.

2. Radicalism and Liberalism in the Age of Aquarius

*J*ohn Updike wrote that the 1970s were the time that the 1960s
percolated down to everybody, but it might just as well have
been Irving Kristol or Daniel Patrick Moynihan. For the assault on
traditional values and bourgeois modes of living that was launched in the
1960s disseminated in numerous ways in the years that followed. The
neoconservatives, predicting the collapse of liberalism long before most
others suspected there was a problem, were especially well equipped to
confront the revolution of the 1960s and its by-products. Always believers in the power of ideas, the neoconservatives had a special interest in
the university—the place where the ideas that govern men are formulated, incubated, and developed. They knew that the consequences of the
student revolts in the 1960s would not be limited to the elite campuses
but would, after a short interval, reverberate throughout the culture at
large.

Nathan Glazer's "The Campus Crucible" presents the neoconservative case against student radicalism in an age where the university served as
a battleground between traditional liberals who had a fundamental allegiance to American society and civilization and the left-liberals who
wanted revolution. Midge Decter's "A Letter to the Young (and their
parents)," demonstrates the consequences of the radical ideas that Glazer
condemned, and shows—as the liberal anticommunists had shown twenty

years before—how liberalism's inability to establish moral authority and to distinguish between the tolerable and the intolerable results in its self-destruction.

When the reforms of the New Deal gave way to the revolution of the Great Society, many neoconservatives began to assess the effects of large government programs on the people they intended to help. The Public Interest *was founded in 1965 by Irving Kristol and Daniel Bell to study the burgeoning government programs and to ascertain their practical effects. The early issues of* The Public Interest *were rationalistic, promoting the belief that the right men, using the right instruments, could make society work better. But as time went on, the studies this journal reported and analyzed called this belief into question and neoconservative views changed. Neoconservative writings began to refer to "the law of unintended consequences," reflecting the idea articulated by Aaron Wildavsky, in 1979, that "Unanticipated consequences are the rule, not the exception, of social action." In his essay "Government and the People" Wildavsky illustrates the intellectual dislocation that comes to a people who expect government to perform tasks and assume duties that are simply beyond its control.*

After penning a widely read Commentary *essay, "The United States in Opposition," that was especially favored by President Ford and Secretary of State Henry Kissinger, Daniel Patrick Moynihan was appointed the U.S. Ambassador to the United Nations in 1975. He was there when Idi Amin's infamous "Zionism Is Racism" resolution was passed, and responded with a speech that became one of the proudest moments in American diplomatic history. It is reprinted here.*

The Campus Crucible: Student Politics and the University

Nathan Glazer

*I*T IS SCARCELY POSSIBLE to write anything about students and the university crisis now without looking back at what one has written over the past five years—and I began to write on this subject in December, 1964, reviewing the first climax of the Berkeley student crisis.

This has the usual sobering effect on human presumption. It turns out one was about half wrong and half right. Both the areas where one was wrong and the areas where one was right are of some interest.

Where I was right: at the beginning I, and others, argued that the issue at Berkeley (and elsewhere) was not one of free speech. Free speech existed at Berkeley, and we argued that very early in the first crisis two other issues had in effect replaced it. One was, would the university become the protected recruiting and launching ground for radical political activity directed to various ends, among them the overthrow of the basic system of operation of a democratic society? And second, would the student tactics of disruption, mild as they appear now in the perspective of four and a half years of increasing escalation, be applied to the basic concerns of the university itself (teaching and research), as well as to such peripheral matters as the political activities permitted on campus?

Those of us who by December, 1964, had decided the free-speech issue was solved, and was then spurious, considered these two issues the dominant ones; those who opposed us thought we were ridiculously exaggerating the most distant possible dangers to free speech, free research, and free teaching. They emphasized on the contrary the facts (with which we all agreed) that the student rebels themselves strongly resisted any tendency toward totalitarianism or even central control in their own movement; that

Reprinted from the Atlantic Monthly, *July 1969.*

the student leaders had found their political orientation in fighting for the rights of Negroes in the South, and for job opportunities for them in the Bay Area; and that young radical civil libertarians, not Communists, were the center of the radical movement. And they pointed out—and this was a very powerful argument indeed—that the young rebels had brought a refreshing sense of community, one that joined students and faculty as well as student with student, into an institution that had been marked by a far too strong concern simply with professional and academic standards, and which had done almost nothing to feed essential needs for close sharing with others, participation, joint action, and common facing of dangers.

These were certainly serious arguments in those distant days, and I doubt that those who in the end voted *against* a faculty resolution which sanctioned the student revolution felt at all easy with their position. Could one really believe that these attractive young people, many of whom had risked their lives in the South, who had taken up so many causes without concern for their own personal future, themselves carried any possible danger to free speech, free teaching, free research? In the end, both sides consulted their feelings—those who had felt the chill of a conformity flowing from an ostensible commitment to freedom voted one way; those who felt the warmth of a community united in common action voted the other. (This is extravagant, of course; there were many other reasons for going one way or another.)

After these chaotic four and a half years, I have no doubt that on this point my friends and I were right. The Free Speech Movement, which stands at the beginning of the student rebellion in this country, seems now almost to mock its subsequent course. In recent years, the issue has been how to *defend* the speech, and the necessary associated actions, of others. The right of unpopular political figures to speak without disruption on campus; the right of professors to give courses and lectures without disruption that makes it impossible for others to listen or to engage in open discussion; the right of professors to engage in research they have freely chosen; the right of government and the corporations to come onto the campus to give information and to recruit personnel; the right of students to prepare themselves as officers on the campus: all these have been attacked by the young apostles of freedom and their heirs.

The organizations that defend academic freedom, the AAUP and the ACLU, and the others, which have so long pointed their heavy guns toward the outside—for defense against conservative trustees, newspapers, legislators, and vigilante communities—are now with some reluctance swinging them around so they face inward. Anyone who has experienced the concrete situation in American universities knows that the threat to free speech, free teaching, free research, comes from radical white students, from militant black students, and from their faculty defenders. The trustees of the University of California may deny credit to a course in which Eldridge Cleaver is the chief lecturer, but radical students in many places (including campuses of the University of California) have effectively intimidated professors so they cannot give courses they were prepared to give. It is a peculiar sign of the times that the denial of credit seems to many a more monstrous act than the denial of freedom to teach.

Thus, we were right in pointing to the dangers. Where were we wrong? Our gravest mistake was that we did not see what strength and plausibility would soon be attached to the argument that this country was ruled by a cruel and selfish oligarchy devoted to the extension of the power and privileges of the few and denying liberty and even life to the many; and to the further assertion that the university was an integral part of this evil system. It was not possible to predict, in December, 1964, that the spring of 1965 would see an enormous expansion of the American role in Vietnam, and would involve us in a large-scale war that was to be fought by this country with unparalleled, one-sided devastation of an innocent civilian population and its land. We had never been in this position before. Where we were overwhelmingly powerful—as against Spain in 1898—there was no occasion or opportunity or capacity to engage in such horrible destruction; where we were horribly destructive—as in Europe and Japan in 1944 and 1945—it was against powerful opponents who had, in the eyes of most Americans, well merited destruction. There were some excuses even for the atom bombs of Hiroshima and Nagasaki. There were some mitigating circumstances. There were hardly any in Vietnam, unfortunately, except for the arguments, which became less and less impressive over time, that we were after all a democratic society, and had gotten involved in such a war through democratic processes; and the further arguments that our strategy was designed to save a small nation from subversion, and our tactics were intended to save American lives.

The Split Between Liberals and Radicals

We have to examine this moment in American history with the greatest care if we are ever to understand what happened afterward, why Berkeley

1964 did not remain an isolated incident, and why the nascent split that appeared there between liberals and radicals became a chasm which has divided American intellectuals more severely even than the issue of Stalinism and Communism in the thirties and forties. What happened to professors at Berkeley happened to liberals and radicals everywhere. And since intellectuals, including professors, played a far larger role in American society in the sixties than in the thirties and forties, this split became far more important than any possible argument among the intellectuals and their associated professors twenty-five years earlier. (One of the differences between the two periods was that so many intellectuals of the sixties, as against the earlier period, were *in* the universities. Compare the writers, circulation, and influence of *Partisan Review* with that of the *New York Review of Books*.)

It may be argued that no split *really* developed in 1964; that the intellectuals who approved of the United States were ambushed by new events that did not fit into their approach, and by an uprising of suppressed intellectuals who had been silenced by McCarthy, who had harbored for a long time some version of the Marxist view of the United States, and who now—by a series of disasters, mistakes, or demonstrations of the country's basic character and tendencies, take your pick—had been given their chance. This is in large measure true. But we forget how closely those who were to become so divided were linked before 1964.

Some political events of those days now seem so unlikely as to be hallucinatory; thus Paul Jacobs (who was to run in 1968 as a candidate for the Peace and Freedom Party), S. M. Lipset (the liberal sociologist of pluralism, now at Harvard), and Philip Selznick (the Berkeley sociologist who was to become one of the strong defenders of student protest at Berkeley) were linked in defending dissident members of Harry Bridges' union in San Francisco and in attacking what they considered the Communist proclivities of various groups in the Bay Area. Lewis Feuer, who became one of the most forceful critics of student radicalism (in his article in the *Atlantic* and in his book *The Conflict of Generations*), was in 1960 the chairman of a committee to defend the students who had put on a vocal (and, it was charged, a disruptive) demonstration against the House Un-American Activities Committee in San Francisco—this event is considered one of the important precursors of the Berkeley student rebellion. Or, if we want to mount a larger stage, consider who wrote for the *New York*

Review of Books in its trial issues of 1963, and consider how many of them now see each other as political enemies.

Thus, to my mind, if we are to understand the student rebellion, we must go back to 1965 and reconstruct the enormous impact of Vietnam, and we will see that the same lines that began to divide friends on student rebellion reappeared to divide them on Vietnam.

Among all those who were horrified by the beginning of the bombing of the North, and by the increasingly destructive tactics in the South—the heavy bombing, the burning of villages, the defoliation of the country-side—a fissure rapidly developed. It could be seen when, for example, Berkeley radicals sat down in front of trains bringing recruits to the Oak-land induction station. Those of us who opposed such tactics argued they would alienate the moderate potential opponents of the war, whose sup-port was needed to bring a change in policy. We argued that to equate Johnson with Hitler and America with Nazi Germany would make it impossible to develop a wide alliance against the war. But actually, the principled basis of our opposition was more important. We did believe there were profound differences between this country and Nazi Germany, Johnson and Hitler, that we lived in a democracy, and that the authority of a democratic government, despite what it was engaged in in Vietnam, should not be undermined, because only worse would follow: from the right, most likely, but also possibly from a general anarchy. Perhaps we were wrong. The reaction from the right was remarkably moderate. The radical tactics did reach large numbers and played finally a major role in changing American policy in Vietnam. But all the returns are not yet in: conceivably the erosion of the legitimacy of a democratic government is a greater loss than what was gained. Conceivably, too, a movement oriented to gaining wide support—along the lines of early SANE—might have been even more effective.

At Berkeley, the liberal split on Vietnam replicated the liberal split on student rebellion in the university and was paralleled by splits on the question of the summer riots and the whole problem of black violence. Again and again the issues were posed in terms of tactics—yes, we are for university reform of political rules, but we are against sit-ins and the degradation of university authorities; yes, we are against the war in Viet-nam, but we will not attack or undermine the legitimacy of a democratic government; yes, we are for expanded opportunities and increased power and wealth for Negroes, but we are against violence and destruction to get them. But of course the split was not really over tactics.

Behind that there was a more basic disagreement. What kind of society, government, and university did we have?, what was owed to them?, to what extent were they capable of reform and change without resort to civil disobedience, disruption, and violence? The history and analysis of this basic division have scarcely been begun. But there is hardly any question as to which side has won among intellectual youth. We have witnessed in the past four or five years one of the greatest and most rapid intellectual victories in history. In the press addressed to the young (whether that press is elite or mass or agitational) a single view of the society and what is needed to change it is presented. Violence is extolled in the *New York Review of Books*, which began with only literary ambitions; Tom Hayden, who urges his audiences to kill policemen, is treated as a hero by *Esquire*; Eldridge Cleaver merits an adulatory *Playboy* interview; and so it goes, all the way, I imagine, down to *Eye*.

The Power of Radical Thinking

When I say *we* were wrong, I mean that we never dreamed that a radical critique of American society and government could develop such enormous power, to the point where it becomes simply the new convention. Even in the fraternities and sororities, conservative opinion has gone underground; the formerly hip conservatism of the *National Review* is as unfashionable on the campus as the intellectualism of *Commentary*. We were not only wrong in totally underestimating the power of radical thinking to seize large masses again; we were also in the position of William Phillips sputtering to Kenneth Tynan, "I know the answer to that, but I've forgotten it." We had forgotten the answers, it was so long ago. When the questions came up again—imperialism, capitalism, exploitation, alienation—those of us who believed that the Marxist and anarchist critiques of contemporary society were fundamentally wrong could not, it seems, find the answers—at least the ones that worked.

Of course, some of the intellectuals of the forties and fifties had never forgotten the old questions (Paul Goodman, Hannah Arendt), and while they looked with some distance, even from the beginning, at the new recruits to their old concerns, they managed with amazing intellectual success the precarious task of combining basic criticism of a liberal society with basic support of the liberal values of free development, human variety, and protection for the individual. Those who had *really* forgotten nothing, neither the problems nor the answers, such as Herbert Marcuse, have been, of course, even more successful in relating to radical youth.

But were we wrong only in underestimating the appeal of old and outworn political ideologies, or were we wrong in considering them outworn, inadequate explanations of the world? In other words, was the issue really some fundamental bent in American society that added up to military adventurism abroad, lack of concern with the rights or lives of those of other skin color, the overwhelming dominance of mindless bureaucracies in determining economic and political policies, the human meaninglessness of the roles these bureaucracies prescribed for people, and the inability of the society and the state to correct these bents under any pressures short of violence, destruction, and rebellion?

The University as Part of Society

One must begin, I am afraid, with these larger questions in speaking about the university today. One's attitude toward it, the role of students within it, and the danger of its possible destruction, as a collection of physical facilities and as an institution, can scarcely be determined without attention to these larger questions. For the university *is* implicated in the society. It is a rare university that can for any period of time stand aside from a society, following a totally independent and critical course. Universities are almost always to some extent independent (one wonders, though, about Russia, China, and Cuba), but their insatiable demands for resources inevitably impose on them the need to relate themselves to the major concerns and interests of the society.

Yet at the same time a university's work *is* in large measure quite independent of the faults or characteristics of any state or government. There is a realm of scholarship beyond political stands and divisions. The science that is taught in the United States is not very different from the science that is taught in the Soviet Union, or in Cuba, or even in China— though at that point we reach the limits of my generalization. Even the scholarship of the humanities bears a great deal in common. I have often been surprised by the degree to which the work of the universities is common across radically different political frontiers. The passion of the Russians and Chinese, under Communism, for archaeology, for the exact restoration of early buildings and structures, and for early philology is evidence of the scholarly and scientific validity and usefulness of archaeology, linguistic reconstruction, art history.

It is only when one approaches the social sciences that the cross-political scientific validity of research and teaching can successfully be challenged, for we do find enormous variations between social science under one political outlook and another. History is perhaps worst off. Consider how Russians or Americans, and among Americans, established or revisionist historians, interpret our past. Sociology is almost as badly off. Yet some parts of it (for example, the statistical methodology of opinion research) seem to have developed wide acceptance across disparate political and cultural frontiers. Economics seems to share some of the universal acceptance of the natural sciences.

I record these truisms to emphasize that the university is not *simply* the creature of social and political systems, and that scientific and scholarly investigation and teaching have some general value divorced from politics, since totally opposed and distinct social systems accept its importance and give it support and prestige. (China is the one great society to break with this general acceptance, and we don't know whether this is only the aberration of a few years.) But certainly the university is in large measure the creature of distinct social and political systems. The degree to which higher education is considered a right of all; the degree to which its credentials are considered essential for jobs and positions of all kinds; the degree to which its research is affected by state determination and the availability of state support; the degree to which university education is seen as part of a service to the state, and to which it is integrated with other kinds of service, such as military service: all these show considerable variation between states, but most modern states tend to converge in answering these questions, and the convergence is in the form of a closer and more complex relationship between university, society, and state. And if one is impressed by fatal flaws in the society and state, one may not be overly impressed with whatever measure of university function is independent of deep involvement with a given society and a given political system. At that point, one may well see the university as only the soft underbelly of the society.

Anger Against the State

What the liberal critics of student disruption in 1964 did not see was that a storm of violent antipathy to the United States—and indeed to any stable industrial society, which raises other questions—could be aroused in the youth and the intellectuals, and that it could be maintained and strengthened year after year until it became the underpinning of the dominant style, political and cultural, among the youth. The question I find harder to answer is whether we failed to see fundamental defects and faults both in the society and state and the associated universities which had inevitably to lead anyone committed to life and freedom to such a ferocious anger.

Vietnam, of course, could justify anything. And yet the same ferocity can be seen in countries such as Germany, Italy, and Japan, which are really scarcely involved, allies though they are in other respects, in our war in Vietnam, and in a country like France, which actively disapproves of our role. Undoubtedly Vietnam has enormously strengthened the movement of antipathy and anger, and not only because our powerful nation was engaged in the destruction—whatever the reasons for it—of a small and poor one. There were other reasons. Vietnam placed youth in a morally insupportable position. The poor and the black were disproportionately subjected to the draft. The well-favored, as long as they stayed in school, and even out of it, were freed from it. The fortunate middle-class youth, with strong emotional and ideological reasons to oppose violently our war in Vietnam, could escape as long as they stayed in college, just as prisoners could escape as long as they were in jail. They undoubtedly felt guilty because those with whom they wanted to be allied, whom they hoped to help, had to go and fight in Vietnam. In this ridiculous moral position, the university became to many a repulsive prison, and prison riots were almost inevitable—whatever else contributed to them.

And yet, where there was no Vietnam, students could create their own, as in France, or the real Vietnam could serve to make them just as angry at their own, in this case hardly guilty, government.

But the question remains: how do we evaluate the role of Vietnam in directly creating frustrations that led to anger at the university? Did Vietnam serve to teach or remind students, with the assistance of critics of capitalism, that they lived in a corrupt society? Or was it itself the major irritant? How was Vietnam related to the larger society? Was it an appropriate symbol or summary of its major trends or characteristics? Or was it itself an aberration, correctable without "major social change"? The dominant tone of student radicalism was increasingly to take the first position—it reflected the society, and could be used as an issue to mobilize people against it.

Those of us who took the position we did in 1964 have stuck with it, and are stuck with it. We took a position of the defense of institutions that we thought worked well enough, which could be changed, and which in the face of radical attack could and would crumble, to be replaced with something worse. I will not defend this position here—I have done so elsewhere (in "The New Left and Its Limits," *Commentary*, July 1968). I will admit to some discomfort with it. We seem to find it impossible to modify our inhuman tactics in Vietnam (even though I understand we adopt them to save American lives), we seem to find it impossible to reduce the enormous military budget or to make effective steps in reducing the atomic arms race (though I am aware another side is involved too), we seem to find it difficult or impossible to move rapidly in the reform of certain inadequate institutions—for example, the system of punishment, the welfare system, the public schools, the universities, the police— without the spur of the disruption and violence I decry. But the disruption and violence, even if they produce reforms, will in the end, I believe, produce a society that we would find less human than the unreformed society. So I have stuck to this not fully adequate position, for I find it sounder, more adapted to reality, and more congenial than the alternative: the despairing view that we have solved no problems, that selfish and overwhelmingly powerful forces prevent us from solving any, that the society and its institutions respond only to disruption and violence.

Of course, this position has never been one that was uncritical of universities and colleges. Many who defend universities and the institu- tions of a democratic society against the radicals—for example, Daniel Bell and David Riesman—have been among the most forceful critics of colleges and universities. (I myself wrote, a year or two before Berkeley, an article critical of college and university education, and joined the small band of educational reformers when I came to Berkeley in 1963.) But rarely was the main force of these critics linked to a basic criticism of the society. Their criticism was directed at the structure of the university or college; it spoke of the university as an educational institution and faulted it for educational failure. What this criticism did *not* do was to subordinate the educational criticism to a devastating criticism of the *society*, its distribution of power, forms of socialization, its role in the world.

University Reform

Early in the American student revolt it seemed reasonable that educational issues were at the heart of the matter. People spoke of the size of Berkeley, the anonymity of the student, the dominance of education by the disciplines, and the graduate departments and their needs. But there was a key difference between the critics of higher education and the student radicals: to the critics educational reform was, if not of major or exclusive concern, a matter of some significance in itself, worth taking seriously on its own terms; to the student radicals, it was immediately subordinated to the larger social criticism—educational reform was valuable if it meant the universities could be moved toward becoming a training ground for revolutionaries, or if it meant that revolutionaries would achieve greater power within it, or if it meant that the university could be used so as to produce "radicalizing confrontations" with "reactionary" forces.

THE EIGHT STUDENT DEMANDS

. . . We have been having tremendous student riots. They began at Petrovski Academy, where the authorities banned the admission of young ladies into student quarters, suspecting these latter not only of prostitution but also of political activity. From the academy it spread to the university, where, surrounded by Hectors and Achilleses heavily armed and mounted, and equipped with lances, the students are making the following demands:

1. Complete autonomy of the universities.
2. Complete freedom of teaching.
3. Free access to the university without distinction of creed, nationality, sex, or social background.
4. Admission of Jews to the university without restriction and equal rights for them with the other students.
5. Freedom of assemblage and recognition of student associations.
6. Establishment of a university and student tribunal.
7. Abolition of the police function of the inspectors.
8. Lowering of fees for courses.

This I have copied from a manifesto, with some abridgments. I think most of the fuss had been kicked up by the bunch of [. . .] and the sex that craves admission to the university, although it is five times worse prepared than the male. The latter is miserably enough prepared as it is, and its university career is, with rare exceptions, inglorious.

—Anton Chekhov to Alexei Suvorin—1890
From *The Selected Letters of Anton Chekhov,*
edited by Lillian Hellman

In other words, university reform was a tactic. I make the distinction too sharply, of course, because to many of the student radicals, university reform was not a tactic; it was a goal of value in itself. Among the student radicals were, and are, to be found many serious students and critics of university education, with strong commitment to change and experiment. And yet again and again the *tactical* use of educational change became dominant.

Thus, consider the case of the course in which Eldridge Cleaver was to lecture at Berkeley, a course organized under the liberalized procedures that permitted students to initiate courses of interest to them. The Regents moved, against this course, that lecturers not members of the regular faculty could give only one guest lecture a quarter in a given course. If the students wanted to hear Eldridge Cleaver give his planned nine lectures, they would have to take the course without credit.

This led to the occupation of the building housing the offices of the College of Letters and Science and the philosophy department by unreconciled radicals (including the ubiquitous Tom Hayden, who can add to his honors his presence in Moses Hall at Berkeley as well as in the mathematics building at Columbia), and to considerable damage. The "revolutionary" slogan, the demands for which the radicals fought, were summed up on a button, "For credit, on campus, as planned!" It would be hard to argue that the radical students were moved by the opportunity to hear Eldridge Cleaver on campus, an opportunity that was available to them every day, if Cleaver had enough time or energy, and it seems quite clear that this educational innovation was now becoming a tactic, a counter in the revolutionary struggle that would (hopefully) activate the students to strike, to occupy buildings, and to disrupt the university.

If we go across the country, we can find a similar development in the enormously successful course that radical students conduct under the auspices of the social relations department of Harvard University, for credit. Some members of the department preferred to move the course elsewhere, into social sciences. The faculty member under whose formal authority the course was given denounced this as an effort to destroy the course, and he and those conducting sections in the course organized to fight the move, insisting it was political, and issued threats as to what would happen if the social relations department tried to disengage itself from this albatross. Thus, it was suggested, other social relations courses would be disrupted in protest.

Everything can be explained, if we are so inclined, as the effort of students devoted to education to save an experimental and rewarding course from destruction, and this certainly was part of the motivation. Reading the statements, I cannot escape the cynical conclusion that the course was being used as a club to threaten a "conservative" department, and the threat was being used to organize and radicalize students. There is enough to suggest that this objective loomed far larger in the minds of the organizers of the course than any concern with education as such.

Of course the organizers would argue, as student radicals argue everywhere, that there is no difference between radicalization and education. Everything else is "miseducation." To understand properly the nature of social relations, or power relations, of the structure of the society, the political system, and the economy is to become radical, and become imbued with the passion to destroy the status quo. Thus, they argue, any so-called "objective" or "scientific" education is really a fraud—if it's not educating people to overthrow the status quo, then it must be educating people to support it, for even inaction (when one could be active against) is a form of support. Thus, the outraged defenders of Social Relations 149 argued that all the other courses were conservative (clearly, for they weren't formally "radical"), and therefore their own radical course was a necessary and valuable effort to redress the balance.

The argument is not new. It is in effect the argument that was fought out in Russia over the question of whether all education and all science must reflect "dialectical materialism," and whether any scholarship that did not was by that fact alone "counterrevolutionary" and "bourgeois." Or the battle that was fought out in Nazi Germany over "Aryan" science and "non-Aryan" (and therefore "Jewish" science). It is understandable why we sputter, "I know the answers, but I've forgotten them." For these positions became so outrageous and untenable in the eyes of Western intellectuals that to have to defend again the possibility and reality of objective science and scholarship means to call into play parts of our minds that have long lain quiescent and unused. But called into play they must be, because the possibility of pursuing and disseminating knowledge freely is now quite seriously threatened.

The Attacks on Freedom

We have to learn the answers to the arguments that are now used to defend attacks on freedom—they are widely used, and in the present cultural atmosphere are repeated in the same form on a hundred campuses. Thus, if ROTC is prevented from operating, and the argument is that students should be free to take it if they wish, the answer is, "But the South Vietnamese are not allowed their freedom—why should students be allowed the freedom to join ROTC and the armed forces, which deny the South Vietnamese their freedom?" If a faculty member is not allowed to give the course he has scheduled, and faculty members criticize the black students who have prevented him from teaching, the answer is, "But this has been a racist institution for a long time, and 'academic freedom' is only a ploy to defend racism and the status quo." If some students engage in violence against others, the argument is, "But the violence of the police at Chicago is far greater, and what about the silent violence of starvation in the South, not to mention the violence of ghetto merchants who over-charge, and of social investigators who ask degrading questions?" We must remember what we have forgotten—for example, the old joke about the man who is being shown the wonderful new Moscow subway, and after a while asks, "But where are the trains?" The Russian answers, "But what about lynching in the South?" It's no joke any longer.

In other words, when I think of the student rebellion today, and of the disasters threatening and in some measure already actual on the campuses today—the massed battles between students and police, the destruction of card catalogues and lecture halls (and the threat to major research libraries), the destruction of computer tapes and research notes, the arming of many black students and the terrorization in many cases of other black and white students—I do not think initially in terms of the major reforms that are required on the university campus, but I think of the politics, and even the tactics, that would defend the university. For I have made some commitments: that an orderly democracy is better than government by the expressive and violent outbursts of the most committed; that the university embodies values that transcend the given characteristics of a society or the specific disasters of an administration; that the faults of our society, grave as they are, do not require—indeed, would in no way be advanced by—the destruction of those fragile institutions which have been developed over centuries to transmit and expand knowledge. These are strongly held commitments, so strongly that my first reaction to student disruption—and it is not only an emotional one—is to consider how the disrupters can be isolated and weakened, how their influence, which is now enormous among students, can be reduced, how dissension among them can be encouraged, and how they can be finally removed from a community they wish to destroy.

I know the faults of the universities as well as any of its critics do, and have worked and continue to work to correct them. But I take this position because I do not believe the character of the university as an institution—its teaching, its research, its government—is really the fundamental issue raised by student radicalism on the campus, or that changes in the government and education and research of the university, important as they are on many grounds, will do much to mitigate or deflect the radical onslaught. Again and again we have seen *political* uprisings on the campus—*political* acts based on a certain interpretation of American society to which one can either adhere or not, as one wishes, in the university—and in response to these political acts, we have seen an effort to shape a response in the *educational* or *administrative* area. This, I suggest, is a completely inappropriate and ineffective response.

Thus, if students attack Columbia for its ties to IDA and its building of a gymnasium in a park adjacent to Harlem, we end up by "restructuring" Columbia, with endless committees, with elected student representatives, with student participation being argued over in every setting, and all the rest—the university turned into committees and tribunals. Now, the fact is that the cause of the uprising was not dissatisfaction with the government of Columbia. The cause was the ceaseless search of the Students for a Democratic Society to find means of attacking the basic character and mode of operation of a society and government they wished to transform, "by any means possible," to use the prevailing rhetoric. IDA and the gymnasium we have been told by SDS activists—and we must take this seriously—were *tactical*.

The cause of the uprising at Columbia was not the system of government, for *any* system of government for that university might in the fifties and sixties have involved ties with IDA and might have undertaken the building of a gymnasium in the park. (Who, after all, objected to these things when they were begun?) And indeed, even Columbia's system of government, archaic as it was, was quite capable of responding to changed attitudes, and was engaged in the process of cutting the ties to IDA, before the student uprising. As to the gymnasium, the fact was that aside from the protests of defenders of New York parkland, and design (I am among them), who objected violently to the gymnasium, there was little other protest. Even the Harlem community was either indifferent to or actually supported the project.

With IDA and the gymnasium alone, as we all now know, the SDS at Columbia would have gotten nowhere. But then there comes the illegal seizure, the successful confrontation, the battle with the police, and *new* issues arise. The radicals are now joined by the liberals. The latter are concerned with due process, with government, with participation, with education. The liberals are much less concerned with the revolutionary change in the society that the radicals insist is necessary. The liberals demand amnesty for the protesters, due process before punishment, a new role for students and faculty, a change in "governance."

The script was played out before Columbia, at Berkeley in 1964 and 1966; and it is now being played out at Harvard. In 1966 at Berkeley, radical students blocked military recruiters. Police were called onto the campus to eject and arrest them. What was the faculty's response? To set up a commission on governance.

Making New Radicals

The logic of these events is truly wonderful. The blocking of recruiters on campus has nothing to do with the governance of an educational institution. Whether it was run by the state, the trustees, the faculty, the students, or the janitors, any university might consider it reasonable to give space for recruiters to talk to students, and if these were blocked, any administration might well decide at some point to call police. But then the liberal students and faculty move into action. First, shocked at the calling of police, they demand that new governance arrangements be created. Then, because they dislike the tactics chosen to remove the disrupters, they demand amnesty for them. Finally, because they have been forced into a tactical alliance with the disrupters—after all, the liberals are defending them against the administration—they begin to find the original positions of the disrupters, with which the liberals had very possibly originally disagreed, more attractive.

We are all aware that calling in the police radicalizes the students and faculty (so aware that many students and faculty protesting President Pusey's action at Harvard said, "Why did he do it, he knows it radicalizes us"—they spoke as if they knew that, according to the scenario, they were *supposed* to be outraged, and they were). We are less aware that the radicalization extends not only to the police issue and the governance issue but to the content of the original demands. A demand to which one can remain indifferent or opposed suddenly gains enormously, greater moral authority after one has been hit on the head by the police for it. Thus, the first mass meeting of the moderate student element after the police bust, in Memorial Church, refused to take a position on ROTC and asked only for a student referendum, and referenda, as we know, generally turn out in favor of retaining ROTC in some form on campus. It is for this as well as for other reasons that SDS denounces votes and majority rule as "counter-revolutionary." But the second meeting of the moderate students, in the Soldiers Field Stadium a few days later, adopted a far more stringent position, hardly different from SDS's. And a few days after that, the distinguished faculty, which had devoted such lengthy attention to ROTC only a short time before, returned to discuss it again, and also took a more severe position.

The recourse to violence by the radical students at Harvard was therefore successful. The issue of ROTC, which was apparently closed, was reopened. The issue of university expansion, which excited few people, became a major one. The issue of black studies, which everyone had thought had been settled for a time, and decently, with the acceptance of the Rosovsky report, was reopened by the black students. It might have been anyway, but certainly the SDS action encouraged the reopening.

The SDS takes the position that these are no victories—by the nature of their analysis of the structure of society, government, and university in this country, there can be no victories, short of the final, indefinable "basic social change." Thus, the fact that the university faculty and corporation have now adopted a resolution which will remove the ROTC from campus entirely (even the rental of facilities, according to the mover of the new faculty resolution, would be improper) demonstrates, according to SDS, that the university has not given an inch. Why? Because the resolution says the university will facilitate student efforts to take ROTC as an outside activity, off campus, presumably in the way it facilitates student efforts to find jobs or nearby churches. "Abolish ROTC," the SDS ROTC slogan, it now appears, means that not only must students not be allowed to take ROTC on campus; the university must not give them the address where they might take it off campus. One can be sure that if this "facilitating" clause were not in the resolution, the SDS would find other means of claiming that the university is intransigent—by definition, the power structure must be—and that there has been no victory.

On university expansion, the corporation and the various schools of the university have come up with the most detailed account to demonstrate that the direct impact of the university on housing has been minor and moderated. The indirect impact is hardly controllable—psychoanalysts want to live in Cambridge, millionaires' children want to live in Cambridge (and some of those after all contribute to radicals' causes), students want to live there, and faculty members want to live there. Any reasonable attempt to moderate the situation—as, for example, Harvard's effort to build low-cost or moderate-cost housing—is denounced by the radicals. Could there be any more convincing demonstration that the demands are tactical, not designed to improve the housing situation (if it were, it might prevent the anger that hopefully leads to the revolution), but to serve as a rallying slogan whereby liberals can be turned into radicals?

The issue of the black demands is a different matter; these are raised by the black students and are not tactical. They are deeply felt, if often misguided. Thus, the key demand of formal student equality in recruiting faculty goes against one of the basic and most deeply held principles of the university—that the faculty consists of a body of scholars who recruit themselves without outside interference, whether from government, trustees, or students. For the purpose of maintaining a body of scholars, students *are* an "outside" force—they are *not* part of the body of scholars. But if the black demands are not raised tactically by the black students, they are adopted tactically by the white radicals—as they were at Harvard, with the indescribably simple phrase, "accept all Afro demands."

Once again, this is the kind of slogan that is guaranteed to create the broadest measure of disruption, disorder, and radicalization. Just as in the case of "abolish ROTC" or "no expansion," "accept all Afro demands" has a wonderful accordion-like character, so that no matter what the university does in response, the SDS can insist that nothing really has been accomplished, the ruling class and the corporation still stand supreme, and the work of building toward the revolution must continue.

There is only one result of a radical action that means success for the radicals—making new radicals. In this sense, the Harvard action has been an enormous success. Those who know something of the history of Marxism and Leninism will be surprised to see this rather esoteric definition of success for true radical movements now emerging full-blown in the midst of the SDS, which began so proudly only a few years ago by breaking with all previous ideology and dogma. "Build the cadres" was the old slogan: "build, the cadres," because any *reform* will only make the peasants and workers happier or more content with their lot, and will thus delay the final and inevitable revolution.

The aim of action, therefore, is never its ostensible end—the slogan is only a tactic—but further radicalization, "building the cadres," now "the movement." The terrible effect of such an approach is to introduce corruption into the heart of the movement, and into the hearts of those who work for it, because the "insiders" know that the *ostensible* slogans are only tactical, that one can demand anything no matter how nonsensical, self-contradictory, and destructive, because the aim is not the fulfillment of demands, but the creation of new radicals who result from the process that follows the putting forward of such demands: violence by the revolutionaries, counterviolence by the authorities, radicalization therefore of the bystanders, and the further "building of the movement."

What justifies this process, of course, is the irredeemable corruption of the society and all its institutions, and therefore the legitimacy of any means to bring it all down.

The Failure of the Liberals

Liberals like to make the distinction between themselves and radicals by saying to radicals, "We approve of your aims but disapprove of your means." This in effect is what the liberal student body and faculty of Harvard did. It disagreed with the occupation of University Hall, the physical ejection of the deans, the breaking into the files. But it said, in effect, by its actions, we think the issues you raised are legitimate ones. Thus, we will revise our carefully thought out position on ROTC, and we will change our position on black studies.

On university expansion, the faculty acted just as a faculty should; it accepted the proposals of a committee that had been set up some time before, a committee on the university and the city, chaired by Professor James Q. Wilson. It followed its agenda and its procedures rather than the agenda set for it by the radicals. It received neither more nor less abuse for this action than for its efforts to accommodate radical demands on ROTC. I think the proper liberal response was: "We disagree totally with your means, which we find abhorrent, we disagree totally with your ends, which are the destruction of any free and civil society; some of the slogans you have raised to advance your ends nevertheless point to real faults which should be corrected by this institution, which has shown by its past actions on various issues that it is capable of rational change without the assistance of violence from those who wish to destroy it, and we will consider them."

Oddly enough, the discussion of the ostensible aims, even though the liberal position was that the aims *were* valid, was terribly muted. The liberals were hampered in their discussion first by lack of knowledge of the issues (how many had gone into the intricacies of relocation and the provision of housing for the poor?), and second by the feeling that some of these issues were not really the business of the faculty. In the case of ROTC, the key issue, the faculty tried to find an "educational" component to justify the action that might assuage the passions of student radicals. Thus, the argument on ROTC was carefully separated from any position on the Vietnam War, and a resolution was passed ostensibly for educational purposes, simply because it had been determined that ROTC did not have any place in a university.

This was nonsense. The educational reasons for action against ROTC were settled when it was determined the courses should not get academic credit and the ROTC instructors should not get faculty standing. Why was it necessary to go on and specify that no facilities should be provided? Space is given or rented for all sorts of noneducational purposes on the campus—religious, athletic, social, and so on. What had happened was that under the guise of responding as an educational body to political demands, the faculty had accepted a good part of the political demands, and implicitly a good part of the political analysis, that led to them. It would have been more honest to denounce the Vietnam War than to remove ROTC. After all, what role has ROTC played in getting us into that quagmire? It was civilians, such as Presidents Kennedy and Johnson, who did that.

By denying to students the right previously established to take military training on the campus, the faculty was in effect taking the position that all the works of the United States government, and in particular its military branches, are abhorrent, which is exactly the position that SDS wishes to establish. It wishes to alienate students from their society and government to the point that they do not consider how it can be reformed, how it can be changed, how it can be prevented from making mistakes and doing evil, but only how people can be made to hate it.

This may appear an extravagant view of the action of the Harvard College faculty, and yet the fact is that there was little faculty debate on the demands. The liberals implicitly took the stand, "We agree with your aims, we disagree only with your tactics," and in taking this stand were themselves then required to figure out how by their procedures they could reach those aims without violence.

But the aims themselves were really never discussed. The "Abolish ROTC" slogan was never analyzed by the faculty. It was only acted upon. All the interesting things wrapped up in that slogan were left unexplored: the rejection of majority rule (explicit in SDS's rejection of the legitimacy of a referendum on ROTC); the implication that American foreign policy is made by the military; the assumption that the American military is engaged in only vile actions; the hope that by denying the government access to the campus it can be turned into a pariah—and once we manage to turn someone by our actions into a pariah, we can be sure the proper emotions will follow.

The expansion demand was never really discussed, or at any rate insufficiently discussed. It never became clear how different elements contributed to the housing shortage and to the rise of rents in Cambridge. It was never pointed out that the popular demand for rent control would inevitably mean under-the-table operations in which the wealthier Harvard students and faculty could continue to outbid the aged and the workers. The issues of the inevitable conflicts over alternative land uses, and the means whereby they could be justly and rationally resolved, were never taken up.

The faculty did most to argue against the new demand for equal student participation in the committee developing the program of Afro-American studies and recruiting faculty. Even there, one can hardly be impressed with the scale and detail of the faculty discussion, though individual statements, such as Henry Rosovsky's speech, were impressive and persuasive. The key questions of the nature of a university, the role of students within it, the inevitable limits that must be set on democracy and participation if an institution designed to achieve the best, in scholarship and in teaching, is to carry out its functions—all these played hardly any role in the discussion. The students were not educated. To their eyes, reasonable and sensible demands were imposed by force on a reluctant faculty. They were right about the force. This was hardly a manly posture for the faculty—at least they should have argued.

There was thus to my mind a serious educational failure at Harvard. All the education, after the occupation and the police bust, was carried on by the radicals. They spoke to the issues they had raised; others did not, or countered them poorly. They established that these issues were important, and thus in the minds of many students their tactics were justified. By student, faculty, and corporation response, their view that the university reacts only to violent tactics was given credence. If this was a failure, of course the chief blame must rest on the faculty. It is their function to educate the students, and the corporation follows their lead and their analysis, when they give one.

There were of course administration failures, too, in not consulting sufficiently widely with students and faculty, and perhaps in calling the police. But these did not justify the faculty in its failure to analyze and argue with the radical demands, and in giving up positions it had just adopted.

I agree with the SDS that the issues should have been discussed—ROTC, campus expansion, black demands. But more than that should have been discussed. The reasons SDS had raised the issues should have been discussed. The basic analysis they present of society and government should have been discussed. The consequences of their analysis and the actions they take to achieve their demands should have been discussed. They should have been engaged in debate. They were not. Instead, they were given an open field and all possible facilities for spreading their view of the world, a view that to my mind is deficient in logic, based on ignorance and passion, contradictory, committed to unattainable aims, and one in which a free university could not possibly operate.

The university now suffers from the consequences of an untempered and irrational attack on American society, government, and university, one to which we as academics have contributed, and on which we have failed to give much light. The students who sat in, threw out the deans, and fought with the police have, after all, been taught by American academics such as C. Wright Mills, Herbert Marcuse, Noam Chomsky, and many, many others. All these explained how the world operated, and we failed to answer effectively. Or we had forgotten the answers. We have to start remembering and start answering.

A Letter to the Young
(and to their parents)

Midge Decter

MY DEAR CHILDREN:

I salute you this way despite the fact that as the world has always reckoned these things you are no longer entitled to be called children. Most of you are in your twenties by now, some perhaps even in your thirties. Some of you have children of your own. Yet you are still our children, not only in terms of the technical definition of a generation, but because we are still so far from having closed our parental accounts with you. We are still so far, that is, from having completed that rite of passage after which, having imparted to you the ways of our tribe, we feel free to invite you to join the company of its fully accredited adults.

I am a member of what must be called America's professional, or enlightened, liberal middle class. Though you were once taken to represent the whole of your age group, it is no longer a secret that perhaps the most celebrated youth in history—you, variously known as "our young people," "the kids," or simply "the young"—are none other than the offspring, both literally and figuratively, of this class. Not all of us, to be sure, are professionals. Some of us are businessmen or the employees of businessmen, some the employees of government, and some ladies and gentlemen of leisure. Yet it is as certain that we are members of a common group—social critics have taken to calling us, usefully if not precisely, the "new class"—as it is that you are our children. You, indeed, and our common property in you, are the primary means by which we make known our connection to one another. You all recognize this, of course, at least unconsciously (unconsciously is the only way most Americans permit themselves to know

Reprinted from The Atlantic Monthly, *February 1975.*

what they truly know about class). Thus you would have little reason to take in any way but perfectly for granted my preoccupation with you here.

This preoccupation, indeed, is a nearly universal one among the members of my class. Two women, barely acquainted, meet over a luncheon table. "How is your son X or your daughter Y?" one of them, in an ordinary effort at polite conversation, asks the other. With the reply, My son is in San Francisco, or perhaps, My son is in Arizona, or My daughter has left school, or has returned to school, or has returned home and is thinking about what she might do—with whatever reply might be forthcoming, the two women will suddenly have come upon a common ground of empathy and interest. They may share nothing else, but between them now—with regard to what was once the most intimate, but has become the most readily available, of subjects—there has collected a whole unspoken but highly meaningful set of references. One of these women is telling the other what the other might, with only a minor adjustment of details, in turn be telling her: the children, having had every advantage pressed upon them, having suffered no hardship, beloved, encouraged, supported, sympathized with, heaped with largesse both of the pocketbook and of the spirit, the children yet cannot find themselves. The children are not, for some reason—may God please tell them what it is—in good shape.

A group of husbands and wives, old friends, spend an evening together. They have no need to ask one another the kind of polite questions asked by the women at lunch. On the contrary, they attempt to shut out the subject of children, for they have come together for a bit of fun. And in any case, they already know the answers. So-and-so's boy, he who once made his parents the envy of all the rest, handsome, healthy, gifted, well-mannered, winner of a scholarship to Harvard, languishes now in a hospital where the therapists feel that in another few months he might attempt a few simple tasks, and ultimately—for the prognosis is good—even hold down a job, provided it is not of the sort to make him feel too challenged or tense. Another of the sons of this group has lately sent a postcard to his sister announcing that he has taken up photography, and that as soon as he gets some work he plans to buy himself a piece of land and build himself a house on it. Yet another—his parents should be grateful by comparison with some others they know, and are frequently troubled with the realization that they do not feel so—is in business; he has organized some friends into a firm of handymen and movers and, to his astonishment and theirs, the firm is prospering. So-and-so's elder daughter is living, unmarried, with a divorced man and looking after his two adolescent children, while the younger has just set off in pursuit of her third—or is it her fourth?—postgraduate degree. Someone else's daughter, who lives at home, has taken and lost or abandoned five jobs within two years, and now finds that she wishes to work only part time so that she might paint. Still another, married and the mother of two small children, has discovered a marriage encounter group. She and her husband, she says, wish to broaden the range of their relationship, and they believe that everyone, including their parents, ought to do the same. One couple in this group has a son in Sweden, where he exiled himself to avoid the draft. He writes to them weekly, demanding that they find some way to secure him an unconditional amnesty, for he wishes to return home; under no circumstances, he underscores, will he agree to submit himself to a term of compensatory public service. His younger brother has decided to give up farming in Vermont and enter law school. His parents, people of rather modest circumstances, are delighted to "lend" him the fifteen thousand dollars that will enable him to devote himself to his studies and at the same time provide for his wife and young baby; they have mailed him the proceeds of the re-mortgage on their house, and vacillate wildly between relief and the irrepressible gnawing fear that he may not, even yet, remain content. The sister of these two, a schoolteacher, participant in a long series of painfully inconclusive love affairs, has taken to spending all her free time on various projects for raising her consciousness to a full perception of the injustices that have been wreaked upon her. She has grown surly, neglects her appearance, and is in an odd new way touchy and difficult to get along with.

As you know better than anyone, these are not extraordinary cases, these women at lunch, these couples gathered for an evening's recreation, unable *not* to talk about their children. Such conversations are taking place in the homes and communities in which you have grown up, and they are taking place concerning you, or at least concerning a good many of the people you know.

Fundamentally, the question your parents have not dared address in so many words, either to themselves or to their friends—and yet cannot any longer keep hidden behind some false front of approving good cheer or resigned hopes for the future—is the question that must surely, at two o'clock in the morning, be growing upon some of you as well. It is, Why have you, the children, found it so hard to take your rightful place in the world? Just that. Why have your parents' hopes for you come to seem so impossible of attainment?

Some of their expectations were, to be sure, exalted. As children of this peculiar, enlightened class, you were expected one day to be manning a more than proportional share of the positions of power and prestige in this society; you would be its executives, its professionals, its artists and intellectuals, among its business and political leaders; you would think its influential thoughts, tend its major institutions, and reap its highest rewards.

But not all our expectations were of this nature. Beneath these throbbing ambitions were all the ordinary—if you will, mundane—hopes that all parents harbor for their children: that you would grow up, come into your own, and with all due happiness and high spirit, carry forward the normal human business of mating, home-building, and reproducing—replacing us, in other words, in the eternal human cycle. And it is here that we find ourselves to be most uneasy, both for you and about you.

Of course, you would see, or would claim to see, in this concern of ours for you, merely another confirmation of the leading attitude of the youth culture: that we are incapable of seeing you as you are. It has, after all, been a major assertion of the songs you sing, the books you read and write, the films you devour, that we are too bound up by our timid, sickly assumptions about life to open ourselves to the range of the new human possibility that you have engendered. And for a long time, we ourselves tried to believe in your explanation for our feelings. We permitted ourselves to be soothed and distracted by the idea that we were in the presence of a revolution, that you were not, as you might have seemed, displaying an incapacity to get on with your lives in an orderly fashion, but rather that you were creating a new kind of order, alien to and superseding our own.

This consoling deception about you came from many sources. Your professors, for instance, told you—they also told themselves and the rest of us—that you were the brightest, most gifted generation they or the world had ever seen. We should have been delighted. Why, then, were we not? For we were not—not you, not we, and least of all those who made the claim. You were surely bright and gifted—that was plain to see—but you seemed so infernally content to remain exactly as you were, so passive and resisting in the face of all the exciting possibility that the world around you ought to have represented to you. You were bright and gifted, but you were also taking yourselves out of school in numbers and under circumstances that first bewildered and then alarmed us.

The answer, we were told, was that you were too good to suffer all the uninspired, dreary, conventional impositions being made upon your minds and spirits. Your professors said that your indictment of your studies, and particularly of the institutions in which you were pursuing them, was a just one. It was your very wisdom, they proclaimed, which had brought you to make the indictment in the first place. Moreover, they hurried to abet you, those of you who managed to remain in school, in your demand to be taught only that which would reflect and deepen your own sense of yourselves.

Yet still you did not prosper—nor did we, nor did they. For as it happens, your indictment of your studies was *not* a just one. Nor could it have accounted for the malaise that you as students were suffering from. In any case, what your admiring professors did not tell you was that your attitude toward the university was helping to reflect and deepen *their* sense of themselves. In your challenge to the value of their work they found the echo of some profound bad conscience, some need to be disburdened of an unfulfilled responsibility to you. Thus the comfort of their self-abasing tolerance was cold comfort indeed. And what in the end—one may well ask—did it avail you?

Or take another case, in some ways a more important and interesting one: that of all the journalists and critics and commentators who spent the better part of a decade discussing you. They told you, they told themselves, they told the rest of us, that you were the most idealistic generation they or the world had ever seen. Everything about you, everything you did, was ascribed to an unprecedented new accession of idealistic zeal. You were the "constituency of conscience"; no longer willing, like your corrupt and self-serving elders, to countenance injustice. Some of these critics and commentators said you were actually a new breed of people, the result of a strange and wonderful new stage in social evolution. You had come, they told us, to lead our society out of evil—the evil of a rampant, heedless materialism that was threatening to infect the whole world with a frenzied quest for ever and ever greater wealth, up to the point of extinguishing life itself. You had come also, it was said, to bring to an end the mindless violence, lust, and greed that had sickened Western society through the long centuries of its ascent into technological splendor and spiritual squalor.

But if you were out to remake the world, you seemed on the other hand to be unsuited for its most rudimentary forms of challenge. Your philosophy of existence called for a level of private demand coupled with a regimen of self-scrutiny and self-expression such as, when acted upon, threatened fairly to blot out the very materiality of others; and you were taking yourselves off into rural, or urban—or simply psychic—wildernesses where you sometimes literally could not even be found, let alone followed. And above all, you seemed to find it difficult, if not impossible, to touch the world at just those tangents where its real work was being done and its real decisions being made.

It was your very superiority, said the critics and commentators, your very refusal to tolerate the cruelty and inhumanity of the acquisitive life which had brought you to turn your backs on it. What the pundits did not tell you was that their passionate advocacy of your attitudes was the material with which they themselves were attempting to forge a powerful and well-paid position in the world. Your hanging back from the contest, in other words, had become the stuff of their own determined effort to win it. No wonder they beatified you; and no wonder your anxiety persisted.

Finally, there was our deception, your parents' deception, of you, the most kindly meant but cruelest deception of all. We told you, we told ourselves, and we told one another that the so-called new style of life you were inventing for yourselves was some kind of great adventure in freedom. However we responded to it, whether with approval, anger, or anguished tears, we consented to call your expression of attitude toward us and toward the world we were offering you by the name of rebellion. You were indeed speaking in the language of rebellion, and making certain of its gestures. But if you were, as you liked to put it, busily intent on "doing your own thing," you were also continuing to allow us to pay your bills. No matter how high or far you flew, you and we together had seen to it that our parental net would be stretching beneath you—a financial net, a physical, and above all an emotional one. The truth is that your freedom, your rebellion, even your new "lifestyles," were based on a fiction, the kind of fiction that gets constructed between people who are, for their own separate reasons, engaged in denying the facts. We wrung our hands in the fictional pose of those abandoned, and continued to write out our checks and proffer the abundance of our homes and hands, no questions asked.

Were you dropping out of school or otherwise refusing the blandishments of prosperity, security, and privilege? That was because you were attempting to fulfill a need, quite murderously neglected by us and our society, to return to the sources of natural being. Did you appear, from our point of view at first quite mysteriously, to be turning your backs on the kind of striving for excellence in all things for which you had been so unstintingly and expensively brought up? That was because you were engaged in transcending the mean competitiveness to which everyone in America had mindlessly been made hostage, and were moving on to a new plane of gentleness and fraternal feeling. Did you seem to be getting dangerously attached to the use of drugs? That was because you were seeking to intensify the quality of experience; because—unlike us, hypocritically engaged in our own use of alcohol and drugs to still the mind and deaden the emotion—you were daring to recover the passional and sensory world so long denied to Western man. Did your initiation into sex seem to us curiously uneventful and haphazard, without moment or weight? That was because you were freeing yourselves from our own crippling obsessions with sex, and restoring the process to its proper, inconsequent, exuberant animal function.

Such were the things we told one another, and tried to tell ourselves, about you for a long time. They were popular things to say; to speak otherwise branded us not only as enemies of the young but as enemies of all things virtuous in the liberal culture, of which the youth revolution had become a cornerstone. They were also self-flattering things to say, putting us, as they did, squarely on your side, and as such, on the side of all things new, daring, and open to the future. Above all, however, these ideas about you protected us, if only temporarily, from the sense of failure that had come to stalk us by day and by night.

Well, some of us may continue to say them to one another—though fewer every day—but none of us any longer says them to himself. And you? Some of you are still prone to go on as before, declaiming your superiority to the meannesses and the hypocrisies of the achieving society and your sensitive refusal to have a hand in its crushing of the human spirit (although those of you who speak this way are doing so less noisily than you once did). But what are you truly, in the privacy of genuine self-confrontation, saying to yourselves?

You are adults now—or should be—no longer in process of formation or unfolding, no longer *in potentia*, but fully here. Thus there are things to be observed about your generation on which the count is already in, things that can no longer be denied by us, that are the real and hard ground from which you must now proceed.

The first thing to be observed about you is that taken all together, you are more than usually incapable of facing, tolerating, or withstanding difficulty of any kind. From the time of your earliest childhood, you have stood in a relation to the world that can only be characterized as a refusal to be tested. This refusal was announced, sometimes literally, sometimes cloaked in the assertions of a higher creativity, in your schools. It shaped your attitude to play, to sports, to sex, to the reading of difficult books and the clarification of difficult ideas, to the assumption of serious roles within your families and communities, and to the consideration of possibilities for your future. It lent enormous impact to your experience of drugs, whose greatest seduction for you lay in their power to create the sensation of well-being with little or no effort on your part. Later, when you were either in or out of college, this refusal took on all the convenient coloration of ideology. The idea that the system was evil, and engaged in an evil war, provided cover for a number of your far deeper impulses to retreat from, or to circumvent, the demand that you take on distasteful tasks—whether to endure a bit of necessary boredom, or to serve in the army, or to overcome the anxieties of normal ambition. The word most frequently on your lips, in the days when you were said to be mounting your relentless campaign against evil, was "hassle." To be "hassled" meant to be subjected to difficulty of, from your point of view, an incomprehensible as well as intolerable sort. And everything, you assured us over and over again, everything we had either to offer or to impose upon you was a "hassle."

In the city where I live, which is New York, there are certain interesting ways in which a number of you have latterly taken to making your living: you are pushcart vendors, taxi drivers, keepers of small neighborhood shops that deal in such commodities as dirty comic books and handmade candles; you are house painters, housecleaners, and movers of furniture. Let us leave aside the larger social significance of this—in American history, at least, unprecedented—voluntary downward mobility. In purely personal terms, all these unexpected occupations of yours have one large feature in common: they are the work of private, and largely unregulated, entrepreneurs—full of their own kind of woe, you have no doubt learned, but free of all that patient overcoming and hard-won new attainment that attend the conquest of a professional career. And they are free, most of all, from any judgments that would be meaningful to *you* as judgments of success or failure. Customers may irritate, and unpaid bills oppress, you as they do any private entrepreneurs; but there hangs over you no shadow of the requirement that you measure, ever so minutely and carefully, the distance of your progression from yesterday to today. In the pushcart—many-layered symbol!—is bodied forth the notion that you might, if sufficiently displeased, simply move on to some new stand.

The second thing to be observed about you is that you are, again taken as a whole, more than usually self-regarding. No one who has dealt with you, neither parent, nor teacher, nor political leader, nor even one of the countless panderers to or profiteers from your cyclonically shifting appetites, can have failed to notice the serenity—the sublime, unconscious, unblinking assurance—with which you accept their attentions to you. A thinker or a book with ideas to impart that you do not already understand and agree with is immediately dubbed "boring" or "irrelevant," and must immediately forfeit all claims upon you. For some reason, it seems never to occur to you that a failure to comprehend, to appreciate, to grasp a subtlety not already present in your own considerations, might be a failure of your own. (In this respect, you very closely resemble that Middle American philistine known to my generation as Babbitt, superiority to whom has been a prime tenet of your, as well as our, self-definition.) What is more important, no member of the so-called adult community appears to have been deemed by you too imposing, too intimidating, or merely too plain busy to be the recipient of those endless discourses upon yourselves by which you make known certain delicate daily calibrations of the state of your feeling. The thought that some attitude or experience of your own might be less formed, less distilled in the twin refineries of time and intellection, less valid, than those of your elders, even those of your elders whom you have elected to call master, seems never to have crossed your minds.

Thus the entire world of thought and art comes to you filtered through a single supreme category of judgment: has it succeeded or has it failed, by your own lights, to move you? To use your own parlance for this category of judgment, does it or does it not "turn you on"? Anyone or anything that leaves you unsatisfied in the way of private, self-generating response is remanded to obscurity. On the other hand, anyone or anything that touches or confirms what you already think and feel, no matter how lacking in any other virtue, is automatically important. Do you find yourselves peculiarly touched, say, by the songs of Bob Dylan? Well, then, he is among the great poets of the ages. Do you have a taste for movies in which the sound track has assumed equal significance with the images? Well, then, the true art form of the age has been discovered. Are you disinclined to do certain kinds of work? Well, then, the very nature and organization of society is due for a complete overhaul. In short, you, and only you, are the ultimate measure of all that you survey.

And the third thing to be observed about you—it is really in some sense a concomitant of the first two—is that you are more than usually dependent, more than usually lacking in the capacity to stand your ground without reference, whether positive or negative, to your parents. So many of your special claims on this society are claims not on the distribution of its power but on the extension of its tolerance; what you so frequently seem to demand is not that the established community make way for you but that it approve of you. Take the case of your conduct with respect to sex. You have, you say, created a revolution in sexual behavior, particularly adolescent sexual behavior. But this revolution is not something you have done, it is something you have requested your parents and schools and other parental authorities to do for you. It is in the apartments that we have rented for you, in the dormitories that we have sexually integrated for you, and in the climate of toleration that we have surrounded you with that you have pursued, in all passive supplication, your alleged revolution.

Or, to state the case in the obverse, take the fashions in dress and personal habit that were so recently rife among you. Being children of the aspiring middle and upper-middle classes, you had been raised by your parents with the expectation that you would be well dressed; therefore you dressed yourselves in rags. (Indeed, a little noted feature of your sartorial fashion is how often it has been a kind of half-grown version of the games of "dress-up" played by little children in their mommies' and daddies' cast-off finery.) You were raised with the expectation that you would be clean and healthy, after the privileged condition of the class into which you were born; therefore you cultivated the gaudiest show of slovenliness and the most unmistakable signs of sickliness. You were raised on the premise that you would be prompt and energetic, and reasonably prudent, and mindful of your manners; therefore you compounded a group style based on nothing so much as a certain weary, breathless vagueness and incompetence—enriched by the display of a deep, albeit soft-spoken, disrespect for the sensibilities and concerns of others. That the key to this entire assertion of style lay in an exact reverse translation of what your parents had taken for granted on your behalf is only one mark of how necessary we were in all your efforts to define yourselves.

Another mark of how necessary we were to your self-definition—only apparently a contradictory one—is that, withal, you were never so adamant, never so energetic, never so articulate as in your demands that we lend our assent to it. Not for nothing did you call the collective products of your search for group style and group meaning by the name of "the counter-culture." For it was a search that utterly depended on, and was positively defined by, that which it opposed. We had little cause to doubt that sooner or later many of you, having had one sort of fling or another out there in the wide world, would return home to us, either from time to time for a brief sojourn or for what in some cases seems to have become a permanent stay. Where but at home were you to find the true nourishment for your illusory sense of adventure? In overcoming us, it seems, has lain your major, perhaps your only, possibility for tasting the joys of triumph.

In any case, whatever you are lately in a mood to say to yourselves, it is such thoughts about you that inform and focus our own new mood as parents. Yet surely, if a whole generation of our grown children have been left with such a great deal to undo in themselves before they can take on what we all know, deep down, to be the essential requirements of membership in the adult tribe—surely, in such a case, no one's shortcomings and failures are better reflected than our own. If you have a low tolerance for difficulty, that is because we were afflicted with a kind of cosmic hubris, which led us to imagine that we were bringing up children as all our ancestors on earth before us had not had the wisdom or the purity of heart to do.

In the life we promised ourselves to give you, there would be no pain we had not the power to assuage, no heartache we had not come upon the correct means to deal with, and no challenges that could not be met voluntarily and full of joy. There can have been no more arrant disrespec-ters of the past, of the sorrows of the past and its accumulated wisdoms, than we members of the enlightened liberal community. And in nothing can our assurance of being superior to our own parents—wiser, kinder, healthier of mind and outlook, cleverer, more perceptive, and in better control of the dark side of our natures—have played a more crucial role than in the theories and practices which we brought to the task of parenthood. So we imagined, and taught you to believe, that pain and heartache and fear were to be banished from your lives.

If you are self-regarding, this is because we refused to stand for ourselves, for both the propriety and the hard-earned value of our own sense of life. Our contentions with you were based on appeal, not on authority. Believing you to be a new phenomenon among mankind—children raised exclusively on a principle of love, love unvaryingly acted out on our side and freely and voluntarily offered on yours—we enthroned you as such. We found our role more attractive this way, more suited to our self-image of enlightenment, and—though we would have died on the rack before confessing it—far easier to play. In other words, we refused to assume, partly on ideological grounds, but partly also, I think, on aesthetic grounds, one of the central obligations of parenthood: to make ourselves the final authority on good and bad, right and wrong, and to take the consequences of what might turn out to be a lifelong battle. It might sound a paradoxical thing to say—for never has a generation of children occupied more sheer hours of parental time—but the truth is that we neglected you. We allowed you a charade of trivial freedoms in order to avoid making those impositions on you that are in the end both the training ground and the proving ground for true independence. We pronounced you strong when you were still weak in order to avoid the struggles with you that would have fed your true strength. We proclaimed you sound when you were foolish in order to avoid taking part in the long, slow, slogging effort that is the only route to genuine maturity of mind and feeling.

Have you been, perhaps, the most indulged generation in history? Yes, but in many ways you have also been the most abandoned, by the very people who endlessly professed how much they cared.

Government and the People

Aaron Wildavsky

W E SHALL NEVER LEARN what needs to be learned about the American political system until we understand not only what the system does to the people, but what the people do to the system. Political institutions are no different from other organizations: to the great question of organizational life—who will bear the costs of change?—the answer, in the public as in the private sphere, is, "someone else, not me." The universal tendency to make life easy for ourselves and to impose difficulties on others applies equally to politicians, and when they find their lives intolerable no one should be surprised that they react by seeking to lay their burdens on the shoulders of others.

Especially during the past decade, almost our whole attention as citizens has been devoted to the ways in which politicians have failed to serve the people. Few have asked how politicians manage to live in the world, because it is assumed that they are doing fine and that the problem is to make them behave decently toward us—almost as if politicians lived somehow apart from American life. Yet it would be strange indeed if our politicians were a special breed, uninfluenced by their milieu, springing full-born like Minerva from the head of Jove in a world they never made, but on which they work their mythical powers.

Politicians are like other animals; indeed their behavior, like our own, can often be analogized to that observed in lower forms of life. Laboratory experiments show that rats who are consistently given contradictory commands become neurotic, if not psychotic. The same phenomenon is readily visible among politicians. Give them incompatible commands, insist that they fulfill contradictory impulses at the same time, and they too will show the classical symptoms—withdrawal, self-mutilation, random activ-

Reprinted from Commentary *(August 1973).*

ity, and other forms of bizarre behavior unrelated to the ostensible task at hand. An occasional deviant is even known to lash out at his experimenters, or at least at the apparatus in which he is enmeshed, though he remains quite incapable of understanding why he worked so hard to accomplish so little, or why life is so bitter when it should be so sweet.

We are all, in fact, doing better and feeling worse.* Every standard of well-being, from housing to health, shows that every sector of the population, however defined, including all racial, religious, and ethnic groupings, has improved its lot in past decades. Even the twin problems of crime and drugs, areas in which we are vividly conscious of recent deterioration, have been considerably reduced in severity, so far as we are able to judge, since the turn of the century. When heroin was legal there were proportionately more addicts in the population; when the nation was younger and poorer there were more criminals, or at least a correspondingly greater degree of crime. Why, then, do so many feel so bad—and why do they continue to feel so bad when, of the two causes reflexively invoked to explain this feeling, the first, the Vietnam War, has come to an end while the second, racial inequity, has clearly and visibly diminished? I cannot pursue this subject in all its ramifications here. Instead I wish to add another element to the puzzle—the manufacture of incompatible policy demands that impose burdens on government which no government can meet.

The fact that the public demands on government in the various areas of policy are contradictory, in the sense that pursuing one policy inevitably means prohibiting the enactment of another, does not mean that an evil genius has been at work programming the political system for a nervous breakdown. Coordination need not require a coordinator; it can be tacit and informal as well as overt. Men coordinate their activities through adherence to a common body of assumptions or through the sharing of a common world view. Quite the same kinds of contradictions can be created by various people in different places making vocal demands that turn out to be mutually opposed. The lack of central direction, in fact, is an advantage because it adds to the general confusion: politicians are given a hard time but they do not know on whom to vent their own frustration. For our

---

* See my essays, "The Empty-head Blues: Black Rebellion and White Reaction," *Public Interest*, No. 11, Spring 1968; "The Revolt Against the Masses," in *The Revolt Against the Masses and Other Essays on Politics and Public Policy* (Basic Books, 1971); "The Search for the Oppressed," *Freedom at Issue*, No. 16, November-December 1972.

purposes it is not necessary to know whether demands on government are made by those who wish to see it fail, and therefore delight in giving it tasks it cannot manage, or who wish to see it succeed, and take pleasure in asking it to perform feats hitherto unaccomplished. Whether it stems from those who love government too little or from those who love it too much, the results of this pressure are the same: government is asked to perform wonders, but the attainment of one wonder often automatically precludes the possibility of attaining another, or many others.

The incompatibility of policy demands is a manifestation of a more general withdrawal of sovereignty from government in America. The rights of government and of politicians are being systematically whittled down. Public officials and professional politicians can no longer organize their political parties as they please, or hold meetings in closed sessions, or keep their papers secret, or successfully sue others for slandering them—even when they can show the allegations to be false—or make the smallest decisions without being hauled into court to convince judge and attorney they have followed standards of due process, considered every conceivable alternative, consulted all who might possibly be injured, or otherwise abandoned virtually every sense of what it used to mean to rule by enforcing binding regulations. We demand more of government but we trust it less. Angered and annoyed by evident failures, our reaction is not to reduce our expectations of what government can accomplish but to decrease its ability to meet them. That is how a society becomes ungovernable.

The legislation proposed by Lyndon Johnson and enacted during the first eighteen months of his Presidency wiped out the New Deal and destroyed both the historical coalition and the universe of common assumptions on the basis of which American citizens and political activists alike had long understood what was happening in the national life. By enacting every piece of social legislation it could lay its hands on, Congress obliterated all the old issues; where once a citizen knew on which side of a given question he stood, now all was confusion.

The passage of the Great Society legislation, in addition, had a devastating effect on many sectors of the federal bureaucracy. The second worst thing that can happen to anybody is to strive for a lifetime and fail to get what he wants. The first worst thing is to strive and to get and to discover that it is not good. Think of people who spent, say, twenty years in the Department of Health, Education and Welfare and its predecessors, trying desperately to secure huge federal appropriations for education. In the mid-1960s they got them; they still have them, but they have discovered that the ground has shifted and that the clientele whose interests they thought they were serving is not the clientele the new policies are aimed at. So they fail and they are bewildered.

In the past, the clients of the New Deal had been the temporarily depressed but relatively stable lower and middle classes, people who were on the whole willing and able to work but who had been restrained by the economic situation; if a hand were extended to them or if the economic picture brightened, things improved for them right away. It hardly mattered one way or the other what government did or did not do in their behalf. Now, however, government policy was being designed to deal not with such people but with the *severely* deprived, those who actually needed not merely an opportunity but continuing, long-term assistance. No previous government had ever attempted to do for this sector of the population—those whom Marx had called the lumpenproletariat—what the American government set out to do. Yet nobody knew *how* to go about it, either. In the field of education, for example, no one had the faintest clue as to what amount of "input" would produce the desired result, and so vast amounts of money and even vaster amounts of enthusiasm were poured into various programs that ultimately ended in failure and bewilderment (as it turns out, we have learned that variations in expenditures of almost four to one make absolutely no difference—or only slight difference—in student performance, and that other variables, known and unknown, must be taken into account).

Far from giving up in the face of such complex ignorance, the tendency instead was to place the emphasis on those variables that did seem controllable. This led to the concept of community action. If no solutions were available and no one had the foggiest notion of how to do anything, it *was* possible to increase the demand for solutions, to create pressure from below that would effect the release of ever increasing amounts of federal money. But the fact that government was trying to deal with a different clientele and that no one knew how to do it meant that an awful lot of money was invested without accomplishing very much. The escalation of demands together with the lack of knowledge of solutions meant a multiplication of programs, each under- or over-financed, each justified by the notion that it was somehow an experiment that would prove something.

There is perhaps nothing new in all this, but the political consequences have not been seen as clearly as they might be. Welfare today has become a political albatross. In the past, those who paid for welfare may not have liked it while those who received it, if they did not love it, at least found it preferable to the alternative. Government got credit from those who received the money and demerits from those who had to pay. Since the poor were more numerous than the wealthy, a political trade-off was effected and things seemed to work out. Today the taxpayers curse and the welfare recipients tell government where to get off. The welfare system gets credit nowhere.

People who are involved in revolutions are usually the last to recognize what has been happening all around them. While the War on Poverty was being waged, those fighting the battles understandably lacked the time, energy, or discernment to see anything like the full implications of their actions. Like good soldiers everywhere, they went from skirmish to skirmish, leaving the grand strategy to generals who, as every classic account of warfare tells us, understood less than anyone else. First, as noted, the generals radiated a sense of hope: wonderful things could be done. On this basis many new programs were launched and even more were proposed, to capitalize on the new potential for eliminating poverty. Second, also as noted, they generated a sense of despair: hardly anything seemed to be working. Out of this was born a new determination to overcome obstacles—in the form of new programs. Third, whether one had hoped or despaired, it became almost a reflex action to call on government to justify the hope or overcome the despair. One consistent trend in this concatenation was the proliferation of demands on government from all quarters. Another trend, seldom noticed, was the incompatibility of the demands.

This particular characteristic of the public-policy debate of the 1960s is still very much with us, and it can be seen at work in areas as diverse as welfare and election reform. Thus the same people who demand that government increase the levels of support and the numbers of people on welfare are just as likely to assert in the next breath that welfare is a total failure, that it costs too much, and that it should be scrapped. Similarly, the demand that the political parties be "democratized" and made more representative is often linked to the demand that the costs of elections be reduced so that the rich will not control the democratic process. As Nelson Polsby has pointed out, it is impossible to do both: democratization in practice means more primaries, more conventions, more meetings—in other words, increased costs.

Or consider employment. There have basically been two objectives in this area of policy: employ the hard-core and create jobs at reasonable costs. It is very expensive to train the hard-core; that is why they are hard-core. It is also very discouraging, because many will not get jobs and many others will not keep them. But in addition, if a government agency has actually been able to show that it created a number of jobs that people filled and stayed in for a while at some kind of reasonable cost (by reasonable cost I mean that it has cost less than it would have just to give them the money), it has then been criticized for dealing with people who were too employable. This is known as "creaming," getting jobs for the best of the worst, so that anyone who has actually found a job was, ipso facto, as Groucho Marx might have said, not the right kind of person to have tried to employ in the first place.

Consider housing, where the demand has been to give preference to the worst-off and provide a better environment. That has led to such monstrosities as the Pruitt Igoe project in St. Louis, finally dynamited in order to reduce the incidence of social evil. Or consider the environment. It is tempting to condemn both pollution and high prices, but there is an intimate connection between the two. Today we expect our government to provide pure air and use less energy: it cannot do both at the same time.

How about community action? We demand widespread participation and we want fast action on the problems of the poor. Participation, however, requires built-in delays; the more committees, the more levels, the more people, the more time lost. It may not really be time wasted if greater participation results, but few remember the original impetus when frustration sets in.

The mischiefs unwittingly created by placing the phrase "maximum feasible participation" in legislation have been amply documented so far as government agencies are concerned. The documentation, however, is incomplete. Efforts to implement the spirit of the phrase have also wreaked havoc with the minority communities themselves. The idea was to facilitate the emergence of indigenous leadership, but, as Judith May has persuasively demonstrated,* the paradoxical result has been to delegitimate

---

* Judith V. May, *The Struggle for Authority: Four Poverty Programs in Oakland* (doctoral dissertation in progress, University of California, Berkeley).

virtually everyone in black communities who could claim to be a leader because there is always some criterion he does not meet. If poor, he may not live exactly in the right neighborhood. If professional, he may not be poor enough. And so forth. Thus the only people who fit the prescription are those who are poor and are in no danger of getting rich, who have lived in the neighborhood for a long time and who cannot get out, and who often care so little they seldom attend meetings of the numerous poverty programs. Such people, it has turned out, have precisely the characteristics—lack of motivation, lack of experience, lack of ability—that do not commend them to their neighbors.

The essential perversity of the policy milieu is its ability to frustrate nearly everyone at the same time. Few programs, for instance, are more noble in intent than those calling for the provision of extra resources and services to the educationally deprived. Since there is not enough money to go around to all who might be considered poor, amendments have been passed at the federal and state level requiring that the most severely deprived be given substantial additional increments so that the massing of resources will have some palpable effect on them. It is difficult to argue with this sensible point of view, but the political impact on the near-poor, who are too well off to receive aid but poor enough to need it, has been severe. They are more easily helped because they have a bit more with which to begin. As they observe extra resources going to the very poor, who are most in need but least likely to be helped, they cannot help but wonder why they, who need less help but can use it more, are being left out. Their dissatisfaction with government is bound to rise as they watch the competition to gather up the funds for which they cannot qualify. And so is government dissatisfaction with itself bound to rise, for officials are asked to aid the least able and to sacrifice the more able.

The political ramifications are potentially disastrous: rising discontent on the part of both those who pay the costs and those who get the benefits. The have-littles are plunged into conflict with the have-nots (the working and lower-middle classes with the poor) because compensatory mechanisms fail to help the one, and do not stretch far enough to reach the other. Observing dissatisfaction on the part of those receiving extra resources, the people who pay are likely to call it ingratitude. Part of the secret of winning, as any football coach knows, lies in arranging an appropriate schedule. Governmental performance depends not only on the ability to solve problems but on selecting problems government knows how to solve.

What are the consequences of constructing and defining issues so as to pose incompatible demands on decision-makers? Both the kinds of policies that we get from government and the kinds of attention paid to the various realms of policy are affected. Within the executive branch a greater emphasis will naturally come to be placed on foreign than on domestic policy because the foreign realm seems less forbidding to Presidents and even given a random occurrence of events it seems likely that some good can be achieved—for which, moreover, credit may accrue to the President. In domestic policy, on the other hand, Presidents have come to see little for which they will be applauded, and much for which they will be condemned for even attempting.

When a government does not expect that anything it does will garner credit it tends to push for form over substance. This comes out in the various "funny money" policies we have become accustomed to recently. An official thinks he has money for model housing—but is that not the money he should have spent three years ago and did not? Is it the money that was allocated for something else; that he thought he had but never received; that he once spent but was returned? Or is there actually a dollar or two of real money? It becomes increasingly difficult to know.

There are also substantive consequences of having incompatible demands made on government. One is a growing stress by analysts on an incomes policy as opposed to a services policy for the poor. Why should government continue to administer a welfare system that everyone hates when one of the few things that can really be done well in Washington is programming a computer to write checks? If guarded with exceptional closeness such a machine will actually write the checks it is supposed to write and people will actually receive them. In this way government does away with the middle men, the agitators for welfare rights. It may spend more money, but it will reduce the size of the bureaucracy and may actually make it possible for people to realize that the help they are getting has come from the government. Another policy consequence is revenue sharing, a bone thrown to cities and towns with a warning attached that if the bone should taste bad or if indigestion should ensue they have no one to blame but themselves. Cities are now beginning to understand that they are getting a little money and a lot of trouble. Increasingly *they* become the center of demand and lack the capacity to respond.

Making incompatible demands on government is bound to have an impact on the federal system. When there is no way to garner credit, when everything attempted is clearly slated to fail, an effort will be made by government to rid itself of the source of anxiety—namely, its responsibility for policy. Any time the federal government can trade trouble for money, it will. Miniature revenue-sharing proposals in the fields of health and welfare are now being seriously considered. The consequences, of course, need not all be bad: people with demands to make will find it more worthwhile to approach the cities and states because these will have more to give. But in a federal system in which each level deliberately seeks to pass its worst problems on to the next, in which blaming the other party has become a national pastime, it will become harder than it is already to know who is responsible for not solving our latest set of insoluble problems.

Fairly construed, the government's record on social policy during the last decade has been one of vigorous effort and some noteworthy if nevertheless defective accomplishments. Food stamps do feed the hungry (as well as the hippies), and public housing is better than its alternatives. Steps have been taken in numerous areas to meet the needs of those who had previously been neglected. The men who have contended with these confusing times deserve compassion rather than contempt, and even a measure of applause. Yet it is only now, when programs are threatened with reductions, that a chorus of concern arises—and this, from quarters that had previously denounced the nation's social programs as too little, too late, misguided, or even positively harmful. It is in any event certain that these programs will die unless those who benefit from them (or who identify with the beneficiaries) come forward with vocal support. The critics of social policy have overplayed their hand; they wanted more and better, instead they are getting less and worse. The Nixon administration eventually came to the conclusion that since no visible credit was forthcoming from the presumptively natural supporters of social programs, it might as well gain whatever benefits it could from the conservatives who opposed them. Like any other institution that wishes to remain solvent, governmental bodies must reestablish their credit when their policies begin to earn a deficit of political support.

"Government," Alfred Marshall wrote, "is the most precious of human possessions; and no care can be too great to be spent on enabling it to do its work in the best way: a chief condition to that end is that it should not be set to work for which it is not specially qualified, under the conditions of time and place." Once government is given not just one or two things it cannot do, but a whole host, the effects will be felt throughout the political system. Voters, for instance, have begun to lose their sense of identification with the major political parties, because they, like the government, cannot deliver on their promises. The nature of political campaigns has also changed. In 1972, instead of defending their record, the leaders of government concentrated on the alleged horrors about to be perpetrated by the opposition—or that had been perpetrated by their own party's past. "Elect me," promised Richard Nixon in effect, "and I will save you from that fellow who created a $33 billion deficit. Elect me, and I will protect you from my Justice Department's former position on busing. Elect me, and I will save you from quotas imposed by my Department of Health, Education and Welfare." The President was running against himself, monopolizing the advantages of incumbency while at the same time pretending he had never been in office. No doubt future challengers will learn the wisdom of being vague, lest their promises, rather than the government's performance, become the focal point of the campaign.

If parties cannot make good on the promises of their candidates for office, what can they make good on? Party structure, for one thing; they can promise to organize themselves in a given way, if only because this is something over which they can exercise control. Thus parties, like politicians, move more strongly into the realm of the expressive and the symbolic rather than of substantive policy. The Democratic party can arrange itself in order to contain certain proportions of this or that ethnic group or gender. It can conduct endless meetings, primaries, conventions, all the while gradually shifting the definition of a party from an instrument seeking to govern the nation to an instrument seeking to govern itself. What parties contribute to the nation, then, is not so much candidates attached to a policy as procedures that meet certain visible but internal norms.

Politicians, too, are shifting emphasis from substantive policy to personal political style. They talk of basic changes in the political process, but move into action only when this consists of a form of opposition. They offer adherence to proclaimed moral principle, where they cannot fail, instead of offering innovation in policy, where they cannot succeed. They are often "against" what is happening but see themselves under no obligation to suggest viable alternatives. A sign of the political times is the growing proportion of Presidential candidates who come from the United States Senate, for that is the office which combines the longest term and the highest national visibility with the least responsibility. When people are angry they may picket mayors and shout down governors, but they rarely advance on the Senate or its occupants. The Senate is the place where a man can say his piece while others worry about the responsibilities of office.

Not only the Senate but the House as well, Congress as a whole, is involved in the dilemma of acting responsibly at a time when substantive achievements are hard to come by. The quandary in which Congressmen find themselves is illustrated in the controversy over impoundment. It is all too easy to blame the conflict entirely on the President; he had ample discretionary powers under the Anti-Deficiency Act of 1951, but he chose instead to throw down the gauntlet by saying that he might refuse to spend money in appropriations bills even after they were passed over his veto. That bit of arrogance deserves what it got. But underneath the surface clash of personalities lies a deepseated unwillingness in Congress to accept responsibility for raising the revenues required to support its own spending desires. It is easier to vote for this or that while laying the burden of reduced expenditures, or of finding new revenues, at the door of the President. The growing practice of Presidential impoundment may be part of a tacit agreement that Congress will get credit for voting the funds while the President takes Congress off the hook by refusing to spend. By allowing impoundment to go on for as long as it did and to cover so extensive a range of policies, Congress demonstrated its apparent willingness to see spending cut if only the blame could be placed elsewhere.

Of all our institutions, the Presidency has been the one most deeply affected by government's inability to get credit for domestic policy, because it is the single most visible source of authority and hence the most obvious target of demands. Even the Watergate affair, about which it is plausible to argue that the mentality that produced it is of a singular kind attributable only to President Nixon and his close associates, may be seen to have connections with the fate of the Presidency as an institution in recent years. This is hardly to deny, much less to excuse, the element of personal pathology, or criminality, involved, but even so extreme a series of events as those surrounding the Watergate affair may be clarified by reference to the general issue of the impact of public policy on the Presidency in the past decade.

The climate of opinion that made Watergate and its cover-up possible is part of (and will contribute further to) the delegitimation of government that I alluded to earlier. Although it is convenient now to forget this, from the middle 1960s onward, national leaders of government have been subject to a crescendo of attack and even personal abuse. They have been shouted down, mobbed, and vilified in public. It was not possible for men like President Lyndon Johnson and Vice President Hubert Humphrey to speak where they wished in safety, or to travel where they wished without fear. Not merely their conduct as individuals, but the political system of which they were a part, has been condemned as vicious, immoral, and depraved. This, after all, was the justification offered for the stealing of government documents—that the government from which they were taken had no right to be doing what it was doing, that it was not legitimate. The rationale offered by Daniel Ellsberg for taking and publishing government documents was the same as that offered by the Watergate conspirators—national interest, a higher law than that applying to ordinary citizens.

Watergate emerged, in my opinion, out of an environment in which people who identified with government sought to delegitimate the opposition just as they believed the opposition had sought to delegitimate government. Presumably no one, in their view, had a right to beat President Nixon in 1972, so they sought to get Senator Muskie out of the race.* They broke into Watergate ostensibly to find evidence that the Democrats were being financed by Cuban (Communist) money, as if to say that their own illegality was permissible because the Democrats were not then a legitimate American political party. The blame, to be sure, is not the same. Ellsberg was not entrusted with the care of government, and the Watergate conspirators were. But they cohere in the same syndrome; the one is a reaction to the other, each party rationalizing its exceptional behavior on the grounds of its enemy's illegitimacy.

Watergate is a curious scandal by American standards, in that it is not concerned with money; nor is it, like a British scandal, concerned with sex. By contrast, it resembles a French scandal, one in which small groups of

---

* I pass over the intriguing question of what lesson the Democratic party might learn when its worst enemies conspire to nominate the candidate it was bent on selecting itself.

conspirators make and execute their clandestine plans in the service of ideologies held by no more than 1 or 2 percent of the population. Watergate may thus represent another step in the "Frenchification" of American political life begun in the mid-1960s, a mode of politics in which apparently inexplicable behavior is found to derive from attachment to ideologies of which the vast bulk of the citizenry knows little and cares less. We may have to accustom ourselves to men on the Left out to save us from Fascism and men on the Right from Communism, men who point to one another's activities as justification for illegal acts.

The French analogy gains strength in light of the entire pattern of President Nixon's conduct before Watergate. Seemingly disparate occurrences fall into place once we understand that Nixon had adopted a plebiscitary view of the Presidency, a view that has echoes in the American past but none in the contemporary Western world except in the Presidency of Charles de Gaulle and his successor in France. From this perspective the position of Nixon's Attorney General on executive privilege, with its suggestion that the Presidency exists wholly apart from other institutions, becomes more explicable. So does Nixon's march on the media. For if the Presidency is not part of a separation of powers with Congress, but of a unity of power with the people, then its survival is critically dependent on direct access to them. His victory at the polls in 1972 seems to have inspired in him the conviction that as the embodiment of the national will he should brook no opposition from Congress. If he said "no" on spending and the legislature said "yes," so much the worse for *it*. Even the Republican party could not share in his triumph—it neither ran his campaign nor got any of its leaders appointed to high positions—lest it become another unwanted intermediary between the President and the people; Vice President Agnew and the Republican National Committee owe their spotless reputations on Watergate (apart from their undoubted integrity) to having been kept out of (or away from) the Presidential branch of government. It was his plebiscitary view of the Presidency that led Nixon to attempt to run a foreign and defense policy without the Senate, a budget policy without the House, and a domestic-security policy without the courts.†

---

† Nixon did not have these views when he came into office. It was his experience in office that led him to such desperate expedients. No doubt each man comes bringing his own desperation with him. But Nixon was already President. To go so far after four years in office he must have been more frustrated than anyone knew.

I have momentarily digressed on the subject of Watergate only to suggest that there was more than personal idiosyncrasy at work here, and that there is reason to look upon Nixon's Presidency as the continuation and exemplification of a number of long-term trends in the political system as a whole. In like fashion, the organization of the executive office under Nixon continues an ever-growing trend toward bureaucratization, a reaction in turn to the perceived failure of the Presidential office to influence public policy in ways that will redound to its credit. And just as President Kennedy's and President Johnson's associates sought to lay the blame for bad public policy on the regular bureaucracy, so Nixon's men were following precedent when they sought to debureaucratize the bureaucracy while themselves becoming more bureaucratic. For bureaucratization is a way of seeking shelter from a stormy world.

The Presidential office has, as everybody can now see, become a bureaucracy in the same sense that Max Weber meant by the term: it has grown greatly in size and it is characterized by specialization, division of labor, chain of command, and hierarchy. At the same time it criticizes, castigates, and blames the regular federal bureaucracy and attempts to circumvent it and intervene directly in the political process at lower and lower levels. From the perhaps three secretaries that Franklin Roosevelt inherited, the executive bureaucracy has risen to several thousand. There are (or recently were) two specialized organizations for dealing with the media, one to handle daily press relations and the other concerned with various promotional ventures. There is a specialized bureaucracy for dealing with foreign policy, begun when John F. Kennedy appointed McGeorge Bundy to the White House; Henry Kissinger's shop now boasts a staff of about one hundred. There is a domestic council to deal with policy at home, started by Richard Nixon. And there is also the Congressional liaison machinery instituted by President Eisenhower. Since 1965 the growth of the executive office of the President has been geometric. The largest increases of all occurred in Nixon's first term, but he was merely accelerating a trend, not initiating it.

Because President Nixon, especially at the start of his second term, apparently set out to alienate every national elite—the press, Congress, the Republican National Committee—the fact that he had long been attacking his own federal bureaucracy has escaped notice. Such incidents abound, however. At ceremonies establishing the special Action Office for Drug

Abuse Control, for example: "the President told an audience of 150 legislators and officials that 'heads would roll' if 'petty bureaucrats' obstruct the
efforts of the office's director, Dr. Jerome H. Jaffe. . . . The President said that
above all the law he just signed put into the hands of Dr. Jaffe full authority to
'knock heads together' and prevent 'empire building' by any one of the many
agencies concerned" (*New York Times*, March 22, 1972). President Nixon
also "informed a group of Western editors in Portland that he had told Secretary Morton 'we should take a look at the whole bureaucracy with regard to
the handling of Indian affairs and shake it up good.' The President blamed
the bureaucracy for Indian problems, saying that 'the bureaucracy feeds on
itself, defends itself, and fights for the status quo. And does very little, in my
opinion, for progress in the field' " (*New York Times*, September 29, 1971).

Here too, Nixon was not so much initiating as continuing a trend.
Much the same hostility to the bureaucracy had been manifested by his
immediate predecessors. Accounts of staff men under Johnson and Kennedy frequently reveal a sense of indignation, if not outrage, at the very
idea of the separation of powers; federalism is an anathema to agents of the
executive branch. Who are all those people out there thwarting us? they
ask all but explicitly. Who do they think they are in the Congress and the
state capitals? Strongest of all is the condemnation of the bureaucracy. The
White House staff has great ideas, marvelous impulses, beautiful feelings,
and these are suppressed, oppressed, crushed by the bureaucratic mind.

Why is it that the President on the one hand seeks to bureaucratize his
own office, while on the other hand he holds the bureaucracy to blame for all
his ills? In the end we return to our beginnings. Presidents have been impelled
to attempt stabilization of their own office and destabilization of the regular
bureaucracy because of radical changes in public policy demands. The structure of domestic political issues is now such that no government, and hence
no President, can get the credit for what is done. Like all the other actors in
this drama the President and his men head for cover in the White House
stockade and shoot at others more vulnerable than themselves.

It would appear amazing, in retrospect, that we thought about the
Presidency as if it were uncaused, as if the things that affected and afflicted us
as citizens had no impact on the men who occupy public office. How long did
we expect attacks on the man and the institution to go on before there was a
response? Nixon's counterattack, it now appears, may have threatened our
liberties. Did the growing popularity of the idea that illegality was permissible for a good cause have no impact on the men surrounding the President?

Did this political peril have nothing to do with the demands we make on our Presidents but only with their designs on us? John F. Kennedy struggled mightily with a sense of failure before he was assassinated. Lyndon B. Johnson was forced to deny himself the chance for reelection. Now Richard Nixon fights for a chance to serve out his term. One or two more experiences like these and someone may think it is more than coincidence.

It might be argued that my portrait of the Presidential office in particular, and of politicians in general, treats public officials as if they were the innocent victims of social pressures rather than active participants in the political process capable of shaping it to their own ends. Politicians, moreover, have faced conflicting demands in the past, and might reasonably be expected to face them successfully in the future. Problems arising from incompatible goals are what leaders are there to help solve. A purpose of leadership, after all, is to clarify what can and cannot be done, to set priorities, and to gain some agreement on a schedule of accomplishment. Is this too much to ask of a politician who wants to make a career out of leadership?

It is not. My thesis, however, is that the problems being allocated to government are not just a random sample of those ordinarily associated with governing, some of which, at least, are eminently soluble, given hard work and good judgment, but that government is increasingly getting a skewed distribution of problems that are insoluble precisely because people demand of government what government cannot do. What remains to be explained is how politicians have become strapped to this particular wheel and why they are so maladroit in getting off it.

Politicians are Americans and they, too, are caught up in American optimism. Just as the Vietnam War was a symptom of the optimistic belief in the boundless possibilities of American intervention abroad, so, too, the War on Poverty was a symptom of an optimistic belief in the boundless possibilities of government intervention at home. By the time public officials began to realize they could not do everything all at once, or even some things at all, they had become committed to a broad new range of social programs. And they did not call a halt to these indecisive engagements because they were liberals, that is, Americans.

America lacks an intellectually respectable conservative tradition. It has always, as Louis Hartz has sought to show, had a liberal tradition. For present purposes this means that equality, no matter how abused or disused, has always been the prevailing American norm; the long tradition of hypocrisy on the issue is itself eloquent testimony to its power. The new social and political programs, whether designed for increased participation in decision-making or a greater share in the good things of life, came into the world bearing the banner of the liberal concept of equality. It was hard to oppose, or even think clearly about opposing, these programs without appearing to be against equality or in favor of inequality. Individual politicians might have doubts, a few deviants might voice them, but there was too much guilt engendered by the rhetoric of equality to make collective action possible.

After the deed comes the rationalization. John Rawls's distinguished book on equality, *A Theory of Justice*, though long in the making, appears now as a gloss on the domestic programs of the 1960s. Its guiding principle is that no inequality is justified unless it helps those who are worse off. Armed with this communitarian thrust to liberal principle, one can defend any sort of policy which proclaims its purpose as that of aiding the worst off but which does not bother to balance smaller benefits to some against larger benefits to others. A few pundits aside, there is not now, if there ever was, a social stratum able to support a conservative ethic against the forces in favor of pushing public policy over the egalitarian precipice. Under the Nixon administration, instead of a social response we got a pitiful outbreak (or break-in) like Watergate.

The American politician, like the American political system, has been attacked at the most vulnerable point. The system is being asked to make good on its most ancient and deeply held beliefs, and it hovers between an inability to abandon its faith and an inability to make its faith manifest to the believers. This is the American crisis of confidence, evident in professors who do not profess, scientists who call for alternative approaches to science that smack of witchcraft, and politicians who condemn politics.

The expectations created by the body politic (or by a small but influential part of it), the rewards and punishments it administers, go far to shape the successes and failures of public officials. Anyone who writes or speaks or thinks seriously about public policy has a special obligation to consider what his contribution, even when placed in the context of many others, implies for the ability of government to perform adequately. Otherwise, private vices will become public vices as well (to reverse Mandeville), and government, seeing that the game is rigged, will respond once again by secretly attempting to change the rules.

Statement by Ambassador Daniel P. Moynihan, United States Representative to the United Nations, in Plenary, in Response to the United Nations Resolution Equating Zionism with Racism and Racial Discrimination, November 10, 1975.

Daniel Patrick Moynihan

THE UNITED STATES rises to declare before the General Assembly of the United Nations, and before the world, that it does not acknowledge, it will not abide by, it will never acquiesce in this infamous act.

Not three weeks ago, the United States Representative in the Social, Humanitarian, and Cultural Committee pleaded in measured and fully considered terms for the United Nations not to do this thing. It was, he said, "obscene." It is something more today, for the furtiveness with which this obscenity first appeared among us has been replaced by a shameless openness.

There will be time enough to contemplate the harm this act will have done the United Nations. Historians will do that for us, and it is sufficient for the moment only to note one foreboding fact. A great evil has been loosed upon the world. The abomination of anti-Semitism—as this year's Nobel Peace Laureate Andrei Sakharov observed in Moscow just a few days ago—the abomination of anti-Semitism has been given the appearance of international sanction. The General Assembly today grants symbolic amnesty—and more—to the murderers of the six million European Jews. Evil enough in itself, but more ominous by far is the realization that now presses upon us—the realization that if there were no General Assembly, this could never have happened.

As this day will live in infamy, it behooves those who sought to avert it to declare their thoughts so that historians will know that we fought here, that we were not small in number—not this time—and that while we lost, we fought with full knowledge of what indeed would *be* lost.

Nor should any historian of the event, nor yet any who have participated in it, suppose that we have fought only as governments, as chancelleries, and on an issue well removed from the concerns of our respective peoples. Others will speak for their nations: I will speak for mine.

In all our postwar history there has not been another issue which has brought forth such unanimity of American opinion. The President of the United States has from the first been explicit: This must not happen. The Congress of the United States, in a measure unanimously adopted in the Senate and sponsored by 436 of 437 Representatives in the House, declared its utter opposition. Following only American Jews themselves, the American trade union movement was first to the fore in denouncing this infamous undertaking. Next, one after another, the great private institutions of American life pronounced anathema on this evil thing—and most particularly, the Christian churches have done so. Reminded that the United Nations was born in the struggle against just such abominations as we are committing today—the wartime alliance of the United Nations dates from 1942—the United Nations Association of the United States has for the first time in its history appealed directly to each of the 141 other delegations in New York not to do this unspeakable thing.

The proposition to be sanctioned by a resolution of the General Assembly of the United Nations is that "Zionism is a form of racism and racial discrimination." Now this is a lie. But as it is a lie which the United Nations has now declared to be a truth, the actual truth must be restated.

The very first point to be made is that the United Nations has declared Zionism to be racism—without ever having defined racism. "Sentence first—verdict afterwards," as the Queen of Hearts said. But this is not wonderland, but a real world, where there are real consequences to folly and to venality. Just on Friday, the President of the General Assembly warned not only of the trouble which would follow from the adoption of this resolution but of its essential irresponsibility—for, he noted, members have wholly different ideas as to what they are condemning. "It seems to me," he said, and to his lasting honor he said it when there was still time, "It seems to me that before a body like this takes a decision they should agree very clearly on what they are approving or condemning, and it takes more time."

Lest I be unclear, the United Nations has in fact on several occasions defined "racial discrimination." The definitions have been loose, but recognizable. It is "racism"—incomparably the more serious charge—which has never been defined. Indeed, the term has only recently appeared in United Nations General Assembly documents. The one occasion on which we know its meaning to have been discussed was the 1644th meeting of the Third Committee on December 16, 1968, in connection with the report of the Secretary-General on the status of the international convention on the elimination of all forms of racial discrimination. On that occasion—to give some feeling for the intellectual precision with which the matter was being treated—the question arose, as to what should be the relative positioning of the terms "racism" and "Nazism" in a number of the "preambular paragraphs." The distinguished delegate from Tunisia argued that "racism" should go first because "Nazism was merely a form of racism. . . ." Not so, said the no less distinguished delegate from the Union of Soviet Socialist Republics. For, he explained, "Nazism contained the main elements of racism within its ambit and should be mentioned first." This is to say that racism was merely a form of Nazism.

The discussion wound to its weary and inconclusive end, and we are left with nothing to guide us, for even this one discussion of "racism" confined itself to word orders in preambular paragraphs, and did not at all touch on the meaning of the words as such. Still, one cannot but ponder the situation we have made for ourselves in the context of the Soviet statement on that not so distant occasion. *If*, as the distinguished delegate declared, racism is a form of Nazism—and *if*, as this resolution declares, Zionism is a form of racism—*then* we have step by step taken ourselves to the point of proclaiming—the United Nations is solemnly proclaiming—that Zionism is a form of Nazism.

What we have here is a lie—a political lie of a variety well known to the twentieth century, and scarcely exceeded in all that annal of untruth and outrage. The lie is that Zionism is a form of racism. The overwhelmingly clear truth is that it is not.

The word "racism" is a creation of the English language, and relatively new to it. It is not, for instance, to be found in the Oxford English Dictionary. The term derives from relatively new doctrines—all of them discredited—concerning the human population of the world, to the effect that there are significant biological differences among clearly identifiable groups, and that these differences establish, in effect, different levels of humanity. Racism, as defined by Webster's Third New International Dictionary, is "The assumption that . . . traits and capacities are determined by biological race and that races differ decisively from one another." It further involves "a belief in the inherent superiority of a particular race and its right to domination over others."

This meaning is clear. It is equally clear that this assumption, this belief, has always been altogether alien to the political and religious movement known as Zionism. As a strictly political movement, Zionism was established only in 1897, although there is a clearly legitimate sense in which its origins are indeed ancient. For example many branches of Christianity have always held that from the standpoint of the biblical prophets, Israel would be reborn one day. But the modern Zionist movement arose in Europe in the context of a general upsurge of national consciousness and aspiration that overtook most other people of Central and Eastern Europe after 1848, and that in time spread to all of Africa and Asia. It was, to those persons of the Jewish religion, a Jewish form of what today is called a national liberation movement. Probably a majority of those persons who became active Zionists and sought to emigrate to Palestine were born within the confines of Czarist Russia, and it was only natural for Soviet Foreign Minister Andrei Gromyko to deplore, as he did in 1948, in the 299th meeting of the Security Council, the act by Israel's neighbors of "sending their troops into Palestine and carrying out military operations aimed"—in Mr. Gromyko's words—"at the suppression of the National Liberation Movement in Palestine."

Now it was the singular nature—if I am not mistaken, it was the unique nature—of this National Liberation Movement that in contrast with the movements that preceded it, those of that time and those that have come since, it defined its members in terms not of birth, but of belief. That is to say, it was not a movement of the Irish to free Ireland, or of the Polish to free Poland, not a movement of Algerians to free Algeria, nor of Indians to free India. It was not a movement of persons connected by historic membership in a genetic pool of the kind that enables us to speak loosely but not meaninglessly, say, of the Chinese people, nor yet of diverse groups occupying the same territory which enables us to speak of the American people with no greater indignity to truth. To the contrary, Zionists defined themselves merely as Jews, and declared to be Jewish anyone born of a Jewish mother or—and this is the absolutely crucial fact—anyone who converted to Judaism. Which is to say, in the terms of the International

Convention on the elimination of all forms of racial discrimination, adopted by the 20th General Assembly, *anyone*—regardless of "race, colour, descent, or national or ethnic origin. . . ."

The State of Israel, which in time was the creation of the Zionist Movement, has been extraordinary in nothing so much as the range of "racial stocks" from which it has drawn its citizenry. There are black Jews, brown Jews, white Jews, Jews from the Orient and Jews from the West. Most such persons could be said to have been "born" Jews, just as most Presbyterians and most Hindus are "born" to their faith, but there are many Jews who are converts. With a consistency in the matter which surely attests to the importance of this issue to that religious and political culture, Israeli courts have held that a Jew who converts to another religion is no longer a Jew. In the meantime the population of Israel also includes large numbers of non-Jews, among them Arabs of both the Muslim and Christian religions and Christians of other national origins. Many of these persons are citizens of Israel, and those who are not can become citizens by legal procedures very much like those which obtain in a typical nation of Western Europe.

Now I should wish to be understood that I am here making one point, and one point only, which is that whatever else Zionism may be, it is not and cannot be "a form of racism." In logic, the State of Israel could be, or could become many things, theoretically including many things undesirable, but it could not be and could not become racist unless it ceased to be Zionist.

Indeed, the idea that Jews *are* a "race" was invented not by Jews but by those who hated Jews. The idea of Jews as a race was invented by nineteenth-century anti-Semites such as Houston Steward Chamberlain and Edouard Drumont, who saw that in an increasingly secular age, which is to say an age which made for fewer distinctions between people, the old religious grounds for anti-Semitism were losing force. New justifications were needed for excluding and persecuting Jews, and so the new idea of Jews as a race—rather than as a religion—was born. It was a contemptible idea at the beginning, and no civilized person would be associated with it. To think that it is an idea now endorsed by the United Nations is to reflect on what civilization has come to.

It is precisely a concern for civilization, for civilized values that are or should be precious to all mankind, that arouses us at this moment to such special passion. What we have at stake here is not merely the honor and the legitimacy of the State of Israel—although a challenge to the legitimacy of any member nation ought always to arouse the vigilance of all members of the United Nations. For a yet more important matter is at issue, which is the integrity of that whole body of moral and legal precepts which we know as human rights.

The terrible lie that has been told here today will have terrible consequences. Not only will people begin to say, indeed they have already begun to say, that the United Nations is a place where lies are told. Far more serious, grave and perhaps irreparable harm will be done to the cause of human rights. The harm will arise first because it will strip from racism the precise and abhorrent meaning that it still precariously holds today. How will the peoples of the world feel about racism, and about the need to struggle against it, when they are told that it is an idea so broad as to include the Jewish National Liberation Movement?

As this lie spreads, it will do harm in a second way. Many of the members of the United Nations owe their independence in no small part to the notion of human rights, as it has spread from the domestic sphere to the international sphere and exercised its influence over the old colonial powers. We are now coming into a time when that independence is likely to be threatened again. There will be new forces, some of them arising now, new prophets and new despots, who will justify their actions with the help of just such distortions of words as we have sanctioned here today. Today we have drained the word "racism" of its meaning. Tomorrow, terms like "national self-determination" and "national honor" will be perverted in the same way to serve the purposes of conquest and exploitation. And when these claims begin to be made—as they already have begun to be made—it is the small nations of the world whose integrity will suffer. And how will the small nations of the world defend themselves, on what grounds will others be moved to defend and protect them, when the language of human rights, the only language by which the small can be defended, is no longer believed and no longer has a power of its own?

There is this danger, and then a final danger that is the most serious of all. Which is that the damage we now do to the idea of human rights and the language of human rights could well be irreversible. The idea of human rights as we know it today is not an idea which has always existed in human affairs. It is an idea which appeared at a specific time in the world, and under very special circumstances. It appeared when European philosophers of the seventeenth century began to argue that man was a being whose existence was independent from that of the State, that he need join a political community only if he did not lose by that association more than he gained. From this very specific political philosophy stemmed the idea of political rights, of claims that the individual could justly make against the State; it was because the individual was seen as so separate from the State that he could make legitimate demands upon it.

That was the philosophy from which the idea of domestic and international rights sprang. But most of the world does not hold with that philosophy now. Most of the world believes in newer modes of political thought, in philosophies that do not accept the individual as distinct from and prior to the State, in philosophies that therefore do not provide any justification for the idea of human rights and philosophies that have no words by which to explain their value. If we destroy the words that were given to us by past centuries, we will not have words to replace them, for philosophy today has no such words.

But there are those of us who have not forsaken these older words, still so new to much of the world. Not forsaken them now, not here, not anywhere, not ever.

The United States of America declares that it does not acknowledge, it will not abide by, it will never acquiesce in this infamous act.

3. Capitalism's Moment

Until the 1970s, one of the few areas of social thought mostly ignored by the neoconservatives was economics. Irving Kristol changed this; he became a serious student of economics in the early 1970s. He studied capitalism from a sociological perspective—as a way of organizing human societies, unlike most economists. Working with his colleagues at the American Enterprise Institute and The Wall Street Journal, *Kristol became the philosophical father of supply-side economics, the governing policy of the nation during the Reagan years. Although he embraced capitalism, Kristol was never what he called a "free market enthusiast," instead severely criticizing libertarians for embracing a simpleminded and desiccated view of human nature. His writings on economics were published on the editorial page of* The Wall Street Journal *during the 1970s and are collected in his second book of essays,* Two Cheers for Capitalism.*

Along with Kristol, the leading neoconservative economic theorists were Michael Novak and George Gilder. Michael Novak's book The Spirit of Democratic Capitalism, *which is excerpted here, is a classic. Widely read all over the world, it became an underground best-seller in the Communist countries of Eastern Europe. George Gilder, the author of the best-seller* Wealth and Poverty *and numerous celebratory essays on capitalism, found beauty and virtue in the workings of the free market. His essay "Moral Sources of Capitalism," reprinted here, deftly encapsulates his defense of capitalism.*

"When Virtue Loses All Her Loveliness"—Some Reflections on Capitalism and "The Free Society"

Irving Kristol

WHEN WE LACK the will to see things as they really are, there is nothing so mystifying as the obvious. This is the case, I think, with the new upsurge of radicalism that is now shaking much of Western society to its foundations. We have constructed the most ingenious sociological and psychological theories—as well as a few disingenuously naive ones—to explain this phenomenon. But there is in truth no mystery here. Our youthful rebels are anything but inarticulate; and though they utter a great deal of nonsense, the import of what they are saying is clear enough. What they are saying is that they dislike—to put it mildly—the liberal, individualist, capitalist civilization that stands ready to receive them as citizens. They are rejecting this offer of citizenship and are declaring their desire to see some other kind of civilization replace it.

That most of them do not always put the matter as explicitly or as candidly as this is beside the point. Some of them do, of course; we try to dismiss them as "the lunatic fringe." But the mass of dissident young are not, after all, sufficiently educated to understand the implications of everything they say. Besides, it is so much easier for the less bold among them to insist that what they find outrageous are the defects and shortcomings of the present system. Such shortcomings undeniably exist and are easy polemical marks. And, at the other end, it is so much easier for the adult generations to accept such polemics as representing the sum and substance of their dissatisfaction. It is consoling to think that the turmoil among them is provoked by the extent to which our society falls short of realizing its ideals. But the plain truth is that it is these ideals themselves that are being

Reprinted from The Public Interest *(Fall 1970).*

rejected. Our young radicals are far less dismayed at America's failure to become what it ought to be than they are contemptuous of what it thinks it ought to be. For them, as for Oscar Wilde, it is not the average American who is disgusting; it is the ideal American.

This is why one can make so little impression on them with arguments about how much progress has been made in the past decades, or is being made today, toward racial equality, or abolishing poverty, or fighting pollution, or whatever it is that we conventionally take as a sign of "progress." The obstinacy with which they remain deaf to such "liberal" arguments is not all perverse or irrational, as some would like to think. It arises, rather, out of a perfectly sincere, if often inchoate, animus against the American system itself. This animus stands for a commitment—*to* what, remains to be seen, but *against* what is already only too evident.

Capitalism's Three Promises

Dissatisfaction with the liberal-capitalist ideal, as distinct from indignation at failures to realize this ideal, are coterminous with the history of capitalism itself. Indeed, the cultural history of the capitalist epoch is not much more than a record of the varying ways such dissatisfaction could be expressed—in poetry, in the novel, in the drama, in painting, and today even in the movies. Nor, again, is there any great mystery why, from the first stirrings of the romantic movement, poets and philosophers have never had much regard for the capitalist civilization in which they lived and worked. But to understand this fully, one must be able to step outside the "progressive" ideology which makes us assume that liberal capitalism is the "natural" state of man toward which humanity has always aspired. There is nothing more natural about capitalist civilization than about many others that have had, or will have, their day. Capitalism represents a sum of human choices about the good life and the good society. These choices inevitably have their associated costs, and after two hundred years the conviction seems to be spreading that the costs have got out of line.

What did capitalism promise? First of all, it promised continued improvement in the material conditions of all its citizens, a promise without precedent in human history. Secondly, it promised an equally unprecedented measure of individual freedom for all of these same citizens. And lastly, it held out the promise that, amidst this prosperity and liberty, the individual could satisfy his instinct for self-perfection—for leading a virtuous life that satisfied the demands of his spirit (or, as one used to say, his soul)—and that the free exercise of such individual virtue would aggregate into a just society.

Now, it is important to realize that, though these aims were in one sense more ambitious than any previously set forth by a political ideology, in another sense they were far more modest. Whereas, as Joseph Cropsey has pointed out, Adam Smith defined "prudence" democratically as "the care of the health, of the fortune, of the rank of the individual," Aristotle had defined that term aristocratically, to mean "the quality of mind concerned with things just and noble and good for man." By this standard, all pre-capitalist systems had been, to one degree or another, Aristotelian: they were interested in creating a high and memorable civilization even if this were shared only by a tiny minority. In contrast, capitalism lowered its sights, but offered its shares in bourgeois civilization to the entire citizenry. Tocqueville, as usual, astutely caught this difference between the aristocratic civilizations of the past and the new liberal capitalism he saw emerging in the United States:

> In aristocratic societies the class that gives the tone to opinion and has the guidance of affairs, being permanently and hereditarily placed above the multitude, naturally conceives a lofty idea of itself and man. It loves to invent for him noble pleasures, to carve out splendid objects for his ambition. Aristocracies often commit very tyrannical and inhuman actions, but they rarely entertain groveling thoughts. . . .
>
> [In democracies, in contrast] there is little energy of character but customs are mild and laws humane. If there are few instances of exalted heroism or of virtues of the highest, brightest, and purest temper, men's habits are regular, violence is rare, and cruelty almost unknown. . . . Genius becomes rare, information more diffused. . . . There is less perfection, but more abundance, in all the productions of the arts.

It is because "high culture" inevitably has an aristocratic bias—it would not be "high" if it did not—that, from the beginnings of the capitalist era, it has always felt contempt for the bourgeois mode of existence. That mode of existence purposively depreciated the very issues that were its *raison d'être*. It did so by making them, as no society had ever dared or desired to do, matters of personal taste, according to the prescription of Adam Smith in his *Theory of Moral Sentiments*:

Though you despise that picture, or that poem, or even that system of philosophy, which I admire, there is little danger of our quarreling upon that account. Neither of us can reasonably be much interested about them. They ought all of them to be matters of great indifference to us both; so that, though our opinions may be opposite, our affections shall be very nearly the same.

In short, an amiable philistinism was inherent in bourgeois society, and this was bound to place its artists and intellectuals in an antagonistic posture toward it. This antagonism was irrepressible—the bourgeois world could not suppress it without violating its own liberal creed; the artists could not refrain from expressing their hostility without denying their most authentic selves. But the conflict could, and was, contained so long as capitalist civilization delivered on its three basic promises. It was only when the third promise, of a virtuous life and a just society, was subverted by the dynamics of capitalism itself, as it strove to fulfill the other two—affluence and liberty—that the bourgeois order came, in the minds of the young especially, to possess a questionable legitimacy.

From Bourgeois Society to a "Free Society"

I can think of no better way of indicating the distance that capitalism has travelled from its original ideological origins than by contrasting the most intelligent defender of capitalism today with his predecessors. I refer to Friederich von Hayek, who has as fine and as powerful a mind as is to be found anywhere, and whose *Constitution of Liberty* is one of the most thoughtful works of the last decades. In that book, he offers the following argument against viewing capitalism as a system that incarnates any idea of justice:

> Most people will object not to the bare fact of inequality but to the fact that the differences in reward do not correspond to any recognizable differences in the merit of those who receive them. The answer commonly given to this is that a free society on the whole achieves this kind of justice. This, however, is an indefensible contention if by justice is meant proportionality of reward to moral merit. Any attempt to found the case for freedom on this argument is very damaging to it, since it concedes that material rewards ought to be made to correspond to recognizable merit and then opposes the conclusion that most people will draw from this by an

assertion which is untrue. The proper answer is that in a free society it is neither desirable nor practicable that material rewards should be made generally to correspond to what men recognize as merit and that it is an essential characteristic of a free society that an individual's position should not necessarily depend on the views that his fellows hold about the merit he has acquired. . . . A society in which the position of the individual was made to correspond to human ideas of moral merit would therefore be the exact opposite of a free society. It would be a society in which people were rewarded for duty performed instead of for success. . . . But if nobody's knowledge is sufficient to guide all human action, there is also no human being who is competent to reward all efforts according to merit.

This argument is admirable both for its utter candor and for its firm opposition to all those modern authoritarian ideologies, whether rationalist or irrationalist, which give a self-selected elite the right to shape men's lives and fix their destinies according to its preconceived notions of good and evil, merit and demerit. But it is interesting to note what Hayek is doing: he is opposing a *free* society to a *just* society—because, he says, while we know what freedom is, we have no generally accepted knowledge of what justice is. Elsewhere he writes:

Since they [i.e., differentials in wealth and income] are not the effect of anyone's design or intentions, it is meaningless to describe the manner in which the market distributed the good things of this world among particular people as just or unjust. . . . No test or criteria have been found or can be found by which such rules of "social justice" can be assessed. . . . They would have to be determined by the arbitrary will of the holders of power.

Now, it may be that this is the best possible defense that can be made of a free society. But if this is the case, one can fairly say that "capitalism" is (or was) one thing, and a "free society" another. For capitalism, during the first hundred years or so of its existence, did lay claim to being a just social order, in the meaning later given to that concept by Paul Elmer More: "Such a distribution of power and privilege, and of property as the symbol and instrument of these, as at once will satisfy the distinctions of reason among the superior, and will not outrage the feelings of the inferior." As a matter of fact, capitalism at its apogee saw itself as the most just social order the world has ever witnessed, because it replaced all arbitrary (e.g., inherited) distributions of power, privilege, and property with a distribution that was directly and intimately linked to personal merit—this latter term being inclusive of both personal abilities and personal virtues.

Writing shortly before the Civil War, George Fitzhugh, the most gifted of Southern apologists for slavery, attacked the capitalist North in these terms:

> In a free society none but the selfish virtues are in repute, because none other help a man in the race of competition. In such a society virtue loses all her loveliness, because of her selfish aims. Good men and bad men have the same end in view—self-promotion and self-elevation.

At the time, this accusation was a half-truth. The North was not yet "a free society," in Hayek's sense or Fitzhugh's. It was still in good measure a bourgeois society in which the capitalist mode of existence involved moral self-discipline and had a visible aura of spiritual grace. It was a society in which "success" was indeed seen as having what Hayek has said it ought never to have: a firm connection with "duty performed." It was a society in which Theodore Parker could write of a leading merchant: "He had no uncommon culture of the understanding or the imagination, and of the higher reason still less. But in respect of the *greater faculties*—in respect of conscience, affection, the religious element—he was well born, well bred." In short, it was a society still permeated by the Puritan ethic, the Protestant ethic, the capitalist ethic—call it what you will. It was a society in which it was agreed that there was a strong correlation between certain personal virtues—frugality, industry, sobriety, reliability, piety—and the way in which power, privilege, and property were distributed. And this correlation was taken to be the sign of a just society, not merely of a free one. Samuel Smiles or Horatio Alger would have regarded Professor Hayek's writings as slanderous of his fellow Christians, blasphemous of God, and ultimately subversive of the social order. I am not sure about the first two of these accusations, but I am fairly certain of the validity of the last.

This is not the place to recount the history and eventual degradation of the capitalist ethic in America. Suffice it to say that, with every passing decade, Fitzhugh's charge, that "virtue loses all her loveliness, because of her selfish aims," became more valid. From having been a *capitalist, republican community*, with shared values and a quite unambiguous claim to the title of a just order, the United States became a *free, democratic society* where the will to success and privilege was severed from its moral moorings.

Three Current Apologia

But can men live in a free society if they have no reason to believe it is also a just society? I do not think so. My reading of history is that, in the same way as men cannot for long tolerate a sense of spiritual meaninglessness in their individual lives, so they cannot for long accept a society in which power, privilege, and property are not distributed according to some morally meaningful criteria. Nor is equality itself any more acceptable than inequality—neither is more "natural" than the other—if equality is merely a brute fact rather than a consequence of an ideology or social philosophy. This explains what otherwise seems paradoxical: that small inequalities in capitalist countries can become the source of intense controversy while relatively larger inequalities in socialist or communist countries are blandly overlooked. Thus, those same young radicals who are infuriated by trivial inequalities in the American economic system are quite blind to grosser inequalities in the Cuban system. This is usually taken as evidence of hypocrisy or self-deception. I would say it shows, rather, that people's notions of equality or inequality have extraordinarily little to do with arithmetic and almost everything to do with political philosophy.

I believe that what holds for equality also holds for liberty. People feel free when they subscribe to a prevailing social philosophy; they feel unfree when the prevailing social philosophy is unpersuasive; and the existence of constitutions or laws or judiciaries have precious little to do with these basic feelings. The average working man in nineteenth-century America had far fewer "rights" than his counterpart today; but he was far more likely to boast about his being a free man.

So I conclude, despite Professor Hayek's ingenious analysis, that men cannot accept the historical accidents of the marketplace—seen merely as accidents—as the basis for an enduring and legitimate entitlement to power, privilege, and property. And, in actual fact, Professor Hayek's rationale for modern capitalism is never used outside a small academic enclave; I even suspect it cannot be believed except by those whose minds have been shaped by overlong exposure to scholasticism. Instead, the arguments offered to justify the social structure of capitalism now fall into three main categories:

1) The Protestant Ethic. This, however, is now reserved for the lower socioeconomic levels. It is still believed, and it is still reasonable to believe, that worldly success among the working class, lower-middle class, and even middle class has a definite connection with personal virtues such as diligence, rectitude, sobriety, honest ambition, etc., etc. And, so far as I can see, the connection is not only credible but demonstrable. It does seem that the traditional bourgeois virtues are efficacious among these classes—at least, it is rare to find successful men emerging from these classes who do not to a significant degree exemplify them. But no one seriously claims that these traditional virtues will open the corridors of corporate power to anyone, or that the men who now occupy the executive suites are—or even aspire to be—models of bourgeois virtue.

2) The Darwinian Ethic. This is to be found mainly among small business-men who are fond of thinking that their "making it" is to be explained as "the survival of the fittest." They are frequently quite right, of course, in believing the metaphor appropriate to their condition and to the ways in which they achieved it. But it is preposterous to think that the mass of men will ever accept as legitimate a social order formed in accordance with the laws of the jungle. Men may be animals, but they are political animals—and, what comes to not such a different thing, moral animals too. The fact that for several decades after the Civil War, the Darwinian ethic, as popularized by Herbert Spencer, could be taken seriously by so many social theorists represents one of the most bizarre and sordid episodes in American intellectual history. It could not last; and did not.

3) The Technocratic Ethic. This is the most prevalent justification of corporate capitalism today and finds expression in an insistence on "performance." Those who occupy the seats of corporate power, and enjoy the prerogatives and privileges thereof, are said to acquire legitimacy by their superior ability to achieve superior "performance"—in economic growth, managerial efficiency, technological innovation. In a sense, what is claimed is that these men are accomplishing social tasks, and fulfilling social responsibilities, in an especially efficacious way.

There are, however, two fatal flaws in this argument. First, if one defines "performance" in a strictly limited and measurable sense, then one is applying a test that any ruling class is bound, on fairly frequent occasions, to fail. Life has its ups and downs; so do history and economics; and men who can only claim legitimacy *via* performance are going to have to spend an awful lot of time and energy explaining why things are not going as well as they ought to. Such repeated, defensive apologias, in the end, will be hollow and unconvincing. Indeed, the very concept of "legitimacy," in its historical usages, is supposed to take account of and make allowances for all those rough passages a society will have to navigate. If the landed gentry of Britain during those centuries of its dominance, or the business class in the United States during the first century and a half of our national history, had insisted that it be judged by performance alone, it would have flunked out of history. So would every other ruling class that ever existed.

Secondly, if one tries to avoid this dilemma by giving the term "performance" a broader and larger meaning, then one inevitably finds oneself passing beyond the boundaries of bourgeois propriety. It is one thing to say with Samuel Johnson that men honestly engaged in business are doing the least mischief that men are capable of; it is quite another thing to assert that they are doing the greatest good—this is only too patently untrue. For the achievement of the greatest good, more than successful performance in business is necessary. Witness how vulnerable our corporate managers are to accusations that they are befouling our environment. What these accusations really add up to is the statement that the business system in the United States does not create a beautiful, refined, gracious, and tranquil civilization. To which our corporate leaders are replying: "Oh, we can perform that mission too—just give us time." But there is no good reason to think they can accomplish this noncapitalist mission; nor is there any reason to believe that they have any proper entitlement even to try.

"Participation" or Leadership?

It is, I think, because of the decline of the bourgeois ethic, and the consequent drainage of legitimacy out of the business system, that the issue of "participation" has emerged with such urgency during these past years. It is a common error to take this word at its face value—to assume that, in our organized and bureaucratized society, the average person is more isolated, alienated, or powerless than ever before, and that the proper remedy is to open new avenues of "participation." We are then perplexed when, the avenues having been open, we find so little traffic passing through. We give college students the right to representation on all sorts of committees—and then discover they never bother to come to meetings. We create new popularly elected "community" organizations in the ghettos—and then discover that ghetto residents won't come out to vote. We decentralize New York City's school system—only to discover that the populace is singularly uninterested in local school board elections.

I doubt very much that the average American is actually more isolated or powerless today than in the past. The few serious studies that have been made on this subject indicate that we have highly romanticized notions of the past—of the degree to which ordinary people were ever involved in community activities—and highly apocalyptic notions of the present. If one takes membership in civic-minded organizations as a criterion, people are unquestionably more "involved" today than ever before in our history. Maybe that's not such a good criterion; but it is a revealing aspect of this whole problem that those who make large statements on this matter rarely give us any workable or testable criteria at all.

But I would not deny that more people, even if more specifically "involved" than ever before, also feel more "alienated" in a general way. And this, I would suggest, is because the institutions of our society have lost their vital connection with the values which are supposed to govern the private lives of our citizenry. They no longer exemplify these values; they no longer magnify them; they no longer reassuringly sustain them. When it is said that the institutions of our society have become appallingly "impersonal," I take this to mean that they have lost any shape that is congruent with the private moral codes which presumably govern individual life. (That presumption, of course, may be factually weak; but it is nonetheless efficacious so long as people hold it.) The "outside" of our social life has ceased being harmonious with the "inside"—the mode of distribution of power, privilege, and property, and hence the very principle of authority, no longer "makes sense" to the bewildered citizen. And when institutions cease to "make sense" in this way, all the familiar criteria of success or failure become utterly irrelevant.

As I see it, then, the demand for "participation" is best appreciated as a demand for authority—for leadership that holds the promise of reconciling the inner and outer worlds of the citizen. So far from its being a hopeful reawakening of the democratic spirit, it signifies a hunger for authority that leads toward some kind of plebiscitary democracy at best, and is in any case not easy to reconcile with liberal democracy as we traditionally have known it. I find it instructive that such old-fashioned populists as Hubert Humphrey and Edmund Muskie, whose notions of "participation" are both liberal and traditional, fail to catch the imagination of our dissidents in the way that Robert Kennedy did. The late Senator Kennedy was very much a leader—one can imagine Humphrey or Muskie participating in an old-fashioned town meeting, one can only envision Kennedy dominating a town rally. One can also envision those who "participated" in such a rally feeling that they had achieved a kind of "representation" previously denied them.

A Case of Regression

For a system of liberal, representative government to work, free elections are not enough. The results of the political process and of the exercise of individual freedom—the distribution of power, privilege, and property— must also be seen as in some profound sense expressive of the values that govern the lives of individuals. An idea of self-government, if it is to be viable, must encompass both the private and the public sectors. If it does not—if the principles that organize public life seem to have little relation to those that shape private lives—you have "alienation," and anomie, and a melting away of established principles of authority.

Milton Friedman, arguing in favor of Hayek's extreme libertarian position, has written that the free man "recognizes no national purpose except as it is the consensus of the purposes for which the citizens severally strive." If he is using the term "consensus" seriously, then he must be assuming that there is a strong homogeneity of values among the citizenry, and that these values give a certain corresponding shape to the various institutions of society, political and economic. Were that the case, then it is indeed true that a "national purpose" arises automatically and organically out of the social order itself. Something like this did happen when liberal capitalism was in its prime, vigorous and self-confident. But is that our condition today? I think not—just as I think Mr. Friedman doesn't really mean "consensus" but rather the mere aggregation of selfish aims. In such a blind and accidental arithmetic, the sum floats free from the addenda, and its legitimacy is infinitely questionable.

The inner spiritual chaos of the times, so powerfully created by the dynamics of capitalism itself, is such as to make nihilism an easy temptation. A "free society" in Hayek's sense gives birth in massive numbers to "free spirits"—emptied of moral substance but still driven by primordial moral aspirations. Such people are capable of the most irrational actions. Indeed, it is my impression that, under the strain of modern life, whole classes of our population—and the educated classes most of all—are entering what can only be called, in the strictly clinical sense, a phase of infantile regression. With every passing year, public discourse becomes sillier and more petulant, while human emotions become, apparently, more ungovernable. Some of our most intelligent university professors are now loudly saying things that, had they been uttered by one of their students twenty years ago, would have called forth gentle and urbane reproof.

The Reforming Spirit and the Conservative Ideal

And yet, if the situation of liberal capitalism today seems so precarious, it is likely nevertheless to survive for a long while, if only because the modern era has failed to come up with any plausible alternatives. Socialism, communism, and fascism have all turned out to be either utopian illusions or sordid frauds. So we shall have time—though not an endless amount of it, for we have already wasted a great deal. We are today in a situation not very different from that described by Herbert Croly in *The Promise of American Life* (1912):

> The substance of our national Promise has consisted . . . of an improving popular economic condition, guaranteed by democratic political institutions, and resulting in moral and social amelioration. These manifold benefits were to be obtained merely by liberating the enlightened self-enterprise of the American people. . . . The fulfillment of the American Promise was considered inevitable because it was based upon a combination of self-interest and the natural goodness of human nature. On the other hand, if the fulfillment of our national Promise can no longer be considered inevitable, if it must be considered as equivalent to a conscious national purpose instead of an inexorable national destiny, the implication necessarily is that the trust reposed in individual self-interest has been in some measure betrayed. No pre-established harmony can then exist between the free and abundant satisfaction of private needs and the accomplishment of a morally and socially desirable result.

Croly is not much read these days. He was a liberal reformer with essentially conservative goals. So was Matthew Arnold, fifty years earlier—and he isn't much read these days, either. Neither of them can pass into the conventional anthologies of liberal or conservative thought. I think this is a sad commentary on the ideological barrenness of the liberal and conservative creeds. I also think it is a great pity. For if our private and public worlds are ever again, in our lifetimes, to have a congenial relationship—if virtue is to regain her lost loveliness—then some such combination of the reforming spirit with the conservative ideal seems to me to be what is most desperately wanted.

I use the word "conservative" advisedly. Though the discontents of our civilization express themselves in the rhetoric of "liberation" and "equality," one can detect beneath the surface an acute yearning for order and stability—but a legitimate order, of course, and a legitimized stability. In this connection, I find the increasing skepticism as to the benefits of economic growth and technological innovation most suggestive. Such skepticism has been characteristic of conservative critics of liberal capitalism since the beginning of the nineteenth century. One finds it in Coleridge, Carlyle, and Newman—in all those who found it impossible to acquiesce in a "progressive" notion of human history or social evolution. Our dissidents today may think they are exceedingly progressive; but no one who puts greater emphasis on "the quality of life" than on "mere" material enrichment can properly be placed in that category. For the idea of progress in the modern era has always signified that the quality of life would inevitably be improved by material enrichment. To doubt this is to doubt the political metaphysics of modernity and to start the long trek back to premodern political philosophy—Plato, Aristotle, Thomas Aquinas, Hooker, Calvin, etc. It seems to me that this trip is quite necessary. Perhaps there we shall discover some of those elements that are most desperately needed by the spiritually impoverished civilization that we have constructed on what once seemed to be sturdy bourgeois foundations.

From The Spirit of Democratic Capitalism

Michael Novak

Capitalism, Socialism, and Religion—An Inquiry into the Spiritual Wealth of Nations

Of all the systems of political economy which have shaped our history, none has so revolutionized ordinary expectations of human life—lengthened the life span, made the elimination of poverty and famine thinkable, enlarged the range of human choice—as democratic capitalism. Recall the societies of the Roman Empire and Carolingian period. Contemplate the Catholic and Protestant powers of the seventeenth century, colonial and mercantilist. Examine the many forms of socialism in the present day. Each of these systems of political economy has had its theological admirers. Yet no theologian, Christian or Jewish, has yet assessed the theological significance of democratic capitalism. Consider, by contrast, the importance Marx and Engels attached to the capitalist revolution:

> The bourgeoisie, during its rule of scarce one hundred years, has created more massive and more colossal productive forces than have all preceding generations together. Subjection of Nature's forces to man, machinery, application of chemistry to industry and agriculture, steam-navigation, railways, electric telegraphs, clearing of whole continents for cultivation, canalization of rivers, whole populations conjured out of the ground—what earlier century had even a presentiment that such productive forces slumbered in the lap of social labor.[1]

Excerpt from the Spirit of Democratic Capitalism *(1981).*

This book, then, is about the life of the spirit which makes democratic capitalism possible. It is about its theological presuppositions, values, and systemic intentions.

What do I mean by "democratic capitalism"? I mean three systems in one: a predominantly market economy; a polity respectful of the rights of the individual to life, liberty, and the pursuit of happiness; and a system of cultural institutions moved by ideals of liberty and justice for all. In short, three dynamic and converging systems functioning as one: a democratic polity, an economy based on markets and incentives, and a moral-cultural system which is pluralistic and, in the largest sense, liberal. Social systems like those of the United States, West Germany, and Japan (with perhaps a score of others among the world's nations) illustrate the type.

The premise of this book may startle some. In the conventional view, the link between a democratic political system and a market economy is merely an accident of history. My argument is that the link is stronger: political democracy is compatible in practice only with a market economy. In turn, both systems nourish and are best nourished by a pluralistic liberal culture. It is important to give attention to all three systems. The full implications of a system which is threefold, rather than unitary, are developed through all the pages of this book.

To begin with, modern democracy and modern capitalism proceed from identical historical impulses. These impulses had moral form before institutions were invented to realize them; they aimed (1) to limit the power of the state, in defense against tyranny and stagnation; and (2) to liberate the energies of individuals and independently organized communities. Such impulses gave birth to modern European cities, whose first citizens took as their battle cry "City air makes men free."[2] Such citizens sought liberation from the crippling taxation, heavy bureaucracy, and dreary regulations of state and church. The moral vision of such citizens demanded forms of self-government in "city republics" and "free cities." It led them to cherish economies based upon free markets, incentives, and contracts. Gradually, such citizens developed polities based upon covenants, suffrage, the separation of powers, and the declaration of individual rights. The two revolutions—political and economic—in practice, but also in theory, nourished each other.[3] Karl Marx recognized this link in his term of contempt: "bourgeois democracy," he called it. Both spring from the same logic, the same moral principles, the same nest of cultural values, institutions, and presuppositions.

While bastard forms of capitalism do seem able for a time to endure without democracy, the natural logic of capitalism leads to democracy.[4] For economic liberties without political liberties are inherently unstable. Citizens economically free soon demand political freedoms. Thus dictatorships or monarchies which permit some freedoms to the market have a tendency to evolve into political democracies, as has happened in recent years in Greece, Portugal, Spain, and other nations. On the other side, the state which does not recognize limits to its power in the economic sphere inevitably destroys liberties in the political sphere. There are, as yet, no instances of dictatorial socialist states becoming democratic (although in 1981 one watched Poland with fascination). Democratic states which are sometimes described as socialist (Sweden, Israel, West Germany) invariably retain large components of private property, markets, and incentives.

Another point must be noted. Democratic polities depend upon the reality of economic growth. No traditional society, no socialist society—indeed, no society in history—has ever produced strict equality among individuals or classes. Real differences in talent, aspiration, and application inexorably individuate humans. Given the diversity and liberty of human life, no fair and free system can possibly guarantee equal outcomes. A democratic system depends for its legitimacy, therefore, not upon equal results but upon a sense of equal opportunity. Such legitimacy flows from the belief of all individuals that they can better their condition. This belief can be realized only under conditions of economic growth. Liberty requires expanse and openness.

In addition, liberty also requires social mobility. While statistical differences between strata necessarily remain, *individuals* must be free to rise from one level to another. Many move from poverty to reasonable economic sufficiency; some move to wealth. Others move up and down in many ways over a lifetime. A graduate student may be classified as "poor" on a graduate student's income, and again after retirement, yet in between may have high status and high income.

The reality of economic growth breaks one vicious circle; social mobility for individuals breaks another. The same democracy which without growth manifests self-destructive tendencies, leads to "balkanization," and inspires factional struggle acquires under conditions of growth a peaceable, generous character and is buoyant and expectant in each of its parts. It yields freedom to dream and realistic fulfillment of dreams. In the trap of a zero-sum economy, the Hobbesian "war of all against all" makes democracy come to seem unworkable. Liberated by economic growth, democracy wins common consent.

Not only do the logic of democracy and the logic of the market economy strengthen one another. Both also require a special moral-cultural base. Without certain moral and cultural presuppositions about the nature of individuals and their communities, about liberty and sin, about the changeability of history, about work and savings, about self-restraint and mutual cooperation, neither democracy nor capitalism can be made to work. Under some moral-cultural conditions, they are simply unachievable.

"Democratic capitalism" is a complex concept, depending in theory and in practice upon a threefold system. In its complexity, democratic capitalism is unlike both the historical societies which preceded it and the collectivized planned society that some wish to build in the future. Many who cherish it sense but cannot state the source of its originality.

The Historical Achievements of Democratic Capitalism

Consider the world at the beginning of the democratic capitalist era. The watershed year was 1776. Almost simultaneously, Adam Smith published *An Inquiry into the Nature and Causes of the Wealth of Nations* and the first democratic capitalist republic came into existence in the United States. Until that time, the classical pattern of political economy was mercantilist. Famines ravaged the civilized world on the average once a generation.[5] Plagues seized scores of thousands. In the 1780s, four fifths of French families devoted 90 percent of their incomes simply to buying bread—only bread—to stay alive. Life expectancy in 1795 in France was 27.3 years for women and 23.4 for men. In the year 1800, in the whole of Germany fewer than a thousand people had incomes as high as $1,000.[6]

"The poor you will always have with you," Christ tells us. At the beginning of the nineteenth century who could doubt it? Travelers from Europe, inured to homegrown poverty, were appalled by the still more unspeakable conditions they found in Africa and Asia. In most places, elementary hygiene seemed unknown. In Africa, the wheel had never been invented. Medical practice in vast stretches of the world was incantatory. Illiteracy was virtually universal. Most of the planet was unmapped. Hardly any of the world's cities had plumbing systems. Potable water was mostly unavailable. Ignorance was so extreme that most humans did not know that unclean water spreads disease. Except in Adam Smith's book, the concept of development did not exist. In 1800, a judgment like that of Ecclesiastes, "There is nothing new under the sun," blanketed a mostly torpid world.

In 1800, popular self-government was uncommon. Democracies (notably Great Britain and the United States) were few. Nearly all states were authoritarian. In most regions, economic enterprises stagnated. In 1800, there were more private business corporations in the infant United States (population: four million) than in all of Europe combined.[7] Liberty of religion and speech was rare. In most cultures, absolute rulers reigned simultaneously over political, economic, and moral-cultural matters. In such a world, in most places, traditional Christianity and Judaism lived under severe constraints.

The invention of the market economy in Great Britain and the United States more profoundly revolutionized the world between 1800 and the present than any other single force. After five millennia of blundering, human beings finally figured out how wealth may be produced in a sustained, systematic way. In Great Britain, real wages doubled between 1800 and 1850, and doubled again between 1850 and 1900. Since the population of Great Britain quadrupled in size, this represented a 1600 percent increase within one century.[8] The gains in liberty of personal choice—in a more varied diet, new beverages, new skills, new vocations—increased accordingly.[9]

The churches did not understand the new economics. Officially and through the theologians, they often regarded "the new spirit of capitalism" as materialistic, secular, and dangerous to religion, as in many respects—being in and of the world—it was. They often protested the rising spirit of individualism. They seldom grasped the new forms of cooperation indispensable to the new economics. They tried to douse the new fire.

Pope Pius XI said that the tragedy of the nineteenth century was the loss of the working classes to the church.[10] An even deeper tragedy lay in the failure of the church to understand the moral-cultural roots of the new economics. Standing outside, it did not infuse. Attached to the past, the church did not leaven the new order with the same combination of critical distance and sympathetic hope with which it had inspired the feudal order, the guilds, and the civic life of medieval Europe.

Yet the possibilities of the new order are manifold. Theology is sustained reflection upon God and his dealings with the human race: *logos* and *theos*, systematic inquiry about God. Judaism and Christianity are distinctive among the world religions because they understand salvation as a vocation in history. It is the religious task of Jews and Christians to change the world as well as to purify their own souls; to build up "the Kingdom of God" in their own hearts and through the work of their hands. At several points, Old and New Testaments alike name Jahweh "Providence," the Provider, and speak in metaphor of "the economy of salvation." Both Jews and Christians are pilgrim peoples. Both in their long history have experienced many different forms of political economy. Both see their religious task as working in and through the institutions of this world. It is the vocation of laypersons, in particular, to fire the iron of politics, economics, and culture to Jahweh's vision.

The Lord of History is purposive. Through his word, human existence aspires upward. Robert Nisbet in his brilliant *History of the Idea of Progress* (1980) shows, against J. B. Bury, that the sense of a future different from the past was crucial to Judaic and Christian theology.[11] Religions like Judaism and Christianity require "historical consciousness," for they are going somewhere, being narrative religions which live by memory and hope. The tentative efforts of the last fifteen years to bring theology to "political consciousness" may yield too much to Marx but do, at least, show concern for shaping history. St. Augustine wrestled to make the City of God discernible in the City of Man. Aquinas attended carefully to the rule of princes, natural law, and civic virtue. Sophistication about history and politics avails little today, however, without sophistication about economics. Yet in no major sphere of life have the traditions of theology fallen further behind. For many centuries, of course, there was no science of economics and no sustained economic growth. So the lack was hardly felt. Today it is a scandal.

From Practice to Theory

For two centuries, democratic capitalism has been more a matter of practice than of theory. This practicality has been deliberate. After the divisiveness and bitterness of the religious wars of the seventeenth century, writers like Montesquieu, Smith, and Madison wished to avoid theological disputes. They were eager to describe methods of collaboration which would not entail prior metaphysical agreement. They wished to construct a pluralistic system open to persons of all faiths and visions. Furthermore, their specific genius lay in the practical order. They sought as much as possible to invent methods of compromise and adjustment. They wanted the "new order" they envisaged to grow by experience, by concrete collaboration, and by trial and error. They wrote constantly of their project as "an experiment." Eagerly they referred one another to obscure accounts of practical experiments which one or another came upon in dusty libraries. They were a new breed: philosophers of practice. The system they championed quite naturally rewarded practitioners more than theoreticians. Two centuries later, Jacques Maritain could still write:

> You are advancing in the night, bearing torches toward which mankind would be glad to turn; but you leave them enveloped in the fog of a merely experiential approach and mere practical conceptualization, with no universal ideas to communicate. For lack of an adequate ideology, your lights cannot be seen.[12]

For many generations, the practical superiority of democratic capitalism was as evident as the commercial proverb "Build a better mousetrap and the world will beat a path to your door." The superiority of practical men to theoretical men seemed verified by history. But there is another proverb, equally potent: "Without vision, the people perish." Furthermore, in a world of instantaneous, universal mass communications, the balance of power has now shifted. Ideas, always a part of reality, have today acquired power greater than that of reality. One of the most astonishing characteristics of our age is that ideas, even false and unworkable ideas, even ideas which are no longer believed in by their official guardians, rule the affairs of men and run roughshod over stubborn facts. Ideas of enormous destructiveness, cruelty, and impracticality retain the allegiance of elites that benefit from them. The empirical record seems not to jut through into consciousness to break their spell. The class of persons who earn their livelihood from the making of ideas and symbols seems both unusually bewitched by falsehoods and absurdities and uniquely empowered to impose them upon hapless individuals.

In previous generations, taking its spiritual inheritance for granted, democratic capitalism felt no acute need for a theory about itself. It did not seem to need a moral theory, a theory about the life of the spirit, since it—erroneously—relied upon its own moral-cultural leaders to maintain one. The age of such innocence has long since passed. The glaring inadequacies of actual socialist societies do not seem to discourage newborn socialists. Entire nations, like Gadarene herds, cast themselves over the precipice. Within democratic capitalist societies as well, humans do not live by bread alone. Inattention to theory weakens the life of the spirit and injures the capacity of the young to dream of noble purposes. Irving Kristol in *Two Cheers for Capitalism* describes a moral vision "desperately needed by the spiritually impoverished civilization that we have constructed on what once seemed to be sturdy bourgeois foundations." He discerns the loss suffered by "a capitalist, republican community, with shared values and a quite unambiguous claim to the title of a just order" when it does not rethink its spiritual foundations and is thoughtlessly "severed from its moral moorings."[13]

The first of all moral obligations is to think clearly. Societies are not like the weather, merely given, since human beings are responsible for their form. Social forms are constructs of the human spirit.

Is there, then, a form for political economy most consonant with Judaic tradition and the Christian gospels? In *Integral Humanism* (1936), Jacques Maritain tried to express such a "proximate ideal," not yet realized by any human society and yet within the reach of human achievement. In other books, he tried to elucidate its presuppositions and its principles. Most astonishingly of all, in *Reflections on America* (1958), written after his firsthand experience of the United States, he admitted, to his own surprise, that the actual form of American society closely resembled the proximate ideal he had sketched in *Integral Humanism*, far more so than he had anticipated.[14] His chapter on the American economic system is especially important. Maritain saw the need for a new theory about the American system, but never gave sustained reflection to it himself. Neither has any other philosopher or theologian. John Courtney Murray, S.J., assayed the political system in *We Hold These Truths* (1960). Walter Lippmann tried to fill the gap with *The Public Philosophy* (1955). Reinhold Niebuhr in *The Irony of American History* (1952) and in other books also blazed a trail across deserts and mountains, but stopped short of the vision.[15]

Such books give me confidence that my own intuitions have not been eccentric. No society in the long history of the Jewish and Christian people owes more than our own to the inspiration of Jewish, Christian, and humanistic traditions. By no means is the political economy of the United States to be identified with the Kingdom of God, which transcends any historical political economy. It is not the "City of God." The transcendent religious commitments of Jews and Christians call us beyond the status quo, are always a source of judgment upon the status quo, and demand ever more profound reforms. Indeed, they transcend any conceivable achievement of reform and place all of history, even the most perfect form of human life, under the judgment of God.

Virtuous Self-Interest

R. H. Tawney described the age of capitalism as the age of acquisitiveness. Marx described it as the reduction of every human relation to the cash nexus. Pamphleteers for generations have denounced its licensing of greed. Yet simple reflection upon one's own life and the life of others, including the lives of those critics who denounce the system from within, suggests that there are enormous reservoirs of high motivation and moral purpose among citizens in democratic capitalist societies. The history of democratic capitalism is alive with potent movements of reform and idealistic purpose. As the world goes, its people do not in fact seem to be more greedy, grasping, selfish, acquisitive, or anarchic than citizens in traditional or in socialist societies. If democratic capitalism is to be blamed for sins it permits to flourish, the virtues it nourishes also deserve some credit.

In practice, the bone of contention seems most often to be the central concept of self-interest. A system committed to the principle that individuals are best placed to judge their real interests for themselves may be accused of institutionalizing selfishness and greed—but only on the premise that individuals are so depraved that they never make any other choice.

The founders of democratic capitalism did not believe that such depravity is universal. Furthermore, they held that the laws of free economic markets are such that the real interests of individuals are best served in the long run by a systematic refusal to take short-term advantage. Apart from internal restraints, the system itself places restraints upon greed and narrowly constructed self-interest. Greed and selfishness, when they occur, are made to have their costs. A firm aware of its long-term fiduciary responsibilities to its shareholders must protect its investments for future generations. It must change with the times. It must maintain a reputation for reliability, integrity, and fairness. In one large family trucking firm, for example, the last generation of owners kept too much in profits and invested too little in new technologies and new procedures, with the result that their heirs received a battered company unable to compete or to solve its cash-flow problems. Thus a firm committed to greed unleashes social forces that will sooner or later destroy it. Spasms of greed will disturb its own inner disciplines, corrupt its executives, anger its patrons, injure the morale of its workers, antagonize its suppliers and purchasers, embolden its competitors, and attract public retribution. In a free society, such spasms must be expected; they must also be opposed.

The real interests of individuals, furthermore, are seldom merely self-regarding. To most persons, their families mean more than their own interests; they frequently subordinate the latter to the former. Their communities are also important to them. In the human breast, commitments to benevolence, fellow-feeling, and sympathy are strong. Moreover, humans have the capacity to see themselves as others see them, and to hold themselves to standards which transcend their own selfish inclinations. Thus the "self" in self-interest is complex, at once familial and communitarian as well as individual, other-regarding as well as self-regarding, cooperative as well as independent, and self-judging as well as self-loving. Understood too narrowly, self-interest destroys firms as surely as it destroys personal lives. Understood broadly enough, as a set of realistic limits, it is a key to all the virtues, as prudence is.

Like prudence in Aristotelian thought, self-interest in democratic capitalist thought has an inferior reputation among moralists. Thus it is necessary to stress again that a *society* may not work well if all its members act always from benevolent intentions. On the other hand, democratic capitalism as a system deliberately enables many persons to do well by doing good (or even purporting to do good). It offers incentives of power, fame, and money to reformers and moralists.[16]

The economic system of democratic capitalism depends to an extraordinary extent upon the social capacities of the human person. Its system of inheritance respects the familial character of motivation. Its corporate pattern reflects the necessity of shared risks and shared rewards. Its divisions both of labor and of specialization reflect the demands of teamwork and association. Its separated churches and autonomous universities reflect the importance of independent moral communities. The ideology of individualism, too much stressed by some proponents and some opponents alike, disguises the essential communitarian character of its system.

Regrettably, the theory of democratic capitalism was left too long to economists. While economists are entitled to specialize, theologians also have such rights. A theology of democratic capitalism requires a larger view, of which economists freely concede the legitimacy. Thus, Milton and Rose Friedman in their bestselling *Free to Choose* consciously stress the broad meaning that must be attached to the concept of "self-interest." Narrow preoccupation with the economic market has led to a narrow interpretation of self-interest as myopic selfishness, as exclusive concern with immediate material rewards. Economics has been berated for allegedly drawing far-reaching conclusions from a wholly unrealistic "economic man" who is little more than a calculating machine, responding only to monetary stimuli. That is a great mistake. Self-interest is not myopic selfishness. It is whatever it is that interests the participants, whatever they value, whatever goals they pursue. The scientist seeking to advance the frontiers of his discipline, the missionary seeking to convert infidels to the true faith, the philanthropist seeking to bring comfort to the needy—all are pursuing their interests, as they see them, as they judge them by their own values.[17]

Under self-interest, then, fall religious and moral interests, artistic and scientific interests, and interests in justice and peace. The interests of the self define the self. In a free society, persons are free to choose their own interests. It is part of the function of a free economy to provide the abundance which breaks the chains of the mere struggle for subsistence, and to permit individual persons to "find themselves," indeed to define themselves through the interests they choose to make central to their lives.

In brief, the term "self-interest" encodes a view of human liberty that far exceeds self-regard, selfishness, acquisitiveness, and greed. Adam Smith attempted to suggest this by speaking of *rational* self-interest, by which he meant a specification of human consciousness not only intelligent and judgmental, beyond the sphere of mere desire or self-regard, but also guided by the ideal of objectivity. In *The Theory of Moral Sentiments* (1759), he argued that what is truly rational must be seen to be so not merely from the point of view of the self-interested party but from that of a disinterested rational observer as well. He called the achievement of such realistic judgment "the perfection of human nature." The whole system, as he imagined it, is aimed toward the acquisition of such realism: "We endeavour to examine our own conduct as we imagine any other fair and impartial spectator would examine it." Again: "To feel much for others, and little for ourselves ... to restrain our selfish, and to indulge our benevolent, affections, constitutes the perfection of human nature."[18]

Democratic capitalism, then, rests on a complex theory of sin. While recognizing ineradicable sinful tendencies in every human, it does not count humans depraved. While recognizing that no system of political economy can escape the ravages of human sinfulness, it has attempted to set in place a system which renders sinful tendencies as productive of good as possible. While basing itself on something less than perfect virtue, reasoned self-interest, it has attempted to draw from self-interest its most creative potential. It is a system designed for sinners, in the hope of achieving as much moral good as individuals and communities can generate under conditions of ample liberty.

Can human society imitate Providence?

Profit and Commercial Values

While markets encourage the exercise of choice, they stand accused of corrupting morals. Money, markets, and profits are this worldly, not other-worldly, terms. They seem to symbolize Mammon, and to run against the perfectionist strain in Christianity. As Irving Kristol has pointed out, certain Christian traditions reflect hostility to commerce unknown in Jewish traditions.[19] Just as some forms of Christianity have harbored excessively negative attitudes toward sex, so some also harbor negative attitudes toward monetary commerce. In particular, the long tradition of hostility toward lending money for profit ("usury")[20] seems to have spilled over into moral antipathy toward profit. "Is the profit motive compatible with humane purposes?" is for some a slow-pitch question whose answer is in the resounding negative.

Yet commerce is not without its own moral structure. The inventors of democratic capitalism—Montesquieu, John Adams, Adam Smith, Benjamin Franklin, Benjamin Rush, James Madison, Thomas Jefferson, and others were not themselves primarily men of commerce or manufacturing. They saw clearly both the perennial abuses typical of commercial life and the deficiencies even of its virtues. Such matters, known to Homer and Vergil, are reflected in ancient proverbs like *Caveat emptor* (Let the buyer beware). In trying to imagine a "new order," the founders of democratic capitalism considered the historical record. They found serious structural difficulties in the civic orders of ancient Greece and Rome, in those of the Holy Roman Empire, and in the various anciens régimes of their experience. In the old regimes, "the king had his glory, the nobles their honor, the Christians their salvation, the citizens of pagan antiquity their ambition."[21] In all such orders, privileges were preserved for too few. Contemplating the historical parade of aristocratic pretension, religious persecution, cults of heroism and glory, and the public presumption of deference to the powerful, the founders of democratic capitalism thought these bred "extravagant rashness and folly," and were at bottom "absurd."[22] Although each of the old orders of political economy appealed to high ideals of disinterestedness, nobility, and honor, these masked much "avidity and injustice" in high places. Based upon human ideals too high for the ordinary mundane business of life, their perfectionism was out of touch with reality. Under their influence, over many centuries, the lot of the ordinary mass of humanity had scarcely advanced at all.

The old orders endowed each man of high birth and inherited status with false notions of "self-sufficiency and absurd conceit of his own superiority."[23] They sold too short the capacities of commoners to direct their own activities, to form their own practical judgments, and to make their own choices. Moreover, they overlooked the tremendous economic potential of practicality, inventiveness, and enterprise on the part of free individuals.

Aristocratic pride produces no wealth, Adam Smith argued.[24] Even from situations of great original wealth, it produces laziness, extravagance, poverty, and ruin. Spain and Portugal did not become rich from the enormous wealth they expropriated from the mines of South America; they were propelled, instead, upon historical decline. Aristocratic taste with its preference for elegance may generate high art, works of beauty, palaces and churches ornately decorated in silver and gold. But, corrupting practical wisdom, it in the end impoverishes.

Thus, the founding fathers rejected aristocratic morals in favor of the common, the useful, the mundane. Favorite words in their new vocabulary were "common sense" and "utility," which they thought to be in tune with the plain teaching of the gospels. In the essay of which I have been making extensive use in this section, Ralph Lerner speaks not of democratic capitalism but of "the commercial republic," a republic which places the moral qualities required for successful commerce at the center of its social life. In such a republic, commerce is by no means the whole of life. Yet in it commerce is given greater freedom, and its prospering is made to be more central to the purposes of the state than in any previous form of civic order.

The ethic of commerce furnishes a school of virtue favorable to democratic governance. This ethic is not pretentious in its conception of reason and human nature. It enhances the cooperative spirit, since economic tasks cannot be accomplished by one person alone. It increases attention to law. It singles out the self-determination of the individual as the main source of social energy. It places limits on the state and other authorities. It incites imagination and industry. It disciplines all to common sense. It teaches respect for "an exact attention to small savings and small gains"[25] which, in turn, are the single most significant engine of sustained economic growth, since progress takes place at the margins and depends upon increments of new investment and new invention. It breaks the grip of those high utopian ideals of earlier civic orders which, while pretending to represent Reason in one or another of its lofty forms, proved in fact to be so impoverishing for real people. It is a system in tune with emergent probability, the limitations of human intelligence, and the unreliability of the human heart. The ethic of commerce is proportioned to man as he is, not as dreams would have him, and plainly appeared to the founders to support "the natural system of liberty and justice."

Early travelers to America observed this "new order" in practice. De Tocqueville noted that everywhere in America citizens were "calculating and weighing and computing."[26] Since practical intelligence yields tangible progress, men and women had an incentive to acquire it, to become savvy, to develop each of their crafts to new heights of inventiveness and effect. In Europe, the code of the gentleman required that one not appear to be too industrious, intent, or sweaty in one's work; everything, it was thought, ought to appear effortless, spontaneous, natural. In America, the market taught men and women to roll up their sleeves, to dirty their hands, and to shrug off "that inconsiderate contempt for practice" typical of aristocrats.[27] European attitudes may have required contempt for crass practicalities and respect for loftiness of station. In America, even the landed gentry took pride in physical labor and attention to practical detail.

Religion, too, was brought down to earth by the new American order. De Tocqueville commented, "In the very midst of their zeal one generally sees something so quiet, so methodical, so calculated that it would seem that the head rather than the heart leads them to the foot of the altar."[28] Montesquieu blamed churchmen for their centuries-long condemnations of commerce and the misfortunes they thus visited upon common people. He blamed them even more for fanning the flames of intolerance, including the persecution of the Jews, and for glorifying ideals too perfectionist for ordinary life. John Adams was equally hard on the emphasis of the ancient Greeks upon virtue, particularly of an aristocratic sort; Sparta, in particular, distorted humans beyond recognizable shape, "destitute of all business, pleasure, and amusement, but war and politics, pride and ambition."[29]

"Commerce cures destructive prejudices," Montesquieu wrote; it "polishes and softens barbaric morals." It makes men less provincial and more humane. "The spirit of commerce unites nations." Commercial nations seek gain, not conquest, and gain in the long term rests on mutual satisfaction through voluntary exchange. Commerce obliges nations to be "pacific from principle."[30] Commerce "diminishes the spirit both of patriotism and military defense," Thomas Paine wrote.[31] Benjamin Rush viewed it as "the means of uniting the different nations of the world together by the ties of mutual writs and obligations."[32] David Hume wrote that in a commercial civilization, as opposed to a martial, aristocratic, or religious civilization, "Factions are then less inveterate, revolutions less tragical, authority less severe, and seditions less frequent."[33] Free to pursue their own happiness, he hoped, individuals would become less ferocious and brutish than their ancestors. He believed that commerce gives "authority and consideration to that middling rank of men, who are the best and firmest in public liberty."[34] For Adam Smith, whereas men had before "lived almost in a continual state of war with their neighbors, and of servile dependency upon their supervisors," under a system committed to commerce they might enjoy "order and good government and, with them, the liberty and security of individuals."[35]

A commercial civilization breaks the monopoly of public service enjoyed by the great. Even the humblest person has opportunity both to improve his station and to enrich the republic. Ambition courses through millions who, under other regimes, would seem sullen and inert. Individuals set goals for themselves—to be a master carpenter, or foreman, or linesman, whatever each might rationally aspire to—and enjoy the satisfaction of self-improvement, whereas the aristocrat "shudders with horror at the thought of . . . continued and long exertion of patience, industry, fortitude and application of thought."[36] More romantic social orders stimulate great passions, de Tocqueville observed, but citizens in a commercial republic exhibit love of order, regard for conventional morality, distrust of genius, and preference for the practical over the theoretical. "Violent political passions have little hold on men whose whole thoughts are bent on the pursuit of well being. Their excitement about small matters makes them calm about great ones."[37] But this is not exactly right. For trade and navigation are seen to be surrogates for war. Great deeds and heroic exertions are borne, not solely for the self, but usually for family and often for the pure achievement of the thing. The man of commerce treats all of life "like a game of chance, a time of revolution, or the day of a battle."[38] Building industries where none stood before yields creative satisfactions.

In the new order, ordinary people feel a lift in self-esteem. Their aspirations realistically reach higher than their fathers'. Their efforts, not in every case but in a sufficiently large number of cases, have continued to be rewarded. Their personal goals, if proportional to their abilities, have a good chance of being realized. Self-realization becomes a common aim. Commerce also teaches that no one can be right all the time, since nearly all sometimes experience failure. The market puts a ceiling on ambition, proportional to each. Not all succeed equally. Luck and timing play important roles. The market raises up many who under other regimes were last, and tumbles many who in earlier regimes were first. New cycles of progress and technological development continue this process. The resulting social system is highly mobile and fluid, compared to others.

A market system entails great human losses. For realists, this was a foregone conclusion. Montesquieu counted the cost of old communal ties, which would be replaced by the less effective ties of mutual interests in liberty and order.[39] Adam Smith was even more aware of the human losses to be expected. The new order would narrow and demean the human spirit, such that the "heroic spirit" would be "almost entirely extinguished."[40] The rapacity of some merchants would lead them to try to close open markets through monopolistic practices. Competitive markets are not sustained by magic; they must be maintained through vigilance on the part of the public and the state.[41] The division of labor would force some into tasks that would mutilate their minds, encourage gross ignorance and stupidity, and corrupt "the nobler parts of human character."[42] Society would have to find compensatory means to redress these injustices; the market alone would not do that. Moreover, since every virtue may be corrupted, the commercial virtues may degenerate into avarice, social meanness, cowardice, and hedonism. Since the greater dangers lay in the indolence and extravagance of aristocracy, in the intolerance of the clergy, and in the despotism of the state, these costs can be borne; but they must be seen to be costs.

Finally, the success of democratic capitalism in producing prosperity and liberty is its own greatest danger. The virtues required to "increase the wealth of nations" are less easily observed once wealth is attained. Parents brought up under poverty do not know how to bring up children under affluence. Moreover, as more and more citizens are taken from productive work and their own non-profit work is supported by the productivity of others, new vested interests are established. A new sort of social aristocracy is born, not through inherited status, but through professional interests and ambitions. As "the new class" of commerce took center stage in 1776, so later a "new class" of intellectuals—so Schumpeter saw[43]—would try to dominate the commercial class by seizing the power of the state. De Tocqueville had foreseen that the passion for equality inherent in the new order might lead, in time, "to servitude or freedom, knowledge or barbarism, prosperity or wretchedness."[44]

The commercial virtues are not, then, sufficient to their own defense. A commercial system needs taming and correction by a moral-cultural system independent of commerce. At critical points, it also requires taming and correction by the political system and the state. The founding fathers did not imagine that the institutions of religion, humanism, and the arts would ever lose their indispensable role. They did not imagine that the state would wither away. Each of the three systems needs the other.

Yet they did understand that an economic system without profit is merely spinning its wheels, providing neither for the unmet needs of the poor nor for progress. Even "small gains and small savings" have extraordinary impact. A growth rate averaging just 2 percent a year was sustained in Great Britain from 1780 until 1914,[45] and made that tiny nation the world's leading power. To have invented a system capable of such sustained development was a gain for humanity. For in the wake of economic development came political and moral-cultural developments of great importance, including a great flowering of individual possibility, the arts, and good works (including many not for profit).

Thus, neither commercial virtues nor profits are merely economic in their character or in their effects. On the other hand, they are not sufficient for a full human life. They play an indispensable role in the achievement of the common good, and societies which lack them struggle in swamps of hopelessness unknown to those that possess them. One may believe the commercial virtues to be less than the highest of virtues, but it is not contrary to biblical faith to honor them for their instrumental role.

Community in Practice

Between individualism and collectivism, there is a third way: a rich pattern of association. Just because individuals are not collectivized it does not follow that they are not communal.

Thus, the Catholic philosopher Jacques Maritain reported his own shock on coming to know the United States. For him, capitalism had always been an evil word. In *Reflections on America*, he wrote: "The American economy is growing beyond capitalism, in the proper classical sense of this word." The United States has discovered a new direction "beyond capitalism and beyond socialism . . . personalist and community-minded at the same time." Under democratic capitalism—one from among the names he suggested to describe the new reality—"free enterprise and private ownership function now in a social context."[46]

Maritain's witness is important.[47] America as he experienced it was not as he had read about it. Like Maritain, each of us in our families has through experience a fund of knowledge about the system which is independent of books. Beyond ideology, there is experience. In a pluralistic system, such experience is amazingly various. The experience of the Irish in the United States is not exactly like that of the Poles, Italians, or Hispanics. The experience of individuals is more various still. Yet all such experience points to community.

For example, my wife and I found a memoir written some ninety years ago by an ancestor of hers. He was Charles E. Brown, the first Baptist missionary in the Iowa Territory, who journeyed westward with his family from Upstate New York in 1842. One of the most stunning features of his memoir is that nearly all the daily activities he reports were cooperative and fraternal.[48] Families helped each other putting up homes and barns. Together, they built churches, schools, and common civic buildings. They collaborated to build roads and bridges. They took pride in being free persons, independent, and self-reliant; but the texture of their lives was cooperative and fraternal.

These pioneer experiences of fraternity were not unlike those of later waves of immigrants, who began coming to America about 1870, notably to the minefields and smaller industrial cities of the northeast. They too lived richly communal lives. They built fraternals, lodges, and associations of many sorts. They too built many of their own homes and common buildings. While it is true that many of them left Europe as individuals, breaking from their own families, their lives in America continued to be intensely familial and associative. Many were active in the labor unions. Virtually all were active in churches, clubs, and many other associations. The experience of my wife's family and mine were not, then, those of "rugged individuals" alone.

It is true that life in America was rather less tribal, less limited to kin, and less homogeneous than in Europe. Neighborhoods and villages tended to be "melting pots" or, as some were later to say, "little leagues of nations." Both the public and the parochial schools tended to unite persons of many diverse backgrounds and linguistic traditions. The idea of fraternity was sharply real. It was not without friction.

The great mobility and patterns of opportunity in America began, however, to change the nature and meaning of community. For many, there still remained many forms of *Gemeinschaft*, that closeness of belonging, kinship, and common memory and faith which their ancestors had known in Europe. Yet every American family has also known the experience of uprooting, often more than once, and virtually all have been aware that their neighbors and friends in the New World belong to kinship networks, cultures, religions, and races different from their own. Pluralism is part of everyday experience. The huge dislocations of World War II, moreover, dramatically introduced even previously distant groups of Americans to one another in military service, in travel, at work. Lads from mining towns and city ghettoes took basic training in the South, visited California, served abroad.

In the years following World War II, mobility and interchange increased. Through these changes, the American people in all their variety continued to manifest loyalties to family, to civic life, and to countless forms of association. Yet in their freedom they have also experienced much rupture of close ties, many separations, and significant loneliness.

One reason problems of community are so acute among Americans is that most of us live between two experiences. More than is commonly thought, a great many of us have known a strong familial, neighborhood, and village life. We are fairly close to the experience of traditional societies known to our grandparents. On the other hand, we know new liberties. This is especially true of those more highly educated professionals whose jobs may carry them anywhere in the nation or the world. Such freedom disciplines the human spirit to the kind of "detachment" which religious superiors used to preach to young priests and religious. The latter's frequent changes of assignment, they were instructed, would oblige them to be uprooted often and to disrupt close human associations many times. They would accept these disciplines for the common good and for their own inner development.

This example shows that "community" is a reality of many kinds. My wife often teases me that I could be happy anywhere, as long as I could have my books and some writing paper. This made me recognize that many of my best friends and kindred spirits—whose books I lug with me from place to place—have been dead for hundreds of years. There are real communities of the spirit, which we carry with us even in solitude. At the Catholic Mass, as in the Jewish sabbath services, one recalls consciously that one is part of a community stretching across thousands of years. Intimate proximity is not essential to community.

In our sentimental age, however, there is a tendency to desire a different sort of community, less a community of the spirit and the inner life than a community of sentiment, emotional support, and often expressed intimacy. Such communities are no doubt precious, but they are also often dubious, cloying, and imprisoning. Community is not a simple reality. The much celebrated "loss of community" is not, correspondingly, all loss.

There is one form of community worth stressing here. It is a community of colleagueship, task-oriented, goal-directed, freely entered into and freely left. Its members have much respect for each other, learn much from each other, come to expect truth from each other, and treat one another fairly. Still, they may not have much emotional attachment to each other, spend much time looking into each other's eyes for moral support, or be particularly intimate with one another. They may enjoy comradeship in fighting the same battles, in enduring together the slings of hostile fortune, and in taking up each other's necessities.

Such community is not like the closeness of medieval villagers, nor does it require having the same faith, worldview, or vision of reality. There are "bands of brothers" who do not occupy the same metaphysical ground. Add to this form of community many years of comradeship, growing mutual esteem, and the competitive urging of each other to new heights of development, and one experiences within it a form of friendship not unknown to the ancients, yet quite distinctively modern. For much modern work requires intense collaboration over long periods of time with skilled and dedicated colleagues. Democratic capitalism is not, I think, inferior in nurturing many such communities. Sports offer an approximation through extended experiences of teamwork. Later life goes far beyond sports.

Thus, in discussing community, I have found it useful to ask: According to which ideal? The sorts of community known to villages and neighborhoods are quite admirable, but they have their own limitations and liabilities. Affective communities which seek to vibrate together on compatible wavelengths also have their attractions and their limits. Collective solidarity seems strong and ennobling; yet it renders dissent and individual difference suspect. Communities of "joy, love and hope"—to cite the words of one contemporary Catholic hymn—inspire gladness but seem superficial. (Psalms of grief, enmity, and despair strike me as truer, deeper, more reliable.)

In order to experience the community of colleagueship, one needs an ethos deeper than individualism and collectivism, an ethos of association, teamwork, and collaboration, oriented by tasks and goals, voluntarily entered into. The ethos of democratic capitalism is rich in such encouragement. This is not the only form of community, but it is a noble one. It is not, however, given. It must be created.

Thus the social life of Americans remains so associative that it is often difficult to get parents and children to sit down together for one meal each day. Eight-year-olds belong to more groups than two parents can supply drivers for. During political campaigns, strangers from all parts of the country converge on states like Iowa and New Hampshire and, without delay, establish patterns of teamwork and swift cooperation.

Some critics accuse Americans of too little individualism. They sometimes describe Americans as too highly organized, too quick to be "joiners," too socially activist, too conformist. David Riesman's famous book *The Lonely Crowd* suggested that too few Americans show that firm inner backbone, that inner-directedness, which used to be the hallmark of one type of individualism.[49] Many are too "other-directed," too quick to take their signals from their associates. The group instinct is too strong.

I have had occasion to visit my mother's family high in the mountains of eastern Slovakia. From the hilltops, on a clear day, one can see into Poland toward Krakow, at one time the greatest trading center in Europe. By sheer chance, I discovered in a sheepherder's hut at some distance from the village some colored pages from an old Sears catalog nailed to the rude walls. The shepherd offered me a cut of goat's cheese on his knife. As he talked, he revealed that he had been born in America in the same hospital in the same city in the same year as I had. His father had brought him home to Slovakia as a child, and the war had prevented their return.

It was impossible not to know that there had been significant transformations between the life forms of those rural villages and those of the cities of the United States (or of Kosice or Bratislava, for that matter). Yet I could not bring myself to feel that the advantages of living in the United States were solely material. I know and value the quality of the lives of those I met in the villages of Brutovce and Dubrava. Yet I felt profoundly grateful to my migrant grandparents for *spiritual* privileges, precisely for a thicker and richer social existence than was possible in the mountain villages of my ancestors.

I do not mean to pen a rhapsody to the social life of America. There is much wrong with it. Yet it would be wrong to be entirely silent about the distinctive forms of community it does build. The experiences America has given to my family, and to many millions of other families, have been so rich in opportunity, in possibility, in dream, that they cannot easily be fathomed. The enormous wealth produced by a free system sometimes masks these social benefits from our sight.

In *Socialism*, Michael Harrington observes that many of the spiritual realities intended by the name "socialism" have been realized under another name, the name "America."[50] Among these are not only political democracy and opportunity, but also marvelously strong traditions of family and association, cooperation and fraternity. A pluralistic society, in particular, draws out in each of us skills in tolerance, collaboration, and mutual respect that are all the more remarkable when compared to the still-bitter antagonisms between groups, religions, and cultures in the lands from which we are derived.

Still, the transition from the village life we remember through our parents and grandparents to the looser associations of our own lives is hard on all of us. Many teenagers seem overwhelmed by the confusing freedoms of their futures and by loss of regular contact with adults. The inroads of crime and drugs are alarming. The horrid *busyness* of nearly everybody's life kills the more relaxed forms of community even our universities used to know. The mobility and travel which, on the one hand, stimulate our minds and enlarge our perceptions leave us, on the other, frayed and seldom fully "present," our whole restful attention available to those among whom we find ourselves. Our moral and cultural traditions have not kept pace with our economic possibilities. We try to match new demands with a spiritual life not designed for them. Democratic capitalism suffers from the underdevelopment of guidance for a spiritual life appropriate to its highly developed political and economic life. To some extent, the leaders of our moral-cultural institutions must accept the blame. They have too often been followers, arriving breathless on battlefields only in time to erect monuments.

In any era, in any culture, it is difficult to become all that one can become. In our time it is exceedingly difficult, because the guiding voices are contradictory, and because one loses so much time groping up so many wrong alleys into so many deadends. Societies as hugely free as ours create enormous problems for individuals seeking to "find themselves" and result in much aimless wandering. One feels, sometimes, like those dry leaves Dante saw swirling outside the gates, more blown than choosing. We desperately need teachers, models, guides—not those who steal our freedom from us but those who teach us to grasp it surehandedly. The life of the spirit is far from stifled by democratic capitalism, but in the absence of strong moral guidance, it is often squandered. Our moral-cultural institutions do their job less well than our economic institutions do theirs. The twain are not yet matched. We need a spirituality appropriate for democratic capitalism as it is, and we do not have it.

Some common misperceptions seem to block us from even starting to acquire it. When I think of the many families in America known to me, most of the descriptions of Americans common to sociological and literary conventions do not seem to fit. In particular, descriptions like "the consumer society," "greed," and "materialism" seem very wide of the mark. These are not saintly families, only ordinary human beings. Yet the more one knows about them, the deeper and more worthy of respect they seem to be. If we would help them to become better than they are, we must at least come to know them as they are. Their generosity may be historically unparalleled. It is a generosity not of financial giving only but of an enormous network of volunteer activities. Faced with a problem, Americans almost by instinct form a committee. Their contributions to humanitarian purposes around the world and to their neighbors are not inferior to those of traditional or socialist societies.[51]

It is tempting to believe that the instinct for community so vital and alive among Americans—"caring," "compassion," "sensitivity," and even "love" are words used so often in American public life as to have become cloying—is due mainly to the political culture of democracy and to the moral-cultural values of Jewish, Christian, and humanistic inheritance. No doubt this is largely true. On the other hand, the specific forms of capitalist *economic* life are actually experienced by most Americans in ways far from "the cash nexus." With respect to their own private lives, money is an almost taboo subject among Americans. Most often, one does not know the salaries of one's associates and, beyond that, whatever financial resources they may have inherited. It would be gross to inquire. At universities, the children of the wealthy seem to be among the most diffident about wealth, the most eager to hide advantages. John Barron reports in his book on the KGB that the Soviets find it almost impossible to recruit American agents through ideology or political conviction; their recruiters are advised that, in approaching Americans, money is the only safe avenue.[52] The Soviets attribute this to capitalist greed. It seems far more attributable to the American sense that a transaction reduced to money seems mundane and innocent.

It is sometimes said that capitalism introduces a "competitive" system, a "rat race," "dog-eat-dog." One does not notice that athletes from socialist nations are any less competitive than those from democratic capitalist lands. Nor is the competition for political power in socialist states any less fearsome than the competition for the more various forms of power open to the citizens of democratic capitalist societies. Still, most persons in America do *not* seem to want to rise to the top. Many compete mostly with themselves. They set goals for themselves and try to realize them in their own way and at their own pace. Taking it easy, playing it as it comes, easy does it—these attributes seem to be at least as widely celebrated and realized as the competitive drive. Individuals choose their own roads—even children from one family go in multiple directions.

The ideal of a democratic capitalist society is to guarantee the right of each person to pursue happiness. (Happiness itself is not guaranteed.) Thus the system as a whole must be open to enormous variety. It must afford satisfactions at work as well as in free time. Since it is in the nature of humans to be social, the ideal is also to build decent and even affectionate relations among those who work together. For many Americans, there is almost as much friendship and mutuality with colleagues or buddies on the job as in the family. Indeed, for some, there may be a larger store of shared values with workmates than with the whole extended family at Thanksgiving dinner, at which they must sit down with persons whose politics they abhor, whose religious views they cannot abide, and whose occupational biases, ideas, values, and even social class may be far removed from their own. We may within limits choose our communities.

In short, even the economic system within democratic capitalism has its own internal impulses toward community, though of a different sort than any known before. Concerning these, we need far more careful thought than anywhere is yet in evidence. They have produced a new type of human being, the communitarian individual. Perhaps we have not seen what is around us because we are too close to it—and have learned too many clichés about the bourgeois man and woman, the middle class, ourselves.

The New Anticapitalism

Antipathy to capitalism is of legendary proportions, especially among the classes whose status is higher under aristocracies and dictatorships: aristocrats, clergy, scholars, artists, and of course government officials. Working people tend to prefer democratic capitalism which, as the Italian Marxist Antonio Gramsci pointed out, quickly raises them into the middle class. Thus, even now that Marxism has been discredited as a social ideal, we may expect new forms of anticapitalism to appear. Eric Voegelin once pointed out that Marxism is a species of gnosticism, that is, a perfectionism ("the paradise of the proletariat") access to which depends upon a privileged form of knowledge (*gnosis*, in this case "scientific socialism") that makes a certain elite superior to everybody else. Gnosticism also implies a certain impatience with the human body, with imperfections, with democratic politics and the slow procedures of persuasion, with compromise, and (in short) with the human condition. Now that Marxism is no longer a credible vehicle for this underlying passion, what will replace it?

In 1990, it seems already clear that antimodern passions run high; even a passion for primitivism is again in evidence. Similar signs were present in the Romantic Movement of the nineteenth century, notably in the operas of Richard Wagner. In the origins of totalitarianism, especially in Italy and Germany, the call of the primitive was quite important, including the cult of unspoiled nature. No doubt, the passions of National Socialism are as dead as the passions of communism. But the underlying sensibility is still very much alive. Capable of assuming a great many shapes, perhaps the cult of nature will be put to creative use in the environmental movement. That movement, however, has already shown many signs of hatred for business corporations, industry, property, and even—on a different plane of reality—the idea of "progress." Its tendency to turn to the power of the state to enforce its own passions is also manifest. One can predict with some certainty that environmentalism is likely to replace Marxism as the main carrier of gnosticism (and anticapitalism) in the near future.

This is not, of course, inevitable. Environmentalists could conclude that the new forms of awareness they are teaching the public can best be served by a free and inventive economy. Whatever the public wants, industry has an incentive to invent a way of supplying. Given the widespread desire for environmental protection now growing in the public mind, a shrewd investor might even anticipate on the part of business corporations an outpouring of new technologies, approaches, products, and processes, around which entire new environmental-minded industries may come into existence. As the public becomes willing to pay for environmental enhancement, ways to achieve it will be swiftly invented. That is already happening. The newer the factory, the cleaner it tends to be; the more recent the product, the more "environment friendly." Meanwhile, the public as a whole will not wish to abolish the benefits of modernity—the medical benefits especially—even though some extremists might. Environmental activists will want television for their messages and pleas, and airplanes to carry them to international conferences. An environmentally conscious industry will thus have plenty to do; the question is only whether environmentalists will perceive it as an ally or not.

Many environmentalists are, of course, conservatives quite committed to the capitalist economy, but many others are hostile to capitalism. The latter might wish to consider two points: First, the dire state of environmental protections both in socialist and in traditionalist (third world) countries; and, second, the fact that no other system is as likely to produce the wealth necessary for environmental protections as democratic capitalist systems.

Thus, it remains useful to reflect on the anticapitalist leanings present even in those who enjoy the benefits of democratic capitalist societies. Even today such powerful anticapitalist leanings affect the vision of those traditionalists who borrow their ideals from the aristocratic classes. For example, if someone says to you that you have aristocratic tastes, or are a prince of a man, you will probably feel complimented. But if someone says to you that you have bourgeois tastes, you will probably feel insulted. But stop for a moment. Is this bias not entirely out of tune with reality? Nearly all the beautiful things patronized by aristocrats and princes down the ages were actually created by those first skilled craftsmen, who were neither serfs nor aristocrats, the burghers who owned their own shops in the towns; in short, the first bourgeoisie. Most of the best wines, the best lace, the silver, the armor, the carved wooden furniture, the paintings and the tapestries that set the world's standards of taste were made by these bourgeois craftsmen.

Another frequently overlooked source of this anticapitalist leaning is the ancient and medieval experience of wealth as a zero-sum game: What some gained, others lost. Wealth was then thought to lie solely in land and gold coin and precious objects, and was usually acquired by plunder, conquest, or favor. In this context such aphorisms arose as *Radix malorum est cupiditas* ("Cupidity is the root of evils"); "Property is theft"; and "The rich get richer, the poor poorer."

A third strain of this anticapitalist leaning is communicated through illusions about the precapitalist system. Not much had changed in the harsh life of the poor from the time of Christ until the realities of France as described by Victor Hugo in *Les Miserables*. Similarly, before 1989 critics of capitalism seldom counted the moral and economic costs of socialism; they gave it the benefit of their dreams. Admittedly, the morality of democratic capitalist systems is low when compared with the supernatural standards of Christianity and other codes of spiritual perfection. But its daily practice in supplying opportunity to the poor is superior to the daily practice of any other historical system, traditional or socialist. It does not pretend to offer a moral paradise, only greater liberties and more flexible supports for moral living than any other system. It brings temptations, but also incredibly high moral possibilities. That is why people migrate in such numbers and with such passion toward it.

A fourth source of this anticapitalist leaning is to associate capitalism solely with material things, with commodities, with objects. This is the usage of Karl Marx; it is also the usage adopted by Pope John Paul II in his encyclical *Laborem Exercens*. (The Vatican tends to define capitalism as an abstract ideology, as in the term "economism," rather than as the tacit wisdom embodied in concrete practices.) If one accepts this usage, how could one do other than to reject capitalism? To take this approach, however, is to overlook the spirit of capitalism, its dynamic principle, its central commitment to practical intellect: to invention, discovery, reasoned cooperation, and the intellectual and moral virtue of enterprise. Were the impulse of capitalism solely materialistic, the system would have long since fallen into narcissism, hedonism, and death. This was the theory of Marx; namely that the alienation inherent in the system would drive the workers to "narcissism" or, in the current Marxist lingo, "consumerism." Instead, the spirit of capitalism seems constantly to reinvigorate itself, to work revolution after revolution in technological possibility (mechanical, industrial, and electronic), and to inspire creativity in every sphere of life. It is a system designed to arouse and to liberate, not the body, but the creative soul. It arouses even the high ideals of those who disdain the "consumerism" they think affects others.

Moreover, so high are the spiritual demands of democratic capitalism that the virtues necessary to such a system may require generations to learn. Alexis de Tocqueville himself noted how difficult and long is the school of democracy. To learn the moral habits necessary to a capitalist order is at least equally demanding. Indeed, the populations of Eastern Europe, Latin America, and Africa are now learning at some cost just how high the moral demands of a democratic, capitalist, and pluralistic order are. The lassitude, corruption, nepotism, cronyism, and other habits instilled in them by traditionalist and socialist orders are not easy to overcome.

It is not at all certain, for example, that the once-communist countries of Eastern Europe and the USSR will be able to make the difficult transition from communism to the free society in less than three generations, and without terrible internal convulsions. Communism taught citizens to respect one moral principle alone: total subjection to the power of party rule. Nothing else mattered, neither truth nor fairness nor competence. However lazy, incompetent, immoral, or even criminal one's behavior might be judged under other systems, under communism no burden of guilt had to be borne for it, so long as one was recognized as a loyal, obedient follower of the party.

The polluting of the natural environment of Eastern Europe, the corruption of the moral ethos, and the relentless spending down of the capital stock of the communist countries has left behind a wasteland—except for one thing. Somehow the love for liberty survived. Human nature has asserted itself, like green shoots at the end of winter. How to give moral nurture to those shoots is now on the world's agenda. A huge moral task lies before us.

Let me state it this way: A revolution in the direction of democracy and capitalism must have moral depth, or it cannot long endure. Citizens must gain respect for the creativity that the Creator Himself has endowed in their nature. More and more of them must exercise their own inalienable capacity for economic initiative. Despite difficulties, all must learn to respect in others the same image of God that they respect in themselves. They must learn afresh to approach each other with respect for each other's liberty, and to address each other through reasoned conversation and voluntary cooperation. These are signs of depth of character; they are also requirements for making a free society work.

Such a political economy must meet high moral standards. To overlook its moral aspirations—to concede merely its pragmatic efficacy—is both to mutilate it and to doom it to destruction. Citizens who live in democratic capitalist nations need the inspiration of the system's own internal standards. They need the practical moral guidance implicit in the system's traditions and evolutionary design. For in its actual historical embodiments, the spirit of democratic capitalism has been morally driven. This inner drive must today be rendered explicit; it must be strengthened; it must be deepened. The democratic capitalist revolution is moral, or not at all.

NOTES

1. Karl Marx and Frederick Engels, *The Communist Manifesto* (New York: International Publishers, 1948), pp. 13–14.

2. See Max Weber, *The City*, trans. D. Martindale and G. Neuwirth (New York: The Free Press, 1958), p. 94.

3. In conceptual logic, *socialism* and *democracy* are mutually compatible. The problem of realizing both at the same time arises from the conditions of actual history. In the real world, a socialism which is rationally planned and coercively imposed by a state bureaucracy is not likely to arise from popular interests, unless one supposes an incredibly passive, docile, and homogeneous populace. Another type of socialism, decentralized and participatory, must deal with the refractoriness of individual agents and groups. If it reconciles diverse interests, it is unlikely to be "rational." If it is "rational," it is unlikely to express diverse interests. Thus democratic socialism, while possible in the world of logic, appears to be incoherent in actual history.

By contrast, *democracy* and *markets* do not mutually entail each other in the world of conceptual logic. One may imagine democracy without markets, and a market system without democracy. But in the real world of actual experience, a polity which recognizes individual rights is bound to be drawn to an economic system which empowers individual agency. Similarly, an economic system based upon markets and individual incentives is, over time, bound to be drawn to a political system recognizing individual rights and liberties.

I call such entailments "dialectical," to suggest the tendencies and preconditions which are operative in the real world of history, as distinct from the merely conceptual necessities of the world of logic.

4. Robert Lekachman writes: "Political democracy seems to be consistent only with some versions of capitalism. Capitalism, embarrassingly, flourishes in places like Chile, Brazil, South Korea, Taiwan, the Philippines, Indonesia, and other bastions of repression. In the past, it has been comfortable in fascist Italy, Spain, Portugal, Greece and elsewhere. In short, capitalism has certainly existed without political democracy and without free play for intermediate organizations. In fairness, of course, one must say that it is difficult to find examples of democratic socialism without some significant degree of capitalism." "The Promise of Democratic Socialism," in *Democracy and Mediating Structures*, ed. Michael Novak (Washington: American Enterprise Institute, 1980), p. 35.

The nations Professor Lekachman points to are not fully formed examples of democratic capitalism. Their economic systems may be more free than their political systems, although even the latter, as he generously suggests, provide a wider range of liberties than those available in neighboring socialist societies (North Korea, Cuba, etc.). Their political authoritarianism, however, diminishes liberty, social mobility, and the circulation of elites. Their typical patterns of corruption, favoritism, nepotism, and other vices violate economic and moral ideals. Thus, to liberate the economy from the state is a necessary but not a sufficient step toward the attainment of fully formed democratic capitalism.

It is true that in Germany, for example, a certain form of capitalism has survived for more than a hundred years under regimes as various as those of Bismarck, the Kaiser, the Weimar Republic, National Socialism, and the Federal Republic of Germany. Still, the economic liberties presupposed in a genuinely broad diffusion of capitalism are best served by the political liberties and individual rights guaranteed under democracy.

In Great Britain, the historical situation seems to have been in some ways the reverse: First there was democracy and, only gradually, capitalism. Still, the political liberties which were so long the rights of Englishmen had as their natural expression the broadening of such rights in the economic sphere. Economic rights and liberties could not forever be beholden to charters and privileges meted out solely by the Crown. There are many interpretations as to how and why capitalism first arose in Great Britain. Yet rights in the political sphere seem also to have encouraged limits upon the state in the economic sphere.

My intention is not to simplify the many underlying schemes of causation, but only to call attention to the underlying consonance of political and economic liberties, and to note, further, their common source in liberties of conscience, morals, and culture.

5. Henry Hazlitt, *The Conquest of Poverty* (New Rochelle, N.Y.: Arlington House, 1973), pp. 13–18.

6. See Paul Johnson, "Has Capitalism a Future?" in *Will Capitalism Survive?* ed. Ernest W. Lefever (Washington, D.C.: Ethics and Public Policy Center, 1979), p. 5.

7. Oscar Handlin, "The Development of the Corporation," in *The Corporation: A Theological Inquiry*, eds. Michael Novak and John W. Cooper (Washington, D.C.: American Enterprise Institute, 1981), p. 2.

8. Johnson, "Has Capitalism a Future?"

9. "One of the merits of the factory system was that it offered, and required, regularity of employment and hence greater stability of consumption. During the period 1790–1830 factory production increased rapidly. A greater proportion of the people came to benefit from it both as producers and as consumers. The fall in the price of textiles reduced the price of clothing. . . . Boots began to take the place of clogs, and hats replaced shawls, at least for wear on Sundays. Miscellaneous commodities, ranging from clocks to pocket handkerchiefs, began to enter into the scheme of expenditure, and after 1820 such things as tea and coffee and sugar fell in price substantially. . . . In 1837 or 1838 Thomas Holmes, an old man of eighty-seven born in 1760 [*sic*], gave . . . his impressions of the changes that had taken place since his youth . . . 'There has been a very great increase in the consumption of meat, wheaten bread, poultry, tea and sugar. But it has not reached the poorest, except tea, sugar and wheaten bread. The poorest are not so well fed. But they are better clothed, lodged and provided with furniture, better taken care of in sickness and misfortune. So they are gainers.' " T. S. Ashton, "The Standard of Life of the Workers in England, 1780–1830," in *Capitalism and the Historians*, ed. F. A. Hayek (Chicago: University of Chicago Press, 1954), pp. 152–54, n. 26.

10. In March 1925, receiving Monsignor Joseph Cardijn of Belgium. See John Tracy Ellis, *American Catholicism* (Chicago: University of Chicago Press, 1956), p. 106.

11. "J. B. Bury, in his *Idea of Progress*, also denied the existence of the idea of progress in Greek and Roman thought (and in Christian thought as well) on the grounds, first, that their philosophers lacked awareness of a long historical past within which progress could be discerned; second, that they were victims of their own belief in a theory of historical degeneration (with the story of mankind perceived as one long decline from an original golden age); and third, that Greek and Roman philosophers were generally committed to an envisagement of human history as endlessly and recurrently cyclical, thus making any thought of linear advancement through the ages quite impossible. . . . Weighty testimony indeed. But the truth, I believe, lies in the opposite corner." Robert Nisbet, *History of the Idea of Progress* (New York: Basic Books, 1980), pp. 10–11.

12. Jacques Maritain, *Reflections on America* (New York: Charles Scribner's Sons, 1958), p. 118.

13. Irving Kristol, *Two Cheers for Capitalism* (New York: Basic Books, 1978), pp. 262, 270.

14. See Jacques Maritain, *Integral Humanism*, trans. Joseph W. Evans (New York: Charles Scribner's Sons, 1968); *Christianity and Democracy*, trans. Doris C. Anson (New York: Charles Scribner's Sons, 1944); *The Person and the Common Good*, trans. John J. Fitzgerald (New York: Charles Scribner's Sons, 1947); and *Man and the State* (Chicago: University of Chicago Press, 1951).

In 1958, Maritain wrote: "I would like to refer to one of my books, *Humanisme Intégral*, which was published twenty years ago. When I wrote this book, trying to outline a concrete historical ideal suitable to a new Christian civilization, my perspective was definitely European. I was in no way thinking in American terms, I was thinking especially of France, and of Europe, and of their historical problems, and of the kind of concrete prospective image that might inspire the activity, in the temporal field, of the Catholic youth of my country.

"The curious thing in this connection is that, fond as I may have been of America as soon as I saw her, and probably because of the particular perspective in which *Human-*

isme Intégral was written, it took a rather long time for me to become aware of the kind of congeniality which existed between what is going on in this country and a number of views I had expressed in my book.

"Of course the book is concerned with a concrete historical ideal which is far distant from any present reality. Yet, what matters to me is the *direction* of certain essential trends characteristic of American civilization. And from this point of view I may say that *Humanisme Intégral* appears to me now as a book which had, so to speak, an affinity with the American climate by anticipation." Maritain, *Reflections on America*, pp. 174–75 (italics his).

15. See John Courtney Murray, S.J., *We Hold These Truths* (New York: Sheed & Ward, 1960); and Walter Lippmann, *The Public Philosophy* (New York: New American Library, 1955). Reinhold Niebuhr wrote: "If the experiences of America as a world power, its responsibilities and concomitant guilt, its frustration and its discovery of the limits of power, constitute an ironic refutation of some of the most cherished illusions of a liberal age, its experiences in domestic politics represent an ironic form of success. Our success in establishing justice and insuring domestic tranquility has exceeded the characteristic insights of a bourgeois culture. Frequently our success is due to social and political policies which violate and defy the social creed which characterizes a commercial society." *The Irony of American History* (New York: Charles Scribner's Sons, 1952), p. 89.

European writers have also tried to capture the unique American spirit. See Jean-Francois Revel, *Without Marx or Jesus*, trans. J. F. Bernard (New York: Doubleday, 1971), chaps. 1, 14, 16; Raymond L. Bruckberger, *Image of America* (New York: Viking Press, 1959); and J.-J. Servan-Schreiber, *The American Challenge*, trans. Ronald Steel (New York: Avon, 1969).

16. See Kathleen Nott, *The Good Want Power: An Essay in the Psychological Possibilities of Liberalism* (New York: Basic Books, 1977).

17. Milton and Rose Friedman, *Free to Choose* (New York: Harcourt Brace Jovanovich, 1980), p. 27.

18. Adam Smith, *The Theory of Moral Sentiments* (Indianapolis: Liberty Classics, 1969), pp. 204, 71.

19. See Irving Kristol, "The Spiritual Roots of Capitalism and Socialism," in *Capitalism and Socialism: A Theological Inquiry*, ed. Michael Novak (Washington, D.C.: American Enterprise Institute, 1979), p. 1.

20. See Noonan, *The Scholastic Analysis of Usury*, chap. 3.

21. Ralph Lerner, "Commerce and Character: The Anglo-American as New-Model Man," *William and Mary Quarterly* 36 (January 1979); 3–26; see p. 5. See also Stephen Miller, "Adam Smith and the Commercial Republic," *Public Interest* 61 (Fall 1980): 106–22. In what follows, I have borrowed extensively from Lerner's argument; for several quotations the author and title only are given, along with the page number of the Lerner article where the quotation appears. For convenient reference, the Lerner article also appears in *Liberation South, Liberation North* (Washington, D.C.: American Enterprise Institute, 1981).

22. Adam Smith, *The Theory of Moral Sentiments* (Indianapolis: Liberty Classics, 1969), pp. 407, 416.

23. Ibid., p. 416.

24. In the New World, two contrasting experiments in political economy caught the attention of Adam Smith. Whereas the colonies of Spain and Portugal in South America

imitated the existing social orders of southern Europe, he wrote, the frugal, simple, yet decent civil and ecclesiastical establishments in the North American colonies displayed "an ever memorable example at how small an expense three millions of people may not only be governed, but well-governed." By contrast, the oppressive practices of South America plunged all but a very few into unnecessary poverty. Smith disdained the "numerous race of mendicant friars, whose beggary" placed "a most grievous tax upon the poor people." The elaborate ceremonials of the South American rich perpetuated "ruinous taxes of private luxury" already well known in Europe. Smith, *Wealth of Nations*, p. 541.

25. Ibid., p. 364.

26. See de Tocqueville, *Democracy in America*, pp. 400–07. Ralph Lerner properly stresses the deliberate lowliness of the commercial republic: "This way of getting rid of a kind of unreason did not presuppose that men at large would use their reason more. Far from seconding the proud aspirations of Reason to grasp the whole of society and to direct its complex workings in detail, the commercial republicans counseled humility. They thought human behavior was adequately accounted for by dwelling upon the wants by which men are driven—wants that are largely, though not exclusively, physical; wants that cannot in most cases be satisfied. Butchers, bakers, prelates and professors—all could be understood in more or less the same way. Once the similitude of our passions was recognized (however much the objects of those passions varied from man to man), our common neediness and vulnerability became apparent." "Commerce and Character," p. 8.

27. De Tocqueville, *Democracy in America*, quoted by Lerner, p. 10. Another early visitor to America, J. Hector St. John Crèvecoeur, saw a new type of human being shaped by the new civic order: "Urged by a variety of motives, here they came. Everything has tended to regenerate them; new laws, a new mode of living, a new social system; here they are become men: in Europe they were as so many useless plants; wanting vegetative mould, and refreshing showers, they withered, and were mowed down by want, hunger, and war; but now by the power of transplantation, like all other plants they have taken root and flourish! Formerly they were not numbered in any civil lists of their country, except in those of the poor; here they rank as citizens. By what invisible power has this surprising metamorphosis been performed? By that of the laws and that of their industry. The laws, the indulgent laws, protect them as they arrive, stamping on them the symbol of adoption; they receive ample rewards for their labours; these accumulated rewards procure them lands; those lands confer on them the title of freemen, and to that title every benefit is affixed which men can possibly require. This is the great operation daily performed by our laws." *Letters from an American Farmer* (New York: Fox, Duffield & Co., 1904; reprint of 1782 ed.), pp. 52–53.

28. De Tocqueville, *Democracy in America*, see Lerner, p. 10.

29. Charles Francis Adams, ed., *The Works of John Adams*, see Lerner, p. 12.

30. Montesquieu, *Esprit de lois*, see Lerner, p. 14.

31. Thomas Paine, "Common Sense," see Lerner, p. 14.

32. Benjamin Rush, "Of the Mode of Education Proper in a Republic," see Lerner, p. 15.

33. David Hume, *Essays*, see Lerner, p. 15.

34. Ibid., see Lerner, p. 15.

35. Smith, *Wealth of Nations*, p. 385.

36. Smith, *The Theory of Moral Sentiments*, see Lerner, p. 16.

37. De Tocqueville, *Democracy in America*, see Lerner, pp. 16–17.

38. Ibid., p. 404.

39. Montesquieu, *Esprit de lois*, see Lerner, p. 21.

40. Smith, *Wealth of Nations*, see Lerner, p. 22. Elsewhere Smith criticizes certain landlords with withering contempt: "All for ourselves, and nothing for other people, seems, in every age of the world, to have been the vile maxim of the masters of mankind." *Wealth of Nations*, pp. 388–89.

41. "Commerce and manufactures can seldom flourish long in any state which does not enjoy a regular administration of justice, in which the people do not feel themselves secure in the possession of their property, in which the faith of contracts is not supported by law, and in which the authority of the state is not supposed to be regularly employed in enforcing the payment of debts from all those who are able to pay." Smith, *Wealth of Nations*, p. 862.

42. Smith, *Wealth of Nations*, see Lerner, p. 22.

43. See Joseph A. Schumpeter, *Capitalism, Socialism and Democracy*, 3d ed. (New York: Harper & Row, 1950), esp. the section entitled "The Sociology of the Intellectual," pp. 145–55.

44. De Tocqueville, *Democracy in America*, p. 705.

45. See Paul Johnson, "Has Capitalism a Future?" in *Will Capitalism Survive?* ed. Ernest W. Lefever (Washington, D.C.: Ethics and Public Policy Center, 1979), p. 4.

46. Jacques Maritain, *Reflections on America* (New York: Charles Scribner's Sons, 1958), pp. 178–79, 101. Maritain also observed: "This industrial civilization, which I had learned to know in Europe, appeared to me, here, both as gigantically developed (like many things transplanted from Europe over here) and as a kind of ritual dedicated to some foreign goddess. Its inner logic, as I knew it—originally grounded as it was on the principle of the fecundity of money and the absolute primacy of individual profit—was, everywhere in the world, inhuman and materialistic" (p. 21).

47. While visiting America, Maritain noticed "the sense of human fellowship" prominent in the country, and observed that attributes of "human reliability, good will, devotion, [and] helpfulness" are characteristic of Americans. "Hence, that American kindness which is so striking a feature to foreign visitors. Americans are ready to help. They are on equal terms of comradeship with everybody. And why? Simply because everybody is a human being. A fellow man. That's enough for him to be supposed worthy of assistance and sympathy—sometimes of exceedingly thoughtful and generous attention." *Reflections on America*, pp. 72, 67–68. I have written further on Maritain's views in "The Economic System: The Evangelical Basis of a Social Market Economy," *Review of Politics* 43 (July 1981): 355–80.

48. See Charles E. Brown, *Personal Recollections of Rev. Charles E. Brown, 1813–1893 (and the Family Record, 1767–1907)* (Ottumwa, Iowa: Ottumwa Stamp Works Press, 1907). Brown writes: "Pioneer life on the far western border had its compensations as well as its hardships, privations and trials. The early settlers were proverbially hospitable. Neighbors were sociable, kindly, sympathetic and helpful; and people who lived this life, as a rule loved it and preferred it to any other" (p. 48). "With our neighbors we at once began work on a log school house, a few rods south of our cabin, where without floor, doors or windows, we opened a Sunday School" (p. 32).

"In 1845 the Maquoketa people began to plan for an Academy, and Mr. Goodenow, always public spirited, generous and enterprising, donated a handsome site for the building. In 1849 the work was taken up and vigorously prosecuted.

"Early in the fall of that year at the instance of the trustees, I went to Eastern New York to solicit funds. Many of the early settlers came from that section and had friends and acquaintances there. . . . Business was dull, times hard and money scarce, and very little could be done in the way of obtaining aid for the Maquoketa Academy. But in spite of discouragement the work went on, and the building, handsome and commodious for the time and place, was completed.

"Mechanics and laborers engaged on the work were boarded in the families of enterprising citizens to help along, the pioneer wives and mothers cheerfully contributing time and toil in the good cause. Competent teachers were employed and many of the children of the Maquoketa settlers laid there the substantial foundation for their education" (pp. 52–53).

49. David Riesman et al., *The Lonely Crowd* (New Haven, Conn.: Yale University Press, 1961).

50. See Michael Harrington, *Socialism* (New York: Saturday Review Press, 1972), p. 118.

51. In 1978 Americans contributed $39.6 billion in private philanthropic funds, including $32.8 billion contributed by individuals, and the remainder by foundations, corporations, and bequests; see U.S. Bureau of the Census, *Statistical Abstract of the United States: 1979*, 100th ed. (Washington, D.C.: 1979), table 582.

52. See John Barron, *KGB* (New York: Reader's Digest Press, 1974), Appendix C, "Recruiting Americans in the U.S.A. and Third Countries."

Moral Sources of Capitalism

George Gilder

"*B*USINESSMEN ARE BASTARDS": This crude view of men of commerce, once pronounced by President John F. Kennedy, sums up the sentiments of socialist thinkers in America and around the world, from Jane Fonda to the remaining followers of the late Chairman Mao. In fact, the idea that businessmen are bastards is such a cliché among the progressive and enlightened men of the Left that most of them would be hurt and startled if a businessman responded by calling them the bigots they objectively are.

Early in 1980, however, the same words were uttered vehemently by a conservative professor of economics at a major American college. Yet conservatives are considered to be the friends of business. In fact, this economist in particular was wearing a handsome Adam Smith necktie and imagined himself to be staunchly defending private enterprise at the very time he made his rude remark about businessmen.

What is most extraordinary about this economist's view is not its extremity, vehemence, or apparent incongruity, but the fact that it was a perfectly ordinary statement for such a man to make. It sums up what has been the prevailing attitude of the leading defenders of free enterprise ever since the time of Adam Smith. Although Smith himself did not use such bawdy language, he insisted that businessmen were in general an unattractive lot who "seldom gather together except to conspire against the public interest." According to Smith the motive force of a capitalist economy is self-concern, which is a more polite way of depicting what a leftist would call avarice or greed. "Not from benevolence," said Smith, "do we expect our bread from the baker," but from self-interest. "As by an invisible hand," Smith immortally maintained, these individual acts of avarice flow together to promote the general welfare, even though few of the businessmen are concerned with any aim beyond their own enrichment.

Reprinted from Society *(September/October 1981).*

These arguments of Adam Smith, espoused in *The Wealth of Nations,* the masterwork of capitalist economics, recur in various forms throughout the literature of free enterprise and lend to many of these writings a strangely antibusiness cast. The general idea is that businessmen are useful sorts but you wouldn't want your daughter to marry one. Just as English aristocrats still sometimes express disdain for people "in trade," so American intellectuals, even on the Right, often depict capitalists as crude, boorish, and predatory figures.

Although one might suppose that such men should be kept on a short rein by government, the conservatives argue on the contrary that governments should keep out of the fray and allow the disciplines of the free market to keep the predators in line. In essence, these economists answer President Kennedy by saying, "Yes, businessmen are bastards, but the best thing to do is let them loose, to fight it out among themselves, and may the best bastard win."

Needless to say, conservative economists offer many other, more sophisticated arguments against the growth of the state. Most of what they say about the virtues of free markets is luminously true. Nonetheless, their essential view of the nature and motivation of capitalists, inherited from Adam Smith, is insidiously false and fails to explain in any convincing way the sources of economic growth and progress. It will no longer do to suggest that businessmen are bad guys, or ambitious dolts, or self-serving money grubbers, and then conclude that if they are given maximum freedom, they will build the new Jerusalem: a good and bountiful society. Capitalism needs no such labored and paradoxical defense. The fact is that capitalism is good and successful not because it miraculously transmutes personal avarice and ambition into collective prosperity, but because it calls forth, propagates, and relies upon the best and most generous of human qualities.

Capitalism begins with giving. This is a growing theme of "economic anthropology," from Melville Herskovits's pioneering book by that name to Marvin Harris's *Cannibals and Kings.* The capitalists of primitive society were tribal leaders who vied with one another in giving great feasts. Similarly, trade began with offerings from one family to another or from one tribe to its neighbor. The gifts, often made in the course of a religious rite, were presented in hopes of an eventual gift in return. The compensation was not defined beforehand. But in the feasting process it was expected to be a return with interest, as another "big man," or *mumi* as he was called among the Siuai in the Solomon Islands, would attempt to exceed the offerings of the first. Harris describes the process by which a young man demonstrates his capacity to become a *mumi* by working hard, limiting his own consumption of meat and coconuts, and eliciting the help of his family in the preparation of his first feast. If that feast is successful, his circle of supporters expands, and he prepares a still more generous feast. With each successful feast, the number of people willing to work for the success of the next one grows, and he will become a *mumi*. Although more sumptuous feasts make more irksome demands on his supporters, the overall volume of production increases.

Helen Codere describes potlatching, a similar sequence of work and saving, capital accumulation and feasting, performed among the Kwakiutl of the northwestern United States: "The public distribution of property by an individual is a recurrent climax to an endless series of cycles of accumulating property—distributing it in a potlatch—being given property—again accumulating and preparing." The piles of food and other gifts and ceremonial exchanges could mount to dumbfounding quantities. One South Sea offering mentioned by Herskovits consisted of 10,000 coconuts and ten baskets of fish.

These competitions in giving are contests of altruism. A gift will only elicit a greater response if it is based on an understanding of the needs of others. In the most successful and catalytic gifts, the giver fulfills an unknown need or desire in a surprising way. The recipient is startled and gratified by the inspired and unexpected sympathy of the giver and is eager to repay him. In order to repay him, however, the receiver must come to understand the giver. Thus the contest of gifts leads to an expansion of human sympathies. The circle of giving (the profits of the economy) will grow as long as the gifts are consistently valued more by the receivers than by the givers.

What the tribal givers were doing, by transcending barter, was inventing a kind of money: a mode of exchange that by excluding exact contractual planning allowed for freedom and uncertainty. Money consists of liabilities, debts, or promises. By giving someone a dollar, you both acknowledge a debt to him of a certain value, and you pass on to him an acknowledgment of debt given to you by someone else. But the process has to start somewhere, with a giver and a gift, a feast and a *mumi*, an investment and an investor.

By giving a feast, the *mumi* imposed implicit debts on all his guests.

By attending it, they accepted a liability to him. Through the gifts or investments of primitive capitalism, man created and extended obligations. These obligations led to reciprocal gifts and further obligations in a growing fabric of economic creation and exchange, with each giver hoping for greater returns but not assured of them, and with each recipient pushed to produce a further favor. This spreading out of debts could be seen as expanding the money supply. The crucial point is that for every liability (or feeling of obligation on the part of the guest), there was a previous asset (meal) given to him. The *mumi*, as a capitalist, could not issue demands or impose liabilities or expand money without providing commensurate supplies. The demand was inherent in the supply—in the meal.

The next step above potlatching was the use of real money. The invention of money enabled the pattern of giving to be extended as far as the reach of faith and trust—from the *mumi*'s tribe to the world economy. Among the most important transitional devices was the Chinese *Hui*. This became the key mode of capital formation for the overseas Chinese in their phenomenal successes as tradesmen and retailers everywhere they went, from San Francisco to Singapore. A more sophisticated and purposeful development of the potlatching principle, the *Hui* began when the organizer needed money for an investment. He would raise it from a group of kin and friends and commit himself to give a series of ten feasts for them. At each feast a similar amount of money would be convivially raised and given by lot or by secret bidding to one of the other members. The rotating distribution would continue until every member had won a collection. Similar systems, called the *Ko* or *Tanamoshi*, created savings for the Japanese; and the West African *Susu* device of the Yoruba, when transplanted to the West Indies, provided the capital base for Caribbean retailing. This mode of capital formation also emerged prosperously among West Indians when they migrated to American cities. All these arrangements required entrusting money or property to others and awaiting returns in the uncertain future.

That supply creates its own demand is a principle of classical economics called Say's Law. It has come to be expressed, and refuted, in many interesting technical forms. But its essential point is potlatching. Capitalism consists of providing first and getting later. The demand is implicit in the supply. Without a monetary economy, such gifts were arrayed in expectation of an immediate profit in prestige and a later feast of interest, and they could be seen as a necessary way to escape the constraints of barter, to obviate the exact coincidence of wants and values required by simple trading. In most cases, the feasts and offerings were essentially entrepreneurial. They entailed the acquisition of goods at a known cost with the intention of acquiring in exchange—in this case, over an extended period—goods of unknown value. As devices of savings and investment, they depended for success on the continued honesty and economic returns of all members. Entrepreneurs succeed only to the extent they are sensitive to the needs of others, and to the extent that others succeed. Altruism is the essence of capitalism.

Capitalist production entails faith—in one's neighbors, in one's society, and in the compensatory logic of the cosmos. Search and you shall find, give and you will be given unto, supply creates its own demand. It is this cosmology, this sequential logic, that essentially distinguishes the free from the socialist economy. The socialist economy proceeds from a rational definition of needs or demands to a prescription of planned supplies. In a socialist economy, one does not supply until the demands have already been determined and specified. Rationality rules, and it rules out the awesome uncertainties and commensurate acts of faith that are indispensable to an expanding and innovative system.

The gifts of advanced capitalism in a monetary economy are called investments. One does not make gifts without some sense, possibly unconscious, that one will be rewarded, whether in this world or the next. Even the biblical injunction affirms that the giver will be given unto. The essence of giving is not the absence of all expectation of return, but the lack of a predetermined return. Like gifts, capitalist investments are made without a predetermined return.

These gifts or investments are experimental in that the returns to the giver are unknown; and whether gains or losses, they are absorbed by him. Because the vast majority of investments fail, the moment of decision is pregnant with doubt and promise and suffused to some degree with faith. Because the ventures are experiments, however, even the failures in a sense succeed, even the waste is often redeemed. In the course of time, perhaps even with the passage of generations, the failures accumulate as new knowledge, the most crucial kind of capital, held by both the entrepreneurs themselves and the society at large.

This new knowledge is a deeper kind than is taught in schools or acquired in the controlled experiments of social or physical science, or gained in the experience of socialist economies. For entrepreneurial experiments are also adventures, with the future livelihood of the investor at stake. He participates with a heightened consciousness and passion and an alertness and diligence that greatly enhance his experience of learning. The experiment may reach its highest possibilities, and its crises and surprises may be exploited to the utmost.

This motivational advantage will often decide the success or failure of enterprises or nations otherwise equally endowed. Harvey Leibenstein of Harvard has presented a large body of experience which shows that the key factor in productivity differences among firms and between countries is neither the kind of allocational efficiency stressed in economic texts nor any other measurable input in the productive process. The differences derive from management, motivation, and spirit; from a factor he cannot exactly identify but which he calls *X-efficiency*. He quotes Tolstoy in *War and Peace*:

> Military science assumes the strength of an army to be identical to its numbers. . . . [In fact it] is the product of its mass and some unknown x . . . the spirit of the army. . . . To define and express the significance of this unknown factor . . . is a problem for science . . . only solvable if we cease arbitrarily to substitute for the unknown x itself the conditions under which that force becomes apparent— such as the commands of the general, the equipment employed and so on . . . and if we recognize this unknown quantity in its entirety as being the greater or lesser desire to fight and to face danger.

In other words, measurable inputs, such as those that can be calcu- lated in a planned economy, do not determine output. Leibenstein shows that productivity differences between workers doing the same job in a particular plant are likely to vary as much as four to one, that differences as high as 50 percent can arise between plants commanding identical equip- ment and the same size labor force paid identically. Matters of manage- ment, motivation, and spirit—and their effects on willingness to innovate and seek new knowledge—dwarf all measurable inputs in accounting for productive efficiency, both for individuals and groups and for management and labor. A key difference is always in the willingness to transform vague information or hypotheses into working knowledge: willingness, in Tolstoy's terms, transferred from the martial to the productive arts, "to fight and face danger," to exert efforts and take risks.

Socialism presumes that we already know most of what we need to know to accomplish our national goals. Capitalism is based on the idea that we live in a world of unfathomable complexity, ignorance, and peril, and that we cannot possibly prevail over our difficulties without constant efforts of initiative, sympathy, discovery, and love. One system maintains that we can reliably predict and elicit the outcomes we demand. The other asserts that we must give long before we can know what the universe will return. One is based on empirically calculable human power; the other, on optimism and faith. These are the essential visions that compete in the world and determine our fate.

When faith dies, so does enterprise. It is impossible to create through the mechanisms of rational self-interest a system of collective regulation and safety that does not finally deaden the moral sources of the willingness to face danger and fight, that does not dampen the spontaneous flow of gifts and experiments which extend the dimensions of the world and the circles of human sympathy.

Walter Lippmann was much closer to the truth of the system than many of its more conservative apologists when in 1936, in the midst of the Great Depression, he wrote that capitalism is based on "an ideal that for the first time in human history" gave men "a way of producing wealth in which the good fortune of others multiplied their own." At long last, "the Golden Rule was economically sound . . . and for the first time men could conceive a social order in which the ancient moral aspiration of liberty, fraternity, and equality was consistent with the abolition of poverty and the increase of wealth." Once "the worldly policy was to be predatory. The claims of the spirit were otherworldly." But with the rise of capitalism "the vista was opened at the end of which men could see the possibility of the good society on this earth. At long last the ancient schism between the world and the spirit . . . was potentially closed."

To defend capitalism, even to understand it, one has to comprehend that businessmen are not bastards, but the heroes of the modern age—crucial vessels of those generous and creative impulses that give hope to an ever more populous humanity in overcoming its continuing scarcities and conflicts. In a world always divided in part between the givers and the takers, businessmen are among the most persistent and ingenious of donors; and all of us who benefit should be thankful.

How is it then that the contrary view is so prevalent in the world—that most observers of capitalism see businessmen not as givers but as takers? There are many reasons, including envy, ignorance, and the corruption of many businessmen by the snares of the state. But the key source of confusion is what can be called the materialist fallacy: the belief that wealth consists chiefly not of human knowledge and creativity, generosity and love, but of a limited fund of "natural resources," always in danger of running out, and the accumulated inheritance of physical capital embodied in farms, factories, and machines.

This belief is one of the oldest of human delusions, from the period of empire when men imagined that wealth was land, to the era of mercantilism when they fantasized that it was gold, won through a favorable balance of trade, and continuing on to today when the world believes that wealth is oil, and grasps at real estate and gold as well. Contemporary economists, liberal and conservative, make a similar error when they define wealth as physical property and capital assets and measure it in quantitative terms.

As long experience should show us, however, resources and machines are nearly useless without entrepreneurs and willing workers. Iran before the revolution was replete with oil and factories, but all their resources availed them little, because they lacked in the generosity and discipline of entrepreneurs. Hong Kong and Taiwan have little material endowment, but their businessmen provide wealth for the world. Japan and Germany possess few natural resources and saw much of their material capital destroyed during World War II, but they have thrived by liberating enterprise. Throughout history, most of mankind have lived cramped and impoverished lives in materially affluent countries because of an absence of the metaphysical capital that is most crucial to progress: the trust in others, the hope for the future, the faith in a providential God that allows freedom and prompts the catalytic gifts of capitalism.

Without these essentially spiritual dimensions, the success of capitalism is inexplicable except where it is already occurring. The great flaw of the bastard capitalism theory is that it cannot explain economic growth under the conditions where it is most needed: a depressed and impoverished economy in which there is little to take and, as John Kenneth Galbraith has written, the most "rational" course is to accept one's poverty rather than to fight hopelessly against it. This perception has prompted Galbraith and many other leftist thinkers to give up on further world development and predict "lean years" of scarcity, entropy, and decay. A blindness to the spiritual sources of wealth thus is leading many "progressive" writers into a strange revival of the dismal science of nineteenth-century economics. No Ricardian law of rents, no Malthusian cycle of population was ever more coldly remorseless in its rejection of the dreams of the poor than Richard Barnet's "entropy theory" or Barry Commoner's "closing circle" of ecological limits to growth.

Adam Smith's self-interest, however, is little more persuasive than Marxist ideas of exploitation and taking as an explanation of capitalist prosperity. The pursuit of self-interest would lead not to the always risky and unpromising ventures of capitalism in an uncertain and perilous world, but to the quest for safety and security in an ever growing welfare state. The only way to escape the vicious cycles of poverty is through the expanding circles of creative giving, the investments of brave men with hope for the future, trust in their fellow men, and faith in providence. This impulse of philanthropy is the prime gift of business success.

Capitalism can be summed up in the language of scripture: *Give and you will be given unto, search and you shall find. . . . Cast your bread upon the waters and it will return to you many fold*. Or even in the language of economics: *supply creates its own demand*. Capitalism is not impugned but affirmed in the biblical parables: the parable of the talents, in which Jesus praises the man who invests and multiplies his money, or even in the parable of the rich man, who is told to give away rather than hoard his wealth.

"Where your treasure is, so your heart is also." It is Marxism and statism that are based on the materialist fallacy, that believe in the treasure of things. It is capitalism that is based on the treasure of ideas and spirit. To the extent that capitalists are bastards—predatory and materialistic, hoarding and miserly, hedonistic and prodigal—they betray the essence of capitalism and balk its growth. The fable of Midas is the story not of perils and contradictions of capitalist wealth but of the pitfalls of materialism itself. The real capitalists have the anti-Midas touch, turning the hoards of gold and liquidity, through an alchemy of creative spirit, into the productive capital of real wealth. And the foundation of wealth is always giving, not taking. The deepest truths of capitalism are faith, hope, and love.

4. Security and Freedom: Making the World Safe with Ronald Reagan

*M*ost neoconservatives opposed the Vietnam War, but their opposition was refined and targeted. They thought the war an error, but were adamant that it set no precedent for future American military involvement around the world. America, they consistently claimed, was the same great country it had been before the war—and had the same responsibility to defend freedom, intellectually, politically, and militarily. In the late 1960s and in the 1970s, the neoconservatives saw that their view was not widely shared; in fact, they feared what Norman Podhoretz, in 1977, termed "a culture of appeasement." As they saw it, the world was gravely threatened by a totalitarian Soviet Union with aggressive outposts around the world and a Third World corrupted by vicious anti-Semitism, racism, and Communist influence. The world was, as Daniel Patrick Moynihan put it in the title of his 1977 book, "a dangerous place," and the United States was the only power with the moral and military resources to guarantee freedom and security in the world. If the United States let the Vietnam experience sap her self-confidence and damage her will, the fragile forces of freedom would be vanquished. The neoconservatives determined to supply the requisite intellectual ammunition to ensure that this did not happen.

Jeane Kirkpatrick's classic essay "Dictatorships and Double Standards" is perhaps the greatest neoconservative anticommunist essay. She explains why Communism is the most formidable enemy of freedom in the world, and why the United States must sometimes make alliances with unsavory nations to counter the totalitarian threat from the Soviet Union. Governor Ronald Reagan of California read this 1979 essay, and on several occasions he discussed its themes with Mrs. Kirkpatrick. When Reagan became president, he made the author of "Dictatorships and Double Standards" U.S. ambassador to the United Nations.

A major project of Moynihan, Kirkpatrick, and other neoconservatives in and out of government was the defense of Israel. In the late 1960s and in the 1970s, they found themselves lonely in this support; few others in the intellectual world were willing to join in their strong defense of the Jewish state. The Left's traditional support of Israel eroded after Israel's astounding victory in the 1967 war. With Israel no longer seen as the "victim," the support from the Left quickly evaporated. Numerous articles in Commentary lamented this precipitous shifting of allegiances and its attendant consequences. By the mid-1970s, Israel was also under fire from the Soviet Union and the Third World and much of the West. The United States was the one exception, and the neoconservatives—stressing that Israel was a just, democratic state constantly threatened by vicious and aggressive neighbors—sought to deepen and strengthen this support. Ruth Wisse's 1981 essay, "The Delegitimation of Israel," was perhaps the best expression of these views.

Dictatorships and Double Standards

Jeane Kirkpatrick

T HE FAILURE of the Carter administration's foreign policy is now clear to everyone except its architects, and even they must entertain private doubts, from time to time, about a policy whose crowning achievement has been to lay the groundwork for a transfer of the Panama Canal from the United States to a swaggering Latin dictator of Castroite bent. In the thirty-odd months since the inauguration of Jimmy Carter as President there has occurred a dramatic Soviet military buildup, matched by the stagnation of American armed forces, and a dramatic extension of Soviet influence in the Horn of Africa, Afghanistan, Southern Africa, and the Caribbean, matched by a declining American position in all these areas. The United States has never tried so hard and failed so utterly to make and keep friends in the Third World.

As if this were not bad enough, in the current year the United States has suffered two other major blows—in Iran and Nicaragua—of large and strategic significance. In each country, the Carter administration not only failed to prevent the undesired outcome; it actively collaborated in the replacement of moderate autocrats friendly to American interests with less friendly autocrats of extremist persuasion. It is too soon to be certain about what kind of regime will ultimately emerge in either Iran or Nicaragua, but accumulating evidence suggests that things are as likely to get worse as to get better in both countries. The Sandinistas in Nicaragua appear to be as skillful in consolidating power as the Ayatollah Khomeini is inept, and leaders of both revolutions display an intolerance and arrogance that do not bode well for the peaceful sharing of power or the establishment of constitutional governments, especially since those leaders have made clear that they have no intention of seeking either.

It is at least possible that the SALT debate may stimulate new scrutiny

Reprinted from Commentary *(November 1979).*

of the nation's strategic position and defense policy, but there are no signs that anyone is giving serious attention to this nation's role in Iranian and Nicaraguan developments—despite clear warnings that the United States is confronted with similar situations and options in El Salvador, Guatemala, Morocco, Zaire, and elsewhere. Yet no problem of American foreign policy is more urgent than that of formulating a morally and strategically acceptable, and politically realistic, program for dealing with nondemocratic governments who are threatened by Soviet-sponsored subversion. In the absence of such a policy, we can expect that the same reflexes that guided Washington in Iran and Nicaragua will be permitted to determine American actions from Korea to Mexico—with the same disastrous effects on the U.S. strategic position. (That the administration has not called its policies in Iran and Nicaragua a failure—and probably does not consider them such—complicates the problem without changing its nature.)

There were, of course, significant differences in the relations between the United States and each of these countries during the past two or three decades. Oil, size, and proximity to the Soviet Union gave Iran greater economic and strategic import than any Central American "republic," and closer relations were cultivated with the Shah, his counselors, and family than with President Somoza, his advisers, and family. Relations with the Shah were probably also enhanced by our approval of his manifest determination to modernize Iran regardless of the effects of modernization on traditional social and cultural patterns (including those which enhanced his own authority and legitimacy). And, of course, the Shah was much better looking and altogether more dashing than Somoza; his private life was much more romantic, more interesting to the media, popular and otherwise. Therefore, more Americans were more aware of the Shah than of the equally tenacious Somoza.

But even though Iran was rich, blessed with a product the United States and its allies needed badly, and led by a handsome king, while Nicaragua was poor and rocked along under a long-tenure president of less striking aspect, there were many similarities between the two countries and our relations with them. Both these small nations were led by men who had not been selected by free elections, who recognized no duty to submit themselves to searching tests of popular acceptability. Both did tolerate limited opposition, including opposition newspapers and political parties, but both were also confronted by radical, violent opponents bent on social and political revolution. Both rulers, therefore, sometimes invoked martial law to arrest, imprison, exile, and occasionally, it was alleged, torture their opponents. Both relied for public order on police forces whose personnel were said to be too harsh, too arbitrary, and too powerful. Each had what the American press termed "private armies," which is to say, armies pledging their allegiance to the ruler rather than the "constitution" or the "nation" or some other impersonal entity.

In short, both Somoza and the Shah were, in central ways, traditional rulers of semitraditional societies. Although the Shah very badly wanted to create a technologically modern and powerful nation and Somoza tried hard to introduce modern agricultural methods, neither sought to reform his society in the light of any abstract idea of social justice or political virtue. Neither attempted to alter significantly the distribution of goods, status, or power (though the democratization of education and skills that accompanied modernization in Iran did result in some redistribution of money and power there).

Both Somoza and the Shah enjoyed long tenure, large personal fortunes (much of which were no doubt appropriated from general revenues), and good relations with the United States. The Shah and Somoza were not only anticommunist; they were positively friendly to the United States, sending their sons and others to be educated in our universities, voting with us in the United Nations, and regularly supporting American interests and positions even when these entailed personal and political cost. The embassies of both governments were active in Washington social life, and were frequented by powerful Americans who occupied major roles in this nation's diplomatic, military, and political life. And the Shah and Somoza themselves were both welcome in Washington, and had many American friends.

Though each of the rulers was from time to time criticized by American officials for violating civil and human rights, the fact that the people of Iran and Nicaragua only intermittently enjoyed the rights accorded to citizens in the Western democracies did not prevent successive administrations from granting—with the necessary approval of successive Congresses—both military and economic aid. In the case of both Iran and Nicaragua, tangible and intangible tokens of U.S. support continued until the regime became the object of a major attack by forces explicitly hostile to the United States.

But once an attack was launched by opponents bent on destruction, everything changed. The rise of serious, violent opposition in Iran and Nicaragua set in motion a succession of events which bore a suggestive resemblance to one another and a suggestive similarity to our behavior in China before the fall of Chiang Kai-shek, in Cuba before the triumph of Castro, in certain crucial periods of the Vietnamese war, and, more recently, in Angola. In each of these countries, the American effort to impose liberalization and democratization on a government confronted with violent internal opposition not only failed, but actually assisted the coming to power of new regimes in which ordinary people enjoy fewer freedoms and less personal security than under the previous autocracy—regimes, moreover, hostile to American interests and policies.

The pattern is familiar enough: an established autocracy with a record of friendship with the United States is attacked by insurgents, some of whose leaders have long ties to the Communist movement, and most of whose arms are of Soviet, Chinese, or Czechoslovak origin. The "Marxist" presence is ignored and/or minimized by American officials and by the elite media on the ground that U.S. support for the dictator gives the rebels little choice but to seek aid "elsewhere." Violence spreads and American officials wonder aloud about the viability of a regime that "lacks the support of its own people." The absence of an opposition party is deplored and civil-rights violations are reviewed. Liberal columnists question the morality of continuing aid to a "rightist dictatorship" and provide assurances concerning the essential moderation of some insurgent leaders who "hope" for some sign that the United States will remember its own revolutionary origins. Requests for help from the beleaguered autocrat go unheeded, and the argument is increasingly voiced that ties should be established with rebel leaders "before it is too late." The President, delaying U.S. aid, appoints a special emissary who confirms the deterioration of the government position and its diminished capacity to control the situation and recommends various measures for "strengthening" and "liberalizing" the regime, all of which involve diluting its power.

The emissary's recommendations are presented in the context of a growing clamor for American disengagement on grounds that continued involvement confirms our status as an agent of imperialism, racism, and reaction; is inconsistent with support for human rights; alienates us from the "forces of democracy"; and threatens to put the United States once more on the side of history's "losers." This chorus is supplemented daily by interviews with returning missionaries and "reasonable" rebels.

As the situation worsens, the President assures the world that the United States desires only that the "people choose their own form of government"; he blocks delivery of all arms to the government and undertakes negotiations to establish a "broadly based" coalition headed by a "moderate" critic of the regime who, once elevated, will move quickly to seek a "political" settlement to the conflict. Should the incumbent autocrat prove resistant to American demands that he step aside, he will be readily overwhelmed by the military strength of his opponents, whose patrons will have continued to provide sophisticated arms and advisers at the same time the United States cuts off military sales. Should the incumbent be so demoralized as to agree to yield power, he will be replaced by a "moderate" of American selection. Only after the insurgents have refused the proffered political solution and anarchy has spread throughout the nation will it be noticed that the new head of government has no significant following, no experience at governing, and no talent for leadership. By then, military commanders, no longer bound by loyalty to the chief of state, will depose the faltering "moderate" in favor of a fanatic of their own choosing.

In either case, the United States will have been led by its own misunderstanding of the situation to assist actively in deposing an erstwhile friend and ally and installing a government hostile to American interests and policies in the world. At best we will have lost access to friendly territory. At worst the Soviets will have gained a new base. And everywhere our friends will have noted that the United States cannot be counted on in times of difficulty and our enemies will have observed that American support provides no security against the forward march of history.

No particular crisis conforms exactly with the sequence of events described above; there are always variations on the theme. In Iran, for example, the Carter administration—and the President himself—offered the ruler support for a longer time, though by December 1978 the President was acknowledging that he did not know if the Shah would survive, adding that the United States would not get "directly involved." Neither did the United States ever call publicly for the Shah's resignation. However, the President's special emissary, George Ball, "reportedly concluded that the Shah cannot hope to maintain total power and must now bargain with a moderate segment of the opposition" and was "known to have discussed various alternatives that would effectively ease the Shah out of total power" (*Washington Post*, December 15, 1978). There is, furthermore, not much doubt that the United States assisted the Shah's departure and helped arrange the succession of Bakhtiar. In Iran, the Carter administration's commitment to nonintervention proved stronger than strategic considerations or national pride. What the rest of the world regarded as a stinging American defeat, the U.S. government saw as a matter to be settled by Iranians. "We personally prefer that the Shah maintain a major role in the government," the President acknowledged, "but that is a decision for the Iranian people to make."

Events in Nicaragua also departed from the scenario presented above both because the Cuban and Soviet roles were clearer and because U.S. officials were more intensely and publicly working against Somoza. After the Somoza regime had defeated the first wave of Sandinista violence, the United States ceased aid, imposed sanctions, and took other steps which undermined the status and the credibility of the government in domestic and foreign affairs. Between the murder of ABC correspondent Bill Stewart by a National Guardsman in early June and the Sandinista victory in late July, the U.S. State Department assigned a new ambassador who refused to submit his credentials to Somoza even though Somoza was still chief of state, and called for replacing the government with a "broadly based provisional government that would include representatives of Sandinista guerrillas." Americans were assured by Assistant Secretary of State Viron Vaky that "Nicaraguans and our democratic friends in Latin America have no intention of seeing Nicaragua turned into a second Cuba," even though the State Department knew that the top Sandinista leaders had close personal ties and were in continuing contact with Havana, and, more specifically, that a Cuban secret-police official, Julian Lopez, was frequently present in the Sandinista headquarters and that Cuban military advisers were present in Sandinista ranks.

In a manner uncharacteristic of the Carter administration, which generally seems willing to negotiate anything with anyone anywhere, the U.S. government adopted an oddly uncompromising posture in dealing with Somoza. "No end to the crisis is possible," said Vaky, "that does not start with the departure of Somoza from power and the end of his regime. No negotiation, mediation, or compromise can be achieved any longer with a Somoza government. The solution can only begin with a sharp break from the past." Trying hard, we not only banned all American arms sales to the government of Nicaragua but pressured Israel, Guatemala, and others to do likewise—all in the name of insuring a "democratic" outcome. Finally, as the Sandinista leaders consolidated control over weapons and communications, banned opposition, and took off for Cuba, President Carter warned us against attributing this "evolutionary change" to "Cuban machinations" and assured the world that the United States desired only to "let the people of Nicaragua choose their own form of government."

Yet despite all the variations, the Carter administration brought to the crises in Iran and Nicaragua several common assumptions each of which played a major role in hastening the victory of even more repressive dictatorships than had been in place before. These were, first, the belief that there existed at the moment of crisis a democratic alternative to the incumbent government; second, the belief that the continuation of the status quo was not possible; third, the belief that any change, including the establishment of a government headed by self-styled Marxist revolutionaries, was preferable to the present government. Each of these beliefs was (and is) widely shared in the liberal community generally. Not one of them can withstand close scrutiny.

Although most governments in the world are, as they always have been, autocracies of one kind or another, no idea holds greater sway in the mind of educated Americans than the belief that it is possible to democratize governments, anytime, anywhere, under any circumstances. This notion is belied by an enormous body of evidence based on the experience of dozens of countries which have attempted with more or less (usually less) success to move from autocratic to democratic government. Many of the wisest political scientists of this and previous centuries agree that democratic institutions are especially difficult to establish and maintain—because they make heavy demands on all portions of a population and because they depend on complex social, cultural, and economic conditions.

Two or three decades ago, when Marxism enjoyed its greatest prestige among American intellectuals, it was the economic prerequisites of democracy that were emphasized by social scientists. Democracy, they argued, could function only in relatively rich societies with an advanced economy, a substantial middle class, and a literate population, but it could be expected to emerge more or less automatically whenever these conditions prevailed. Today, this picture seems grossly oversimplified. While it surely helps to have an economy strong enough to provide decent levels of well-being for all, and "open" enough to provide mobility and encourage achievement, a pluralistic society and the right kind of political culture—and time—are even more essential.

In his essay on *Representative Government*, John Stuart Mill identified three fundamental conditions which the Carter administration would do well to ponder. These are "One, that the people should be willing to receive it [representative government]; two, that they should be willing and able to do what is necessary for its preservation; three, that they should be willing and able to fulfill the duties and discharge the functions which it imposes on them."

Fulfilling the duties and discharging the functions of representative government make heavy demands on leaders and citizens, demands for participation and restraint, for consensus and compromise. It is not necessary for all citizens to be avidly interested in politics or well-informed about public affairs—although far more widespread interest and mobilization are needed than in autocracies. What *is* necessary is that a substantial number of citizens think of themselves as participants in society's decision-making and not simply as subjects bound by its laws. Moreover, leaders of all major sectors of the society must agree to pursue power only by legal means, must eschew (at least in principle) violence, theft, and fraud, and must accept defeat when necessary. They must also be skilled at finding and creating common ground among diverse points of view and interests, and correlatively willing to compromise on all but the most basic values.

In addition to an appropriate political culture, democratic government requires institutions strong enough to channel and contain conflict. Voluntary, nonofficial institutions are needed to articulate and aggregate diverse interests and opinions present in the society. Otherwise, the formal governmental institutions will not be able to translate popular demands into public policy.

In the relatively few places where they exist, democratic governments have come into being slowly, after extended prior experience with more limited forms of participation during which leaders have reluctantly grown accustomed to tolerating dissent and opposition, opponents have accepted the notion that they may defeat but not destroy incumbents, and people have become aware of government's effects on their lives and of their own possible effects on government. Decades, if not centuries, are normally required for people to acquire the necessary disciplines and habits. In Britain, the road from the Magna Carta to the Act of Settlement, to the great Reform Bills of 1832, 1867, and 1885, took seven centuries to traverse. American history gives no better grounds for believing that democracy comes easily, quickly, or for the asking. A war of independence, an unsuccessful constitution, a civil war, a long process of gradual enfranchisement marked our progress toward constitutional democratic government. The French path was still more difficult. Terror, dictatorship, monarchy, instability, and incompetence followed on the revolution that was to usher in a millennium of brotherhood. Only in the twentieth century did the democratic principle finally gain wide acceptance in France and not until after World War II were the principles of order and democracy, popular sovereignty and authority, finally reconciled in institutions strong enough to contain conflicting currents of public opinion.

Although there is no instance of a revolutionary "socialist" or Communist society being democratized, right-wing autocracies do sometimes evolve into democracies—given time, propitious economic, social, and political circumstances, talented leaders, and a strong indigenous demand for representative government. Something of the kind is in progress on the Iberian peninsula and the first steps have been taken in Brazil. Something similar could conceivably have also occurred in Iran and Nicaragua if contestation and participation had been more gradually expanded.

But it seems clear that the architects of contemporary American foreign policy have little idea of how to go about encouraging the liberalization of an autocracy. In neither Nicaragua nor Iran did they realize that the only likely result of an effort to replace an incumbent autocrat with one of his moderate critics or a "broad-based coalition" would be to sap the foundations of the existing regime without moving the nation any closer to democracy. Yet this outcome was entirely predictable. Authority in traditional autocracies is transmitted through personal relations: from the ruler to his close associates (relatives, household members, personal friends) and from them to people to whom the associates are related by personal ties resembling their own relation to the ruler. The fabric of authority unravels quickly when the power and status of the man at the top are undermined or eliminated. The longer the autocrat has held power, and the more pervasive his personal influence, the more dependent a nation's institutions will be on him. Without him, the organized life of the society will collapse, like an arch from which the keystone has been removed. The blend of qualities that bound the Iranian army to the Shah or the national guard to Somoza is typical of the relationships—personal, hierarchical, nontransferable—that support a traditional autocracy. The speed with which armies collapse, bureaucracies abdicate, and social structures dissolve once the autocrat is removed frequently surprises American policy makers and journalists accustomed to public institutions based on universalistic norms rather than particularistic relations.

The failure to understand these relations is one source of the failure of U.S. policy in this and previous administrations. There are others. In Iran and Nicaragua (as previously in Vietnam, Cuba, and China) Washington overestimated the political diversity of the opposition—especially the strength of "moderates" and "democrats" in the opposition movement; underestimated the strength and intransigence of radicals in the movement; and misestimated the nature and extent of American influence on both the government and the opposition.

Confusion concerning the character of the opposition, especially its intransigence and will to power, leads regularly to downplaying the amount of force required to counteract its violence. In neither Iran nor Nicaragua did the United States adequately appreciate the government's problem in maintaining order in a society confronted with an ideologically extreme opposition. Yet the presence of such groups was well known. The State Department's 1977 report on human rights described an Iran confronted

> with a small number of extreme rightist and leftist terrorists operating within the country. There is evidence that they have received substantial foreign support and training ... [and] have been responsible for the murder of Iranian government officials and Americans.

The same report characterized Somoza's opponents in the following terms:

> A guerrilla organization known as the Sandinista National Liberation Front (FSLN) seeks the violent overthrow of the government, and has received limited support from Cuba. The FSLN carried out an operation in Managua in December 1974, killing four people,

taking several officials hostage, ... since then, it continues to challenge civil authority in certain isolated regions.

In 1978, the State Department's report said that Sandinista violence was continuing—after the state of siege had been lifted by the Somoza government.

When U.S. policy makers and large portions of the liberal press interpret insurgency as evidence of widespread popular discontent and a will to democracy, the scene is set for disaster. For if civil strife reflects a popular demand for democracy, it follows that a "liberalized" government will be more acceptable to "public opinion."

Thus, in the hope of strengthening a government, U.S. policy makers are led, mistake after mistake, to impose measures almost certain to weaken its authority. Hurried efforts to force complex and unfamiliar political practices on societies lacking the requisite political culture, tradition, and social structures not only fail to produce desired outcomes; if they are undertaken at a time when the traditional regime is under attack, they actually facilitate the job of the insurgents.

Vietnam presumably taught us that the United States could not serve as the world's policeman; it should also have taught us the dangers of trying to be the world's midwife to democracy when the birth is scheduled to take place under conditions of guerrilla war.

If the administration's actions in Iran and Nicaragua reflect the pervasive and mistaken assumption that one can easily locate and impose democratic alternatives to incumbent autocracies, they also reflect the equally pervasive and equally flawed belief that change per se in such autocracies is inevitable, desirable, and in the American interest. It is this belief which induces the Carter administration to participate actively in the toppling of noncommunist autocracies while remaining passive in the face of Communist expansion.

At the time the Carter administration came into office it was widely reported that the President had assembled a team who shared a new approach to foreign policy and a new conception of the national interest. The principal elements of this new approach were said to be two: the conviction that the cold war was over, and the conviction that, this being the case, the United States should give priority to North-South problems and help less developed nations achieve their own destiny.

More is involved in these changes than originally meets the eye. For, unlikely as it may seem, the foreign policy of the Carter administration is guided by a relatively full-blown philosophy of history which includes, as philosophies of history always do, a theory of social change, or, as it is currently called, a doctrine of modernization. Like most other philosophies of history that have appeared in the West since the eighteenth century, the Carter administration's doctrine predicts progress (in the form of modernization for all societies) and a happy ending (in the form of a world community of developed, autonomous nations).

The administration's approach to foreign affairs was clearly foreshadowed in Zbigniew Brzezinski's 1970 book on the U.S. role in the "technetronic era," *Between Two Ages*. In that book, Brzezinski showed that he had the imagination to look beyond the cold war to a brave new world of global politics and interdependence. To deal with that new world a new approach was said to be "evolving," which Brzezinski designated "rational humanism." In the new approach, the "preoccupation" with "national supremacy" would give way to "global" perspectives, and international problems would be viewed as "human issues" rather than as "political confrontations." The traditional intellectual framework for dealing with foreign policy would have to be scrapped:

> Today, the old framework of international politics . . . with their spheres of influence, military alliances between nation states, the fiction of sovereignty, doctrinal conflicts arising from 19th-century crisis—is clearly no longer compatible with reality.*

Only the "delayed development" of the Soviet Union, "an archaic religious community that experiences modernity existentially but not quite

---

* Concerning Latin America, Brzezinski observed: "Latin American nationalism, more and more radical as it widens its popular base, will be directed with increasing animosity against the United States unless the United States rapidly shifts its own posture. Accordingly, it would be wise for the United States to make an explicit move to abandon the Monroe Doctrine and to concede that in the new global age geographic or hemispheric contiguity no longer need be politically decisive. Nothing could be healthier for Pan-American relations than for the United States to place them on the same level as its relations with the rest of the world, confining itself to emphasis on cultural-political affinities (as it does with Western Europe) and economic-social obligations (as it does with less developed countries)."

yet normatively," prevented wider realization of the fact that the end of Lideology was already here. For the United States, Brzezinski recommended "a great deal of patience," a more detached attitude toward world revolutionary processes, and a less anxious preoccupation with the Soviet Union. Instead of engaging in ancient diplomatic pastimes, we should make "a broader effort to contain the global tendencies toward chaos," while assisting the processes of change that will move the world toward the "community of developed nations."

The central concern of Brzezinski's book, as of the Carter administration's foreign policy, is with the modernization of the Third World. From the beginning, the administration has manifested a special, intense interest in the problems of the so-called Third World. But instead of viewing international developments in terms of the American national interest, as national interest is historically conceived, the architects of administration policy have viewed them in terms of a contemporary version of the same idea of progress that has traumatized Western imaginations since the Enlightenment.

In its current form, the concept of modernization involves more than industrialization, more than "political development" (whatever that is). It is used instead to designate "the process through which a traditional or pretechnological society passes as it is transformed into a society characterized by machine technology, rational and secular attitudes, and highly differentiated social structures." Condorcet, Comte, Hegel, Marx, and Weber are all present in this view of history as the working out of the idea of modernity.

The crucial elements of the modernization concept have been clearly explicated by Samuel P. Huntington (who, despite a period at the National Security Council, was assuredly not the architect of the administration's policy). The modernization paradigm, Huntington has observed, postulates an ongoing process of change: complex, because it involves all dimensions of human life in society; systemic, because its elements interact in predictable, necessary ways; global, because all societies will, necessarily, pass through the transition from traditional to modern; lengthy, because time is required to modernize economic and social organization, character, and culture; phased, because each modernizing society must pass through essentially the same stages; homogenizing, because it tends toward the convergence and interdependence of societies; irreversible, because the direction of change is "given" in the relation of the elements of the process;

progressive, in the sense that it is desirable, and in the long run provides significant benefits to the affiliated people.

Although the modernization paradigm has proved a sometimes useful as well as influential tool in social science, it has become the object of searching critiques that have challenged one after another of its central assumptions. Its shortcomings as an analytical tool pale, however, when compared to its inadequacies as a framework for thinking about foreign policy, where its principal effects are to encourage the view that events are manifestations of deep historical forces which cannot be controlled and that the best any government can do is to serve as a "midwife" to history, helping events to move where they are already headed.

This perspective on contemporary events is optimistic in the sense that it foresees continuing human progress; deterministic in the sense that it perceives events as fixed by processes over which persons and policies can have but little influence; moralistic in the sense that it perceives history and U.S. policy as having moral ends; cosmopolitan in the sense that it attempts to view the world not from the perspective of American interests or intentions but from the perspective of the modernizing nation and the "end" of history. It identifies modernization with both revolution and morality, and U.S. policy with all three.

The idea that it is "forces" rather than people which shape events recurs each time an administration spokesman articulates or explains policy. The President, for example, assured us in February of this year:

> The revolution in Iran is a product of deep social, political, religious, and economic factors growing out of the history of Iran itself.

And of Asia he said:

> At this moment there is turmoil or change in various countries from one end of the Indian Ocean to the other; some turmoil as in Indochina is the product of age-old enmities, inflamed by rivalries for influence by conflicting forces. Stability in some other countries is being shaken by the process of modernization, the search for national significance, or the desire to fulfill legitimate human hopes and human aspirations.

Harold Saunders, Assistant Secretary for Near Eastern and South Asian Affairs, commenting on "instability" in Iran and the Horn of Africa, states:

> We, of course, recognize that fundamental changes are taking place across this area of western Asia and northeastern Africa—economic modernization, social change, a revival of religion, resurgent nationalism, demands for broader popular participation in the political process. These changes are generated by forces within each country.

Or here is Anthony Lake, chief of the State Department's Policy Planning staff, on South Africa:

> Change will come in South Africa. The welfare of the people there, and American interests, will be profoundly affected by the way in which it comes. The question is whether it will be peaceful or not.

Brzezinski makes the point still clearer. Speaking as chief of the National Security Council, he has assured us that the struggles for power in Asia and Africa are really only incidents along the route to modernization:

> all the developing countries in the arc from northeast Asia to southern Africa continue to search for viable forms of government capable of managing the process of modernization.

No matter that the invasions, coups, civil wars, and political struggles of less violent kinds that one sees all around do not *seem* to be incidents in a global personnel search for someone to manage the modernization process. Neither Brzezinski nor anyone else seems bothered by the fact that the political participants in that arc from northeast Asia to southern Africa do not *know* that they are "searching for viable forms of government capable of managing the process of modernization." The motives and intentions of real persons are no more relevant to the modernization paradigm than they are to the Marxist view of history. Viewed from this level of abstraction, it is the "forces" rather than the people that count.

So what if the "deep historical forces" at work in such diverse places as Iran, the Horn of Africa, Southeast Asia, Central America, and the United Nations look a lot like Russians or Cubans? Having moved past what the President calls our "inordinate fear of Communism," identified by him with the cold war, we should, we are told, now be capable of distinguishing Soviet and Cuban "machinations," which anyway exist mainly in the minds of cold warriors and others guilty of oversimplifying the world, from evolutionary changes, which seem to be the only kind that actually occur.

What can a U.S. President faced with such complicated, inexorable, impersonal processes *do*? The answer, offered again and again by the President and his top officials, is, not much. Since events are not caused by human decisions, they cannot be stopped or altered by them. Brzezinski, for example, has said: "We recognize that the world is changing under the influence of forces no government can control." And Cyrus Vance has cautioned: "The fact is that we can no more stop change than Canute could still the waters."

The Carter administration's essentially deterministic and apolitical view of contemporary events discourages an active American response and encourages passivity. The American inability to influence events in Iran became the President's theme song:

> Those who argue that the U.S. should *or could* intervene directly to thwart [the revolution in Iran] are wrong about the realities of Iran. . . . We have encouraged *to the limited extent of our own ability* the public support for the Bakhtiar government. . . . How long [the Shah] will be out of Iran, we have no way to determine. Future events and his own desires will determine that. . . . It is impossible for anyone to anticipate all future political events. . . . Even if we had been able to anticipate events that were going to take place in Iran or in other countries, obviously our ability to determine those events is very limited. (Emphasis added.)

Vance made the same point:

> In Iran our policy throughout the current crisis has been based on the fact that only Iranians can resolve the fundamental political issues which they now confront.

Where once upon a time an American President might have sent Marines to assure the protection of American strategic interests, there is no room for force in this world of progress and self-determination. Force, the President told us at Notre Dame, does not work; that is the lesson he extracted from Vietnam. It offers only "superficial" solutions. Concerning Iran, he said:

Certainly we have no desire or ability to intrude massive forces into Iran or any other country to determine the outcome of domestic political issues. This is something that we have no intention of ever doing in another country. We've tried this once in Vietnam. It didn't work, as you well know.

There was nothing unique about Iran. In Nicaragua, the climate and language were different but the "historical forces" and the U.S. response were the same. Military intervention was out of the question. Assistant Secretary of State Viron Vaky described as "unthinkable" the "use of U.S. military power to intervene in the internal affairs of another American republic." Vance provided parallel assurances for Africa, asserting that we would not try to match Cuban and Soviet activities there.

What *is* the function of foreign policy under these conditions? It is to understand the processes of change and then, like Marxists, to align ourselves with history, hoping to contribute a bit of stability along the way. And this, administration spokesmen assure us, is precisely what we are doing. The Carter administration has defined the U.S. national interest in the Third World as identical with the putative end of the modernization process. Vance put this with characteristic candor in a recent statement when he explained that U.S. policy vis-à-vis the Third World is "grounded in the conviction that we best serve our interest there by supporting the efforts of developing nations to advance their economic well-being and preserve their political independence." Our "commitment to the promotion of constructive change worldwide" (Brzezinski's words) has been vouchsafed in every conceivable context.

But there is a problem. The conceivable contexts turn out to be mainly those in which noncommunist autocracies are under pressure from revolutionary guerrillas. Since Moscow is the aggressive, expansionist power today, it is more often than not insurgents, encouraged and armed by the Soviet Union, who challenge the status quo. The American commitment to "change" in the abstract ends up by aligning us tacitly with Soviet clients and irresponsible extremists like the Ayatollah Khomeini or, in the end, Yasir Arafat.

So far, assisting "change" has not led the Carter administration to undertake the destabilization of a *Communist* country. The principles of self-determination and nonintervention are thus both selectively applied.

We seem to accept the status quo in Communist nations (in the name of "diversity" and national autonomy), but not in nations ruled by "right-wing" dictators or white oligarchies. Concerning China, for example, Brzezinski has observed: "We recognize that the PRC and we have different ideologies and economic and political systems. . . . We harbor neither the hope nor the desire that through extensive contacts with China we can remake that nation into the American image. Indeed, we accept our differences." Of Southeast Asia, the President noted in February:

> Our interest is to promote peace and the withdrawal of outside forces and not to become embroiled in the conflict among Asian nations. And, in general, our interest is to promote the health and the development of individual societies, not to a pattern cut exactly like ours in the United States but tailored rather to the hopes and the needs and desires of the peoples involved.

But the administration's position shifts sharply when South Africa is discussed. For example, Anthony Lake asserted in late 1978:

> We have indicated to South Africa the fact that if it does not make significant progress toward racial equality, its relations with the international community, including the United States, are bound to deteriorate.
>
> Over the years, we have tried through a series of progressive steps to demonstrate that the U.S. cannot and will not be associated with the continued practice of apartheid.

As to Nicaragua, Hodding Carter III said in February 1979:

> The unwillingness of the Nicaraguan government to accept the [OAS] group's proposal, the resulting prospects for renewal and polarization, and the human-rights situation in Nicaragua . . . unavoidably affect the kind of relationships we can maintain with that government.

And Carter commented on Latin American autocracies:

> My government will not be deterred from protecting human rights, including economic and social rights, in whatever ways we can. We prefer to take actions that are positive, but where nations persist in serious violations of human rights, we will continue to demon-

strate that there are costs to the flagrant disregard of international standards.

Something very odd is going on here. How does an administration that desires to let people work out their own destinies get involved in determined efforts at reform in South Africa, Zaire, Nicaragua, El Salvador, and elsewhere? How can an administration committed to nonintervention in Cambodia and Vietnam announce that it "will not be deterred" from righting wrongs in South Africa? What should be made of an administration that sees the U.S. interest as identical with economic modernization and political independence and yet heedlessly endangers the political independence of Taiwan, a country whose success in economic modernization and egalitarian distribution of wealth is unequaled in Asia? The contrast is as striking as that between the administration's frenzied speed in recognizing the new dictatorship in Nicaragua and its continuing refusal to recognize the elected government of Zimbabwe Rhodesia, or its refusal to maintain any presence in Zimbabwe Rhodesia while staffing a U.S. Information Office in Cuba. Not only are there ideology and a double standard at work here; the ideology neither fits nor explains reality, and the double standard involves the administration in the wholesale contradiction of its own principles.

Inconsistencies are a familiar part of politics in most societies. Usually, however, governments behave hypocritically when their principles conflict with the national interest. What makes the inconsistencies of the Carter administration noteworthy are, first, the administration's moralism—which renders it especially vulnerable to charges of hypocrisy; and, second, the administration's predilection for policies that violate the strategic and economic interests of the United States. The administration's conception of national interest borders on doublethink: it finds friendly powers to be guilty representatives of the status quo and views the triumph of unfriendly groups as beneficial to America's "true interests."

This logic is quite obviously reinforced by the prejudices and preferences of many administration officials. Traditional autocracies are, in general and in their very nature, deeply offensive to modern American sensibilities. The notion that public affairs should be ordered on the basis of kinship, friendship, and other personal relations rather than on the basis of objective "rational" standards violates our conception of justice and efficiency. The preference for stability rather than change is also disturbing to Americans whose whole national experience rests on the principles of change, growth, and progress. The extremes of wealth and poverty characteristic of traditional societies also offend us, the more so since the poor are usually *very* poor and bound to their squalor by a hereditary allocation of role. Moreover, the relative lack of concern of rich, comfortable rulers for the poverty, ignorance, and disease of "their" people is likely to be interpreted by Americans as moral dereliction pure and simple. The truth is that Americans can hardly bear such societies and such rulers. Confronted with them, our vaunted cultural relativism evaporates and we become as censorious as Cotton Mather confronting sin in New England.

But if the politics of traditional and semitraditional autocracy is nearly antithetical to our own—at both the symbolic and the operational level—the rhetoric of progressive revolutionaries sounds much better to us; their symbols are much more acceptable. One reason that some modern Americans prefer "socialist" to traditional autocracies is that the former have embraced modernity and have adopted modern modes and perspectives, including an instrumental, manipulative, functional orientation toward most social, cultural, and personal affairs; a profession of universalistic norms; an emphasis on reason, science, education, and progress; a de-emphasis of the sacred; and "rational," bureaucratic organizations. They speak our language.

Because socialism of the Soviet/Chinese/Cuban variety is an ideology rooted in a version of the same values that sparked the Enlightenment and the democratic revolutions of the eighteenth century; because it is modern and not traditional; because it postulates goals that appeal to Christian as well as to secular values (brotherhood of man, elimination of power as a mode of human relations), it is highly congenial to many Americans at the symbolic level. Marxist revolutionaries speak the language of a hopeful future while traditional autocrats speak the language of an unattractive past. Because left-wing revolutionaries invoke the symbols and values of democracy—emphasizing eglitarianism rather than hierarchy and privilege, liberty rather than order, activity rather than passivity— they are again and again accepted as partisans in the cause of freedom and democracy.

Nowhere is the affinity of liberalism, Christianity, and Marxist socialism more apparent than among liberals who are "duped" time after time into supporting "liberators" who turn out to be totalitarians, and among

Left-leaning clerics whose attraction to a secular style of "redemptive community" is stronger than their outrage at the hostility of socialist regimes to religion. In Jimmy Carter—egalitarian, optimist, liberal, Christian—the tendency to be repelled by frankly nondemocratic rulers and hierarchical societies is almost as strong as the tendency to be attracted to the idea of popular revolution, liberation, and progress. Carter is, *par excellence*, the kind of liberal most likely to confound revolution with idealism, change with progress, optimism with virtue.

Where concern about "socialist encirclement," Soviet expansion, and traditional conceptions of the national interest inoculated his predecessors against such easy equations, Carter's doctrine of national interest and modernization encourages support for all change that takes place in the name of "the people," regardless of its "superficial" Marxist or anti-American content. Any lingering doubt about whether the United States should, in case of conflict, support a "tested friend" such as the Shah or a friendly power such as Zimbabwe Rhodesia against an opponent who despises us is resolved by reference to our "true," our "long-range" interests.

Stephen Rosenfeld of the *Washington Post* described the commitment of the Carter administration to this sort of "progressive liberalism":

> The Carter administration came to power, after all, committed precisely to reducing the centrality of strategic competition with Moscow in American foreign policy, and to extending the United States' association with what it was prepared to accept as legitimate wave-of-the-future popular movements around the world— first of all with the victorious movement in Vietnam. . . .
>
> Indochina was supposed to be the state on which Americans could demonstrate their "post-Vietnam" intent to come to terms with the progressive popular element that Kissinger, the villain, had denied.

In other words, the Carter administration, Rosenfeld tells us, came to power resolved not to assess international developments in the light of "cold war" perspectives but to accept at face value the claim of revolutionary groups to represent "popular" aspirations and "progressive" forces— regardless of the ties of these revolutionaries to the Soviet Union. To this end, overtures were made looking to the "normalization" of relations with Vietnam, Cuba, and the Chinese People's Republic, and steps were taken to cool relations with South Korea, South Africa, Nicaragua, the Philippines, and others. These moves followed naturally from the conviction that the United States had, as our enemies said, been on the wrong side of history in supporting the status quo and opposing revolution.

One might have thought that this perspective would have been undermined by events in Southeast Asia since the triumph of "progressive" forces there over the "agents of reaction." To cite Rosenfeld again:

> In this administration's time, Vietnam has been transformed for much of American public opinion, from a country wronged by the U.S. to one revealing a brutal essence of its own.
>
> This has been a quiet but major trauma to the Carter people (as to all liberals) scarring their self-confidence and their claim on public trust alike.

Presumably, however, the barbarity of the "progressive" governments in Cambodia and Vietnam has been less traumatic for the President and his chief advisers than for Rosenfeld, since there is little evidence of changed predispositions at crucial levels of the White House and the State Department. The President continues to behave as before—not like a man who abhors autocrats but like one who abhors only right-wing autocrats.

In fact, high officials in the Carter administration understand better than they seem to the aggressive, expansionist character of contemporary Soviet behavior in Africa, the Middle East, Southeast Asia, the Indian Ocean, Central America, and the Caribbean. But although the Soviet/Cuban role in Grenada, Nicaragua, and El Salvador (plus the transfer of MIG-23s to Cuba) had already prompted resumption of surveillance of Cuba (which in turn confirmed the presence of a Soviet combat brigade), the President's eagerness not to "heat up" the climate of public opinion remains stronger than his commitment to speak the truth to the American people. His statement on Nicaragua clearly reflects these priorities:

> It's a mistake for Americans to assume or to claim that every time an evolutionary change takes place in this hemisphere that somehow it's a result of secret, massive Cuban intervention. The fact in Nicaragua is that the Somoza regime lost the confidence of the people. To bring about an orderly transition there, our effort was to let the people of Nicaragua ultimately make the decision on who

would be their leader—what form of government they should have.

This statement, which presumably represents the President's best thinking on the matter, is illuminating. Carter's effort to dismiss concern about military events in this specific country as a manifestation of a national proclivity for seeing "Cuban machinations" under every bed constitutes a shocking effort to falsify reality. There was no question in Nicaragua of "evolutionary change" or of attributing such change to Castro's agents. There was only a question about the appropriate U.S. response to a military struggle in a country whose location gives it strategic importance out of proportion to its size or strength.

But that is not all. The rest of the President's statement graphically illustrates the blinding power of ideology on his interpretation of events. When he says that "the Somoza regime lost the confidence of the people," the President implies that the regime had previously rested on the confidence of "the people," but that the situation had now changed. In fact, the Somoza regime had never rested on popular will (but instead on manipulation, force, and habit), and was not being ousted by it. It was instead succumbing to arms and soldiers. However, the assumption that the armed conflict of Sandinistas and Somozistas was the military equivalent of a national referendum enabled the President to imagine that it could be, and should be, settled by the people of Nicaragua. For this pious sentiment even to seem true the President would have had to be unaware that insurgents were receiving a great many arms from other non-Nicaraguans; and that the United States had played a significant role in disarming the Somoza regime.

The President's mistakes and distortions are all fashionable ones. His assumptions are those of people who want badly to be on the progressive side in conflicts between "rightist" autocracy and "leftist" challenges, and to prefer the latter, almost regardless of the probable consequences.

To be sure, neither the President, nor Vance, nor Brzezinski *desires* the proliferation of Soviet-supported regimes. Each has asserted his disapproval of Soviet "interference" in the modernization process. But each, nevertheless, remains willing to "destabilize" friendly or neutral autocracies without any assurance that they will not be replaced by reactionary totalitarian theocracies, totalitarian Soviet client states, or worst of all, by murderous fanatics of the Pol Pot variety.

The foreign policy of the Carter administration fails not for lack of good intentions but for lack of realism about the nature of traditional versus revolutionary autocracies and the relation of each to the American national interest. Only intellectual fashion and the tyranny of Right/Left thinking prevent intelligent men of good will from perceiving the *facts* that traditional authoritarian governments are less repressive than revolutionary autocracies, that they are more susceptible of liberalization, and that they are more compatible with U.S. interests. The evidence on all these points is clear enough.

Surely it is now beyond reasonable doubt that the present governments of Vietnam, Cambodia, Laos are much more repressive than those of the despised previous rulers; that the government of the People's Republic of China is more repressive than that of Taiwan, that North Korea is more repressive than South Korea, and so forth. This is the most important lesson of Vietnam and Cambodia. It is not new but it is a gruesome reminder of harsh facts.

From time to time a truly bestial ruler can come to power in either type of autocracy—Idi Amin, Papa Doc Duvalier, Joseph Stalin, Pol Pot are examples—but neither type regularly produces such moral monsters (though democracy regularly prevents their accession to power). There are, however, *systemic* differences between traditional and revolutionary autocracies that have a predictable effect on their degree of repressiveness. Generally speaking, traditional autocrats tolerate social inequities, brutality, and poverty while revolutionary autocracies create them.

Traditional autocrats leave in place existing allocations of wealth, power, status, and other resources which in most traditional societies favor an affluent few and maintain masses in poverty. But they worship traditional gods and observe traditional taboos. They do not disturb the habitual rhythms of work and leisure, habitual places of residence, habitual patterns of family and personal relations. Because the miseries of traditional life are familiar, they are bearable to ordinary people who, growing up in the society, learn to cope, as children born to untouchables in India acquire the skills and attitudes necessary for survival in the miserable roles they are destined to fill. Such societies create no refugees.

Precisely the opposite is true of revolutionary Communist regimes. They create refugees by the million because they claim jurisdiction over the whole life of the society and make demands for change that so violate internalized values and habits that inhabitants flee by the tens of thousands in the remarkable expectation that their attitudes, values, and goals will "fit" better in a foreign country than in their native land.

The former deputy chairman of Vietnam's National Assembly from 1976 to his defection early in August 1979, Hoang Van Hoan, described recently the impact of Vietnam's ongoing revolution on that country's more than one million Chinese inhabitants:

> They have been expelled from places they have lived in for genera-tions. They have been dispossessed of virtually all possessions—their lands, their houses. They have been driven into areas called new economic zones, but they have not been given any aid.
>
> How can they eke out a living in such conditions reclaiming new land? They gradually die for a number of reasons—diseases, the hard life. They also die of humiliation.

It is not only the Chinese who have suffered in Southeast Asia since the "liberation," and it is not only in Vietnam that the Chinese suffer. By the end of 1978 more than six million refugees had fled countries ruled by Marxist governments. In spite of walls, fences, guns, and sharks, the steady stream of people fleeing revolutionary utopias continues.

There is a damning contrast between the number of refugees created by Marxist regimes and those created by other autocracies: more than a million Cubans have left their homeland since Castro's rise (one refugee for every nine inhabitants) as compared to about 35,000 each from Argentina, Brazil, and Chile. In Africa more than five times as many refugees have fled Guinea and Guinea Bissau as have left Zimbabwe Rhodesia, suggesting that civil war and racial discrimination are easier for most people to bear than Marxist-style liberation.

Moreover, the history of this century provides no grounds for expect-ing that radical totalitarian regimes will transform themselves. At the moment there is a far greater likelihood of progressive liberalization and democratization in the governments of Brazil, Argentina, and Chile than in the government of Cuba; in Taiwan than in the People's Republic of China; in South Korea than in North Korea; in Zaire than in Angola; and so forth.

Since many traditional autocracies permit limited contestation and participation, it is not impossible that U.S. policy could effectively encour-age this process of liberalization and democratization, provided that the effort is not made at a time when the incumbent government is fighting for its life against violent adversaries, and that proposed reforms are aimed at producing gradual change rather than perfect democracy overnight. To accomplish this, policy makers are needed who understand how actual democracies have actually come into being. History is a better guide than good intentions.

A realistic policy which aims at protecting our own interest and assisting the capacities for self-determination of less developed nations will need to face the unpleasant fact that, if victorious, violent insurgency headed by Marxist revolutionaries is unlikely to lead to anything but totalitarian tyranny. Armed intellectuals citing Marx and supported by Soviet-bloc arms and advisers will almost surely not turn out to be agrarian reformers, or simple nationalists, or democratic socialists. However incomprehensible it may be to some, Marxist revolutionaries are not contemporary embodiments of the Americans who wrote the Declaration of Independence, and they will not be content with establishing a broad-based coalition in which they have only one voice among many.

It may not always be easy to distinguish between democratic and totalitarian agents of change, but it is also not too difficult. Authentic democratic revolutionaries aim at securing governments based on the consent of the governed and believe that ordinary men are capable of using freedom, knowing their own interest, choosing rulers. They do not, like the current leaders in Nicaragua, assume that it will be necessary to postpone elections for three to five years during which time they can "cure" the false consciousness of almost everyone.

If, moreover, revolutionary leaders describe the United States as the scourge of the twentieth century, the enemy of freedom-loving people, the perpetrator of imperialism, racism, colonialism, genocide, war, then they are not authentic democrats or, to put it mildly, friends. Groups which define themselves as enemies should be treated as enemies. The United States is not in fact a racist, colonial power, it does not practice genocide, it does not threaten world peace with expansionist activities. In the last decade especially we have practiced remarkable forbearance everywhere and undertaken the "unilateral restraints on defense spending" recommended by Brzezinski as appropriate for the technetronic era. We have also moved further, faster, in eliminating domestic racism than any multiracial society in the world or in history.

For these reasons and more, a posture of continuous self-abasement and apology vis-à-vis the Third World is neither morally necessary nor politically appropriate. No more is it necessary or appropriate to support vocal enemies of the United States because they invoke the rhetoric of popular liberation. It is not even necessary or appropriate for our leaders to forswear unilaterally the use of military force to counter military force. Liberal idealism need not be identical with masochism, and need not be incompatible with the defense of freedom and the national interest.

The Delegitimation of Israel

Ruth R. Wisse

WHAT WAS IT about European Jewry that made possible its extermination? Historians, psychologists, theologians, thoughtful people everywhere will continue to ask this question and to grope for partial answers. For no less troubling than the barbarism of the Germans and other Europeans who assisted in the destruction was their prior success in selecting the Jews as the target of their murderous enmity. How did it come about that the Jews, who were neither bellicose nor numerous, and who had contributed not a little to European well-being, were transformed into the very essence of satanic evil—the image which the Nazis projected onto them and which so much of Europe seemed to accept as true?

The history of European anti-Semitism is not a study in mere opposition to Jews. Religions and nations have opposed one another since the record of mankind began. We take it for granted that religions stand in competition with each other, and that nations vie for territory and influence. Opposition to the Jews was something else; from the beginning of the Christian era, it took the special form of delegitimation.

"Since the days of the Church Fathers," the late historian H. H. Ben-Sasson has written, "the Church had claimed that the true image befitting Israel, which had refused to recognize Jesus and had slain him, was that of Cain who had murdered his brother." Ben-Sasson traces the evolution of this idea in the theory of Jewish "servitude" in the Middle Ages, which justified the humiliation of the Jews on theological grounds and made them, in practice, increasingly prey to the whim of political authority. Protected by charters with limited rights of residence and economic activity, they were granted only temporary exemption from the punishment that was considered deservedly theirs.

Reprinted from Commentary *(October 1981).*

One might have thought the negative definition of the Jew would have disappeared with the Enlightenment challenge to Christianity, or with the Emancipation; but it merely assumed a more elegant, rationalist form. It was now considered reasonable for the Jew to be granted equal status as a citizen; in return, it was considered reasonable to expect him to forfeit his special status as a Jew. When Jews, "intransigent" and "ungrateful," persisted in their distinctiveness, anti-Semitism was the logical reaction. Modern anti-Semitism, writes the historian Arthur Hertzberg, is "chastisement for the sin of imperfect assimilation and the goad toward the messianic day when the Jews, by completely refashioning themselves in the image of proper Westerners, would have won the acceptance that they then would merit."

By the end of the nineteenth century it was obvious to Jews and non-Jews of both Western and Eastern Europe that the "Jewish question" was not about to evaporate. The delegitimation of the Jew had become one of Christianity's most lasting legacies to the modern world, infecting the political Left and Right alike. For socialists, the Jew became the symbol of evil capitalism; for nationalists, of racial defilement. By the time Adolf Hitler isolated the Jew as the corrupting feature of European civilization, he was able to draw on a considerable body of both Christian and post-Christian mythology, which he then translated into a positive ideal— extermination. In Hitler's formulation, if the Jews were illegitimate and evil, destroying them was not murder but a benefaction to the continent and the world.

Long before the emergence of the Third Reich, European Jews had recognized their vulnerability in secularized Christian societies, where distrust of them was no longer tempered by the religious inhibitions that had characterized the Church at its best, or by the economic requirements of feudalism which had preserved for them a designated place in the hierarchy. Whether out of positive attraction or an instinct for collective survival, modern Jews tried to adapt the emerging ideologies of socialism and nationalism to their own situation.

There were many creative thinkers among the Jews in these years, and almost as many proffered solutions to the "Jewish question." Common to all was the desire for a normalization of status among the peoples of the world, so that Jews should no longer be held subject to a double standard of judgment. Zionists of all factions placed the main emphasis on normalization through territory: a people with its own land would be guaranteed equal status among nations. The socialists aimed at normalization through socioeconomic transformation: Jews would be at home in the world once divisiveness gave way to class solidarity. Though many Jewish socialists tried to reconcile their particularist and universalist loyalties, they were never rewarded with the harmony they sought.

The pressure of anti-Semitism was not only greater in modern times, it also put a greater internal pressure on Jews. The traditional Jew derived his sense of legitimacy from his religion, which provided its own deep and serene justification. But when a modern, secular Jew, having jettisoned the armor of his faith, was attacked as illegitimate, he felt obligated to prove his worthiness. How could this be done? The contest was hardly equal. The Germans, Poles, Ukrainians, among others, were seeking to eliminate a minority from within their midst, while the Jews wanted simply to be allowed to live as that minority. Perhaps it was only natural that the aggression of anti-Semitism from without should have generated habits of defensiveness and apology within.

By the 1930's, before the combined onslaught of fascist anti-Semitism and, in the East, Communist efforts at deracination, Jews found themselves at a loss to refute charges that were becoming ever more twisted and venal. Since the disseminators of the hatred remained beyond their reach, Jews redirected the better part of their efforts at self-justification, which also meant, in practice, denouncing those of their fellow Jews whom they considered politically misguided, a provocation to their enemies, chauvinists, fascists, traitors, collaborators, and all the rest. There is a demonstrable correspondence between the pitch of the propaganda directed against them and the factional fury among Jews themselves.

This progressive demoralization is not difficult to explain in its historical context, but it is not a noble story. If, after the war, the heroic struggle of the Warsaw Ghetto was taken by survivors as the symbol by which the destruction of the Jews should be remembered, the impulse derived at least in part from a desire to erase the memory of the years of internecine conflict that preceded it. As for the record of American Jews during this period, it can be found in the pages of the Yiddish and Anglo-Jewish press until 1943. No one will ever boast of it.

The war against the Jews, as Lucy S. Dawidowicz has called what others enshroud in the term "Holocaust," was from the point of view of its perpetrators and collaborators successful beyond belief. In the aftermath of the war, during a period of international realignment, when the dead still seemed to haunt the conscience, the Zionist goal of Jewish normalization through territorial stability was realized. The state of Israel was declared and, though left to fend for itself, was welcomed by most of the community of nations.

In theory, that should have been the end of anti-Semitism, and the Jews may in any case be pardoned for feeling that they had earned a moment of rest in history. But the Arab states did not acknowledge the existence of the Jewish state. They refused to accept partition and they refused to accept its consequence. In the intervening decades they have launched repeated wars against Israel and ignored repeated opportunities for peace. Even the peace treaty of unprecedented generosity which Israel has struck with Egypt has failed to move the other rejectionist states from their insistence on Arab hegemony and Arab hegemony alone in the Middle East.

In addition to resorting to force of arms, the Arabs and their abettors on the international scene have tried to delegitimate the Jewish state in other ways—to accomplish in the political arena what Christianity did on the theological plane. UN Resolution 3379 equating Zionism with racism, passed by the General Assembly in 1975 to its eternal disgrace, institutionalized anti-Semitism in international politics. Allegations of Israel's racism, and blatant anti-Semitic slander, are by now so common at the United Nations and other international gatherings as to attract little notice. As Michael Novak, the United States Representative to the Commission on Human Rights, recently observed, they are a form of Orwellian speech, which "uses words to mean their opposite, and then repeats such words over and over, in the hope that truth can be manufactured from untruth solely by repetition." The clear purpose of this doublespeak, Novak went on, "is to undermine the legitimacy and the existence of the state of Israel."

Sober people think they can guard against such distortions, but the success of the Arabs in their campaign of doublespeak is everywhere visible. They have transformed their obdurate refusal to accept Israel into an alleged Israeli war of aggression against *them*. They have won from Western governments a policy of evenhandedness—which dictates that as much weight be given to the war against the existence of Israel as to the struggle to maintain it. Normally, when countries go to war—Britain and Argentina, for example—each acknowledges the legitimacy of the other's existence even as they both try to change the balance of power between them. The Arab rejectionists have yet to acknowledge Israel's existence; a policy of evenhandedness applied to the conflict between them amounts to a license to pursue Israel's destruction.

The cynicism of Arab policy would provoke indignation except that a further achievement of Orwellian speech, when it is used long enough, is that it withers the habit of indignation, and even turns it against the victim. Thus, Saudi Crown Prince Fahd could speak last August of a "just and comprehensive settlement" in the Middle East and not raise an eyebrow when he later denied that he had ever intended to recognize Israel. A London-based Arab newspaper financed by Saudi Arabia, *Al Shark el-Assouti*, was more honest in saying that "one should recognize the Israelis, but only in their tomb." Thirty-four years after its establishment, and with the exception of Egypt, Israel has yet to be dignified by its neighbors with the simple fact of recognition. Its neighbors feel free to call for the destruction of Israel without concern for political repercussions or even moral censure. And the same Western calculations of expediency that grant the Arab oil-producing countries a near-immunity from criticism also allow them to spread their lies as truth.

Arab progress in delegitimating Israel is not limited to the United Nations. American public opinion is still very much in support of Israel, and will continue to be, so long as both countries remain proud and independent democracies. But Arab propaganda has made great inroads on this continent, with an inevitably damaging consequence to Israel.

A recent report on centers for Middle East studies at American universities, deliberately moderate in its tone, exposes a sharp trend toward the delegitimation of Israel at the very heart of academic study of the area. The report, prepared for the American Jewish Committee, deals with seven of the largest centers, all supported by heavy federal funding and some by gifts from Arab governments or pro-Arab corporations. As the obvious training ground of teachers, government workers, and businessmen, these graduate programs shape the knowledge and views of future experts and decision makers.

The report finds that there is a general absence of courses on Israel or Zionism in the curricula of the Middle East centers and that Israel is omitted from or minimized in the literature put out by some of the centers. The numbers of Jewish graduate students in general Middle East programs are dwindling; to avoid the often inimical atmosphere of the Middle East centers, such graduate students tend to cluster instead in Jewish studies programs, "primarily in cultural or in purely linguistic areas." The centers themselves increasingly manifest the subliminal if not the overt influence of their sources of income.*

Part of the imbalance can be traced to the decision of the federal government to exclude Hebrew from those languages designated as essential to the national defense and security, and thus deserving of federal aid. The original argument was that sufficient numbers of students, mainly Jewish, would take Hebrew anyway. In fact, however, this denial of federal funding in an otherwise very heavily subsidized area has meant a near-exclusion of Hebrew-language students from Middle East programs. At the University of Michigan, for example, where one of the largest of these programs is located, there were 336 undergraduate enrollments in Hebrew in 1980, mostly at the introductory level, but only 4 graduate enrollments. By contrast, the number of undergraduates and graduates studying Arabic was almost equal, 124 and 109; of the twenty National Defense Education Act fellowships, the bulk were for graduate students of Arabic.

The lack of graduate students specializing in Israel and Zionism, or incorporating such study as part of their curriculum, is only the smaller part of the problem. More serious by far is the redefinition of the Middle East as an area in which Israel does not necessarily figure. What does it mean for a Middle East program to be "pro-Israel," as Berkeley's was reputed to be before its radical reorganization in 1976? It means that Israel is considered part of the Middle East and is reflected in the academic study of the center. What does it mean for such a program to be "evenhanded"? It means the virtual elimination of Israel from the curriculum—just as being "evenhanded" in international politics means, as we have seen, giving serious regard to the aim of eliminating Israel physically. Thus, when Berkeley's Middle East program was "pro-Israel" it produced, between 1974 and 1976, a total of six dissertations on Israeli history, anthropology, and political science. Since it turned "evenhanded" in 1976 there has been no sign of a single social-science dissertation on contemporary Israel.

---

* "Middle East Centers at Selected American Universities," by Gary S. Schiff. In a recent development, Harvard University accepted $1 million from a Saudi businessman for a professorship in Arab studies even though the gift was linked by the donor to the appointment of a known PLO sympathizer to a research position at Harvard's Center for Middle Eastern Studies (New York *Times*, June 6, 1982).

The attitude of faculty to this corruption of the academic enterprise reflects the difficulty of countering a campaign of delegitimation. Liberal professors, with their laudable commitment to intellectual freedom, see no reason why the "Arab cause" should not receive as much play as the Israeli cause. Perhaps within the category of normal intellectual and territorial conflict they would be correct; indeed, one of the great gains of Arab propaganda has been to define the Middle East conflict as "normal" in this sense. But as long as the Arab cause remains the destruction of the state of Israel, the elimination of a neighbor state, the academy that bends to this bias gives license to intentions of genocide. The ideal of the university is based on mutual respect for ideas and persons, and true liberals are those with the courage to uphold that ideal.

The discrediting of Israel proceeds through isolation and omission, as in the case of the Middle East centers; contrariwise, it also proceeds through an unceasing barrage of attention, mostly from the media. There are many reasons for the volume of attention, not least among them the availability of information on Israel as compared with the general dearth of information about all other countries in the area. But there are other, less neutral reasons. The difficulty encountered in filming and then showing *Death of a Princess*, a rather mild documentary on the rough justice of Saudi Arabia, is not likely to encourage others to expose that country's weaknesses.

Media pressure on Israel no doubt attests to the press freedoms guaranteed there, as opposed to the absolute censorship practiced by its neighbors, but the result has been a double standard of judgment which soon becomes an instrument of incrimination. This takes its most egregious form among liberal editorial writers and columnists supposedly concerned with helping Israel live up to its moral promise and with protecting it from its own "suicidal folly." A longstanding practitioner of this art of solicitous incrimination is Anthony Lewis of the *New York Times*, who plays the good cop to the Arab states' bad cop by helpfully exposing alleged Israeli malfeasance with an air of charitable concern.

On a recent trip to the Middle East Lewis sought out local critics of the Israeli government so that he could bare before his readers all the unpleasant facts that Israel (like any open society) can yield. A victim of Lewis's strictures later described this method of "investigative reporting" as a simple pattern of prejudice: "If they look at our water problems, then we are stealing the Arab wells. If they look at our hospitals, then we are

letting Arab babies die while saving ours in the Hadassah respirators."
Reading Lewis lately, one wonders how long it will be before he will be
accusing the Israelis of *poisoning* the wells.

Lewis's most recent effort at improving Israel's wayward conduct
concerned the subject of alleged book-banning by Israeli occupation authorities in Gaza and what was, between 1922 and King Hussein's greedy
invasion of Jerusalem in 1967, the West Bank of Jordan. Quoting Justice
Brandeis, "the great American Zionist of his day," Lewis accused the Israeli
authorities of various acts of censorship, including the banning of Palestinian poetry because it contains nationalist images. All this, he wrote, is
part of Israel's attempt to suppress political feeling among the Palestinians,
part of the "apparatus of repression in the occupied territories." Lewis
concluded with the twisted logic that has become his trademark:

> In this country too there are those who would silence the truth
> about the occupation. Things as bad or worse happen in other
> countries, they say. To criticize any Israeli policy is to weaken that
> harassed state; people should stop finding fault with Israel.
>
> How Justice Brandeis would have scorned such arguments. He
> did not work for a Jewish state so it could be compared with the
> tyrannies of the earth; he expected it to be a beacon of freedom. He
> knew that wise government does not flourish in silence; it needs
> truth, however painful. And he would see now, in the West Bank
> and Gaza, *proof that repression breeds hate* (emphasis added).

Israel's Ministry of Foreign Affairs, taking the defensive—
unfortunately either its fated or its adopted role—issued a point-by-point
refutation of Lewis's charges, which were based on sources he did not
check in the first place but simply lifted from the writing of a local opposition critic. Melvin Lasky, editor of the British journal, *Encounter*, who was
alerted to Lewis's article because of the mischief it had done in *Egyptian*
intellectual circles, determined to get to the root of the matter. He found the
entire charge to be based on misinformation and error which had been
rectified years earlier, as Lewis could easily have determined had he not
been intent on believing, and repeating, the worst.

Actually, it is not Israel's but Lewis's abuse of freedom which should
be at issue here. By what moral right does an American journalist exploit a
country's democratic guarantees of free speech to smear it with allegations
he has made no effort to check? And if freedom of political expression

among the *Arabs* is in question, there is only one point to be made: the great irony of the Middle East, if this new disciple of Justice Brandeis has ever noticed, is that Arabs throughout Israel, emphatically including the occupied territories, enjoy greater freedom of expression and access to information than in any Arab country in the world.

Why, if Lewis is so concerned for the Palestinian poets, did he not investigate their political rights when he was in Jordan? Hath not an Arab eyes? Shall the students and writers of Arab countries, where there are no Jews to "oppress" them with the rights of free speech, and no Jewish critics to needle the government on their behalf, be doomed to a lifetime of self-censorship and silence? It is the peculiar evil of this double standard of judgment not merely to apply an absolute moral criterion to the Jews alone, and use it as a bludgeon against the Jewish state, but to discard moral standards altogether when it comes to other nations in the region.

When Mobil and Aramco try to pretty up the Arab position, at least one knows their objectives and their justification. Their business is oil. Their suppliers must be wooed. Their economic interests in the Arab states outweigh any consideration they may have for the state of Israel. Business sometimes makes such shabby compromises in the name of business.

Lewis's voluntary enlistment in the war of delegitimation against Israel has no such obvious basis, but his capitulation to the Arabs is no less obsequious. The sign of it is that he twists historical facts into the shape of the big lie, for the Israeli presence in the West Bank is not the cause of Arab hatred, as in Lewis's corrupted formula, but its *result*. The policies of Begin, indeed the fact that Begin was elected to head the government of Israel, are the consequence of Arab intentions, not the cause of them. But in deference to the greater strength and obduracy of the Arab rejectionists in the region, Lewis's political pleasure, immoral though it be, is to urge concessions on Israel. The political claims of the Arabs he accepts at face value, while of the Israelis he demands that they prove their moral right to exist, "as a beacon of freedom"—or else.

Just as the cycle of hatred and rejection began with the Arabs, so it will have to be resolved by the Arabs. The American "liberal" press would do well, in one respect, to pay heed to Edward Said's chidings on the folly of thinking others too exotic to be held accountable. The Arabs deserve to be judged by no less stringent a set of expectations than the Israelis. They deserve to be bound by the same ideals, the same standard of morality. Far from resenting the moral scrutiny of such as Anthony Lewis, the friends of

Israel are unwilling to be its sole beneficiaries. Since the conflict in the Middle East will be ended when the Arabs decide to end it, it is time they be credited where credit is, undeniably, due.

Unhappily, the greatest gains in the Arab war of delegitimation are in evidence among American Jews, some of whom have begun to see themselves through the eyes of their accusers, and to bow to the accusation. The rapid demoralization of Jews in the face of anti-Zionism attests to the dangerous level the abuse has reached. It also shows the depth of the influence of the past, for many have yet to achieve the simple self-respect that has been eluding the Jews collectively since the dawn of modernity.

To be sure, when the vulnerability of Israel is directly involved, as in the case of the sale of sophisticated weaponry to Saudi Arabia, American Jews act persuasively and effectively, even if they are not always successful against competing lobbies and far greater resources of influence than they can muster.* But against the campaign to delegitimate Israel, American Jews have been impotent and silent.

On college campuses, even those with large and vocal Jewish populations, there are more and more unopposed attacks on Israel. PLO pamphlets flood the dormitories. Exhibits of Israeli "aggression" are presented under the guise of Arab culture. In the classroom itself there is systematic dissemination of libelous falsehood, which has been noted and documented by dozens of witnesses who say they do not consider it important enough to publicize and expose, but who, one suspects, are actually afraid to commit themselves to the process of sustained prosecution. At international and academic conferences, the terms "Zionist-racist" and "Zionist-fascist" are shrugged off as unexceptional by Jewish participants who pretend the slurs do not warrant public objection, but who are more likely embarrassed to stand up and defend their people's dignity.

Of the United Nations resolution on Zionism/racism, which forces Jews into the position of Cain not in the eyes of Christianity alone but within the entire community of nations, many American Jews pretend to take no note. "Only Jews pay attention to the United Nations," a Jewish

---

* See Murray Friedman, "AWACS and the Jewish Community," *Commentary*, April 1982, and the articles by Steven Emerson in the *New Republic*, "The Petrodollar Connection" (February 17, 1982) and "The Aramco Connection" (May 19, 1982).

intellectual answered when asked why he did not take a stand against the defamation. Yet the UN is not a parochial playpen, and real enemies do not evaporate when ignored. Instead of tirelessly challenging defamatory libels whenever they occur, so that none can hurl them with impunity, Jews have too often adopted the simpler tactic of silence—with the consequence that they have forfeited much ground in the propaganda battle to discredit Zionism.

Some, however, have felt the edge of assault so keenly they have begun to speak after all—in the language of their debasers. Organized opposition to Israel government policy on the part of American Jews began, in fact, about the same time as the UN resolution defining Zionism as a form of racism. Ironically, this opposition has always lauded itself for daring to break a community-wide "silence" concerning Israel's misdeeds. When Breira, a college-based group of American Jews, began advocating Jewish criticism of Israel five years ago, it claimed heroically to be "breaking a taboo." This formulation has been adopted by each successor to Breira, which disbanded as an organization but bequeathed its program to a much broader constituency.

A World Jewish Congress report on the *Implications of Israel-Arab Peace* (sic!), conceived in 1979 and issued in the winter of 1981, echoes much of the Breira platform, incorporating too the notion of its own courageousness. The report compliments itself on relieving the pent-up pressures of self-restraint—restraint not from criticism of the Arabs (which would have been courageous indeed) but from criticism of Israel. According to the report the most important trend in recent years has been the increasing strain in the relation of American Jews with Israel. No connection is made, however, between the oil crisis and rising Arab influence in America, between rising Arab influence in America and consequent pressure on Israel, between pressure on Israel and the strain on those who feel obliged to defend an increasingly unpopular cause. Instead, the analysis treats the struggle for Israel and Zionism as though the faults of the Jews were the reason for the enmity being directed against them. In this way certain American Jews manage to evade the unpleasant and difficult task of upholding Israel's right to self-determination, and to call themselves heroes in the process.

At first, Jewish groups were still hesitant about embarking upon this program, although from the outset the American press loved the idea of man bites dog—Jews versus Israel. At the 1979 General Assembly of the

Council of Jewish Federations and Welfare Funds, the largest working gathering of Jews in America among hundreds of workshops and sessions reflecting every cultural, religious, organizational, and political concern, the *New York Times* featured only an impromptu briefing called by Peace Now representatives, the successors of Breira in America, to encourage open criticism of Israel. That pattern of "coverage" has never changed. American Jewish critics of Israel, emboldened by media acclaim, now regularly call into question the morality of the rest of the Jewish community, which is "silent" in the face of Israeli miscreancy. This has had its inevitable effect. "When I'm accused of standing up for Israel," a professor said at a recent meeting of the local chapter of the Canadian Professors for Peace in the Middle East, "I no longer know what to say in my defense."

American Jewish attempts to discredit the policies of the Begin government obviously take pains to disavow any hostility to Israel as a whole, but they cannot help serving the purposes of such hostility. In the first place, since Begin heads a democratic state, he cannot be discredited without calling into question the country that has elected him. The critics, unable to deal effectively with this knot, end by falsifying the facts and impugning Israeli democracy; they ignore the wide base of support that Likud enjoys on university campuses and in the army, and they assert that Begin was put into power by North African immigrants, Soviet émigrés, and religious Jews, as if these voters, on account of their ethnic origins and beliefs, were untrustworthy at the polls. The implications of this line of argument should be obvious to democracy's proponents and opponents alike.

More disturbing still are the terms of the American Jewish attack upon Begin, which simply echo the Arab language of delegitimation. The critics do not merely contrast the political aims of Likud with those of the Labor party—which, as it happens, initiated the policy of West Bank settlements—but raise the specter of satanic evil. Thus, no less a Zionist than Arthur Hertzberg, writing in the pages of the *New York Review of Books*, concludes a piece on the threat posed by Menachem Begin with the incredible exhortation, "The Jews of the world can no longer choose to be silent." This puts Begin in the gallery of all those—may their names be blotted out—against whose murderous intentions Jews should have been expected to raise their voices in the past and should be raising their voices now.

Hertzberg uses the standard formula of inversion to transform the global reality of which Israel is a part into a hand-to-hand Jewish combat. American Jews "fear" Begin, he says, because he is destroying the glorious vision of Israel created by David Ben-Gurion. The American Jewish community "was persuaded to support Zionism after 1945 by the vision of a Jewish state that would *redeem* the victims of Hitler and build a *benign* society that could be a *light unto the nations*" (emphasis added). Now Begin, heir to a counter-tradition of Jewish zealotry that wants to bring Jews into the world of "real power," perverts the moral cause of the state. He is "frightening" and "dangerous," and the claims he is advancing to the land of Israel threaten to bring about a "confrontation between Jews and Gentiles."

Hertzberg, who (as we have seen) is a perceptive historian of the process of Jewish delegitimation since the Enlightenment, thus falls neatly into its trap. He pleads for the higher Israel as if Israel's moral behavior, and not its existence, were the source of the difficulty it faces in the Middle East, and as if it has taken Begin and the Likud to bring about the threat of "a confrontation between Jews and Gentiles."

It is far too convenient, as well as demonstrably deceptive, to pretend that Begin is the cause of the fears that are experienced by American Jews. They are frightened because of the tremendous rise of *Arab* "real power" and prestige since the establishment of the state of Israel; because of the unanticipated return of anti-Semitism in the mask of anti-Zionism; because of the hammering to which Israel is subjected, even by countries it has benefited at considerable cost of effort to itself. This frightens American Jews, as indeed it should, because it puts them into a position of responsibility for a vulnerable and unpopular brother.*

As for the West Bank, it is simple historical fact that the Arabs who fled Palestine in 1948–49 were left by *their* brothers to rot in refugee camps, a superior breeding ground for terrorism. (At the same time, Jews fleeing from Arab countries, in equal numbers, were absorbed by Israel imperfectly but with genuine and often self-sacrificing initiative.) The use to which the Arab refugees of 1948 have been put by their respective host

---

* In an article in *Commentary*, "The Exposed American Jew," Nathan Glazer wrote of these fears with a keen grasp of their true source—and that was in June 1975, two years before Begin's election. See also my "The Anxious American Jew," *Commentary* (September 1978).

countries has created a terrible force in the Middle East, and it is no comfort to Israel or to the Jews that the Arab countries are themselves, to some extent, reaping the harvest of hatred. What frightens Jews is that decades of callous Arab neglect should now be laid to their conscience, and history rewritten at Arab will. It also begins to be frightening that a Jewish historian of Hertzberg's caliber lends his hand to the process.

Contrary to Hertzberg's claim, and that of Anthony Lewis as well, American Jews after 1945 were "persuaded to accept" no glorious dream of Israel as a light unto the nations, or even the promise of a Labor Zionist homeland. With the same guilt and relief that prompted America itself to consent to the birth of a Jewish state (one that would, among other things, absorb the burden of hundreds of thousands of broken refugees who might otherwise have applied *here*), American Jews accepted and then came to support Israel as an assurance of the normalization of Jewish existence— which meant that their own place would be more comfortable as a result.

Nor was that "acceptance" quite as wholehearted as Hertzberg pretends. The left-wing intellectuals, the assimilationists, some of the Bundists and Communists and their children, never altogether made peace with a national Jewish presence in the world, certainly not one to which they might be expected to owe moral or spiritual allegiance. They accepted Israel with the proviso that it remain true to their own prior political orientation, their secular outlook, and their preference for Western culture. Indeed, the more honest among them have expressed over the years the conditional nature of that acceptance, as if one gives birth to a country, as to a child, on condition that it vote socialist and stay out of the synagogue. Now that attacks on Israel are becoming de rigueur among the cosmopolitan intelligentsia, many old-time opponents of Jewish "chauvinism" are resurfacing to add their outcry to the general din.

Hertzberg would have been on more solid ground had he pointed out that most American Jews would not have voted for Begin and are not in favor of either his domestic or his foreign policies. But this in itself is hardly surprising. In the absence of a strong, autonomous Jewish press in America, there is relatively little day-to-day neutral information on Israel, and even the Jewish press has been anti-Begin from the start, that is, since the 1940's, and more and more so since his election in 1977. The putative "silence" of the Jews has been mostly found among those who support Begin, not those who oppose him.

If the views of Israelis and American Jews did coincide for several decades, it was because they were both so close to the same source, both largely products of a common East European experience of modernization, discrimination, and emigration. Yet the historical and geographic pressures on the two communities are so different that the cultural gap between them cannot help but widen with the years, and just as the attitudes of American Jews reflect what they think is good for them, so the attitudes of Israelis, freely expressed in frequent elections and public-opinion polls, declare what they think is good for *them*. Jews in both America and Israel may be equally afraid of the debilitating consequence of Arab rejectionism and the attempt at delegitimation; Israeli voters happen to think for the moment that the Likud coalition is a better instrument for dealing with the problem, even if American Jews, from their privileged distance, think otherwise. In any case, it ill becomes individuals who oppose Begin's religious rhetoric to employ, as Hertzberg does, the messianic language of redemption in making known their own political preferences.

Jews who advocate attacking the government of Israel rather than the Arab rejectionists ask us to believe in the anguish of their concern. Only Israel's great moral danger and suicidal folly, they say, prompt them to switch from defense to offense. Yet one may question the sincerity of these self-justifications, for morality is measured by the demands one places upon oneself, not on others. American Jews who want an Israel shaped in their image know that the Law of Return enables them to act upon their desire, and to vote in the next Israeli election. What critics call the "cosmopolitan minority" in Israel is shrinking because cosmopolitans who could form the majority do not immigrate to Israel with the same staying power or in the same numbers as do the Orthodox, the supporters of Gush Emunim, and Soviet émigré antisocialists. Yet it is fully within the power of American Jews, the most numerous Jewish community in the world, to reclaim the land for whatever social or political purpose they have the dedication to shape. The new American Jewish "idealists" who fear so greatly for the future of the state might demand of themselves no less than they credit to the Zionists whom they cite as their heroes.

In the meantime, the withdrawal of support from Israel becomes ever more selfish and debased. Leonard Fein, editor of *Moment* magazine, has vowed (from the banks of the Charles) to topple the Begin government. In the most recent issue of his magazine, to the accompaniment of the usual expressions of pain and anguish, he suggests that American Jews *boycott* travel to Judea and Samaria—the West Bank—to show their opposition to Israeli policy in that area. It does not appear to have occurred to Fein that Jews attempting to influence Israeli policy in this manner are no different from President Hosni Mubarak who refuses to come to Israel's capital city of Jerusalem—for does not he object to Israeli "occupation" with the same righteous vehemence as they? Belligerents boycott one another. American Jews, who until recently tried to prevent the penetration of the Arab boycott to these shores, are now invited instead to declare themselves a new category of belligerent, and to initiate a boycott of their own. Not only are Jews taking over from the Arabs their arguments, Fein wants to adopt their tactics as well.

The Arab campaign to discredit Zionism caught the Jews before they had altogether regained their self-respect in the context of the modern age. There are many who do not know how to resist that campaign, others who lack the power and the will, still others who have moved preemptively to join the attack, renaming their fear as fear of their fellow Jews, and their anger as a righteous anger with their fellow Jews. Thus a rabbi recently announced to his congregation from the pulpit *as a fact* that the Israeli army had dressed an insane man in uniform and sent him armed into the Al Aksa mosque during prayer time to shoot innocent Arabs. No one rose to "silence" this rabbi, certainly not his numb congregation. The result of all this is to magnify internal conflict, and leave the campaign of delegitimation untouched at its source.

The Jews of Israel—doves and hawks, religious and secular alike—have learned that whether or not a people can be purer than others, "a light unto the nations," it must first be considered as good as others, unexceptional by the standards of the international community, normally designated on the map of enemies, neutrals, and friends. The state of Israel has shown itself capable of defending its borders, and also of readjusting them in exchange for political security. The American Jewish community, beneficiary of the process of Jewish normalization in the world, has been proud to assist it in a minor way. Now that Arab influence spreads to this continent, and concentrates the campaign of discreditation in the United States, American Jews are being asked to bear the brunt of resistance.

Indeed, they may now have come once again to a severe time of testing. As this article goes to press, Israeli forces have entered Lebanon to secure the northern sector of their country from continual harassment. In the past, such actions by Israel, though successful from a military point of view, have invariably unleashed waves of hypocritical diplomatic reproach, and the early responses at the UN and elsewhere this time show every sign of conforming to the usual pattern. It remains to be seen how the American Jewish community will stand up to a renewed and potentially even more virulent attack on the legitimacy of Israel.

5. Social Obligations and the Welfare State

*T*hroughout the 1950s and 1960s, the liberal anticommunists, soon to be labeled neoconservatives, were political liberals. They were strong supporters of Franklin Roosevelt's New Deal, which they champion to this day. Most neoconservatives backed an active, energetic government, but one that respects traditional values and local mores. The juxtaposition of two Irving Kristol columns, his 1978 essay, "Human Nature and Social Reform," and his 1993 essay, "A Conservative Welfare State," capture the neoconservative vision for the modern welfare state.

Though they gradually became disillusioned with the welfare state, the neoconservatives never reverted to a libertarian individualism. Strong believers in the importance of communities, the neoconservatives focused on what they called "mediating structures." Mediating structures are voluntary associations—churches, synagogues, bowling leagues, soccer associations, charitable organizations—in which people interact for a common purpose, often to serve a greater good. Modern American discourse on the importance of civil society was launched by Richard John Neuhaus and Peter Berger's landmark 1976 American Enterprise Institute monograph, "To Empower People," which is excerpted here.

For the neoconservatives, perhaps the worst manifestation of the liberal welfare state is the idea of racial classification through affirmative *action and its measuring stick, quotas. The neoconservatives saw affirmative action as anathema not only to the ideal of a color-blind society, but ultimately destructive to societal cohesion. Thomas Sowell's masterful essay, "Affirmative Action: A Worldwide Disaster," summarizes these unintended consequenses of affirmative action and many other reasons why, in his view, it is a failed policy.*

Human Nature and Social Reform

Irving Kristol

W E ARE LIVING through a period of much disillusionment with social reform, at least on the part of the majority of the American people. An energetic and articulate minority, to be sure, is still willing to defend the dozens of Great Society programs of the last fifteen years, lamenting only the "niggardliness" with which they were conceived and executed. But even the media—always the last to know—no longer put much stock in any such apologias. "Throwing money at problems" is the way these programs are now described (and dismissed). And even though we continue to do just that, it is all done in a rather mechanical and half-hearted way, simply because we feel we must do something.

What is missing is any kind of serious reflection on our experience with social policy. We seem uninterested in learning from this rich—at least expensive—experience. We are curiously reluctant to analyze why some reforms work, others do not.

Not all social reforms fail. Let me point to one which has been an extraordinary success, though it is practically never mentioned in the literature on the subject. I refer to night school, at the secondary and postsecondary level. For many decades now, night schools have permitted millions of working class Americans to acquire an education, and eventually to improve their condition, while supporting themselves and/or their families. Not everyone goes to night school, of course; and many go only quickly to drop out. But these people do not thereby constitute any kind of social problem. In night school, you get only no effects or good effects.

An "Opportunity Program"

Now, why is this program so successful? The answer is obvious (though not at all trivial): It builds on existing motivations. It doesn't try to reform

Reprinted from The Wall Street Journal, *September 18, 1978.*

or rehabilitate the individual. It offers him (or her) an opportunity to achieve an ambition. Let us call this kind of program an "opportunity program," and of such programs we can say flatly: They always work. They may not work as well as we wish or hope. But they are never counterproductive.

All of us of a certain age are familiar enough with such opportunity programs, though we don't always recognize them as such. Alcoholics Anonymous, for example, is exactly such a program. In it, people who wish to cease being alcoholics can achieve that goal. As for those who prefer to remain alcoholics—well, there is no program on God's earth which can reform them. Motivation is all.

What is true for alcoholism is also true for drug addiction, juvenile delinquency, and adult criminality. Those who wish to move out of these conditions will be helped by programs that "hook on" to this motivation. The rest will be unaffected by any program.

Juvenile delinquency is probably the most interesting of these cases, since most adults would like to think that all young people, in the proper environment, will respond positively to love and care and affection. Well, not all do. We have had for over a century now, in this country and elsewhere, an infinite variety of juvenile delinquency programs. They have all been studied exhaustively by sociologists, criminologists, and social workers, and the findings are dismal. Not a single such program works better than no program at all.

This does not mean, fortunately, that all juvenile delinquents are irretrievably doomed to a life of crime. In fact, most juvenile delinquents do not grow up to be professional criminals. The reason is that, as they grow older, their motivations change. Indeed, for these maturing delinquents society does offer an opportunity program that is extraordinarily successful. It is called marriage. Falling in love creates new motivations more powerful (and more benign) than the old. Nothing creates more joy in the heart of a parole officer than the news that one of his charges is getting married.

The case of adult criminals is not so very different. Here, too, we have had hundreds of experiments, in dozens of countries, with prison reform aiming at the rehabilitation of habitual criminals. Not a single such program works better than no program at all, as measured by the rates of recidivism. Once again: If there were such a program you would have heard all about it by now.

But, once more again, this does not mean that criminals are a breed apart from the rest of mankind. Their motivations, too, can change. Getting married ("settling down with a good woman") can do it. Religious conversion can do it (which is why it is deplorable that so many prisoners now read law books instead of the Bible). And the weariness of older age— nature's opportunity program, if you will—can do it. Very little else, apparently, can.

What it comes down to is this: There can be no successful social program which does not take seriously, is not realistically attentive to, people's motivations. There is one important exception to this rule. The issue of motivation is irrelevant to people who are dependent by nature (i.e., whose dependency is simply not open to question). I refer, of course, to the old, the halt, the blind, the infirm. Programs that "throw money" at such people are perfectly appropriate. True, one can recklessly if generously throw too much money at them. But that is a question of economic prudence, not of social policy. In principle, all such programs, for such people, work. The reason they work for such people is because their only problem is the lack of money, not the lack of any kind of motivation.

But the issue of motivation certainly does arise in connection with our welfare population, whose dependency is social, not natural. The reason our welfare policy has been such a disaster—disastrous, above all, to the people it is supposed to help—is because our reformers thought it would be a slander against human nature even to permit the question of motivation to enter their thinking.

Almost 150 years ago, Alexis de Tocqueville visited England and was quickly struck by the paradox that the wealthiest nation in the world was preeminently perplexed by a massive "pauper problem." Investigating, he soon discovered the explanation for this paradox. Welfare rates had been set so high as to compete successfully with the job rates for unskilled labor. Many people, who preferred nonwork to work, were therefore leaving (or refusing to enter) the labor force. This population, now dependent, was soon corrupted and demoralized by its own unnatural dependency, and manifested all the familiar symptoms of social pathology: abandoned families, drunkenness, sloth, criminality, and so on.

This is precisely what has happened in the United States in these past fifteen years. (It didn't happen in France, incidentally, which, having no generous welfare program, had no welfare problem.) Why didn't we realize what was happening?

The reason, so far as I can see, has to do with the metaphysics behind modern social thought and the modern impulse to social reform. Our reformers evidently don't much care about opportunity programs—they speak little of them, devise few of them. They care very much, on the other hand, about what we may call "environmental programs"—that is, programs that enable us (in theory) to change everyone's motivations for the better, through the practical exercise of our unadulterated compassion, our universal benevolence, our gentle paternalistic authority.

What it comes down to is that our reformers simply cannot bring themselves to think realistically about human nature. They believe it to be not only originally good, but also incorruptible (hence the liberal tolerance for pornography).

Wreckers at Work

When a slum population wrecks a brand-new housing project, it is the designers of the project who are blamed, never the inhabitants. Those inhabitants are promptly relocated in other housing—which they will also wreck, since there are no rewards or punishments attached to existing motivations. There is thought to be no need for such rewards or punishments, since officials at HEW and our liberal social scientists know that poor people have only good motivations.

They know this as a matter of faith—by liberal revelation, as it were. To question this principle of the original goodness of human nature—and its corollary: the ease of improvement of human nature—would also set limits to that most profound of liberal passions, the passion of self-righteous compassion. It is this passion that defines the very essence of modern liberalism, and which—not so incidentally—legitimates the liberal exercise of intrusive authority over our social and economic life. So it is not surprising that, with such a secure anchor in both secular faith and self-interest, the liberal motivation is, of all motivations, the least responsive to messages from the real world.

Still, reality will not be denied. What we call the "neoconservative" impulse today—so evident in both our political parties—is basically a disillusionment with, and disengagement from, the strategy of environmental reform. This does not mean the end of reform itself, as many liberals insist and some conservatives claim. But it does indeed signify a profound shift in the climate of ideas within which reform will henceforth be conceived.

From To Empower People: The Role of Mediating Structures in Public Policy

Richard John Neuhaus and Peter Berger

Mediating Structures and the Dilemmas of the Welfare State

Two seemingly contradictory tendencies are evident in current thinking about public policy in America. First, there is a continuing desire for the services provided by the modern welfare state. Partisan rhetoric aside, few people seriously envisage dismantling the welfare state. The serious debate is over how and to what extent it should be expanded. The second tendency is one of strong animus against government, bureaucracy, and bigness as such. This animus is directed not only toward Washington but toward government at all levels. Although this essay is addressed to the American situation, it should be noted that a similar ambiguity about the modern welfare state exists in other democratic societies, notably in Western Europe.

Perhaps this is just another case of people wanting to eat their cake and have it too. It would hardly be the first time in history that the people wanted benefits without paying the requisite costs. Nor are politicians above exploiting ambiguities by promising increased services while reducing expenditures. The extravagant rhetoric of the modern state and the surrealistic vastness of its taxation system encourage magical expectations that make contradictory measures seem possible. As long as some of the people can be fooled some of the time, some politicians will continue to ride into office on such magic.

But this is not the whole story. The contradiction between wanting more government services and less government may be only apparent.

Excerpted from To Empower People: The Role of Mediating Structures in Public Policy *(Washington, D.C.: American Enterprise Institute, 1976), 1–33.*

More precisely, we suggest that the modern welfare state is here to stay, indeed that it ought to expand the benefits it provides—but that *alternative mechanisms are possible to provide welfare-state services.*

The current antigovernment, antibigness mood is not irrational. Complaints about impersonality, unresponsiveness, and excessive interference, as well as the perception of rising costs and deteriorating service—these are based upon empirical and widespread experience. The crisis of New York City, which is rightly seen as more than a fiscal crisis, signals a national state of unease with the policies followed in recent decades. At the same time there is widespread public support for publicly addressing major problems of our society in relieving poverty, in education, health care, and housing, and in a host of other human needs. What first appears as contradiction, then, is the sum of equally justified aspirations. The public policy goal is to address human needs without exacerbating the reasons for animus against the welfare state.

Of course there are no panaceas. The alternatives proposed here, we believe, can solve *some* problems. Taken seriously, they could become the basis of far-reaching innovations in public policy, perhaps of a new paradigm for at least sectors of the modern welfare state.

The basic concept is that of what we are calling mediating structures. The concept in various forms has been around for a long time. What is new is the systematic effort to translate it into specific public policies. For purposes of this study, mediating structures are defined as *those institutions standing between the individual in his private life and the large institutions of public life.*

Modernization brings about an historically unprecedented dichotomy between public and private life. The most important large institution in the ordering of modern society is the modern state itself. In addition, there are the large economic conglomerates of capitalist enterprise, big labor, and the growing bureaucracies that administer wide sectors of the society, such as in education and the organized professions. All these institutions we call the *megastructures.*

Then there is that modern phenomenon called private life. It is a curious kind of preserve left over by the large institutions and in which individuals carry on a bewildering variety of activities with only fragile institutional support.

For the individual in modern society, life is an ongoing migration between these two spheres, public and private. The megastructures are typically alienating, that is, they are not helpful in providing meaning and identity for individual existence. Meaning, fulfillment, and personal identity are to be realized in the private sphere. While the two spheres interact in many ways, in private life the individual is left very much to his own devices, and thus is uncertain and anxious. Where modern society is "hard," as in the megastructures, it is personally unsatisfactory; where it is "soft," as in private life, it cannot be relied upon. Compare, for example, the social realities of employment with those of marriage.

The dichotomy poses a double crisis. It is a crisis for the individual who must carry on a balancing act between the demands of the two spheres. It is a political crisis because the megastructures (notably the state) come to be devoid of personal meaning and are therefore viewed as unreal or even malignant. Not everyone experiences this crisis in the same way. Many who handle it more successfully than most have access to institutions that *mediate* between the two spheres. Such institutions have a private face, giving private life a measure of stability, and they have a public face, transferring meaning and value to the megastructures. Thus, mediating structures alleviate each facet of the double crisis of modern society. Their strategic position derives from their reducing both the anomic precariousness of individual existence in isolation from society and the threat of alienation to the public order.

Our focus is on four such mediating structures—neighborhood, family, church, and voluntary association. This is by no means an exhaustive list, but these institutions were selected for two reasons: first, they figure prominently in the lives of most Americans and, second, they are most relevant to the problems of the welfare state with which we are concerned. The proposal is that, if these institutions could be more imaginatively recognized in public policy, individuals would be more "at home" in society, and the political order would be more "meaningful."

Without institutionally reliable processes of mediation, the political order becomes detached from the values and realities of individual life. Deprived of its moral foundation, the political order is "delegitimated." When that happens, the political order must be secured by coercion rather than by consent. And when that happens, democracy disappears.

The attractiveness of totalitarianism—whether instituted under left-wing or right-wing banners—is that it overcomes the dichotomy of private and public existence by imposing on life one comprehensive order of meaning. Although established totalitarian systems can be bitterly disappointing to their architects as well as their subjects, they are, on the historical record, nearly impossible to dismantle. The system continues quite effectively, even if viewed with cynicism by most of the population—including those who are in charge.

Democracy is "handicapped" by being more vulnerable to the erosion of meaning in its institutions. Cynicism threatens it; wholesale cynicism can destroy it. That is why mediation is so crucial to democracy. Such mediation cannot be sporadic and occasional; it must be institutionalized in *structures*. The structures we have chosen to study have demonstrated a great capacity for adapting and innovating under changing conditions. Most important, they exist where people are, and that is where sound public policy should always begin.

This understanding of mediating structures is sympathetic to Edmund Burke's well-known claim: "To be attached to the subdivision, to love the little platoon we belong to in society, is the first principle (the germ as it were) of public affections." And it is sympathetic to Alexis de Tocqueville's conclusion drawn from his observation of Americans: "In democratic countries the science of association is the mother of science; the progress of all the rest depends upon the progress it has made." Marx too was concerned about the destruction of community, and the glimpse he gives us of postrevolutionary society is strongly reminiscent of Burke's "little platoons." The emphasis is even sharper in the anarcho-syndicalist tradition of social thought.

In his classic study of suicide, Emile Durkheim describes the "tempest" of modernization sweeping away the "little aggregations" in which people formerly found community, leaving only the state on the one hand and a mass of individuals, "like so many liquid molecules," on the other. Although using different terminologies, others in the sociological tradition—Ferdinand Toennies, Max Weber, Georg Simmel, Charles Cooley, Thorstein Veblen—have analyzed aspects of the same dilemma. Today Robert Nisbet has most persuasively argued that the loss of community threatens the future of American democracy.

Also, on the practical political level, it might seem that mediating structures have universal endorsement. There is, for example, little political mileage in being antifamily or antichurch. But the reality is not so simple. Liberalism—which constitutes the broad center of American politics, whether or not it calls itself by that name—has tended to be blind to the political (as distinct from private) functions of mediating structures.

The main feature of liberalism, as we intend the term, is a commitment to government action toward greater social justice within the existing system. (To revolutionaries, of course, this is "mere reformism," but the revolutionary option has not been especially relevant, to date, in the American context.)

Liberalism's blindness to mediating structures can be traced to its Enlightenment roots. Enlightenment thought is abstract, universalistic, addicted to what Burke called "geometry" in social policy. The concrete particularities of mediating structures find an inhospitable soil in the liberal garden. There the great concern is for the individual ("the rights of man") and for a just public order, but anything "in between" is viewed as irrelevant, or even an obstacle, to the rational ordering of society. What lies in between is dismissed, to the extent it can be, as superstition, bigotry, or (more recently) cultural lag.

American liberalism has been vigorous in the defense of the private rights of individuals, and has tended to dismiss the argument that private behavior can have public consequences. Private rights are frequently defended *against* mediating structures—children's rights against the family, the rights of sexual deviants against neighborhood or small-town sentiment, and so forth. Similarly, American liberals are virtually faultless in their commitment to the religious liberty of individuals. But the liberty to be defended is always that of privatized religion. Supported by a very narrow understanding of the separation of church and state, liberals are typically hostile to the claim that institutional religion might have public rights and public functions. As a consequence of this "geometrical" outlook, liberalism has a hard time coming to terms with the alienating effects of the abstract structures it has multiplied since the New Deal. This may be the Achilles heel of the liberal state today.

The Left, understood as some version of the socialist vision, has been less blind to the problem of mediation. Indeed the term "alienation" derives from Marxism. The weakness of the Left, however, is its exclusive or nearly exclusive focus on the capitalist economy as the source of this evil, when in fact the alienations of the socialist states, insofar as there are socialist states, are much more severe than those of the capitalist states. While some theorists of the New Left have addressed this problem by using elements from the anarcho-syndicalist tradition, most socialists see mediating structures as something that may be relevant to a postrevolutionary future, but that in the present only distracts attention from the struggle toward building socialism. Thus the Left is not very helpful in the search for practical solutions to our problem.

On the Right of the political broad center, we also find little that is helpful. To be sure, classical European conservatism had high regard for mediating structures, but, from the eighteenth century on, this tradition has been marred by a romantic urge to revoke modernity—a prospect that is, we think, neither likely nor desirable. On the other hand, what is now called conservatism in America is in fact old-style liberalism. It is the laissez-faire ideology of the period before the New Deal, which is roughly the time when liberalism shifted its faith from the market to government. *Both* the old faith in the market *and* the new faith in government share the abstract thought patterns of the Enlightenment. In addition, today's conservatism typically exhibits the weakness of the Left in reverse: it is highly sensitive to the alienations of big government, but blind to the analogous effects of big business. Such one-sidedness, whether Left or Right, is not helpful.

As is now being widely recognized, we need new approaches free of the ideological baggage of the past. The mediating structures paradigm cuts across current ideological and political divides. This proposal has met with gratifying interest from most with whom we have shared it, and while it has been condemned as right-wing by some and as left-wing by others, this is in fact encouraging. Although the paradigm may play havoc with the conventional political labels, it is hoped that, after the initial confusion of what some social scientists call "cognitive shock," each implication of the proposal will be considered on its own merits. . . .

Neighborhood

"The most sensible way to locate the neighborhood," writes Milton Kotler in *Neighborhood Government* (Bobbs-Merrill, 1969) "is to ask people where it is, for people spend much time fixing its boundaries. Gangs mark its turf. Old people watch for its new faces. Children figure out safe routes between home and school. People walk their dogs through their neighborhood, but rarely beyond it."

At first blush, it seems the defense of neighborhood is a motherhood issue. The neighborhood is the place of relatively intact and secure existence, protecting us against the disjointed and threatening big world "out there." Around the idea of neighborhood gravitate warm feelings of nostalgia and the hope for community. It may not be the place where we are entirely at home, but it is the place where we are least homeless.

While no doubt influenced by such sentiments, the new interest in neighborhoods today goes far beyond sentimentality. The neighborhood should be seen as a key mediating structure in the reordering of our national life. As is evident in fears and confusions surrounding such phrases as ethnic purity or neighborhood integrity, the focus on neighborhood touches some of the most urgent and sensitive issues of social policy. Indeed, many charge that the "rediscovery" of the neighborhood is but another, and thinly veiled, manifestation of racism.

Against that charge we contend—together with many others, both black and white, who have a strong record of commitment to racial justice—that strong neighborhoods can be a potent instrument in achieving greater justice for all Americans. It is not true, for example, that all-black neighborhoods are by definition weak neighborhoods. As we shall see, to argue the contrary is to relegate black America to perpetual frustration or to propose a most improbable program of social revolution. To put it simply, real community development must begin where people are. If our hopes for development assume an idealized society cleansed of ethnic pride and its accompanying bigotries, they are doomed to failure.

While social policy that can be morally approved must be attuned to the needs of the poor—and in America that means very particularly the black poor—the nonpoor also live in and cherish the values of neighborhood. The neighborhood in question may be as part-time and tenuous as the many bedroom communities surrounding our major cities; it may be the ethnic and economic crazy quilt of New York's East Village; it may be the tranquil homogeneity of the east side of Cisco, Texas. Again, a neighborhood is what the people who live there say is a neighborhood.

For public policy purposes, there is no useful definition of what makes a good neighborhood, though we can agree on what constitutes a bad neighborhood. Few people would choose to live where crime is rampant, housing deteriorated, and garbage uncollected. To describe these phenomena as bad is not an instance of imposing middle-class, bourgeois values upon the poor. No one, least of all the poor, is opposed to such "middle class" values as safety, sanitation, and the freedom of choice that comes with affluence. With respect to so-called bad neighborhoods, we have essentially three public policy choices: we can ignore them, we can attempt to dismantle them and spread their problems around more equitably, or we can try to transform the bad into the better on the way to becoming good. The first option, although common, should be intolerable. The second is massively threatening to the nonpoor, and therefore not feasible short of revolution. The third holds most promise for a public policy that can gain the support of the American people. And, if we care more about consequence than about confrontation, the third is also the most radical in long-range effect.

Because social scientists and planners have a penchant for unitary definitions that cover all contingencies, there is still much discussion of what makes for a good neighborhood. Our approach suggests that the penchant should be carefully restrained. It is not necessarily true, for example, that a vital neighborhood is one that supplies a strong sense of social cohesion or reinforces personal identity with the group. In fact many people want neighborhoods where free choice in association and even anonymity are cherished. That kind of neighborhood, usually urban, is no less a neighborhood for its lack of social cohesion. Cohesion exacts its price in loss of personal freedom; freedom may be paid for in the coin of alienation and loneliness. One pays the price for the neighborhood of one's choice. Making that choice possible is the function of the *idea* of neighborhood as it is embodied in many actual neighborhoods. It is not possible to create the benefits of each kind of neighborhood in every neighborhood. One cannot devise a compromise between the cohesion of a New England small town and the anonymity of the East Village without destroying both options.

Nor is it necessarily true that progress is marked by movement from the neighborhood of cohesion to the neighborhood of elective choice. Members of the cultural elite, who have strong influence on the metaphors by which public policy is designed, frequently feel they have escaped from the parochialisms of the former type of neighborhood. Such escapes are one source of the continuing vitality of great cities, but this idea of liberation should not be made normative. The Upper West Side of New York City, for example, the neighborhood of so many literary, academic, and political persons, has its own forms of parochialism, its taboos and restrictions, approved beliefs and behavior patterns. The urban sophisticate's conformity to the values of individual self-fulfillment and tolerance can be as intolerant of the beliefs and behavior nurtured in the community centered in the St. Stanislaus American Legion branch of Hamtramck, Michigan, as the people of Hamtramck are intolerant of what is called liberation on the Upper West Side.

Karl Marx wrote tellingly of "the idiocy of village life." Important to our approach, however, is the recognition that what looks like idiocy may in fact be a kind of complexity with which we cannot cope or do not wish to be bothered. That is, the movement from the community of cohesion to cosmopolitanism, from village to urban neighborhood, is not necessarily a movement from the simple to the complex. In fact, those who move toward the cosmopolitan may be simplifying their lives by freeing themselves from the tangled associations—family, church, club, and so forth—that dominate village life. It is probably easier for an outsider to become a person of political and social consequence in New York City than in most small towns. In a large city almost everyone is an outsider by definition. To put it another way, in the world of urban emigrés there are enough little worlds so that everyone can be an insider somewhere. Against the urban and universalizing biases of much social thought, the mediating structures paradigm requires that we take seriously the structures, values, and habits by which people order their lives in neighborhoods, wherever those neighborhoods may be, and no matter whether they are cohesive or individualistic, elective or hereditary. There is no inherent superiority in or inevitable movement toward the neighborhood whose life gravitates around the liberal Democratic club rather than around the parish church or union hall. The goal of public policy should be to sustain the diversity of neighborhoods in which people can remain and to which they can move in accord with what "fits" their self-understanding and their hopes for those about whom they care most.

The empowerment of people in neighborhoods is hardly the answer to all our social problems. Neighborhoods empowered to impose their values upon individual behavior and expression can be both coercive and cruel. Government that transcends neighborhoods must intervene to protect elementary human rights. Here again, however, the distinction between public and private spheres is critically important. In recent years an unbalanced emphasis upon individual rights has seriously eroded the community's power to sustain its democratically determined values in the public sphere. It is ironic, for example, to find people who support landmark commissions that exercise aesthetic censorship—for example, by forbidding owners of landmark properties to change so much as a step or a bay window without legal permission—and who, at the same time, oppose public control of pornography, prostitution, gambling, and other "victim-less crimes" that violate neighborhood values more basic than mere aesthetics. In truth, a strong class factor is involved in this apparent contradiction. Houses in neighborhoods that are thought to be part of our architectural heritage are typically owned by people to whom values such as architectural heritage are important. These are usually not the people whose neighborhoods are assaulted by pornography, prostitution, and drug trafficking. In short, those who have power can call in the police to reinforce their values while the less powerful cannot.

This individualistic and neighborhood-destroying bias is reinforced by court judgments that tend to treat all neighborhoods alike. That is, the legal tendency is to assume that there is a unitary national community rather than a national community composed of thousands of communities. Thus, the people of Kokomo, Indiana, must accept public promotions of pornography, for instance, because such promotions are protected by precedents established in Berkeley, California, or in Times Square. It is just barely arguable that the person who wants to see a live sex show in downtown Kokomo would be denied a constitutional right were such shows locally prohibited. It is a great deal clearer that the people of Kokomo are now denied the right to determine democratically the character of the community in which they live. More careful distinctions are required if we are to stay the rush toward a situation in which civil liberties are viewed as the enemy of communal values and law itself is pitted against the power of people to shape their own lives. Such distinctions must reflect a greater appreciation of the differences between public and private behavior.

One reason for the present confusion about individual and communal rights has been the unreflective extension of policies deriving from America's racial dilemma to other areas where they are neither practicable nor just. That is, as a nation, and after a long, tortuous, and continuing agony, we have solemnly covenanted to disallow any public regulation that discriminates on the basis of race. The national decision must in no way be compromised. At the same time, the singularity of America's racial history needs to be underscored. Public policy should be discriminating about discriminations. Discrimination is the essence of particularism and particularism is the essence of pluralism. The careless expansion of anti-discrimination rulings in order to appease every aggrieved minority or individual will have two certain consequences: first, it will further erode local communal authority and, second, it will trivialize the historic grievances and claims to justice of America's racial minorities.

In terms of communal standards and sanctions, deviance always exacts a price. Indeed, without such standards, there can be no such thing as deviance. Someone who engages in public and deviant behavior in, say, Paducah, Kentucky, can pay the social price of deviance, can persuade his fellow citizens to accept his behavior, or can move to New York City. He should not be able to call in the police to prevent the people of Paducah from enforcing their values against his behavior. (Obviously, we are not referring to the expression of unpopular political or religious views, which, like proscriptions against racial discrimination, is firmly protected by national law and consensus.) The city—variously viewed as the cesspool of wickedness or the zone of liberation—has historically been the place of refuge for the insistently deviant. It might be objected that our saying "he can move to the city" sounds like the "love it or leave it" argument of those who opposed antiwar protesters in the last decade. The whole point, however, is the dramatic difference between a nation and a neighborhood. One is a citizen of a nation and lays claim to the rights by which that nation is constituted. Within that nation there are numerous associations such as neighborhoods—more or less freely chosen—and membership in those associations is usually related to affinity. This nation is constituted as an exercise in pluralism, as the *unum* within which myriad *plures* are sustained. If it becomes national policy to make the public values of Kokomo or Salt Lake City indistinguishable from those of San Francisco or New Orleans, we have as a nation abandoned the social experiment symbolized by the phrase "E Pluribus Unum." . . .

With respect to the connection between neighborhood and race, we would draw a sharp distinction between a society of *pro*scription and a society of *pre*scription. We have as a society covenanted to proscribe racial discrimination in the public realm. That proscription must be tirelessly implemented, no matter how frustrating the efforts at implementation sometimes are. But it is quite another matter to pursue policies of *pre*scription in which government agencies prescribe quotas and balances for the redistribution of people and wealth. Pushed far enough, the second course invites revolutionary reaction, and it would almost certainly be revolution from the right. Pushed as far as it is now being pushed, it is eroding community power, distracting from the tasks of neighborhood development, and alienating many Americans from the general direction of domestic public policy. . . .

Family

There are places, especially in urban areas, where lifestyles are largely detached from family connections. This is, one hopes, good for those who choose it. Certainly such lifestyles add to the diversity, the creativity, even the magic, of the city. But since a relatively small number of people inhabit these areas, it would be both foolish and undemocratic to take such lifestyles as guidelines for the nation. For most Americans, neighborhood and community are closely linked to the family as an institution.

The family may be in crisis in the sense that it is undergoing major changes of definition, but there is little evidence that it is in decline. High divorce rates, for example, may indicate not decline but rising expectations in what people look for in marriage and family life. The point is underscored by high remarriage rates. It is noteworthy that the counterculture, which is so critical of the so-called bourgeois family, uses the terminology of family for its new social constructions, as do radical feminists pledged to "sisterhood." For most Americans, the evidence is that involvement in the bourgeois family, however modified, will endure.

Of course, modernization has already had a major impact on the family. It has largely stripped the family of earlier functions in the areas of education and economics, for example. But in other ways, modernization has made the family more important than ever before. It is the major institution within the private sphere, and thus for many people the most valuable thing in their lives. Here they make their moral commitments, invest their emotions, plan for the future, and perhaps even hope for immortality.

There is a paradox here. On the one hand, the megastructures of government, business, mass communications, and the rest have left room for the family to be the autonomous realm of individual aspiration and fulfillment. This room is by now well secured in the legal definitions of the family. At the same time, the megastructures persistently infringe upon the family. We cannot and should not eliminate these infringements entirely. After all, families exist in a common society. We can, however, take positive measures to protect and foster the family institution, so that it is not defenseless before the forces of modernity.

This means public recognition of the family *as an institution*. It is not enough to be concerned for individuals more or less incidentally related to the family as institution. Public recognition of the family as an institution is imperative because every society has an inescapable interest in how children are raised, how values are transmitted to the next generation. Totalitarian regimes have tried—unsuccessfully to date—to supplant the family in this function. Democratic societies dare not try if they wish to remain democratic. Indeed they must resist every step, however well intended, to displace or weaken the family institution.

Public concern for the family is not antagonistic to concern for individual rights. On the contrary, individuals need strong families if they are to grow up and remain rooted in a strong sense of identity and values. Weak families produce uprooted individuals, unsure of their direction and therefore searching for some authority. They are ideal recruits for authoritarian movements inimical to democratic society.

Commitment to the family institution can be combined, although not without difficulty, with an emphatically libertarian view that protects the private lives of adults against public interference of any kind. Public interest in the family is centered on children, not adults; it touches adults insofar as they are in charge of children. The public interest is institutional in character. That is, the state is to view children as members of a family. The sovereignty of the family over children has limits—as does any sovereignty in the modern world—and these limits are already defined in laws regarding abuse, criminal neglect, and so on. The onus of proof, however, must be placed on policies or laws that foster state interference rather than on those that protect family autonomy. In saying this we affirm what has been the major legal tradition in this country.

Conversely, we oppose policies that expose the child directly to state intervention, without the mediation of the family. We are skeptical about much current discussion of children's rights—especially when such rights are asserted *against* the family. Children do have rights, among which is the right to a functionally strong family. When the rhetoric of children's rights means transferring children from the charge of families to the charge of coteries of experts ("We know what is best for the children"), that rhetoric must be suspected of cloaking vested interests—ideological interests, to be sure, but, also and more crudely, interest in jobs, money, and power.

Our preference for the parents over the experts is more than a matter of democratic conviction—and does not ignore the existence of relevant and helpful expertise. It is a bias based upon the simple, but often overlooked, consideration that virtually all parents love their children. Very few experts love, or can love, most of the children in their care. Not only is that emotionally difficult, but expertise generally requires a degree of emotional detachment. In addition, the parent, unike the expert, has a long-term, open-ended commitment to the individual child. Thus the parent, almost by definition, is way ahead of the expert in sheer knowledge of the child's character, history, and needs. The expert, again by definition, relates to the child within general and abstract schemata. Sometimes the schemata fit, but very often they do not.

We have no intention of glorifying the bourgeois family. Foster parents, lesbians and gays, liberated families, or whatever—all can do the job *as long as* they provide children the loving and the permanent structure that traditional families have typically provided. Indeed, virtually any structure is better for children than what experts or the state can provide.

Most modern societies have in large part disfranchised the family in the key area of education. The family becomes, at best, an auxiliary agency to the state, which at age five or six coercively (compulsory school laws) and monopolistically (for the most part) takes over the child's education. Of course there are private schools, but here class becomes a powerful factor. Disfranchisement falls most heavily on lower-income parents who have little say in what happens to their children in school. This discrimination violates a fundamental human right, perhaps the most fundamental human right—the right to make a world for one's children.

Our purpose is not to deprive upper-income families of the choices they have. The current assault on private schools in Britain (there called public schools) is not a happy example. Our purpose is to give those choices to those who do not now have decision-making power. When some are freezing while others enjoy bright fires, the solution is not to extinguish all fires equally but to provide fires for those who have none.

There is yet a further class discrimination in education. By birth or social mobility, the personnel of the education establishment are upper middle class, and this is reflected in the norms, the procedures, and the very cultural climate of that establishment. This means the child who is not of an upper-middle-class family is confronted by an alien milieu from his or her first day at school. In part this may be inevitable. The modern world is bourgeois and to succeed in a bourgeois world means acquiring bourgeois skills and behavior patterns. We do not suggest, as some do, that the lower-class child is being culturally raped when taught correct English. But there are many other, sometimes unconscious, ways in which the education establishment systematically disparages ways of life other than those of the upper middle class. Yet these disparaged ways of life are precisely the ways in which parents of millions of American children live. Thus schools teach contempt for the parents and, ultimately, self-contempt.

In a few metropolitan areas, the education establishment has responded to these problems, sometimes creatively. But monopolies endowed with coercive powers do not change easily. The best way to induce change is to start breaking up the monopoly—to empower people *to shop elsewhere*. We trust the ability of low-income parents to make educational decisions more wisely than do the professionals who now control their children's education. To deny this ability is the worst class bias of all, and in many instances it is racism as well.

To affirm empowerment against tutelage, irrespective of economic or social status, is hardly a wildly radical position. That it may seem so to some is a measure of the elitist and essentially antidemocratic effects of the bureaucratization and professionalization of American society.

Against the politics of resentment, empowerment is not a zero-sum game. That is, lower-income people can be enfranchised without disfranchising or impoverishing the better off. But this process does assume a lower limit of poverty beyond which efforts at empowerment are futile. Any humane and effective social policy must place a floor of decency under everyone in the society. The relative merits of income maintenance programs—guaranteed income, negative income tax, and so forth—are beyond the scope of this essay, but the whole argument assumes that a floor of decency must be established. Aside from moral imperatives, such a floor can strengthen mediating structures, notably here poor families, by helping them break out of present patterns of dependency upon a confused and confusing welfare system.

Church

Religious institutions form by far the largest network of voluntary associations in American society. Yet, for reasons both ideological and historical, their role is frequently belittled or totally overlooked in discussions of social policy. Whatever may be one's attitude to organized religion, this blind spot must be reckoned a serious weakness in much thinking about public policy. The churches and synagogues of America can no more be omitted from responsible social analysis than can big labor, business corporations, or the communications media. Not only are religious institutions significant "players" in the public realm, but they are singularly important to the way people order their lives and values at the most local and concrete levels of their existence. Thus they are crucial to understanding family, neighborhood, and other mediating structures of empowerment.

The view that the public sphere is synonymous with the government or the formal polity of the society has been especially effective in excluding religion from considerations of public policy. We shall return to some of the church/state controversies that have reflected and perpetuated this view; but for the moment it should be obvious that our whole proposal aims at a complex and nuanced understanding of the public realm that includes many "players" other than the state. Also, much modern social thought deriving from Enlightenment traditions has operated on one or two assumptions that tend to minimize the role of religion. The first assumption is that education and modernization make certain the decline of allegiance to institutional religion. That is, there is thought to be an inevitable connection between modernization and secularization. The second assumption is that, even if religion continues to flourish, it deals purely with the private sphere of life and is therefore irrelevant to public policy. Both assumptions need to be carefully reexamined.

The evidence, at least in America, does not support the hypothesis of the inevitable decline of religion. Although the decline is perennially announced—its announcement being greeted with both cheers and lamentations—it is likely that religion is at least as institutionally intact as some other major institutions (such as, for example, higher education). It is worth noting that in recent years the alleged decline of religion has been measured by comparison with the so-called religious boom of the late 1950s. The comparison with that unprecedented period of institutional growth offers a very skewed perspective. But, even when the vitality of religion is measured by that misleading comparison, it is notable that in the past few years the indexes are again on the upswing. Church attendance, claimed affiliation, financial contributions, and other indicators all suggest that whatever decline there was from the apex of the late 1950s has now stopped or been reversed. It is perhaps relevant to understanding American society to note that on any given Sunday there are probably more people in churches than the total number of people who attend professional sports events in a whole year—or to note that there are close to 500,000 local churches and synagogues voluntarily supported by the American people.

This is not the place for a detailed discussion of various secularization theories. We are keenly aware of the need to distinguish between institutions of religion and the dynamic of religion as such in society. Let it suffice that our approach raises a strong challenge to the first assumption mentioned above, namely, that in the modern world allegiance to institutional religion must perforce decline. Public policies based upon that highly questionable, if not patently false, assumption will continue to be alienated from one of the most vital dimensions in the lives of many millions of Americans.

The second assumption—that religion deals purely with the private sphere and is therefore irrelevant to public policy—must also be challenged. Although specifically religious activities have been largely privatized, the first part of the proposition overlooks the complex ways in which essentially religious values infiltrate and influence our public thought. But even to the extent that the first part of the proposition is true, it does not follow that religion is therefore irrelevant to public policy. The family, for example, is intimately involved in the institution of religion, and since the family is one of the prime mediating structures (perhaps the prime one), this makes the church urgently relevant to public policy. Without falling into the trap of politicizing all of life, our point is that structures such as family, church, and neighborhood are all public institutions in the sense that they must be taken seriously in the ordering of the polity.

The church (here meaning all institutions of religion) is important not only to the family but also to families and individuals in neighborhoods and other associations. For example, the black community, both historically and at present, cannot be understood apart from the black church. Similarly, the much discussed ethnic community is in large part religiously defined, as are significant parts of American Jewry (sometimes, but not always, subsumed under the phenomenon of ethnicity). And of course the role of religion in small towns or rural communities needs no elaboration. In none of these instances should the religious influence be viewed as residual. Few institutions have demonstrated and continue to demonstrate perduring power comparable to that of religion. It seems that influence is residual only to the extent that the bias of secularizing culture and politics is determined to act as though it is residual. Again, these observations seem to us to be true quite apart from what we may or may not *wish* the influence of religion to be in American society. We are convinced that there is a profoundly antidemocratic prejudice in public policy discourse that ignores the role of religious institutions in the lives of most Americans.

In the public policy areas most relevant to this discussion—health, social welfare, education, and so on—the historical development of programs, ideas, and institutions is inseparable from the church. In some parts of the country, notably in the older cities of the Northeast, the great bulk of social welfare services function under religious auspices. For reasons to be discussed further in the next section, the religious character of these service agencies is being fast eroded. Where government agencies are not directly taking over areas previously serviced by religious institutions, such institutions are being turned into quasi-governmental agencies through the powers of funding, certification, licensing, and the like. The loss of religious and cultural distinctiveness is abetted also by the dynamics of professionalization within the religious institutions and by the failure of the churches either to support their agencies or to insist that public policy respect their distinctiveness. The corollary to the proposition that government responsibilities must be governmentally implemented—a proposition we challenge—is that public is the opposite of sectarian. In public policy discourse "sectarian" is usually used as a term of opprobrium for anything religious. We contend that this usage and the biases that support it undermine the celebration of distinctiveness essential to social pluralism.

The homogenizing consequences of present patterns of funding, licensing, and certification are intensified by tax policies that have a "chilling effect" upon the readiness of religious institutions to play their part in the public realm. The threatened loss of tax exemption because of excessive "political activity" is a case in point. Even more ominous is the developing notion of tax expenditures. Most recently what has been called tax reform has aimed at driving a wedge between churches as such and their church-related auxiliaries, making the latter subject to disclosure, accountability, and therefore greater control by the state. These directions are, we believe, fundamentally wrongheaded. Pushed far enough, they will likely provoke strong reaction from a public that will not countenance what is perceived as an attack on religion. But public policy decision makers should not wait for that reaction to supply a corrective to present tendencies. It is precisely in the interest of public policy to advance a positive approach to the church as a key mediating structure.

Obviously all these questions touch on the complex of issues associated with separation of church and state. We believe, together with many scholars of jurisprudence, that the legal situation of church/state questions is today bogged down in conceptual confusions and practical contradictions. "The wall of separation between church and state" (Jefferson's phrase, not the Constitution's) is a myth long overdue for thorough rethinking. We are deeply committed to the religion clauses of the First Amendment. They should not be understood, however, as requiring absolute separationism; such absolute separationism is theoretically inconceivable and practically contrary to the past and present interaction of church and state. It is yet another of those grand abstractions that have had such a debilitating effect upon the way society's institutions relate to one another and upon the way in which people actually order their own lives.

In brief, "no establishment of religion" should mean that no religious institution is favored by the state over other religious institutions. "Free exercise of religion" should mean that no one is forced to practice or profess any religion against his will. Where there is neither favoritism nor coercion by the state there is no violation of the separation of church and state. While the subject is more complicated than suggested here, and while the courts will no doubt take time to disentangle themselves from the confusions into which they have been led, it is to be hoped that public policy will, in general, more nearly approximate "the Kurland rule" (named after Philip Kurland of the University of Chicago), namely, that if a policy furthers a legitimate secular purpose it is a matter of legal indifference whether or not that policy employs religious institutions. Clearly, this has far-ranging implications in the areas of education, child care, and social services generally.

The danger today is not that the churches or any one church will take over the state. The much more real danger is that the state will take over the functions of the church, except for the most narrowly construed definition of religion limited to worship and religious instruction. It is not alarmist but soberly necessary to observe that the latter has been the totalitarian pattern of modern states, whether of the Left or of the Right. Pluralism, including religious pluralism, is one of the few strong obstacles to that pattern's success. While those who advance this pattern may often do so inadvertently, it would be naive to ignore the fact that many of them— sundry professionals, bureaucrats, politicians—have a deep vested interest in such state expansion. The interest is not only ideological, although that is no doubt the primary interest in many cases; it is also and very practically an interest in jobs and power.

From the beginning, we have emphasized the importance of mediating structures in generating and maintaining values. We have already discussed the function of the family in this connection. Within the family, and between the family and the larger society, the church is a primary agent for bearing and transmitting the operative values of our society. This is true not only in the sense that most Americans identify their most important values as being religious in character, but also in the sense that the values that inform our public discourse are inseparably related to specific religious traditions. In the absence of the church and other mediating structures that articulate these values, the result is not that the society is left without operative values; the result is that the state has an unchallenged monopoly on the generation and maintenance of values. Needless to say, we would find this a very unhappy condition indeed.

With respect to our minimalist proposition, that public policy should not undercut mediating structures, a number of implications become evident. Already mentioned are aspects of taxation and regulation, which we will treat more fully in the next section because they affect not only the church but all voluntary associations. More specific to religious institutions is the demand for "right to equal access," a notion that cannot help but undercut particularism. Here again we run into the problem of not being discriminating about discriminations or, to put it differently, of failing to distinguish between discrimination and discretion. It seems to us, for example, there is nothing wrong with an elderly Italian Roman Catholic woman wanting to live in a nursing home operated and occupied by Italian Roman Catholics. To challenge that most understandable desire seems to us, quite frankly, perverse. Yet challenged it is—indeed, it is made increasingly impossible—by depriving such a "sectarian" or "discriminatory" institution of public funds. The same obviously holds true for Methodists, atheists, Humanists, and Black Muslims. Public policy's legitimate secular purpose is to ensure that old people have proper care. It should also be public policy that such care be available as much as possible within the context that people desire for themselves and for those whom they care most about. Again, the unique proscription relevant to public policy is against racial discrimination. (To contend that, since there are few black Italian Roman Catholics or few white Black Muslims, this constitutes racial discrimination *in result* is the kind of absurd exercise in social abstraction that plagues too much policy thinking today.)

A most poignant instance of public policy's undercutting the mediating structure of religion is that of present litigation aimed at prohibiting adoption and foster-care agencies from employing a religious criterion. That is, it is proposed to outlaw agencies designed to serve Jewish, Protestant, or Catholic children, if those agencies receive public funds (which of course they do). The cruel and dehumanizing consequences of this are several. First, the parent putting a child up for adoption or surrendering a child to foster care is deprived of the most elementary say in how that child is to be reared. As mentioned in the last section, this is among the most basic of human rights and should not be denied except under the most pressing necessity, especially when one considers that the surrender of children to such agencies is not always entirely voluntary. Another consequence is that the motivation of paid and volunteer workers in such agencies is severely undercut. In many, if not most, instances that motivation is to live out and explicitly transmit religious conviction. Yet a further consequence, perhaps the most important, is that the child is deprived of religious training. This may well be construed as a denial of free exercise of religion. The state has no rightful authority to decide that this is not a serious deprivation. What is necessary to rearing the child should be left to those who bear the children and those who care for them. Except for cases of criminal neglect or other injury, the state should have no authority to intervene. Again, the legitimate secular purpose is that the children be cared for.

It might be objected that leaving such a wide range of social services to religious and other voluntary associations would mean that the many people who did not belong to such groups would go unserved. The objection is revealed as specious, however, when it is recalled that public funds would be made available to almost every conceivable kind of group so long as it were prepared to carry out the public policy purpose. Such agencies might espouse one religion, all religions, or none. Almost everyone belongs to some group that can, with public funds, facilitate public policy in the area of social services. In truth, if we are really concerned for those individuals who fall between the cracks, it is worth noting that the most anomic individuals in our society, the denizens of skid row for example, are cared for almost exclusively by voluntary associations, usually religious in character. Government bureaucracies—indeed, by definition, all bureaucracies—demonstrate little talent for helping the truly marginal who defy generalized categories. The Salvation Army needs no lessons from the state on how to be nonsectarian in its compassion for people. The raison d'être of the Salvation Army is seriously undercut, however, if its workers cannot preach to those to whom they minister.

Still on the minimalistic side of the proposition, the mediating structures paradigm opposes the growing trend toward legally enforced symbolic sterility in public space. A Christmas tree or Hanukkah lights on the town common is a good case in point. Voluntary prayer in public schools is another. "In God We Trust" inscribed on coins is another. Little things these may be, perhaps, but of myriad such little things the public ethos is formed. Reaching toward absurdity, a California court recently ruled that it was unconstitutional to have a state holiday on Good Friday. Presumably there is no objection to the previous Friday, since the secular purpose is to give another day off to state workers. But when secular purpose is combined with religious significance it is apparently beyond the pale of constitutionality.

Our proposition assumes that nobody has a right to be unaffected by the social milieu of which he or she is part. If someone walks naked down Main Street, citizens now have the right to call in the police and have the offensive behavior stopped. Such regulations dealing with community values are of course undergoing change in many places. Change is a constant in the definition of community standards, and the authors probably tend to be more libertarian than most on the question of tolerating deviant behavior in public. The point here is that there must also be limits on the ability of individuals to call in the police to prevent behavior that is communally approved—for example, the Christmas tree on the town common. Nobody has a legal right not to encounter religious symbols in public places and thus to *impose his aversion* to such symbols on the community that cherishes them. As long as public space is open to the full range of symbols cherished in that community, there is no question of one religion being "established" over another. Public policy is presently biased toward what might be called the symbolic nakedness of the town square. Again, social abstractions have resulted in antidemocratic consequences, antidemocratic because they deny the democratically determined will of the people to celebrate themselves—their culture and their beliefs—in public, and, just as important, consequences that are antidemocratic because they give to the state a monopoly on public space and on the values to be advanced in that space.

"Affirmative Action":
A Worldwide Disaster

Thomas Sowell

ARGUMENTS FOR AND AGAINST "affirmative action" have raged for about twenty years in the United States. Similar arguments have provoked controversy—and even bloodshed—for a longer or a shorter period, in the most disparate societies, scattered around the world. India, Nigeria, Australia, Guyana, Malaysia, Sri Lanka, Pakistan, and Indonesia are just some of the countries where some groups receive official, government-sanctioned preferences over others. While the American phrase "affirmative action" is used in Australia and Canada, other countries have used a variety of other phrases, such as "positive discrimination" (India), "sons of the soil" preferences (Indonesia, Malaysia), "standardization" (Sri Lanka), or "reflecting the federal character" of the country (Nigeria). The same general principle of government apportionment of coveted positions, to supersede the competition of the marketplace or of academia, was of course also embodied in the *numerus clausus* laws used to restrict the opportunities of Jews in prewar Central and Eastern Europe.

The countries with preferential policies have varied enormously in cultural, political, economic, and other ways. The groups receiving preferences have likewise varied greatly, from locally or nationally dominant groups in some countries to the poorest and most abject groups, such as the untouchables of India. Such vast disparities in settings and people make it all the more striking that there are common patterns among these countries—patterns with serious implications for "affirmative-action" policies in the United States. Among these patterns are the following:

1. Preferential programs, even when explicitly and repeatedly defined as "temporary," have tended not only to persist but also to

Reprinted from Commentary *(December 1989).*

expand in scope, either embracing more groups or spreading to wider realms for the same groups, or both. Even preferential programs established with legally mandated cut-off dates, as in India and Pakistan, have continued far past those dates by subsequent extensions.

2. Within the groups designated by government as recipients of preferential treatment, the benefits have usually gone disproportionately to those members already more fortunate.

3. Group polarization has tended to increase in the wake of preferential programs, with nonpreferred groups reacting adversely, in ways ranging from political backlash to mob violence and civil war.

4. Fraudulent claims of belonging to the designated beneficiary groups have been widespread and have taken many forms in various countries.

In the United States, as in other countries around the world, the empirical consequences of preferential policies have received much less attention than the rationales and goals of such policies. Too often these rationales and goals have been sufficient unto themselves, both in the political arena and in courts of law. Without even an attempt at empirical assessment of costs versus benefits, with no attempt to pinpoint either losers or gainers, discussions of preferential policies are often exercises in assertion, counter-assertion, and accusation. Illusions flourish in such an atmosphere. So do the disappointments and bitterness to which illusions lead.

Foremost among these illusions is the belief that group "disparities" in "representation" are suspect anomalies that can be corrected by having the government temporarily apportion places on the basis of group membership. Every aspect of this belief fails the test of evidence, in country after country. The prime moral illusion is that preferential policies compensate for wrongs suffered. This belief has been supported only by a thin veneer of emotional rhetoric, seldom examined but often reiterated.

The Assumptions of "Affirmative Action"

"Temporary" Policies

When U.S. Supreme Court Justice William J. Brennan described the "affirmative-action" plan in the *Weber* case as "a temporary measure," he was echoing a view widely held, not only in the United States but also around the world. Britain's Lord Scarman likewise said:

We can and for the present must accept the loading of the law in favor of one group at the expense of others, defending it as a temporary expedient in the balancing process which has to be undertaken when and where there is social and economic inequality.

The rhetoric of transience and the reality of persistence and proliferation are both international features of preferential policies. "Affirmative-action" plans initially justified in the United States by the unique historic sufferings of blacks have been successively extended, over the years, to groups that now add up to several times as many people as the black population—and more than half of the total American population. These include not only American Indians, Hispanics, and Asians, but also women. A very similar pattern emerged in India, where official preferences were established more than forty years ago for untouchables, for some tribal groups, and for unspecified "other backward classes." Since then, so many groups have managed to get themselves included under "other backward classes" that they now outnumber the untouchables and the tribal peoples put together.

Even where no new groups are added to those legally entitled to official preferences, new occupations, institutions, and sectors of the society can fall under the coverage of preferential policies. Malays were granted preferential employment in government back in colonial Malaya under the British. After Malaya became independent Malaysia, and especially after the "New Economic Policy" announced in 1969, preferences spread to university admissions, government loans, occupational licenses, and employment in private businesses, both local and foreign-owned. The island nation of Sri Lanka has followed a pattern much like that of Malaysia. Preferences for the Sinhalese have not spread to other groups but have simply become more pronounced and more widespread over time.

Perhaps the classic example of preferences that spread far beyond their initial group and their original rationale have been the preferences in Pakistan. The desperately poor Bengalis of East Pakistan were "underrepresented" in the civil service, the military business, and the professions. Even the administration of East Pakistan was filled with West Pakistanis. Preferential policies to correct this were advocated in 1949 as "temporary" expedients to be phased out in five to ten years. In reality, however, these policies have lasted decades beyond this time and in 1984 were extended to

1994 by the late President Zia. Not only did preferential quotas spread well beyond people from the East Pakistan region; they persisted long after East Pakistan broke away in 1971 to form the independent nation of Bangladesh. In other words, those who provided the initial rationale for preferential policies have now disappeared by secession but the policies themselves have acquired a political life of their own.

Despite such patterns in these and other countries, the word "temporary" continues to be used in discussions of preferential policies—judicial and scholarly, as well as popular and political. No argument seems to be considered necessary to show that this transience can be enforced, so that the word "temporary" will be something more than political decoration. Indeed, few seem to feel a need to specify whether the dimensions of "temporary" are to be measured in actual units of time or by the attainment of some preconceived social results. If the latter, then the distinction between "temporary" and "eternal" can be wholly illusory in practice. In short, the nebulousness of the concept of "temporary" preference has matched its futility.

Statistical Disparities

Equally nebulous are the assumptions about the statistical "disparities" and "imbalances" that preferential policies are supposed to correct.

The idea that large statistical disparities between groups are unusual—and therefore suspicious—is commonplace, but only among those who have not bothered to study the history of racial, ethnic, and other groups in countries around the world. Among leading scholars who have in fact devoted years of research to such matters, a radically different picture emerges. Donald L. Horowitz of Duke University, at the end of a massive and masterful international study of ethnic groups—a study highly praised in scholarly journals—examined the idea of a society where groups are "proportionately represented" at different levels and in different sectors. He concluded that "few, if any, societies have ever approximated this description."

A worldwide study of military forces and police forces by Cynthia Enloe of Clark University likewise concluded that "militaries fall far short of mirroring, even roughly, the multi-ethnic societies" from which they come. Moreover, just "as one is unlikely to find a police force or a military that mirrors its plural society, so one is unlikely to find a representative bureaucracy." One reason is that "it is common for different groups to rely on different mobility ladders." Some choose the military, some the bureau-cracy, and some various parts of the private sector. Even within the military, different branches tend to have very different racial or ethnic compositions—the Afrikaners, for example, being slightly underrepresented in the South African navy and greatly overrepresented in the South African army, though their utter dominance in the government ensures that they cannot be discriminated against in either branch. Powerless minorities have likewise been greatly overrepresented or even dominant in particular branches of the military or the police—the Chinese in Malaysia's air force and among detectives in the police force, for example.

In the private sector as well, it is commonplace for minorities to be overrepresented, or even dominant, in competitive industries where they have no power to prevent others from establishing rival businesses. Jewish prominence in the clothing industry, not only in the United States, but in Argentina and Chile as well, did not reflect any ability to prevent other Americans, Argentines, or Chileans from manufacturing garments, but simply the advantages of the Jews' having brought needle-trade skills and experience with them from Eastern Europe. The fact that Jews owned more than half the clothing stores in mid-nineteenth-century Melbourne likewise reflected that same advantage, rather than any ability to forbid other Australians from selling clothes. In a similar way, German minorities have been dominant as pioneers in piano manufacturing in colonial America, czarist Russia, Australia, France, and England. Italian fishermen, Japanese farmers, and Irish politicians have been among many other minority groups with special success in special fields in various countries, without any ability to keep out others.

Another distinguished scholar who has studied multi-ethnic societies around the world, Myron Weiner of MIT, refers to "the universality of ethnic inequality." He points out that those inequalities are multidimensional:

> All multi-ethnic societies exhibit a tendency for ethnic groups to engage in different occupations, have different levels (and, often, types) of education, receive different incomes, and occupy a different place in the social hierarchy.

Yet the pattern Professor Weiner has seen, after years of research, as a "universality" is routinely assumed to be an *anomaly*, not only by preferential-policy advocates, but also by the intelligentsia, the media, legislators, and judges—all of whom tend to assume, as a *norm*, what Professor Horowitz has found to exist (or even to be approximated) in "few, if any, societies." That what exists widely across the planet is regarded as an anomaly, while what exists virtually nowhere is regarded as a norm, is a tribute to the effectiveness of sheer reiteration in establishing a vision—and of the difficulties of dispelling a prevailing vision by facts.

Some might try to salvage the statistical argument for discrimination by describing discrimination as also being universal. But, to repeat, groups who are in no position to discriminate against anybody have often been overrepresented in coveted positions—the Chinese in Malaysian universities, the Tamils in Sri Lankan universities, the southerners in Nigerian universities, all during the 1960's, and Asians in American universities today being just some of the minorities of whom this has been true. All sorts of other powerless minorities have dominated particular industries or sectors of the economy, the intellectual community, or government employment. Among businessmen, India's Gujaratis in East Africa, the Lebanese in West Africa, the Chinese in Southeast Asia, the Jews in Eastern Europe, and Koreans and Vietnamese in black ghettos across the United States are just some examples. Among high government officials, the Germans were greatly over-represented in czarist Russia, as were Christians in the Ottoman Empire. Among intellectuals, the Scots were as dominant in eighteenth- and nineteenth-century Britain as the Jews have been in other parts of Europe. In short, large statistical disparities have been commonplace, both in the presence of discrimination and in its absence. Indeed, large disparities have been commonplace in the utilization of preferential programs designed to reduce disparities.

The intellectual and political *coup* of those who promote the randomness assumption is to put the burden of proof entirely on others. It is not merely the individual employer, for example, who must disprove this assumption in his own particular case in order to escape a charge of discrimination. All who oppose the randomness assumption find themselves confronted with the task of disproving an elusive plausibility, for which no evidence is offered. As for counter-evidence, no enumeration of the myriad ways in which groups are grossly disparate—in age of marriage, alcohol consumption, immigration patterns, performance in sports, performance on tests—can ever be conclusive, even when extended past the point where the patience of the audience is exhausted.

Those viscerally convinced of the pervasiveness of discrimination and its potency as an explanation of social disparities—and convinced also of the effectiveness of preferential policies as a remedy—are little troubled by the logical shakiness of the statistical evidence. That is all the more reason for others to be doubly troubled—not simply because an incorrect policy may be followed but also, and more importantly, because actions ostensibly based on the rule of law are in substance based on visceral convictions, the essence of lynch law.

Statistical "Control" and "Explanation"

Those who regard income differences or occupational differences among groups as evidence of discrimination recognize that groups also differ in education, job experience, and other factors that affect such results as incomes and occupations. However, by comparing individuals with the same education, the same job experience, etc., who belong to different racial or ethnic groups, they treat the remaining differentials in pay or occupational status as evidence of discrimination and as a rough measure of its magnitude. In principle, this process of statistically controlling variables that affect outcomes is logical and reasonable. It is only in practice that serious problems arise because we simply do not know enough to do what we are trying to do or claiming to do.

A 1982 study by the U.S. Commission on Civil Rights, for example, recognized that differences in age and education affect incomes but considered that its study of intergroup economic differences was "controlling for such factors" when it compared individuals of the same age and with the same number of years of schooling. Unfortunately, education is one of many *multidimensional* variables. Education varies not only in number of years, but also qualitatively, according to the caliber of the institution in which the education was received, the performance of the student receiving the education, and the kind of field in which the student specializes. Seldom are statistical data sufficiently detailed to permit holding all these dimensions of education constant. Moreover, qualitative variables such as the caliber of the institution are difficult to quantify and impossible to quantify with precision.

One way of dealing with this complication is to ignore the multidimensional nature of education, by either explicitly or implicitly assuming that these individual variations more or less cancel out when comparing thousands of people. However, individuals from different racial or ethnic groups differ not only randomly but also systematically. For example, groups with significantly lower quantities of education tend to have lower qualities of education as well, whether quality is measured by individual performance, institutional ranking, or the prestige and remuneration of the fields of specialization. This pattern is found, whether comparing Chinese versus Malays in Malaysia, Tamils versus Sinhalese in Sri Lanka, European and American Jews versus North African and Middle Eastern Jews in Israel, caste Hindus versus untouchables in India, or whites versus blacks or Hispanics in the United States. Thus, what is called the "same" education in intergroup statistical comparisons is often not even approximately the same education in reality.

The difference that these multiple dimensions can make may be illustrated by one of the few studies that attempted to control the qualitative dimensions of education—a study comparing the salaries of faculty members from different racial backgrounds. Among its variables were (1) possession or non-possession of a Ph.D.; (2) the professional ranking of the department from which the Ph.D. was obtained; (3) the field of specialization; and (4), the number of articles published by the faculty member. In gross terms—that is, controlling for none of these variables—white faculty had a higher average salary than black faculty. But when blacks and whites in the same field were compared, blacks had higher salaries than whites in the social sciences and the natural sciences, while whites had higher salaries in the humanities. When comparing blacks and whites who both had Ph.D.'s from highly rated departments, blacks earned more than whites in all three areas. Among faculty members with Ph.D.'s from lower-ranked departments, however, whites still had higher salaries than blacks. Blacks with Ph.D.'s earned higher salaries in the social sciences and whites with Ph.D.'s earned more in the natural sciences. Among faculty members with Ph.D.'s and five or more articles published, blacks had higher salaries than whites in all three fields, when both had their doctorates from the same quality level of institution.

In short, the very same raw data can tell not only a different story, but even an opposite story, according to how much they are disaggregated or how many variables are held constant. Ultimately the researcher is limited by the available data and the dimensions they cover. These particular data happened to cover qualitative dimensions that are often lacking. This good fortune resulted from the long-standing practice of academic professions to rank graduate departments in their own respective fields. What is more generally relevant to the use of statistics in preferential-policy analysis is that individuals with apparently the "same" education along one dimension may have very different education along other dimensions. Put another way, groups are not distributed randomly or the same among the various dimensions. In this particular example, black faculty had a Ph.D. less than half as frequently as white faculty, the Ph.D.'s received by black faculty were from high-quality institutions less than half as often, and were concentrated in fields with lower average earnings. Finally, black faculty published far less than white faculty.

These data also happened to include Asian faculty members. Their distribution in all these respects differed substantially from the distributions of either blacks or whites. Such multidimensional differences among groups are commonplace around the world, however often random or proportionate distribution is *assumed* in discussions of preferential policy. In India, for example, an attempt to compare untouchable medical-school students and caste Hindu medical-school students of the same social characteristics proved futile when individuals from the two groups who were similar in specified characteristics turned out, during lengthy interviews, to be very dissimilar in characteristics not specified at the outset but clearly relevant to their medical education.

Beginning with untouchable and caste Hindu "students matched individually" by "some important background characteristics" such as father's occupation, income, or language, Indian scholar P. R. Velaskar later discovered that "the match group is not perfectly matched as originally planned"—a considerable understatement, for the illiteracy rate among the fathers and grandfathers of the untouchable medical-school students was several times as high as among the other medical-school students' fathers and grandfathers. Understandably, the untouchable students had had parental guidance in their education less often than the other students had, the homes from which they came contained far fewer books, and their pre-college schools were not as good. They were not meaningfully the same, even though the same on the particular socioeconomic characteristics initially specified. Untouchable students in India's medical, engineering, and other institutions of higher learning have had disastrously higher failure rates and drop-out rates.

Multidimensional differences are not statistically "controlled" by holding one dimension constant, even when that is the only dimension on which data are available. Moreover, not all differences are quantifiable, or all non-quantifiable differences negligible in their effect on outcomes. Where statistics are able to capture only some of the relevant dimensions—to "control" only some of the variables—the assumption that remaining disparities represent discrimination is implicitly an assumption that groups are distributed similarly in the unexamined dimensions, however disparately they are distributed in the variables for which we have data.

Just as statistical "controls" for variables that differ among groups often fail to control, so statistical "explanations" often fail to explain in any but the most narrow definitional sense used by statisticians. When two groups differ in some way—in income, for example—and 20 percent of that difference is eliminated by holding constant some factor x (years of education, for instance), then *in a purely definitional sense* statisticians say that factor x "explains" 20 percent of the difference between the groups. Unfortunately, as arguments develop, their initial special definitions and assumptions tend to fade into the background, with the statistical results becoming correspondingly inflated as to their scope and validity.

The potential for misleading explanations can be illustrated with a simple example. Shoe size undoubtedly correlates with test scores on advanced mathematics examinations, in the sense that people with size-3 shoes probably cannot, on average, answer as many questions correctly as people with size-12 shoes—the former being much more likely to be younger children and the latter more likely to be older children or adults. Thus shoe size "explains" part of the math-score difference—in the special sense in which statisticians use the word. But nobody can expect to do better on a math test by wearing larger shoes on the day it is taken. In the real sense of the word, shoe size *explains* nothing.

When a statistician testifies in court that his data can "explain" only 40 percent of income disparities between groups by "controlling" for age, education, urbanization, and whatever other variable may be cited, the judge and jury may not realize how little the words "explain" and "control" mean in this context. Judge and jury may conclude that the other 60 percent must represent discrimination. But virtually no statistical study can control for all the relevant variables simultaneously, because the in-depth data, especially along qualitative dimensions, are often simply not available. By controlling for the available variables and implicitly assuming that the unaccounted-for variables do not differ significantly between groups, one can generate considerable residual "unexplained" statistical disparity. It is arbitrary to call that residual "discrimination."

Looked at another way, groups with visible, quantifiable disadvantages often have other, not-so-visible, not-so-quantifiable disadvantages as well. If statistics manage to capture the effect of the first kinds of disadvantages, the effects of the second kind become part of an unexplained residual. It is equating that residual with discrimination that is the fatal leap in logic. There may in fact be real discrimination—but the crude statistics currently available neither demonstrate its presence nor measure its magnitude.

Statistical Trends

Where the benefits of "affirmative action" are not simply regarded as axiomatic, they are too often based on a partial reading of statistical trends. "Before" and "after" comparisons abound, to show that minority representation in this or that institution or sector—or in desirable jobs throughout the economy—has increased in the wake of preferential policies. This might be valid in a static world, to which "change" was added— which seems to be the kind of world envisioned by those using that approach. However, such a vision bears little resemblance to the real world, in which affirmative action has been just one of innumerable social changes, including many going back much farther than preferential policies.

The proportions of blacks in professional and other high-level occupations increased substantially in the decade following passage of the Civil Rights Act of 1964—a fact often cited as evidence of its effectiveness in the economy. What is almost never cited is the fact that the proportions of blacks in such occupations rose even more substantially in the decade *preceding* passage of the Civil Rights Act of 1964. Nor were blacks unique. The incomes of Chinese Americans, Japanese Americans, and Mexican Americans all rose, both absolutely and relative to the incomes of whites, in the decade preceding passage of the Civil Rights Act of 1964. This was not a static world, to which "change" was added, but a world of trends already in motion. Moreover, the kinds of social trends that preceded preferential policies were by no means unique to the United States.

In a number of countries around the world, it has been precisely the rise of a newly-educated and upwardly-mobile class among previously lagging groups that provided the political impetus to demands for preferential policies. In Bombay, capital of India's state of Maharashtra, the "marked advancement of the Maharashtrians occurred prior to the stringent policy measures adopted by the state government" to promote preferential hiring, according to a scholarly study. In part this reflected a prior "enormous growth in school enrollments" in Maharashtra and a "rapid expansion in college enrollment"—also prior to preferences. A similar growth of an indigenous, newly-educated class in Poland, Czechoslovakia, and Lithuania during the years between the two world wars led to demands for preferential policies in the form of group quotas to relieve them from having to compete with Jews. Likewise, in Nigeria, it was the recent growth of an educated class in the north that led to demands for preferential policies to relieve them from having to compete with more educated southern Nigerians. This same pattern of a rising educated class prior to the preferential policies that they promote can also be found in Indonesia, Sri Lanka, Malaysia, the Quebec province of Canada, and much of sub-Saharan Africa.

A serious assessment of preferential policies cannot ignore preexisting trends. Neither can it generalize from trends in particular sectors to national trends. Even in countries where nationwide data on the economic position of officially preferred groups show little or no improvement, nevertheless improvements in particular sectors may be dramatic. For example, increased employment of officially preferred groups at higher levels may be much more striking in government agencies and in government-related parts of the private sector than in the economy as a whole. This pattern has been visible at various periods in India, Poland, Malaysia, Hungary, Sri Lanka, and the United States. But this is hardly decisive evidence of the effectiveness of such policies when nationwide data tell a very different story.

In the United States, stories and statistics abound as to how the number of blacks employed in particular institutions increased dramatically during the 1970's—often in government agencies or in firms with government contracts that made them subject to federal "guidelines." However, the employment of blacks by private firms without government contracts actually declined between 1970 and 1980. What were, from the viewpoint of the economy, *transfers* of people were seen from the viewpoint of particular institutions as dramatic *increases*. It is one of the elementary fallacies to generalize from a part to the whole, whether it is called "the fallacy of composition" or the story of the blind men feeling different parts of an elephant.

Assumptions as Law

Flaws in logic or evidence are unfortunate in intellectual speculation but they are far more serious in courts of law, where major penalties may be inflicted on those whose employees or students, for example, do not have a racial or ethnic composition that meets the preconceptions of other people. Some U.S. Supreme Court Justices have repeatedly treated statistical disparities as tantamount to discrimination and assumed the task of restoring groups to where they would have been otherwise. Even where group disparities in "representation" reflect demonstrable performance disparities, these performance disparities themselves have been taken as proof of societal discrimination. Thus, in the *Weber* case, Justice Harry Blackmun declared that there could be "little doubt that any lack of skill" on the part of minority workers competing with Brian Weber "has its roots in purposeful discrimination of the past." In the *Bakke* case, four Justices declared that the failure of minority medical-school applicants to perform as well as Allan Bakke "was due principally to the effects of past discrimination." The Court's task, therefore, was one of "putting minority applicants in the position they would have been in if not for the evil of racial discrimination."

All this presupposes a range of knowledge that no one has ever possessed. Ironically, this sweeping assumption of knowledge has been combined with an apparent ignorance of vast disparities in performance, disparities favoring groups with no power to discriminate against anybody. From such judicial speculation it is only a short step to the idea of restoring groups to where they would have been—and *what* they would have been—but for the offending discrimination.

What would the average Englishman be like today "but for" the Norman conquest? What would the average Japanese be like "but for" the enforced isolation of Japan for two-and-a-half centuries under the Tokugawa shoguns? What would the Middle East be like "but for" the emergence of Islam? In any other context besides preferential-policy issues, the presumption of knowing the answers to such questions would be regarded as ridiculous, even as intellectual speculation, much less as a basis for serious legal action.

To know how one group's employment, education, or other pattern differs statistically from another's is usually easy. What is difficult to know are the many variables determining the interest, skill, and performance of those individuals from various groups who are being considered for particular jobs, roles, or institutions. What is virtually impossible to know are the patterns that would exist in a non-discriminatory world—the deviations from which would indicate the existence and magnitude of discrimination.

Age distribution and geographic distribution are only two very simple factors which can play havoc with the assumption that groups would be evenly or randomly distributed in occupations and institutions, in the absence of discrimination. When one group's median age is a decade younger than another's—not at all uncommon—that alone may be enough to cause the younger group to be statistically "overrepresented" in sports, crime, and entry-level jobs, as well as in those kinds of diseases and accidents that are more prevalent among the young, while the older group is overrepresented in homes for the elderly, in the kinds of jobs requiring long years of experience, and in the kinds of diseases and accidents especially prevalent among older people.

Another very simple factor operating against an even "representation" of groups is that many ethnic groups are distributed geographically in patterns differing from one another. It would be unlikely that American ethnic groups concentrated in cold states like Minnesota and Wisconsin would be as well represented among citrus growers and tennis players as they are on hockey teams and among skiers. It is also unlikely that groups concentrated in land-locked states would be equally represented in maritime activities, or that groups from regions lacking mineral deposits would be as well-represented among miners or in other occupations associated with extractive industries as groups located in Pennsylvania or West Virginia.

Differences in geographic concentrations among racial and ethnic groups are by no means confined to the United States. In Brazil, people of German and Japanese ancestry are concentrated in the south. In Switzerland, whole regions are predominantly French, German, or Italian. In countries around the world, an overwhelming majority of the Chinese or the Jewish population is heavily concentrated in a few major cities—often in just one city in a given country. Group differences in geographical distribution can reach right down to the neighborhood level or even to particular streets. In Buenos Aires, people of Italian ancestry have concentrated in particular neighborhoods or on particular streets, according to the places of their own or their ancestral origins in Italy. In Bombay, people from different parts of India are likewise concentrated in particular neighborhoods or on particular streets.

Lest the point be misunderstood, while these two simple and obvious factors—age and location—are capable of disrupting the even "representation" that many assume to exist in the absence of discrimination, there are also innumerable other factors, of varying degrees of complexity and influence, that can do the same. Moreover, differences in age and location may play a significant role in explaining *some* socioeconomic differences between *some* groups but not other socioeconomic differences between those groups, or among other groups. The purpose here is not to pinpoint the reasons for intergroup differences—or even to assume that they can all be pinpointed—but rather to show how arbitrary and unfounded is the assumption that groups would be evenly "represented," in the absence of discrimination. Precisely because the known differences among groups are large and multidimensional, the presumption of weighing these differences so comprehensively and accurately as to know where some group would be "but for" discrimination approaches hubris.

Even the more modest goal of knowing the *general direction* of the deviation of a group's position from where it would have been without discrimination is by no means necessarily achievable. What are the "effects" of centuries of injustice, punctuated by recurring outbursts of lethal mass violence, against the overseas Chinese in Southeast Asia or against the Jews in Europe? Both groups are generally more prosperous than their persecutors. Would they have been still more prosperous in the absence of such adversity? Perhaps—but many people with a long history of peace, and with prosperity supplied by nature itself, have quietly stagnated. This is not to say that the Jews and the Chinese would have done so. It is only to say that *we do not know and cannot know*. No amount of good intentions will make us omniscient. No fervent invocation of "social justice" will supply the missing knowledge.

Incentives and Results

"Affirmative-action" policies assume not only a level of knowledge that no one has ever possessed but also a degree of control that no one has ever exercised. Proponents of preferential policies have tended to reason in terms of the rationales and goals of such policies—not in terms of the *incentives* these policies create. Yet these incentives acquire a life of their own, independent of—and often counter to—the avowed goals of preferential policies. Nor are these simply isolated "mistakes" that can be "corrected." They are the fruition of fundamental misconceptions of the degree of control that can be maintained over a whole galaxy of complex social interactions.

At the individual level, the potential beneficiary and the potential loser are not mere blocks of wood passively placed where the policy dictates. Nor are they automatons who continue acting as before, except for modifications specified for them by others. Rather, they respond *in their own ways* to preferential policies. One of these ways was exemplified by a question raised by a group activist seeking preferential hiring in India's city of Hyderabad: "Are we not entitled to jobs just because we are not as qualified?" A Nigerian wrote of "the tyranny of skills." The sense of entitlement—independent of skills or performance—has long been an accompaniment of preferential policies, for the most disparate groups in the most disparate societies.

The late South African economist W. H. Hutt pointed out long ago that the most "virulent" white supporters of early racial-preferential policies in the mines were "those who had not troubled to qualify themselves for promotion," and who therefore relied on being white instead. Today, in the Virgin Islands, even schoolchildren excuse their own substandard academic and behavioral performance by pointing out that government jobs will be waiting for them as U.S. citizens—jobs for which their better-behaved and better-performing West Indian classmates are ineligible. In Malaysia, likewise, "Malay students, who sense that their future is assured, feel less pressure to perform," according to a study there. A study of black colleges in the United States similarly noted that even students planning postgraduate study often showed no sense of urgency about needing to be prepared "because they believed that certain rules would simply be set aside for them." In India, even a fervent advocate of the untouchables, and of preferential policies for them, has urged untouchable students in medical and engineering schools to abandon their "indifference."

The disincentives created by group preferences apply to both preferred and non-preferred groups. As W. H. Hutt wrote of the South African "color bar," these racial preferences "have vitiated the efficiency of the non-whites by destroying incentives" and have also "weakened incentives to efficiency on the part of the whites who have been featherbedded." A very similar principle is found in the very different setting of Jamaica, after it became independent and black-run. There it was the whites who faced the disincentives of the non-preferred. Many withdrew from the competition for public office because they "felt that the day of the black man had come and questioned why they had to make the effort if the coveted job or the national honor would go to the blacks, despite their qualifications." The upshot is that preferential policies represent not simply a transfer of benefits from one group to another, but can also represent a net loss, as both groups perform less well as a result.

Those who initiate preferential policies cannot sufficiently control the reactions of either preferred or non-preferred groups to ensure that such policies will have the desired effect, or even move in the desired direction. Counterproductive reactions that reduce national prosperity or social tranquility adversely affect even members of the preferred group, who are also members of the general society. Whether their gains in one role exceed their losses in the other role is an empirical question whose answer depends on the specifics of each situation. One of the clearly undesired and uncontrolled consequences of preferential policies has been a backlash by non-preferred groups. This backlash has ranged from campus racial incidents in the United States to a bloody civil war in Sri Lanka.

Honors

Nowhere is control more illusory than in the awarding of honors, whose very meaning and effect depend upon other people's opinions. Preferential honors for members of particular groups can easily render suspect not only those particular honors but also honors fully merited and awarded after free and open competition. If one-fifth of the honors received by preferred groups are awarded under double standards, the other four-fifths are almost certain to fall under a cloud of suspicion as well, if only because some of those who lost out in the competition would prefer to believe that they were not bested fairly. It is by no means clear that more real honors—which are ultimately other people's opinions—will come to a group preferentially given awards. Preferential honors can in practice mean a moratorium on recognition of the group's achievements, which can be confounded with patronage or pay-offs. This need not inevitably be so. The point is that the matter is out of the control of those who decide award policy, and in the hands of others observing the outcomes and deciding what to make of them.

Honor is more than a sop to personal vanity. It is a powerful incentive which accomplishes many social tasks, including tasks that are too arduous and dangerous to be compensated by money—even inducing individuals in crisis situations to sacrifice their lives for the greater good of others. In more mundane matters, honor and respect from one's colleagues and subordinates are important and sometimes indispensable aids, without which even the most talented and conscientious individuals sometimes cannot fulfill their promise. To jeopardize the respect and recognition of individuals from preferred groups by rewarding "honors" tainted with double standards is not only to downgrade their own achievements but also to downgrade their chances of accomplishing those achievements in the first place. For example, minority faculty members have often complained about a lack of intellectual and research interaction with their colleagues, and of being thought of as "affirmative-action" professors. After the media revealed that black students were admitted to the Harvard Medical School with lower qualifications, white patients began to refuse to be examined by such students. The negative effects of tainted honors are by no means limited to academia.

Partial Preferences

The illusion of control includes the belief that preferential policies can be extended *partway* into a process while maintaining equal treatment in the remainder of the process. For example, in the early days of "affirmative action" in the United States, it was sometimes asserted that special efforts to recruit minority employees or minority students would be followed by equal treatment at the actual selection stage and afterward. Special concern for particular groups might also mean only special scrutiny to see that they were treated equally. President John F. Kennedy's Executive Order No. 10,925 required that employers who were government contractors "take affirmative action to ensure that the applicants are employed, and that employees are treated during employment without regard to race, creed, color, or national origin." That is virtually the antithesis of what "affirmative action" has come to mean today, either in the United States or in other countries where the term refers to statistical results viewed precisely *with regard* to race, color, creed, or national origin.

The concept of preferential concern stopping partway into a process is not confined to employment or to the United States. In India, a government minister has urged a small lowering of university-admissions standards for students from scheduled castes (untouchables) and scheduled tribes, with the proviso that "he was recommending relaxation for admission and not for passing or grading." Similar views were once expressed in the United States, where special recruitment programs for minority students quickly led to lower admission standards for them—and this in turn sometimes led to "affirmative grading," to prevent excessive failures by minority students. Double standards in grading may originate with the individual professor or be a result of administrative pressures. Halfway around the world—in Soviet Central Asia—professors are also pressured to give preferential grading to Central Asian students. In Malaysia, preferential grading is virtually institutionalized. As Gordon P. Means puts it:

> Although grading is supposed to be without reference to ethnicity, all grades must be submitted to an evaluation review committee having heavy Malay representation. Individual faculty members report various instances when grades were unilaterally raised, apparently for purposes of "ethnic balance."

Sometimes preferential grading takes the less direct form of creating special or easier subjects for particular groups, such as Maori Studies in New Zealand, Malay Studies in Singapore, or a variety of ethnic studies in the United States.

Whether in employment, education, or other areas, carefully limited or fine-tuned preferences have repeatedly proved to be illusory. Neither time limitations nor other limitations have in fact stopped their persistence and spread.

A wide variety of moral arguments has been used to justify preferential policies. Some of these arguments have little in common, except for being largely unexamined in the excitement of crusading zeal—and being successful politically. Among the reasons given for preferences are that (1) the group is indigenous; (2) the group has been historically wronged; and (3) the group happens to be less well represented in desirable institutions or occupations, for whatever reason, so that this "imbalance" must be "corrected."

Whatever the arguments for preferential policies, these preferences (as we have seen) can long outlive the validity of those arguments, whether the degree of validity be zero or 100 percent, or anywhere in between. A genuinely disadvantaged group can cling to preferences, or seek more, long after their disadvantages have been redressed. The moral question, therefore, is not simply whether particular groups deserve particular benefits for particular periods of time, or until particular social conditions are achieved. The real question is whether the *actual consequences of the particular processes* being initiated are likely to be justified, morally or otherwise.

Indigenousness

The logic that turns indigenousness into a moral claim is by no means obvious. Claims of being indigenous evoke a sense of solidarity within the beneficiary group—and often also feelings of moral support from outside the beneficiary group. The question is what basis there is for anyone who is not indigenous to take seriously such moral claims by those who are.

Where an indigenous group was once invaded, dispossessed of its lands, or otherwise mistreated by conquerors, the moral condemnation of the latter is based on their actions, not on the indigenousness of the victims. Had they done the same things to people who had settled within the prior century, that would not make it any more right or wrong. Moreover, claims of indigenous preference are not limited to such situations. Malays today claim privileges based on being "sons of the soil"—not against the British, who were the colonial power, but against the Chinese and the Indians, who were not. Similar preferential claims have been advanced by the indigenous peoples of Fiji, Burma, Uganda, and other countries, against groups who never conquered them or even tried to.

One reason indigenous victims may seem especially wronged is that the toil of untold generations may have gone into producing what was taken from them. But, again, this may be equally true (or more true) of people who cannot claim to be indigenous. Were England to be invaded, conquered, and plundered, that would be widely condemned, even though no one familiar with their history would claim that the English are the indigenous people of England. Moreover, in many parts of the world, the indigenous peoples have built few material things of a lasting nature and the conquerors have built much, so that a reconquest by descendants of the original inhabitants would represent more plunder than the original conquest. So too would a governmental transfer of what has been created in the meantime.

One of the recurring themes in moral arguments for indigenous preferences is the linkage of the indigenous peoples to their native soil. Phrases like "sons of the soil," in various countries, evoke this image. However, human beings have not created land. Whether indigenous or not, their occupation of it as a group has largely been based on force. When one conquering people is in turn conquered by another, observers may deplore the bloodshed and plunder, but it is difficult to see what moral claim the losing side has against the winners, who have simply been more efficient or more lucky in pursuing the same goals as themselves. Here as elsewhere, where injustice has been done, it is the injustice that is morally significant, not the indigenousness of the victim.

Even in places and times where no credible claim of conquest or plunder can be made against a non-native, non-preferred group, there is often still a feeling that the indigenous people are entitled to preferential treatment in their own homeland. Little or no argument is usually offered for this assertion. At most there may be an allusion to the fact that most peoples "rule the roost" in their own homelands, and that there is psychic discomfort when "foreigners" (even many generations resident in the country) are unduly prominent in the economy or society. This is essentially an argument that what *is* in most places is what *ought* to be in all places. In addition to being a *non sequitur*, this assertion attributes to indigenousness a power that is usually due to being a numerical majority. At its worst, it is an argument that might makes right or an evocation of tribalism that need not be shared by observers who are not of that tribe, and which has no moral basis in any case.

Historical Compensation

The wrongs of history have been invoked by many groups in many countries as a moral claim for contemporary compensation. Much emotional fervor goes into such claims but the question here is about their logic or morality. Assuming for the sake of argument that the historical claims are factually correct, which may not be the case in all countries, to transfer benefits between two groups of living contemporaries because of what happened between two sets of dead people is to raise the question whether any sufferer is in fact being compensated. Only where both wrongs and compensation are viewed as collectivized and inheritable does redressing the wrongs of history have a moral, or even a logical, basis.

The biological continuity of the generations lends plausibility to the notion of group compensation—but only if guilt can be inherited. Otherwise there are simply windfall gains and windfall losses among contemporaries, according to the accident of their antecedents. Moreover, few people would accept this as a general principle to be applied consistently, however much they may advocate it out of compassion (or guilt) over the fate of particular unfortunates. No one would advocate that today's Jews are morally entitled to put today's Germans in concentration camps, in compensation for the Nazi Holocaust. Most people would not only be horrified at any such suggestion but would also regard it as a second act of gross immorality, in no way compensating the first, but simply adding to the sum total of human sins.

Sometimes a more sociological, rather than moral, claim is made that living contemporaries are suffering from the *effects* of past wrongs and that it is these effects which must be offset by compensatory preferences. Tempting as it is to imagine that the contemporary troubles of historically wronged groups are due to those wrongs, this is confusing causation with morality. The contemporary socioeconomic position of groups in a given society often bears no relationship to the historic wrongs they have suffered. Both in Canada and in the United States, the Japanese have significantly higher incomes than the whites, who have a documented history of severe anti-Japanese discrimination in both countries. The same story could be told of the Chinese in Malaysia, Indonesia, and many other countries around the world, of the Jews in countries with virulent anti-Semitism, and a wide variety of other groups in a wide variety of other countries. Among poorer groups as well, the level of poverty often has little correlation with the degree of oppression. No one would claim that the historic wrongs suffered by Puerto Ricans in the United States exceed those suffered by blacks, but the average Puerto Rican income is lower than the average income of blacks.

None of this proves that historic wrongs have no contemporary effects. Rather, it is a statement about the limitations of our knowledge, which is grossly inadequate to the task undertaken and likely to remain so. To pretend to disentangle the innumerable sources of intergroup differences is an exercise in hubris rather than morality.

As one contemporary example of how easy it is to go astray in such efforts, it was repeated for years that the high rate of single-parent, teenage pregnancy among blacks was "a legacy of slavery." Evidence was neither asked nor given. But when serious scholarly research was finally done on this subject, the evidence devastated this widely held belief. The vast majority of black children grew up in two-parent homes, even under slavery itself, and for generations thereafter. The current levels of single-parent, teenage pregnancy are a phenomenon of the last half of the twentieth century and are a disaster that has also struck groups with wholly different histories from that of blacks. Passionate commitment to "social justice" can never be a substitute for knowing what you are talking about.

Those who attribute any part of the socioeconomic fate of any group to factors internal to that group are often accused of "blaming the victim." This may sometimes be part of an attempt to salvage the historical-compensation principle but it deserves separate treatment.

"Blame" and "Victims"

The illusion of morality is often confused with the reality of causation. If group A originates in a country where certain scientific and technological skills are widespread and group B originates in a country where they are not, then when they immigrate to the same third country, they are likely to be statistically "represented" to very different degrees in occupations and institutions requiring such skills. There is nothing mysterious about this, in causal terms. But those who wish to attribute this disparity to institutional discrimination are quick to respond to any mention of group B's lesser scientific-technological background as a case of "blaming the victim." By making the issue *who* is to blame, such arguments evade or preempt the more fundamental question—whether this is a matter of blame in the first place.

Clearly today's living generation—in any group—cannot be *blamed* for the centuries of cultural evolution that went on before they were born, often in lands that they have never seen. Nor can they be blamed for the fact that the accident of birth caused them to inherit one culture rather than another. In causal terms, it would be a staggering coincidence if cultures evolving in radically different historical circumstances were equally effective for all purposes when transplanted to a new society. Blame has nothing to do with it.

Grievance versus "Justice"

Moralism confuses issues in many ways. For example, justifiable compassion for less fortunate people often shades off into an unjustifiable romanticizing of such people, their leaders, or their leaders' ideas and rhetoric. Groups seeking preferential treatment almost invariably say that they are seeking "justice," whether they are a majority or a minority, previously favored or disfavored, currently better off or worse off than others. When people want *more*, they call *more* "justice." But when groups with a sense of grievance acquire power, locally or nationally, they seldom stop at redressing grievances and seldom exhibit justice toward others.

Nothing is more common than for previously oppressed groups to oppress others when they get the chance. When Poles and Hungarians acquired their own independent nations after World War I, they inaugurated a savage escalation of anti-Semitism. Similarly, after World War II, newly independent nations began oppressing their respective minorities from Indonesia to Sri Lanka to almost all of sub-Saharan Africa. This has included not only the usual forms of discrimination but also mob violence that has killed hundreds in Indonesia and Malaysia, thousands in Sri Lanka, and tens of thousands in Nigeria.

South Africa's white Afrikaners have long been a "grievance-fed" people, as W. H. Hutt called them. Their leaders have kept alive for generations the grievances that caused them to launch a great trek away from British authority to settle new land in the nineteenth century, the grievances growing out of the two Boer wars they lost against the British, and the economic resentments they felt as a predominantly lower class in an economy dominated by British and Jewish businessmen and financiers. Some of these historic grievances were quite valid—for example, the 25,000 Afrikaner women and children who died in British concentration camps during the second Boer war. However, as Hutt observed: "Races which grumble about the 'injustices' or 'oppressions' to which they are subjected can often be observed to be inflicting not dissimilar injustices upon other races." The Afrikaners' escalation of anti-black laws when they first came to power in a coalition government in 1924 was only a foretaste of the evils of full-scale apartheid which they later imposed after they achieved unchallenged political dominance in 1948.

Similar patterns have existed in the United States. Just as the long-oppressed Irish became one of the groups most hostile to blacks, so today Koreans and Vietnamese refugees operating small businesses in black ghettos in cities around the country are targets of racist propaganda and violence from local black leaders and those whom they incite. The arguments and demands made against them are the same as those made against the Jewish businessmen in the same ghettos a generation earlier or against the Chinese businessmen in Southeast Asia, the Lebanese in Sierre Leone, or small retailing minority groups in countries around the world. What is different is that such racism on the part of some black leaders is passed over in silence by those who normally condemn racism, because their vision automatically casts blacks in the role of victims. But people do not cease being human beings just because they are labeled victims—and if the history of human beings shows anything, it shows repeatedly the desire for self-aggrandizement at the expense of others.

A sense of group grievance is seldom a prelude to just treatment of others. More often it heralds a "Now it's our turn" attitude. No one felt or promoted a sense of being historically aggrieved more than Adolf Hitler.

"Underrepresentation" and "Life Chances"

Quite aside from claims of historic wrongs, the argument has often been made—on grounds of morality as well as political or social expediency— that the "under-representation" of particular groups in desirable roles is an "imbalance" to be "corrected." Majorities have pressed such claims as readily as minorities, in circumstances where their only disadvantages were their own lack of skills or interest, as well as where a plausible case could be made that imposed disabilities have handicapped them.

Among the many unexamined assumptions behind preferential policies is the belief that intergroup friction is a function of the magnitude of income gaps, so that more social harmony can be achieved by reducing these gaps. As with so much that has been said in this area, evidence has been neither asked nor given, while counter-evidence is plentiful, varied, and ignored.

In Bombay, the hostility of the Maharashtrians has been directed primarily at the South Indians, who are somewhat ahead of them economically, rather than against the Gujaratis, who are far ahead of them. Throughout sub-Saharan Africa, there has historically been far more hostility directed by Africans against Asians than against Europeans, who are economically far ahead of both. A similar pattern is found *within* African groups. In Nigeria, for example, the Yoruba were far ahead of the Ibo economically in 1940, while there was a much smaller gap at that time between the Hausa and the Ibo. Yet the hostility and violence between Hausa and Ibo in that era greatly exceeded any friction between either of these groups and the Yoruba. Later, as the Ibos rose, narrowing the gap between themselves and the Yoruba, it was precisely then that Ibo-Yoruba outbreaks of violence occurred.

Advocates of preferential policies often express a related belief, similarly unsupported by evidence, that an even distribution of groups across sectors of the economy tends to reduce social frictions and hostility. Much history suggests the opposite, that (in the words of Professor Horowitz) "the ethnic division of labor is more a shield than a sword."

The utter dominance of particular sectors by particular minority groups has been quietly accepted for generations in many countries—until a specific, organized campaign has been whipped up against the minority, often by members of the majority who are seeking to enter the minority-dominated sector and are finding their competition very formidable. Often majority-group customers or suppliers actually prefer dealing with the minority-run entrepreneurs. Even in the midst of ethnic riots against other groups certain middleman minorities have been spared—the Greeks in the Sudan, Hindus in Burma, Marwaris in Assam. Organized boycotts of minority businessmen have been spearheaded by majority-group business rivals, from Uganda and Kenya to the Philippines and the United States. Contrary to what is widely (and lightly) assumed, neither an even representation of groups nor mass resentment at unevenness is "natural."

Repeatedly, in countries scattered around the world, it has been precisely the rise of newly emerging ethnic competitors—whether in business, government, or the professions—which has produced not only friction with groups already dominant in the sectors concerned but also, and much more importantly, has led the newcomers to whip up their whole group emotionally against the already established group. A Sri Lankan legislator noted this pattern early in that country's inter-ethnic troubles:

> University graduates and people like that are the cause of all the trouble—not the vast mass of the Sinhalese people. It is those men, these middle-class unemployed seeking employment, who are jealous of the fact that a few Tamils occupy seats of office in government—these are the people who have gone round the countryside, rousing the masses and creating this problem.

Halfway around the world a similar charge was made, that "the educated Nigerian is the worst peddler of tribalism." In the very different setting of Hungary in the 1880's, the promotion of anti-Semitism was largely the work of students, intellectuals, and sections of the middle classes, while the Hungarian peasant masses remained relatively unresponsive.

Advocates of preferential policies often see these policies as not only promoting social harmony by reducing gaps in income and "representation," but also as part of a more general attempt to "equalize life chances." Much effort is expended establishing the moral desirability of this goal and the extent to which we currently fall short of it, while little or no effort goes into establishing our *capability* to accomplish such a staggering task. One clue to the magnitude and difficulty of what is being attempted are the various ways in which first-born children excel their siblings. A completely disproportionate number of the famous individuals in history were either firstborn or the only child. In more mundane achievements as well, the first-born tend to excel. A study of National Merit Scholarship finalists showed that, even in five-child families, the first-born became finalists more often than all the other siblings combined. The same was true in two-, three-, and four-child families. Such disparities, among people born of the same parents and raised under the same roof, mock presumptions of being able to equalize life chances across broader and deeper differences among people in a large, complex, and, especially, multi-ethnic society.

The abstract moral desirability of a goal cannot preempt the prior question of our capacity to achieve it. This is not even a question of falling short of all that might be hoped for. It is a question of risking counterproductive, disastrous, and even bloody results.

Beneficiaries and Losers

Part of the moral aura surrounding preferential policies is due to the belief that such policies benefit the less fortunate. The losers in this presumed redistribution are seldom specified, though the underlying assumption seems to be that they are the more fortunate.

Empirical evidence for such assumptions is largely lacking and the a priori case for believing them is unconvincing. For example, the effects of preferential policies depend on the costs of complementary factors required to use the preferences. These costs can obviously be borne more readily by those who are already more fortunate. Benefits set aside for businessmen of the preferred group are of no use to members of that group who do not happen to own a business, or possess the capital to start one. Preferential admission to medical school is a benefit only to those who have already gone to college. Because preferential benefits tend to be concentrated on more lucrative or prestigious things, they are often within striking distance only for the fortunate few who have already advanced well beyond most other members of the preferred group. In Third World countries, where the great demand is for clerical jobs in the government, the poorer groups in these countries often have difficulty reaching even the modest level of education required for such employment.

Preferential scholarships for Malays in Malaysia are a classic example. Students from families in the lower-income brackets—63 percent of the population—received 14 percent of the university scholarships, while students whose families were in the top 17 percent of the income distribution received more than half of the scholarships. In India, preferential programs for both untouchables and "other backward classes" show the same pattern. In the state of Haryana, 37 different untouchable castes were entitled to preferential scholarships but only 18 actually received any—and just one of these received 65 percent of the scholarships at the graduate levels and 80 percent at the undergraduate level. Similar patterns are found in other parts of the country. In the state of Tamil Nadu, the highest of the so-called "backward classes" (11 percent of the total) received nearly half of all jobs and all university admissions set aside for such classes. The bottom 12 percent received no more than 2 percent of the jobs and university admissions.

In some cases—including the United States—the less fortunate members of a preferred group may actually retrogress while the more fortunate advance under preferential policies. After "affirmative-action" policies took hold in the early 1970s, blacks with little education and little job experience fell further behind the general population—and indeed further behind whites with little education and little job experience. Meanwhile, blacks with college education or substantial job experience advanced economically, both absolutely and relative to whites with the same advantages. Yet another example of the benefits of "affirmative action" to those already more fortunate are the business "set-asides" that give minority entrepreneurs preferential access to government contracts under Section 8(a) of the Small Business Act. Minority businessmen who participate in this program have an average net worth of $160,000. This is not only far higher than the average net worth of the groups they come from, but also higher than the average net worth of Americans in general.

This pattern of simultaneous advance at the top and retrogression at the bottom is not confined to the United States. In India, the era of preferential policies has seen the proportion of untouchables increase significantly among high-level government officials, while the proportion of untouchables who work as landless agricultural laborers has also increased. In Malaysia, the representation of Malays on corporate boards of directors has increased significantly, while the proportion of Malays among the population living below the official poverty level has also increased.

Just as the advocates of preferential policies arbitrarily assume that such policies will benefit the "disadvantaged," so they arbitrarily assume that this will be at the expense of the "privileged." They neither offer evidence of this in advance nor are so impolitic as to collect data on this point after preferential programs have been inaugurated. Such evidence as exists points in the opposite direction. In Bombay, preferential policies to put Maharashtrians into the ranks of business executives had only minor effects on the Gujaratis who were dominant in that occupation, reducing the proportion of Gujarati executives from 52 percent to 44 percent. Among the South Indians, however, their 25-percent representation among Bombay executives was cut in half, to 12 percent. A similar pattern appeared in the very different setting of prewar Hungary, where policies favoring Gentiles had relatively little effect on the Jewish financial and industrial elite but imposed real hardships on the Jewish middle class and lower middle class. In the United States, despite voluminous official statistics on all sorts of racial and ethnic matters, no one seems to have collected data on the actual losers under "affirmative action." It may be significant, however, that those who have protested their losses all the way up to the U.S. Supreme Court have not been named Adams, Cabot, or Rockefeller, but DeFunis, Bakke, and Weber.

The Illusion of Compensation

What makes compensation an illusion is not only that sufferers are not in fact compensated, or the effects of historic wrongs redressed—or even accurately identified and separated from innumerable other social factors at work simultaneously. Both the principle of compensation and the particular form of compensation via preferential policies require careful examination.

The Principle of Compensation

Given the mortality of human beings, often the only compensation for historic wrongs that is within the scope of our knowledge and control is purely symbolic compensation—taking from individuals who inflicted no harm and giving to individuals who suffered none. In addition to the moral shakiness and social dangers of such a policy, it also promotes a kind of social irredentism, a set of a priori grievances against living people, whether or not they have ever inflicted harm on those who feel aggrieved. In view of the futile but bitter and bloody struggles engendered by territorial irredentism, there is little good to hope for by applying this same principle in a new field.

The factual reality that actual benefits from compensatory preferences tend to be concentrated in the already more fortunate elites among the preferred groups makes the moral case for such policies weaker and the social dangers greater. The more educated, articulate, and more politically sophisticated elites have every incentive to whip up group emotions in favor of more and better preferences, despite the increasing group polarization this may produce, and to be intransigent against any suggestion that any such preferences should ever be reduced or ended. This has been a common pattern in the most disparate countries.

In principle, compensation can take many forms, beginning with a simple transfer of money from one group to another. In practice, however, preferential policies are the form taken in many countries around the world. The implications of that particular form, and of its alternatives, raise still more troubling questions.

The Form of Compensation

If, notwithstanding all philosophic objections to the principle of group compensation, such a policy is in fact chosen, then the particular form of the compensation can make a major difference in the costs and the consequences of compensatory policies. When resources, or the benefits they create, are transferred from group A to group B, this is not necessarily—or even likely—a zero-sum process, in which the value of what is lost by one is the same as the value of what is gained by the other. What is transferred may be subjectively valued differently by the losers and the recipients. There may also be objectively discernible differences in the use of the same resources by the two groups.

Compensatory policies may, in theory, take place through transfers of money, transfers of in-kind benefits, or through differential applications of rules and standards. In Australia, for example, various money and in-kind transfers to the aborigines add up to more than $2,000 annually for every aboriginal man, woman, and child. Such transfers arouse relatively little political opposition or social backlash. Similarly, in the United States, monetary compensation for Japanese Americans interned during World War II aroused relatively little controversy—and even that little controversy quickly subsided, once the decision was made.

Such monetary transfers are less costly to individual members of the majority population the more the majority outnumbers the minority receiving the transfer. Obviously, if group A is 100 times as large as group B, each member of group B can receive $100 at a cost of only one dollar to each member of group A. However, even where the losses sustained by one group are significant, monetary transfers may still be efficient, in the narrowly economic sense that what is lost by one group as a whole is gained by another group, with no direct net loss to society as a whole. Whatever the merits or demerits of the particular transfer on other grounds, it is not inefficient. Politically and socially, the opposition to such transfers is therefore unlikely to be as great as opposition to the same net transfers in forms that cost more to the losers than is gained by the gainers. Preferential policies often cost the losers more than is gained by the gainers. Preferential policies, by definition, involve a differential application of rules and standards to individuals originating in different groups. Even where the preferences are not stated in terms of differential rules or standards, but rather in terms of numerical quotas, "goals," or "targets," differences in the qualifications of the respective pools of applicants can readily make numerical similarities amount to differences in standards. This is a very common result in countries around the world. In Nigeria, programs to have college-student populations reflect "the federal character" of the country—i.e., tribal quotas under regional names—led to a situation where cut-off scores for admission to the same college varied substantially between students from different tribes or regions. In Sri Lanka, demographic "standardization" policies led to similar disparities in qualification requirements for individuals from different regions of the country. In India, attempts to meet quotas for untouchable students led to drastic reductions in the qualifications they needed for admission to various institutions. Where applicant pools in different groups are different in qualifications, numerical quotas are equivalent to different standards. Therefore preferential policies in general, however phrased, are essentially an application of different rules or standards to individuals from different groups. The question then is: what are the effects of transfers between groups in this particular form?

There are many ways in which intergroup transfers through differential standards can become negative-sum processes, in which what is lost by one group exceeds what is gained by another, thus representing a direct loss to society as a whole—as well as causing indirect losses, due to a larger resistance or backlash than if the recipient group had obtained the same value or benefit in some other form. An obvious example is when a particular group, in which 90 percent of the students admitted to college succeed in graduating, loses places to another group in which only 30 percent of the students graduate. Group A must lose 900 graduates, in order for group B to gain 300 graduates. It might be objected that this overstates the net loss, since there may be some marginal benefit simply from having attended college, even without graduating. Offsetting this, however, is the fact that groups with lower qualifications tend to specialize in easier and less remunerative fields, whether in India, Malaysia, the Soviet Union, or the United States. Therefore group A may lose 900 graduates largely concentrated in mathematics, science, and engineering, while group B gains 300 graduates largely concentrated in sociology, education, and ethnic studies.

The *apparent* losses to one group under preferential policies may also far exceed the real losses, thereby further raising the indirect social costs of backlash and turmoil. For example, an observer of India's preferential policies for untouchables (known officially as "scheduled castes") has commented:

> ... we hear innumerable tales of persons being deprived of appointments in favor of people who ranked lower than they did in the relevant examinations. No doubt this does happen, but if all these people were, in fact, paying the price for appointments to Scheduled Castes, there would be many more SC persons appointed than there actually are. To illustrate: supposing that 300 people qualify for ten posts available. The top nine are appointed on merit but the tenth is reserved, so the authorities go down the list to find an SC applicant. They find one at 140 and he is appointed. Whereupon all 131 between him and the merit list feel

aggrieved. He has not taken 131 posts; he has taken one, yet 131 people believe they have paid the price for it. Moreover, the remaining 159 often also resent the situation, believing that their chances were, somehow, lessened by the existence of SC reservations.

Where certain opportunities are rigidly "set aside" for particular groups, in the sense that members of other groups cannot have them, even if these opportunities remain unused, then there is the potential for a maximum of grievance for a minimum of benefit transfer. Admission to medical school in India's state of Gujarat operates on this principle—and has led repeatedly to bloody riots in which many people have died. Reservations or "set-asides" in general tend to provoke strong objections. The first major setback for "affirmative action" in the U.S. Supreme Court was based on objections to reserved-admissions places for minority applicants in the 1978 *Bakke* case. A later major setback occurred in *City of Richmond* v. *Croson* (1989), where minority business set-asides were struck down by the Supreme Court. Similarly, in India, an exhaustive, scholarly legal study of preferential policies found: "Virtually all of the litigation about compensatory discrimination has involved reservations, even though preferences in the form of provisions of facilities, resources, and protections directly affect a much larger number of recipients." This litigation has been initiated mostly by non-preferred individuals who complain of being adversely affected. In some ultimate sense, non-preferred individuals are just as much adversely affected by preferences in other forms that direct resources away from them and toward preferred groups. But it is preference in the specific form of "reservation" or "set-aside" that seems most to provoke both violence and litigation.

By contrast, resource transfers designed to enable disadvantaged groups to meet standards are accepted while attempts to bring the standards down to them are overwhelmingly rejected. In the United States, preferential policies have repeatedly been rejected in public-opinion polls. However, the same American public has strongly supported "special educational or vocational courses, free of charge, to enable members of minority groups to do better on tests." More than three-fifths of all whites even support "requiring large companies to set up special training programs for members of minority groups." The issue is not simply whether one is for or against the advancement of particular groups or is willing to see transfers of resources for their betterment. The method by which their betterment is attempted matters greatly in terms of whether such efforts have the support or the opposition of others.

Replacing Illusions

With all the empirical weaknesses, logical flaws, and social dangers of preferential policies, why have they become so popular and spread so rapidly around the world? One reason is that their *political* attractions are considerable. They offer an immediate response—a quick fix—at relatively little government expense, to the demands of vocal, aroused, and often organized elites, speaking in the name of restive masses. This restiveness of the masses is by no means incidental. Violence has frequently preceded preferences, from the American ghetto riots of the 1960's to the Malay and Indonesian riots against the Chinese at about the same time, to terrorism in India, and massive mob violence against the Tamils in Sri Lanka. This violence by the masses is typically used politically to promote elite purposes via preferential policies. An international study of ethnic conflicts concluded:

> Preferences tend to respond to middle-class aspirations almost entirely. They do little or nothing about the resentments of those who do not aspire to attend secondary school or university, to enter the modern private sector or the bureaucracy, or to become businessmen. Although lower-class resentments are often profound— it is not, after all, the middle class that typically participates in ethnic violence—the resentments may have nothing to do with occupational mobility and preferences do not address them.

Preferential policies, then, are politically attractive as a response, however socially ineffective or counterproductive such policies may later prove to be in practice. At a sufficiently superficial level, the moral attractions of preferential policies are considerable as well. Even in South Africa, moral appeals were made on behalf of a "civilized labor policy"— protecting European workers' customary standard of living from being undercut by Africans and Indians accustomed to living on less—and clergy, intellectuals, and others not personally benefiting joined in support of these policies on that basis. Preferential policies allow intellectuals as well as politicians to be on the side of the angels (as locally defined at the time) at low cost—or rather, at a low down payment, for the real costs come later, and have sometimes been paid in blood.

The last refuge of a failed policy is "the long run," in which it will supposedly be a success. In other words, those who predicted the short run wrongly ask to be trusted with the much harder task of predicting the long run rightly. This argument, used to defend the counterproductive effects of preferential policies, is far less defensible in an international perspective where older preferential policies (as in India or Sri Lanka) have progressed from intergroup political hostility to bloodshed in the streets and deaths by the thousands, while newer programs (as in the United States) are still in the process of increasing group polarization, and the even more recent preferential policies taking shape in Australia and New Zealand are still at the stage of optimistic predictions.

Even the most damning indictment of a policy is almost certain to be met with the response: "But what would you replace it with?" However effective as a political tactic, such a question confuses rather than clarifies. It is like an arbitrary prohibition against saying that the emperor has no clothes, until a complete wardrobe has been designed. The question misconceives policy, and human actions in general, in yet another way: no one who extinguishes a forest fire or removes a cancer has to "replace" it with anything. We are well rid of evils.

This is not to say that none of the aspects of social issues raised during "affirmative-action" controversies should ever be addressed by public policy. The case for public policy in general, or for a particular public policy, must be made on the individual merits of the particular issues raised—but not as a general "replacement" for some discredited policy.

What must be replaced are the social illusions and misconceptions underlying preferential policies, for any alternative policy based on the same illusions and misconceptions will have the same fatal weaknesses in its structure. In some countries and for some purposes social policy may wish to ameliorate the lot of the less fortunate or make it possible for individuals or groups to acquire the knowledge and skills necessary for their own advancement. It is infinitely more important that such efforts be based on facts and logic than that there be one particular scheme selected from innumerable possibilities as the uniquely designated "replacement" for existing policy.

We may or may not be able to agree on what the ideal, or even a viable, policy must be. What we can agree on is far more fundamental: We can agree to *talk sense*. That will mean abandoning a whole vocabulary of political rhetoric which preempts factual questions by arbitrarily calling statistical disparities "discrimination," "exclusion," "segregation," and the like. It will mean confronting issues instead of impugning motives. It will mean specifying goals and defending those specifics, rather than speaking in terms of seeking some nebulously unctuous "change" or "social justice." Perhaps more than anything else, talking sense will mean examining policies in terms of the incentives they create, and the results to which these incentives lead, rather than the hopes they embody. It will mean that evidence takes precedence over assertion and reiteration.

Incentives versus Hopes

"Temporary" Preferences
Many of the factual findings of this study will be surprising only because incentives have not usually been the focus of discussions of preferential policies. For example, given the incentives, it can hardly be surprising that preferential policies do not become temporary merely because their proponents use the word "temporary." The incentives are to do exactly what has been done, in country after country: extend and expand both the preferences and the list of beneficiaries, not to mention those individuals who make themselves beneficiaries through fraud.

Once we face up to the fact that "temporary" preferences are not likely to be temporary in reality, and that the group whose history provides the moral rationale for initiating preferential policies is unlikely to remain the sole group preferred in a multi-ethnic society, the real issue then becomes: what are the probable consequences of an enduring policy of group preferences for the whole range of groups that will probably get them? The answer to that question will depend, not on what rationales there are for preferences, but rather on what *incentives* these policies create—including incentives for members of the preferred group, for members of other groups likely to seek preferences, for members of groups likely to resent and react to preferences, and for a whole group-consciousness industry that acquires a vested interest in agitating emotional issues in an ever more tense, polarized, and even explosive atmosphere.

The moral issue is then no longer whether group A or B deserves compensatory preferences, but whether groups C, D, E, etc., also deserve such preferences—especially if these latter groups are larger, more educated, or otherwise better-positioned to use the preferences, thereby diluting or destroying the value of preferences for group A or B, who may have stronger moral claims or more urgent social needs. As the cases of untouchables in India and blacks in the United States both illustrate, it is all too easy for a tragically unfortunate group of people to be used simply as an entering wedge to create benefits going largely to others in much more fortunate circumstances, whether those others are within their own racial or social group or numerous outsiders to whom the preferential principle is successively extended. Clearly, no recitation of the historic oppressions suffered by blacks can justify preferences for white, middle-class women, whom some believe to be the principal beneficiaries of the acceptance of the preferential principle.

Both in India and in the United States, a point is ultimately reached where the initially designated beneficiaries of preferential policies begin to object to the continued extension of that status to others. Thus blacks objected to legislation in the Louisiana House of Representatives which extended "minority" status to Cajuns. In India, untouchable leader Dr. B. R. Ambedkar fought successfully against the extension of central-government preferences to members of the "other backward classes" in the Indian constitution.

An analysis of preferential policies in terms of the incentives they create cannot treat preferences as simply a benefit added to existing social processes. Preferential policies change the very nature of processes—whether these be hiring processes, college-admissions processes, or other social processes. An employer who was once free to choose among job applicants on the basis of his own assessments of their ability to do the job must, after preferential policies, consider also how readily his decision can be justified to third parties, in terms that will be understood and accepted by those who are less knowledgeable about his business, who were not present at the interview, and who would have less experience on which to base an assessment such as he made. "Objective" criteria in general and educational credentials in particular are likely to gain more weight under these circumstances because third parties can understand such things, even if other qualities are in fact more important on the job. The growth of credentialism can further disadvantage less fortunate groups, especially if preferences have also been extended to other groups with more credentials—e.g., middle-class white women in America as compared to black males. There can be *fewer* job opportunities for less educated black males after preferential policies that extend far beyond them to encompass groups better able to play the game under the new rules.

Where preferential policies apply not only to the initial intake (hiring, college admissions) but also to subsequent progress (promotions, college grades, honors), the incentives created can operate at cross purposes. For example, the requirement that initial intake numbers be reported to third parties tends, by itself, to create incentives to hire more of the designated group. However, the knowledge that this group's subsequent progress must also be reported—and can become the basis for costly litigation and large damage awards—inhibits the hiring of individuals from the preferred group, unless they seem more "safe" than individuals who can be readily demoted or terminated because they come from groups without legal preferences. Which of these contending tendencies will predominate in the actual decisions can vary with the industry or activity, the nature of the pools of applicants, the policies and practices of the third-party observers, and whether the decision-maker is spending his own money or the tax-payers' money. The point here is that, once more, the changes in the nature of the process induced by preferential processes need not increase the opportunities of the officially preferred group—and may, on net balance, *reduce* those opportunities. Where the existence of preferential policies also leads to a slackening of efforts among the preferred group, then the dangers of counterproductive results are further increased.

Abstract possibilities of counterproductive results from preferential policies are by no means conclusive. However, they do make it easier to understand empirical patterns observed in the United States, India, and Malaysia, where (as noted above) the poorer members of the preferred group have actually *retrogressed* during the same span of time when the group's elite has advanced dramatically. Preferential policies unequivocally create an increased demand for the "safe" and credentialed members of the preferred group, while making the less educated, less skilled, and less experienced members a more risky gamble for an employer than they would be in the absence of preferences. This is especially so in the United States, where preferences are predicated on prior discrimination and on continuing dangers of discrimination, with statistical disparities often be-ing equated with such discrimination in courts of law, which can make multimillion-dollar damage awards to those judged to be victims.

Evasions of Preferences

Given the differing costs of discrimination to those in government who impose preferential policies and businessmen in the private sector who are required to carry them out, it can hardly be surprising that both opposition and evasions have been aroused against such policies in country after country.

In the absence of an understanding of incentives, explanations tend to account for evasion or opposition to preferential policies by a hostility to the particular groups designated as beneficiaries of these policies. Clearly this cannot explain widespread white evasions of policies designed to help whites, as in South Africa, where for years the government has been fining white businessmen for hiring more blacks and in higher occupations than they are legally allowed to. Economic incentives, rather than humanitarianism, have been behind such widespread evasions of the "color bar" in South Africa in times past and of apartheid laws more recently. Once the *multiple* sources of resistance to preferential policies are admitted, it is no longer possible to attribute automatically the failures of such policies to "institutional racism," "unconscious bias," or similar explanations, *without evidence*. Circular reasoning cannot substitute for evidence.

Incentives allow discussions to proceed in terms of the actual decision-makers involved, individual or institutional, seeking their own specific self-interest rather than in terms of some arbitrarily collectivized "society," "power structure," or other such construct not corresponding to any empirically demonstrable decision-making unit. The poetic license of speaking of "society" as acting this way or that is a declaration of intellectual bankruptcy, as far as empirical evidence is concerned. Such metaphors are an evasion of crucial questions about incentives and causation.

Incentives of Activists

Unelected "spokesmen" who speak boldly to the media in the name of groups seeking or receiving preferential policies are a common social phenomenon from New Zealand to Britain to North America. There are also common patterns in their pronouncements, reflecting common incentives facing them. Any fundamental reexamination of the assumptions behind preferential policies—and still more so, any resulting change of policies—can expect to encounter their vocal, bitter, and determined opposition, including inevitable charges of racism against outsiders, labels of "traitor" put on any members of their own group who disagree publicly with them, and whatever other claims or charges seem likely to be politically effective.

The common thread of group activists around the world is separatism. Insofar as their group, whether a majority or a minority, reaches a modus vivendi with other groups, there is less of a role for group activists. Accordingly, group activists often seek separate languages, separate institutions, and even separate territories. Even where most of the group already speaks the language of the surrounding society, as among the Maoris of New Zealand, group activists seek to reconstitute artificially a separate language community. In Australia, all-aborigine schools have been established, emphasizing the teaching of the aboriginal languages.

Unrealizable demands are another common feature of group activists, whether these demands are for massive "reparations" payments for slavery for blacks in the United States or for making the Maori language the official language of New Zealand. While demands that can be met might benefit the group, demands that cannot be met benefit the group activist. The point is "to create the appropriate climate for bitter recriminations," as an observer of Australian aboriginal activists put it. Sometimes, through miscalculation, a demand may be made that can be and is met—in which case, what is conceded must then be denounced as paltry and insultingly inadequate, however important it may have been depicted as being when it seemed unattainable.

Threats of catastrophe if their demands are not met are another common tactic of group activists. An aboriginal activist in Australia described the aborigines as being of a radically different culture, as "totally frustrated and angry with white society," so that unless whites get rid of their "inbuilt bias and prejudice," he predicted "there's going to be an absolute disaster in Australia." He concluded: "We've got to find alternative principles if humanity is to survive." By contrast, one of the few aborigines actually *elected* by aborigines depicted his people as sharing many of the values and aspirations of white Australians, offered no such apocalyptic view of the future, and declared that many of the activists' ideas were foreign to aboriginal culture, though congenial to "the trendy middle classes."

A key factor in the success of vocal activists around the world is their ability to strike a responsive chord in the "trendy middle classes" in the name of a group which has not elected them and which often has views radically different from theirs. Such activists are not "leaders" of their people in any meaningful sense. That fact can only become more painfully clear if a fundamental change in public policy makes the internal development of the group the prime focus. In such a situation today's group activists would have little role to play except that of attempting to discredit or sabotage the effort. They may be politically very formidable in that role, however.

Presumptions versus People

Preferential policies are generally intended to favor groups currently "underrepresented" in desirable occupations or institutions. Both majorities and minorities have equated statistical inequalities with moral inequities. In extreme cases—not necessarily rare cases—the presumption that groups would be evenly represented in various sectors and levels of society, in the absence of discrimination, has become a belief almost hermetically sealed off from any logical or empirical argument. Criticism is dismissed as malevolently motivated, evidence as culturally biased, criteria as irrelevant.

Evidence that clearly contradicts the vision has often been hidden by redefinition. For example, where the assumption is that the lower economic position of non-whites is due to discrimination by whites, non-white groups who have been successful in the same society are an obvious embarrassment to the proponents of the theory. In Britain, this has led to a redefinition of all non-white groups, including Asians, as "black." Thus Asians disappear as a separate group by verbal sleight-of-hand, as the collective economic, educational, and other performances of "blacks" as a whole are compared to those of whites. In the United States, a similar burying of discordant evidence is achieved by using the ponderous phrase "people of color" to encompass all non-whites, thereby swamping the above-average income statistics of Chinese and Japanese Americans under the larger numbers of below-average income statistics from blacks and other low-income, non-white groups. In Canada, the lumping-together phrase is "visible minorities." It too helps conceal the fact that some non-white groups in Canada are more prosperous than some white groups. The particular words used to lump disparate groups together differ from country to country but the tactic is the same.

In short, no matter what the evidence says, the vision is protected from it. Such heads-I-win-and-tails-you-lose arguments have become as commonplace among group activists in Britain as in the United States.

Implicit in this vision is the assumption that the respective pools of potential group "representatives" are not substantially different or that the differences are not relevant. This assumption is contradicted by objective evidence from around the world as to the large variations—both qualitative and quantitative—in educational achievement between groups in the same society, whether India, Israel, Sri Lanka, Nigeria, Malaysia, or the United States.

Non-quantifiable differences are not necessarily any less important factors in statistical disparities, though such differences are often dismissed as "stereotypes." However, so-called "stereotypes" about group behavior often show a certain consistency between what group members say about themselves and what others say about them, though the connotations may differ. Many backward groups from Burma to Guyana "view themselves as the major obstacle to their own advancement," as Donald Horowitz's study showed. Nor can these groups be dismissed as brainwashed minorities, full of "self-hate." Majorities in charge of their own preferential programs have also confronted their own behavior as a factor inhibiting the progress they wish to make. This was perhaps nowhere more candidly stated than in an official Malaysian government publication which criticized the Malays' "unwillingness to work and take risks," their lack of "skills and initiative," and their "practice of assigning to others for specific remuneration the use of licenses granted to them."

In the very different setting of Hungary, in 1940, Hungary's longtime regent, Admiral Miklós Horthy, wrote to the Prime Minister:

> As regards the Jewish problem, I have been an anti-Semite through all my life. I have never had contact with Jews. I have considered it intolerable that here in Hungary every factory, bank, large fortune, business, theater, press, commercial enterprise, etc., should be in the hands of Jews, and that Jews should be the image reflected of Hungary, especially abroad. Since, however, one of the most important tasks of the government is to raise the living standards (i.e., we have to acquire wealth), it is impossible, in a year or two, to eliminate the Jews, who have everything in their hands, and to replace them by incompetent, most unworthy big-mouth elements, for we would become bankrupt. This requires a generation at least.

Surely Malays and Hungarian Gentiles are not the only people on this planet whose own behavior patterns have been among the factors inhibiting their progress. Yet any such candid recitation of such patterns among many other groups in other countries would automatically be denounced as "blaming the victim"—not only by political activists but even by scholars. Any suggestion of difficulties in finding qualified members of any group for any job is likely to be dismissed as a lame excuse, even in courts of law. In the United States, the unbridled vilification of the Moynihan Report in 1965 marked virtually the beginning of the end of candid discussions of minority groups. Ironically, the Moynihan Report was a plea for more government help for blacks, and what it said about social conditions within the black community had already been said by black scholars, including some who joined in the vilification of Moynihan. Moreover, the candor of the Moynihan Report did not begin to approach the painful frankness of *Black Bourgeoisie* by E. Franklin Frazier, the outstanding black sociologist.

Any policy that attempts to advance the interests of any group in any country must begin with the reality of their situation—not with hermetically sealed visions that offer psychic comfort or politically useful illusions benefiting a relative handful of elite or activist individuals. It is far more important to understand what a viable policy must be based on than to narrow arbitrarily the range of such possible policies to one specified "solution."

Denial of any group's internal problems can mean denying a history of long and sometimes heroic efforts to overcome those problems. The role of the Catholic Church in socially uplifting the Irish in America is just one of these historic efforts leading to the transformation of a people. Both blacks and whites participated in successful efforts to develop an educated class among blacks in the first generation after slavery and on into the twentieth century. The "Jewish Enlightenment" in Europe and the spectacular rise of the Scots in the eighteenth century are other examples of a kind of valuable human experience that is often ignored today because to admit that there were internal problems in the first place would shatter the hermetically sealed vision.

One symptom of the determined refusal to examine the characteristics of a group nominated for preferences is the setting of numerical "goals" *without the slightest mention* of the size of the pool of qualified people from whom these goals are to be met. Where the problem of pool size is even obliquely acknowledged, it is often in the context of establishing numerical goals for the pool itself—which simply pushes the same issue back one stage. Ultimately, this logically leads back to childhood and the values of the home and the group. When Maori students, admitted under preferential policies at New Zealand's University of Auckland, fail to show up for tutorials as often as other students, their academic failures cannot be attributed automatically to institutional racism or to not having enough "role models"—not if the purpose is to advance Maoris rather than to score ideological points.

Politics versus Progress

The ingredients of political success and the ingredients of social progress are not only different but often antithetical. Nothing was more politically successful than the preferential policies which led Sri Lanka into race riots, atrocities, and civil war. Even Marxist parties, ideologically opposed to ethnic-group preferences, were forced by electoral disasters to advocate such policies as the price of political survival. Preferential policies in Pakistan were politically robust enough to survive and flourish after their initial beneficiary group, the East Bengalis, seceded to form the separate nation of Bangladesh. Preferential policies in Nigeria began before independence and survived in varying forms through changes in constitutions, military coups, and a civil war that took over a million lives. The political success of preferential policies in Guyana, India, and Malaysia has likewise been impressive.

What has been far less impressive is the social record of preferential policies. However beneficial to the elites of preferred groups, such policies have helped raise the masses from poverty to prosperity only in South Africa, where the once urgent "poor-white" problem among the Afrikaners has been solved by the ruthless sacrifice of the interests of the vastly larger non-white population and the relentless suppression of their resistance. Yet it is by no means clear that the long-run costs of this social "success" will prove to be worth it, even for South African whites, many of whom have begun emigrating to other countries in anticipation of trouble in the years ahead.

The reasons for the political success of preferential policies highlight the political difficulties of alternative policies designed to enable genuinely unfortunate people to advance. Preferential policies allow large promises about the future to be made by politicians at small immediate cost to the government. Such policies reward vocal leaders of the preferred groups by creating benefits focused on their class and flatter the group as a whole that its problems are caused by other people, whose wrongdoing or unfair advantages will be suppressed by government. This approach fits in neatly with various "liberation" themes, whose essential message is that other people are to blame for one's troubles. With the complex difficulties and painful trade-offs involved in social advancement reduced to the simple level of group conflict, the issue can be presented and its goals defined in terms politically comprehensible to all. Conflict has obvious media appeal as well and moralists and intellectuals can choose the side considered to be that of the angels. Politicians benefit by gaining the political support of the beneficiary groups. Where those groups do not constitute a majority, then the preferential policies can nevertheless succeed politically by keeping a low profile, by being redefined as antidiscrimination efforts, or by being justified by such moral rationales as will mollify the majority.

Consider, by contrast, the political situation facing a program which genuinely intends to aid the advancement of less fortunate people by improving those people's education, skills, and habits. Such a program must take far more time, probably cost far more money, and cannot provide either the group conflict so useful to the media or the sense of moral superiority so much in demand by crusaders or others who want to be on the side of the angels. The scope and pace of genuine advancement for less fortunate masses cannot produce as dramatic results as a doubling or tripling of group members in a few elite positions within a few years under preferential policies. If thousands more minority women who might have become maids become secretaries instead, that is still not as dramatic as having three minority cabinet members instead of one, even though far more people would be benefited by the former, including people far more in need of help. Politically, symbolic representation in visible high-level positions "sells." Preferential policies can deliver that better and faster than any policy of helping less fortunate masses advance. Most important of all, it can deliver before the next election.

Education is widely recognized as a key factor in the advancement of individuals and groups. Whether in India or the United States or in other countries, the tendency is to focus efforts at the visible, high-level end of education—at the colleges and universities, including postgraduate education. Obviously, the genuinely less fortunate seldom reach these levels. If they are to be helped, the help must come much earlier in the educational process and the task will be infinitely more difficult than lowering admissions standards in higher education to achieve statistical representation. Moreover, the struggle will not be the kind of struggle between groups, or between good and evil, that the media can dramatize but instead a harder, slower, and less glamorous struggle between the inherent requirements of quality education and the habits, attitudes, and beliefs of people who have not had to deal with such requirements before. School disrupters will have to be dealt with as problems to be gotten rid of, rather than as victims to be defended by in-group organizations or "public-interest" lawyers from the general society.

Even assuming that all of these educational difficulties can be overcome and high-quality students begin to emerge from the system, they will not emerge from high school for another twelve years, from college for sixteen years, or from postgraduate education and professional apprenticeship levels for twenty years. Such time spans are simply beyond the horizon of politicians whose focus is the next election. Genuine educational improvement is at a clear disadvantage politically in competing with preferential policies that can offer a "quick fix" before the voters go to the polls. Even if there are early signs that a program is starting to work, rising test scores in Harlem elementary schools will never carry the same political weight as appointing a few more high-level minority officials or even increasing the number of minority students admitted to the city's colleges and universities without meeting the standards required of others.

Could some judicious blend of preferential programs and programs designed to improve the performances of less educated groups work? Here the problem is that the two kinds of programs create incentives that work at cross-purposes, even if their goals are the same. Forcing students to meet higher standards—a painful process for them and their teachers alike—will be made all the more difficult if the students know that these standards are unnecessary for them to reach whatever educational or employment goals they have, or even to be promoted to the next grade. If group-representation statistics are the standard by which institutions will be judged, other standards will be sacrificed for the sake of body count. This is true not only of educational institutions but of other institutions as well.

Political feasibility is the greatest obstacle to new policies with an overriding goal of advancing the less fortunate because time is the key ingredient in such advancement on a large scale. Even in the extreme case of South Africa, where massive transfers of the nation's resources were focused on a small minority of its people, in *addition* to preferential policies pursued in utter disregard of the losses and even tragedies suffered by others as a result, it was decades before the Afrikaner "poor whites" became middle-class. Only in terms of political appearances are preferential policies a "quick fix." The dangers of an actual retrogression among the masses of the beneficiary group cannot be dismissed, either from an analytical or an empirical perspective. Even greater dangers have materialized in countries that have experienced bloodshed in the wake of group polarization brought on by preferential policies.

While current political feasibility may be the touchstone of the professional politician, it cannot be the last word for others. In many countries, what is most politically feasible are policies that further a continued drift in the direction of group polarization and the dangers and disasters this entails. Specific alternative policies will differ for different groups and different countries. What is crucial is that these alternatives be examined in terms of the *incentives* they create and the results to which such incentives can be expected to lead—regardless of the rationales, aspirations, or symbolism of these policies. Determining in this way what *should* be done is not an exercise in utopianism, for once there is a consensus on what needs to be done, that in itself changes what is politically feasible.

The starting point for rethinking and reform must be a recognition that "affirmative action" has been a failure in the United States and a disaster in other countries that have had such policies longer. Indeed, a growing polarization and increasing numbers of ugly racial incidents (especially on campuses that are strongholds of "affirmative action") may be early warnings that we too may be moving from the stage of mere failure to the stage of social disaster.

A Conservative Welfare State

Irving Kristol

I HAD IT COMING. In my last article in this newspaper, I challenged conservatives in general, and the Republican Party in
particular, to come up with their ideas for a reformed welfare state. Inevitably, my challenge redounded upon me. "Well," my friends, associates, and
many correspondents replied, "where are your ideas? Stop sermonizing
and get down to specifics." I now rise to that challenge, though with
apprehension, since my ideas happen to be rather controversial, and I fear
many conservatives will be unappreciative of their merits.

Let me lay down the basic principles—the basic deficiency, some
will say—of my approach. I shall, to begin with, assume that the welfare
state is with us, for better or worse, and that conservatives should try to
make it better rather than worse. And I shall pay no attention to the
economics of the welfare state, which I regard as a secondary issue. What
conservatives ought to seek, first of all, is a welfare state consistent with
the basic moral principles of our civilization and the basic political principles of our nation. The essential purpose of politics, after all, is to
transmit to our children a civilization and a nation that they can be proud
of. This means we should figure out what we want before we calculate
what we can afford, not the reverse, which is the normal conservative
predisposition. In this respect, public finance differs fundamentally from
household economics.

It has long been my opinion that the conservative hostility to Social
Security, derived from a traditional conservative fiscal monomania, leads
to political impotence and a bankrupt social policy. Our Social Security
system is enormously popular. If the American people want to be generous
to their elderly, even to the point of some extravagance, I think it is very
nice of them. After all, the elderly are such wonderful, unproblematic

Reprinted from The Wall Street Journal, *June 14, 1993.*

citizens. They are patriotic, they do not have illegitimate children, they do not commit crimes, they do not riot in the streets, their popular entertainments are decent rather than degrading, and if they find themselves a bit flush with funds, they happily distribute the money to their grandchildren.

So, in my welfare state, we leave Social Security alone—except for being a bit more generous, perhaps. Certainly, all restrictions on the earnings of the elderly should be abolished, as a matter of fairness. As for Medicare—well, conservatives believe in honoring thy father and mother, and the Good Book does not say that such honor should be limited only to parents (or grandparents) who are in good health and do not live too long. Medicare's cost is not a conservative problem, except for those conservatives whose Good Book is the annual budget.

As with the elderly, so with children. Ever since World War II, weak-minded and budget-conscious Republican administrations have conspired with liberals to cheat the children of middle-class and working-class households. The income tax deduction for children, now $2,500, would now be $7,500 had it been indexed for inflation. The next Republican administration should address this scandal, giving it the highest priority. The budget consequences are considerable, so perhaps we would want to phase in the indexed increase over a five-year period. But nothing less than that, I would say.

The charms of this reform would, from the conservative point of view, be significant and various. It would be enormously popular, which is no small thing. But it would also be much more than that. These households represent the conservative ideal of the normal household—the household that exemplifies "family values"—and we wish to encourage such households instead of adding to their financial difficulties, as we have been doing. One could also contemplate unanticipated benefits, instead of the unanticipated ills that are so characteristic of liberal reform. After all, one of the things these parents could do is use the money for the children's education, thereby making "school choice" an actuality, not merely an advocated possibility.

Now for the more contentious part. It is easy and attractive to discriminate in favor of large sections of the population. It is far less attractive, and makes us all uneasy, to discriminate against any section of the population. Yet such discrimination is absolutely necessary if we are to change the welfare state into something more deserving of that name.

This issue, of "discriminating against," is most sharply posed when we consider the reform of welfare itself. The problem with our current welfare programs is not that they are costly—which they are—but that they have such perverse consequences for the people they are supposed to benefit. The emergence of a growing and self-perpetuating "underclass" that makes our cities close to uninhabitable is a demonstrable consequence of the present, liberal-inspired welfare system. The system breeds social pathologies—crime, juvenile delinquency, illegitimacy, drug addiction and alcoholism, along with the destruction of a once functioning public school system.

The neoliberal response, advocated by Mr. Clinton during his campaign, which calls for "two years and out" for all able-bodied welfare recipients, is a fantasy. It will not happen. We are not going to see state legislatures and the huge welfare establishment ruthlessly dumping welfare families onto the streets. Public opinion will not stand for it, liberal politicians will not be able to stomach it. It is merely a rhetorical diversionary tactic, and conservatives who are now attracted to it will end up distancing themselves from it as fast as they can.

The key to a conservative reform would be (a) to discourage young women from having an illegitimate child in the first place and (b) to discriminate between "welfare mothers" and "mothers on welfare." Such discrimination must have a clear moral basis.

"Mothers on welfare" includes married women with children who have been divorced or widowed or abandoned by their husbands. Most such women have little connection with any kind of underclass. For the most part, they have middle-class aspirations, subscribe to "family values," and create no intergenerational class of welfare dependents. Their stay on welfare is usually less than two years—they don't like being on welfare. They exit from the welfare population by reason of remarriage or getting a job (sometimes after diligently taking vocational training). They are not a problem population, and deserve our generous assistance as well as our sympathy.

"Welfare mothers," on the other hand, usually end up on welfare as a result of their own actions. Young girls permit themselves to get pregnant, and to bear a child, because the prospect of going on welfare does not frighten them. Welfare permits them to leave homes that are often squalid or worse. It provides them with support, in cash and kind (food stamps, housing allowances, Medicaid), that is in many ways superior to what they could earn working at the minimum wage.

These girls should be made to look upon welfare not as an opportunity, but as a frightening possibility. It follows that they should receive no housing allowance—this is probably the most important change of all. Having your own apartment, in which you can raise your child, can be seen as "fun." Living with your child in your parents' home is a lot less alluring. This would especially be the case if the mother received no food stamps and was ineligible for Medicaid. (She would have to rely on the hospital clinic.) The child, on the other hand, would be eligible for food stamps and Medicaid, as well as a children's cash allowance. But the net effect of such reforms would be to reduce the mother's income by 30 percent to 50 percent—at which point there is little to be said in favor of welfare, from her point of view. There is, of course, the danger that she won't spend the money on the child. But that is true of the present system as well.

In addition, able-bodied men and mentally healthy men would have no entitlement whatever to welfare. If they are alcoholics or drug addicts or just allergic to responsibilities, they can rely on private charities. (Remember the Salvation Army.) The general rule has to be: If it is your own behavior that could land you on welfare, then you don't get it, or you get very little of it.

Such a reform of welfare as I am proposing will surely be denounced as cruel and "judgmental." It would indeed be cruel—and unfair, too—if all those currently on welfare, their situations and characters formed by the current system, were summarily incorporated in the new system. A "phasing out" procedure would have to be invented. But I would argue that it is crueler to entice people into the blind alley of welfare, where their very humanity is dissipated and degraded, than to sternly warn them off. In social policy, consequences ought always to trump intentions, however benign.

The "judgmental" issue, however, does get to the heart of the matter. A conservative welfare state should express conservative moral values, just as a liberal welfare state tries to impose liberal moral values upon us. It should discriminate in favor of satisfactory human results, not humane intentions. In the end, the American people will have ample political opportunity to decide what kind of society they wish to live in, what kind of welfare state they wish to live with. But they will never have such a choice if conservatives fail to offer them a conservative vision.

6. Bourgeois Critiques and Culture Wars

*T*he central tenet of the neoconservative case for capitalism is that it must be supported by the bourgeois virtues. During the 1980s and 1990s, the neoconservatives became concerned that the moral capital upon which the American system of democratic capitalism depends was being depleted. The neoconservatives turned their attention to the culture, and produced some of their richest and most important work.

Irving Kristol began this quest with what is perhaps his best known work, "Pornography, Obscenity and the Case for Censorship." James Q. Wilson's essay "The Rediscovery of Character: Private Virtue and Public Policy" describes how and why the rationalism of early neoconservatism gave way to an investigation of the deeper question of character and values. One of Wilson's most acclaimed articles, "Broken Windows: The Police and Neighborhood Safety," which he co-wrote with George Kelling, is a quintessential Wilsonian intellectual consideration of community life, merged with the larger ideas of public philosophy and the hard realities of social science. This essay has had a major impact on public policy, serving, for example, as a blueprint for the efforts of Mayor Rudolph Giuliani to combat street crime in New York City.

Leon Kass is a medical doctor, philosopher, and biblical scholar. His essay in this volume considers the biblical story of the rape of Dinah and *the lessons it has for relations between the sexes for Americans in the wake of the sexual revolution.*

In the summer of 1993, Senator Daniel Patrick Moynihan published "Defining Deviancy Down" in The American Scholar. *In that major essay, he illustrates how our conceptions of deviancy and normalcy have changed enormously in the past generation. Using several prominent examples in American culture, Moynihan illustrates how changes in our definitions of deviancy have had significant social consequences. Charles Krauthammer, building upon Moynihan's work, published "Defining Deviancy Up" several months later. He argues that Moynihan is correct, but captures only half of the story. While we have made the traditionally deviant normal in many ways, Krauthammer writes that just as much damage has been done by making the normal deviant. To understand the neoconservative diagnosis of the social crisis and intellectual dislocation facing modern American society, there is no better place to turn than these twin essays, published together for the first time in these pages.*

The Rediscovery of Character:
Private Virtue and Public Policy

James Q. Wilson

T HE MOST IMPORTANT CHANGE in how one defines the public interest that I have witnessed—and experienced—over the last twenty years has been a deepening concern for the development of character in the citizenry. An obvious indication of this shift has been the rise of such social issues as abortion and school prayer. A less obvious but I think more important change has been the growing awareness that a variety of public problems can only be understood—and perhaps addressed—if they are seen as arising out of a defect in character formation.

The Public Interest began publication at about the time that economics was becoming the preferred mode of policy analysis. Its very first issue contained an article by Daniel Patrick Moynihan hailing the triumph of macroeconomics: "Men are learning how to make an industrial economy work" as evidenced by the impressive ability of economists not only to predict economic events accurately but to control them by, for example, delivering on the promise of full employment. Six months later I published an essay suggesting that poverty be dealt with by direct income transfers in the form of a negative income tax or family allowances. In the next issue, James Tobin made a full-scale proposal for a negative income tax and Virginia Held welcomed program planning and budgeting to Washington as a means for rationalizing the allocative decisions of government, a topic enlarged upon the following year by a leading practitioner of applied economics, William Gorham. Meanwhile, Thomas C. Schelling had published a brilliant economic analysis of organized crime and Christopher Jencks a call for a voucher system that would allow parents to choose

Reprinted from The Public Interest *(Fall 1985).*

among public and private purveyors of education. In a later issue, Gordon Tullock explained the rise in crime as a consequence of individuals responding rationally to an increase in the net benefit of criminality.

There were criticisms of some of these views. Alvin L. Schorr, James C. Vadakian, and Nathan Glazer published essays in 1966, 1968, and 1969 attacking aspects of the negative income tax, and Aaron Wildavsky expressed his skepticism about program budgeting. But the criticisms themselves often accepted the economic assumptions of those being criticized. Schorr, for example, argued that the negative income tax was unworkable because it did not resolve the conflict between having a strong work incentive (and thus too small a payment to many needy individuals) and providing an adequate payment to the needy (and thus weakening the work incentive and making the total cost politically unacceptable). Schorr proposed instead a system of children's allowances and improved social security coverage, but he did not dissent from the view that the only thing wrong with poor people was that they did not have enough money and the conviction that they had a "right" to enough. Tobin was quick to point out that he and Schorr were on the same side, differing only in minor details.

A central assumption of economics is that "tastes" (which include what non-economists would call values and beliefs, as well as interests) can be taken as given and are not problematic. All that is interesting in human behavior is how it changes in response to changes in the costs and benefits of alternative courses of action. All that is necessary in public policy is to arrange the incentives confronting voters, citizens, firms, bureaucrats, and politicians so that they will behave in a socially optimal way. An optimal policy involves an efficient allocation—one that purchases the greatest amount of some good for a given cost, or minimizes the cost of a given amount of some good.

This view so accords with common sense in countless aspects of ordinary life that, for many purposes, its value is beyond dispute. Moreover, enough political decisions are manifestly so inefficient or rely so excessively on issuing commands (instead of arranging incentives) that very little harm and much good can be done by urging public officials to "think economically" about public policy. But over the last two decades, this nation has come face to face with problems that do not seem to respond, or respond enough, to changes in incentives. They do not respond, it seems, because the people whose behavior we wish to change do not have the right "tastes" or discount the future too heavily. To put it plainly, they lack character. Consider four areas of public policy: schooling, welfare, public finance, and crime.

Schooling

Nothing better illustrates the changes in how we think about policy than the problem of finding ways to improve educational attainment and student conduct in the schools. One of the first reports of the 1966 study on education by James Coleman and his associates appeared in this magazine. As every expert on schooling knows, that massive survey of public schools found that differences in the objective inputs to such schools—pupil-teacher ratios, the number of books in the library, per pupil expenditures, the age and quality of buildings—had no independent effect on student achievement as measured by standardized tests of verbal ability.

But as many scholars have forgotten, the Coleman Report also found that educational achievement was profoundly affected by the family background and peer-group environment of the pupil. And those who did notice this finding understandably despaired of devising a program that would improve the child's family background or social environment. Soon, many specialists had concluded that schools could make no difference in a child's life prospects, and so the burden of enhancing those prospects would have to fall on other measures. (To Christopher Jencks, the inability of the schools to reduce social inequality was an argument for socialism.)

Parents, of course, acted as if the Coleman Report had never been written. They sought, often at great expense, communities that had good schools, never doubting for a moment that they could tell the difference between good ones and bad ones or that this difference in school quality would make a difference in their child's education. The search for good schools in the face of evidence that there was no objective basis for that search seemed paradoxical, even irrational.

In 1979, however, Michael Rutter and his colleagues in England published a study that provided support for parental understanding by building on the neglected insights of the Coleman Report. In *Fifteen Thousand Hours,* the Rutter group reported what they learned from following a large number of children from a working-class section of inner London as they moved through a dozen non-selective schools in their community. Like Coleman before him, Rutter found that the objective features of the schools made little difference; like almost every other scholar, he found that differences in verbal intelligence at age ten were the best single predictor of educational attainment in the high school years. But unlike Coleman, he looked at differences in that attainment across schools, holding individual ability constant. Rutter found that the schools in inner London had very different effects on their pupils, not only in educational achievement but also in attendance, classroom behavior, and even delinquency. Some schools did a better job than others in teaching children and managing their behavior.

The more effective schools had two distinctive characteristics. First, they had a more balanced mix of children—that is, they contained a substantial number of children of at least average intellectual ability. By contrast, schools that were less effective had a disproportionate number of low-ability students. If you are a pupil of below average ability, you do better, both academically and behaviorally, if you attend a school with a large number of students who are somewhat abler than you. The intellectual abilities of the students, it turned out, were far more important than their ethnic or class characteristics in producing this desirable balance.

Second, the more effective schools had a distinctive ethos: an emphasis on academic achievement, the regular assignment of homework, the consistent and fair use of rewards (especially praise) to enforce generally agreed-upon standards of conduct, and energetic teacher involvement in directing classroom work. Subsequent research by others has generally confirmed the Rutter account, so much so that educational specialists are increasingly discussing what has come to be known as the "effective schools" model.

What is striking about the desirable school ethos is that it so obviously resembles what almost every developmental psychologist describes as the desirable family ethos. Parents who are warm and caring but who also use discipline in a fair and consistent manner are those parents who, other things being equal, are least likely to produce delinquent offspring. A decent family is one that instills a decent character in its children; a good school is one that takes up and continues in a constructive manner this development of character.

Teaching students with the right mix of abilities and in an atmosphere based on the appropriate classroom ethos may be easier in private than in public schools, a fact which helps explain why Coleman (joined now by Thomas Hoffer and Sally Kilgore) was able to suggest in the 1982 book, *High School Achievement*, that private and parochial high schools may do somewhat better than public ones in improving the vocabulary and mathematical skills of students and that this private-school advantage may be largely the result of the better behavior of children in those classrooms. In the authors' words, "achievement and discipline are intimately inter-twined." Public schools that combine academic demands and high disci-plinary standards produce greater educational achievement than public schools that do not. As it turns out, private and parochial schools are better able to sustain these desirable habits of work behavior—this greater dis-play of good character—than are public ones.

Welfare

Besides the Coleman Report, another famous document appeared at about the time this magazine was launched—the Moynihan Report on the prob-lems of the black family (officially, the U.S. Department of Labor docu-ment entitled *The Negro Family: The Case for National Action*). The storm of controversy that report elicited is well-known. Despite Moynihan's efforts to keep the issue alive by publishing in these pages several essays on the welfare problem in America, the entire subject of single-parent families in particular and black families in general became an occasion for the exchange of mutual recriminations instead of a topic of scientific inquiry and policy entrepreneurship. Serious scholarly work, if it existed at all, was driven underground, and policy makers were at pains to avoid the matter except, occasionally, under the guise of "welfare reform" which meant (if you were a liberal) raising the level of benefits or (if you were a conserva-tive) cutting them. By the end of the 1960s, almost everybody in Washing-ton had in this sense become a conservative; welfare reform, as Moynihan remarked, was dead.

Twenty years after the Moynihan Report, Moynihan himself could deliver at Harvard a lecture in which he repeated the observations he had made in 1965, but this time to an enthusiastic audience and widespread praise in the liberal media. At the same time, Glenn C. Loury, a black economist, could publish in these pages an essay in which he observed that almost everything Moynihan had said in 1965 had proved true except in one sense—today, single-parent families are twice as common as they were when Moynihan first called the matter to public attention. The very title of Loury's essay suggested how times had changed: Whereas leaders once spoke of "welfare reform" as if it were a problem of finding the most cost-effective way to distribute aid to needy families, Loury was now prepared to speak of it as "The Moral Quandary of the Black Community."

Two decades that could have been devoted to thought and experimentation had been frittered away. We are no closer today than we were in 1965 to understanding why black children are usually raised by one parent rather than by two or exactly what consequences, beyond the obvious fact that such families are very likely to be poor, follows from this pattern of family life. To the extent the matter was addressed at all, it was usually done by assuming that welfare payments provided an incentive for families to dissolve. To deal with this, some people embraced the negative income tax (or as President Nixon rechristened it, the Family Assistance Plan) because it would provide benefits to all poor families, broken or not, and thus remove incentive for dissolution.

There were good reasons to be somewhat skeptical of that view. If the system of payments under the program for Aid to Families of Dependent Children (AFDC) was to blame for the rise in single-parent families, why did the rise occur so dramatically among blacks but not to nearly the same extent among whites? If AFDC provided an incentive for men to beget children without assuming responsibility for supporting them, why was the illegitimacy rate rising even in states that did not require the father to be absent from the home for the family to obtain assistance? If AFDC created so perverse a set of incentives, why did these incentives have so large an effect in the 1960s and 1970s (when single-parent families were increasing by leaps and bounds) and so little, if any, such effect in the 1940s and 1950s (when such families scarcely increased at all)? And if AFDC were the culprit, how is it that poor, single-parent families rose in number during a decade (the 1970s) when the value of AFDC benefits in real dollars was declining?

Behavior does change with changes in incentives. The results of the negative income tax experiments certainly show that. In the Seattle and Denver experiments, the rate of family dissolution was much higher among families who received the guaranteed annual income than among similar families who did not—36 percent higher in the case of whites, 42 percent higher in the case of blacks. Men getting the cash benefits reduced their hours of work by 9 percent, women by 20 percent, and young males without families by 43 percent.

Charles Murray, whose 1984 book, *Losing Ground,* has done so much to focus attention on the problem of welfare, generally endorses the economic explanation for the decline of two-parent families. The evidence from the negative income tax experiments is certainly consistent with his view, and he makes a good case that the liberalization of welfare eligibility rules in the 1960s contributed to the sudden increase in the AFDC caseload. But as he is the first to admit, the data do not exist to offer a fully tested explanation of the rise of single-parent families; the best he can do is to offer a mental experiment showing how young, poor men and women might rationally respond to the alternative benefits of work for a two-parent family and welfare payments for a one-parent one. He rejects the notion that character, the *Zeitgeist,* or cultural differences are necessary to an explanation. But he cannot show that young, poor men and women in fact responded to AFDC as he assumes they did, nor can he explain the racial differences in rates or the rise in caseloads at a time of declining benefits. He notes an alternative explanation that cannot be ruled out: During the 1960s, a large number of persons who once thought of being on welfare as a temporary and rather embarrassing expedient came to regard it as a right that they would not be deterred from exercising. The result of that change can be measured: Whereas in 1967, 63 percent of the persons eligible for AFDC were on the rolls, by 1970 91 percent were.

In short, the character of a significant number of persons changed. To the extent one thinks that change was fundamentally wrong, then, as Loury has put it, the change creates a moral problem. What does one do about such a moral problem? Lawrence Mead has suggested invigorating the work requirement associated with welfare, so that anyone exercising a "right" to welfare will come to understand that there is a corresponding obligation. Murray has proposed altering the incentives by increasing the difficulty of getting welfare or the shame of having it so as to provide positive rewards for not having children, at least out of wedlock. But nobody has yet come to grips with how one might test a way of using either obligations or incentives to alter character so that people who once thought it good to sire or bear illegitimate children will now think it wrong.

Public Finance

We have a vast and rising governmental deficit. Amidst the debate about how one might best reduce that deficit (or more typically, reduce the rate of increase in it), scarcely anyone asks why we have not always had huge deficits.

If you believe that voters and politicians seek rationally to maximize their self-interest, then it would certainly be in the interest of most people to transfer wealth from future generations to present ones. If you want the federal government to provide you with some benefit and you cannot persuade other voters to pay for your benefit with higher taxes, then you should be willing to have the government borrow to pay for that benefit. Since every voter has something he would like from the government, each has an incentive to obtain that benefit with funds to be repaid by future generations. There are, of course, some constraints on unlimited debt financing. Accumulated debt charges from past generations must be financed by this generation, and if these charges are heavy there may well develop some apprehension about adding to them. If some units of government default on their loans, there are immediate economic consequences. But these constraints are not strong enough to inhibit more than marginally the rational desire to let one's grandchildren pay (in inflation-devalued dollars) the cost of present indulgences.

That being so, why is it that large deficits, except in wartime, have been a feature of public finance only in the past few decades? What kept voters and politicians from buying on credit heavily and continuously beginning with the first days of the republic?

James M. Buchanan, in his 1984 presidential address to the Western Economic Association, has offered one explanation for this paradox. He has suggested that public finance was once subject to a moral constraint—namely, that it was right to pay as you go and accumulate capital and wrong to borrow heavily and squander capital. Max Weber, of course, had earlier argued that essential to the rise of capitalism was a widely shared belief (he ascribed it to Protestantism) in the moral propriety of deferring present consumption for future benefits. Buchanan has recast this somewhat: He argues that a Victorian morality inhibited Anglo-American democracies from giving in to their selfish desire to beggar their children.

Viewed in this way, John Maynard Keynes was not simply an important economist, he was a moral revolutionary. He subjected to rational analysis the conventional restraints on deficit financing, not in order to show that debt was always good but to prove that it was not necessarily bad. Deficit financing should be judged, he argued, by its practical effect, not by its moral quality.

Buchanan is a free-market economist, and thus a member of a group not ordinarily given to explaining behavior in any terms other than the pursuit of self-interest narrowly defined. This fact makes all the more significant his argument that economic analysts must understand "how morals impact on choice, and especially how an erosion of moral precepts can modify the established functioning of economic and political institutions."

A rejoinder can be made to the Buchanan explanation of deficit financing. Much of the accumulated debt is a legacy of having fought wars, a legacy that can be justified on both rational and moral grounds (who wishes to lose a war, or to leave for one's children a Europe dominated by Hitler?). Another part of the debt exists because leaders miscalculated the true costs of desirable programs. According to projections made in 1965, Medicare was supposed to cost less than $9 billion a year in 1990; in 1985, the bill was already running in excess of $70 billion a year. Military pensions seemed the right thing to do when men were being called to service; only in retrospect is their total cost appreciated. The Reagan tax cuts were not designed to impose heavy debts on our children but to stimulate investment and economic growth; only later did it become obvious that they have contributed far more to the deficit than to economic growth. The various subsidies given to special interest groups long seemed like a small price to pay for insuring the support of a heterogeneous people for a distant government; no one could have foreseen their cumulative burden.

No doubt there is some truth in the proposition that our current level of debt is the result of miscalculation and good intentions gone awry. But what strengthens Buchanan's argument, I believe, is the direction of these miscalculations (if that is what they were) and the nature of these good intentions. In almost every instance, leaders proposing a new policy erred in the direction of understating rather than overstating future costs; in almost every instance, evidence of a good intention was taken to be government action rather than inaction. Whether one wishes to call it a shift in moral values or not, one must be struck by the systematic and consistent bias in how we debated public programs beginning in the 1930s but especially in the 1960s. It is hard to remember it now, but there once was a time, lasting from 1789 to well into the 1950s, when the debate over almost any new proposal was about whether it was *legitimate* for the government to do this at all. These were certainly the terms in which Social Security, civil rights, Medicare, and government regulation of business were first addressed. By the 1960s, the debate was much different: how much should we spend (not, should we spend anything at all); how can a policy be made cost-effective (not, should we have such a policy in the first place). The character of public discourse changed and I suspect in ways that suggest a change in the nature of public character.

Crime

I have written more about crime than any other policy issue, and so my remarks on our changing understanding of this problem are to a large degree remarks about changes in my own way of thinking about it. On no subject have the methods of economics and policy analysis had greater or more salutary effect than on scholarly discussions of criminal justice. For purposes of designing public policies, it has proved useful to think of would-be offenders as mostly young males who compare the net benefits of crime with those of work and leisure. Such thinking, and the rather considerable body of evidence that supports it, leads us to expect that changes in the net benefits of crime affect the level of crime in society. To the extent that policy makers and criminologists have become less hostile to the idea of altering behavior by altering its consequences, progress has been made. Even if the amount by which crime is reduced by these measures is modest (as I think in a free society it will be), the pursuit of these policies conforms more fully than does the rehabilitative idea to our concept of justice—namely, that each person should receive his due.

But long-term changes in crime rates exceed anything that can be explained by either rational calculation or the varying proportion of young males in the population. Very little in either contemporary economics or conventional criminology equips us to understand the decline in reported crime rates during the second half of the nineteenth century and the first part of the twentieth despite rapid industrialization and urbanization, a large influx of poor immigrants, the growing ethnic heterogeneity of society, and widening class cleavages. Very little in the customary language of policy analysis helps us explain why Japan should have such abnormally low crime rates despite high population densities, a history that glorifies samurai violence, a rather permissive pattern of child-rearing, the absence of deep religious convictions, and the remarkably low ratio of police officers to citizens.

In an essay in this magazine in 1983 I attempted to explain the counterintuitive decline in crime during the period after the Civil War in much the same terms that David H. Bayley had used in a 1976 article dealing with crime in Japan. In both cases, distinctive cultural forces helped restrain individual self-expression. In Japan, these forces subject an individual to the informal social controls of family and neighbors by making him extremely sensitive to the good opinion of others. The controls are of long standing and have so far remained largely intact despite the individualizing tendencies of modernization. In the United States, by contrast, these cultural forces have operated only in certain periods, and when they were effective it was as a result of a herculean effort by scores of voluntary associations specially created for the purpose.

In this country as well as in England, a variety of enterprises—Sunday schools, public schools, temperance movements, religious revivals, YMCAs, the Children's Aid Society—were launched in the first half of the nineteenth century that had in common the goal of instilling a "self-activating, self-regulating, all-purpose inner control." The objects of these efforts were those young men who, freed from the restraints of family life on the farms, had moved to the boardinghouses of the cities in search of economic opportunities. We lack any reliable measure of the effect of these efforts, save one—the extraordinary reduction in the per capita consumption of alcoholic beverages that occurred between 1830 (when the temperance efforts began in earnest) and 1850 and that persisted (despite an upturn during and just after the Civil War) for the rest of the century.

We now refer to this period as one in which "Victorian morality" took hold; the term itself, at least as now employed, reflects the condescension in which that ethos has come to be regarded. Modernity, as I have argued elsewhere, involves, at least in elite opinion, replacing the ethic of self-control with that of self-expression. Some great benefits have flowed from this change, including the liberation of youthful energies to pursue new ideas in art, music, literature, politics, and economic enterprise. But the costs are just as real, at least for those young persons who have not already acquired a decent degree of self-restraint and other-regardingness.

The view that crime has social and cultural as well as economic causes is scarcely new. Hardly any layperson, and only a few scholars, would deny that family and neighborhood affect individual differences in criminality. But what of it? How, as I asked in 1974, might a government remake bad families into good ones, especially if it must be done on a large scale? How might the government of a free society reshape the core values of its people and still leave them free?

They were good questions then and they remain good ones today. In 1974 there was virtually no reliable evidence that any program seeking to prevent crime by changing attitudes and values had succeeded for any large number of persons. In 1974 I could only urge policy makers to postpone the effort to eliminate the root causes of crime in favor of using those available policy instruments—target hardening, job training, police deployment, court sentences—that might have a marginal effect at a reasonable cost on the commission of crime. Given what we knew then and know now, acting as if crime is the result of individuals freely choosing among competing alternatives may be the best we can do.

In retrospect, nothing I have written about crime so dismayed some criminologists as this preference for doing what is possible rather than attempting what one wishes were possible. My purpose was to substitute the experimental method for personal ideology; this effort has led some people to suspect I was really trying to substitute my ideology for theirs. Though we all have beliefs that color our views, I would hope that everybody would try to keep that coloration under control by constant reference to the test of practical effect. What works?

With time and experience we have learned a bit more about what works. There are now some glimmers of hope that certain experimental projects aimed at preparing children for school and equipping parents to cope with unruly offspring may reduce the rate at which these youngsters later commit delinquent acts. Richard J. Herrnstein and I have written about these and related matters in *Crime and Human Nature*. Whether further tests and repeated experiments will confirm that these glimmers emanate from the mother lode of truth and not from fool's gold, no one can yet say. But we know how to find out. If we discover that these ideas can be made to work on a large scale (and not just in the hands of a few gifted practitioners), then we will be able to reduce crime by, in effect, improving character.

Character and Policy

The traditional understanding of politics was that its goal was to improve the character of its citizens. The American republic was, as we know, founded on a very different understanding—that of taking human nature pretty much as it was and hoping that personal liberty could survive political action if ambition were made to counteract ambition. The distinctive nature of the American system has led many of its supporters (to say nothing of its critics) to argue that it should be indifferent to character formation. Friend and foe alike are fond of applying to government Samuel

Goldwyn's response to the person who asked what message was to be found in his films: If you want to send a message, use Western Union.

Since I yield to no one in my admiration for what the Founders created, I do not wish to argue the fundamental proposition. But the federal government today is very different from what it was in 1787, 1887, or even 1957. If we wish it to address the problems of family disruption, welfare dependency, crime in the streets, educational inadequacy, or even public finance properly understood, then government, by the mere fact that it defines these states of affairs as problems, acknowledges that human character is, in some degree, defective and that it intends to alter it. The local governments of village and township always understood this, of course, because they always had responsibility for shaping character. The public school movement, for example, was from the beginning chiefly aimed at moral instruction. The national government could afford to manage its affairs by letting ambition counteract ambition because what was originally at stake in national affairs—creating and maintaining a reasonably secure commercial regime—lent itself naturally to the minimal attentions of a limited government operated and restrained by the reciprocal force of mutual self-interest.

It is easier to acknowledge the necessary involvement of government in character formation than it is to prescribe how this responsibility should be carried out. The essential first step is to acknowledge that at root, in almost every area of important public concern, we are seeking to induce persons to act virtuously, whether as schoolchildren, applicants for public assistance, would-be lawbreakers, or voters and public officials. Not only is such conduct desirable in its own right, it appears now to be necessary if large improvements are to be made in those matters we consider problems: schooling, welfare, crime, and public finance.

By virtue, I mean habits of moderate action; more specifically, acting with due restraint on one's impulses, due regard for the rights of others, and reasonable concern for distant consequences. Scarcely anyone favors bad character or a lack of virtue, but it is all too easy to deride a policy of improving character by assuming that this implies a nation of moralizers delivering banal homilies to one another.

Virtue is not learned by precept, however; it is learned by the regular repetition of right actions. We are induced to do the right thing with respect to small matters, and in time we persist in doing the right thing because now we have come to take pleasure in it. By acting rightly with respect to small things, we are more likely to act rightly with respect to large ones. If this view sounds familiar, it should; it is Aristotle's. Let me now quote him directly: "We become just by the practice of just actions, self-controlled by exercising self-control."

Seen in this way, there is no conflict between economic thought and moral philosophy: The latter simply supplies a fuller statement of the uses to which the former can and should be put. We want our families and schools to induce habits of right conduct; most parents and teachers do this by arranging the incentives confronting youngsters in the ordinary aspects of their daily lives so that right action routinely occurs.

What economics neglects is the important subjective consequence of acting in accord with a proper array of incentives: people come to feel pleasure in right action and guilt in wrong action. These feelings of pleasure and pain are not mere "tastes" that policy analysts should take as given; they are the central constraints on human avarice and sloth, the very core of a decent character. A course of action cannot be evaluated simply in terms of its cost-effectiveness, because the consequence of following a given course—if it is followed often enough and regularly enough—is to teach those who follow it what society thinks is right and wrong.

Conscience and character, naturally, are not enough. Rules and rewards must still be employed; indeed, given the irresistible appeal of certain courses of action—such as impoverishing future generations for the benefit of the present one—only some rather draconian rules may suffice. But for most social problems that deeply trouble us, the need is to explore, carefully and experimentally, ways of strengthening the formation of character among the very young. In the long run, the public interest depends on private virtue.

Pornography, Obscenity, and the Case for Censorship

Irving Kristol

BEING FRUSTRATED IS DISAGREEABLE, but the real disasters in life begin when you get what you want. For almost a century now, a great many intelligent, well-meaning, and articulate people—of a kind generally called liberal or intellectual, or both—have argued eloquently against any kind of censorship of art and/or entertainment. And within the past ten years, the courts and the legislatures of most Western nations have found these arguments persuasive—so persuasive that hardly a man is now alive who clearly remembers what the answers to these arguments were. Today, in the United States and other democracies, censorship has to all intents and purposes ceased to exist.

Is there a sense of triumphant exhilaration in the land? Hardly. There is, on the contrary, a rapidly growing unease and disquiet. Somehow, things have not worked out as they were supposed to, and many notable civil libertarians have gone on record as saying this was not what they meant at all. They wanted a world in which *Desire under the Elms* could be produced, or *Ulysses* published, without interference by philistine busybodies holding public office. They have got that, of course; but they have also got a world in which homosexual rape takes place on the stage, in which the public flocks during lunch hours to witness varieties of professional fornication, in which Times Square has become little more than a hideous market for the sale and distribution of printed filth that panders to all known (and some fanciful) sexual perversions.

But disagreeable as this may be, does it really matter? Might not our unease and disquiet be merely a cultural hangover—a "hang-up," as they say? What reason is there to think that anyone was ever corrupted by a book?

This last question, oddly enough, is asked by the very same people

Reprinted from the New York Times Magazine, *March 28, 1971.*

who seem convinced that advertisements in magazines or displays of violence on television do indeed have the power to corrupt. It is also asked, incredibly enough and in all sincerity, by people—for example, university professors and schoolteachers—whose very lives provide all the answers one could want. After all, if you believe that no one was ever corrupted by a book, you have also to believe that no one was ever improved by a book (or a play or a movie). You have to believe, in other words, that all art is morally trivial and that, consequently, all education is morally irrelevant. No one, not even a university professor, really believes that.

To be sure, it is extremely difficult, as social scientists tell us, to trace the effects of any single book (or play or movie) on an individual reader or any class of readers. But we all know, and social scientists know it too, that the ways in which we use our minds and imaginations do shape our characters and help define us as persons. That those who certainly know this are nevertheless moved to deny it merely indicates how a dogmatic resistance to the idea of censorship can—like most dogmatism—result in a mindless insistence on the absurd.

I have used these harsh terms—"dogmatism" and "mindless"—advisedly. I might also have added "hypocritical." For the plain fact is that none of us is a complete civil libertarian. We all believe that there is some point at which the public authorities ought to step in to limit the "self-expression" of an individual or a group, even where this might be seriously intended as a form of artistic expression, and even where the artistic transaction is between consenting adults. A playwright or theatrical director might, in this crazy world of ours, find someone willing to commit suicide on the stage, as called for by the script. We would not allow that—any more than we would permit scenes of real physical torture on the stage, even if the victim were a willing masochist. And I know of no one, no matter how free in spirit, who argues that we ought to permit gladiatorial contests in Yankee Stadium, similar to those once performed in the Colosseum at Rome—even if only consenting adults were involved.

The basic point that emerges is one that Walter Berns has powerfully argued: No society can be utterly indifferent to the ways its citizens publicly entertain themselves.* Bearbaiting and cockfighting are prohibited

---

* This is as good a place as any to express my profound indebtedness to Walter Berns's superb essay "Pornography vs. Democracy," in the Winter 1971 issue of *The Public Interest*.

only in part out of compassion for the suffering animals; the main reason they were abolished was because it was felt that they debased and brutalized the citizenry who flocked to witness such spectacles. And the question we face with regard to pornography and obscenity is whether, now that they have such strong legal protection from the Supreme Court, they can or will brutalize and debase our citizenry. We are, after all, not dealing with one passing incident—one book, or one play, or one movie. We are dealing with a general tendency that is suffusing our entire culture.

I say pornography *and* obscenity because, though they have different dictionary definitions and are frequently distinguishable as "artistic" genres, they are nevertheless in the end identical in effect. Pornography is not objectionable simply because it arouses sexual desire or lust or prurience in the mind of the reader or spectator; this is a silly Victorian notion. A great many nonpornographic works—including some parts of the Bible—excite sexual desire very successfully. What is distinctive about pornography is that, in the words of D. H. Lawrence, it attempts "to do dirt on [sex]. . . . [It is an] insult to a vital human relationship."

In other words, pornography differs from erotic art in that its whole purpose is to treat human beings obscenely, to deprive human beings of their specifically human dimension. That is what obscenity is all about. It is light years removed from any kind of carefree sensuality—there is no continuum between Fielding's *Tom Jones* and the Marquis de Sade's *Justine*. These works have quite opposite intentions. To quote Susan Sontag: "What pornographic literature does is precisely to drive a wedge between one's existence as a full human being and one's existence as a sexual being—while in ordinary life a healthy person is one who prevents such a gap from opening up." This definition occurs in an essay *defending* pornography—Miss Sontag is a candid as well as gifted critic—so the definition, which I accept, is neither tendentious nor censorious.

Along these same lines, one can point out—as C. S. Lewis pointed out some years back—that it is no accident that in the history of all literatures obscene words, the so-called four-letter words, have always been the vocabulary of farce or vituperation. The reason is clear; they reduce men and women to some of their mere bodily functions—they reduce man to his animal component, and such a reduction is an essential purpose of farce or vituperation.

Similarly, Lewis also suggested that it is not an accident that we have no offhand, colloquial, neutral terms—not in any Western European language at any rate—for our most private parts. The words we do use are either (1) nursery terms, (2) archaisms, (3) scientific terms, or (4) a term from the gutter (i.e., a demeaning term). Here I think the genius of language is telling us something important about man. It is telling us that man is an animal with a difference: He has a unique sense of privacy, and a unique capacity for shame when this privacy is violated. Our "private parts" are indeed private, and not merely because convention prescribes it. This particular convention is indigenous to the human race. In practically all primitive tribes, men and women cover their private parts; and in practically all primitive tribes, men and women do not copulate in public.

It may well be that Western society, in the latter half of the twentieth century, is experiencing a drastic change in sexual mores and sexual relationships. We have had many such "sexual revolutions" in the past—the bourgeois family and bourgeois ideas of sexual propriety were themselves established in the course of a revolution against eighteenth-century "licentiousness"—and we shall doubtless have others in the future. It is, however, highly improbable (to put it mildly) that what we are witnessing is the Final Revolution which will make sexual relations utterly unproblematic, permit us to dispense with any kind of ordered relationships between the sexes, and allow us freely to redefine the human condition. And so long as humanity has not reached that utopia, obscenity will remain a problem.

One of the reasons it will remain a problem is that obscenity is not merely about sex, any more than science fiction is about science. Science fiction, as every student of the genre knows, is a peculiar vision of power: What it is really about is politics. And obscenity is a peculiar vision of humanity: What it is really about is ethics and metaphysics.

Imagine a man—a well-known man, much in the public eye—in a hospital ward, dying an agonizing death. He is not in control of his bodily functions, so that his bladder and his bowels empty themselves of their own accord. His consciousness is overwhelmed and extinguished by pain, so that he cannot communicate with us, nor we with him. Now, it would be, technically, the easiest thing in the world to put a television camera in his hospital room and let the whole world witness this spectacle. We do not do it—at least we do not do it as yet—because we regard this as an *obscene* invasion of privacy. And what would make the spectacle obscene is that we would be witnessing the extinguishing of humanity in a human animal.

Incidentally, in the past our humanitarian crusaders against capital punishment understood this point very well. The abolitionist literature goes into great physical detail about what happens to a man when he is hanged or electrocuted or gassed. And their argument was—and is—that what happens is shockingly obscene, and that no civilized society should be responsible for perpetrating such obscenities, particularly since in the nature of the case there must be spectators to ascertain that this horror was indeed being perpetrated in fulfillment of the law.

Sex—like death—is an activity that is both animal and human. There are human sentiments and human ideals involved in this animal activity. But when sex is public, the viewer does not see—cannot see—the sentiments and the ideals. He can only see the animal coupling. And that is why, when men and women make love, as we say, they prefer to be alone—because it is only when you are alone that you can make love, as distinct from merely copulating in an animal and casual way. And that, too, is why those who are voyeurs, if they are not irredeemably sick, also feel ashamed at what they are witnessing. When sex is a public spectacle, a human relationship has been debased into a mere animal connection.

It is also worth noting that this making of sex into an obscenity is not a mutual and equal transaction but rather an act of exploitation by one of the partners—the male partner. I do not wish to get into the complicated question as to what, if any, are the essential differences—as distinct from conventional and cultural differences—between male and female. I do not claim to know the answer to that. But I do know—and I take it as a sign that has meaning—that pornography is, and always has been, a man's work; that women rarely write pornography; and that women tend to be indifferent consumers of pornography.* My own guess, by way of explanation, is that a woman's sexual experience is ordinarily more suffused with human emotion than is man's, that men are more easily satisfied with autoerotic activities, and that men can therefore more easily take a more "technocratic" view of sex and its pleasures. Perhaps this is not correct. But whatever the explanation, there can be no question that pornography is a form of "sexism," as the women's liberation movement calls it, and that the instinct of women's liberation has been unerring in perceiving that when

---

* There are, of course, a few exceptions. *L'Histoire d'O*, for instance, was written by a woman. It is unquestionably the most *melancholy* work of pornography ever written. And its theme is precisely the dehumanization accomplished by obscenity.

pornography is perpetrated, it is perpetrated against them, as part of a conspiracy to deprive them of their full humanity.

But even if all this is granted, it might be said—and doubtless will be said—that I really ought not to be unduly concerned. Free competition in the cultural marketplace—it is argued by people who have never otherwise had a kind word to say for laissez-faire—will automatically dispose of the problem. The present fad for pornography and obscenity, it will be asserted, is just that, a fad. It will spend itself in the course of time; people will get bored with it, will be able to take it or leave it alone in a casual way, in a "mature way," and, in sum, I am being unnecessarily distressed about the whole business. The *New York Times,* in an editorial, concludes hopefully in this vein.

> In the end . . . the insensate pursuit of the urge to shock, carried from one excess to a more abysmal one, is bound to achieve its own antidote in total boredom. When there is no lower depth to descend to, ennui will erase the problem.

I would like to be able to go along with this line of reasoning, but I cannot. I think it is false, and for two reasons, the first psychological, the second political.

The basic psychological fact about pornography and obscenity is that it appeals to and provokes a kind of sexual regression. The sexual pleasure one gets from pornography and obscenity is autoerotic and infantile; put bluntly, it is a masturbatory exercise of the imagination, when it is not masturbation pure and simple. Now, people who masturbate do not get bored with masturbation, just as sadists do not get bored with sadism, and voyeurs do not get bored with voyeurism.

In other words, infantile sexuality is not only a permanent temptation for the adolescent or even the adult—it can quite easily become a permanent, self-reinforcing neurosis. It is because of an awareness of this possibility of regression toward the infantile condition, a regression which is always open to us, that all the codes of sexual conduct ever devised by the human race take such a dim view of autoerotic activities and try to discourage autoerotic fantasies. Masturbation is indeed a perfectly natural autoerotic activity, as so many sexologists blandly assure us today. And it is precisely because it is so perfectly natural that it can be so dangerous to the mature or maturing person, if it is not controlled or sublimated in some way. That is the true meaning of Portnoy's complaint. Portnoy, you will recall, grows up to be a man who is incapable of having an adult sexual relationship with a woman; his sexuality remains fixed in an infantile mode, the prisoner of his autoerotic fantasies. Inevitably, Portnoy comes to think, in a perfectly *infantile* way, that it was all his mother's fault.

It is true that, in our time, some quite brilliant minds have come to the conclusion that a reversion to infantile sexuality is the ultimate mission and secret destiny of the human race. I am thinking in particular of Norman O. Brown, for whose writings I have the deepest respect. One of the reasons I respect them so deeply is that Mr. Brown is a serious thinker who is unafraid to face up to the radical consequences of his radical theories. Thus, Mr. Brown knows and says that for his kind of salvation to be achieved, humanity must annul the civilization it has created—not merely the civilization we have today, but all civilization—so as to be able to make the long descent backward into animal innocence.

And that is the point. What is at stake is civilization and humanity, nothing less. The idea that "everything is permitted," as Nietzsche put it, rests on the premise of nihilism and has nihilistic implications. I will not pretend that the case against nihilism and for civilization is an easy one to make. We are here confronting the most fundamental of philosophical questions, on the deepest levels. In short, the matter of pornography and obscenity is not a trivial one, and only superficial minds can take a bland and untroubled view of it.

In this connection, I must also point out, those who are primarily against censorship on liberal grounds tell us not to take pornography or obscenity seriously; while those who are for pornography and obscenity on radical grounds take it very seriously indeed. I believe the radicals—writers like Susan Sontag, Herbert Marcuse, Norman O. Brown, and even Jerry Rubin—are right, and the liberals are wrong. I also believe that those young radicals at Berkeley, some seven years ago, who provoked a major confrontation over the public use of obscene words, showed a brilliant political instinct. And once Mark Rudd could publicly ascribe to the president of Columbia a notoriously obscene relationship to his mother, without provoking any kind of reaction, the SDS [Students for a Democratic Society] had already won the day. The occupation of Columbia's buildings merely ratified their victory. Men who show themselves unwilling to defend civilization against nihilism are not going to be either resolute or effective in defending the university against anything.

I am already touching upon a political aspect of pornography when I suggest that it is inherently and purposefully subversive of civilization and its institutions. But there is another and more specifically political aspect, which has to do with the relationship of pornography and/or obscenity to democracy, and especially to the quality of public life on which democratic government ultimately rests.

Though the phrase "the quality of life" trips easily from so many lips these days, it tends to be one of those clichés with many trivial meanings and no large, serious one. Sometimes it merely refers to such externals as the enjoyment of cleaner air, cleaner water, cleaner streets. At other times it refers to the merely private enjoyment of music, painting, or literature. Rarely does it have anything to do with the way the citizen in a democracy views himself—his obligations, his intentions, his ultimate self-definition.

Instead, what I would call the "managerial" conception of democracy is the predominant opinion among political scientists, sociologists, and economists, and has, through the untiring efforts of these scholars, become the conventional journalistic opinion as well. The root idea behind this managerial conception is that democracy is a "political system" (as they say) which can be adequately defined in terms of—can be fully reduced to—its mechanical arrangements. Democracy is then seen as a set of rules and procedures, and *nothing but* a set of rules and procedures, whereby majority rule and minority rights are reconciled into a state of equilibrium. If everyone follows these rules and procedures, then a democracy is in working order. I think this is a fair description of the democratic idea that currently prevails in academia. One can also fairly say that it is now the liberal idea of democracy par excellence.

I cannot help but feel that there is something ridiculous about being this kind of a democrat, and I must further confess to having a sneaking sympathy for those of our young radicals who also find it ridiculous. The absurdity is the absurdity of idolatry—of taking the symbolic for the real, the means for the end. The purpose of democracy cannot possibly be the endless functioning of its own political machinery. The purpose of any political regime is to achieve some version of the good life and the good society. It is not at all difficult to imagine a perfectly functioning democracy which answers all questions except one—namely, why should anyone of intelligence and spirit care a fig for it?

There is, however, an older idea of democracy—one which was fairly common until about the beginning of this century—for which the conception of the quality of public life is absolutely crucial. This idea starts from the proposition that democracy is a form of self-government, and that if you want it to be a meritorious polity, you have to care about what kind of people govern it. Indeed, it puts the matter more strongly and declares that if you want self-government, you are only entitled to it if that "self" is worthy of governing. There is no inherent right to self-government if it means that such government is vicious, mean, squalid, and debased. Only a dogmatist and a fanatic, an idolater of democratic machinery, could approve of self-government under such conditions.

And because the desirability of self-government depends on the character of the people who govern, the older idea of democracy was very solicitous of the condition of this character. It was solicitous of the individual self, and felt an obligation to educate it into what used to be called "republican virtue." And it was solicitous of that collective self which we call public opinion and which, in a democracy, governs us collectively. Perhaps in some respects it was nervously oversolicitous—that would not be surprising. But the main thing is that it cared, cared not merely about the machinery of democracy but about the quality of life that this machinery might generate.

And because it cared, this older idea of democracy had no problem in principle with pornography and/or obscenity. It censored them—and it did so with a perfect clarity of mind and a perfectly clear conscience. It was not about to permit people capriciously to corrupt themselves. Or, to put it more precisely: In this version of democracy, the people took some care not to let themselves be governed by the more infantile and irrational parts of themselves.

I have, it may be noticed, uttered that dreadful word censorship. And I am not about to back away from it. If you think pornography and/or obscenity is a serious problem, you have to be for censorship. I will go even further and say that if you want to prevent pornography and/or obscenity from becoming a problem, you have to be for censorship. And lest there be any misunderstanding as to what I am saying, I will put it as bluntly as possible: If you care for the quality of life in our American democracy, then you have to be for censorship.

But can a liberal be for censorship? Unless one assumes that being a liberal *must* mean being indifferent to the quality of American life, then the answer has to be yes, a liberal can be for censorship—but he ought to favor a liberal form of censorship.

Is that a contradiction in terms? I do not think so. We have no problem in contrasting *repressive* laws governing alcohol and drugs and tobacco with laws *regulating* (i.e., discouraging the sale of) alcohol and drugs and tobacco. Laws encouraging temperance are not the same thing as laws that have as their goal prohibition or abolition. We have not made the smoking of cigarettes a criminal offense. We have, however, and with good liberal conscience, prohibited cigarette advertising on television, and may yet, again with good liberal conscience, prohibit it in newspapers and magazines. The idea of restricting individual freedom, in a liberal way, is not at all unfamiliar to us.

I therefore see no reason why we should not be able to distinguish repressive censorship from liberal censorship of the written and spoken word. In Britain, until a few years ago, you could perform almost any play you wished, but certain plays, judged to be obscene, had to be performed in private theatrical clubs, which were deemed to have a "serious" interest in theater. In the United States, all of us who grew up using public libraries are familiar with the circumstances under which certain books could be circulated only to adults, while still other books had to be read in the library reading room, under the librarian's skeptical eye. In both cases, a small minority that was willing to make a serious effort to see an obscene play or read an obscene book could do so. But the impact of obscenity was circumscribed and the quality of public life was only marginally affected.*

I am not saying it is easy in practice to sustain a distinction between liberal and repressive censorship, especially in the public realm of a democracy, where popular opinion is so vulnerable to demagoguery. Moreover, an acceptable system of liberal censorship is likely to be exceedingly difficult to devise in the United States today, because our educated classes, upon whose judgment a liberal censorship must rest, are so convinced that there is no such thing as a problem of obscenity, or even that there is no such thing as obscenity at all. But, to counterbalance this, there is the further, fortunate truth that the tolerable margin for error is quite large, and single mistakes or single injustices are not all that important.

This possibility of error, of course, occasions much distress among artists and academics. It is a fact, one that cannot and should not be denied,

---

* It is fairly predictable that someone is going to object that this point of view is "elitist"—that, under a system of liberal censorship, the rich will have privileged access to pornography and obscenity. Yes, of course, they will—just as, at present, the rich have privileged access to heroin if they want it. But one would have to be an egalitarian maniac to object to this state of affairs on the grounds of equality.

that any system of censorship is bound, upon occasion, to treat unjustly a particular work of art—to find pornography where there is only gentle eroticism, to find obscenity where none really exists, or to find both where its existence ought to be tolerated because it serves a larger moral purpose. Though most works of art are not obscene, and though most obscenity has nothing to do with art, there are some few works of art that are, at least in part, pornographic and/or obscene. There are also some few works of art that are in the special category of the comic-ironic "bawdy" (Boccaccio, Rabelais). It is such works of art that are likely to suffer at the hands of the censor. That is the price one has to be prepared to pay for censorship—even liberal censorship.

But just how high is this price? If you believe, as so many artists seem to believe today, that art is the only sacrosanct activity in our profane and vulgar world—that any man who designates himself an artist thereby acquires a sacred office—then obviously censorship is an intolerable form of sacrilege. But for those of us who do not subscribe to this religion of art, the costs of censorship do not seem so high at all.

If you look at the history of American or English literature, there is precious little damage you can point to as a consequence of the censorship that prevailed throughout most of that history. Very few works of literature—of real literary merit, I mean—ever were suppressed; and those that were, were not suppressed for long. Nor have I noticed, now that censorship of the written word has to all intents and purposes ceased in this country, that hitherto suppressed or repressed masterpieces are flooding the market. Yes, we can now read *Fanny Hill* and the Marquis de Sade. Or, to be more exact, we can now openly purchase them, since many people were able to read them even though they were publicly banned, which is as it should be under a liberal censorship. So how much have literature and the arts gained from the fact that we can all now buy them over the counter, that, indeed, we are all now encouraged to buy them over the counter? They have not gained much that I can see.

And one might also ask a question that is almost never raised: How much has literature lost from the fact that everything is now permitted? It has lost quite a bit, I should say. In a free market, Gresham's Law can work for books or theater as efficiently as it does for coinage—driving out the good, establishing the debased. The cultural market in the United States today is being preempted by dirty books, dirty movies, dirty theater. A pornographic novel has a far better chance of being published today than a nonpornographic one, and quite a few pretty good novels are not being published at all simply because they are not pornographic, and are therefore less likely to sell. Our cultural condition has not improved as a result of the new freedom. American cultural life was not much to brag about twenty years ago; today one feels ashamed for it.

Just one last point, which I dare not leave untouched. If we start censoring pornography or obscenity, shall we not inevitably end up censoring political opinion? A lot of people seem to think this would be the case—which only shows the power of doctrinaire thinking over reality. We had censorship of pornography and obscenity for 150 years, until almost yesterday, and I am not aware that freedom of opinion in this country was in any way diminished as a consequence of this fact. Fortunately for those of us who are liberal, freedom is not indivisible. If it were, the case for liberalism would be indistinguishable from the case for anarchy; and they are two very different things.

But I must repeat and emphasize: What kinds of laws we pass governing pornography and obscenity, what kind of censorship—or, since we are still a federal nation, what kinds of censorship—we institute in our various localities may indeed be difficult matters to cope with; nevertheless the real issue is one of principle. I myself subscribe to a liberal view of the enforcement problem: I think that pornography should be illegal *and* available to anyone who wants it so badly as to make a pretty strenuous effort to get it. We have lived with under-the-counter pornography for centuries now, in a fairly comfortable way. But the issue of principle, of whether it should be over or under the counter, has to be settled before we can reflect on the advantages and disadvantages of alternative modes of censorship. I think the settlement we are living under now, in which obscenity and democracy are regarded as equals, is wrong; I believe it is inherently unstable; I think it will, in the long run, be incompatible with any authentic concern for the quality of life in our democracy.

Broken Windows: The Police and Neighborhood Safety

James Q. Wilson and George L. Kelling

*I*N THE MID-1970s, the state of New Jersey announced a "Safe and Clean Neighborhoods Program," designed to improve the quality of community life in twenty-eight cities. As part of that program, the state provided money to help cities take police officers out of their patrol cars and assign them to walking beats. The governor and other state officials were enthusiastic about using foot patrol as a way of cutting crime, but many police chiefs were skeptical. Foot patrol, in their eyes, had been pretty much discredited. It reduced the mobility of the police, who thus had difficulty responding to citizen calls for service, and it weakened headquarters control over patrol officers.

Many police officers also disliked foot patrol, but for different reasons: it was hard work, it kept them outside on cold, rainy nights, and it reduced their chances for making a "good pinch." In some departments, assigning officers to foot patrol had been used as a form of punishment. And academic experts on policing doubted that foot patrol would have any impact on crime rates; it was, in the opinion of most, little more than a sop to public opinion. But since the state was paying for it, the local authorities were willing to go along.

Five years after the program started, the Police Foundation, in Washington, D.C., published an evaluation of the foot-patrol project. Based on its analysis of a carefully controlled experiment carried out chiefly in Newark, the foundation concluded, to the surprise of hardly anyone, that foot patrol had not reduced crime rates. But residents of the foot-patrolled neighborhoods seemed to feel more secure than persons in other areas, tended to believe that crime had been reduced, and seemed to take fewer

Reprinted from the Atlantic Monthly, *March 1982.*

steps to protect themselves from crime (staying at home with the doors locked, for example). Moreover, citizens in the foot-patrol areas had a more favorable opinion of the police than did those living elsewhere. And officers walking beats had higher morale, greater job satisfaction, and a more favorable attitude toward citizens in their neighborhoods than did officers assigned to patrol cars.

These findings may be taken as evidence that the skeptics were right—foot patrol has no effect on crime: it merely fools the citizens into thinking that they are safer. But in our view, and in the view of the authors of the Police Foundation study (of whom Kelling was one), the citizens of Newark were not fooled at all. They knew what the foot-patrol officers were doing, they knew it was different from what motorized officers do, and they knew that having officers walk beats did in fact make their neighborhoods safer.

But how can a neighborhood be "safer" when the crime rate has not gone down—in fact, may have gone up? Finding the answer requires first that we understand what most often frightens people in public places. Many citizens, of course, are primarily frightened by crime, especially crime involving a sudden, violent attack by a stranger. This risk is very real, in Newark as in many large cities. But we tend to overlook or forget another source of fear—the fear of being bothered by disorderly people. Not violent people, nor, necessarily, criminals, but disreputable or obstreperous or unpredictable people: panhandlers, drunks, addicts, rowdy teenagers, prostitutes, loiterers, the mentally disturbed.

What foot-patrol officers did was to elevate, to the extent they could, the level of public order in these neighborhoods. Though the neighborhoods were predominantly black and the foot patrolmen were mostly white, this "order-maintenance" function of the police was performed to the general satisfaction of both parties.

One of us (Kelling) spent many hours walking with Newark foot-patrol officers to see how they defined "order" and what they did to maintain it. One beat was typical: a busy but dilapidated area in the heart of Newark, with many abandoned buildings, marginal shops (several of which prominently displayed knives and straight-edged razors in their windows), one large department store, and, most important, a train station and several major bus stops. Though the area was run-down, its streets were filled with people, because it was a major transportation center. The good order of this area was important not only to those who lived and worked there but also to many others, who had to move through it on their way home, to supermarkets, or to factories.

The people on the street were primarily black; the officer who walked the street was white. The people were made up of "regulars" and "strangers." Regulars included both "decent folk" and some drunks and derelicts who were always there but who "knew their place." Strangers were, well, strangers, and viewed suspiciously, sometimes apprehensively. The officer—call him Kelly—knew who the regulars were, and they knew him. As he saw his job, he was to keep an eye on strangers, and make certain that the disreputable regulars observed some informal but widely understood rules. Drunks and addicts could sit on the stoops, but could not lie down. People could drink on side streets, but not at the main intersection. Bottles had to be in paper bags. Talking to, bothering, or begging from people waiting at the bus stop was strictly forbidden. If a dispute erupted between a businessman and a customer, the businessman was assumed to be right, especially if the customer was a stranger. If a stranger loitered, Kelly would ask him if he had any means of support and what his business was; if he gave unsatisfactory answers, he was sent on his way. Persons who broke the informal rules, especially those who bothered people waiting at bus stops, were arrested for vagrancy. Noisy teenagers were told to keep quiet.

These rules were defined and enforced in collaboration with the "regulars" on the street. Another neighborhood might have different rules, but these, everybody understood, were the rules for *this* neighborhood. If someone violated them, the regulars not only turned to Kelly for help but also ridiculed the violator. Sometimes what Kelly did could be described as "enforcing the law," but just as often it involved taking informal or extra-legal steps to help protect what the neighborhood had decided was the appropriate level of public order. Some of the things he did probably would not withstand a legal challenge.

A determined skeptic might acknowledge that a skilled foot-patrol officer can maintain order but still insist that this sort of "order" has little to do with the real sources of community fear—that is, with violent crime. To a degree, that is true. But two things must be borne in mind. First, outside observers should not assume that they know how much of the anxiety now endemic in many big-city neighborhoods stems from a fear of "real" crime and how much from a sense that the street is disorderly, a source of distasteful, worrisome encounters. The people of Newark, to judge from their behavior and their remarks to interviewers, apparently assign a high value to public order, and feel relieved and reassured when the police help them maintain that order.

Second, at the community level, disorder and crime are usually inextricably linked, in a kind of developmental sequence. Social psychologists and police officers tend to agree that if a window in a building is broken *and is left unrepaired,* all the rest of the windows will soon be broken. This is as true in nice neighborhoods as in run-down ones. Window-breaking does not necessarily occur on a large scale because some areas are inhabited by determined window-breakers whereas others are populated by window-lovers; rather, one unrepaired broken window is a signal that no one cares, and so breaking more windows costs nothing. (It has always been fun.)

Philip Zimbardo, a Stanford psychologist, reported in 1969 on some experiments testing the broken-window theory. He arranged to have an automobile without license plates parked with its hood up on a street in the Bronx and a comparable automobile on a street in Palo Alto, California. The car in the Bronx was attacked by "vandals" within ten minutes of its "abandonment." The first to arrive were a family—father, mother, and young son—who removed the radiator and battery. Within twenty-four hours, virtually everything of value had been removed. Then random destruction began—windows were smashed, parts torn off, upholstery ripped. Children began to use the car as a playground. Most of the adult "vandals" were well-dressed, apparently clean-cut whites. The car in Palo Alto sat untouched for more than a week. Then Zimbardo smashed part of it with a sledgehammer. Soon, passersby were joining in. Within a few hours, the car had been turned upside down and utterly destroyed. Again, the "vandals" appeared to be primarily respectable whites.

Untended property becomes fair game for people out for fun or plunder, and even for people who ordinarily would not dream of doing such things and who probably consider themselves law-abiding. Because of the nature of community life in the Bronx—its anonymity, the frequency with which cars are abandoned and things are stolen or broken, the past experience of "no one caring"—vandalism begins much more quickly than it does in staid Palo Alto, where people have come to believe that private possessions are cared for, and that mischievous behavior is costly. But vandalism can occur anywhere once communal barriers—the sense of mutual regard and the obligations of civility—are lowered by actions that seem to signal that "no one cares."

We suggest that "untended" behavior also leads to the breakdown of community controls. A stable neighborhood of families who care for their homes, mind each other's children, and confidently frown on unwanted intruders can change, in a few years or even a few months, to an inhospitable and frightening jungle. A piece of property is abandoned, weeds grow up, a window is smashed. Adults stop scolding rowdy children; the children, emboldened, become more rowdy. Families move out, unattached adults move in. Teenagers gather in front of the corner store. The merchant asks them to move; they refuse. Fights occur. Litter accumulates. People start drinking in front of the grocery; in time, an inebriate slumps to the sidewalk and is allowed to sleep it off. Pedestrians are approached by panhandlers.

At this point it is not inevitable that serious crime will flourish or violent attacks on strangers will occur. But many residents will think that crime, especially violent crime, is on the rise, and they will modify their behavior accordingly. They will use the streets less often, and when on the streets will stay apart from their fellows, moving with averted eyes, silent lips, and hurried steps. "Don't get involved." For some residents, this growing atomization will matter little, because the neighborhood is not their "home" but "the place where they live." Their interests are elsewhere; they are cosmopolitans. But it will matter greatly to other people, whose lives derive meaning and satisfaction from local attachments rather than worldly involvement; for them, the neighborhood will cease to exist except for a few reliable friends whom they arrange to meet.

Such an area is vulnerable to criminal invasion. Though it is not inevitable, it is more likely that here, rather than in places where people are confident they can regulate public behavior by informal controls, drugs will change hands, prostitutes will solicit, and cars will be stripped. That the drunks will be robbed by boys who do it as a lark, and the prostitutes' customers will be robbed by men who do it purposefully and perhaps violently. That muggings will occur.

Among those who often find it difficult to move away from this are the elderly. Surveys of citizens suggest that the elderly are much less likely to be the victims of crime than younger persons, and some have inferred from this that the well-known fear of crime voiced by the elderly is an exaggeration: perhaps we ought not to design special programs to protect older persons; perhaps we should even try to talk them out of their mistaken fears. This argument misses the point. The prospect of a confrontation with an obstreperous teenager or a drunken panhandler can be as fear-inducing for defenseless persons as the prospect of meeting an actual robber; indeed, to a defenseless person, the two kinds of confrontation are often indistinguishable. Moreover, the lower rate at which the elderly are victimized is a measure of the steps they have already taken—chiefly, staying behind locked doors—to minimize the risks they face. Young men are more frequently attacked than older women, not because they are easier or more lucrative targets but because they are on the streets more.

Nor is the connection between disorderliness and fear made only by the elderly. Susan Estrich, of the Harvard Law School, has recently gathered together a number of surveys on the sources of public fear. One, done in Portland, Oregon, indicated that three fourths of the adults interviewed cross to the other side of a street when they see a gang of teenagers; another survey, in Baltimore, discovered that nearly half would cross the street to avoid even a single strange youth. When an interviewer asked people in a housing project where the most dangerous spot was, they mentioned a place where young persons gathered to drink and play music, despite the fact that not a single crime had occurred there. In Boston public housing projects, the greatest fear was expressed by persons living in the buildings where disorderliness and incivility, not crime, were the greatest. Knowing this helps one understand the significance of such otherwise harmless displays as subway graffiti. As Nathan Glazer has written, the proliferation of graffiti, even when not obscene, confronts the subway rider with the "inescapable knowledge that the environment he must endure for an hour or more a day is uncontrolled and uncontrollable, and that anyone can invade it to do whatever damage and mischief the mind suggests."

In response to fear, people avoid one another, weakening controls. Sometimes they call the police. Patrol cars arrive, an occasional arrest occurs, but crime continues and disorder is not abated. Citizens complain to the police chief, but he explains that his department is low on personnel and that the courts do not punish petty or first-time offenders. To the residents, the police who arrive in squad cars are either ineffective or uncaring; to the police, the residents are animals who deserve each other. The citizens may soon stop calling the police, because "they can't do anything."

The process we call urban decay has occurred for centuries in every city. But what is happening today is different in at least two important respects. First, in the period before, say, World War II, city dwellers— because of money costs, transportation difficulties, familial and church connections—could rarely move away from neighborhood problems. When movement did occur, it tended to be along public-transit routes. Now mobility has become exceptionally easy for all but the poorest or those who are blocked by racial prejudice. Earlier crime waves had a kind of built-in self-correcting mechanism: the determination of a neighborhood or community to reassert control over its turf. Areas in Chicago, New York, and Boston would experience crime and gang wars, and then normalcy would return, as the families for whom no alternative residences were possible reclaimed their authority over the streets.

Second, the police in this earlier period assisted in that reassertion of authority by acting, sometimes violently, on behalf of the community. Young toughs were roughed up, people were arrested "on suspicion" or for vagrancy, and prostitutes and petty thieves were routed. "Rights" were something enjoyed by decent folk, and perhaps also by the serious professional criminal, who avoided violence and could afford a lawyer.

This pattern of policing was not an aberration or the result of occasional excess. From the earliest days of the nation, the police function was seen primarily as that of a night watchman: to maintain order against the chief threats to order—fire, wild animals, and disreputable behavior. Solving crimes was viewed not as a police responsibility but as a private one. In the March 1969 *Atlantic*, one of us (Wilson) wrote a brief account of how the police role had slowly changed from maintaining order to fighting crimes. The change began with the creation of private detectives (often ex-criminals), who worked on a contingency-fee basis for individuals who had suffered losses. In time, the detectives were absorbed into municipal police agencies and paid a regular salary; simultaneously, the responsibility for prosecuting thieves was shifted from the aggrieved private citizen to the professional prosecutor. This process was not complete in most places until the twentieth century.

In the 1960s, when urban riots were a major problem, social scientists began to explore carefully the order-maintenance function of the police, and to suggest ways of improving it—not to make streets safer (its original function) but to reduce the incidence of mass violence. Order-maintenance became, to a degree, coterminous with "community relations." But, as the crime wave that began in the early 1960s continued without abatement throughout the decade and into the 1970s, attention shifted to the role of the police as crime-fighters. Studies of police behavior ceased, by and large, to be accounts of the order-maintenance function and became, instead, efforts to propose and test ways whereby the police could solve more crimes, make more arrests, and gather better evidence. If these things could be done, social scientists assumed, citizens would be less fearful.

A great deal was accomplished during this transition, as both police chiefs and outside experts emphasized the crime-fighting function in their plans, in the allocation of resources, and in deployment of personnel. The police may well have become better crime-fighters as a result. And doubtless they remained aware of their responsibility for order. But the link between order-maintenance and crime-prevention, so obvious to earlier generations, was forgotten.

That link is similar to the process whereby one broken window becomes many. The citizen who fears the ill-smelling drunk, the rowdy teenager, or the importuning beggar is not merely expressing his distaste for unseemly behavior; he is also giving voice to a bit of folk wisdom that happens to be a correct generalization—namely, that serious street crime flourishes in areas in which disorderly behavior goes unchecked. The unchecked panhandler is, in effect, the first broken window. Muggers and robbers, whether opportunistic or professional, believe they reduce their chances of being caught or even identified if they operate on streets where potential victims are already intimidated by prevailing conditions. If the neighborhood cannot keep a bothersome panhandler from annoying passersby, the thief may reason, it is even less likely to call the police to identify a potential mugger or to interfere if the mugging actually takes place.

Some police administrators concede that this process occurs, but argue that motorized-patrol officers can deal with it as effectively as foot-patrol officers. We are not so sure. In theory, an officer in a squad car can observe as much as an officer on foot, in theory, the former can talk to as many people as the latter. But the reality of police–citizen encounters is powerfully altered by the automobile. An officer on foot cannot separate himself from the street people; if he is approached, only his uniform and his personality can help him manage whatever is about to happen. And he can never be certain what that will be—a request for directions, a plea for help, an angry denunciation, a teasing remark, a confused babble, a threatening gesture.

In a car, an officer is more likely to deal with street people by rolling down the window and looking at them. The door and the window exclude the approaching citizen; they are a barrier. Some officers take advantage of this barrier, perhaps unconsciously, by acting differently if in the car than they would on foot. We have seen this countless times. The police car pulls up to a corner where teenagers are gathered. The window is rolled down. The officer stares at the youths. They stare back. The officer says to one, "C'mere." He saunters over, conveying to his friends by his elaborately casual style the idea that he is not intimidated by authority. "What's your name?" "Chuck." "Chuck who?" "Chuck Jones." "What'ya doing, Chuck?" "Nothin'," "Got a P.O. [parole officer]?" "Nah." "Sure?" "Yeah." "Stay out of trouble, Chuckie." Meanwhile, the other boys laugh and exchange comments among themselves, probably at the officer's expense. The officer stares harder. He cannot be certain what is being said, nor can he join in and, by displaying his own skill at street banter, prove that he cannot be "put down." In the process, the officer has learned almost nothing and the boys have decided the officer is an alien force who can safely be disregarded, even mocked.

Our experience is that most citizens like to talk to a police officer. Such exchanges give them a sense of importance, provide them with the basis for gossip, and allow them to explain to the authorities what is worrying them (whereby they gain a modest but significant sense of having "done something" about the problem). You approach a person on foot more easily, and talk to him more readily, than you do a person in a car. Moreover, you can more easily retain some anonymity if you draw an officer aside for a private chat. Suppose you want to pass on a tip about who is stealing handbags, or who offered to sell you a stolen TV. In the inner city, the culprit, in all likelihood, lives nearby. To walk up to a marked patrol car and lean in the window is to convey a visible signal that you are a "fink."

The essence of the police role in maintaining order is to reinforce the informal control mechanisms of the community itself. The police cannot, without committing extraordinary resources, provide a substitute for that informal control. On the other hand, to reinforce those natural forces the police must accommodate them. And therein lies the problem.

Should police activity on the street be shaped, in important ways, by the standards of the neighborhood rather than by the rules of the state? Over the past two decades, the shift of police from order-maintenance to law-enforcement has brought them increasingly under the influence of legal restrictions, provoked by media complaints and enforced by court decisions and departmental orders. As a consequence, the order-maintenance functions of the police are now governed by rules developed to control police relations with suspected criminals. This is, we think, an entirely new development. For centuries, the role of the police as watch-men was judged primarily not in terms of its compliance with appropriate procedures but rather in terms of its attaining a desired objective. The objective was order, an inherently ambiguous term but a condition that people in a given community recognized when they saw it. The means were the same as those the community itself would employ, if its members were sufficiently determined, courageous, and authoritative. Detecting and apprehending criminals, by contrast, was a means to an end, not an end in itself; a judicial determination of guilt or innocence was the hoped-for result of the law-enforcement mode. From the first, the police were expected to follow rules defining that process, though states differed in how stringent the rules should be. The criminal-apprehension process was always understood to involve individual rights, the violation of which was unacceptable because it meant that the violating officer would be acting as a judge and jury—and that was not his job. Guilt or inno-cence was to be determined by universal standards under special pro-cedures.

Ordinarily, no judge or jury ever sees the persons caught up in a dispute over the appropriate level of neighborhood order. That is true not only because most cases are handled informally on the street but also because no universal standards are available to settle arguments over disorder, and thus a judge may not be any wiser or more effective than a police officer. Until quite recently in many states, and even today in some places, the police make arrests on such charges as "suspicious person" or "vagrancy" or "public drunkenness"—charges with scarcely any legal meaning. These charges exist not because society wants judges to punish vagrants or drunks but because it wants an officer to have the legal tools to remove undesirable persons from a neighborhood when informal efforts to preserve order in the streets have failed.

Once we begin to think of all aspects of police work as involving the application of universal rules under special procedures, we inevitably ask what constitutes an "undesirable person" and why we should "criminalize" vagrancy or drunkenness. A strong and commendable desire to see that people are treated fairly makes us worry about allowing the police to rout persons who are undesirable by some vague or parochial standard. A growing and not-so-commendable utilitarianism leads us to doubt that any behavior that does not "hurt" another person should be made illegal. And thus many of us who watch over the police are reluctant to allow them to perform, in the only way they can, a function that every neighborhood desperately wants them to perform.

This wish to "decriminalize" disreputable behavior that "harms no one"—and thus remove the ultimate sanction the police can employ to maintain neighborhood order—is, we think, a mistake. Arresting a single drunk or a single vagrant who has harmed no identifiable person seems unjust, and in a sense it is. But failing to do anything about a score of drunks or a hundred vagrants may destroy an entire community. A particular rule that seems to make sense in the individual case makes no sense when it is made a universal rule and applied to all cases. It makes no sense because it fails to take into account the connection between one broken window left untended and a thousand broken windows. Of course, agencies other than the police could attend to the problems posed by drunks or the mentally ill, but in most communities—especially where the "deinstitutionalization" movement has been strong—they do not.

The concern about equity is more serious. We might agree that certain behavior makes one person more undesirable than another, but how do we ensure that age or skin color or national origin or harmless mannerisms will not also become the basis for distinguishing the undesirable from the desirable? How do we ensure, in short, that the police do not become the agents of neighborhood bigotry?

We can offer no wholly satisfactory answer to this important question. We are not confident that there *is* a satisfactory answer, except to hope that by their selection, training, and supervision, the police will be inculcated with a clear sense of the outer limit of their discretionary authority. That limit, roughly, is this—the police exist to help regulate behavior, not to maintain the racial or ethnic purity of a neighborhood.

Consider the case of the Robert Taylor Homes in Chicago, one of the largest public-housing projects in the country. It is home for nearly 20,000 people, all black, and extends over ninety-two acres along South State Street. It was named after a distinguished black who had been, during the 1940s, chairman of the Chicago Housing Authority. Not long after it opened, in 1962, relations between project residents and the police deteriorated badly. The citizens felt that the police were insensitive or brutal; the police, in turn, complained of unprovoked attacks on them. Some Chicago officers tell of times when they were afraid to enter the Homes. Crime rates soared.

Today, the atmosphere has changed. Police–citizen relations have improved—apparently, both sides learned something from the earlier experience. Recently, a boy stole a purse and ran off. Several young persons who saw the theft voluntarily passed along to the police information on the identity and residence of the thief, and they did this publicly, with friends and neighbors looking on. But problems persist, chief among them the presence of youth gangs that terrorize residents and recruit members in the project. The people expect the police to "do something" about this, and the police are determined to do just that.

But do what? Though the police can obviously make arrests whenever a gang member breaks the law, a gang can form, recruit, and congregate without breaking the law. And only a tiny fraction of gang-related crimes can be solved by an arrest; thus, if an arrest is the only recourse for the police, the residents' fears will go unassuaged. The police will soon feel helpless, and the residents will again believe that the police "do nothing." What the police in fact do is to chase known gang members out of the project. In the words of one officer, "We kick ass." Project residents both know and approve of this. The tacit police–citizen alliance in the project is reinforced by the police view that the cops and the gangs are the two rival sources of power in the area, and that the gangs are not going to win.

None of this is easily reconciled with any conception of due process or fair treatment. Since both residents and gang members are black, race is not a factor. But it could be. Suppose a white project confronted a black gang, or vice versa. We would be apprehensive about the police taking sides. But the substantive problem remains the same: how can the police strengthen the informal social-control mechanisms of natural communities in order to minimize fear in public places? Law enforcement, per se, is no answer. A gang can weaken or destroy a community by standing about in a menacing fashion and speaking rudely to passersby without breaking the law.

We have difficulty thinking about such matters, not simply because the ethical and legal issues are so complex but because we have become accustomed to thinking of the law in essentially individualistic terms. The law defines *my* rights, punishes *his* behavior, and is applied by *that* officer because of *this* harm. We assume, in thinking this way, that what is good for the individual will be good for the community, and what doesn't matter when it happens to one person won't matter if it happens to many. Ordinarily, those are plausible assumptions. But in cases where behavior that is tolerable to one person is intolerable to many others, the reactions of the others—fear, withdrawal, flight—may ultimately make matters worse for everyone, including the individual who first professed his indifference.

It may be their greater sensitivity to communal as opposed to individual needs that helps explain why the residents of small communities are more satisfied with their police than are the residents of similar neighborhoods in big cities. Elinor Ostrom and her co-workers at Indiana University compared the perception of police services in two poor, all-black Illinois towns—Phoenix and East Chicago Heights—with those of three comparable all-black neighborhoods in Chicago. The level of criminal victimization and the quality of police–community relations appeared to be about the same in the towns and the Chicago neighborhoods. But the citizens living in their own villages were much more likely than those living in the Chicago neighborhoods to say that they do not stay at home for fear of crime, to agree that the local police have "the right to take any action necessary" to deal with problems, and to agree that the police "look out for the needs of the average citizen." It is possible that the residents and the police of the small towns saw themselves as engaged in a collaborative effort to maintain a certain standard of communal life, whereas those of the big city felt themselves to be simply requesting and supplying particular services on an individual basis.

If this is true, how should a wise police chief deploy his meager forces? The first answer is that nobody knows for certain, and the most prudent course of action would be to try further variations on the Newark experiment, to see more precisely what works in what kinds of neighborhoods. The second answer is also a hedge—many aspects of order-maintenance in neighborhoods can probably best be handled in ways that involve the police minimally, if at all. A busy, bustling shopping center and a quiet, well-tended suburb may need almost no visible police presence. In both cases, the ratio of respectable to disreputable people is ordinarily so high as to make informal social control effective.

Even in areas that are in jeopardy from disorderly elements, citizen action without substantial police involvement may be sufficient. Meetings between teenagers who like to hang out on a particular corner and adults who want to use that corner might well lead to an amicable agreement on a set of rules about how many people can be allowed to congregate, where, and when.

Where no understanding is possible—or if possible, not observed—citizen patrols may be a sufficient response. There are two traditions of communal involvement in maintaining order. One, that of the "community watchmen," is as old as the first settlement of the New World. Until well into the nineteenth century, volunteer watchmen, not policemen, patrolled their communities to keep order. They did so, by and large, without taking the law into their own hands—without, that is, punishing persons or using force. Their presence deterred disorder or alerted the community to disorder that could not be deterred. There are hundreds of such efforts today in communities all across the nation. Perhaps the best known is that of the Guardian Angels, a group of unarmed young persons in distinctive berets and T-shirts, who first came to public attention when they began patrolling the New York City subways but who claim now to have chapters in more than thirty American cities. Unfortunately, we have little information about the effect of these groups on crime. It is possible, however, that whatever their effect on crime, citizens find their presence reassuring, and that they thus contribute to maintaining a sense of order and civility.

The second tradition is that of the "vigilante." Rarely a feature of the settled communities of the East, it was primarily to be found in those frontier towns that grew up in advance of the reach of government. More than 350 vigilante groups are known to have existed; their distinctive feature was that their members did take the law into their own hands, by acting as judge, jury, and often executioner as well as policeman. Today, the vigilante movement is conspicuous by its rarity, despite the great fear expressed by citizens that the older cities are becoming "urban frontiers." But some community-watchmen groups have skirted the line, and others may cross it in the future. An ambiguous case, reported in the *Wall Street Journal,* involved a citizens' patrol in the Silver Lake area of Belleville, New

Jersey. A leader told the reporter, "We look for outsiders." If a few teen-agers from outside the neighborhood enter it, "we ask them their business," he said. "If they say they're going down the street to see Mrs. Jones, fine, we let them pass. But then we follow them down the block to make sure they're really going to see Mrs. Jones."

Though citizens can do a great deal, the police are plainly the key to order-maintenance. For one thing, many communities, such as the Robert Taylor Homes, cannot do the job by themselves. For another, no citizen in a neighborhood, even an organized one, is likely to feel the sense of responsibility that wearing a badge confers. Psychologists have done many studies on why people fail to go to the aid of persons being attacked or seeking help, and they have learned that the cause is not "apathy" or "selfishness" but the absence of some plausible grounds for feeling that one must personally accept responsibility. Ironically, avoiding responsibility is easier when a lot of people are standing about. On streets and in public places, where order is so important, many people are likely to be "around," a fact that reduces the chance of any one person acting as the agent of the community. The police officer's uniform singles him out as a person who must accept responsibility if asked. In addition, officers, more easily than their fellow citizens, can be expected to distinguish between what is necessary to protect the safety of the street and what merely protects its ethnic purity.

But the police forces of America are losing, not gaining, members. Some cities have suffered substantial cuts in the number of officers available for duty. These cuts are not likely to be reversed in the near future. Therefore, each department must assign its existing officers with great care. Some neighborhoods are so demoralized and crime-ridden as to make foot patrol useless; the best the police can do with limited resources is respond to the enormous number of calls for service. Other neighborhoods are so stable and serene as to make foot patrol unnecessary. The key is to identify neighborhoods at the tipping point—where the public order is deteriorating but not unreclaimable, where the streets are used frequently but by apprehensive people, where a window is likely to be broken at any time, and must quickly be fixed if all are not to be shattered.

Most police departments do not have ways of systematically identifying such areas and assigning officers to them. Officers are assigned on the basis of crime rates (meaning that marginally threatened areas are often stripped so that police can investigate crimes in areas where the situation is hopeless) or on the basis of calls for service (despite the fact that most citizens do not call the police when they are merely frightened or annoyed). To allocate patrol wisely, the department must look at the neighborhoods and decide, from firsthand evidence, where an additional officer will make the greatest difference in promoting a sense of safety.

One way to stretch limited police resources is being tried in some public-housing projects. Tenant organizations hire off-duty police officers for patrol work in their buildings. The costs are not high (at least not per resident), the officer likes the additional income, and the residents feel safer. Such arrangements are probably more successful than hiring private watchmen, and the Newark experiment helps us understand why. A private security guard may deter crime or misconduct by his presence, and he may go to the aid of persons needing help, but he may well not intervene—that is, control or drive away—someone challenging community standards. Being a sworn officer—a "real cop"—seems to give one the confidence, the sense of duty, and the aura of authority necessary to perform this difficult task.

Patrol officers might be encouraged to go to and from duty stations on public transportation and, while on the bus or subway car, enforce rules about smoking, drinking, disorderly conduct, and the like. The enforcement need involve nothing more than ejecting the offender (the offense, after all, is not one with which a booking officer or a judge wishes to be bothered). Perhaps the random but relentless maintenance of standards on buses would lead to conditions on buses that approximate the level of civility we now take for granted on airplanes.

But the most important requirement is to think that to maintain order in precarious situations is a vital job. The police know this is one of their functions, and they also believe, correctly, that it cannot be done to the exclusion of criminal investigation and responding to calls. We may have encouraged them to suppose, however, on the basis of our oft-repeated concerns about serious, violent crime, that they will be judged exclusively on their capacity as crime-fighters. To the extent that this is the case, police administrators will continue to concentrate police personnel in the highest-crime areas (though not necessarily in the areas most vulnerable to criminal invasion), emphasize their training in the law and criminal apprehension (and not their training in managing street life), and join too quickly in campaigns to decriminalize "harmless" behavior (though public drunkenness, street prostitution, and pornographic displays can destroy a community more quickly than any team of professional burglars).

Above all, we must return to our long-abandoned view that the police ought to protect communities as well as individuals. Our crime statistics and victimization surveys measure individual losses, but they do not measure communal losses. Just as physicians now recognize the importance of fostering health rather than simply treating illness, so the police—and the rest of us—ought to recognize the importance of maintaining, intact, communities without broken windows.

Regarding Daughters and Sisters: The Rape of Dinah

Leon R. Kass

*E*VER SINCE I was a boy, long before I had a wife and daughters, I have always thought and keenly felt that rape is a capital offense, a crime worse even than murder. For the rapist, says the book of Deuteronomy, "death by stoning." It has never seemed to me too cruel or excessive a punishment.

No one taught me to feel this way; indeed, I am sure I never discussed such topics with anyone until well after I was a family man. Though it seems incredible in these shameless times, nice people forty or even thirty years ago did not talk much about sex in any form, let alone chatter away in lurid detail about rape, incest, or sodomy. A certain decorousness prevailed, both in deed and in speech, at the center of which was a high regard for womanly modesty, itself an inarticulate yet profound tribute to the awesome procreative power central to the silent mystery of womanliness. Paradoxically, the very sense of shame that inhibited explicit speech about sex silently taught us the enormity of the crime of rape.

What exactly is the crime, and why is it so heinous? According to Blackstone's *Commentaries,* rape is defined as "carnal knowledge of a woman forcibly and against her will." Thus, the crime against the woman has three elements: sexual intercourse; the use (or threat) of force; her unwillingness. Accordingly, there are three coincident "offenses": one against her specifically female sexual nature; one against her bodily integrity; one against her will. Traditionally, our understanding of the crime focused largely on the first. Rape, though it involves the use of force and is

Reprinted from Commentary *(April 1992).*

always against the will, is not—either in common law or in common sense—just a special case of assault and battery. It is a *sexual* crime, a violation of a woman's sexual (and therefore *generative*) nature. The purity of woman's sexual being—and, therewith, also the purity of marriage and the clarity of lineage—was the primary concern of the law, as it was of sexual morality in general.

In Roman law, according to Blackstone,

> stealing a woman from her parents or guardians, and debauching her, is equally penal by the emperor's edict, whether she consent or is forced. . . . And this, in order to take away from women every opportunity of offending in this way; whom the Roman law supposes never to go astray, without the seduction and arts of the other sex; and therefore by restraining and making so highly penal the solicitations of the men, they meant to secure effectually the honor of the women.

It was English common law that introduced an emphasis on lack of consent, yet not because it came to regard rape as a crime against the will, but for reasons of fairness and prudence:

> But our English law does not entertain quite such sublime ideas of the honor of either sex, as to lay the blame of a mutual fault on one of the transgressors only: and therefore, makes it a necessary ingredient in the crime of rape, that it must be against the woman's will.

And whereas the Roman law did not recognize the rape of a prostitute or common harlot, "not allowing any punishment for violating the chastity of her, who hath indeed no chastity at all, or at least hath no regard to it," the law of England—still concerned with chastity but more willing to allow for personal reform—"holds it to be felony to force even a concubine or harlot; because the woman may have forsaken that unlawful course of life."

By contrast, today's discussions of rape, largely led by feminist critics of this allegedly patriarchal tradition of law and sexual morality, focus almost exclusively on the absence of the woman's clear consent. Rape is regarded primarily as a violation of the will, not a violation of womanliness. To be sure, we still distinguish rape from other forms of unconsented touching. But since the entire view of relations between the sexes is increasingly seen solely through the lens of power, rape is viewed merely as a most egregious example of the generalized male tendency to dominate and violate women. It follows that the remedy is female empowerment rather than womanly shame and gentlemanly respect; karate lessons and campaigns to "take back the night" rather than a restoration of a proper regard for the deeper meanings of sexuality, love, and intimacy. The empowered woman can have it all: sexual freedom without any risks or dangers. From men she no longer wants or needs the righteous indignation and the courage that will defend a lady's (or a sister's or a daughter's) honor, but simply a willingness to let "no" mean "no."

What should thoughtful students of human affairs, both male and female, think about this new dispensation? Does it properly understand the meaning of rape? Does it offer an effective strategy to prevent it? Does it properly understand the meaning of our sexuality? Does it counsel well about how we should educate and care for daughters and sisters in these matters? To help us consider these questions, let us examine one of our tradition's oldest stories about rape and about fathers and daughters, brothers and sisters: the biblical tale of the rape of Dinah, daughter of Jacob and Leah.

The story of the rape of Dinah (Genesis 34) is remarkable in many ways, and not only because (as the commentator in the Soncino edition of the Pentateuch remarks) it is "an exception to the series of peaceful scenes from patriarchal life and character—a tale of dishonor, wild revenge, and indiscriminate slaughter." It is one of the few stories in Genesis about a woman, and the only one about a daughter and a sister. Only in this story can we see how the founders of Israel regard and treat a daughter: for Dinah is the only daughter born to the patriarchs, Abraham, Isaac, and Jacob. Only in this story can we see how young Israelites regard and treat a sister: for Dinah has brothers galore who unite to defend her honor. Indeed, the brothers' response comprises nearly the whole of the tale; the bulk of the account reports how they plot and execute revenge on the entire manhood of the city of Shechem. By thus exploring relations between the Israelites and their neighbors—including prospects for peaceful coexistence or enmity, for separateness or intermarriage—the story also raises questions regarding the chances for the long-term survival and integrity of the people of the covenant.

Why are all these matters presented in one story? Why make the one tale about daughters the story of a rape? Why merge the personal story of a rape with the political question of foreign relations? Is the story of the rape merely incidental, serving mainly as a vehicle for launching (and exploring) the political confrontation between Israel and its neighbors? Are relations among nations best explored by considering controversies over women? Or, conversely, does the political context of the story illuminate also the very *meaning* of rape? Could it be that rape, though a horrible personal crime, is finally intelligible only culturally and politically? Can one best read the character of a people in how they respond to rape in particular and to the dignity of women in general? Does this story point to the distinctive view of woman that will come to characterize the way of Israel?

The story which provokes these questions does not explicitly answer them. In the book of Genesis, the author does not go in for direct moralizing; the voice of the (textual) narrator rarely pronounces judgment. (One exception: "Thus did Esau despise his birthright.") And we must not accept as authoritative a judgment rendered by any one character, no matter how worthy. The stories are supposed to speak for themselves; they "teach," but not directly or didactically. Thus they invite thought and require interpretation and judgment. Their meaning must be sought in light of the textual context and the special circumstances in which the characters find themselves, and we must be careful not to project onto the text our current prejudices: things which strike *us* as harsh or immoral may not in fact be so, at least under the circumstances. At the same time, necessity does not simply justify: even where circumstances require harsh or cruel conduct, that conduct is not simply accepted. Throughout Genesis, the moral ambiguity of human actions—and its lasting effects—is vividly portrayed, rarely more powerfully than in the present tale.

Our story interrupts a series of remarkable successes for the house of Jacob. Returning to Canaan from Paddan-Aram after having made peace with Laban, his household intact and rich in cattle, Jacob has just achieved two great triumphs: he has successfully wrestled the man-angel, winning a blessing and gaining a new name; and he has accomplished a peaceful reunion with his brother Esau, who (it seems to us) was willing to abandon a twenty-year-old grudge. Made wiser, through his adventures, regarding the ways of man and God, and reminded by his limp of his encounter with the divine, Jacob appears ready to settle down and to allow his now swollen tribe to cross the threshold into nationhood. He builds a house in Succoth, the first immobile dwelling of the patriarchs. He makes booths for his cattle. He then buys land from the ruler of Shechem, the first purchase of land other than the cave which Abraham had purchased for the limited purpose of burial. Jacob establishes himself in the promised land.

Though his conduct is certainly understandable, hindsight reveals it to be unwise. Very likely, Jacob's successes have gone to his head. His conflicts with Laban are past; he has escaped a fratricidal encounter with Esau; his rivalrous wives are not making trouble; his beloved Rachel has at last borne a son; he has returned to Canaan a prosperous man. He thinks everything is now settled, so he settles. He deliberately encamps "before the city"—literally *in-the-face-of* the city—of Shechem, a move that we readers should regard with apprehension, given what we have learned about the character of cities. Jacob does not return to Beth-El (cf. 28:20–22; 31:13), from whence he left promising to return, and to which God will send him in the sequel; instead, he takes up a place among—in the face of—the nations of Canaan.

Upon purchasing the land he erects there an altar which he calls *El-Elohe-Israel*, "God, the God of Israel." Pious readers may take this to be Jacob's profession of monotheism and his faith in the one true God; but, in the context, it could rather express an anxious appeal to his own *personal* deity (for "Israel" here means only Jacob), a deity whose assistance he will need now that he is settling among strangers, people with different ways and *other* gods.* In the immediate sequel, an unexpected encounter with these Canaanite neighbors straightaway upsets the peace and exposes the foolishness—or at least the insufficiency—of Jacob's plans.

Dinah initiates the encounter: "And Dinah, the daughter of Leah, whom she had borne unto Jacob, went out to see the daughters of the land." This is all that Dinah did, and all we know about it. Yet it is not difficult to understand her intentions and to guess at her motives. One daughter among eleven sons, she may well have been lonely and eager for

---

* Jacob has forgotten the pillar he had anointed in Beth-El, and his vow that "this stone, which I have set up as a pillar, shall be God's house; and of all that Thou shalt give me I will surely give the tenth unto Thee" (28:22).

female company; it is the *daughters* of the land she goes out to see. Alternatively, she may have been curious, attracted not by similarity but by difference, the difference between "the daughter *of Leah*" and "the daughters *of the land*"; this would not be the first time in Genesis that we meet a woman who is curious and who finds "outside" matters attractive, "a delight to the eyes" (cf. 3:6).

It seems that Dinah does not go merely to see, in detached beholding, but rather to visit: in Hebrew idiom, "to see, to look upon" means "to make friendship with." Perhaps she wishes to join with the daughters in matters of seeing: to see *"and be seen"* adds the Samaritan text. For how else might a single young woman, living at home in a houseful of men, ever come to the notice of prospective suitors? Her mother,* after all, could have taught her, from painful experience, what it meant to be passed over and unloved. And from her father's less than equal regard for her mother and his clear preference for the more beautiful Rachel, Dinah might well have concluded that it is only good looks and being seen that truly count.

The text leaves Dinah's motives unclear, as motives often are in such matters. But, more likely, the text is not interested in motives, but rather in the action itself and its meaning. For Dinah's deed has a meaning quite apart from her intention, a meaning of which she was likely entirely innocent. Whatever her motive, she did indeed "go out" and she did indeed go "to see." She left the home—and the customs and ways—of her mother and father, under the aegis of *El-Elohe-Israel,* and went *out* into alien territory. She went out *alone,* without security, perhaps even without permission. She went to *town,* to the city, never—not even today—a safe place for an innocent, attractive, unprotected, and vulnerable young woman. And, willy-nilly, in going *to see* she would necessarily look upon— and be initiated into—ways that were not her own, as happens to every young person who goes abroad (or even off to college) "to see for myself." Actions taken in innocence are often far from innocent.

---

* The eleventh-century commentator Rashi here makes much of the connection of Dinah to her mother: "The daughter of Leah—so Scripture calls her; why not the daughter of Jacob? But just because she 'went out' she is called Leah's daughter, since she too was fond of 'going out' [Midrash Genesis Rabbah, 80], as it is said [30:16], 'and Leah went out to meet him.' With an allusion to her they formulated the proverb: 'Like mother, like daughter.' "

This is not to blame the victim: Dinah would be culpable only if these were her intentions or if she went against advice and with foreknowledge of the dangers. If blame is to be meted out, it should go instead to Jacob. For Jacob knows from personal experience what can happen to a man confronted with a beautiful woman: it was he, a stranger in a strange land, who defied men's customs (at the well) to be alone with Rachel (29:7); it was he who lost his wits and forgot to make a contract with Laban for Rachel, so infatuated was he with her beauty; it was he, lusting or perhaps just drunk on his wedding night, who did not even recognize the substitution of Leah for his beloved Rachel. Shrewd and wise in the ways of the world, Jacob certainly should have taken precautions to instruct and protect his daughter—unless, of course, he was lulled into a false sense of security by his many recent successes and by his peaceful real-estate transactions with the ruling house of the town, or, worse, unless he had not yet learned *that* and *how* one must care for daughters. Just as Abraham needed help learning the importance and meaning of "wife"—one cannot innocently pass her off as one's sister—so Jacob (and, through him, we readers) must learn, painfully, the importance and meaning of "daughter."

Dinah went out to see the daughters. But it was she who was seen, and not by daughters: "And saw her Shechem the son of Hamor the Hivite, the prince of the land, and he took her and he lay with her and he defiled her." Dinah was seen by Shechem, the prince of Shechem, the leading young Shechemite, the first and finest young man in the town. The coincidence of the name of man and town announces that this is the paradigmatic encounter between these two "cultures" (much like the story of the sons of God and the daughters of men; 6:2). Without a word, immediately upon seeing Dinah, Shechem took, lay with, and defiled—or "humbled" or "abased" (*'anâh*, "to put down, to depress")—her. He had complete power over her, and he exercised it. About Dinah's response the text is silent. The brute fact is all we are asked to see: Dinah was raped.

Dinah's defilement will haunt us throughout; but it makes no difference to Shechem, who now finds that "his soul did cleave to Dinah the daughter of Jacob, and he loved the damsel, and he spoke to the heart of the damsel [*na'arâh*, a girl from infancy to adolescence: damsel, maiden]." We may, if we wish, take at face value Shechem's professed love for Dinah. But we know how readily some men rationalize their lusts, how a woman they found "good in bed" suddenly seems lovable, how a man sweet-talks a woman into accepting his aggressive advances—even to reassure her, his lust now being sated, after he has raped her. Her abasement means nothing; new love will conquer all. True, she needs comforting; but, says he to himself, speech to the heart will overcome her regret or sorrow.* Defilement is just a state of mind, alterable by a change of heart. While sweet-talking the damsel, Shechem tells his father to *get him* this girl for a wife, and his father, the ruling prince Hamor, will oblige.

To defend Shechem's conduct, the reader can appeal only to cultural relativity. Predatory behavior—"take first, ask later"—seems to be the customary way of the Shechemites; the ruling prince does not upbraid his son for rape. The desire to make an "honest woman" of Dinah, now that he loves her, seems to be all that is needed to make prior abasement and defilement null and void. Woman is for the ravishing.

Not so in the house of Jacob. As Hamor goes out to gain his son's desire, Jacob hears and concentrates only on his daughter's defilement (a new word: *tâmê*, to be foul, contaminated, polluted, unclean). But as his sons are in the field with his cattle, he bides his time, awaiting their return. Jacob's silence has long puzzled readers, because of what we know of his previous energy, resourcefulness, and shrewdness. Perhaps, Robert Sacks suggests,

> Jacob, who dealt successfully with his brother when facing the problems of an earlier generation, decided not to intervene in the present affair. The relation between Israel and its neighbors once a house had been built became the problems of another generation. Therefore he remained silent and waited for Dinah's brothers to arrive.†

But we must also consider the possibility that Jacob was thoroughly nonplussed, astonished at what had occurred, guilty over his own failure to prevent it, overwhelmed by sadness at the pollution of his household, or

---

* Rashi reads similarly: he spoke "words that would appeal to her heart: see how much money your father has lavished for a small plot of field. I will marry you and you will then possess the city and all its fields."

† "The Lion and the Ass: A Commentary on the Book of Genesis (Chapters 31–34)," *Interpretation,* January 1983.

unsure of what one must do under such circumstances. No one he knew had faced the question of daughters before.* Whatever the reason, Jacob holds his peace until the sons return.

What began as an interpersonal matter between a prince and a damsel now quickly becomes a political issue between peoples. But the interests, concerns, and attitudes of the two sides differ sharply. The Hivite ruler and his son are eager to obtain Dinah as Shechem's wife; Jacob and his sons are preoccupied with her defilement. As soon as they hear the news, Jacob's sons return from the fields, grieved and very angry, as the narrator reports, "because he had done a vile deed in Israel in lying with Jacob's daughter which thing ought not to be done" (34:7). Though laws against rape had not yet been explicitly promulgated, not even among the Israelites, the sons intuitively understood it as an immoral, even a heinous, deed. What is more, they took it as an outrage not only against Dinah but against the entire clan and its ways.

Indeed, one might even say that the clan here acts to define itself: we are a community which unites to defend a woman's honor. This first action of Israel's (Jacob's) sons, to avenge a vile deed committed against Israel's daughter, gives birth to the *people* of Israel, now defined morally and politically, and no longer merely genealogically and economically. This moral-political unification of an otherwise potentially fractious and rivalrous band of men may be what Jacob shrewdly had in mind when he waited for his sons to return before responding.

Unification in the face of a common enemy is the oldest political story. There are even famous accounts of such political self-definition in defense of women and to avenge a rape. The Trojan War united the Achaians, who fought to avenge the rape of Helen by Paris while he was the guest of her husband Menelaus. But many other cultures do not take rape this seriously. The ancient Persians, in justifying themselves for their invasion of

---

* This is not quite true. His father-in-law, Laban, had shown him a certain high-handed way with daughters, substituting the elder, Leah, for the younger, Rachel, in what Jacob thought was his marriage to Rachel. Having lain with Leah, Jacob was then compelled to marry her, and she later bore him Dinah. Jacob, who—according to Laban—had tried to ignore local customs regarding marriageable daughters, was unwittingly and unwillingly trapped into a "shotgun marriage." The sins of the fathers are sometimes visited also on the daughters.

Greece, blame the war on the Greeks and the revenge they took for Helen. Herodotus presents their reasons:

> It is the work of unjust men, we think, to carry off women at all; but once they have been carried off, to take seriously the avenging of them is the part of fools, as it is the part of sensible men to pay no heed to the matter; clearly, the women would not have been carried off had they no mind to be." The Persians say that they, for their part, made no account of the women carried off from Asia but that the Greeks, because of a Lacedaemonian woman [i.e., Helen], gathered a great army, came straight to Asia, and destroyed the power of Persia, and from that time forth the Persians regarded the Greek people as their foes.

On closer inspection, the grounds of Greek and Israelite collective action appear to differ significantly. In the Trojan War the crime avenged was understood to be a crime against hosts and hospitality; it is a perversion of hospitality to take the wife of one's host. In avenging the rape of Dinah, the sons of Israel regard it as a crime against the maiden herself. This concern with the dignity of woman as such—*not* as the possession of the husband or father—will later become emblematic of Israelite collective self-understanding.

Hamor begins to make his case in strictly personal terms, pleading in the name of love: "The soul of my son longeth for your daughter. I pray you give her unto him to wife" (34:8). But he soon appeals to what he assumes is Israelite self-interest and makes a pitch for thoroughgoing intermarriage. (Hamor would certainly have noticed that Jacob had eleven sons, already or soon to be in need of wives.) Hamor generously invites Jacob to "*give* your daughters unto us"—if and when and to whom *you* please—and to "*take* our daughters unto you"—again, presumably, whomever *you* please. There is no allusion to compulsion or force; indeed, there is not even a whiff of Hivite *taking-as-they*-please, let alone taking without prior paternal consent. (Needless to say, for the Canaanites, the consent of the *daughter* will play no part in arranging marriages.) Appealing still further to self-interest, Hamor proposes that the Israelites may then dwell among his people, trade freely in the land, and gain possessions there.

In short, if they cooperate, the Israelites may get them wives and (other) valuable goods, through free and peaceful trade. At this point, Shechem adds his own personal appeal, promising to pay whatever bride-price is asked, if only they will give him the damsel to wife; he, too, shows no shame or remorse, and makes no mention that he has already taken lustfully by force what he now proposes to buy generously with gifts.

We, fathers of daughters or brothers of sisters, listening to this plea and this proposal—how do we react to such a generous and useful and profitable offer? Shall we be swayed by professions of love and promises of peaceful trade and coexistence? Shall we overlook injustice for the sake of gain, overlook an assault on our daughter (sister) so that we might easily get wives for all of our sons? Or shall we side with the moral indignation of the sons of Israel, who see only the defilement of their sister and who craftily plot revenge?

Outnumbered by the Shechemites, Jacob's sons have no alternative but to proceed with guile. The device they use is ingenious—not only strategically, but especially morally and symbolically:

> We cannot do this thing, to give our sister to one that is uncircum-
> cised; for that were a reproach unto us. Only on this condition will
> we consent unto you: if ye will be as we are, that every male of you
> be circumcised; then will we give our daughters unto you and we
> will take your daughters to us, and we will dwell with you, and *we
> will become one people.* But if ye will not hearken unto us, to be
> circumcised, then we will take our daughter and we will be gone.
> (34:14–17; emphasis added)

The sons ignore the personal side of the request and treat the matter entirely politically. Just as they saw that the crime against Dinah was a crime also against Israel, so they see that the union of man and woman anticipates children and, therefore, the question of perpetuating one's ways and beliefs. They make explicit the assimilationist meaning that was merely implicit in the Shechemite proposal for intermarriage; for freely to exchange daughters means, culturally, *to become one people.* The question is, whose ways will the assimilated populace adopt? Shall they still be the people of the covenant, whose sign is marked in the flesh by circumcision? Confronted with this question, the sons of Israel assert and insist upon the difference of their ways, a difference which reminds always of God and His promise to Abraham.

To be sure, the use of circumcision here serves mainly as part of the strategy for revenge. Almost certainly, the sons do not intend to go through with the agreement for intermarriages. Many readers will even blame the sons for their deceit, all the more because it exploits and perhaps abuses for violent purposes the sacred sign of the covenant. Still, the demand for circumcision carries moral meaning on its own, regardless of the deceitful intention and bloody outcome. For it reveals still more deeply the differences between the peoples and their different attitudes toward women and sexuality.

The Israelites are, of course, not the only people who practice male circumcision. But with them, the ritual has a high and special meaning: it is the sign of the covenant God made with Abraham, the founder. A brief backward glance at that story will deepen our understanding of the present one.

The story of God's new covenant is the immediate sequel to the story of the birth of Ishmael, Abraham's long-awaited first-born son, whom Hagar bore when Abraham was eighty-six years old, eleven years after he left Haran in search of God's rich promise. Now that Abraham has a son, the crucial task of perpetuation begins in earnest. As Ishmael approaches young manhood (age thirteen), God, looking to the future, proposes a new covenant, telling Abraham to "walk before Me and be thou wholehearted. And I will make My covenant between thee and Me, and will multiply thee exceedingly" (17:1–2). The covenant is announced in explicit relation to the theme of procreation and perpetuation.

God's part of the covenant is very generous and full: He promises Abraham that He will make him exceedingly fruitful, the father of nations and the progenitor of kings; He will make an everlasting covenant with the seed of Abraham to be their God; He will give unto them the land of Canaan as an everlasting possession. As for Abraham (and his seed), the obligation is simple: keeping the covenant simply means *remembering* it, that is, marking its token or sign in the flesh of every male throughout the generations, by the act of circumcision.

Why circumcision? We can think of many possible reasons, all of them apt. Unlike the rainbow, the sign of God's covenant with Noah and all life after the Flood, which demanded nothing from man in return, circumcision is an *un*-natural sign—both artificial and conventional. It is the memorial of an agreement that deems it necessary (hence, conventional); it must be made by man (hence, artificial); yet it is marked in the organ of generation (hence, also natural). The world as given, and life even when secure ("No more floods"), are not yet completed; the best way to live remains hidden and must be revealed by additional human effort, exercised in the face of powerful human drives that lead us astray.

Circumcision emphasizes, even as it also restricts and transcends, the natural and the generative, sanctifying them in the process: under God's command, men willingly produce in their living and generational flesh the mark of their longing for God, of their desire for His benevolence and care. Though it is the child who bears the mark, the obligation falls rather on the parents; it is a perfect symbol of the relation among the generations, for the deeds of parents are always inscribed, often heritably, into the lives of their children.

The obligation of circumcision calls parents to the parental task. Performed soon after birth, it circumcises their pride, reminding them that children are a gift, for which they are not themselves creatively responsible. More importantly, they are called from the start to assume the obligations of transmission. They are compelled to remember, now when it counts, that they belong to a long line of descent, beginning with Abraham who was called and who sought to walk before God and to be wholehearted. They are reminded that bearing the child is the easy part, that rearing him well is the real vocation. They are summoned to continue the chain by rearing their children looking up to the sacred and the divine, by initiating them into God's chosen ways. And they are made aware of the consequences for their children—now and hereafter—of a failure to hearken to the call: "And the uncircumcised male . . . that soul shall be cut off from his people; he hath broken My covenant." With circumcision, the child, and all *his* potential future generations, are symbolically offered to the way of God.

But why a rite applicable only to the male children? Because males especially need extra inducements to undertake the parental role. Freed by nature from the consequences of their sexuality, probably both less fitted and less interested by nature than women for the work of nurture and rearing, men need to be acculturated to the work of transmission. Virility and potency are, from the Bible's point of view, much less important than decency, righteousness, and holiness. The father is re-called to this teaching, and, accordingly, symbolically remakes his son's masculinity for generations to come. When he comes of age, the son will also come to understand the meaning of the mark of his fathers and their covenant with

God; presumably, it will decisively affect how he uses his sexual powers and how he looks on the regenerative and nurturing powers of woman.

Shechem, the rapist, was psychically as well as physically uncircumcised. First, he acted as if his *lust* entitled him to have his way with Dinah. Afterward, the ground of his claim shifted to his *desire,* to his longing for her. The generative meaning of sexuality and the attendant reverence owed to womanly shame he understood not at all; much less did he have in mind a right partner for the future work of transmission. And, as we shall see, he will soon lead his entire city into destruction, just so that he can satisfy his heart's desire. The Shechemites, like Shechem himself, will submit to circumcision, but with no understanding of what it means, in itself and, especially, to the Israelites. Shechemite circumcision turns out to be a parody of the covenant, just as Shechem's request to be given a bride whom he had already taken and defiled was a parody of a proper marriage proposal.

Hamor and Shechem are well pleased with the proposal of Jacob's sons, and Shechem hastens to the deed: "And the young man deferred not to do the thing, *because he had delight in Jacob's daughter.* And he was honored above all the house of his father" (34:19). But the proposal required that *all* the men of Shechem submit to circumcision. How could they be persuaded? To win the hearts of their fellow Shechemites, Hamor and Shechem smoothly talk business:

> These men are peaceable with us; therefore let them dwell in the land, and trade therein; for, behold, the land is large enough for them; let us *take their* daughters to us for wives, and let us *give* them *our* daughters. (34:21; emphasis added)

The appeal begins quietly: the men (i.e., Jacob's clan) are not warlike or troublesome, and, as there is enough land, let them live here and trade. Even better, *we* can *take* their daughters (whomever *we* like) and we can *give* them—*if* and when *we* like—our daughters; in speaking to their own, Hamor and Shechem cast the liberalities differently from when they spoke to Jacob and his sons. But the cost of this bargain in spousing has yet to be mentioned, and, to pay it, the people will require an even better reward:

> Only on this condition will the men consent unto us to dwell with us, *to become one people,* if every male among us be circumcised,

as they are circumcised. *Shall not their cattle and their substance
and all their beasts be ours?* Only let us consent unto them, and
they will dwell with us. (34:22–23; emphasis added)

The appeal succeeds: every able-bodied man is circumcised, presumably the married as well as the unmarried. Some, perhaps, are tempted by
the promise of prospective brides; others—probably the majority—more
greedy than lustful, are moved by the promise of capturing through assimilation all of the Israelite wealth and cattle, so confident are they that their
superior numbers and ways will prevail. The Shechemites are culturally
open to all customs, provided that they increase the gross national product.
    As it turns out, their leaders have made false promises, or, at best,
have exposed their own deviousness. For, at least for the time being, Jacob
and Israel have no marriageable daughters but Dinah, and she is (in many
senses) "taken" (note well: she has not been returned to her people, but
remains in Shechem's house). The appeal to gain and greed is perhaps a
disingenuous promise to the rabble—hiding from view that only Shechem
himself will profit from their acquiescence. Otherwise, if honest, the appeal
to the Shechemites betrays a rather sordid view of the entire proposal to
"become one people." In any case, the Shechemites circumcise themselves
wholeheartedly for gain, not—as did Abraham—to gain wholehearted-
ness. What they gain, in fact, is their own death and the ruin of their city.

    This is not to justify the excessive harshness of the penalty exacted by
Dinah's (full) brothers, Simeon and Levi, who steal into the city "post-
operatively," while the men are in pain, and slay all the males, and take
Dinah from Shechem's house. But it does suggest the (at least partial)
fitness of collective punishment, bearing out the earlier suggestion that
Prince Shechem is somehow representative of his entire city—both as
paradigm and as head. Here is a nation indifferent to rape and the defilement of women, eager for intermarriage, keen upon gain, coveting both its
neighbors' wives and its neighbors' cattle—equally regarded as objects for
possession. Here is a people that will accept circumcision as a price for
profit, to gain a woman or to win a herd of cattle, not as a reminder of the
importance of rearing your children in a spirit of reverence. No one is
moved by this self-inflicted act on the genitals to reflect—or to suffer pangs
of conscience—on the rape or on the proper use of one's sexuality. No one
is moved to feel awe or reverence for the divine. Insufficiently respectful of

women, with corruption in their hearts, the Shechemites cannot be kept from being cut off as a people by mere circumcision in the flesh. It is no justification of their slaughterers to say that the Shechemites are not fit to survive.

The slaughter of the entire manhood of Shechem could, in fact, be perhaps defended as a matter of necessity and on grounds of Realpolitik. Limited revenge taken upon the young prince alone would unquestionably have resulted in counter-vengeance: one could hardly expect the Shechemites to regard his killing as just ("once women had been carried off, to take seriously the avenging of them is the part of fools"); and, justice aside, they would certainly have struck back in defense of their own first family. Greatly outnumbered, Jacob's sons would have stood little chance in an all-out battle; and while the Lord's intercession might have given them the upper hand, they would have had no good reason to count on divine aid in the fighting. Besides, Dinah, their sister, was still in Shechemite hands. Guile, deception, and stealth, followed by a massive "surgical" strike of "protective reaction," would be a sound strategy under the circumstances.

Yet it is unlikely that the sons of Jacob are ruled simply by such shrewd and cool calculation. Most likely, they are driven by rage and by the desire to visit the harshest possible punishment on Shechem and his entire kind. They do not cease with killing the men. They spoil the entire city "because *they* had defiled their sister." They take everything, both from the city and the fields—flocks, herds, asses, and all their wealth they spoil; all their children and all their wives they take captive. (This last, of course, could be recommended on grounds of policy: to obliterate the possibility of future generations that will come looking for revenge.) Their zeal for revenge knows no limits: the innocent suffer with the guilty. Worse, the avengers profit from their revenge. Even if justified or necessary, the attack reeks of barbaric cruelty. The most Machiavellian of readers experiences the horror of these "necessary" actions.

Jacob, too, is horrified, but for different reasons. The collective action, taken by his sons, has backfired; it has made it impossible for him to settle peacefully in the land as he had planned. Worse, his entire tribe is now at risk; his sons, in their zeal, have failed to consider that there are other Canaanite tribes who will not ignore the slaughter of their kinsmen:

> Ye have troubled me, to make me odious unto the inhabitants of
> the land, even unto the Canaanites and the Perizzites, and I being

few in number, they will gather themselves together against me and smite me; and I shall be destroyed, I and my house. (34:30)

Later, at the end of his life, Jacob, in blessing his sons, will heap moral opprobrium and curses upon Simeon and Levi.* But here, after the deed itself, his concerns are strictly political-prudential, and mainly self-preservative. He is now a pariah and, worse, a likely victim, in the land of his fathers, a land which, the reader knows, was promised to his ancestors and their seed.

But Jacob's sons have the last word. They reject his rebuke and his utilitarian and survivalist concerns, in the name of morality:

As with a harlot should one deal with our sister? (34:31)

This rhetorical question, especially because it is the story's last word, reverberates in our minds: "As with a harlot should one deal with our sister?" What does this mean? And why is this the last word?

The word translated "like a harlot" comes from the verb *zânâh*, from a primitive root meaning "highly fed," and, therefore, "wanton." It means "to commit adultery" (especially for the female) or "to play the harlot," and, in the causative, "to cause to commit fornication" or "to cause to be [or to play] the whore." But it also easily acquires the (figurative) meaning "to commit idolatry," "to whore after false gods," on the understanding that Israel is betrothed solely to God. Both meanings can be heard in the brothers' rejoinder to Jacob.

At first glance, the brothers seem to be equating rape with harlotry, or, at least, suggesting that what Shechem did to Dinah might have been overlooked—or at least mitigated—were Dinah a whore. Similar sorts of arguments are, to this day, advanced in defense of accused rapists: "Look how she dresses." "She sleeps around." "What was she doing in his apartment, or in that fraternity house?" "She was asking for it." Even granting their possible relevance, such complaints of "provocation" never constitute

---

* "Simeon and Levi are brethren; weapons of violence their kinship. Let my soul not come into their council; unto their assembly let my glory not be united; for in their anger they slew men, and in their self-will they houghed oxen. Cursed be their anger, for it was fierce, and their wrath, for it was cruel; I will divide them in Jacob, and scatter them in Israel" (49:5–7).

an adequate defense for rape—though they might make it more difficult to determine whether what transpired was in fact rape and not, say, seduction. For this reason, we must not construe the "motto" of Jacob's sons to mean that it would be permissible to rape a harlot. Rather, the sons are asserting that *their failure to defend their sister's honor* would be tantamount to regarding her as if she were a harlot. Worse, to practice "turning the other cheek" would mean (tacitly) to share, by acquiescence, in her defilement. The sons see very clearly that *in rape—and in indifference to rape—a man, or a community, treats a woman the way a harlot treats herself.*

Regardless of their divergent motives, the deeds of rapist and harlot have a convergent inner meaning. Both are without modesty, shame, or sexual self-restraint. Both are indifferent to the generative meaning of (especially female) sexuality, both regard sex purely as a matter of present and private (especially male) gratification. Both are indifferent to the fact that sex points to future generations, those to whom we give life and nurture, paying back, in the only way we can, our debts to our own forebears. Both are especially indifferent to marriage and family, those conventional institutions whose main purpose is to provide a true home for fruitful and generous love and for the proper rearing of children. And both are indifferent to the moral, cultural, and religious beliefs of the sexual partner, so crucial for the preservation of lineage and the perpetuation of one's ways.

Whether or not they understand fully what they are saying, Jacob's sons remind Jacob (who had hoped for peaceful coexistence)—as they instruct the reader—that the alternative to defending the virtue of one's sisters is to abandon them, and all future generations, to the realm of false gods. Rape—like harlotry and the indiscriminate intermarriage proposed by the Shechemites—means the spiritual defilement of an entire people. The defense of chastity and the transmission of holiness are part of a single package.

Fair-minded readers of the story are left with nagging questions. We wonder about the practice of deceit and the merely cunning exploitation of the holy rite of circumcision. We are troubled by the difficulty of practicing proper vengeance, for one may not be able to finish what one has started, or one may, in heat, be led to cruel extremes. We see the terrible dilemmas of settling in a land amid people who are not God-fearing, especially if one has imprudent and zealous offspring. We see how zeal in defense of God's ways can lead men into war, and how, should they prove successful, the spoils of war can lead them, ironically, *away* from God's ways. Yet we are inclined to believe, with Jacob's sons, that a culture that will make war to defend the virtue of its women, against a culture that dishonors other people's women, proves itself—by this very fact of fighting—to be not only superior in justice but also more fit to survive and flourish.

It would seem, from the sequel, that God does not disagree. For it is He who has the genuinely last word. Right after the speech of the sons, God speaks to Jacob:

> Arise, go up to Beth-El, and dwell there; and make there an altar
> unto God, Who appeared unto thee when thou didst flee from the
> face of Esau thy brother. (35:1)

Jacob, who had tried to settle permanently in the face of Shechem, is told now to complete his journey. Jacob must return to Beth-El, "the house of God," where Abraham had built an altar and first called upon the name of the Lord, and where Jacob himself had dreamed his famous dream of the ladder just before his departure into Paddan-Aram. Jacob now understands that he has been called to spiritual repurification. He commands his household and all that are with him to "put away the strange gods that are among you, and purify yourselves, and change your garments; and let us arise, and go up to Beth-El . . ." (35:2–3). He collects and buries the foreign gods and the earrings (probably from the captive Shechemite women and children but also, perhaps, from Rachel), and the entire clan heads off to Beth-El. And as they journey, "a terror of God was upon the cities that were round about them, and they did not pursue after the sons of Jacob" (35:5).

After Jacob builds the altar at Beth-El, God appears to him again, this time to pronounce His first full divine blessing upon him:

> "Thy name is Jacob; thy name shall not be called any more Jacob,
> but Israel shall be thy name"; and He called his name Israel. And
> God said unto him, "I am God Almighty. Be fruitful and multiply; a
> nation and a company of nations shall be of thee, and kings shall
> come out of thy loins; and the land which I gave unto Abraham and
> Isaac, to thee will I give it, and to thy seed after thee I will give the
> land." (35:10–12)

Context leads us to suspect that God's revelation and great benediction—especially for fecundity and posterity—are, in part, a commentary on the Israelites' demonstrated devotion to the dignity of their daughters. The divine renaming of Jacob now carries also the meaning of the people; it is singularly appropriate that the people are renamed—and morally reborn—after this episode.

Yet despite God's intervention, we must not conclude that our story has a happy ending. Dinah, though avenged, remains defiled. The sons may have satisfaction, but she has shame. In our focus on the vengeance of the brothers, we run the risk of forgetting the sister, the daughter, the maiden. But one should not mistake silence—neither ours nor the story's—for indifference. True, we are told absolutely nothing about Dinah's feelings or thoughts—not about the rape itself, or the aftermath with Shechem and his sweet speeches, or the proposal of marriage, or the bloody slaughter of Shechem and the men of his entire city, not even about her "rescue" by her brothers. We have not one spoken word from her own lips, not before, not after. And we hear no words spoken to her by her father or brothers. In dreadful silence, we can only imagine the terrible consequences for this young maiden—psychic, social, spiritual. As far as we know, she never marries and never bears children. Her name appears only once hereafter in the entire Bible (Genesis 46:15), all alone in the list of names of the household of Jacob who accompanied him on the move to Egypt.*

But do not mistake the reticence: the silence of her shame cries out for our sympathy and searching attention.

Unlike other women we have met in Genesis, Dinah is defined solely by her womanliness. Unlike Sarah who could command her husband, unlike Rebekah, a paragon of tact and prudence,† unlike the rivalrous sisters Leah and Rachel, each with her own capacity for self-defense, Dinah is, for us, merely a maid—exposed, innocent, vulnerable to male predation. Let us not jump to the wrong conclusion: of course, she has thoughts and feelings, motives and desires; of course, she is a person in her own right. But for present purposes, the biblical author abstracts from her inner life; he wants us to concentrate entirely on the fact that Dinah is a *woman,*

---

* Even her mention here in the census is oblique, as if she were only ambiguously present: "These are the sons of Leah whom she bore unto Jacob in Paddan-Aram, and with Dinah his daughter."

† See my essay on Rebekah, "A Woman for All Seasons," *Commentary*, September 1991.

and, more precisely, a young and *unmarried* woman, and, of course, a daughter. Her womanly ancestors we know mainly as wives and mothers. With Dinah we are compelled to think about maidenhood—and about daughters. How should they comport themselves? And what should we, their fathers and their mothers, teach them in matters of men, sex, and marriage? How should we help them avoid the ever-present dangers of rape, harlotry, intermarriage?

Jacob, it seems, did not understand the need for such education and protection. His mind focused (understandably) on other matters, perhaps reassured regarding his future by his having numerous sons, he failed to see that it is reverent and virtuous daughters who safeguard a nation's heritage. No daughters, no nation. He might have known better. He himself had been sent to Paddan-Aram to find a wife, so as not to marry a Canaanite woman; from the stellar example of his own mother, he should have known the importance of woman—both to ensure lineage and to foster proper rearing—and taken steps to protect his daughter's purity. But, though he was in when she went out, he prevented neither her going nor her going alone; he did not even warn her against the dangers. He was, to say the least, insufficiently concerned about her maidenhood—until it was too late.

Yet, with the help of the story, we readers can see the need for a special education and protection of daughters. The circumcision of the males, symbolizing the restraint of male promiscuity and beckoning males to familial responsibility, must have its female counterpart: modesty, caution, refusal, self-reverence, and chastity, all exercised in the service of eventual marriage—love-filled, fruitful, sanctified. This is not, as critics would have it, the infamous double standard. In Israel, it is a single standard, differently applied, as befits the natural differences between men and women.

We Americans, especially the more "enlightened" and emancipated among us, have managed these past three decades to become thoroughly lost in matters sexual. The sexual revolution, made possible by the contraceptive separation of sexual activity from its implicit generative consequences, deliberately sacrificed female virtue on the altar of the god of pleasure now. Not surprisingly, the result was emancipated male predation and exploitation, as men were permitted easy conquests of women without responsibility or lasting intimacy. Unhappy with this outcome, but failing to appreciate its roots in the overthrow of modesty, the liberated women's movement mounted a moralistic political campaign against the "patriarchy," seeking power and respect, mistakenly believing that the respect women need *as women* is based solely on power.

Whatever the benefits in the workplace, the consequences for private life are horrendous. Romance is replaced by relationships; people do not fall in love, they just "come on to" one another—like lice; courtship is nonexistent. Speech is unbelievably crude and explicit, and the greatest heroes of the popular culture, sporting (at best) their underwear on the outside, gyrate obscenely on television. The centuries-old delicate dance of young man and young woman, with its subtle steps and missteps, its whispered secrets and mysterious rhythms, is all but forgotten, replaced if not by explicit crudity then by ideology. Young women, humorless and grim, with jaws clenched and shoulders padded, cut an angry path across the would-be fields of dreams, supported in their demands for empowerment by those oh-so-sensitive males who will defend to the death not a woman's honor but her need to learn the manly art of self-defense. Many lonely women, more than can safely admit it, secretly hope to meet a gentleman; but the vast majority steadfastly refuse to be ladies—indeed, no longer know what it means. Small wonder, then, so much sexual harassment and even rape. When power becomes the name of the game, the stronger will get his way.

Under such circumstances, one cannot exactly blame women for wanting to learn how to defend themselves against sexual attack. But, addressing the symptom not the cause, the remedies of karate and "take back the night"—and, still more, the shallow beliefs about sexual liberation that support these practices—can only complete the destruction of healthy relations between man and woman. For, truth to tell, the night never did and never can belong to women, except for the infamous women-of-the-night. Only a restoration of sexual self-restraint and sexual self-respect—for both men and women—can reverse our rapid slide toward Shechem. Only a recovery of the deeper understanding of sexuality, accessible to us (among other places) in the stories of the Hebrew Bible, can allow true love and family happiness to flourish.

Defining Deviancy Down

Daniel Patrick Moynihan

*I*N ONE OF THE founding texts of sociology, *The Rules of Sociological Method* (1895), Emile Durkheim set it down that "crime
is normal." "It is," he wrote, "completely impossible for any society entirely free of it to exist." By defining what is deviant, we are enabled to
know what is not, and hence to live by shared standards. This aperçu
appears in the chapter entitled "Rules for the Distinction of the Normal
from the Pathological." Durkheim writes:

> From this viewpoint the fundamental facts of criminology appear
> to us in an entirely new light. . . . [T]he criminal no longer appears
> as an utterly unsociable creature, a sort of parasitic element, a
> foreign, inassimilable body introduced into the bosom of society.
> He plays a normal role in social life. For its part, crime must no
> longer be conceived of as an evil which cannot be circumscribed
> closely enough. Far from there being cause for congratulation
> when it drops too noticeably below the normal level, this apparent
> progress assuredly coincides with and is linked to some social
> disturbance.

Durkheim suggests, for example, that "in times of scarcity" crimes of
assault drop off. He does not imply that we ought to approve of crime—
"[p]ain has likewise nothing desirable about it"—but we need to understand its function. He saw religion, in the sociologist Randall Collins's
terms, as "fundamentally a set of ceremonial actions, assembling the
group, heightening its emotions, and focusing its members on symbols of
their common belongingness." In this context "a punishment ceremony
creates social solidarity."

The matter was pretty much left at that until seventy years later when,

Reprinted from The American Scholar *(Summer 1993).*

in 1965, Kai T. Erikson published *Wayward Puritans*, a study of "crime rates" in the Massachusetts Bay Colony. The plan behind the book, as Erikson put it, was "to test [Durkheim's] notion that the number of deviant offenders a community can afford to recognize is likely to remain stable over time." The notion proved out very well indeed. Despite occasional crime waves, as when itinerant Quakers refused to take off their hats in the presence of magistrates, the amount of deviance in this corner of seventeenth-century New England fitted nicely with the supply of stocks and whipping posts. Erikson remarks:

> It is one of the arguments of the . . . study that the amount of deviation a community encounters is apt to remain fairly constant over time. To start at the beginning, it is a simple logistic fact that the number of deviancies which come to a community's attention are limited by the kinds of equipment it uses to detect and handle them, and to that extent the rate of deviation found in a community is at least in part a function of the size and complexity of its social control apparatus. A community's capacity for handling deviance, let us say, can be roughly estimated by counting its prison cells and hospital beds, its policemen and psychiatrists, its courts and clinics. Most communities, it would seem, operate with the expectation that a relatively constant number of control agents is necessary to cope with a relatively constant number of offenders. The amount of men, money, and material assigned by society to "do something" about deviant behavior does not vary appreciably over time, and the implicit logic which governs the community's efforts to man a police force or maintain suitable facilities for the mentally ill seems to be that there is a fairly stable quota of trouble which should be anticipated.
>
> In this sense, the agencies of control often seem to define their job as that of keeping deviance within bounds rather than that of obliterating it altogether. Many judges, for example, assume that severe punishments are a greater deterrent to crime than moderate ones, and so it is important to note that many of them are apt to impose harder penalties when crime seems to be on the increase and more lenient ones when it does not, almost as if the power of the bench were being used to keep the crime rate from getting out of hand.

Erikson was taking issue with what he described as "a dominant strain in sociological thinking" that took for granted that a well-structured society "is somehow designed to prevent deviant behavior from occurring." In both authors, Durkheim and Erikson, there is an undertone that suggests that, with deviancy, as with most social goods, there is the continuing problem of demand exceeding supply. Durkheim invites us to

> imagine a society of saints, a perfect cloister of exemplary individuals. Crimes, properly so called, will there be unknown; but faults which appear venial to the layman will create there the same scandal that the ordinary offense does in ordinary consciousness. If, then, this society has the power to judge and punish, it will define these acts as criminal and will treat them as such.

Recall Durkheim's comment that there need be no cause for congratulations should the amount of crime drop "too noticeably below the normal level." It would not appear that Durkheim anywhere contemplates the possibility of too much crime. Clearly his theory would have required him to deplore such a development, but the possibility seems never to have occurred to him.

Erikson, writing much later in the twentieth century, contemplates both possibilities. "Deviant persons can be said to supply needed services to society." There is no doubt a tendency for the supply of any needed thing to run short. But he is consistent. There can, he believes, be *too much* of a good thing. Hence "the number of deviant offenders a community *can afford* to recognize is likely to remain stable over time" (my emphasis).

Social scientists are said to be on the lookout for poor fellows getting a bum rap. But here is a theory that clearly implies that there are circumstances in which society will choose *not* to notice behavior that would be otherwise controlled, or disapproved, or even punished.

It appears to me that this is in fact what we in the United States have been doing of late. I proffer the thesis that, over the past generation, since the time Erikson wrote, the amount of deviant behavior in American society has increased beyond the levels the community can "afford to recognize" and that, accordingly, we have been re-defining deviancy so as to exempt much conduct previously stigmatized, and also quietly raising the "normal" level in categories where behavior is now abnormal by any earlier standard. This redefining has evoked fierce resistance from defenders of "old" standards, and accounts for much of the present "cultural war" such as proclaimed by many at the 1992 Republican National Convention.

Let me, then, offer three categories of redefinition in these regards: the *altruistic*, the *opportunistic*, and the *normalizing*.

The first category, the *altruistic*, may be illustrated by the deinstitutionalization movement within the mental health profession that appeared in the 1950s. The second category, the opportunistic, is seen in the interest group rewards derived from the acceptance of "alternative" family structures. The third category, the normalizing, is to be observed in the growing acceptance of unprecedented levels of violent crime.

It happens that I was present at the beginning of the deinstitutionalization movement. Early in 1955 Averell Harriman, then the new governor of New York, met with his new commissioner of mental hygiene, Dr. Paul Hoch, who described the development, at one of the state mental hospitals, of a tranquilizer derived from rauwolfia. The medication had been clinically tested and appeared to be an effective treatment for many severely psychotic patients, thus increasing the percentage of patients discharged. Dr. Hoch recommended that it be used systemwide; Harriman found the money. That same year Congress created a Joint Commission on Mental Health and Illness whose mission was to formulate "comprehensive and realistic recommendations" in this area, which was then a matter of considerable public concern. Year after year, the population of mental institutions grew. Year after year, new facilities had to be built. Never mind the complexities: population growth and such like matters. There was a general unease. Durkheim's constant continued to be exceeded. (In *Spanning the Century: The Life of W. Averell Harriman*, Rudy Abramson writes: "New York's mental hospitals in 1955 were overflowing warehouses, and new patients were being admitted faster than space could be found for them. When he was inaugurated, 94,000 New Yorkers were confined to state hospitals. Admissions were running at more than 2,500 a year and rising, making the Department of Mental Hygiene the fastest-growing, most-expensive, most-hopeless department of state government.")

The discovery of tranquilizers was adventitious. Physicians were seeking cures for disorders that were just beginning to be understood. Even a limited success made it possible to believe that the incidence of this particular range of disorders, which had seemingly required persons to be confined against their will or even awareness, could be greatly reduced.

The Congressional Commission submitted its report in 1961; it proposed a nationwide program of deinstitutionalization.

Late in 1961, President Kennedy appointed an interagency committee to prepare legislative recommendations based upon the report. I represented Secretary of Labor Arthur J. Goldberg on this committee and drafted its final submission. This included the recommendation of the National Institute of Mental Health that 2,000 community mental health centers (one per 100,000 of population) be built by 1980. A buoyant Presidential Message to Congress followed early in 1963. "If we apply our medical knowledge and social insights fully," President Kennedy pronounced, "all but a small portion of the mentally ill can eventually achieve a wholesome and a constructive social adjustment." A "concerted national attack on mental disorders [was] now possible and practical." The President signed the Community Mental Health Centers Construction Act on October 31, 1963, his last public bill-signing ceremony. He gave me a pen.

The mental hospitals emptied out. At the time Governor Harriman met with Dr. Hoch in 1955, there were 93,314 adult residents of mental institutions maintained by New York State. As of August 1992, there were 11,363. This occurred across the nation. However, the number of community mental health centers never came near the goal of the 2,000 proposed community centers. Only some 482 received federal construction funds between 1963 and 1980. The next year, 1981, the program was folded into the Alcohol and Other Drug Abuse block grant and disappeared from view. Even when centers were built, the results were hardly as hoped for. David F. Musto of Yale writes that the planners had bet on improving national mental health "by improving the quality of general community life through expert knowledge, not merely by more effective treatment of the already ill." There was no such knowledge.

However, worse luck, the belief that there *was* such knowledge took hold within sectors of the profession that saw institutionalization as an unacceptable mode of social control. These activists subscribed to a redefining mode of their own. Mental patients were said to have been "labeled," and were not to be drugged. Musto says of the battles that followed that they were "so intense and dramatic precisely because both sides shared the fantasy of an omnipotent and omniscient mental health technology which could thoroughly reform society; the prize seemed eminently worth fighting for."

But even as the federal government turned to other matters, the mental institutions continued to release inmates. Professor Fred Siegel of Cooper Union observes: "In the great wave of moral deregulation that began in the mid-1960s, the poor and the insane were freed from the fetters of middle-class mores." They might henceforth sleep in doorways as often as they chose. The problem of the homeless appeared, characteristically defined as persons who lacked "affordable housing."

The *altruistic* mode of redefinition is just that. There is no reason to believe that there was any real increase in mental illness at the time deinstitutionalization began. Yet there was such a perception, and this enabled good people to try to do good, however unavailing in the end.

Our second, or *opportunistic* mode of re-definition, reveals at most a nominal intent to do good. The true object is to do well, a long-established motivation among mortals. In this pattern, a growth in deviancy makes possible a transfer of resources, including prestige, to those who control the deviant population. This control would be jeopardized if any serious effort were made to reduce the deviancy in question. This leads to assorted strategies for re-defining the behavior in question as not all that deviant, really.

In the years from 1963 to 1965, the Policy Planning Staff of the U.S. Department of Labor picked up the first tremors of what Samuel H. Preston, in the 1984 Presidential Address to the Population Association of America, would call "the earthquake that shuddered through the American family in the past twenty years." The *New York Times* recently provided a succinct accounting of Preston's point:

> Thirty years ago, 1 in every 40 white children was born to an unmarried mother; today it is 1 in 5, according to Federal data. Among blacks, 2 of 3 children are born to an unmarried mother; 30 years ago the figure was 1 in 5.

In 1991, Paul Offner and I published longitudinal data showing that, of children born in the years 1967–69, some 22.1 percent were dependent on welfare—that is to say, Aid to Families with Dependent Children—before reaching age eighteen. This broke down as 15.7 percent for white children, 72.3 percent for black children. Projections for children born in 1980 gave rates of 22.2 percent and 82.9 percent respectively. A year later, a *New York Times* series on welfare and poverty called this a "startling finding . . . a symptom of vast social calamity."

And yet there is little evidence that these facts are regarded as a calamity in municipal government. To the contrary, there is general acceptance of the situation as normal. Political candidates raise the subject, often to the point of dwelling on it. But while there is a good deal of demand for symbolic change, there is none of the marshaling of resources that is associated with significant social action. Nor is there any lack of evidence that there is a serious social problem here.

Richard T. Gill writes of "an accumulation of data showing that intact biological parent families offer children very large advantages compared to any other family or non-family structure one can imagine." Correspondingly, the disadvantages associated with single-parent families spill over into other areas of social policy that now attract great public concern. Leroy L. Schwartz, M.D., and Mark W. Stanton argue that the real quest regarding a government-run health system such as that of Canada or Germany is whether it would work "in a country that has social problems that countries like Canada and Germany don't share to the same extent." Health problems reflect ways of living. The way of life associated with "such social pathologies as the breakdown of the family structure" lead to medical pathologies. Schwartz and Stanton conclude: "The United States is paying dearly for its social and behavioral problems," for they have now become medical problems as well.

To cite another example, there is at present no more vexing problem of social policy in the United States than that posed by education. A generation of ever-more ambitious statutes and reforms have produced weak responses at best and a fair amount of what could more simply be called dishonesty. ("Everyone knows that Head Start works." By the year 2000, American students will "be first in the world in science and mathematics.") None of this should surprise us. The 1966 report *Equality of Educational Opportunity* by James S. Coleman and his associates established that the family background of students played a much stronger role in student achievement relative to variations in the ten (and still standard) measures of school quality.

In a 1992 study entitled *America's Smallest School: The Family*, Paul Barton came up with the elegant and persuasive concept of the parent-pupil ratio as a measure of school quality. Barton, who was on the policy planning staff in the Department of Labor in 1965, noted the great increase in the proportion of children living in single-parent families since then. He further noted that the proportion "varies widely among the states" and is related to "variation in achievement" among them. The correlation between the percentage of eighth graders living in two-parent families and average mathematics proficiency is a solid .74. North Dakota, highest on the math test, is second highest on the family compositions scale—that is, it is second in the percentage of kids coming from two-parent homes. The District of Columbia, lowest on the family scale, is second lowest in the test score.

A few months before Barton's study appeared, I published an article showing that the correlation between eighth-grade math scores and distance of state capitals from the Canadian border was .522, a respectable showing. By contrast, the correlation with per pupil expenditure was a derisory .203. I offered the policy proposal that states wishing to improve their schools should move closer to Canada. This would be difficult, of course, but so would it be to change the parent-pupil ratio. Indeed, the 1990 Census found that for the District of Columbia, apart from Ward 3 west of Rock Creek Park, the percentage of children living in single-parent families in the seven remaining wards ranged from a low of 63.6 percent to a high of 75.7. This being a one-time measurement, over time the proportions become asymptotic. And this in the nation's capital. No demand for change comes from that community—or as near to no demand as makes no matter. *For there is good money to be made out of bad schools.* This is a statement that will no doubt please many a hard heart, and displease many genuinely concerned to bring about change. To the latter, a group in which I would like to include myself, I would only say that we are obliged to ask why things do not change.

For a period there was some speculation that, if family structure got bad enough, this mode of deviancy would have less punishing effects on children. In 1991 Deborah A. Dawson, of the National Institutes of Health, examined the thesis that "the psychological effects of divorce and single parenthood on children were strongly influenced by a sense of shame in being 'different' from the norm." If this were so, the effect should have fallen off in the 1980s, when being from a single-parent home became much more common. It did not. "The problems associated with task overload among single parents are more constant in nature," Dawson wrote, adding that since the adverse effects had not diminished, they were "not based on stigmatization but rather on inherent problems in alternative family structures"—*alternative* here meaning other than two-parent families. We should take note of such candor. Writing in the *Journal of Mar-*

riage and the Family in 1989, Sara McLanahan and Karen Booth noted: "Whereas a decade ago the prevailing view was that single motherhood had no harmful effects on children, recent research is less optimistic."

The year 1990 saw more of this lesson. In a paper prepared for the Progressive Policy Institute, Elaine Ciulla Kamarck and William A. Galston wrote that "if the economic effects of family breakdown are clear, the psychological effects are just now coming into focus." They cite Karl Zinsmeister:

> There is a mountain of scientific evidence showing that when families disintegrate children often end up with intellectual, physical, and emotional scars that persist for life. . . . We talk about the drug crisis, the education crisis, and the problems of teen pregnancy and juvenile crime. But all these ills trace back predominantly to one source: broken families.

As for juvenile crime, they cite Douglas Smith and G. Roger Jarjoura: "Neighborhoods with larger percentages of youth (those aged 12 to 20) and areas with higher percentages of single-parent households also have higher rates of violent crime." They add: "The relationship is so strong that controlling for family configuration erases the relationship between race and crime and between low income and crime. This conclusion shows up time and time again in the literature; poverty is far from the sole determinant of crime." But the large point is avoided. In a 1992 essay "The Expert's Story of Marriage," Barbara Dafoe Whitehead examined "the story of marriage as it is conveyed in today's high school and college textbooks." Nothing amiss in this tale.

> It goes like this:
> The life course is full of exciting options. The lifestyle options available to individuals seeking a fulfilling personal relationship include living a heterosexual, homosexual, or bisexual single lifestyle; living in a commune; having a group marriage; being a single parent; or living together. Marriage is yet another lifestyle choice. However, before choosing marriage, individuals should weigh its costs and benefits against other lifestyle options and should consider what they want to get out of their intimate relationships. Even within marriage, different people want different things. For example, some people marry for companionship, some marry in

order to have children, some marry for emotional and financial security. Though marriage can offer a rewarding path to personal growth, it is important to remember that it cannot provide a secure or permanent status. Many people will make the decision between marriage and singlehood many times throughout their life.

Divorce represents part of the normal family life cycle. It should not be viewed as either deviant or tragic, as it has been in the past. Rather, it establishes a process for "uncoupling" and thereby serves as the foundation for individual renewal and "new beginnings."

History commences to be rewritten. In 1992, the Select Committee on Children, Youth, and Families of the U.S. House of Representatives held a hearing on "Investing in Families: A Historical Perspective." A fact sheet prepared by committee staff began:

"INVESTING IN FAMILIES: A HISTORICAL PERSPECTIVE"

FACT SHEET

HISTORICAL SHIFTS IN FAMILY COMPOSITION CHALLENGING CONVENTIONAL WISDOM

While in modern times the percentage of children living with one parent has increased, more children lived with just one parent in Colonial America.

The fact sheet proceeded to list program on program for which federal funds were allegedly reduced in the 1980s. We then come to a summary.

Between 1970 and 1991, the value of AFDC [Aid to Families with Dependent Children] benefits decreased by 41%. In spite of proven success of Head Start, only 28% of eligible children are being served. As of 1990, more than $18 billion in child support went uncollected. At the same time, the poverty rate among single-parent families with children under 18 was 44%. Between 1980 and 1990, the rate of growth in the total Federal budget was four times greater than the rate of growth in children's programs.

In other words, benefits paid to mothers and children have gone down steadily, as indeed they have done. But no proposal is made to restore benefits to an earlier level, or even to maintain their value, as is the case with other "indexed" Social Security programs. Instead we go directly to the subject of education spending.

Nothing new. In 1969, President Nixon proposed a guaranteed income, the Family Assistance Plan. This was described as an "income strategy" as against a "services strategy." It may or may not have been a good idea, but it was a clear one, and the resistance of service providers to it was equally clear. In the end it was defeated, to the huzzahs of the advocates of "welfare rights." What is going on here is simply that a large increase in what once was seen as deviancy has provided opportunity to a wide spectrum of interest groups that benefit from re-defining the problem as essentially normal and doing little to reduce it.

Our *normalizing* category most directly corresponds to Erikson's proposition that "the number of deviant offenders a community can afford to recognize is likely to remain stable over time." Here we are dealing with the popular psychological notion of "denial." In 1965, having reached the conclusion that there would be a dramatic increase in single-parent families, I reached the further conclusion that this would in turn lead to a dramatic increase in crime. In an article in *America*, I wrote:

> From the wild Irish slums of the 19th century Eastern seaboard to the riot-torn suburbs of Los Angeles, there is one unmistakable lesson in American history: a community that allows a large number of young men to grow up in broken families, dominated by women, never acquiring any stable relationship to male authority, never acquiring any set of rational expectations about the future— that community asks for and gets chaos. Crime, violence, unrest, unrestrained lashing out at the whole social structure—that is not only to be expected; it is very near to inevitable.

The inevitable, as we now know, has come to pass, but here again our response is curiously passive. Crime is a more or less continuous subject of political pronouncement, and from time to time it will be at or near the top of opinion polls as a matter of public concern. But it never gets much further than that. In the words spoken from the bench, Judge Edwin Torres of the New York State Supreme Court, Twelfth Judicial District, described how "the slaughter of the innocent marches unabated: subway riders, bodega owners, cab drivers, babies; in laundromats, at cash machines, on elevators, in hallways." In personal communication, he writes: "This numbness, this near narcoleptic state can diminish the human condition to the level of combat infantrymen, who, in protracted campaigns, can eat their battlefield rations seated on the bodies of the fallen, friend and foe alike. A society that loses its sense of outrage is doomed to extinction." There is no expectation that this will change, nor any efficacious public insistence that it do so. The crime level has been *normalized*.

Consider the St. Valentine's Day Massacre. In 1929 in Chicago during Prohibition, four gangsters killed seven gangsters on February 14. The nation was shocked. The event became legend. It merits not one but two entries in the *World Book Encyclopedia*. I leave it to others to judge, but it would appear that the society in the 1920s was simply not willing to put up with this degree of deviancy. In the end, the Constitution was amended, and Prohibition, which lay behind so much gangster violence, ended.

In recent years, again in the context of illegal traffic in controlled substances, this form of murder has returned. But it has done so at a level that induces denial. James Q. Wilson comments that Los Angeles has the equivalent of a St. Valentine's Day Massacre every weekend. Even the most ghastly reenactments of such human slaughter produce only moderate responses. On the morning after the close of the Democratic National Convention in New York City in July, there was such an account in the second section of the *New York Times*. It was not a big story; bottom of the page, but with a headline that got your attention. "3 Slain in Bronx Apartment, but a Baby is Saved." A subhead continued: "A mother's last act was to hide her little girl under the bed." The article described a drug execution; the now-routine blindfolds made from duct tape; a man and a woman and a teenager involved. "Each had been shot once in the head." The police had found them a day later. They also found, under a bed, a three-month-old baby, dehydrated but alive. A lieutenant remarked of the mother, "In her last dying act she protected her baby. She probably knew she was going to die, so she stuffed the baby where she knew it would be safe." But the matter was left there. The police would do their best. But the event passed quickly; forgotten by the next day, it will never make *World Book*.

Nor is it likely that any great heed will be paid to an uncanny reenactment of the Prohibition drama a few months later, also in the Bronx. The *Times* story, page B3, reported:

9 MEN POSING AS POLICE
ARE INDICTED IN 3 MURDERS
Drug Dealers Were Kidnapped for Ransom

The *Daily News* story, same day, page 17, made it *four* murders, adding nice details about torture techniques. The gang members posed as federal Drug Enforcement Administration agents, real badges and all. The victims were drug dealers, whose families were uneasy about calling the police. Ransom seems generally to have been set in the $650,000 range. Some paid. Some got it in the back of the head. So it goes.

Yet, violent killings, often random, go on unabated. Peaks continue to attract some notice. But these are peaks above "average" levels that thirty years ago would have been thought epidemic.

LOS ANGELES, AUG. 24. (Reuters) Twenty-two people were killed in Los Angeles over the weekend, the worst period of violence in the city since it was ravaged by riots earlier this year, the police said today.

Twenty-four others were wounded by gunfire or stabbings, including a 19-year old woman in a wheelchair who was shot in the back when she failed to respond to a motorist who asked for directions in south Los Angeles.

["The guy stuck a gun out of the window and just fired at her," said a police spokesman, Lieut. David Rock. The woman was later described as being in stable condition.

Among those who died was an off-duty officer, shot while investigating reports of a prowler in a neighbor's yard, and a Little League baseball coach who had argued with the father of a boy he was coaching.]

The police said at least nine of the deaths were gang-related, including that of a 14-year old girl killed in a fight between rival gangs.

Fifty-one people were killed in three days of rioting that started April 29 after the acquittal of four police officers in the beating of Rodney G. King.

Los Angeles usually has above-average violence during August, but the police were at a loss to explain the sudden rise. On an average weekend in August, 14 fatalities occur.

Not to be outdone, two days later the poor Bronx came up with a near record, as reported in *New York Newsday*:

> Armed with 9-mm. pistols, shotguns and M-16 rifles, a group of masked men and women poured out of two vehicles in the South Bronx early yesterday and sprayed a stretch of Longwood Avenue with a fusillade of bullets, injuring 12 people.

A Kai Erikson of the future will surely need to know that the Department of Justice in 1990 found that Americans reported only about 38 percent of all crimes and 48 percent of violent crimes. This, too, can be seen as a means of *normalizing* crime. In much the same way, the vocabulary of crime reporting can be seen to move toward the normal-seeming. A teacher is shot on her way to class. The *Times* subhead reads: "Struck in the Shoulder in the Year's First Shooting Inside a School." First of the season.

It is too early, however, to know how to regard the arrival of the doctors on the scene declaring crime a "public health emergency." The June 10, 1992, issue of the *Journal of the American Medical Association* was devoted entirely to papers on the subject of violence, principally violence associated with firearms. An editorial in the issue signed by former Surgeon General C. Everett Koop and Dr. George D. Lundberg is entitled: "Violence in America: A Public Health Emergency." Their proposition is admirably succinct.

> Regarding violence in our society as purely a sociological matter, or one of law enforcement, has led to unmitigated failure. It is time to test further whether violence can be amenable to medical/public health interventions.
>
> We believe violence in America to be a public health emergency, largely unresponsive to methods thus far used in its control. The solutions are very complex, but possible.

The authors cited the relative success of epidemiologists in gaining some jurisdiction in the area of motor vehicle casualties by re-defining what had been seen as a law enforcement issue into a public health issue. Again, this process began during the Harriman administration in New York in the 1950s. In the 1960s the morbidity and mortality associated with automobile crashes was, it could be argued, a major public health problem; the public health strategy, it could also be argued, brought the problem under a measure of control. Not in "the 1970s and 1980s," as the

Journal of the American Medical Association would have us think: the federal legislation involved was signed in 1965. Such a strategy would surely produce insights into the control of violence that elude law enforcement professionals, but whether it would change anything is another question.

For some years now I have had legislation in the Senate that would prohibit the manufacture of .25 and .32 caliber bullets. These are the two calibers most typically used with the guns known as Saturday Night Specials. "Guns don't kill people," I argue, "bullets do."

Moreover, we have a two-century supply of handguns but only a four-year supply of ammunition. A public health official would immediately see the logic of trying to control the supply of bullets rather than of guns.

Even so, now that the doctor has come, it is important that criminal violence not be defined down by epidemiologists. Doctors Koop and Lundberg note that in 1990 in the state of Texas "deaths from firearms, for the first time in many decades, surpassed deaths from motor vehicles, by 3,443 to 3,309." A good comparison. And yet keep in mind that the number of motor vehicle deaths, having leveled off since the 1960s, is now pretty well accepted as normal at somewhat less than 50,000 a year, which is somewhat less than the level of the 1960s—the "carnage," as it once was thought to be, is now accepted as normal. This is the price we pay for high-speed transportation: there is a benefit associated with it. But there is no benefit associated with homicide, and no good in getting used to it. Epidemiologists have powerful insights that can contribute to lessening the medical trauma, but they must be wary of normalizing the social pathology that leads to such trauma.

The hope—if there be such—of this essay has been twofold. It is, first, to suggest that the Durkheim constant, as I put it, is maintained by a dynamic process which adjusts upwards and *downwards*. Liberals have traditionally been alert for upward redefining that does injustice to individuals. Conservatives have been correspondingly sensitive to downward redefining that weakens societal standards. Might it not help if we could all agree that there is a dynamic at work here? It is not revealed truth, nor yet a scientifically derived formula. It is simply a pattern we observe in ourselves. Nor is it rigid. There may once have been an unchanging supply of jail cells which more or less determined the number of prisoners. No longer. We are building new prisons at a prodigious rate. Similarly, the executioner is back. There is something of a competition in Congress to think up new offenses for which the death penalty is seemed the only available deterrent. Possibly also modes of execution, as in "fry the kingpins." Even so, we are getting used to a lot of behavior that is not good for us.

As noted earlier, Durkheim states that there is "nothing desirable" about pain. Surely what he meant was that there is nothing pleasurable. Pain, even so, is an indispensable warning signal. But societies under stress, much like individuals, will turn to painkillers of various kinds that end up concealing real damage. There is surely nothing desirable about *this*. If our analysis wins general acceptance, if, for example, more of us came to share Judge Torres's genuine alarm at "the trivialization of the lunatic crime rate" in his city (and mine), we might surprise ourselves how well we respond to the manifest decline of the American civic order. Might.

Defining Deviancy Up

Charles Krauthammer

*I*N A RECENT ESSAY in *The American Scholar* titled "Defining Deviancy Down," Daniel Patrick Moynihan offers an arresting view of the epidemic of deviancy—of criminality, family breakdown, mental illness—that has come to characterize the American social landscape. Deviancy has reached such incomprehensible proportions, argues Moynihan, that we have had to adopt a singular form of denial: we deal with the epidemic simply by defining away most of the disease. We lower the threshold for what we are prepared to call normal in order to keep the volume of deviancy—redefined deviancy—within manageable proportions.

For example. Since 1960 the incidence of single parenthood has more than tripled. Almost 30 percent of all American children are now born to unmarried mothers. The association of fatherlessness with poverty, welfare dependency, crime and other pathologies points to a monstrous social problem. Yet, as the problem has grown, it has been systematically redefined by the culture—by social workers, intellectuals and most famously by the mass media—as simply another lifestyle choice. Dan Quayle may have been right, but Murphy Brown won the ratings war.

Moynihan's second example is crime. We have become totally inured to levels of criminality that would have been considered intolerable thirty years ago. The St. Valentine's Day massacre, which caused a national uproar and merited two entries in the *World Book Encyclopedia*, involved four thugs killing seven other thugs. An average weekend in today's Los Angeles, notes James Q. Wilson. More than half of all violent crimes are not even reported. We have come to view homicide as ineradicable a part of the social landscape as car accidents.

Reprinted from the New Republic, *November 22, 1993. This article is adapted from the author's Bradley Lecture at the American Enterprise Institute.*

And finally there is mental illness. Unlike family breakdown and criminality, there has probably been no increase in mental illness over the last thirty years. Rates of schizophrenia do not change, but the rate of hospitalization for schizophrenia and other psychoses has changed. The mental hospitals have been emptied. In 1955 New York state asylums had 93,000 patients. Last year they had 11,000. Where have the remaining 82,000 and their descendants gone? Onto the streets mostly. In one generation, a flood of pathetically ill people has washed onto the streets of America's cities. We now step over these wretched and abandoned folk sleeping in doorways and freezing on grates. They, too, have become accepted as part of the natural landscape. We have managed to do that by redefining them as people who simply lack affordable housing. They are not crazy or sick, just very poor—as if anyone crazy and sick and totally abandoned would not end up very poor.

Moynihan's powerful point is that with the moral deregulation of the 1960s, we have had an explosion of deviancy in family life, criminal behavior and public displays of psychosis. And we have dealt with it in the only way possible: by redefining deviancy down so as to explain away and make "normal" what a more civilized, ordered and healthy society long ago would have labeled—and long ago did label—deviant.

Moynihan is right. But it is only half the story. There is a complementary social phenomenon that goes with defining deviancy down. As part of the vast social project of moral leveling, it is not enough for the deviant to be normalized. The normal must be found to be deviant. Therefore, while for the criminals and the crazies deviancy has been defined down (the bar defining normality has been lowered), for the ordinary bourgeois deviancy has been defined up (the bar defining normality has been raised). Large areas of ordinary behavior hitherto considered benign have had their threshold radically redefined up, so that once innocent behavior now stands condemned as deviant. Normal middle-class life then stands exposed as the true home of violence and abuse and a whole catalog of aberrant acting and thinking.

As part of this project of moral leveling, entirely new areas of deviancy—such as date rape and politically incorrect speech—have been discovered. And old areas—such as child abuse—have been amplified by endless reiteration in the public presses and validated by learned reports of their astonishing frequency. The net effect is to show that deviancy is not the province of criminals and crazies but thrives in the heart of the great middle class. The real deviants of society stand unmasked. Who are they? Not Bonnie and Clyde but Ozzie and Harriet. True, Ozzie and Harriet have long been the object of ridicule. Now, however, they are under indictment.

The moral deconstruction of middle-class normality is a vast project. Fortunately, thousands of volunteers are working the case. By defining deviancy up they have scored some notable successes. Three, in particular. And in precisely the areas Moynihan identified: family life, crime and thought disorders.

First, family life. Under the new dispensation it turns out that the ordinary middle-class family is not a warm, welcoming fount of "family values," not a bedrock of social and psychic stability as claimed in conservative propaganda. It is instead a caldron of pathology, a teeming source of the depressions, alienations and assorted dysfunctions of adulthood. Why? Because deep in the family lies the worm, the 1990s version of original sin: child abuse.

Child abuse is both a crime and a tragedy, but is it nineteen times more prevalent today than it was thirty years ago? That is what the statistics offer. In 1963: 150,000 reported cases. In 1992: 2.9 million.

Now, simply considering the historical trajectory of the treatment of children since the nineteenth century, when child labor—even child slavery—was common, it is hard to believe that the tendency toward improved treatment of children has been so radically reversed in one generation.

Plainly it hasn't. What happened then? The first thing that happened was an epidemic of over-reporting. Douglas Besharov points out that whereas in 1975 about one-third of child abuse cases were dismissed for lack of evidence, today about two-thirds are dismissed. New York state authorities may have considered it a great social advance that between 1979 and 1983, for example, reported cases of child abuse increased by almost 50 percent. But over the same period, the number of substantiated cases actually declined. In other words, the 22,000 increase of reported cases yielded a net decrease of real cases.

Note the contrast. For ordinary crime, to which we have become desensitized, we have defined deviancy down. One measure of this desensitization is under-reporting: nearly two out of every three ordinary crimes are never even reported. Child abuse is precisely the opposite. For child abuse, to which we have become exquisitely oversensitized, deviancy has been correspondingly defined up. One of the measures of oversensitization is over-reporting: whereas two out of three ordinary crimes are never reported, two out of three reported cases of child abuse are never shown to have occurred.

The perceived epidemic of child abuse is a compound of many factors. Clearly, over-reporting is one. Changing societal standards regarding corporal punishment is another. But beyond the numbers and definitions there is a new ideology of child abuse. Under its influence, the helping professions, committed to a belief in endemic abuse, have encouraged a massive search to find cases, and where they cannot be found, to invent them.

Consider this advice from one of the more popular self-help books on sex abuse, *Courage to Heal*. "If you are unable to remember any specific instances [of childhood sex abuse] . . . but still have a feeling that something abusive happened to you, it probably did." And "if you think you were abused and your life shows the symptoms, then you were."

If your life shows the symptoms. In a popular culture saturated with tales of child abuse paraded daily on the airwaves, it is not hard to suggest to vulnerable people that their problems—symptoms—are caused by long-ago abuse, indeed, even unremembered abuse. Hence the reductio ad absurdum of the search for the hidden epidemic: adults who present themselves suddenly as victims of child abuse after decades of supposed amnesia—the amnesia reversed and the memory reclaimed thanks to the magic of intensive psychotherapy.

Now, the power of therapeutic suggestion is well-known. Dr. George Ganaway of Emory University points out—and, as a retired psychiatrist, I well remember—how fiction disguised as memory can be created at the suggestion of a trusted therapist whom the patient wants to please.

Why should memories of child abuse please the therapist? Because it fits the new ideology of neurosis. For almost a century Freudian ideology located the source of adult neuroses in the perceived psychosexual traumas of childhood. But Freud concluded after initial skepticism that these psychosexual incidents were fantasy.

Today Freud's conclusion is seen either as a great error or, as Jeffrey Masson and other anti-Freudian crusaders insist, as a great betrayal of what he knew to be the truth. Today's fashion, promoted by a vanguard of therapists and researchers is that the fantasies are true. When the patient presents with depression, low self-esteem or any of the common ailments of modern life, the search begins for the underlying childhood sexual abuse. "Some contemporary therapists," writes Elizabeth Loftus, professor of psychology at the University of Washington, "have been known to tell patients, on the basis of a suggestive history or 'symptom profile,' that they definitely had a traumatic experience. The therapist then urges the patient to pursue the recalcitrant memories."

This new psychology is rooted in and reinforces current notions about the pathology of ordinary family life. Rather than believing, as we did for a hundred years under the influence of Freud, that adult neurosis results from the inevitable psychological traumas of sexual maturation, compounded by parental error and crystallized in the (literally) fantastic memories of the patient, today there is a new dispensation. Nowadays neurosis is the outcome not of innocent errors but of criminal acts occurring in the very bosom of the ordinary-looking family. Seek and ye shall find: the sins of the fathers are visible in the miserable lives of the children. Child abuse is the crime waiting only to be discovered with, of course, the proper therapeutic guidance and bedtime reading. It is the dirty little secret behind the white picket fence. And beside this offense, such once-regarded deviancies of family life as illegitimacy appear benign.

So much for the family. Let us look now at a second pillar of everyday bourgeois life: the ordinary heterosexual relationship. A second vast category of human behavior that until recently was considered rather normal has had its threshold for normality redefined up so as to render much of it deviant. Again we start with a real offense: rape. It used to be understood as involving the use of or threat of force. No longer. It has now been expanded by the concept of date rape to encompass an enormous continent of behavior that had long been viewed as either normal or ill-mannered, but certainly not criminal.

"Some 47 percent of women are victims of rape or attempted rape . . . and 25 percent of women are victims of completed rape." So asserts Catharine MacKinnon on a national television news special. Assertions of this sort are commonplace. A Stanford survey, for example, claims that a third of its women have suffered date rape. The most famous and widely reported study of the rape epidemic is the one done by Mary Koss (and published, among other places, in *Ms.* magazine). Her survey of 6,159 college students found that 15 percent had been raped and another 12 percent subjected to attempted rape. She also reported that in a single year 3,187 college females reported 886 incidents of rape or attempted rape. That is more than one incident for every four women per year. At that rate, about three out of every four undergraduate women would be victims of rape or attempted rape by graduation day.

If those numbers sound high, they are. As Neil Gilbert points out in *The Public Interest*, the numbers compiled by the FBI under the Unified Crime Reporting Program and suitably multiplied to account for presumed unreported cases, yield an incidence of rape somewhere around one in a thousand. As for the college campus, reports from 2,400 campuses mandated by the Student Right-to-Know and Campus Security Act of 1990 showed fewer than 1,000 rapes for 1991. That is about one-half a rape per campus per year. Barnard College, a hotbed of anti-rape and Take Back the Night activity, released statistics in 1991 showing no reports of rape, date or otherwise, among its 2,200 students. Same for Harvard, Yale, Princeton, Brown—and Antioch, author of the strictest, most hilarious sexual correctness code in American academia.

How does one explain the vast discrepancy—1 in 2 differs from 1 in 1,000 by a factor of 500—between the real numbers and the fantastic numbers that have entered the popular imagination? Easy. Deviancy has again been redefined—up. Rape has been expanded by Koss and other researchers to include behavior that you and I would not recognize as rape. And not just you and I—the supposed victims themselves do not recognize it as rape. In the Koss study, 73 percent of the women she labeled as rape victims did not consider themselves to have been raped. Fully 42 percent had further sexual relations with the so-called rapist.

Now, women who have been raped are not generally known for going back for more sex with their assailants. Something is wrong here. What is wrong is the extraordinarily loose definition of sexual coercion and rape. Among the questions Koss asked her subjects were these: "Have you given in to sexual intercourse when you didn't want to because you were overwhelmed by a man's continual arguments and pressure?" and "Have you had sexual intercourse when you didn't want to because a man gave you alcohol or drugs?" The Stanford study, the one that turned up one out of three female students as victims of date rape, rests on respondents' self-report of "full sexual activity when they did not want to."

It is a common enough experience for people (both men and women) to be of two minds about having sex, and yet decide, reluctantly but certainly freely, to go ahead even though they do not really want to. Call that rape and there are few who escape the charge.

The cornerstone of this new and breathtakingly loose definition is the idea of verbal coercion. Consider this definition from the "Nonviolent Sexual Coercion" chapter in *Acquaintance Rape: The Hidden Crime* (John Wiley, 1991): "We define verbal sexual coercion as a woman's consenting to unwanted sexual activity because of a man's verbal arguments, not including verbal threats of physical force." With rape so radically defined up—to include offering a drink or being verbally insistent—it is no surprise that the result is an epidemic of sexual deviancy.

Of course, behind these numbers is an underlying ideology about the inherent aberrancy of all heterosexual relations. As Andrea Dworkin once said, "Romance . . . is rape embellished with meaningful looks." The date rape epidemic is just empirical dressing for a larger theory which holds that because relations between men and women are inherently unequal, sex can never be truly consensual. It is always coercive.

"The similarity between the patterns, rhythms, roles and emotions, not to mention acts, which make up rape (and battery) on the one hand and intercourse on the other, . . ." writes MacKinnon, "makes it difficult to sustain the customary distinctions between pathology and normalcy, violence and sex." And "Compare victims' reports of rape with women's reports of sex. They look a lot alike. . . . In this light, the major distinction between intercourse (normal) and rape (abnormal) is that the normal happens so often that one cannot get anyone to see anything wrong with it." Or as Susan Estrich puts it, "Many feminists would argue that so long as women are powerless relative to men, viewing 'yes' as a sign of true consent is misguided." But if "yes" is not a sign of true consent, then what is? A notarized contract?

And if there is no such thing as real consent, then the radical feminist ideal is realized: all intercourse is rape. Who needs the studies? The incidence of rape is not 25 percent or 33 or 50. It is 100 percent. Then Naomi Wolf can write in *The Beauty Myth* that we have today "a situation among the young in which boys rape and girls get raped *as a normal course of events*." (Her italics.)

Date rape is only the most extreme example of deviancy redefined broadly enough to catch in its net a huge chunk of normal, everyday behavior. It is the most extreme example because it is criminal. But then there are the lesser offenses, a bewildering array of transgressions that come under the rubric of sexual harassment, the definition of which can be equally loose and floating but is always raised high enough to turn innocent behavior into deviancy. As Allan Bloom wrote, "What used to be understood as modes of courtship are now seen as modes of male intimidation."

So much then for the family and normal heterosexual relations. On now to the third great area of the new deviancy: thought crimes.

This summer, I was visited by an FBI agent doing a routine background check on a former employee of mine now being considered for some high administration post. The agent went through the usual checklist of questions that I had heard many times before: questions about financial difficulties, drug abuse, alcoholism. Then he popped a new one: Did this person ever show any prejudice to a group based on race, ethnicity, gender, national origin, etc.? I assumed that he was not interested in whether the person had been involved in any racial incident. The FBI would have already known about that. What he wanted to know about was my friend's deeper thoughts, feelings he might have betrayed only to someone with whom he had worked intimately for two years. This was the point in the interview at which I was supposed to testify whether I had heard my friend tell any sexist or racist jokes or otherwise show signs of hidden prejudice. That is when it occurred to me that insensitive speech had achieved official status as a thought crime.

Now, again we start with real deviance—racial violence of the kind once carried out by the Klan or today by freelancers like the two men in Tampa recently convicted of a monstrous racial attack on a black tourist. These are outlawed and punished. So are the more benign but still contemptible acts of nonviolent racial discrimination, as in housing, for example. But now that overt racial actions have been criminalized and are routinely punished, the threshold for deviancy has been ratcheted up. The project now is to identify prejudiced thinking, instincts, anecdotes, attitudes.

The great arena for this project is the American academy. The proliferation of speech codes on campuses, restrained only by their obvious unconstitutionality, was an attempt by universities to curtail speech that may cause offense to groups designated for special protection. A University of Michigan student, for example, offers the opinion *in class* that homosexuality is an illness, and finds himself hauled before a formal university hearing on charges of harassing students on the basis of sexual orientation.

The irony here is quite complete. It used to be that homosexuality was considered deviant. But now that it has been declared a simple life-style choice, those who are not current with the new definitions, and have the misfortune to say so in public, find themselves suspected of deviancy.

There is, of course, the now-famous case of the Israeli-born University of Pennsylvania student who called a group of rowdy black sorority sisters making noise outside his dorm in the middle of the night "water buffaloes" (his rough translation from the Hebrew *behema*). He was charged with racial harassment. A host of learned scholars was assigned the absurd task of locating the racial antecedents of the term. They could find none. (They should have asked me. I could have saved them a lot of trouble. My father called me behemah so many times it almost became a term of endearment. I don't think he was racially motivated.) Nonetheless, the university, convinced that there was some racial animus behind that exotic term and determined not to let it go unpunished, tried to pressure the student into admitting his guilt. Penn offered him a plea bargain. Proceedings would be stopped if he confessed and allowed himself to be re-educated through a "program for living in a diverse community environment."

Consider: the psychotic raving in the middle of Broadway is free to rave. No one will force him into treatment. But a student who hurls "water buffalo" at a bunch of sorority sisters is threatened with the ultimate sanction at the disposal of the university—expulsion—unless he submits to treatment to correct his deviant thinking.

This may seem ironic but it is easily explained. Under the new dispensation it is not insanity but insensitivity that is the true sign of deviant thinking, requiring thought control and re-education. One kind of deviancy we are prepared to live with; the other, we are not. Indeed, one kind, psychosis, we are hardly prepared to call deviancy at all. As Moynihan points out, it is now part of the landscape.

The mentally ill are not really ill. They just lack housing. It is the rest of us who are guilty of disordered thinking for harboring—beneath the bland niceties of middle-class life—racist, misogynist, homophobic and other corrupt and corrupting insensitivities.

Ordinary criminality we are learning to live with. What we are learning we cannot live with is the heretofore unrecognized violence against women that lurks beneath the facade of ordinary, seemingly benign, heterosexual relations.

The single-parent and broken home are now part of the landscape. It is the Ozzie and Harriet family, rife with abuse and molestation, that is the seedbed of deviance.

The rationalization of deviancy reaches its logical conclusion. The deviant is declared normal. And the normal is unmasked as deviant. That, of course, makes us all that much more morally equal. The project is complete. What real difference is there between us?

And that is the point. Defining deviancy up, like defining deviancy down, is an adventure in moral equivalence. As such, it is the son of an old project that met its demise with the end of the Soviet empire. There once was the idea of moral equivalence between the East and the West. Even though the Soviets appeared to be imperialist and brutal and corrupt and rapacious, we were really as bad as they were. We could match them crime for crime throughout the world.

Well, this species of moral equivalence is now dead. The liberation of the Communist empire, the opening of the archives, the testimony of the former inmates—all these have made a mockery of this version of moral equivalence.

But ideology abhors a vacuum. So we have a new version of moral equivalence: the moral convergence within Western society of the normal and the deviant. It is a bold new way to strip the life of the bourgeois West of its moral sheen. Because once it becomes, to use MacKinnon's words, "difficult to sustain the customary distinctions between pathology and normalcy," the moral superiority to which bourgeois normalcy pretends vanishes.

And the perfect vehicle for exposing the rottenness of bourgeois life is defining deviancy up. After all, the law-abiding middle classes define their own virtue in contrast to the deviant, a contrast publicly dramatized by opprobrium, ostracism and punishment. And now it turns out that this great contrast between normality and deviance is a farce. The real deviants, mirabile dictu, are those who carry the mask of sanity, the middle classes living on their cozy suburban streets, abusing their children, violating their women and harboring deep inside them the most unholy thoughts.

Defining deviancy up is a new way of satisfying an old ideological agenda. But it also fills a psychological need. The need was identified by Moynihan: How to cope with the explosion of real deviancy? One way is denial: defining real deviancy down creates the pretense that deviance has disappeared because it has been redefined as normal. Another strategy is distraction: defining deviancy up creates brand-new deviancies that we can now go off and fight. That distracts us from real deviancy and gives us the feeling that, despite the murder and mayhem and madness around us, we are really preserving and policing our norms.

Helpless in the face of the explosion of real criminality, for example, we satisfy our crime-fighting needs with a crusade against date rape. Like looking for your lost wallet under the street lamp even though you lost it elsewhere, this job is easier even if not terribly relevant to the problem at hand. Defining deviancy up creates a whole new universe of behavior to police, and—a bonus—a higher class of offender. More malleable, too: the guilt-ridden bourgeois, the vulnerable college student, is a far easier object of social control than the hardened criminal or the raving lunatic.

These new crusades do nothing, of course, about real criminality or lunacy. But they make us feel that we are making inroads on deviancy nonetheless. A society must feel that it is policing its norms by combating deviancy. Having given up fighting the real thing, we can't give up the fight. So we fight the new deviancy with satisfying vigor. That it is largely a phantom and a phony seems not to matter at all.

7. The Way Home

*I*n this final section, neoconservatives address the question how a lost culture can recover its moral moorings. In "A De-Moralized Society: The British/American Experience," the social historian Gertrude Himmelfarb offers a dour diagnosis of the American cultural situation and discusses how the adaptation of traditional virtues and time-honored modes of interaction and behavior are essential for a cultural correction. Where do these virtues and modes of interaction and behavior stem from originally; where are their roots? The neoconservatives offer an answer: religion. They have stressed that religious values are essential to public virtue, and in the 1990s many neoconservatives have drawn directly from strong personal Jewish and Christian faith. Their theologies may be different, but to the neoconservatives the values their faiths teach are universal. As Michael Novak has written, "The two [Judaism and Christianity] share an astonishing number of convictions, aims, expectations, perspectives, and criteria of goodness. It is hard to exaggerate how much they have in common." The neoconservatives argue for the importance of bringing those values into the public arena.

Richard John Neuhaus, a Catholic priest, and founder and editor of the influential journal of religion and public life First Things, has been the neoconservative leader in these matters. Neuhaus, in a powerfully argued essay, "A New Order of Religious Freedom," discusses how a forthright religious presence in the public square honors the intent of the framers and speaks to the best part of the American nature. The neoconservatives *realize that many people approach the public display of faith with great skepticism, and have stressed that religious people have a responsibility to articulate their values in the public arena in a universal secular vernacular. George Weigel's article "Christian Conviction and Democratic Etiquette" explains this duty and shows how it should be executed. William Kristol, formerly the chief of staff to Vice President Dan Quayle and now the editor and publisher of* The Weekly Standard, *concludes this section by explaining how the government, through energetic creativity, can aid the unfolding conservative cultural transformation.*

A New Order of Religious Freedom

Richard John Neuhaus

MORE THAN HE WANTED to be remembered for having been President, Mr. Jefferson wanted to be remembered as the author of the Virginia "Bill for Establishing Religious Freedom." In his draft of that bill he wrote: "The opinions of men are not the object of civil government, nor under its jurisdiction." In a republic of free citizens, every opinion, every prejudice, every aspiration, every moral discernment has access to the public square in which we deliberate the ordering of our life together.

"The opinions of men are not the object of civil government, nor under its jurisdiction." And yet civil government is ordered by, and derives its legitimacy from, the opinions of the citizenry. Precisely here do we discover the novelty of the American experiment, the unique contribution of what the Founders called this *novus ordo seclorum*, a new order for the ages. Never before in human history had any government denied itself jurisdiction over that on which it entirely depends, the opinion of its people.

That was the point forcefully made by Lincoln in his dispute with Stephen Douglas over slavery. Douglas stubbornly held to the Dred Scott decision as the law of the land. Lincoln had the deeper insight into how this republic was designed to work. "In this age, and this country," Lincoln said, "public sentiment is every thing. *With* it, nothing can fail; *against* it, nothing can succeed. Whoever moulds public sentiment, goes deeper than he who enacts statutes, or pronounces judicial decisions. He makes possible the inforcement of these, else impossible."

The question of religion's access to the public square is not first of all a question of First Amendment law. It is first of all a question of understand-

Reprinted from First Things *(February 1992). This article is adapted from an address delivered at a conference on Christianity and Democracy at Emory University.*

ing the theory and practice of democratic governance. Citizens are the bearers of opinion, including opinion shaped by or espousing religious belief, and citizens have equal access to the public square. In this representative democracy, the state is forbidden to determine which convictions and moral judgments may be proposed for public deliberation. Through a constitutionally ordered process, the people will deliberate and the people will decide.

In a democracy that is free and robust, an opinion is no more disqualified for being "religious" than for being atheistic, or psychoanalytic, or Marxist, or just plain dumb. There is no legal or constitutional question about the admission of religion to the public square; there is only a question about the free and equal participation of citizens in our public business. Religion is not a reified "thing" that threatens to intrude upon our common life. Religion in public is but the public opinion of those citizens who are religious.

As with individual citizens, so also with the associations that citizens form to advance their opinions. Religious institutions may understand themselves to be brought into being by God, but for the purposes of this democratic polity they are free associations of citizens. As such, they are guaranteed the same access to the public square as are the citizens who comprise them. It matters not at all that their purpose is to advance religion, any more than it matters that other associations would advance the interests of business or labor or radical feminism or animal rights or whatever.

For purposes of democratic theory and practice, it matters not at all whether these religious associations are large or small, whether they reflect the views of a majority or minority, whether we think their opinions bizarre or enlightened. What opinions these associations seek to advance in order to influence our common life is entirely and without remainder the business of citizens who freely adhere to such associations. It is none of the business of the state. Religious associations, like other associations, give corporate expression to the opinions of people and, as Mr. Jefferson said, "the opinions of men are not the object of civil government, nor under its jurisdiction."

It is to be feared that those who interpret "the separation of church and state" to mean the separation of religion from public life do not understand the theory and practice of democratic governance. Ours is not a secular form of government, if by "secular" is meant indifference or hostility to opinions that are thought to be religious in nature. The civil government is as secular as are the people from whom it derives its democratic legitimacy. No more, no less. Indeed a case can be made—and I believe it to be a convincing case—that the very founding principle that removes opinion from the jurisdiction of the state is itself religious in both historical origin and continuing foundation. Put differently, the foundation of religious freedom is itself religious.

"We hold these truths," the Founders declared. And when these truths about the "unalienable rights" with which men are "endowed by their Creator" are no longer firmly held by the American people and robustly advanced in the public square, this experiment will have come to an end. In that unhappy case, this experiment will have turned out to be not a *novus ordo seclorum* but a temporary respite from humanity's penchant for tyranny. Yet in the second century of the experiment, secularized elites in our universities and our courts became embarrassed by the inescapably religious nature of this nation's founding and fortune.

These secularized elites have devoted their energies to explaining why the Founders did not hold the truths that they said they held. They have attempted to strip the public square of religious opinion that does not accord with their opinion. They have labored assiduously to lay other foundations than those laid in the beginning. From John Dewey to John Rawls, and with many lesser imitators in between, they have tried to construct philosophical foundations for this experiment in freedom, only to discover that their efforts are rejected by a people who stubbornly persist in saying with the Founders, "We hold these truths." A theory of democracy that is neither understood nor accepted by the democracy for which it is contrived is a theory of democracy both misbegotten and stillborn. Two hundred years ago, and even more so today, the American people, from whom democratic legitimacy is derived, are incorrigibly religious. This America continues to be, in the telling phrase of Chesterton, "a nation with the soul of a church."

And yet there are those who persist in the claim that "the separation of church and state" means the separation of religion from public life. They raise the alarm about "church-state conflicts" that are nothing of the sort. There are conflicts, to be sure, but they are the conflicts of a robust republic in which free citizens freely contend in the public square. The extreme separationists will tolerate in public, they may even assiduously protect, the expression of marginal religious opinion, of opinion that is not likely to influence our common life. But they take alarm at the voice of the majority. In that voice it is the people that they hear; it is the people that they fear; it is democracy that they fear.

Mr. Jefferson did not say that the civil government has no jurisdiction over opinion *except* when it is religious opinion. He did not say that the civil government has no jurisdiction over opinion *except* when it is expressed through associations called churches or synagogues. He did not say that the civil government has no jurisdiction over opinion *except* when it is majority opinion. He said, "The opinions of men are not the object of civil government, nor under its jurisdiction."

Many worry about the dangers of raw majoritarianism, and well we all should worry. The Founders worried about it, and that is why they devised a constitutional order for *representative* governance, and for the protection of minority opinion and behavior. But, without the allegiance of the majority to that constitutional order, such protections are only, in the words of James Madison, "parchment barriers" to tyranny. As Lincoln observed, without the support of public sentiment, statutes and judicial decisions—including those intended to protect citizens who dissent from public sentiment—cannot be enforced.

In our day, minorities seeking refuge in the protections of the Constitution frequently do so in a manner that pits the Constitution against the American people. That is understandable, but it is a potentially fatal mistake. We must never forget the preamble and irreplaceable premise of the Constitution: "We the people . . . do ordain and establish this Constitution for the United States of America." That is to say, the Constitution and all its protections depend upon the sentiment of "we the people." Majority rule is far from being the only principle of democratic governance, but it is a necessary principle. In the Constitution, the majority imposes upon itself a self-denying ordinance; it promises not to do what it otherwise could do, namely, ride roughshod over the dissenting minorities.

Why, we might ask, does the majority continue to impose such a limitation upon itself? A number of answers suggest themselves. One reason is that most Americans recognize, however inarticulately, a sovereignty higher than the sovereignty of "we the people." They believe there is absolute truth but they are not sure that they understand it absolutely; they are, therefore, disinclined to force it upon those who disagree. It is not chiefly a secular but a religious restraint that prevents biblical believers from coercing others in matters of conscience. For example, we do not kill one another over our disagreements about the will of God because we believe that it is the will of God that we should not kill one another over our disagreements about the will of God. Christians and Jews did not always believe that, but, with very few exceptions, we in this country have come to believe it. It is among the truths that we hold.

Then too, protecting those who differ is in the self-interest of all. On most controverted issues in our public life, there is no stable majority, only ever-shifting convergences and divergences. Non-Christians, and Jews in particular, sometimes see an ominous majoritarian threat in the fact that nearly 88 percent of the American people claim to be Christian. As a matter of practical fact, however, that great majority is sharply divided along myriad lines when it comes to how civil government should be rightly ordered. Furthermore, a growing number of Christians, perhaps most Christians, have a religiously grounded understanding of the respect that is owed living Judaism. Those Christians who argue that "Christian America" should be reconstructed in conformity with a revealed biblical blueprint for civil government are few and marginal, and are likely to remain so.

Father John Courtney Murray observed that, while in theory politics should be unified with revealed truth, "it seems that pluralism is written into the script of history." Some of us would go further and suggest that it is God who has done the writing. Pluralism is our continuing condition and our moral imperative until the End Time, when our disagreements will be resolved in the coming of the Kingdom. The protection against raw majoritarianism, then, depends upon this constitutional order. But this constitutional order depends, in turn, upon the continuing ratification of the majority who are "we the people." Among the truths these people hold is the truth that it is necessary to protect those who do not hold those truths.

It is a remarkable circumstance, this American circumstance. It is also fragile. We may wish that Lincoln was wrong when he observed that "In this age, and this country, public sentiment is every thing." But he was right, and in the conflict over slavery he was to see public sentiment turn against the constitutional order and nearly bring it to irretrievable ruin. We are dangerously deceived if we think that Lincoln's observation about our radical dependence upon public sentiment is one whit less true today.

The question before us, then, is not the access of religion to the public square. The question is the access, indeed the full and unencumbered participation, of men and women, of citizens, who bring their opinions, sentiments, convictions, prejudices, visions, and communal traditions of moral discernment to bear on our public deliberation of how we ought to order our life together in this experiment that aspires toward representative democracy. It is of course an aspiration always imperfectly realized.

I noted at the start that the question before us is not first of all a question of First Amendment law. It is a question, first of all, of understanding the origins, the constituting truths, and the continuing foundations of this republic. That having been said, the question before us is also and very importantly a question of the First Amendment, and of the first liberty of that First Amendment.

The first thing to be said about that first liberty is that liberty is the end, the goal, and the entire rationale of what the First Amendment says about religion. This means that there is no conflict, no tension, no required "balancing" between free exercise and no-establishment. There are not two religion clauses. There is but one religion clause. The stipulation is that "Congress shall make no law," and the rest of the clause consists of participial modifiers explaining what kind of law Congress shall not make. This may seem like a small grammatical point, but it has far-reaching jurisprudential significance.

The no-establishment part of the religion clause is entirely and without remainder in the service of free exercise. Free exercise is the end; no-establishment is a necessary means to that end. No-establishment simply makes no sense on its own. Why on earth should we need a no-establishment provision? The answer is that no-establishment is required to protect the rights of those who might dissent from whatever religion is established. In other words, no-establishment is required for free exercise. It is, one may suggest, more than a nice play on words that Mr. Jefferson's bill of 1779 was called the "Bill for *Establishing* Religious Freedom." The purpose of the non-establishment of religion is to establish religious freedom. It follows that any interpretation of no-establishment that hinders free exercise is a misinterpretation of no-establishment.

In recent history, especially in the last four decades, the priority of free exercise has been dangerously obscured. Indeed, one must go further. The two parts of the religion clause have been quite thoroughly inverted. One gets the distinct impression from some constitutional scholars and, all too often, from the courts that no-establishment is the end to which free exercise is something of a nuisance. To take but one prominent example,

Laurence Tribe writes in his widely used *American Constitutional Law* that there is a "zone which the free exercise clause carves out of the establishment clause for permissible accommodation of religious interests. This carved-out area might be characterized as the zone of permissible accommodation."

There we have the inversion clearly and succinctly stated. Professor Tribe allows—almost reluctantly, it seems—that, within carefully prescribed limits, the *means* that is no-establishment might permissibly accommodate the *end* that is free exercise. This is astonishing, and it is the more astonishing that it no longer astonishes, for Professor Tribe is hardly alone. Scholars and judges have in these few decades become accustomed to having the religion clause turned on its head.

Once we forget that no-establishment is a means and instrument in support of free exercise, it is a short step to talking about the supposed conflict or tension between the two provisions. And from there it is a short step to the claim that the two parts of the religion clause are "pitted against one another" and must somehow be "balanced." And from there it is but another short step to the idea that the no-establishment provision protects "secular liberty" while the free exercise provision protects "religious liberty." When the religion clause is construed according to this curious inversion, it is no surprise that religious liberty comes out the loser. Any impingement of religion upon public life is taken to violate the "secular liberty" of the nonreligious. Thus has no-establishment become the master of the free exercise that it was designed to serve.

We need not speculate about the practical consequences of this curious inversion of the religion clause. The consequences are plainly to be seen all around us. In the name of no-establishment, wherever government advances religion must retreat. And government does inexorably expand its sway over the entire social order. In education, social services, and other dimensions of public life, it is claimed that, for the sake of the nonestablishment of religion, Americans must surrender the free exercise of religion. Those who insist upon the exercise of religious freedom in education, for example, must forego the government support that is available to those who do not so insist. Thus is religious freedom penalized in the name of a First Amendment that was designed to protect religious freedom. Thus has the constitutionally privileged status of religion been turned into a disability. Thus has insistence upon the free exercise of religion been turned into a disqualifying handicap in our public life.

The argument that public policy should not discriminate against citizens who are religious is said to be an instance of special pleading by those who have an interest in religion. That seems very odd in a society where over 90 percent of its citizens claim to be religious. It is more than odd, it is nothing less than grotesque, that we have become accustomed to the doctrine that public policy should not benefit religion. What is this "religion" that must not be benefited? It is the individually and communally expressed *opinion* of a free people. To say that government should not be responsive to religion is to say that government should not be responsive to the opinion of the people. Again, the argument of extreme separationism is, in effect, an argument against democratic governance.

Once more, Mr. Jefferson: "The opinions of men are not the object of civil government, nor under its jurisdiction." The state of current First Amendment jurisprudence is such that the opinions of men and women, when they are religious, have been placed under the jurisdiction of the government. According to the inverted construal of the religion clause, wherever the writ of government runs the voice of religion must be silenced or stifled—and the writ of government runs almost everywhere. No-establishment, the servant of the free exercise of religion, has become the enemy of the free exercise of religion.

To contend for the free exercise of religion is to contend for the perpetuation of a nation "so conceived and so dedicated." It is to contend for the hope "that this nation, under God, shall have a new birth of freedom; and that government of the people, by the people, for the people, shall not perish from the earth." Despite the perverse jurisprudence of recent decades, most Americans still say with the Founders, "We hold these truths." And, with the Founders, they understand those truths to be religious both in their origin and in their continuing power. Remove that foundation and we remove the deepest obligation binding the American people to this constitutional order.

The argument here is not for an unbridled freedom for people to do whatever they will, so long as they do it in the name of religion. That way lies anarchy and the undoing of religious freedom in the name of religious freedom. There are of necessity limits on behavior, as distinct from opinion. But the constitutionally privileged and preferred status of religious freedom is such that, when free exercise is invoked, we must respond with the most diligent caution. The invocation of free exercise is an appeal to a higher sovereignty. The entire constitutional order of limited government is premised upon an acknowledgment of such higher sovereignty.

Sometimes—reluctantly, and in cases of supreme and overriding public necessity—the claim to free exercise protection for certain actions must be denied. Where such lines should be drawn is a matter of both constitutional law and democratic deliberation. It is a matter that engages the religiously grounded moral discernments of the public, without whose support such decisions cannot be democratically implemented. In other words, in this age and this country, the limits on the free exercise of religion must themselves be legitimated religiously.

A morally compelling reason must be given for refusing to allow people to do what is morally compelling. Those who seriously invoke the free exercise of religion claim to be fulfilling a solemn duty. As Madison, Jefferson, and others of the Founders understood, religious freedom is a matter less of rights than of duties. More precisely, it is a matter of rights derived from duties. Denying a person or community the right to act upon such duty can only be justified by appeal to a yet more compelling duty. Those so denied will, of course, usually not find the reason for the denial compelling. Because they may turn out to be right about the duty in question, and because, even if they are wrong, religion bears witness to that which transcends the political order, such denials should be both rare and painfully reluctant.

We have in this last half-century drifted far from the constituting vision of this *novus ordo seclorum*. The free exercise of religion is the irreplaceable cornerstone of that order. In his famed *Memorial and Remonstrance*, James Madison wrote: "It is the duty of every man to render to the Creator such homage, and such only, as he believes to be acceptable to Him. This duty is precedent, both in order of time and in degree of obligation, to the claims of Civil Society."

The great problem today is not the threat that religion poses to public life, but the threat that the state, presuming to embody public life, poses to religion. The entire order of freedom, including all the other freedoms specified in the Bill of Rights, is premised upon what Madison calls the precedent duty that is religion. When the American people can no longer publicly express their obligations to the Creator, it is to be feared that they will no longer acknowledge their obligations to one another—nor to the Constitution in which the obligations of freedom are enshrined. The free exercise of religion is not about mere "access." The free exercise of religion is about the survival of an experiment in which civil government has no jurisdiction over the expression of the higher loyalties on which that government depends.

Debates over the niceties of First Amendment law must and will continue. We should not forget, however, that our real subject is the constituting vision of a constitutional order that, if we have the wit and the nerve for it, may yet turn out to be a new order for the ages.

Christian Conviction and Democratic Etiquette

George Weigel

ACCORDING TO A BIT of street wisdom that has worked its way into the national vocabulary, "You got to walk the walk, not just talk the talk." But since the opposite of everything is frequently, if not always, true, we might, on the matter of explicitly Christian rhetoric and the American public square, consider reversing the injunction and asking the question: How do we talk the talk? How, that is, do we talk so that moral judgments born from Christian religious conviction can be heard and thoughtfully considered by all Americans—or at least by those Americans willing to concede that moral judgment plays a crucial role in the public policy process?

The question of how Christians "talk the talk" in American public life will not go away, because it cannot go away; this is a fact of demographics, as well as a reflection of the nation's historic cultural core. For the foreseeable future the United States will remain at one and the same time a democracy, a deeply religious society, and a vibrantly, gloriously, maddeningly, and, in some respects, depressingly diverse culture. And thus, just as in decades if not centuries past, the 1990s will see a striking diversity of "vocabularies" in the American public square: many of them religious, others determinedly secular.

How, then, to begin with, can Christians of various theological persuasions talk with each other as they deliberate their public responsibilities within the household of faith? And how can those same diverse Christian communities contribute to a public moral discourse that would more closely resemble a reasonable argument than a cacophony? Is there, in other words, a grammar that can bring some discipline to the inevitably polyglot public debate over how we ought to live together?

Reprinted from First Things *(March 1994).*

These questions have been perennials in the garden of American public controversy. But they have been rendered more urgent over the past twenty years by two phenomena, distinct in their provenance but not unrelated in their public consequences.

The first is the return to the public square of conservative, evangelical, and fundamentalist Protestants from the cultural hinterlands to which they were consigned (and to which they often consigned themselves) in the aftermath of the Scopes Trial of 1925. For almost fifty years after that great trek to the margins of the public discourse, "the evangelicals" were content to remain in their enclaves, worshipping and educating their children as they saw fit, asking only to be left alone by the larger society. By the late 1970s, however, the Carter administration's Justice Department and Internal Revenue Service, by their assault on Christian day schools, had demonstrated the impossibility of sustaining that strategy; and the result was the defensive/offensive movement we have come to know as the "religious new right." That this movement dramatically sharpened the debate over the place of Christian conviction in public discourse is too obvious to need further elaboration.

And second, the return of the evangelicals and fundamentalists from cultural exile was paralleled in the 1980s by a new assertiveness on the part of American Roman Catholics (and especially several prominent bishops). On issues such as abortion, pornography, school choice, and the claims of the gay/lesbian/bisexual movement, Catholic bishops, activists, and intellectuals who insisted on acting like Catholics in public soon found themselves engaged not simply in political or electoral battles, but in heated confrontations with several of the key idea-shaping and values-transmitting institutions in our society: among them the prestige press, the academy, and the popular entertainment industry. Perhaps the high (or low) point of this trajectory was reached on the 26th of November, 1989, when a *New York Times* editorial solemnly warned Catholic bishops that their resistance to abortion-on-demand threatened the "truce of tolerance" by which Catholics were permitted to play a part in American public life: a warning that was, even by *Times'* standards, an exercise in brazen chutzpah.

Thus through the evangelical insurgency and the revitalization of the Catholics in the public square—through the activism and interaction of two groups who had long eyed each other with mutual suspicion (if not downright hostility) but who now found themselves in common cause on a host of fevered public issues—American democracy was faced, yet again, with the problem of how it could be an *e pluribus unum* in fact as well as in theory. And for their part, American Christians had to think through the question of how their most deeply held convictions could be brought to bear on public life in ways that were faithful both to those convictions and to the canons of democratic civility. Given that the United States remains, in Chesterton's famous phrase, a nation with the soul of a church, the two questions were not unrelated.

So far as we know, the apostle Paul was not overly vexed about the public policy of Athens in the first century of the common era; but Paul's struggle to "translate" the Christian Gospel into terms that the Athenians could understand and engage suggests that the issue confronting Christians has a venerable history. Paul's invocation of the "unknown god" to the men gathered on the Areopagus was, of course, an evangelical tactic aimed at the religious conversion of his audience; the book of Acts does not suggest that Paul was very much concerned to reform deficit financing, health care, education, or defense appropriations in Greater Athens. But that evangelical instinct which led the apostle to seek a language—a grammar, if you will—through which the Athenians could grasp (and be grasped by) the claims of the Gospel is something on which we might well reflect, as we ponder such decidedly secondary and tertiary questions as deficit financing, health care reform, education, and defense appropriations in the American Republic.

Paul was a man at home with at least two moral-intellectual "grammars": the Judaic, in which he had been rabbinically trained, and the Hellenistic, which dominated elite culture in the eastern Mediterranean at the time. We may be sure that Paul regarded the Judaic grammar as superior to the Hellenistic, but he did not hesitate to employ the latter when he deemed it necessary for the sake of the Gospel.

This grammatical ecumenicity, as we might call it, was memorably captured in Paul's familiar boast, "I have become all things to all men, that I might by all means save some" (1 Corinthians 9:22b). Again, the questions behind this present discussion are questions of considerably less consequence than the salvation of souls. But if, in such a grand cause, the apostle of the gentiles could appeal to his audiences through language and images with which they were most familiar—if, to get down to cases, Paul could expropriate an Athenian idol as an instrument for breaking open the Gospel of Christ, the Son of the Living God—then perhaps it is incumbent upon us, working in the far less dramatic precincts of public policy, to devise means of translating our religious convictions into language and images that can illuminate for all our fellow-citizens the truths of how we ought to live together, as we have come to understand them through faith and reason.

There is danger in this, of course, and it should be squarely faced: Christians eager to be heard in the public square today may, through an excess of grammatical ecumenicity, so attenuate their message that the sharp edge of truth gets blunted, and thus debased. Flaccidity in the cause of a misconceived public ecumenism has been one dimension of the decline of the academic study of religion in America, as it has been a dimension of the decline of mainline/oldline Protestantism. Some would suggest that a similar disposition to excessive public correctness, as that set of attitudes is defined by the tastemakers of our society, has also misshaped certain interpretations of the Roman Catholic "consistent ethic of life."

Moreover, it can often seem as if our cultural moment demands uncompromising confrontation rather than polite dialogue. When unborn children have less legal standing than an endangered species of bird in a national forest; when any conceivable configuration of consenting adults sharing body parts is considered in enlightened circles to constitute a "marriage"; when senior United States Senators bloviate about "sexual harassment" in kindergarten while national illegitimacy rates approach 30 percent of all births: one is reminded of Orwell's observation, two generations ago, that "we have now sunk to a depth at which the restatement of the obvious is the first duty of intelligent men." There are some hard, home truths to be told on the various Mars Hills of the American Republic, and one need not doubt that the telling of such truths, even in a publicly accessible grammar, is going to bring down upon one's head the odium of those committed to the establishment of the Republic of the Imperial Autonomous Self. Under such circumstances, the old country saw which tells us that we may as well get hung for a sheep as for a goat retains its pertinence.

But the good news is that the bad news is not all the news there is. For in certain signs of these times we may also be seeing a new public recognition of the enduring realities of religious conviction and a new willingness to concede a place for religiously based moral argument in the American public square. The warm reception given Professor Stephen L. Carter's recent critique of the secularism of our elite culture, our law, and our politics suggests that seeds first planted by Richard John Neuhaus in *The Naked Public Square* are beginning to flower, however variously or confusedly. The broad bipartisan, ecumenical, and interreligious support that made possible the passage last year of the Religious Freedom Restoration Act is also an important straw in the wind (although it remains to be seen just how the creative minds on the federal bench will bend RFRA to various agendas of their own devising).

Then there is the fact that we have a President who, unlike his predecessor, is unabashedly public about his Christian faith, and who seems to understand that the engagement of differing religious convictions within the bond of democratic civility is good for America. It is far from self-evident that President Clinton's policies (and appointments) are entirely congruent with his religious and moral rhetoric; nor can one dismiss as mere partisanship the suggestion that the President's rhetoric has been designed in part to divide the white evangelical vote and thus secure his reelection in 1996. But politicians will always be politicians, and those of us who take the bully pulpit seriously can still applaud the fact that the President of the United States publicly acknowledges that "we are a people of faith" and that "religion helps to give our people the character without which a democracy cannot survive."* However wide the chasm between the President's talk and his administration's walk, it surely means something that President Clinton experiences no embarrassment about using religious language in public.

---

* The White House, Office of the Press Secretary, "Remarks by the President at Signing Ceremony for the Religious Freedom Restoration Act," November 16, 1993. President Clinton's comments on this and other occasions are in sharp contrast to the discomforts that President Bush experienced in publicly acknowledging religious faith. Some will attribute this, and not without reason, to the cultural differences between Kennebunkport Episcopalians and Little Rock Baptists. But even Bush's most ardent admirers would have to concede that he was, to put it bluntly, terrified by the "religion issue," which he seemed to regard as an expression of that "right-wing agenda stuff" he reportedly deplored. Most memorably, during the 1988 primaries, Bush, asked to recall what he was thinking about when he was floating alone in the Pacific after his plane had been shot down by the Japanese, replied that he had thought about "Mom and Dad, about our country, about God . . . and about the separation of church and state."

At the very least, the President's public appeal to biblical religion ought to remind us just how far from our roots we have strayed when the "naked public square" could even be considered a plausible embodiment of the American democratic experiment. In a nation whose coinage and currency contain the motto, "In God We Trust"; whose Supreme Court sessions open with the plea (admittedly, ever more poignant in recent years) that "God save this honorable court"; whose House of Representatives and Senate begin their daily work with prayer; whose Presidents have, without exception, invoked the blessing of God in their inaugural addresses—it is the proponents of established secularism who should be on the historical, cultural, constitutional, and moral defensive. If President Clinton's use of explicitly religious language does nothing other than make clear who ought to be prosecuting and who defending in this matter of religion and public life, then the President will have done the country a service indeed.

Still, the sheer fact that religiously based public moral argument seems "okay" again in certain influential quarters does not suggest the end of our problem, any more than the widespread celebration of the film *The Age of Innocence*, with its celebration of the superiority of marital fidelity over extramarital sexual passion, suggests the end of the sexual revolution. What we may have today, through a confluence of forces (and not least because the crisis of the urban underclass has finally focused the elite culture on problems of moral formation), is an opening through which to begin the slow and laborious process of reclothing the naked public square. Save in some tenured bunkers where cultural vandals make merry while the cities burn and children shoot children over basketball shoes, it is now widely acknowledged that its nudity has been bad for the country. The question is how, and in what livery, the square will be reclothed.

Abraham Lincoln, and specifically his Second Inaugural Address, provides an important historical model. In this speech, remember, Lincoln interpreted the national agony of a violent and sanguinary civil war in explicitly biblical terms, citing Matthew's Gospel ("Woe unto the world because of offenses; for it must needs be that offenses come; but woe to that man by whom the offense cometh") and the Psalmist ("The judgments of the Lord are true and righteous altogether") to buttress his general hermeneutic claim that the workings-out of the American democratic experiment were caught up in a divinely ordered plan for human history.

Now, can anyone reasonably argue that, in his deliberate choice of biblical language and in his appeal to the notion of a providential purpose in history, Lincoln was excluding anyone from the public debate over the meaning and purpose of the War Between the States? Can it be reasonably contended that Lincoln's attempt to prepare the United States for reconciliation by offering a biblically based moral interpretation of the recent national experience constituted an unconstitutional "imposition" of belief and values on others?

We recognize Lincoln's Second Inaugural as perhaps the greatest speech in American history precisely because, with singular eloquence and at a moment of unparalleled national trauma, it spoke to the entire country in an idiom that the entire country could understand. No one was excluded by Lincoln's use of biblical language and imagery; all, irrespective of confessional conviction (or the lack thereof), were included in the great moral drama whose meaning the President was trying to fix in the national consciousness.

It is arguably true that, even in the midst of civil war, the United States (North and South) was a more culturally coherent nation than our America today; and it is certainly true that no statesman of Lincoln's eloquence and moral imagination is on the horizon of our public life. Yet there is still an important lesson here. And the lesson is that biblical language and imagery in public discourse ought to be used, not to divide, but rather to unite: not to finish off an opponent with a rhetorical coup de grâce, but to call him (and all of us) to a deeper reflection on the promise and perils of the American democratic experiment.

This principle does not preclude hard truth-telling (as the Second Inaugural amply attests). But Lincoln spoke as one who had understood the frailty of all things human, and especially of all things political; he did not suggest, even amidst a civil war, that all righteousness lay on one side, and all evil on another; he knew, and acknowledged, that the nation was under judgment; and he spoke not as a Republican, and not even as a Northerner, but as an American seeking to reach out to other Americans across chasms of division at least as broad and deep as any we face today.

Such an approach—in which Christian conviction speaks through and to the plurality of our national life, such that that plurality is enabled to become a genuine pluralism—ought to commend itself to us, first and foremost, on Christian theological, indeed doctrinal, grounds.

The treasure of the Gospel has been entrusted to the earthen vessels of our humanity for the salvation of the world, not for the securing of partisan advantage. We debase the Gospel and we debase the Body of Christ (which witnesses in history to God's saving work in Christ) when we use the Gospel as a partisan trump card. Our first loyalty—our overriding loyalty—is to God in Christ, in the power of the Holy Spirit. Because of that loyalty, Christians are "resident aliens" in any polis in which they find themselves, as the second-century "Letter to Diognetus" puts it. But it is precisely because our ultimate allegiance is to a Kingdom not of this world that we can make a useful contribution to the working out of an American democratic experiment that has understood itself, from the outset, to be an experiment in limited government, judged by transcendent moral norms, and open to the participation of all men and women who affirm belief in certain "self-evident" truths about human persons and human community.

The experiment could fail; it requires a virtuous people in order to succeed. All of this was implied in the Second Inaugural, and that helps explain the enduring power of Lincoln's address. None of us is Lincoln. But everything we say and do in public should make clear that our purposes are to reunite America through a new birth of freedom, not simply to throw their rascals out and get our rascals in.

And at a far more vulgar level, there are also practical considerations to be weighed here. Playing the Gospel as a trump card is not only offensive to Jews, Muslims, Buddhists, and secularists; it is also offensive to other Christians—even (perhaps especially) to those Christians who may be otherwise inclined to make common cause on public policy issues. In brief, playing the Gospel as a trump card makes us less effective witnesses to the truths we hold about the way in which we ought to live together. (Moreover, and to go back to our primary concern, the suggestion that Christian orthodoxy yields a single answer to virtually every contested issue of public policy is an offense, not simply against political common sense, but against . . . Christian orthodoxy.)

Lincoln's Second Inaugural, and its unchallenged position in the pantheon of American public rhetoric, ought to have secured a place for biblical language and imagery in our public life, the frettings of radical secularists notwithstanding. But, having seen in Lincoln a model for the proper deployment of explicitly biblical language in American public discourse, perhaps a word about natural law is in order.

This is not the place to explore the differences among the various natural law theories, or the points of tangency (and distinction) between Roman Catholic natural law theory and Calvinist concepts of common grace. Rather, the question before us is how Christians contribute to the evolution of a genuine pluralism out of the plurality of vocabularies in American public moral discourse today; the question is how today's cannonading is transformed, in John Courtney Murray's pungent phrase, into a situation of "creeds at war, intelligibly." And the issue is a serious one, for society will descend into a different kind of war, Hobbes's dread war of "all against all," unless we can talk to each other in such a way that we make sense to each other—or at least enough sense to conduct the public argument that is the lifeblood of a democracy.

"Natural law" here means the claim that, even under the conditions of the Fall, there is a moral logic built into the world and into us: a logic that reasonable men and women can grasp by disciplined reflection on the dynamics of human action. The grasping of that logic may be (and Christians would say, most certainly is) aided by the effects of grace at work in human hearts; and it may be the case that the Gospel draws out of the natural law certain behavioral implications that are not so readily discernible with the naked eye (so to speak). But that such a moral logic exists, that it is available to all men through rational reflection, and that it can be intelligibly argued in public, is, I think, a matter of moral common sense.

We saw that logic at work in the American public debate over possible U.S. military action in the Persian Gulf in the months between Iraq's invasion of Kuwait and the beginning of Operation Desert Storm. From one end of the country to the other, and in venues ranging from radio talk shows to taxicabs to barber shops to bars to the halls of Congress, men and women instinctively argued in the natural law categories of the just war tradition in order to debate America's responsibilities in the Gulf: Was ours a just cause? Who could properly authorize the use of force? Did we have a reasonable chance of success? Was military action a last resort? How could innocent civilian lives be protected? The country did not instinctively reach for these questions because the just war tradition had been effectively catechized in our schools over the past generation (alas); rather, we reached for those questions because those are the "natural" questions that any morally reflective person will ask when contemplating the use of lethal force for the common good. Moreover, the rather high level of public moral argument over the Gulf crisis (perhaps the highest since a similar natural law argument had been publicly engaged during the debate over the 1964 Civil Rights Act) suggests that this instinctive moral logic has the perhaps unique capacity to bring grammatical order to the deliberations of a diverse society.

To commend the development of the skills necessary for conducting public debate according to the grammar of the natural law is not to deny explicitly Christian (or Jewish, Muslim, or Buddhist) moral discourse a place in the American public square. All Americans have the right to bring their most deeply held convictions into play in our common life; that is—or rather, ought to be—the commonly accepted meaning of the First Amendment's guarantee of "free exercise." But those convictions will be most readily engaged which are translated into idioms that can be grasped by those whom we are trying to persuade. And one grammar capable of effecting that translation is the natural law tradition. Two examples may help illustrate the point.

The abortion license created by the Supreme Court in 1973 remains the single most bitterly contested issue in American public life. It is self-evident that Christian orthodoxy regards elective abortion as a grave moral evil: as a profound offense against the entire structure of Christian morals. And there is no doubt that the steady proclamation of that truth, in love, has been a crucial factor in the perdurance of the right-to-life movement over the past generation. The overwhelming majority of those active on behalf of the right to life of the unborn are committed to that cause, and have remained committed in the teeth of fierce opposition from the elite culture, because they understand that the Lord requires this of us.

But how are we to make our case to those who do not share that prior religious commitment, or to those Christians whose churches do not provide clear moral counsel on this issue? And how do we do this in a political-cultural-legal climate in which individual autonomy has been virtually absolutized?

The answer is, we best make our case by insisting that our defense of the right to life of the unborn is a defense of civil rights and of a generous, hospitable American democracy. We best make our case by insisting that abortion-on-demand gravely damages the American democratic experiment by drastically constricting the community of the commonly protected. We best make our case by arguing that the private use of lethal violence against an innocent is an assault on the moral foundations of any just society. In short, we best make our case for maximum feasible legal protection of the unborn by deploying natural law arguments that translate our Christian moral convictions into a public idiom more powerful than the idiom of autonomy.

A similar strategy commends itself in the face of the gay and lesbian insurgency. Again, the position of orthodox Christian morality is unambiguously clear: homosexual acts violate the structure of the divinely created form of love by which men and women are to exercise their sexuality in unitive and procreative responsibility. Thus "homosexual marriage" is an oxymoron, and other proposals to grant homosexuality "equal protection" with heterosexuality are an offense against biblical morality: what many would call, unblushingly, an abomination before the Lord.

But given the vast disarray wrought by the sexual revolution, by the plurality of moral vocabularies in America, and by the current confusions attending Fourteenth Amendment jurisprudence, we make a more powerful case against the public policy claims of the gay and lesbian insurgency by arguing on natural law grounds: by arguing that it is in the very nature of governments to make discriminations; that the relevant question is whether any proposed discrimination is invidiously unjust; and that the legal preference given to heterosexual marriage is good for society because it strengthens the basic unit of society, the family, and because it is good for children. Given the fantastic damage done to the urban underclass by the breakdown of family life, this is, alas, an easier argument to make today than it was, say, twenty years ago. But as that asphalt *Via Dolorosa* comes to impress itself more indelibly on the national conscience, we may well find that natural law-based appeals to public responsibility for the welfare of children and families give us a vocabulary superior in political potency to the rhetoric of autonomy. And we just may find a new possibility for building a conservative-liberal coalition on precisely these grounds, facing precisely these issues.

Similar models of argumentation can be developed for other "social issues," including censorship, school curricula, school choice, sex education, and public health. In all these cases, it should be emphasized again, the goal is not to weaken the moral claims or judgments involved, but rather to translate them, through the grammar of natural law, into claims and judgments that can be heard, engaged, and, ultimately, accepted by those who do not share our basic Christian commitment (and, perhaps, even by some of the confused brethren who do).

Finally, a word about democratic etiquette. If patriotism is often the last refuge of scoundrels, then what currently passes for civility can be the last refuge of moral weakness, confusion, or cowardice. Moreover, as Mr. Dooley pointed out a while ago, "pollytics ain't beanbag." That enduring reality, and the gravity of the questions engaged in the American Kulturkampf, remind us that genuine civility is not the same as docility or "niceness."

But there is a truth embedded in the habit of democratic etiquette, and we should frankly acknowledge it. The truth is that persuasion is better than coercion. And that is true because public moral argument is superior—morally and politically—to violence.

All law is, of course, in some measure coercive. But one of the moral superiorities of democracy is that our inevitably coercive laws are defined by a process of persuasion, rather than by princely ukase or politburo decree. And why is this mode of lawmaking morally superior? Because it embodies four truths: that men and women are created with intelligence and free will, and thus as subjects, not merely objects, of power; that genuine authority is the right to command, not merely the power to coerce; that those who are called to obey and to bear burdens have first the right to be heard and to deliberate on whether a proposed burden to be borne is necessary for the common good; and that there is an inherent sense of justice in the people, by which they are empowered to pass judgment on how we ought to live together.

Thus in observing, even as we refine, the rules of democratic etiquette, Christians are helping to give contemporary expression to certain moral understandings that have lain at the heart of the central political tradition of the West since that tradition first formed in Jerusalem, Athens, and Rome (to take symbolic reference points). And, not so inconsequentially, we are thereby taking a stand against the totalitarian temptation that lurks at the heart of every modern state, including every modern democratic state. To be sure, that is not the most important "public" thing we do as Christians. But it is an important thing to do, nonetheless.

Two sets of obstacles make the transition from plurality to genuine pluralism in contemporary America even more difficult than it necessarily is.

The first obstacle is the legal and cultural sediment of the Supreme Court's jurisprudence about the First Amendment religion clause over the past fifty years. There is no space here to review this sorry history in detail.

Suffice it to say that the Court's strange decision to divide what is clearly one religion clause into two religion clauses, and its subsequent tortuous efforts to "balance" the claims of free exercise and no-establishment through Rube Goldberg contraptions like the three-part "Lemon test" have not only led the justices into a jurisprudential labyrinth of exceptional darkness and complexity; they have also created a legal and cultural climate in which the public exercise of religious conviction is too often understood as a quirk to be tolerated, rather than a fundamental human right that any just state is obliged to acknowledge. Which is to say, the justices' increasingly bizarre balancing act has elevated no establishment and subordinated free exercise to the point where a new establishment, the establishment of secularism, threatens the constitutional order. And until the First Amendment's religion clause is sutured together once again, in law and in the popular understanding of the law—until, that is, no-establishment is understood as the means to the goal of free exercise—our law will remain profoundly confused and our political culture too often inhospitable to people of faith.

Thus, for example, one cannot applaud Professor Stephen Carter's suggestion that the answer to the trivialization of religious belief and practice in contemporary American law and politics is something like maximum feasible toleration for religion in public life. No: the free and public exercise of religious conviction is not to be "tolerated"—it is to be accepted, welcomed, indeed celebrated as the first of freedoms and the foundation of any meaningful scheme of human rights. And until we reverse, both in law and in our popular legal-political culture, the inversion of the religion clause that the Court has effected since the *Everson* decision in 1947, the already difficult problem of bringing a measure of democratic order and civility into our public moral discourse will be endlessly exacerbated.

The second obstacle in the path to genuine pluralism is a certain lack of theological and political discipline on the part of the religious right.

Now this may seem a classic case of "blaming the victim"; after all, we have recently witnessed a campaign for lieutenant governor of Virginia in which the Democratic Party and much of the media portrayed the Republican candidate, an avowed Christian, as a high-tech Savonarola panting to impose a theocracy on the great Commonwealth, the Mother of Presidents, through such lurid policies as . . . well, school choice, informed consent prior to an elective abortion, parental notification of a minor's intention to seek an abortion, equalization of the state's personal income tax exemption with that allowed by the federal government, tort reform, and a lid on state borrowing. All of which took place eight brief months after a *Washington Post* reporter, in a magnificently revealing Freudian slip, unselfconsciously described evangelicals as "largely poor, uneducated, and easy to command." Which in turn took place a mere seven months after the prestige press batted nary an eye when Jesse Jackson, at the 1992 Democratic National Convention, told the Christmas story in such a way as to criticize those who would have objected to Mary aborting Jesus. In these circumstances, in which fevered warnings are endlessly issued about the machinations of the religious right and not a word is written or said about the agenda of the religious left (and its influence on no less a personage than Hillary Rodham Clinton), it may seem passing strange to suggest that the necessary challenge to the imposition of an establishment of secularism in America must be complemented by a parallel demand for increased self-discipline on the part of the religious right. Yet that is what is needed. And here is why.

It is needed, first and foremost, for theological reasons. A partisan Gospel is an ideological Gospel; and as many of us insisted against the claims of liberation theology in the 1970s and 1980s, an ideologically driven Gospel is a debasement of the Gospel. "Christian voter scorecards" which suggest that the Gospel provides a "Christian answer" to President Clinton's economic stimulus package, to the administration's tax proposals, to questions of voting rules in the House of Representatives, and to increasing the federal debt ceiling demean the Gospel by identifying it with an ideological agenda.

Another set of concerns arises from democratic theory. One can have no quarrel with describing our current circumstances as an American "culture war." But the suggestion, offered by Patrick J. Buchanan at the 1992 Republican Convention, that a culture war is to be equated, willy-nilly, with a "religious war" must be stoutly resisted. The two are not the same. A culture war can be adjudicated, and a reasonable accommodation reached, through the processes (including electoral and juridical processes) of democratic persuasion; a religious war cannot.

Moreover, the very phrase "religious war" suggests that the answer to the issue at the heart of the culture war—namely, the establishment of officially sanctioned secularism as the American democratic creed—is an alternative sanctified creed. But under the conditions of plurality that seem to be written into the script of history (by God, some of us would say), such a substitution is not and cannot be the answer. The alternative to the naked public square is the reconstitution of civil society in America. And what is "civil society"? Civil society is the achievement of a genuine pluralism in which creeds are "intelligibly in conflict." Genuine pluralism is, as Richard Neuhaus has written on many occasions, not the avoidance of our deepest differences, but the engagement of those differences within the bond of democratic civility.

No serious observer of the American political scene can doubt that any number of forces have declared war on the religious right. For its part, however, the religious right should decline that definition of the conflict, and get on with the task of rebuilding civil society in America—a strategy that is both theologically appropriate and, one suspects, very good politics.

Finally, a greater measure of theological and political self-discipline is to be urged on the religious right because it is just possible that the Right might win, and thus it had better start thinking now about how it wants to win: as a force of reaction, or as a movement for the revitalization of the American experiment. The choice here is going to have a lot to do with how conservatives, evangelical Christian or otherwise, govern in the future.

To say that the religious right might just win is not necessarily to predict the outcome of, say, the 1996 presidential election, or the 1997 Virginia gubernatorial election, or the 1998 congressional elections. Nor can one overlook the possibility that the current moral-cultural ills in this country might lead to a kind of national implosion, perhaps in the next decade. Given the demographic realities and the current sad state of our politics and our law, that might yet happen.

To say that the religious right might win is, rather, to express an intuition about the current correlation of forces in the debate over how we ought to live together. One cannot get over the feeling that Irving Kristol was on to something when he argued (in the *Wall Street Journal* of February 1, 1993) that cultural conservatism is the wave of the future in the United States. The secularization project, for all that it dominates the network airwaves and the academy, has largely failed: Americans are arguably more religious today than they were fifty years ago. And this growth is not to be found in those precincts where mainline/oldline churches have been acquiescing, both morally and theologically, to this secularization. On the contrary, it is precisely the churches making the most serious doctrinal and moral demands on their congregants which are flourishing. All of this on the positive side, coupled with the undeniably disastrous effects of the sexual revolution, the welfare state, and the absolutization of individual autonomy on the negative side, suggests that the revival of "traditional moral values" as the common ethical horizon of our public life in the late twentieth and the early twenty-first century is not an impossibility.

In these circumstances, it is not only appropriate, but indeed obligatory, for the evangelical and fundamentalist components of the religious right to practice the public arts of grammatical ecumenicity: to learn how to translate religiously grounded moral claims into a public language and imagery capable of challenging the hegemony of what Mary Ann Glendon has styled "rights-talk."

For the cultural-conservative coalition that can revitalize American civil society and American politics will be a coalition that includes Christians of Protestant, Roman Catholic, and Orthodox commitment; Jews who have broken ranks with the reflexive secularism and cultural liberalism that have come to inform so much of American Jewry's approach to the public square; a few secular people; and, just perhaps, a considerable number of Muslims. Grammatical ecumenicity within this coalition is essential to maintaining its tensile strength in the cultural and political battles in which this coalition will be engaged. And such ecumenicity will if anything be even more essential in exercising the authority of governance such that the reconstitution of America as a nation *e pluribus unum* involves a deepening, rather than a theologically and democratically inappropriate narrowing, of the *unum*.

In talking the talk, in truth and in charity, with force and with wit, so that others can enter the great conversation over the "oughts" of our common life, the religious right can make a signal contribution to the reclothing of the naked public square in America. And in doing that, it will be serving the Lord who stands in judgment on all the works of our hands, but most especially on our politics. For orthodox Christians politics is, or ought to be, penultimate. Talking the talk in the terms suggested here helps keep politics in its place: and that, too, is no mean contribution to the reconstruction of civil society in America at the end of the twentieth century.

A De-Moralized Society: The British/ American Experience

Gertrude Himmelfarb

T HE PAST IS a foreign country," it has been said. But it is not an unrecognizable country. Indeed, we sometimes experience a "shock of recognition" as we confront some aspect of the past in the present. One does not need to have had a Victorian grandmother, as did Margaret Thatcher, to be reminded of "Victorian values." One does not even have to be English; "Victorian America," as it has been called, was not all that different, at least in terms of values, from Victorian England. Vestigial remains of that Victorianism are everywhere around us. And memories of them persist, even when the realities are gone, rather like an amputated limb that still seems to throb when the weather is bad.

How can we not think of our present condition when we read Thomas Carlyle on the "Condition of England" one hundred and fifty years ago? While his contemporaries were debating "the standard of living question"—the "pessimists" arguing that the standard of living of the working classes had declined in that early period of industrialism, and the "optimists" that it had improved—Carlyle reformulated the issue to read, "the condition of England question." That question, he insisted, could not be resolved by citing "figures of arithmetic" about wages and prices. What was important was the "condition" and "disposition" of the people: their beliefs and feelings, their sense of right and wrong, the attitudes and habits that would dispose them either to a "wholesome composure, frugality, and prosperity," or to an "acrid unrest, recklessness, gin-drinking, and gradual ruin."

In fact, the Victorians did have "figures of arithmetic" dealing with the condition and disposition of the people as well as their economic state.

Reprinted from The Public Interest *(Fall 1994).*

These "moral statistics" or "social statistics," as they called them, dealt with crime, illiteracy, illegitimacy, drunkenness, pauperism, vagrancy. If they did not have, as we do, statistics on drugs, divorce, or teenage suicide, it is because these problems were then so negligible as not to constitute "social problems."

It is in this historical context that we may address our own "condition of the people question." And it is by comparison with the Victorians that we may find even more cause for alarm. For the current moral statistics are not only more troubling than those a century ago; they constitute a trend that bodes even worse for the future than for the present. Where the Victorians had the satisfaction of witnessing a significant improvement in their moral and social condition, we are confronting a considerable deterioration in ours.

The "Moral Statistics": Illegitimacy

In nineteenth-century England, the illegitimacy ratio—the proportion of out-of-wedlock births to total births—rose from a little over 5 percent at the beginning of the century to a peak of 7 percent in 1845. It then fell steadily until it was less than 4 percent at the turn of the century. In East London, the poorest section of the city, the figures are even more dramatic, for illegitimacy was consistently well below the average: 4.5 percent in mid-century and 3 percent by the end of the century. Apart from a temporary increase during both world wars, the ratio continued to hover around 5 percent until 1960. It then began to rise: to over 8 percent in 1970, 12 percent in 1980, and then, precipitously, to more than 32 percent by the end of 1992—a two-and-one-half times increase in the last decade alone and a sixfold rise in three decades. In 1981, a married woman was half as likely to have a child as she was in 1901, while an unmarried woman was three times as likely. (See Figure 1.)

In the United States, the figures are no less dramatic. Starting at 3 percent in 1920 (the first year for which there are national statistics), the illegitimacy ratio rose gradually to slightly over 5 percent by 1960, after which it grew rapidly: to almost 11 percent in 1970, over 18 percent in 1980, and 30 percent by 1991—a tenfold increase from 1920 and a sixfold increase from 1960. For whites alone, the ratio went up only slightly between 1920 and 1960 (from 1.5 percent to a little over 2 percent) and then advanced at an even steeper rate than that of blacks: to almost 6 percent in 1970, 11 percent in 1980, and nearly 22 percent in 1991—

Figure 1
Illegitimacy in England and Wales, 1801–1992

Source: For 1800 to 1840: *Bastardy and Its Comparative History,* ed. Peter Laslett, et al. (Cambridge, Mass., 1980); for 1841 to 1992: United Kingdom Office of Population Censuses and Surveys.

fourteen times the 1920 figure and eleven times that of 1960. If the black illegitimacy ratio did not accelerate as much, it was because it started at a higher level: from 12 percent in 1920 to 22 percent in 1960, over 37 percent in 1970, 55 percent in 1980, and 68 percent by 1991. (See Figure 2.)

Teenage illegitimacy has earned the United States the dubious distinction of ranking first among all industrialized nations, the rate having tripled between 1960 and 1991. In 1990, one in ten teenage girls got pregnant, half of them giving birth and the other half having abortions. England is second only to the United States in teenage illegitimacy, but the rate of increase in the past three decades has been even more rapid. In both countries, teenagers are far more "sexually active" (as the current expression has it) than ever before, and at an earlier age. In 1970, 5 percent of fifteen-year-old girls in the United States had had sexual intercourse; in 1988, 25 percent had.

The "Moral Statistics": Crime

Public opinion polls in both England and the United States show crime as the major concern of the people, and for good reason, as the statistics suggest. Again, the historical pattern is dramatic and disquieting. In England between 1857 and 1901, the rate of indictable offenses (serious offenses, not including simple assault, drunkenness, vagrancy, and the like)

Figure 2
Illegitimacy in the United States, 1920–1991

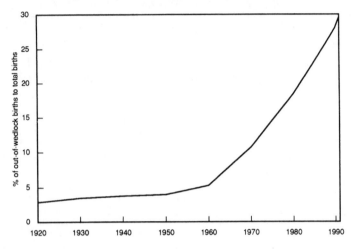

Source: For 1920 to 1930: U.S. Bureau of the Census, *Vital Statistics of the United States, 1940;* for 1940 to 1991: U.S. Department of Health and Human Services, National Center for Health Statistics.

decreased from about 480 per 100,000 population to 250—a decline of almost 50 percent in four decades. The absolute numbers are even more graphic: while the population grew from about 19 million to 33 million, the number of serious crimes fell from 92,000 to 81,000. Moreover, 1857 was not the peak year; it is simply the year when the most reliable and consistent series of statistics starts. The decline (earlier statistics suggest) started in the mid- or late 1840s—at about the same time as the beginning of the decline in illegitimacy. It is also interesting that just as the illegitimacy ratio in the middle of the century was lower in the metropolis than in the rest of the country, so was the crime rate.

The considerable decrease of crime in England is often attributed to the establishment of the police force, first in London in 1829, then in the counties, and, by 1856, in the country at large. Although this undoubtedly had the effect of deterring crime, it also improved the recording of crime and the apprehension of criminals, which makes the lower crime rates even more notable. One criminologist, analyzing these statistics, concludes that deterrence alone cannot account for the decline, that the explanation has to be sought in "heavy generalizations about the 'civilizing' effects of religion, education, and environmental reform."

The low crime rate persisted until shortly before the First World War when it rose very slightly. It fell during the war and started a steady rise in the mid-twenties, reaching 400 per 100,000 population in 1931 (somewhat less than the 1861 rate) and 900 in 1941. During the Second World War, unlike the First (and contrary to popular opinion), crime increased, levelling off or declining slightly in the early 1950s. The largest rise started in the mid-fifties, from under 1,000 in 1955 to 1,750 in 1961, 3,400 in 1971, 5,600 in 1981, and a staggering 10,000 in 1991—ten times the rate of 1955 and forty times that of 1901. Violent crimes alone almost doubled in each decade after 1950. (See Figure 3.) (On the eve of this rise, in 1955, the anthropologist Geoffrey Gorer remarked upon the extraordinary degree of civility exhibited in England, where "football crowds are as orderly as church meetings." Within a few years, those games became notorious as the scene of mayhem and riots.)

There are no national crime statistics for the United States for the nineteenth century and only partial ones (for homicides) for the early twentieth century. Local statistics, however, suggest that, as in England, the decrease of crime started in the latter part of the nineteenth century (except for a few years following the Civil War) and continued into the early twentieth century. There was even a decline of homicides in the larger cities, where they were most common; in Philadelphia, the rate fell from 3.3 per 100,000 population in mid-century to 2.1 by the end of the century.

National crime statistics became available only in 1960, when the rate was under 1,900 per 100,000 population. That figure doubled within the decade and tripled by 1980. A decline in the early 1980s, from almost 6,000 to 5,200, was followed by an increase to 5,800 in 1990; the latest figure, for 1992, is somewhat under 5,700. The rate of violent crime (murder, rape, robbery, and aggravated assault) followed a similar pattern, except that the increase after 1985 was more precipitous and continued until 1992, making for an almost fivefold rise from 1960. In 1987, the Department of Justice estimated that eight of every ten Americans would be a victim of violent crime at least once in their lives. (See Figure 4.)*

Homicide statistics go back to the beginning of the century, when the national rate was 1.2 per 100,000 population. That figure skyrocketed during prohibition, reaching as high as 9.7 by one account (6.5 by another)

---

* Because of differences in the definition and reporting of crimes, the American index of crime is not equivalent to the English rate of indictable offenses. The English rate of 10,000 in 1991 does not mean that England experienced almost twice as many crimes per capita as America did. It is the trend lines in both countries that are significant, and those lines are comparable.

Figure 3
Crime in England and Wales, 1857–1991

Source: For 1857 to 1980: B. R. Mitchell, *British Historical Statistics* (Cambridge,
England, 1988), 776–778; for 1981 to 1991: Home Office *Criminal Statistics.*
Note: I have converted absolute numbers into rate per 100,000 population.

in 1933, when prohibition was repealed. The rate dropped to between 5 and
6 during the 1940s and to under 5 in the fifties and early sixties. In the mid-
sixties, it started to climb rapidly, more than doubling between 1965 and
1980. A decline in the early eighties was followed by another rise; in 1991 it
was just short of its 1980 peak. The rate among blacks, especially in the
cities, was considerably higher than among whites—at one point in the
1920s as much as eight times higher. In the 1970s and early 1980s, the black
rate fell by more than one fourth (from over 40 to under 30), while the white
rate rose by one third (from 4.3 to 5.6); since then, however, the rate for
young black males tripled while that for young white males rose by 50 percent. Homicide is now the leading cause of death among black youths.

For all kinds of crimes the figures for blacks are far higher than for
whites—for blacks both as the victims and as the perpetrators of crime.
Criminologists have coined the term "criminogenic" to describe this phenomenon:

> In essence, the inner city has become a criminogenic community, a
> place where the social forces that create predatory criminals are far
> more numerous and overwhelmingly stronger than the social
> forces that create virtuous citizens. At core, the problem is that
> most inner city children grow up surrounded by teenagers and

Figure 4
Crime in the United States, 1960–1992

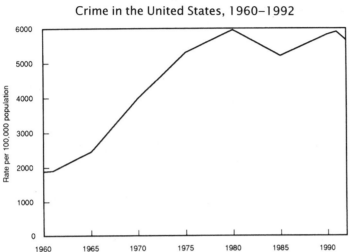

Source: U.S. Department of Justice, Federal Bureau of Investigations.
Note: Because of differences in the definition and reporting of crimes, the American index of crime is not equivalent to the English rate of indictable offenses. They are the only lines in the two countries that are comparable.

adults who are themselves deviant, delinquent, or criminal. At best, these teenagers and adults misshape the characters and lives of the young in their midst. At worst, they abuse, neglect, or criminally prey upon the young.

More Moral Statistics

There are brave souls, inveterate optimists, who try to put the best gloss on the statistics. But it is not much consolation to be told that the overall crime rate in the United States has declined slightly from its peak in the early 1980s, if the violent crime rate has risen in the same period—and increased still more among juveniles and girls (an ominous trend, since the teenage population is also growing). Nor that the divorce rate has fallen somewhat in the past decade, if it had doubled in the previous two decades; if more parents are cohabiting without benefit of marriage (the rate in the United States has increased sixfold since 1970); and if more children are born out of wedlock and living with single parents. (In 1970, one out of ten families was headed by a single parent; in 1990, three out of ten were.) Nor that the white illegitimacy ratio is considerably lower than the black, if the white ratio is rapidly approaching the black ratio of a few decades ago, when Daniel Patrick Moynihan wrote his percipient report about the breakdown of the black family. (The black ratio in 1964, when that report was issued, was 24.5 percent; the white ratio now is 22 percent. In 1964, 50 percent of black teenage mothers were single; in 1991, 55 percent of white teenage mothers were single.)

Nor is it reassuring to be told that two thirds of new welfare recipients are off the rolls within two years, if half of those soon return, and a quarter of all recipients are on for more than eight years. Nor that divorced mothers leave the welfare rolls after an average of five years, if never-married mothers remain for more than nine years, and unmarried mothers who bore their children as teenagers stay on for ten or more years. (Forty-three percent of the longest-term welfare recipients started their families as unwed teenagers.)

Nor is the cause of racial equality promoted by the news of an emerging "white underclass," smaller and less conspicuous than the black (partly because it is more dispersed) but rapidly increasing. If, as has been conclusively demonstrated, the single-parent family is the most important factor associated with the "pathology of poverty"—welfare dependency, crime, drugs, illiteracy, homelessness—a white illegitimacy ratio of 22 percent, and twice that for white women below the poverty line, signifies a new and dangerous trend. In England, Charles Murray has shown, a similar underclass is developing with twice the illegitimacy of the rest of the population; there it is a purely class rather than racial phenomenon.

Redefining Deviancy

The English sociologist Christie Davies has described a "U-curve model of deviance," which applies both to Britain and the United States. The curve shows the drop in crime, violence, illegitimacy, and alcoholism in the last half of the nineteenth century, reaching a low at the turn of the century, and a sharp rise in the latter part of the twentieth century. The curve is actually more skewed than this image suggests. It might more accurately be described as a "J-curve," for the height of deviancy in the nineteenth century was considerably lower than it is today—an illegitimacy ratio of 7 percent in England in the mid-nineteenth century, compared with over 32 percent toward the end of the twentieth; or a crime rate of about 500 per 100,000 population then compared with 10,000 now.

In his *American Scholar* essay, "Defining Deviancy Down," Senator Moynihan has taken the idea of deviancy a step further by describing the downward curve of the *concept* of deviancy. What was once regarded as deviant behavior is no longer so regarded; what was once deemed abnormal has been normalized. As deviancy is defined downward, so the threshold of deviancy rises: behavior once stigmatized as deviant is now tolerated and even sanctioned. Mental patients, no longer institutionalized, are now treated, and appear in the statistics, not as mentally incapacitated but as "homeless." Divorce and illegitimacy, once seen as betokening the break-down of the family, are now viewed more benignly: illegitimacy has been officially rebaptized as "nonmarital childbearing," and divorced and unmarried mothers are lumped together in the category of "single-parent families." And violent crime has become so endemic that we have practically become inured to it. The St. Valentine's Day Massacre in Chicago in 1929, when four gangsters killed seven other gangsters, shocked the nation and became legendary, immortalized in encyclopedias and history books; in Los Angeles today, James Q. Wilson observes, as many people are killed every weekend.

It is ironic to recall that only a short while ago criminologists were accounting for the rise of the crime rates in terms of our "sensitization to violence." As a result of the century-long decline of violence, they reasoned, we had become more sensitive to "residual violence"; thus, more crimes were being reported and apprehended. This "residual violence" has by now become so overwhelming that, as Moynihan points out, we are being desensitized to it.

Charles Krauthammer has proposed a complementary concept in his *New Republic* essay "Defining Deviancy Up." As deviancy is normalized, so the normal becomes deviant. The kind of family that has been regarded for centuries as natural and moral—the "bourgeois" family, as it is invidiously called—is now seen as pathological, concealing behind the facade of respectability the new "original sin," child abuse. While crime is underreported because we have become desensitized to it, child abuse is overreported, including fantasies imagined (often inspired by therapists and social workers) long after the supposed events. Similarly, rape has been "defined up" as "date rape," to include sexual relations that the participants themselves may not at the time have perceived as rape.

The combined effect of defining deviancy up and defining it down has been to normalize and legitimize what was once regarded as abnormal and illegitimate, and, conversely, to stigmatize and discredit what was once normal and respectable. This process, too, has occurred with startling rapidity. One might expect that attitudes and values would lag behind the reality, that people would continue to pay lip service to the moral principles they were brought up with, even while violating those principles in practice. What is startling about the 1960s "sexual revolution," as it has properly been called, is how revolutionary it was, in sensibility as well as reality. In 1965, 69 percent of American women and 65 percent of men under the age of thirty said that premarital sex was always or almost always wrong; in 1972, those figures plummeted to 24 percent and 21 percent. For women over the age of thirty, the figures dropped from 91 percent to 62 percent, and for men from 62 percent to 47 percent—this in seven short years. Thus language, sensibility, and social policy conspire together to redefine deviancy.

Understanding the Causes

For a long time, social critics and policy makers found it hard to face up to the realities of our moral condition, in spite of the evidence of statistics. They criticized the statistics themselves or tried to explain them away. The crime figures, they said, reflect not a real increase of crime but an increase in the reporting of crime; or the increase is a temporary aberration, a blip on the demographic curve representing the "baby boomers" who would soon outgrow their infantile, antisocial behavior; or criminal behavior is a cry for help from individuals desperately seeking recognition and self-esteem; or crime is the unfortunate result of poverty, unemployment, and racism, to be overcome by a more generous welfare system, a more equitable distribution of wealth, and a more aggressive drive against discrimination.

These explanations have some plausibility. The rise and fall of crime sometimes, but not always, corresponds to the increase and decrease of the age group most prone to criminal behavior. And there is an occasional, but not consistent, relation between crime and economic depression and poverty. In England in the 1890s, in a period of severe unemployment, crime (including property crime) fell. Indeed, the inverse relationship between crime and poverty at the end of the nineteenth century suggests, as one study put it, that "poverty-based crime" had given way to "prosperity-based crime."

In the twentieth century, the correlation between crime and unemployment has been no less erratic. While crime did increase in England during the depression of the 1930s, that increase had started some years earlier. A graph of unemployment and crime between 1950 and 1980 shows no significant correlation in the first fifteen years and only a rough correlation thereafter. The crime figures, a Home Office bulletin concludes, would correspond equally well, or even better, with other kinds of data. "Indeed, the consumption of alcohol, the consumption of ice cream, the number of cars on the road, and the Gross National Product are highly correlated with rising crime over 1950–1980."

The situation is similar in the United States. In the high-unemployment years of 1949, 1958, and 1961, when unemployment was 6 or 7 percent, crime was less than 2 percent; in the low-unemployment years of 1966 to 1969, with unemployment between 3 and 4 percent, crime was almost 4 percent. Today in the inner cities there is a correlation between unemployment and crime, but it may be argued that it is not so much unemployment that causes crime as a culture that denigrates or discourages employment, making crime seem more normal, natural, and desirable than employment. The "culture of criminality," it is evident, is very different from the "culture of poverty" as we once understood that concept.

Nor can the decline of the two-parent family be attributed, as is sometimes suggested, to the economic recession of recent times. Neither illegitimacy nor divorce increased during the far more serious depression of the 1930s—or, for that matter, in previous depressions, either in England or in the United States. In England in the 1980s, illegitimacy actually increased more in areas where the employment situation improved than in those where it got worse. Nor is there a necessary correlation between illegitimacy and poverty; in the latter part of the nineteenth century, illegitimacy was significantly lower in the East End of London than in the rest of the country. Today there is a correlation between illegitimacy and poverty, but not a causal one; just as crime has become part of the culture of poverty, so has the single-parent family.

The Language of Morality

These realities have been difficult to confront because they violate the dominant ethos, which assumes that moral progress is a necessary by-product of material progress. It seems incomprehensible that in this age of free, compulsory education, illiteracy should be a problem, not among immigrants but among native-born Americans; or illegitimacy, at a time when sex education, birth control, and abortion are widely available. Even more important is the suspicion of the very idea of morality. Moral principles, still more moral judgments, are thought to be at best an intellectual embarrassment, at worst evidence of an illiberal and repressive disposition.

It is this reluctance to speak the language of morality, far more than any specific values, that separates us from the Victorians.

Most of us are uncomfortable with the idea of making moral judgments even in our private lives, let alone with the "intrusion," as we say, of moral judgments into public affairs. We are uncomfortable not only because we have come to feel that we have no right to make such judgments and impose them upon others, but because we have no confidence in the judgments themselves, no assurance that our principles are true and right for us, let alone for others. We are constantly beseeched to be "nonjudgmental," to be wary of crediting our beliefs with any greater validity than anyone else's, to be conscious of how "Eurocentric" and "culture-bound" we are. *Chacun à son goût*, we say of morals, as of taste; indeed, morals have become a matter of taste.

Public officials in particular shy away from the word "immoral," lest they be accused of racism, sexism, or elitism. When members of the President's cabinet were asked if it is immoral for people to have children out of wedlock, they drew back from that distasteful phrase. The Secretary of Health and Human Services replied, "I don't like to put this in moral terms, but I do believe that having children out of wedlock is just wrong." The Surgeon General was more forthright: "No. Everyone has different moral standards. . . . You can't impose your standards on someone else."

It is not only our political and cultural leaders who are prone to this failure of moral nerve. Everyone has been infected by it, to one degree or another. A moving testimonial to this comes from an unlikely source: Richard Hoggart, the British literary critic and very much a man of the Left, not given to celebrating Victorian values. It was in the course of criticizing a book espousing traditional virtues that Hoggart observed about his own hometown:

> In Hunslet, a working-class district of Leeds, within which I was brought up, old people will still enunciate, as guides to living, the moral rules they learned at Sunday School and Chapel. Then they almost always add, these days: "But it's only my opinion, of course." A late-twentieth-century insurance clause, a recognition that times have changed towards the always shiftingly relativist. In that same council estate, any idea of parental guidance has in many homes been lost. Most of the children there live in, take for granted, a violent, jungle world.

De-moralizing Social Policy

In Victorian England, moral principles and judgments were as much a part of social discourse as of private discourse, and as much a part of public policy as of personal life. They were not only deeply ingrained in tradition; they were also imbedded in two powerful strains of Victorian thought: Utilitarianism on the one hand, Evangelicalism and Methodism on the other. These may not have been philosophically compatible, but in practice they complemented and reinforced each other, the Benthamite calculus of pleasure and pain, rewards and punishments, being the secular equivalent of the virtues and vices that Evangelicalism and Methodism derived from religion.

It was this alliance of a secular ethos and a religious one that determined social policy, so that every measure of poor relief or philanthropy, for example, had to justify itself by showing that it would promote the moral as well as the material well-being of the poor. The distinction between pauper and poor, the stigma attached to the "able-bodied pauper," indeed, the word "pauper" itself, today seem invidious and inhumane. At the time, however, they were the result of a conscious moral decision: an effort to discourage dependency and preserve the respectability of the independent poor, while providing at least minimal sustenance for the indigent.

In recent decades, we have so completely rejected any kind of moral calculus that we have deliberately, systematically divorced welfare from moral sanctions or incentives. This reflects in part the theory that society is responsible for all social problems and should therefore assume the task of solving them; and in part the prevailing spirit of relativism, which makes it difficult to pass any moral judgments or impose any moral conditions upon the recipients of relief. We are now confronting the consequences of this policy of moral neutrality. Having made the most valiant attempt to "objectify" the problem of poverty, to see it as the product of impersonal economic and social forces, we are discovering that the economic and social aspects of that problem are inseparable from the moral and personal ones. And having made the most determined effort to devise social policies that are "value free," we find that these policies imperil both the moral and the material well-being of their intended beneficiaries.

In de-moralizing social policy—divorcing it from any moral criteria, requirements, even expectations—we have demoralized, in the more familiar sense, both the individuals receiving relief and society as a whole. Our welfare system is counterproductive not only because it aggravates the problem of welfare, creating more incentives to enter and remain within it than to try to avoid or escape from it. It also has the effect of exacerbating other, more serious, social problems, so that chronic dependency has become an integral part of the larger phenomenon of "social pathology."

The Supplemental Security Income program is a case in point. Introduced in 1972 to provide a minimum income for the blind, the elderly, and the disabled poor, the program has been extended to drug addicts and alcoholics as the result of an earlier ruling defining "substance abusers" as "disabled" and therefore eligible for public assistance. Apart from encouraging these "disabilities" ("vices," the Victorians would have called them), the program has the effect of rewarding those who remain addicts or alcoholics while penalizing (by cutting off their funds) those who try to overcome their addiction. This is the reverse of the principle of "less eligibility" that was the keystone of Victorian social policy: the principle that the dependent poor be in a less "eligible," less desirable, condition than the independent poor. One might say that we are now operating under a principle of "more eligibility," the recipient of relief being in a more favorable position than the self-supporting person.

Just as many intellectuals, social critics, and policy makers were reluctant for so long to credit the unpalatable facts about crime, illegitimacy, or dependency, so they find it difficult to appreciate the extent to which these facts themselves are a function of values—the extent to which "social pathology" is a function of "moral pathology" and social policy a function of moral principle.

Victims of the Upperclass

The moral divide has become a class divide. The same people who have long resisted the realities of social life also find it difficult to sympathize with those, among the working classes especially, who feel acutely threatened by a social order that they perceive to be in an acute state of disorder. (The very word "order" now sounds archaic.) The "new class," as it has been called, is not in fact all that new; it is by now firmly established in the media, the academy, the professions, and the government. In its denigration of "bourgeois values" and the "Puritan ethic," the new class has legitimized, as it were, the values of the underclass and illegitimized those of the working class, who are still committed to bourgeois values, the Puritan ethic, and other such benighted ideas.

In a powerfully argued book, Myron Magnet has analyzed the dual revolution that led to this strange alliance between what he calls the "Haves" and the "Have-Nots." The first was a social revolution, intended to liberate the poor from the political, economic, and racial oppression that kept them in bondage. The second was a cultural revolution, liberating them (as the Haves themselves were being liberated) from the moral restraints of bourgeois values. The first created the welfare programs of the Great Society, which provided counter-incentives to leaving poverty. And the second disparaged the behavior and attitudes that traditionally made for economic improvement—"deferral of gratification, sobriety, thrift, dogged industry, and so on through the whole catalogue of antique-sounding bourgeois virtues." Together these revolutions had the unintended effect of miring the poor in their poverty—a poverty even more demoralizing and self-perpetuating than the old poverty.

The underclass is not only the victim of its own culture, the "culture of poverty." It is also the victim of the upperclass culture around it. The kind of "delinquency" that a white suburban teenager can absorb with relative (only relative) impunity may be literally fatal to a black inner-city teenager. Similarly, the child in a single-parent family headed by an affluent professional woman is obviously in a very different condition from the child (more often, children) of a woman on welfare. The effects of the culture, however, are felt at all levels. It was only a matter of time before there should have emerged a white underclass with much the same pathology as the black. And not only a white underclass but a white upper class; the most affluent suburbs are beginning to exhibit the same pathological symptoms: teenage alcoholism, drug addiction, crime, and illegitimacy.

By now this "liberated," antibourgeois ethic no longer seems so liberating. The social realities have become so egregious that it is now finally permissible to speak of the need for "family values." President Clinton himself has put the official seal of approval on family values, even going so far as to concede—a year after the event—that there were "a lot of very good things" in Quayle's famous speech about family values (although he was quick to add that the "Murphy Brown thing" was a mistake).

Beyond Economic Incentives

If liberals have much rethinking to do, so do conservatives, for the familiar conservative responses to social problems are inadequate to the present situation. It is not enough to say that if only the failed welfare policies are abandoned and the resources of the free market released, economic growth and incentives will break the cycle of dependency and produce stable families. There is an element of truth in this view, but not the entire truth, for it underestimates the moral and cultural dimensions of the problem. In Britain as in America, more and more conservatives are returning to an older Burkean tradition, which appreciates the material advantages of a free-market economy (Edmund Burke himself was a disciple of Adam Smith) but also recognizes that such an economy does not automatically produce the moral and social goods that they value—that it may even subvert those goods.

For the promotion of moral values, conservatives have always looked to individuals, families, churches, communities, and all the other voluntary associations that Tocqueville saw as the genius of American society. Today they have more need than ever to do that, as the dominant culture—the "counterculture" of yesteryear—becomes increasingly uncongenial. They support "school choice," permitting parents to send their children to schools of their liking; or they employ private security guards to police their neighborhoods; or they form associations of fathers in inner cities to help fatherless children; or they create organizations like the Character Counts Coalition to encourage "puritan" virtues and family values. They look, in short, to civil society to do what the state cannot do—or, more often, to undo the evil that the state has done.

Yet here too conservatives are caught in a bind, for the values imparted by the reigning culture have by now received the sanction of the state. This is reflected in the official rhetoric ("nonmarital childbearing" or "alternative lifestyle"), in mandated sexual instruction and the distribution of condoms in schools, in the prohibition of school prayer, in social policies that are determinedly "nonjudgmental," and in myriad other ways. Against such a pervasive system of state-supported values, the traditional conservative recourse to private groups and voluntary initiatives may seem inadequate.

Individuals, families, churches, and communities cannot operate in isolation, cannot long maintain values at odds with those legitimated by the state and popularized by the culture. It takes a great effort of will and intellect for the individual to decide for himself that something is immoral and to act on that belief when the law declares it legal and the culture deems it acceptable. It takes an even greater effort for parents to inculcate that belief in their children when school officials contravene it and authorize behavior in violation of it. Values, even traditional values, require legitimation. At the very least, they require not to be illegitimated. And in a secular society that legitimation or illegitimation is in the hands of the dominant culture, the state, and the courts.

You cannot legislate morality, it is often said. Yet we have done just that. Civil rights legislation prohibiting racial discrimination has succeeded in proscribing racist conduct not only legally but morally as well. Today moral issues are constantly being legislated, adjudicated, or resolved by administrative fiat (by the educational establishment, for instance). Those who want to resist the dominant culture cannot merely opt out of it; it impinges too powerfully upon their lives. They may be obliged, however reluctantly, to invoke the power of the law and the state, if only to protect those private institutions and associations that are the best repositories of traditional values.

The Use and Abuse of History

One of the most effective weapons in the arsenal of the "counter-counterculture" is history—the memory not only of a time before the counterculture but also of the evolution of the counterculture itself. In 1968, the English playwright and member of Parliament A. P. Herbert had the satisfaction of witnessing the passage of the act he had sponsored abolishing censorship on the stage. Only two years later, he complained that what had started as a "worthy struggle for reasonable liberty for honest writers" had ended as the "right to represent copulation, veraciously, on the public stage." About the same time, a leading American civil liberties lawyer, Morris Ernst, was moved to protest that he had meant to ensure the publication of Joyce's *Ulysses*, not the public performance of sodomy.

In the last two decades, the movements for cultural and sexual liberation in both countries have progressed far beyond their original intentions. Yet few people are able to resist their momentum or to recall their initial principles. In an unhistorical age such as ours, even the immediate past seems so remote as to be antediluvian; anything short of the present state of "liberation" is regarded as illiberal. And in a thoroughly relativistic age such as ours, any assertion of value—any distinction between the publication of *Ulysses* and the public performance of sodomy—is thought to be arbitrary and authoritarian.

It is in this situation that history may be instructive, to remind us of a time, not so long ago, when all societies, liberal as well as conservative, affirmed values very different from our own. (One need not go back to the Victorian age; several decades will suffice.) To say that history is instructive is not to suggest that it provides us with models for emulation. One could not, even if one so desired, emulate a society—Victorian society, for example—at a different stage of economic, technological, social, political, and cultural development. Moreover, if there is much in the ethos of our own times that one may deplore, there is no less in Victorian times. Late-Victorian society was more open, liberal, and humane than early-Victorian society, but it was less open, liberal, and humane than most people today would think desirable. Social and sexual discriminations, class rigidities and political inequalities, autocratic men, submissive women, and overly disciplined children, constraints, restrictions, and abuses of all kinds—there is enough to give pause to the most ardent Victoriaphile. Yet there is also much that might appeal to even a modern, liberated spirit.

Victorian Lessons

The main thing the Victorians can teach us is the importance of values—or, as they would have said, "virtues"—in our public as well as private lives. The Victorians were, candidly and proudly, "moralists." In recent decades, that has almost become a term of derision. Yet, contemplating our own society, we may be prepared to take a more appreciative view of Victorian moralism—of the "Puritan ethic" of work, thrift, temperance, cleanliness; of the idea of "respectability" that was as powerful among the working classes as among the middle classes; of the reverence for "home and hearth"; of the stigma attached to the "able-bodied pauper," as a deterrent to the "independent" worker; of the spirit of philanthropy which made it a moral duty on the part of the donors to give not only money but their own time and effort to the charitable cause, and a moral duty on the part of the recipients to try to "better themselves."

We may even be on the verge of assimilating some of that moralism into our own thinking. It is not only "values" that are being rediscovered but "virtues" as well. That long neglected word is appearing in the most unlikely places: in books, newspaper columns, journal articles, and scholarly discourse. An article in the *Times Literary Supplement*, reporting on a spate of books and articles from "virtue revivalists" on both the Right and the Left of the political spectrum, observes that "even if the news that Virtue is back is not in itself particularly exciting to American pragmatism, the news that Virtue is good for you most emphatically is." The philosopher Martha Nussbaum, reviewing the state of Anglo-American philosophy, focuses upon the subject of "Virtue Revived," and her account suggests a return not to classical ethics but to something very like Victorian ethics: an ethics based on "virtue" rather than "principle," on "tradition and particularity" rather than "universality," on "local wisdom" rather than "theory," on the "concreteness of history" rather than an "ahistorical detached ethics."

If anything was lacking to give virtue the imprimatur of American liberalism, it was the endorsement of the White House, which came when Hillary Rodham Clinton declared her support for a "Politics of Virtue." If she is notably vague about the idea (and if, as even friendly critics have pointed out, some of her policies seem to belie it), her eagerness to embrace the term is itself significant.

In fact, the idea of virtue has been implicit in our thinking about social policy even while it was being denied. When we speak of the "social pathology" of crime, drugs, violence, illegitimacy, promiscuity, pornography, illiteracy, are we not making a moral judgment about that "pathology"? Or when we describe the "cycle of welfare dependency," or the "culture of poverty," or the "demoralization of the underclass," are we not defining that class and that culture in moral terms and finding them wanting in those terms? Or when we propose to replace the welfare system by a "workfare" system, or to provide "role models" for fatherless children, or to introduce "moral education" into the school curriculum, are we not testifying to the enduring importance of moral principles that we had, surely prematurely, consigned to the dustbin of history? Or when we are told that organizations are being formed in black communities to "inculcate values" in the children and that "the concept of self-help is reemerging," or that campaigns are being conducted among young people to promote sexual abstinence and that "chastity seems to be making a comeback," are we not witnessing the return of those quintessentially Victorian virtues?

The Present Perspective

It cannot be said too often: No one, not even the most ardent "virtue revivalist," is proposing to revive Victorianism. Those "good-old"/"bad-old" days are irrevocably gone. Children are not about to return to that docile condition in which they are seen but not heard, nor workers to that deferential state where they tip their caps to their betters (a custom that was already becoming obsolete by the end of the nineteenth century). Nor are men and women going to retreat to their "separate spheres"; nor blacks and whites to a state of segregation and discrimination. But if the past cannot—and should not—be replicated, it can serve to put the present in better perspective.

In this perspective, it appears that the present, not the past, is the anomaly, the aberration. Those two powerful indexes of social pathology, illegitimacy and crime, show not only the disparity between the Victorian period and our own but also, more significantly, the endurance of the Victorian ethos long after the Victorian age—indeed, until well into the present century. The 4 to 5 percent illegitimacy ratio was sustained (in both Britain and the United States) until 1960—a time span that encompasses two world wars, the most serious depression in modern times, the traumatic experiences of Nazism and Communism, the growth of a consumer economy that almost rivals the industrial revolution in its moral as well as material consequences, the continuing decline of the rural population, the unprecedented expansion of mass education and popular culture, and a host of other economic, political, social, and cultural changes. In this sense "Victorian values" may be said to have survived not only the formative years of industrialism and urbanism but some of the most disruptive experiences of our times.

It is from this perspective, not so much of the Victorians as of our own recent past, that we must come to terms with such facts as a sixfold rise of illegitimacy in only three decades (in both Britain and the United States),* or a nearly sixfold rise of crime in England and over threefold in the United States, or all the other indicators of social pathology that are no less disquieting. We are accustomed to speak of the sexual revolution of this period, but that revolution, we are now discovering, is part of a larger, and more ominous, moral revolution.

---

* The present illegitimacy ratio is not only unprecedented in the past two centuries; it is unprecedented, so far as we know, in American history going back to colonial times, and in English history from Tudor times. The American evidence is scanty, but the English is more conclusive. English parish records in the mid-sixteenth century give an illegitimacy ratio of 2.4 percent; by the early seventeenth century it reached 3.4 percent; in the Cromwellian period it fell to 1 percent; during the eighteenth century it rose from 3.1 percent to 5.3 percent; it reached its peak of 7 percent in 1845, and then declined to under 4 percent by the end of the nineteenth century. It is against this background that the present rate of 32 percent must be viewed.

A Society's Ethos

The historical perspective is also useful in reminding us of our gains and losses—our considerable gains in material goods, political liberty, social mobility, racial and sexual equality—and our no less considerable losses in moral well-being. There are those who say that it is all of a piece, that what we have lost is the necessary price of what we have gained. ("No pain, no gain," as the motto has it.) In this view, liberal democracy, capitalism, affluence, and modernity are thought to carry with them the "contradictions" that are their undoing. The very qualities that encourage economic and social progress—individuality, boldness, the spirit of enterprise and innovation—are said to undermine conventional manners and morals, traditions and authorities. This echoes a famous passage in *The Communist Manifesto*:

> The bourgeoisie, wherever it has got the upper hand, has put an end to all feudal, patriarchal, idyllic relations. It has pitilessly torn asunder the motley feudal ties that bound man to his "natural superior," and has left no other bond between man and man than naked self-interest, than callous "cash payment." . . . The bourgeoisie has torn away from the family its sentimental veil, and has reduced the family relation to a mere money relation.

Marx was as wrong about this as he was about so many things. Victorian England was a crucial test case for him because it was the first country to experience the industrial-capitalist-bourgeois revolution in its most highly developed form. Yet that revolution did not have the effects he attributed to it. It did not destroy all social relations, tear asunder the ties that bound man to man, strip from the family its sentimental veil, and reduce everything to "cash payment" (the "cash nexus," in other translations). It did not do this, in part because the free market was never as free or as pervasive as Marx thought (laissez-faire, historians now agree, was less rigorous, both in theory and in practice, than was once supposed); and in part because traditional values and institutions continued to play an important role in society, even in those industrial and urban areas most affected by the economic and social revolution.

Industrialism and urbanism—"modernism," as it is now known—so far from contributing to the de-moralization of the poor, seem to have had the opposite effect. At the end of the nineteenth century, England was a more civil, more pacific, more humane society than it had been in the beginning. "Middle-class" manners and morals had penetrated into large sections of the working classes. The traditional family was as firmly established as ever, even as women began to be liberated from their "separate sphere." And religion continued to thrive, in spite of the premature reports of its death.

If Victorian England did not succumb to the moral and cultural anarchy that are said to be the inevitable consequences of economic individualism, it is because of a powerful ethos that kept that individualism in check. For the Victorians, the individual, or "self," was the ally rather than the adversary of society. Self-help was seen in the context of the community as well as the family; among the working classes, this was reflected in the virtue of "neighbourliness," among the middle classes, of philanthropy. Self-interest stood not in opposition to the general interest but, as Adam Smith had it, as the instrument of the general interest. Self-discipline and self-control were thought of as the source of self-respect and self-betterment; and self-respect as the precondition for the respect and approbation of others. The individual, in short, was assumed to have responsibilities as well as rights, duties as well as privileges.

That Victorian "self" was very different from the "self" that is celebrated today. Unlike "self-help," "self-esteem" does not depend upon the individual's actions or achievements; it is presumed to adhere to the individual regardless of how he behaves or what he accomplishes. Moreover, it adheres to him regardless of the esteem in which he is held by others, unlike the Victorian's self-respect which always entailed the respect of others. The current notions of self-fulfillment, self-expression, and self-realization derive from a self that does not have to prove itself by reference to any values, purposes, or persons outside itself—that simply is, and by reason of that alone deserves to be fulfilled and realized. This is truly a self divorced from others, narcissistic and solipsistic.

This is the final lesson we may learn from the Victorians: that the ethos of a society, its moral and spiritual character, cannot be reduced to economic, material, political, or other factors, that values—or, better yet, virtues—are a determining factor in their own right; so far from being a "reflection," as the Marxist says, of the economic realities, they are themselves, as often as not, the crucial agent in shaping those realities. If in a period of rapid economic and social change, the Victorians showed a substantial improvement in their "condition" and "disposition," it may be that economic and social change do not necessarily result in personal and public disarray. If they could retain and even strengthen an ethos that had its roots in religion and tradition, it may be that we are not as constrained by the material conditions of our time as we have thought. A postindustrial economy, we may conclude, does not necessarily entail a postmodernist society or culture, still less a de-moralized society or culture.

The Politics of Liberty, the Sociology of Virtue

William Kristol

T HE 1994 ELECTION marked the end of an era. In narrow political terms, it ended sixty-two years of Democratic Party dominance.[1] In a broader sense, it marked the end of the New Deal/Great Society era of big government liberalism. It would be too strong to say that the 1994 election represented a repudiation of that era, for much that was accomplished during those years will—and should—survive. But the election did mark the closing of a historic period—a period whose roots in turn lie in the Progressive movement. In a sense, then, November 8, 1994, could be said to cap and conclude the Progressive Era of American history. We have fulfilled the "promise" of Herbert Croly's vision—and in doing so have brought to light its limitations and even its pathologies. We now have a chance to shape a new era, informed by a new promise.

It won't be easy. It is entirely possible that the Progressive Era will simply be followed by an era of deconstruction, and deconstruction not just of progressivism but of much that is solid in American life. We can all too easily imagine an American future consisting of a politics of dealignment, a culture of decomposition, and a society of disenchantment. But perhaps not. Perhaps we can move on and up from progressivism, informed by a new vision that returns, with suitable modifications, to the principles and understandings of the Founders. In Federalist No. Thirty-Nine, Madison refers to "that honorable determination which animates every votary of freedom to rest all our political experiments on the capacity of mankind for self-government."[2] Vindicating the capacity of mankind for self-government implies a political system that protects our liberty, and

From The New Promise of American Life, *ed. Lamar Alexander and Chester E. Finn, Jr. (Indianapolis, IN, Hudson Institute, 1995).*

a society that fosters in its citizens a character capable of self-government, in both the political and moral senses. Self-government therefore implies both a politics of liberty and a sociology of virtue.

The construction (or reconstruction) of a politics of liberty and a sociology of virtue is at the core of the promise of postprogressive America. For as the sociologist Robert Nisbet points out, "a conservative party (or other group) has a double task confronting it. The first is to work tirelessly toward the diminution of the centralized, omnipotent, and unitary state with its ever-soaring debt and deficit." This task—the relimiting of government—is the politics of liberty. "The second and equally important task," says Nisbet, "is that of protecting, reinforcing, nurturing, where necessary, the varied groups and associations which form the true building blocks of the social order."[3] This task—strengthening the institutions of civil society that attend to the character of the citizenry—is the sociology of virtue.

The Politics of Liberty

The phrase "politics of liberty" suggests that the preservation of liberty is a political task. Conservatives and libertarians have on occasion neglected the implications of this fact. We have sometimes acted as if making the theoretical case for liberty, and decrying restrictions on liberty, would convince our fellow citizens to relimit government. But we have given less thought to the matter of structuring institutions and incentives to preserve and strengthen the system of liberty. We have criticized big government's usurpations and lamented its continued growth. Many—a majority of Americans—share this criticism. But how do we go about relimiting government?

In the wake of the election of 1994, this question has come to the fore. It is now clear that there is far more popular support than before for rolling back the huge expansion of government of the past half-century. The American people now believe the federal government is too big, too intrusive, and too meddlesome. They are open to more than criticism of particular government policies; they are now willing to address the issue of the size and scope of government itself. And we have learned that it is not enough simply to make the case against big government; we have to think politically and institutionally about how to rally support and create incentives for limited government.

Such thinking begins with an appreciation of the institutional obstacles to cutting government policies and programs. Electing conservative or Republican presidents in recent years, after all, has not changed things very much. Nor, so far, has the movement of popular opinion toward greater skepticism about government policies and programs. This is because the liberal welfare state has built up sets of relationships and patterns of behavior that are hard to break once they have formed and congealed. George Bernard Shaw said early in this century, "A government that borrows from Peter to pay Paul can always depend on the support of Paul." And if the government doesn't rob Peter *too* much, and if there are a lot of Peters dispersed throughout the society and only a few Pauls, there will be an endless process of little robberies of Peter to give benefits to Paul. And if the Pauls are organized as an interest group, and are strong in several congressional districts, and if, in the name of "progress," the notion of principled limits on governmental action disappears, then the welfare state just keeps on growing.

And yet it has become discredited. Poll data, and the recent election results, show that the American people now have a deep distrust of the federal government. In fact they believe, by substantial margins, that the government is more likely to do harm than good. We now have a public opinion that could support a broad attack on unlimited government. But because particular policies have beneficiaries who will fight to keep them, while the opposition to these particular policies is often diffuse, the best strategy for containing and rolling back the liberal welfare state may be to look for ways to cut the Gordian knot, rather than trying to unwind it one string at a time. Thus the attraction of proposals such as a balanced budget amendment, term limits, tax and spending limitations at several levels of government, the devolution of power to states and localities, and the privatization of government functions. Such policies are radical in the sense that they do not seek simply to contain some of the damage done by the welfare state, or to address its particular pathologies one by one. Rather, they seek to change the patterns of behavior of the political system as a whole to make it more supportive of relimiting government.

Such institutional reforms are, of course, in the spirit of the Founding Fathers' attempts to create structures, incentives, and relationships that would preserve liberty. In this sense, the new politics of liberty is an attempt to find new remedies for diseases that have grown up over our progressive century, as we abandoned the older constraints on government. Some of these new remedies are in fact traditional ones—for example, federalism, or devolution of power. But what conservative reformers now understand is that we do not need more "New Federalism" efforts in which state and local governments simply become ever more dependent extensions of the federal octopus. We need *real* federalism, understood as part of a general program of relimiting government. And that means that the devolution effort must occur at the state level as well. State governments are no more immune to capture by interest groups than the federal government, though they are more constrained by the need to balance the budget and by popular pressure. Teachers' unions in Albany or Sacramento are as strong as they are in Washington, D.C. Thus, it is not enough to kill the federal Department of Education and return power to states and localities; that is but a *step* on the road to real devolution of power to citizens—in this case, to greater parental control of and choice in their children's schools. The point, after all, is not to get power back to the state governments; it is to get power back to parents and citizens.

Similarly, the new politics of liberty does not simply seek to *restore* the old ways of governing. In 1995, the accumulated departures from those ways have acquired such weight that we need to think more imaginatively about cutting through the jungle of the modern welfare state with fresh populist remedies. Most striking in this respect is the emergence of the movement for term limits. This idea, rejected at the Constitutional Convention, had virtually disappeared from our politics for almost two centuries. Today, however, term limits may be the most popular movement in the country. Few in Washington like this idea very much—but voters in all twenty-two states where it has been on the ballot have passed such limits. If the Supreme Court now strikes down state-imposed term limits on federal officials, the issue will be driven to the national level, and could trigger a broader debate about what we want from our representatives and what their relationship to limited government is to be.

The reason for the interest in term limits, after all, is not simply a general belief that Congress will work better if there is greater turnover of its members. The case for term limits rests on a critique of what "representation" has become in the world of big-government/interest-group liberalism, in which "iron triangles" of politicians, bureaucrats, and interest groups establish and benefit from welfare-state and corporatist programs. This triangle seems at once virtually impervious to change from above—from a popular president—and to change from below—from public opinion. Term limits strike at the iron triangle. The incentives for individual congressmen will change under term limits, as the seniority system and committee baronies disintegrate and the balance of power changes within Congress, between Congress and the other branches of government, and between Congress and the electorate. Term limits thus offer the promise of addressing some of the pathological tendencies of interest-group liberalism.

The politics of liberty, therefore, goes beyond a politics informed by a generalized hostility to big government. It means thinking imaginatively about structural, legislative, and constitutional changes that would restore both the principle and the practice of limited government. Above all, the politics of liberty does not imply that we reinvent government; it requires that we relimit it.

We must relimit it not simply because big government is a threat to our economic well-being. It is a threat to free society, because it corrupts such a society by making its people less able to govern themselves. Self-government means that communities and citizens and families are able and willing to govern themselves. This requires the reassertion of the old-fashioned presumption that civil society should exist more or less free of government regulation, even regulation for desirable policy ends. The "pursuit of happiness" will be left primarily to citizens acting freely in civil society; government will secure some of the conditions of such a pursuit, but it will not try to make "happiness"—or even "security" in an extended sense—its direct object. And politicians in this new era will have to be able to articulate and live by this stern message of the limits to proper government action.

The Sociology of Virtue

The sternness of this message can be softened, however, by the hope embodied in the other pillar of the postprogressive agenda, the sociology of virtue. Critics of progressivism have long been concerned with the effect of modern political and social developments on our character, on our virtues. But we have tended to speak primarily of "preserving" our wasting moral capital from the depredations of modern life, of "defending" traditional ideas of law and morality against the assaults launched by a new doctrine of personal liberation, of "shoring up" old institutions that were under modernist assault. Our concern for virtue has been profoundly "conservative," even defensive.

Today's task—and possibility—is radical rather than conservative, proactive rather than defensive: it is to foster a sociology of virtue rather than merely stemming further erosion of virtue's moral capital. That erosion has today gone too far for a merely "conservative" approach. A new sociology of virtue thus implies a thinking through of the ways in which social institutions can be reinvented, restructured, or reformed to promote virtue and foster sound character. This won't happen merely because of a few political victories. Relimiting government would help us deal with our social and moral problems; a successful politics of liberty would make a sociology of virtue easier to pursue. But even a sound political order will not be sufficient for a good society. Such a society also requires a resurgence of efforts within the private and voluntary spheres to grapple directly with our social problems, problems that are ultimately problems of character, problems of virtue.

Such efforts are in fact already happening. They are not waiting for the success of the politics of liberty. Despite all the social destructiveness around us, there is ample evidence of a resurgent sociology of virtue at work. There are efforts by inner-city pastors to relegitimize and redignify fatherhood, for example, as a beginning to solving the terrible problems of our inner cities. There is an authentic religious revival going on in the land, despite the continuing efforts of progressives in the public sphere to delegitimize religion and reduce its role. The right-to-life movement provides counseling and homes for unwed mothers, trying to convince women to shun the exercise of a right they have won thanks to a "progressive" Supreme Court. Citizens are banding together to deal with even so fundamental an area of government responsibility as crime. It is clear that we will see ever more such efforts to deal with our social problems through social and civic actions, efforts that simply leave government aside or incorporate it as one part of a larger enterprise.

These efforts will ultimately have a political effect, of course. Take the area of education. Following on the successful models in Indianapolis and Milwaukee, there are increasing numbers of privately funded voucher programs that enable students from lower-income families to go to a school of their parents' choice. Those who wanted to help young people at risk to escape from dreadful government schools decided they could not wait for the political system to act. But ultimately, this kind of nonpolitical activity does put pressure on the political system to allow school choice, for the evidence of the success of the private efforts is itself a powerful political argument. In fact, such activity in the private sphere may be the most effective way to spur efforts to reform government policies.

This approach might be called the Federal Express model of reform. Critics of the post office tried for decades to reform it, decrying it as an inefficient monopoly dominated by unions. Americans agreed that the post office did not work well, but it seemed impossible to make any progress legislatively or administratively. Then, in the early 1970s, Fred Smith started Federal Express. The post office and its allies made an effort to strangle this upstart in its cradle. But Federal Express prevailed, since it is politically easier to defend a small business from the government than to break up a huge government monopoly. Now, thanks also to technological developments (such as the fax machine), we have a situation where, with no real legal change, the delivery of mail in America has been transformed. The post office is still big, unwieldy, and sluggish, but it is not a major obstacle to American competitiveness; and it is now weaker politically, because of the growth of private-sector competitors and to the demonstrated superiority of the private sector. The opportunities for fundamental political reform are far greater today thanks to autonomous actions in the private sector.

A similar approach can be taken in many other areas. Instead of waiting for success in changing government institutions, citizens simply begin to go around them. As that happens, these institutions either have to reform themselves, or they become relics that ultimately lose political support. Now, as the Federal Express example suggests, political action is often necessary to protect these private-sector efforts from government attempts to suppress them. That is, after all, how religious conservatives became politically active. During the Carter administration the federal government seemed to threaten the tax-exempt status of Christian schools; as a response to this perceived threat, the Moral Majority was founded to protect these private-sector institutions from the government. As this example suggests, defensive efforts on behalf of the institutions of civil society can ultimately become proactive ones that seek also to reform the political system and the political culture.

So while the sociology of virtue implies pursuing virtue primarily in the private sector through our social institutions, it ultimately has political implications. At the very least, it requires the defense of sound social institutions from attempts by a "progressive" polity to suppress or reshape them.

Liberty, Virtue, and the Family

The politics of liberty and the sociology of virtue might be said to be the twin tracks for a postprogressive American politics. They are, on the whole, consistent and complementary tracks—and they influence each other. A politics of liberty can allow for new kinds of common pursuits in the space cleared by the retrenchment of government. Thus these tracks run parallel to one another for a considerable distance, allowing libertarians to limit government and social conservatives to attend to the sociology of virtue.

But the two tracks cannot be kept forever parallel; the two efforts—though basically complementary—do come into some tension, especially around a core set of issues involving the family. Here the politics of liberty runs up against the impossibility of neutrality about the fundamental arrangements of society; and the sociology of virtue runs up against the limits of what can be achieved in the civil sphere without some legal or policy support.

This can perhaps be made clear by reflecting briefly on Charles Murray's famous October 1993 *Wall Street Journal* article, "The Coming White Underclass."[4] Murray argued that the problems of crime, illiteracy, welfare, homelessness, drugs, and poverty all stem from a core problem, which is illegitimacy. Illegitimacy is therefore "the single most important social problem of our time." Doing something about it is not just one more item on the American political and social agenda; it should be at the top of the agenda. The broad and deep response to Murray's article suggests that it struck a chord—and, in fact, it has implications for both the politics of liberty and sociology of virtue.

Murray argues that we need a politics of liberty. We do not need additional progressive social engineering to solve a problem such engineering has in part created; we need the state to stop interfering with the social forces that kept the overwhelming majority of births within marriage for millennia. While Murray is pessimistic about how much government can do (except for getting out of the way), he is optimistic about how little it needs to do. Perhaps government could make the tax code friendlier to families with children; otherwise, a politics of liberty, presumably supplemented by a private-sector sociology of virtue, would seem to be Murray's recommendation.

But near the end of his article Murray adds this: "A more abstract but ultimately crucial step is to make marriage once again the sole legal institution through which parental rights and responsibilities are defined and exercised." Indeed, "a marriage certificate should establish that a man and woman have entered into a unique legal relationship. The changes that have blurred the distinctiveness of marriage are subtly but importantly destructive."[5]

Murray's suggestion that we reverse these changes goes beyond a mere "politics of liberty." It implies legal "discrimination" against illegitimacy or nontraditional family arrangements. In other words, a pure politics of liberty seems insufficient to Murray to combat "the single most important social problem of our time." State welfare policies, for example, cannot today discriminate against illegitimate children. Part of this problem could be solved by undoing welfare as we know it. But if it is essential that the law explicitly support marriage and the family—if we can't depend on civil society in a climate of legal neutrality simply to produce healthy families and to see to it that children are mostly born into intact families— then we come to the point where the politics of liberty and the sociology of virtue intersect. At this intersection, the politics of liberty would have to accommodate the special status of the family, and the sociology of virtue would have to acknowledge its need for political support for the family as a social institution. In other words, the political sphere, whose primary goal is liberty, cannot be entirely inattentive to the claims of virtue; and the social sphere, whose focus is virtue, requires some political support. For the two spheres to accommodate one another, a common view of what is right and just must ultimately underlie and inform both our politics and our society.

To support the family, one must hold a certain view of human nature and possibilities, a view different from that animating the sexual revolution, whose effects Murray laments. Murray thinks that our public policy should lean against the sexual revolution. But Murray also alludes to the (differing) expectations we need to have for "little boys" and "little girls"; he would seem to want our public policy to lean as well against the other powerful revolution of our time, the feminist revolution. For Murray emphasizes that the burden of preserving the family inevitably must fall primarily on women, and he believes public policy has to recognize this fact.

The sexual and feminist revolutions sprang up in civil society, so to speak. Politicians did not invent them. But the policy helped them along by legitimizing them and delegitimizing those who tried to resist them. No politics can simply be neutral between the sexual revolution and those who would resist it, or between radical feminism and those who would resist it. So even though our new American politics should be overwhelmingly a politics of liberty, and the pursuit of virtue should be primarily a "sociological" matter, at the intersection of politics and society—especially at the family—some judgments will have to be made. These judgments will always be more problematic than the relatively clear and mostly separate agendas of the politics of liberty and the sociology of virtue; but they cannot be avoided. We can pursue the politics of liberty and the sociology of virtue for quite a distance before we reach their intersection, but they do come together at a point at which neither our politics nor our sociology can be neutral as to the content of "the laws of Nature and Nature's God." Ultimately, the return to nature, an ascent from the progressive view of history, underlies both the politics of liberty and the sociology of virtue.

NOTES

1. This essay draws substantially on the Bradley Lecture delivered by the author at the American Enterprise Institute for Public Policy Research in December 1993.

2. James Madison, *The Federalist Papers*, ed. Clinton Rossiter (New York: New American Library, 1961), 240.

3. Robert Nisbet, "Still Questing," *Intercollegiate Review*, Fall 1993, 45.

4. Charles Murray, "The Coming White Underclass," *Wall Street Journal*, October 29, 1993, A14.

5. Ibid.

CONTRIBUTORS

Peter L. Berger is a professor of sociology at Boston University and is the president of the Institute on Economic Culture at that institution. He is the author of *The Homeless Mind*, among many other books.

Midge Decter has recently retired as the distinguished fellow at the Institute on Religion and Public Life. She has been an editor at *Commentary, Harper's*, and Basic Books. Ms. Decter is the author of *Liberal Parents, Radical Children*, among other books.

George Gilder is the editor of *Forbes ASAP*, a monthly magazine about technology. He is the author of many books, including *Wealth and Poverty*.

Nathan Glazer is a Professor of Education and Sociology at Harvard University. He is the author of numerous books and articles, notably *Beyond the Melting Pot* (with Daniel Patrick Moynihan), *The Limits of Social Policy*, and *Affirmative Discrimination*.

Gertrude Himmelfarb taught for twenty-three years at Brooklyn College and the graduate school of City University of New York, where she was named Distinguished Professor of History in 1978. She is the author of ten books, most recently *The Demoralization of Society: From Victorian Virtues to Modern Values*.

Leon R. Kass, M.D., is a professor at the University of Chicago and a member of the Committee on Social Thought. He is the author of *Toward a More Natural Science* and, most recently, *The Hungry Soul*.

Jeane Kirkpatrick is a distinguished fellow at the American Enterprise Institute. She is a syndicated columnist and the author of *Political Woman* and *Dictatorships and Double Standards*. From 1981 to 1984, Dr. Kirkpatrick served as the U. S. Representative to the United Nations.

Charles Krauthammer, a psychiatrist by training, is a syndicated columnist. He is the author of a collection of essays, *Cutting Edges*.

Irving Kristol is the editor of *The Public Interest* and the publisher of *The National Interest*. He has published four collections of essays, most recently *Neoconservatism: Autobiography of an Idea*.

William Kristol is editor and publisher of *The Weekly Standard*. A former professor of government at Harvard University and the University of Pennsylvania, Mr. Kristol served in the Reagan and Bush administrations as the chief of staff to Secretary of Education William Bennett and then Vice President Dan Quayle.

Daniel Patrick Moynihan is the senior U.S. senator from New York. Senator Moynihan served in the administrations of Presidents Kennedy, Johnson, Nixon, and Ford. He is the author of *Beyond the Melting Pot* (with Nathan Glazer) and *A Dangerous Place*, among other books.

Richard John Neuhaus is the editor-in-chief of *First Things* and the president of the Institute on Religion and Public Life. Father Neuhaus is the author of *The Naked Public Square* and, most recently, *Doing Well and Doing Good: The Challenge to the Christian Capitalist*.

Michael Novak holds the George Frederick Jewett chair at the American Enterprise Institute. He is the author of *The Spirit of Democratic Capitalism* and, most recently, *The Catholic Ethic and the Spirit of Catholicism*. He was awarded the Templeton Prize in 1994 for his work on religion.

Norman Podhoretz, a senior fellow at the Hudson Institute, was the editor-in-chief of *Commentary* from 1960 to 1985. He is the author of several books, including two memoirs, *Making It* (1967) and *Breaking Ranks* (1979).

Thomas Sowell is a senior fellow at the Hoover Institution. He is the author of *Race and Culture* and, most recently, *The Vision of the Anointed*.

George Weigel is the president of the Ethics and Public Policy Center. He is the author most recently of *Idealism Without Illusions*.

The late **Aaron Wildavsky** taught political science at the University of California, Berkeley. He was one of the most prolific scholars of his generation. His most recent book, published posthumously, is *But Is It True: A Citizen's Guide to the Environment*.

James Q. Wilson is the John C. Anderson Professor of Management at the University of California at Los Angeles. A past president of the American Political Science Association, he is the author of numerous books, including *Thinking About Crime* and *The Moral Sense*.

Ruth Wisse is professor of Yiddish literature and of comparative literature at Harvard University, where she also serves as the director of the Center for Jewish Studies. She is the author of *If I Am Not for Myself: The Liberal Betrayal of the Jews*.

PERMISSION ACKNOWLEDGMENTS

Jeane Kirkpatrick, "Dictatorships and Double Standards." Originally printed in *Commentary*, November 1979. Reprinted by permission of the author.

Ruth Wisse, "The Deligitimation of Israel." Originally printed in *Commentary*, October 1981. Reprinted by permission of the author.

Irving Kristol, "Human Nature and Social Reform." Originally printed in *The Wall Street Journal*, September 18, 1978. Reprinted by permission of the author.

Richard John Neuhaus and Peter Berger, excerpt from *To Empower People: Mediating Structures and Public Policy* (Washington: American Enterprise Institute, 1976). Reprinted by permission of The American Enterprise Institute for Public Policy Research, Washington, D.C.

Thomas Sowell, "Affirmative Action: A Worldwide Disaster." Originally printed in *Commentary*, December 1989. Reprinted by permission of the author.

Irving Kristol, "A Conservative Welfare State." Originally printed in *The Wall Street Journal*, June 14, 1993. Reprinted by permission of the author.

James Q. Wilson, "The Rediscovery of Character: Private Virtue and Public Policy." Originally printed in *Public Interest*, Fall 1985. Reprinted by permission of the author.

Irving Kristol, "Pornography, Obscenity and the Case for Censorship." Originally printed in the *New York Times Magazine*, March 28, 1971. Reprinted by permission of the author.

James Q. Wilson and George Kelling, "Broken Windows: The Police and Neighborhood Safety." Originally printed in the *Atlantic Monthly*, March 1982. Reprinted by permission of the authors.

Leon R. Kass, "Regarding Daughters and Sisters: The Rape of Dinah." Reprinted, with permission of the author, from *Commentary* (April 1992).

Daniel Patrick Moynihan, "Defining Deviance Down." Reprinted from *The American Scholar*, Volume 62, Number 1, Winter 1993. Copyright © 1992 by the author. By permission of the publisher.

Charles Krauthammer, "Defining Deviancy Up." Originally printed in *The*

New Republic, November 22, 1993. Reprinted by permission of the publisher.

Richard John Neuhaus, "A New Order of Religious Freedom." Originally printed in *First Things*, February 1992. Reprinted by permission of the author.

George Weigel, "Christian Conviction and Democratic Etiquette." Originally printed in *First Things*, March 1994. Reprinted by permission of the author.

Gertrude Himmelfarb, "A De-Moralized Society: The British/American Experience." Originally printed in *The Public Interest*, Fall 1994. This essay was adapted from *The De-Moralization of Society: From Victorian Virtues to Modern Values* (New York: Knopf, 1995). Reprinted by permission of the author.

William Kristol, "The Politics of Liberty, the Sociology of Virtue," from *The New Promise of American Life*, edited by Lamar Alexander and Chester Finn, Jr. (Indianapolis, IN: Hudson Institute Press, 1995). Reprinted by permission of the author.

INDEX

Audel™

HVAC Fundamentals
Volume 3
Air-Conditioning, Heat Pumps, and Distribution Systems

All New 4ᵗʰ Edition

James E. Brumbaugh

WILEY

Wiley Publishing, Inc.

Vice President and Executive Group Publisher: Richard Swadley
Vice President and Executive Publisher: Robert Ipsen
Vice President and Executive Publisher: Joseph B. Wikert
Vice President and Publishing
Executive Editor: Carol Long, Katie Mohr
Acquisitions Editor: Katie Malm
Editorial Manager: Kathryn Brown
Development Editor: Kevin Kunkemueller
Production Editor: Vincent Kunkemueller
Text Design & Composition: TechBooks

For Laura, my friend, my daughter.

Contents

Introduction

The purpose of this series is to provide the layman with an introduction to the fundamentals of installing, servicing, troubleshooting, and repairing the various types of equipment used in residential and light-commercial heating, ventilating, and air conditioning (HVAC) systems. Consequently, it was written not only for the HVAC technician and others with the required experience and skills to do this type of work but also for the homeowner interested in maintaining an efficient and trouble-free HVAC system. A special effort was made to remain consistent with the terminology, definitions, and practices of the various professional and trade associations involved in the heating, ventilating, and air conditioning fields.

Volume 1 begins with a description of the principles of thermal dynamics and ventilation, and proceeds from there to a general description of the various heating systems used in residences and light-commercial structures. Volume 2 contains descriptions of the working principles of various types of equipment and other components used in these systems. Following a similar format, Volume 3 includes detailed instructions for installing, servicing, and repairing these different types of equipment and components.

The author wishes to acknowledge the cooperation of the many organizations and manufacturers for their assistance in supplying valuable data in the preparation of this series. Every effort was made to give appropriate credit and courtesy lines for materials and illustrations used in each volume.

Special thanks is due to Greg Gyorda and Paul Blanchard (Watts Industries, Inc.), Christi Drum (Lennox Industries, Inc.), Dave Cheswald and Keith Nelson (Yukon/Eagle), Bob Rathke (ITT Bell & Gossett), John Spuller (ITT Hoffman Specialty), Matt Kleszezynski (Hydrotherm), and Stephanie DePugh (Thermo Pride).

Last, but certainly not least, I would like to thank Katie Feltman, Kathryn Malm, Carol Long, Ken Brown, and Vincent Kunkemueller, my editors at John Wiley & Sons, whose constant support and encouragement made this project possible.

James E. Brumbaugh

About the Author

James E. Brumbaugh is a technical writer with many years of experience working in the HVAC and building construction industries. He is the author of the *Welders Guide, The Complete Roofing Guide,* and *The Complete Siding Guide.*

Chapter 1

Radiant Heating

Heat is lost from the human body through radiation, convection, and evaporation. Radiation heat loss represents the transfer of energy by means of electromagnetic waves. The convection loss is the heat carried away by the passage of air over the skin and clothing. The evaporation loss is the heat used up in converting moisture on the surface of the skin into vapor.

Heat transfer, whether by convection or radiation, follows the same physical laws in the radiant heating system as in any other; that is, heat flows from the warmer to the cooler exposure at a rate directly proportional to the existing temperature difference.

The natural tendency of warmed air to rise makes it apparent that this induced air current movement is greater at the cooler floor and exterior walls of the average heated enclosure than at its ceiling. It is through absorption by these air currents that the radiant panel releases the convection component of its heat transfer into the room air.

The average body heat loss is approximately 400 Btu per hour; total radiation and convection account for approximately 300 to 320 Btu of it. Because this is obviously the major portion, the problem of providing comfort is principally concerned with establishing the proper balance between radiation and convection losses.

It is important to understand that bodily comfort is obtained in radiant heating by maintaining a proper balance between radiation and convection. Thus, if the air becomes cooler and accordingly the amount of heat given off from the body by convection *increases*, then the body can still adjust itself to a sense of comfort if the heat given off from the body by radiation is *decreased*. The amount given off from the body by radiation can be decreased by raising the temperature of the surrounding surfaces, such as the walls, floor, and ceiling. For comfort, the body demands that if the amount of heat given off by convection increases, the heat given off by radiation must decrease, and vice versa.

The principles involved in radiant heating exist in such commonplace sources of heat as the open fireplace, outdoor campfires, electric spot heaters, and similar devices. In each of these examples, no attempt is made to heat the air or enclosing surfaces surrounding the individual. In fact, the temperature of the air and surrounding surfaces may be very low, but the radiant heat from the fireplace or campfire will still produce a sensation of comfort (or even discomfort from excess heat) to those persons within range. This situation can occur even though a conventional thermometer may indicate a temperature well below freezing. Radiant heat rays do not perceptibly heat the atmosphere through which they pass. They move from warm to colder surfaces where a portion of their heat is absorbed.

This chapter is primarily concerned with a description of radiant panel heating, which can be defined as a form of radiant heating in which large surfaces are used to radiate heat at relatively low temperatures. The principal emphasis will be on hydronic and electric radiant floor heating.

Types of Radiant Panel Heating Systems

Radiant panel heating systems use water-filled tubing or electric heating mats or rolls installed in the floors, walls, and ceilings to distribute the heat. Radiant floor heating is by far the most popular installation method in residential and light-commercial construction.

Note
> The word *panel* is used to indicate a complete system of tubing loops in a single room or space in a structure. It may also be used to indicate a premanufactured radiant floor heating panel.

Floor Panel Systems
Floor panels are usually easier to install than either ceiling or wall panels. Using floor panels is the most effective method of eliminating cold floors in slab construction. Another advantage of heating with floor panels is that much of the radiated heat is delivered to the lower portions of the walls. The principal disadvantage of using floor panels is that furniture and other objects block portions of the heat emission.

Floor panels are recommended for living or working areas constructed directly on the ground, particularly one-story structures. Partial ceiling or wall treatment may be used as a supplement wherever large glass or door exposures are encountered. A typical floor installation is shown in Figure 1-1.

Ceiling Panel Systems
The advantage of a ceiling panel is that its heat emissions are not affected by drapes or furniture. As a result, the entire ceiling area can be used as a heating panel. Ceiling panels are recommended for rooms or space with 7-foot ceilings or higher. A ceiling panel should never be installed in a room with a low ceiling (under 7 feet) because it may produce an undesirable heating effect on the head.

Figure 1-1 Diagram of a typical radiant floor heating installation.

In multiple-story construction, the use of ceiling panels appears to be more desirable from both the standpoint of physical comfort and overall economy. The designed utilization of the upward heat transmission from ceiling panels to the floor of the area immediately above will generally produce moderately tempered floors. Supplementing this with automatically controlled ceiling panels will result in a very efficient radiant heating system. Except directly below roofs or other unheated areas, this design eliminates the need for the intermediate floor insulation sometimes used to restrict the heat transfer from a ceiling panel exclusively to the area immediately below. It must be remembered, however, that when intermediate floor insulations are omitted, the space above a heated ceiling will not be entirely independent with respect to temperature control but will necessarily be influenced by the conditions in the space below. A typical ceiling installation is shown in Figure 1-2.

Figure I-2 Diagram of a typical radiant ceiling heating panel.

Apartment buildings and many office and commercial structures should find the ceiling panel method of radiant heating most desirable. In offices and stores, the highly variable and changeable furnishings, fixtures, and equipment favor the construction of ceiling panels, to say nothing of the advantage of being able to make as many partition alterations as desired without affecting the efficiency of the heating system.

Wall Panel Systems

Walls are not often used for radiant heating because large sections of the wall area are often interrupted by windows and doors. Furthermore, the heat radiation from heating coils placed in the lower sections of a wall will probably be blocked by furniture. As a result, a radiant wall installation is generally used to supplement ceiling or floor systems, not as a sole source of heat.

Wall heating coils are commonly used as supplementary heating in bathrooms and in rooms in which there are a number of large picture windows. In the latter case, the heating coils are installed in the walls opposite the windows. Wall heating coils will probably not be necessary if the room has good southern exposure. A typical wall installation is shown in Figure 1-3.

BALANCING AND SHUTOFF
VALVES IN WALL BOX

DIRECTION OF FLOW
SAME AS MAINS

Figure 1-3 Typical wall installation. Panel is installed on wall as high as possible.

Hydronic Radiant Floor Heating

Hydronic radiant floor systems heat water in a boiler, heat pump, or water heater and force it through tubing arranged in a pattern of loops located beneath the floor surface. These systems can be classified as being either wet installations or dry installations depending on how the tubing is installed.

In wet installations, the tubing is commonly embedded in a concrete foundation slab or attached to a subfloor and covered with a lightweight concrete slab. Dry installations are so called because the tubing is not embedded in concrete.

System Components

The principal components of a typical hydronic radiant floor heating system can be divided into the following categories:

1. Boilers, water heaters, and heat pumps
2. Tubing and fittings
3. Valves and related controls
4. Circulator
5. Expansion tank
6. Air separator
7. Heat exchanger
8. Thermostat

Boilers, Water Heaters, and Heat Pumps

The boilers used in hot-water radiant heating systems are the same types of heating appliances as those used in hydronic heating systems. Information about the installation, maintenance, service, and repair of hydronic boilers is contained in Chapter 15 of Volume 1.

Gas-fired boilers are the most widely used heat source in hydronic radiant heating systems. Oil-fired boilers are second in popularity and are used most commonly in the northern United States and Canada. Coal-fired boilers are still found in some hydronic radiant heating systems, but their use has steadily declined over the years.

Note

Hydronic radiant floor heating systems operate in an 85–140°F (29–60°C) temperature range. This is much lower than the 130–160°F (54–71°C) temperature operating range required in other hydronic systems. As a result, the boilers used in floor systems operate at lower boiler temperatures, which results in a much longer service life for the appliance.

The electric boilers used in hydronic radiant floor systems are competitive with other fuels in those areas where electricity costs are low. Their principal advantage is that they are compact appliances that can be installed where space is limited.

Radiant floor systems can also be heated with a geothermal heat pump. In climates where the heating and cooling loads are equal or almost equal in size, a geothermal heat pump will be very cost effective.

Most standard water heaters produce a maximum of 40,000 to 50,000 Btu/h. This is sufficient Btu input to heat a small house or to separately heat a room addition, but it cannot provide the heat required for medium to large houses. As a result, some HVAC manufacturers have developed high-Btu-output dedicated water heaters for radiant heating systems. These water heaters are designed specifically as single heat sources for both the domestic hot water and the space-heating requirements. As is the case with boilers used in hydronic radiant heating systems, they operate in conjunction with a circulating pump and an expansion tank. See Chapter 4 ("Water Heaters") for additional information about combination water heaters.

Tubing and Fittings

The tubing in a radiant heating system is divided into the supply and return lines. The *supply line* extends from the discharge opening of a boiler to the manifold. It carries the heated fluid to the loops (circuits) in the floors, walls, or ceilings. A *return line* extends from the return side of a manifold to the boiler. It carries the water from the heating panels back to the boiler where it is reheated.

Hydronic radiant floor heating systems use copper, plastic (PEX or polybutylene tubing), or synthetic-rubber tubing to form the loops. Because of space limitations, only the two most commonly used types are described in this chapter: copper tubing and PEX (plastic) tubing. Information about the other types of tubing used in hydronic heating systems can be found in Chapter 8 ("Pipes, Pipe Fittings, and Piping Details") of Volume 2.

Loops or Circuits

The words *loop* and *circuit* are synonyms for the length of tubing within a zone. Sometimes both are used in the same technical publication. At other times, one or the other is used exclusively. Many loops or circuits of the same length will form a zone. Circuits also refer to the electrical circuit required to operate the heating system.

Copper Tubing

In most modern radiant floor heating systems, the water is circulated through copper or cross-linked polyethylene (PEX) tubing (see Figure 1-4). The metal coils used in hydronic radiant heating systems commonly are made of copper tubing (both the hard and soft varieties). Steel and wrought-iron pipe also have been used in hydronic floor heating systems, but it is rare to find them in modern residential radiant floor heating systems.

¾-INCH ID

½-INCH ID

⅜-INCH ID

Inside diameters (ID) of commonly used copper tubing in hydronic radiant floor heating systems.

Figure I-4 Copper tubing.

The soft tempered Type L copper tubing is recommended for hydronic radiant heating panels. Because of the relative ease with which soft copper tubes can be bent and shaped, they are especially well adapted for making connections around furnaces, boilers, oil-burning equipment, and other obstructions. This high workability characteristic of copper tubing also results in reduced installation time and lower installation costs. Copper tubing is produced in diameters ranging from ⅛ inch to 10 inches and in a variety of different wall thicknesses. Both copper and brass fittings are available. Hydronic heating systems use small tube sizes joined by soldering.

The size of the pipes or tubing used in these systems depends on the flow rate of the water and the friction loss in the tubing. The *flow rate* of the water is measured in gallons per minute (gpm), and constant *friction loss* is expressed in thousandths of an inch for each foot of pipe length. For a description of the various types of tubing used in hydronic heating systems, see the appropriate sections of Chapter 8 ("Pipes, Pipe Fittings, and Piping Details") in Volume 2.

Most of the fittings used in hydronic radiant heating systems are typical plumbing fittings. They include couplings (standard, slip, and reducing couplings), elbows (both 45° and 90° elbows), male and female adapters, unions, and tees (full size and reducing tees) (see Figure 1-5).

Three special fittings used in hydronic radiant heating systems are the brass adapters, the brass couplings, and the repair couplings. A *brass adapter* is a fitting used to join the end of a length of ¾-inch diameter copper tubing to the end of a length of plastic polyethylene tubing. A *brass coupling*, on the other hand, is a fitting used to join two pieces of plastic heat exchanger tubing. A *repair coupling* is a brass fitting enclosed in clear vinyl protective sheath to prevent concrete from corroding the metal fitting. The fitting is strengthened by double-clamping it with stainless steel hose clamps.

A decoiler bending device or jig should be used to bend metal tubing into the desired coil pattern. Only soft copper tubing can be easily bent by hand. It is recommended that a tube bender of this type be made for each of the different center-to-center spacing needed for the various panel coils in the installation.

Soft copper tubing is commonly available in coil lengths of 40 feet, 60 feet, and 100 feet. When the tubing is uncoiled, it should be straightened in the trough of a straightener jig. For convenience of handling, the straightener should not be more than 10 feet long.

Note

> Most copper tubing leaks will occur at bends or U-turns in the floor loops. These leaks are caused by water or fluids under high pressure flowing through the weakened sections of tubing. The weakened metal is commonly caused by improper bending techniques.

Whenever possible, continuous lengths of tubing should be used with as few fitting connections as possible. Coils of 60 feet or 100 feet

Figure 1-5 Some examples of copper tubing fittings.

are best for this purpose and are generally preferred for floor panels. The spacing between the tubing should be uniform and restricted to 12 inches or less. Use soldered joints to make connections between sections of tubing or pipe.

Cross-Linked Polyethylene (PEX) Tubing

Cross-linked polyethylene (PEX) tubing is commonly used indoors in hydronic radiant heating panels or outdoors embedded beneath the surface of driveways, sidewalks, and patios to melt snow and ice. It is made of a high-density polyethylene plastic that has been subjected to a cross-linking process (see Figures 1-6, 1-7, and 1-8). It is flexible, durable, and easy to install. There are two types of PEX tubing:

- Oxygen barrier tubing
- Nonbarrier tubing

Figure 1-6   PEX tubing. *(Courtesy Watts Radiant, Inc.)*

Oxygen barrier tubing (BPEX) is treated with an oxygen barrier coating to prevent oxygen from passing through the tubing wall and contaminating the water in the system. It is designed specifically to prevent corrosion to any ferrous fittings or valves in the piping system. BPEX tubing is recommended for use in a hydronic radiant heating system.

Nonbarrier tubing should be used in a hydronic radiant heating system only if it can be isolated from the ferrous components by a corrosion-resistant heat exchanger, or if only corrosion-resistant system components (boiler, valves, and fittings) are used.

PEX tubing is easy to install. Its flexibility allows the installer to bend it around obstructions and into narrow spaces. A rigid plastic cutter tool, or a copper tubing cutter equipped with a plastic cutting wheel, should be used to cut and install PEX tubing. Both tools produce a square cut without burrs.

PEX tubing can be returned to its original shape after accidental crimping or kinking by heating it to about 250–275°F. This attribute of PEX tubing makes it possible to perform field repairs without removing the damaged tubing section. This is not the case with polybutylene tubing, which is not cross-linked. Synthetic rubber tubing

Figure 1-7 PEX tubing markings. *(Courtesy Vanguard Piping Systems, Inc.)*

Crimping Fittings

1. Expand the end of the PEX tubing with the expansion tool provided by the PEX tube manufacturer.

2. Insert the brass fitting into the end of the expanded PEX tube.

3. Use the expansion tool to pull the brass sleeve back over the PEX tube and fitting for a tight connection.

Compression Fitting

1. Slide the locking nut and split compression ring up the tubing.

2. Insert the tubing onto the compression fitting.

3. Tighten the nut onto the compression fitting snugly.

4. Re-tighten the fittings after the heat has been turned on and the hot water has circulated through the tubing.

Figure I-8   PEX tubing fittings.
(Courtesy Watts Radiant, Inc.)

is also not cross-linked, but its material composition and its flexibility make it very resistant to crimping or kinking damage.

Manifolds

A *manifold* is a device used to connect multiple tubing lines to a single supply or return line in a hydronic radiant floor heating system (see Figures 1-9 and 1-10). Each heating system has at least two

Manifolds with integral valves should be used as return manifolds unless flow indicators are desired. If both flow indication and electric valve actuators are needed, use manifold with flow indicator valves on their turn and manifold with integral valves on the supply. Apply any desired combination of 2-wire and 4-wire electric actuators.

Figure 1-9   Weil-McLain hydronic radiant heating manifold.

(Courtesy Weil-McLain)

1

RETURN: FLOW INDICATORS
SUPPLY: ELECTRIC VALVES

This combination allows
independent zone control
and easy balancing.

2

RETURN: FLOW INDICATORS
SUPPLY: NO VALVES

This combination provides
easy balancing, but does
not provide independent
zone control.

3

RETURN: ELECTRIC VALVES
SUPPLY: NO VALVES

This combination provides
independent zone control.
Balancing will be more difficult
than combination 1 or 2.

4

RETURN: NO VALVES
SUPPLY: NO VALVES

This combination provides
no balancing means. Use
ball valves in tubing circuits
if balancing is needed.

Figure 1-10 Manifold combinations. (*Courtesy Weil-McLain*) types of manifolds: a supply manifold and a return manifold. A supply manifold receives water from the heating appliance (that is, the boiler, water heater, or heat pump) through a single supply pipe and then distributes it through a number of different tubing lines to the room or space being heated (see Figure 1-11). A return manifold provides the opposite function. It receives the return water from the room or space through as many tubing lines and sends it back to the boiler by a single return pipe. A supply manifold and a return manifold are sometimes referred to jointly as a *manifold station*.

Figure 1-11   Typical manifold location.

Preassembled manifolds are available from manufacturers for installation in most types of heating systems. Customized manifolds can also be ordered, but they are more expensive than the standard, preassembled types.

A *supply manifold*, when operating in conjunction with zone valves, can be used to control the hot water flow to the distribution lines in the radiant heating system. The zone valves, which are usually ball valves, can be manually adjusted or automatically opened and closed with a zone valve actuator. Some zone valves are designed as fully open or fully closed valves. Others are operated by a modulating actuator that can adjust the opening to the heat required by the zoned space.

A supply manifold with zoning capabilities is sometimes called a *zone manifold* or *distribution manifold*. In addition to zone valves, these manifolds also can be ordered to include supply and return water sensors, the circulator, and a control panel with indoor and outdoor sensors.

Depending on the heating system requirements, a manifold may also include inline thermometers or a temperature gauge to measure the temperature of the water flowing through the tubing; check valves or isolation valves to isolate the manifold so that it can be serviced or repaired; drain valves to remove water from the manifold; an air vent to purge air from the system; and pump flanges (for the circulator) plus all the required plumbing connections and hardware.

Manifold balancing valves regulate each zone (loop) to ensure efficient heat distribution and eliminate those annoying cold and hot spots on the floor. These valves can be adjusted to deliver the design flow rate of water in gallons per minute (gpm). Some manifolds are designed to electronically read the flow and temperature of the water in individual tubing loops. This function results in rapid and accurate data feedback for balancing. It also makes troubleshooting problems easier.

Manifolds are available for mounting on walls or installation in concrete slabs. The latter type, sometimes called a *slab manifold*, is made of copper and is available with up to six supply and six return loop connections. Slab manifolds also should be equipped with a pressure-testing feature so that they can be tested for leaks before the slab is poured.

Slab manifolds are installed with a box or form that shields the device from the concrete when it is poured. All connections remain below the level of the floor except for the tops of the supply and return tubing.

Valves and Related Control Devices

Valves and similar control devices are used for a variety of different purposes in a hydronic radiant floor heating system. Some are used as high-limit controls to prevent excessively hot water from flowing through the floor loops. Some are used to isolate system components, such as the circulating pump, so that it can be serviced or removed without having to shut down the entire system. Others are used to regulate the pressure or temperature of the water, to reduce the pressure of the water before it enters the boiler, or to regulate the flow of water.

Many of the different types of valves and control devices used in hydraulic radiant floor heating systems are listed in the sidebar. A brief description of the more commonly used ones is provided in this section. For a fuller, more detailed description of their operation, maintenance, service, and repair, read the appropriate sections of Chapter 9 ("Valves and Valve Installation") of Volume 2. Not all the valves listed in the sidebar or the ones described in this chapter will necessarily be used in the same heating system. The valves chosen will fit the requirements of a specific application (see Figures 1-12, 1-13, and 1-14).

Hydraulic Heating System Valves and Related Control Devices

- Air vent
- Aquastat
- Backflow preventers
- Ball valves
- Boiler drain valve
- Check valves
- Feed water pressure regulator
- Flow control valve
- Gate valve
- Globe valve
- Isolation valve
- Mixing valve
- Motorized zone valve
- Pressure-reducing valve
- Pressure relief valve
- Purge and balancing valves
- Solenoid valve

Air Vent

An air vent is a device used to manually or automatically expel air from a closed hydronic heating system. An automatic air vent valve provides automatic and continuous venting of air from the system. The function of both types is to prevent air from collecting in the piping loops.

1. Air scoop.
2. Backflow preventer.
3. Boiler drain valve.
4. Boiler fill valve.
4a. Combination backflow·preventer
   and boiler fill valve.
5. Bronze check valve.
6. Expansion tank.
7. Flow check valves.
8. Flow control valve.
9. Gate or globe valve.
10. Mixing valve.

11. Purge valve.
12. Pressure relief valve.
13. Hot water safety relief valve.
14. Test plug.
15. Ball valve.
16. Automatic float vent valve.
17. Float vent.
18. Water pressure reducing valve.
19. Service check valve.
20. Combination temperature
   and pressure gauge.
21. Boiler energy saver.

Figure 1-12 Typical locations of valves and related control devices in a hydronic heating system. *(Courtesy Watts Regulator Co.)*

Aquastat

An *aquastat* is a control device consisting of a sensing bulb, a diaphragm, and a switch (see Figure 1-14). As the temperature surrounding the sensing bulb increases, the gas inside the bulb expands and flows into the diaphragm. This action causes the diaphragm to expand and activate the switch controlling the connected device. When temperatures exceed the high-limit setting on

Figure 1-13 Piping diagram of a zoned radiant heating system supplying hot water to both floor panels and baseboards.

Note: Circulating pumps, illustrated in the above applications, circulate tempered water through the system. The aquastat shuts the circulating pump off if the tempered water exceeds the temperature set point, which is normally ± 5°F (± 2°C) of the tempering valve discharge.

Figure 1-14 Piping diagram of a radiant heating system with circulator controlled by aquastat.

the aquastat, it shuts off the circulator or circulators until the problem can be corrected.

The switching contacts of some aquastats can be manually adjusted for temperature settings. In other systems, the switching contacts of an aquastat may be preset at a predetermined temperature setting.

Backflow Preventer

A *backflow preventer* is a valve used to prevent the mixing of boiler hot water with domestic (potable) water (see Figure 1-15). Most systems use an inline backflow preventer. It must be installed with the arrow on the side of the valve facing the direction of water flow. Sometimes a backflow preventer and boiler fill valve are combined in the same unit.

Ball Valve, Gate, and Globe Valves

A *ball valve* can be used to isolate components or lines, or to regulate flow. A *gate valve* is often used to isolate components for service, repair, or replacement. They are not designed to regulate the flow of water. A *globe valve* is used to regulate the flow of water in a radiant heating system.

Note

Use a fully closing ball or gate valve on the supply and return line so that the manifold can be isolated and serviced without interrupting the pressure in the rest of the system.

Figure 1-15   Feed water pressure regulator. *(Courtesy Watts Regulator Co.)*

Boiler Drain Valve

A *boiler drain valve* is a quarter-turn ball valve used to drain water from a boiler. As shown in Figure 1-12, it is located near the bottom of the boiler close to a floor drain.

Check Valves

A *check valve* (also called a shutoff valve) is used to ensure that water is flowing in the correct direction by providing positive shutoff to the flow. Typical locations of check (shutoff) valves are shown in Figures 1-12, 1-13, and 1-14.

A *swing check valve* is designed to prevent the backflow of water. A *flow-control valve* is a check valve used to prevent circulation of the hot water through the heating system when the thermostat has not called for circulation. The flow-control check valve must be used when the radiant panels are located below the boiler.

Note

Flow-control valves should not be used when the radiant floor panel is below the level of the boiler.

Another type of check valve used in a radiant floor heating system is the *isolation valve* (also sometimes called a *service valve*).

The isolation valve is used to isolate a hydronic system component for servicing and/or removal so that it can be repaired or replaced. Isolating the component eliminates the need to drain and refill the system with water.

Caution
> Reduce the system pressure to a safe level before attempting to remove system components.

Caution
> An isolation valve is not designed to isolate a pressure (safety) relief valve or other safety or flow-sensitive components.

Feed Water Pressure Regulators

A feed water pressure regulator is used to fill both the boiler and system piping (including the floor panel loops) with water. A typical location of a feed water pressure regulator in the cold-water return line is illustrated in Figure 1-15. These valves also maintain the water pressure at the required level in the system at all times. If a leak should occur in the system, the feed water pressure regulator is designed to provide the required amount of makeup water. Using the feed water pressure regulator speeds filling and purging of air from the piping during the initial fill procedure.

Disconnect Switch

Two principal types of on-off switches are used to open or close an electrical circuit: the disconnect switch and the thermostat (see *Thermostat* in this section).

The *disconnect switch* is a manually operated on-off switch used to shut down the entire heating system when a problem is beginning to develop. When the switch is in the off position, the circuit opens and the electricity operating the boiler, heat pump, or water heater is shut off. When it is in the on position, the circuit closes (that is, completes itself) and electricity bypasses the boiler, heat pump, or space-heating water heater.

Inline Thermometer

An *inline thermometer* is a device that is used to monitor the water temperature as it circulates through the system. Two inline thermometers are installed in the heating system. One monitors the temperature of the water as it enters the supply line. The other monitors the temperature of the water as it leaves. The difference between these two measurements provides clues to the operating efficiency of the system.

Mixing Valve

A *thermostatic mixing valve* is used in a radiant heating system to recirculate a variable portion of the return water and at the same time add a sufficient quantity of hot boiler water to maintain the required water temperature in the loops. These valves are also called *thermostatic mixing valves, water blending valves, water blenders, water tempering valves,* or *tempering valves.* Typical locations of mixing valves are shown in Figures 1-12, 1-13, and 1-14.

Both manual and automatic modulating mixing valves are used in hydronic heating systems. The manual mixing valve is often used to control the water temperature in a high-mass concrete slab. It is not as accurate as an automatic valve (for example, a thermostatic valve), but the high-mass concrete slab stores it and releases it slowly over a long period of time, making exact temperature control unnecessary.

The three-way and four-way thermostatic mixing valves provide automatic control of the mixed water temperatures. The valve varies the flow of hot water between its hot port and its cold port so that it can deliver through its mixed port a steady flow of water at a constant temperature.

Mixing valves are often used with high-temperature boilers designed to provide water at temperatures of more than 160°F.

Motorized Zone Valve

A *motorized zone valve* is used to control the flow of water through a single zone (see Figure 1-16). It consists of a valve body combined with an electric actuator. A radiant panel heating system will often use a number of motorized zoning valves to maintain a uniform temperature throughout the rooms and spaces in the structure. As shown in Figure 1-17, a motorized zone valve is used to control each zone. Motorized zone valves are controlled by an aquastat, individual thermostats at each loop, or a room thermostat.

Figure I-16 Honeywell V4043 motorized zone valve.

(Courtesy Honeywell, Inc.)

Figure 1-17 A typical control system for a multiple-zone radiant heating system. *(Courtesy Honeywell Tradeline)*

Note

A zone valve simplifies the piping required for a hydronic heating system because it eliminates the need for a flow check valve and relays.

Pressure-Reducing Valve

A *pressure-reducing valve* is designed to reduce the pressure of the water entering the system and to maintain the pressure at a specific minimum setting (usually about 12 lbs). A typical location of a pressure relief valve is shown in Figure 1-12.

Pressure Relief Valve

A *pressure relief valve* (also sometimes called a *safety relief valve*) is used to prevent excessive and dangerous pressure from entering the system. It is located on top of the boiler or very close to it (see Figures 1-12, 1-13, and 1-14).

Purge and Balancing Valves

Purge and balancing valves are used on either the supply or return side of the manifold in systems where multiple manifolds are served by only one circulator. Among its varied functions is (1) to allow adjustments of proper water flow for each loop; (2) to function as a shutoff valve and a drain valve for each zone or loop; (3) to control (balance) water flow through the circulation loop; and (4) to provide a means of expelling air from heating zones during initial loop fill (valve is located on the boiler return piping). If the heating system contains individual loops of unequal length, each should be equipped with a balancing valve.

Circulator

The *circulator* (circulating pump) provides the motive force to circulate the water through the radiant heating system. Sometimes a variable-speed pump is used to maintain a supply water temperature between 90°F and 150°F.

In some zoned systems, a circulator operates in conjunction with a zone thermostat instead of a zoning valve to maintain a uniform floor temperature in each room or space of the structure. The zone thermostat controls the temperature in the zone by turning the circulator on and off. The size of the circulating pump selected for a radiant panel heating system will depend on the pressure drop in the system and the rate at which water must circulate. The circulation rate of the water is determined by the heating load and the *design* temperature drop of the system and is expressed in gallons per minute (gpm). This can be calculated by using the following formula:

$$\text{gpm} \times \frac{\text{Total Heating Load}}{T \times 60 \times 8}$$

The *total heating load* is calculated for the structure and is expressed in Btu per hour. A value of 20°F is generally used for the design temperature drop (T) in most hot-water radiant panel heating systems. The other two values in the formula are the minutes per hour (60) and the weight (in pounds) of a gallon of water (8).

By way of example, the rate of water circulation for a structure with a total heating load of 30,000 Btu per hour may be calculated as follows:

$$\text{gpm} = \frac{30,000 \text{ Btu/hr}}{20 \times 60 \times 8}$$

$$= \frac{30,000}{9600} = 3.13$$

Expansion Tank

An *expansion tank* (also called a *compression tank*) is required for use in all closed hydronic radiant heating systems (see Figure 1-18). Water and other fluids expand when they are heated. The expansion tank provides space to store the increased volume to prevent stress on the system.

Air Separator

An *air separator* (also called an *air scoop* or an *air eliminator*) is a device used in a closed radiant heating system to capture and remove air trapped in the water (see Figure 1-18). Some of these devices are

Figure 1-18 Air separator and expansion tank.

FLOAT VENT

SERVICE CHECK VALVE

AIR SCOOP

SERVICE CHECK VALVE

EXPANSION TANK

equipped with tappings for the installation of an expansion tank and air vent.

Heat Exchanger

A *heat exchanger* is a device used in some radiant heating systems to separate dissimilar fluids such as water mixed with antifreeze (in snow- and ice-melting applications) and water (for radiant floor heating tubing and domestic hot water). Its function is to allow the transfer of heat between the fluids without allowing them to mix and thereby contaminate one another.

Automatic Controls

While any thermostatic method of control will function with a radiant floor heating system, the most desirable method is one based on continuously circulating hot water. The temperature of the water should be automatically adjusted to meet outdoor conditions, but the circulation itself is controlled by interior limiting thermostats instead of the simple off-on method of circulating hot water at a fixed temperature (see Figure 1-19).

Some radiant floor heating systems are designed with a thermostat for each zone (see Figure 1-17). A more common method is to group several rooms or spaces together and control them by a single thermostat. In this approach, the kitchen and dining room may be included in one thermostat-controlled loop, the bedrooms in another, the bathrooms in still another, and so on.

Figure 1-19 Examples of thermostat controls used in hydronic radiant heating systems.

Many HVAC control manufacturers are now producing control consoles such as the one shown in Figure 1-20.

Designing a Hydronic Radiant Floor Heating System

Design of a hydronic radiant floor heating system should be attempted only by those with the qualifications, training, and experience to do it right. It is *very* important that the design of a radiant panel heating system be correct at the outset. The fact that the coils or cables are permanently embedded in concrete, or located beneath

Figure 1-19 *(Continued)*

other materials, makes corrections or adjustments very difficult and expensive.

Many manufacturers of radiant panel heating system equipment have devised simplified and dependable methods for designing this type of heating system. In most cases, the manufacturer will provide any available materials to assist in calculating the requirements of a particular radiant floor heating system. Various design manuals, manufacturer-specific installation guides, and software tools are available for use in designing and sizing radiant floor heating systems.

Tekmar **Universal reset Control 363.** (*Courtesy Tekmar Control Systems, Inc.*)

The control panel operates in conjunction with both indoor and outdoor sensors to control space and heating temperatures (multiple zones or single-zone), domestic hot water supply, slab heat, and snow–melting applications. The control panel uses an outdoor reset to adjust the boiler and mixed loop water temperatures delivered to the heating system. A variable speed driven wet-rotor circulator or a floating action driven mixing valve is used as a mixing device.

Figure 1-19   *(Continued)*

A radiant floor heating system in which there is a constant (uninterrupted) circulation of water is the preferred design. The benefits of constant water circulation through the circuits are as follows:

- It maintains an even floor temperature.
- It prevents hot spots from forming when there is no call for heat.
- It prevents air from entering the system.
- It reduces the risk of the water freezing in systems where antifreeze cannot be used (that is, systems in which the water

Figure 1-20 Watts Boiler Energy Saver and wiring diagrams.

(Courtesy Watts Regulator Company)

heater heats both the water for space heating and the water for cooking and bathing purposes).

The flow of water in some radiant heating systems is controlled by the circulator (pump). When the room thermostat calls for heat, the pump starts and rapidly circulates heated water through the radiant panels until the heat requirement is satisfied. The pump is then shut off by the thermostat. In some systems, a flow-control valve is forced open by the flow of water through the pipes as long as the pump is running, permitting free circulation of heated water through the system. When the pump stops, the control valve closes, preventing circulation by gravity, which might cause overheating. The principal disadvantage of a system with this off-on control is that it results in temperature lag and causes the panels to intermittently heat and cool.

The continuous circulation of water through radiant heating panels is made possible by means of an outdoor-indoor control.

In this arrangement, hot water from the boiler is admitted to the system in modulated quantities when the temperature of the circulating water drops below the heat requirement of the panels. This modulated bleeding of water into the panel is accomplished through a bypass valve. When no additional heat is required, the valve is closed. When more heat is required, the valve is gradually opened by the combined action of the outdoor temperature bulb and a temperature bulb in the supply main. This system gives control by the method of varying the temperature of the water.

Air Venting Requirements

A common defect encountered in hot-water system design is improper venting. The flow of water should be automatically kept free of air binding throughout the system. Air in the pipes or pipe coils almost always results in a reduction of heat.

A practical method of venting is shown in Figure 1-21. The key to this method is the use of automatic air vents. Each air vent should be located in an area readily accessible for repair. The air trap test cock should be placed where it can be easily operated. Both the air trap and the air trap test cock must be located where they are not subject to freeze-up, as both are noncirculating except during venting operation (automatic or manual).

Sizing Calculations

The successful operation of any hot-water heating system requires the incorporation of design provisions that ensure an even and balanced flow of water through the pipes or coils of the installation.

The procedure for designing a hydronic radiant floor heating system may be outlined as follows:

1. Determine the total rate of heat loss per room in the structure.
2. Determine the available area for panels (loops) in each room.
3. Determine the output required by each panel to replace the heat loss.
4. Determine the required surface temperature for each panel.
5. Determine the required heat input to the panel (should equal heat output).
6. Determine the most efficient and economical means of supplying heat to the panel.
7. Install adequate insulation on the reverse side and edges of the panel to prevent undesirable heat loss.
8. Install the panels opposite room areas where the greater heat loss occurs.

Symbols: → Indicates downward grade of tubing. Ⓐ automatic air trap at top of main flow riser; Ⓑ automatic air trap at top of main return riser; Ⓒ automatic air trap at top of special loop Ⓚ required by possible obstruction and when small size vent by-pass is also not permissible at Ⓨ; Ⓓ heater; Ⓔ pump; Ⓕ check valve; Ⓖ drain valve; Ⓗ heating panel coil; Ⓚ loop in main flow (See Ⓒ); Ⓜ trap shut-off valve (for repair); Ⓝ expansion tank; Ⓟ manual test cock (air trap); Ⓡ open and automatic vent tube (½ in. copper).

Note—By reversing direction of grade at Ⓗ air trap Ⓑ can be eliminated. Same riser vent layout should be used for up-feed systems. Test cocks Ⓟ should be located accessible for occasional use. Open ends of vent tubes Ⓡ (normally dry) can discharge visibly into nearest drain or sink.

Figure 1-21   An automatic vent radiant heating system.

Note

Always keep floor temperatures at or slightly below recommended high limits.

Radiant Floor Construction Details

Radiant floor construction can be divided into two broad categories based on the installation method used: (1) wet installation and (2) dry installation. The *wet installation method* involves completely embedding the tubing in a concrete slab or covering it with a thin layer of concrete (commonly a gypsum-based lightweight pour).

The *dry installation method* is so-called because the tubing is installed without embedding it in concrete.

The examples of radiant floor construction described in this section represent the most commonly used forms. They are offered here only as examples, not as planning guides for contractors. The actual construction plans will depend on the design of the hydronic radiant floor heating system, the impact of local building codes and regulations, and other variables.

Slab-on-grade construction

In slab-on-grade construction, the tubing is attached to a wire mesh or special holding fixtures to keep it in place until the concrete is poured around it. The tubing loops are embedded in the middle of the concrete slab and are located approximately 2 inches below the slab surface (see Figure 1-22). A brief summary of the steps involved in slab-on-grade construction is as follows:

1. Compact the soil base to prevent uneven settling of the slab.
2. Cover the compacted soil with a lapped 6-mil vapor barrier.
3. Cover the vapor barrier with 2-inch-thick extruded polystyrene insulation.
4. Install rigid polystyrene insulation vertically on the inside surface of the exterior foundation walls to prevent edgewise (horizontal) heat loss.
5. Lay concrete reinforcing mesh over the insulation.
6. Position the tubing on top of the reinforcement mesh according to the tubing layout plan.
7. Tie the tubing to the reinforcement mesh with tie straps or wire.
8. Cover the tubing with a minimum of 9 inches of concrete.

Thin-Slab Construction

In this type of wet installation, a layer of lightweight concrete or lightweight gypsum is poured over the tubing to form a thin slab (see Figure 1-23). Thin-slab construction is used over a wood subfloor supported by wood framing.

A summary of the steps involved in forming a thin-slab floor system using poured concrete to form the slab may be outlined as follows:

1. Apply a lapped 6-mil polyethylene vapor barrier to the wood subfloor.
2. Position the tubing on the subfloor according to the tubing layout plan.

Figure 1-22   Slab-on-grade construction.

3. Fasten the tubing to the wood subfloor with plastic clips or metal staples.

4. Pour concrete over the tubing and subfloor.

5. Install batt insulation in the joist cavities beneath the subfloor. If lightweight gypsum cement instead of concrete is used to form the slab, pour the gypsum in two stages. The first pour should be no higher than the tops of the tubes. When this first layer dries, it will shrink slightly and pull back from the tubing. Apply a second layer of gypsum to completely cover the first layer and the tops of the tubing.

Sandwich Floor Construction
Sandwich floor construction is available in a number of different configurations (see Figure 1-24). This construction method involves

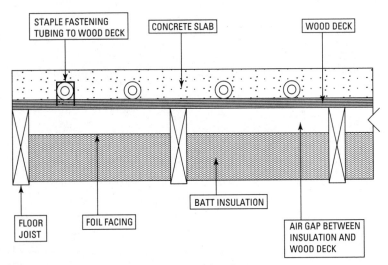

Figure I-23   Thin-slab construction details.

locating the tubing between the subfloor and additional flooring layers. In some cases, aluminum plates are added for heat dispersion. The two layers of a sandwich floor have wood sleepers installed between them for adding the tubing and subsequent flooring layers. These systems all contain less thermal mass than slab systems, and some allow for more rapid temperature responsiveness.

Staple-Up Method
In the staple-up method, the tubing is located below the subfloor. This method of installing tubing is very common in both new construction and remodeling work. Its use is recommended when retrofitting because it avoids the problem and expense of having to remove the existing floor covering.

Note
The staple-up construction method will require drilling holes for the tubing in some of the supporting joists.

The staple-up construction method illustrated in Figure 1-25 is used without heat transfer plates. The tubing is fastened to the bottom of the subfloor in the joist cavities. Install either 3½-inch batts or 2-inch polystyrene rigid insulation in the joist cavities below the tubing with a 1½- to 4-inch air gap between the subfloor and the insulation.

Sandwich construction
over concrete slab with
tubing spaced 6 inches
on centers.

CONCRETE SLAB

TUBING

¾-INCH THICK FACED
RIGID POLYSTYRENE
INSULATION BOARD.

SPACE

TUBING LOOP

¾-INCH PLYWOOD

Sandwich construction
over framing with tubing
spaced 6 inches on centers.

AIR GAP

3½-Inch faced batt
insulation installed
between floor joists
with 2¾-inch air gap.

Figure 1-24 Examples of sandwich floor construction.

(Courtesy Watts Radiant, Inc.)

Figure 1-25 Staple-up method.

The heating efficiency of the staple-up construction method can be greatly improved by adding preformed, grooved aluminum heat transfer plates beneath the subfloor (see Figure 1-26). The plates are stapled to the bottom of the subfloor in the joist cavities, and the tubing is inserted in the preformed plate grooves. Insulation is installed beneath the tubing with a 2- to 4-inch air space between the top of the insulation and the bottom of the subfloor. The heat from the tubing spreads horizontally across the plate surface and then flows upward into the room or space above the floor. Without these plates, a percentage of the heat from the tubing is lost because it flows down into the spaces below the room being heated. To compensate for the heat loss, the heating system must operate at higher temperatures. This results in higher heating costs.

A variation of the staple-up construction method is to hang the tubing several inches below the subfloor in the joist cavities. Aluminum heat-transfer plates are fastened to the bottoms of the floor joists leaving an air gap between the plates and the bottom of the subfloor.

Figure I-26 Staple-up method with heat transfer plates.

Tubing Installed Above the Subfloor

Figure 1-27 illustrates a common dry installation method of installing the tubing above the subfloor. It consists of wood sleepers nailed to the top surface of the wood subfloor with the tubing located in the spaces between the sleepers. Plywood is nailed to the tops of the sleepers to support the floor covering material.

Figure I-27 Tubing installed above the subfloor between sleepers.

Note

> A loose, noninsulating masonry filler poured around the tubing will increase the thermal mass of the floor. Do not use loose fill insulation, such as perlite or vermiculite. These are insulating materials that will interfere with the heat radiation from the tubing. Masonry filler is not an insulating material.

An alternative method is to install heat-transfer plates between the sleepers and use the plates to support (cradle) the tubing. In both cases, a suitable insulation must be installed between the floor joists (see Figure 1-28).

Still another method is to install factory-made, grooved wood panels beneath the finished floor. The dimensions of the panels may vary, depending on the manufacturer. The tubing is inserted in the panel grooves and set flush with the panel surface.

Floor Coverings

Floor covering materials reduce the amount of heat radiation rising into the room or space above the floor. The insulating properties of floor coverings must be considered when designing a hydronic or electric radiant floor heating system. Plush carpets and polyurethane carpet pads should not be installed over a radiant floor heating system. The same holds true for thick wood floors or multiple layers of plywood subfloors. Both have a high thermal resistance.

SLEEPER NAILED TO SUBFLOOR

FLOOR COVERING

SUBFLOOR

FOIL FACED BATT INSULATION

HEAT TRANSFER PLATES STAPLED TO SLEEPERS

TUBING SUPPORTED BY HEAT TRANSFER PLATE

Figure I-28 Tubing installed above the subfloor between sleepers with heat-transfer plates. *(Courtesy Weil-McLain)*

Carpets are commonly installed over a carpet pad. The combined carpet and cushion R-value (that is, its insulating value) should not exceed a maximum of R-4.0. Use either a foam rubber or waffle rubber pad. To reduce the resistance even further, consider eliminating the carpet pad.

Sheet final and tile floor coverings radiate the heat much faster than carpet, thereby reducing the lag time between when the hot water flows through the circuit and the heat is actually delivered to the room or space above.

Coils and Coil Patterns

Hydronic radiant floor heating panels are available as prefabricated units, or they can be constructed at the site. The principal coil patterns used in radiant floor heating systems are the following:

1. Coil pattern for uniform heat distribution.
2. Coil pattern for perimeter heat distribution along two walls.
3. Coil pattern for perimeter heat distribution along one wall.

Counterflow Spiral Tube Layout Pattern

The tube layout illustrated in Figure 1-29 provides the most even and uniform heat distribution for a room in a radiant floor heating system. It accomplishes this by running the supply and return lines parallel to one another. As a result, an average temperature is created between the tubes.

Double Serpentine Layout Pattern

In some rooms, there will be a significant amount of heat loss through two adjacent exterior walls. As shown in Figure 1-30, the supply tubing runs along the perimeter of the walls where the hot water can provide maximum heat transfer. It then turns inward in a series of serpentine-like loops to the center of the room (the area of lowest heat loss) before returning to the manifold.

Single Serpentine Layout Pattern

If a major heat loss occurs along a single exterior wall, the supply tubing runs along the perimeter of that wall before returning in a series of serpentine loops to the return manifold (see Figure 1-31).

In a well-designed hydronic radiant floor heating system, the linear travel from the heating unit and pump should be the same for each of the panels (see Figure 1-32). This will result in the flow through each panel being in natural balance.

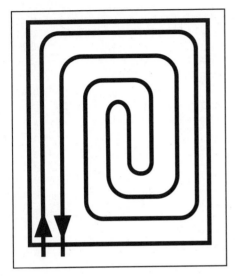

Figure 1-29   Counterflow spiral tube layout pattern.

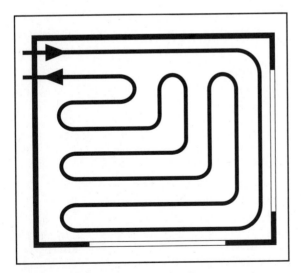

Figure 1-30   Double serpentine layout pattern.

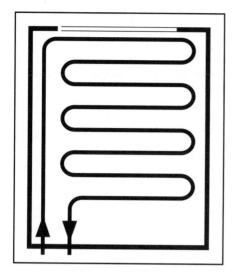

Figure 1-31   Single serpentine layout pattern.

Figure 1-32   Correct and incorrect method of laying out a forced hot-water distribution system. The travel from pump and heater should be the same through P_1, P_2, and P_3 as shown in the correct method.

Installing a Hydronic Radiant Floor Heating System (PEX Tubing)

These installation recommendations are provided for general information only. The architect or HVAC contractor is responsible for all design details and installation procedures for the specific radiant floor heating system. The architect or contractor is also responsible for maintaining the work in compliance with all applicable building codes, local and national.

Note

> Install all the components of a hydronic radiant floor heating system in accordance with the equipment manufacturer's instructions and all applicable codes. Failure to do so could result in severe personal injury, death, or substantial property damage.

Installation Recommendations

The following installation recommendations are provided as a general reference. Each manufacturer will provide instructions specific to its product.

System Inspection

After the PEX tubing has been embedded or concealed, it becomes a relatively permanent part of the structure. Because of the difficulty of servicing embedded or concealed loops, it is essential that a final inspection be performed to make sure the tubing or piping has not been damaged during construction and that all tubing or piping loops have been installed in compliance with local codes and ordinances. Check the following:

- Check to make sure the tubing or piping loops have been installed according to the layout (coil patterns) in the building plan.
- Inspect the tubing or piping for kinks, scrapes, slits, or crush damage.
- Inspect the tubing or piping for correct spacing.
- Make sure all manifolds are correctly located and provide easy access.
- Check to make sure the tubing or piping connections to the manifold are tight.
- Make sure the tubing or piping is properly fastened and there is a correct spacing maintained between the fasteners.

Tubing Length and Diameter

It is important to know the length and inside diameter (ID) of the tubing when creating a circuit (loop). Excessive circuit lengths will result in a significant temperature drop in the circuit. The temperature drop is the difference between the supply (hotter) water entering the circuit and the return (cooler) water leaving the circuit. In residential heating systems, the temperature drop is normally 15–20°F. If the temperature drop is greater than 15–20°F, it will result in insufficient heat and/or uneven heat being delivered to the room or space.

Long loops also result in increased friction in the tubing, which slows the flow rate of the water. This pressure drop must be overcome by the circulator (pump) in order to maintain a uniform flow rate for the water in the tubing.

A typical residential hydronic radiant heating system uses ½-inch-ID tubing. The maximum recommended length for this diameter is 300 feet. Most circuits (loops) in residential heating systems are shorter (about 100 to 250 feet long). Tubing with an ID of ⅝-inch or ¾–inch, on the other hand, can be used in circuits up to a maximum of 450 feet in length.

In addition to the tubing ID, the length of the tubing required per square foot of floor will also be affected by such variables as the type of slab used, the heat load for the structure, the type of appliance (boiler, water heater, or heat pump), the type of controls used, and even the climate.

Tubing Spacing

Another important factor to consider when designing and installing a hydronic radiant floor heating system is the spacing of the tubing in the loops. Most residential heating systems are based on the use of 1 to 1½ linear feet of ½-inch-ID tubing per square foot of floor area with the tubing spaced 9 to 12 inches apart. That is only a general rule, however, because there are situations where the tubing must be spaced closer to increase the heat output (for example, under windows, along cold exterior walls, and so on). A 3-inch to 6-inch spacing of the tubing will require 2 to 4 linear feet of tubing per square foot of heated floor area.

Loop Continuity

The tubing loop extending from the manifold supply port to the manifold return port must be one continuous length. Never splice together two lengths of tubing to form a loop. Doing so will weaken the loop.

Insulation

Install insulation beneath the tubing to prevent the downward loss of a portion of the heat. In uninsulated slab-on-grade construction, for example, a portion of the heat will be lost to the ground. The ground becomes a heat sink if there is no insulation installed. Use 1- to 2-inch-thick rigid polystyrene to insulate a slab-on-grade radiant heating system. Batt and blanket insulation are also in other types of radiant heating systems. See "Radiant System Construction Details" for examples of the use of the different types of insulation.

Vapor Barrier
A vapor barrier of 6-mil polyethylene sheeting should be installed between a thin slab and the wood sheathing to limit the transfer of moisture from the slab to the wood. Check the local building code for the use of a vapor barrier. Not all codes require it.

Panel Testing Procedures
Radiant heating coils should be tested for leaks after they have been secured in position but before they are covered with concrete or some other covering material. Both a compressed-air test and a hydraulic pressure test are used for this purpose.

The compressed-air test requires a compressor, a pressure gauge, and a shutoff valve. The idea is to inject air under pressure into the radiant heating system and watch for a pressure drop on the gauge. A continually dropping pressure is an indication of a leak somewhere in the system.

The pressure gauge is attached to one of the radiant heating coils, and the shutoff valve is placed on the *inlet* side of the gauge in a valve-open position. The air compressor is then connected, and compressed air is introduced into the system under approximately 100 psi. After the introduction of the air, the shutoff valve is closed and the compressor is disconnected. The system is now a closed one. If there are no leaks, the air pressure reading on the gauge will remain at approximately 100 psi. A steady drop in the air pressure reading means a leak exists somewhere in the system. A leak can be located by listening for the sound of escaping air. Another method is to use a solution of soap and water and watch for air bubbles.

The hydraulic pressure test requires that the coils be filled with water and the pressure in the coils be increased to approximately 275 to 300 psi. Care must be taken that *all* air is removed from the coils before the system is closed. The system is then closed, and the gauge is watched for any change in pressure. A leak in the system will be indicated by a steady drop in pressure on the gauge. The source of the leak can be located by watching for the escaping water. If a leak is discovered, the coil should be repaired or replaced and a new test run on the system.

Installation Guidelines

Guidelines
• Run the tubing parallel to the wall or walls with the greatest heat loss. *(continues)*

Guidelines (continued)

- Maintain a 12-inch gap between the outermost tubing and an exterior wall.

- Space tubing 6 inches o.c. between the first two loops along the wall or walls with the greatest heat loss.

- Tie tubing every 3 feet or less with plastic tie wraps. Note: Never tie tubing anywhere within the end of a loop.

- Always use a vapor barrier under the slab. Note: Place the vapor barrier between the ground and insulation, if the latter is used under the slab.

- Place a vapor barrier between the soil and any insulation installed under the slab.

- Insulate under the slab if groundwater comes within 3 feet.

- Always install edge insulation along the foundation walls to prevent edgewise (horizontal) heat loss.

Whenever possible, follow the radiant heating system manufacturer's installation guidelines. The procedure described here for installing a hydronic radiant floor heating system (using PEX tubing) is offered as a general guideline. It may be outlined as follows:

1. Attach the manifold wall brackets to the wall.

2. Assemble the manifold (if it is not a factory-assembled unit) and clamp it into position on the wall brackets.

3. Mount a pipe bend support directly below the manifold to hold the supply pipe.

4. Connect the supply pipe to the manifold and lay out the pipe loop by following the layout plan.

5. Mount a pipe bend support below the manifold to hold the return pipe.

6. Create coil pattern.

7. Cut the return pipe and connect it to the manifold.

8. Mark or number the first loop for identification.

9. Check the length of the first loop against the layout plan by using the length markings on the outside of the pipe. A significant deviation in overall length between the layout plan and the installed pipe loop will require an adjustment of the loop balance settings.

10. Repeat steps 1 through 8 for the remaining loops in the system.

11. Close the supply, return, and shutoff valves on the first manifold.

12. Connect hoses to the end caps on the manifold.

13. Connect the end of one of the hoses to the main and the end of the other hose to a drain.

14. Open the end cap valves for filling and draining the system.

15. Open the supply and return valves on the manifold for the first loop.

16. Turn on the water and allow it to flow through the loop until all the air has been expelled. Purging the air from the system is a very important step. Air trapped in the loops will cause the system to operate inefficiently.

Note

If the water will not flow through the loop, the pipe may be buckled or crimped or there may be a blockage at the manifold connection. Check and repair before proceeding to the next step.

17. Repeat steps 10 through 15 until each loop in the heating system has been filled with water and any air trapped in the piping has been removed.

18. Open all the system valves and perform a pressure test (at 3 to 4 bar pressure). The pressure will drop during the first few hours and then remain stable if there are no leaks and the ambient temperature remains constant.

19. Install the floor covering (cement, carpet, tiles, and so on).

20. Close all the loop valves and open the shutoff valves.

21. Fill the boiler and the supply pipes with water, and purge the air. Open every valve and fixture (faucets and so on) in the system and continue purging until all the air trapped in the pipes has been pushed out of the lines and the water flows freely from the fixtures. Purge the air from the end caps at each end of the manifolds. In a structure with several floors, purge the air from the manifold located at the lowest level first.

Note

There must be shutoff valves on the manifolds to properly purge air from the loops.

22. Open all the loops in the heating system and check to make sure the air has been removed. If there is still air in the tubing, repeat steps 20 and 21 until all air has been removed.

23. Place the system under pressure by starting the boiler and circulator.

Servicing and Maintaining Hydronic Radiant Floor Heating Systems

Hydronic radiant floor heating systems require very little service and maintenance, but this does not mean they should be ignored. The following recommendations apply to all floor heating systems:

- Check the system pressure on a regular basis. An incorrect pressure reading may indicate air trapped in the system. An air pocket or bubble will block the flow of water and cause pressure readings outside the norm.
- Check the system for leakage. If the tubing is attached under the floor to the stud bottoms, access to the tubing or tubing connections to make repairs is relatively easy. If the tubing is embedded in cement above the subfloor, however, locating a leak is more difficult and expensive.
- Check to make sure there is enough water in the system. If not, it may need refilling.

If purging air, repairing leaks, and/or refilling the system with water does not result in maintaining the required pressure in the system, ask for a service call from a certified HVAC technician with experience in hydronic floor radiant heating systems.

Troubleshooting Hydronic Floor Radiant Heating Systems

Problems with hydronic floor radiant heating systems (see Table 1-1) will occur in the following areas:

1. Heating appliance (boiler, heat pump, or water heater)
2. Circulator (circulating pump)
3. Automatic controls
4. Tubing

Most of the troubleshooting and repair procedures for the various components of a hydronic floor radiant heating system have been described in considerable detail in other chapters. Use the volume index to locate those sources of information.

The first step when troubleshooting a radiant floor system is to check the controls. Turn the room thermostat on or off and wait for a few minutes for the system to respond. If the system responds by turning on or off within 2 or 3 minutes, the controls are not the problem.

Table I-I   Troubleshooting Hydronic Floor Radiant Heating Systems

Symptom and Possible Cause	Suggested Remedy
Insufficient heat.	
(a) Slow initial response time.	(a) Normal for hydronic floor heating system.
(b) Insufficient heat generally occurring on design temperature day.	(b) Improper system design; add auxiliary heat.
(c) Boiler or other heat source problem.	(c) Check heat source for problem and correct.
(d) Defective floor sensor.	(d) Replace.
No heat.	
(a) Defective room thermostat and/or floor sensor.	(a) Replace thermostat and/or floor sensor.
(b) Boiler or other heat source problem.	(b) Check heat source for problem and correct.
(c) Defective circulator.	(c) Test; repair or replace.
Floor temperature too hot or too cold.	
(a) Defective mixing valve.	(a) Replace defective valve.
(b) Incorrect mixing valve setting.	(b) Adjust valve setting; change valve setting number according to specifications in manufacturer's installation manual.
(c) Defective outdoor air sensor.	(c) Test and replace.
Floor temperature too cold.	
(a) Boiler or other heat source problem.	(a) Check heat source for problem and correct.
(b) Circulator working against large system temperature drop; not moving enough water.	(b) Check temperature drop when system is warm; circulator is undersized if drop is found to be too large; correct as necessary.

Table 1-1   (continued)

Symptom and Possible Cause	Suggested Remedy
(c) Circulator working against small system temperature drop; water and floor temperatures almost equal, resulting in little heat transfer.	(c) Check temperature drop when system is warm; circulator is oversized if temperatures almost equal; increase floor temperature if less than 85°F to be too large.
Hot spot in floor.	
(a) Excessive high and concentrated temperatures in floor caused by tubing or tubing connection break.	(a) Locate break and repair.

Check the boiler, heat pump, or water heater for a problem. These appliances and their troubleshooting methods are described in Chapter 15 ("Steam and Hydronic Boilers") in Volume 1, Chapter 10 ("Heat Pumps") in Volume 2, and Chapter 4 ("Water Heaters") in Volume 2, respectively.

Note

> Some heating systems have a thermometer installed in the circulation loop. The thermometer displays the temperature of the circulating water. A low fluid temperature displayed *while the circulator is operating* will indicate a problem with the boiler, heat pump, or water pump.

The troubleshooting and repair of circulators (water-circulating pumps) is covered in Chapter 10 ("Steam and Hydronic Line Controls") in Volume 2.

Problems requiring repairs or replacements of the manifolds or loops, especially embedded loops in wet installations, require the expertise of HVAC technicians experienced in the installation and maintenance of floor radiant heating systems.

Hydronic Radiant Heating Snow- and Ice-Melting Systems

Radiant systems used to melt snow and ice on driveways, sidewalks, and other outdoor surfaces are inexpensive to operate because they are used only when required. They begin to operate at a reduced output mode when the outdoor temperatures drop below a certain preset point and then switch to full operation when rain or snow reaches the surface.

The simplest form of control for snow-melting and ice-melting installations is a remote, manually operated on-off switch. The switch is commonly located inside the garage and operated only when required. Some snow- and ice-melting installations are operated by an automatic control system connected to a thermostat and a heating boiler, heat pump, or water heater.

Because the tubes carrying the heated water are located outdoors beneath the driveway surface, an antifreeze solution such as propylene glycol should be added to protect the system from freezing.

Electric Radiant Floor Heating

A number of manufacturers produce electric radiant floor heating systems for use in residential and light commercial construction. They are safe, relatively easy to install, and extremely energy efficient.

Note
> Electric radiant heating produces electromagnetic fields, and these EMFs may cause health problems. The potential health risk from EMFs can be minimized or even eliminated by (1) following the wiring and grounding methods recommended by the *National Electrical Code*; (2) purchasing and installing a radiant heating system that produces very low EMFs (some manufacturers claim zero EMFs for their systems); and (3) avoiding systems that produce EMFs higher than 2 mG at 2 feet.

Most of these electric radiant floor heating systems consist of a thin electric mat or roll applied to the subfloor where it is embedded in a thinset or self-leveling cement. Watts Radiant manufactures heating mats (HeatWeave UnderFloor mats) for installation between the floor joists under the subfloor.

System Components

An electric floor heating system in which electric heating mats or rolls are used will include some or all of the following components, depending on the system design:

1. Heating mats or rolls
2. Thermostat
3. Floor sensor
4. Ground fault circuit interrupter
5. Relay contactor
6. Timer
7. Dimmer switch

Heating Mats or Rolls

The electric mats or rolls used in electric floor radiant heating systems are made of coils of heat resistance wire joined to a supporting material. They are only ⅛ inch thick, which means they can be installed over the subfloor and under the floor covering without significantly raising the floor level (see Figure 1-33). The heating element of a constant-wattage electric heating cable or wire operates on 120 volts or 240 volts.

Electric heating mats or rolls are produced in a wide variety of sizes to fit different floor dimensions. Custom sizes can also be ordered from manufacturers to fit areas with curves, angles, and other nonstandard shapes.

An entire electric radiant floor heating system can be ordered from any one of the manufacturers listed in the sidebar. When ordering the materials for one of these heating systems, send them an installation layout plan listing the exact dimensions of the rooms or spaces to be heated. The plan may be for an entire house, an addition to a house, or a single room or space.

Note

> The manufacturer will cut the mats or rolls to the sizes listed in the installation plan. Once the mats or rolls are cut, they cannot be returned if a mistake is discovered unless it can be shown that the manufacturer was at fault.

The recommended heating capacity for electric resistance heating is specified by the building codes on a watt-per-square-foot-of-living-area basis. The electric heating mats or rolls are designed to draw 8 to 15 watts per square foot. Their operation is very similar to that of an electric blanket.

Manufacturers of Electric Radiant Heating Mats or Rolls

Flextherm, Inc.
2400, de la Province Street
Longueuil, Quebec J4G 1G1
Canada
450-442-9990
800-353-9843
www.flextherm.com

Heatway, Inc. (Watts Heatway, Inc.)
3131 W. Chestnut Express Way
Springfield, MO 65802
800-255-1996
www.heatway.com   (continues)

Manufacturers of Electric Radiant Heating Mats or Rolls (continued)

NuHeat Industries Ltd.
1689 Cliveden Ave.
Delta, BC V3M 6V5
Canada
800-778-9276
604-529-4400
www.nuheat.com

SunTouch Electric Floor Warming
A Division of Watts Radiant, Inc.
3131 W. Chestnut Expressway
Springfield, MO 65802
417-522-6128
www.suntouch.net

WarmlyYours, Inc.
1400 E. Lake Cook Road, Suite 140
Buffalo Grove, Illinois 60089
800-875-5285
www.WarmlyYours.com

Warmzone, Inc.
Salt Lake City, Utah
888-488-9276
801-994-8450
www.warmzone.com

Watts Radiant, Inc.
A Division of Watts Water Technologies, Inc.
31341 West Chestnut Expressway
Springfield, Missouri 65802
800-276-2419
978-688-1811
www.wattsradiant.com

Automatic Controls

The automatic controls of a typical electric radiant floor heating system consist of a thermostat, a GFCI safety breaker, and an optional timer. If a floor-heating thermostat is used instead of a room thermostat, the former is wired to a floor sensor that detects the actual floor temperature. A GFCI and a timer are integral components of a floor-warming thermostat.

Figure 1-33 Construction details of a typical electric heating mat or roll. *(Courtesy Watts Radiant, Inc.)*

Thermostat

The *thermostat* is the controlling device for an electric radiant floor heating system. Most modern systems use a *programmable thermostat*, which contains an integral ground fault circuit interrupter (GFCI) and a manual high-low temperature setback switch (see Figure 1-34). A programmable thermostat is connected to an embedded floor sensor that monitors the floor temperature and transmits it to a digital display on the thermostat. A programmable thermostat can be programmed for four setting changes each day of the week.

Figure 1-34 Programmable thermostat with digital display for an electric radiant floor heating system. *(Courtesy Watts Radiant, Inc.)*

Nonprogrammable thermostats are used commonly for small spot-warming areas. They are also equipped with a GFCI device.

Note
> Never exceed the maximum capacity of the thermostat to heat the floor. If additional power is required, zone with additional programmable thermostats or use a relay contactor.

Floor Sensor
A *floor sensor* is a temperature-monitoring device embedded in the floor and connected to a programmable thermostat. It should be installed in such a way as to give the truest floor temperature. Its installation will also be governed by the type of floor covering.

Many manufacturers will recommend the location of the floor sensor for the different types of floor coverings used with their floor sensor (see Figure 1-35).

Figure 1-35 Floor sensor installed in angled hole drilled in the bottom of the subfloor. *(Courtesy Watts Radiant, Inc.)*

Ground Fault Circuit Interrupter

A *ground fault circuit interrupter* (GFCI) is used to monitor the flow of electricity through the heat resistance wire in the mat or roll for any loss of current. If a loss of current is detected, the GFCI immediately cuts off the electricity to the heating system. This is done to prevent damage to the heat resistance wire in the heating mat or roll. The GFCI is an integral part of a programmable thermostat.

An indicating-type GFCI circuit breaker may be installed to serve as a local disconnect. It should be installed near the end of the line close to the thermostat.

Relay Contactor

A *relay contactor* is a device used in conjunction with a single controller to operate the heating in large rooms or spaces. Both single- and double-relay contactors are used in heating systems.

Timer

A *timer* is an optional device used to control when the heating system is turned on and off. It can be used to program 14 events, or two on-off cycles per day for a 2-day or 5-day period. It also can be used in conjunction with a dimmer switch to regulate floor temperature. It cannot moderate the floor temperature.

Dimmer Switch

A *dimmer switch* is a device with an on-off button and a sliding manual control used in some systems to increase or decrease the floor temperature. It can be used in conjunction with a 7-day programmable timer to program a weekly period repetitively.

Installing Electric Heating Mats or Rolls

Electric heating mats or rolls must be installed in accordance with the manufacturer's instructions and any local codes or ordinances.

Before installing the heating mats or rolls, check the shipment to make sure the manufacturer has included everything. If the order is complete, remove the mats or rolls from their boxes and test the ohm resistance of each to make sure it has not been damaged during shipment.

Note
> This will be the first of three resistance tests. The second resistance test is performed after the mats have been secured to the subfloor, and the third after the floor covering has been applied over the mats.

To perform a resistance test, set a digital multimeter to the 200-ohms setting and connect the mat lead wires to the multimeter probes. Make sure the resistance reading is within the range of plus 10 percent to minus 5 percent of the resistance rating listed on the mat tag.

An insulation test should be performed to make sure there is no short or ground in the mat or roll. To conduct an insulation test, set the digital multimeter to the megohms setting and connect the silver braid (ground) and black lead to the multimeter probes. The multimeter should read "open" or "OL." Check the instructions with the multimeter to confirm which code represents the "open line." Repeat this test between the silver braid (ground) and the white lead wire.

Caution
> The installation of electrical heating systems involves some risk of fire and/or electrical shock that can result in injury or even death. With that in mind, only a qualified, certified electrician or someone with similar training and experience should connect the electric heating mats or rolls to the thermostat and the electrical circuit. Connections should be made in accordance with local codes and ordinances and the provisions in the latest edition of the *National Electrical Code.* The heating mats or rolls must be installed by a qualified contractor or homeowner before the connections to the electrical circuits and control device are made.

Installing Electric Mats or Rolls over Subfloors

Keep a permanent record of the location of the mats or rolls and the floor sensor, if one is installed.

Note

      Do not install solid-based furniture, built-in cabinets, bookcases, room dividers, or plumbing fixtures over heating mats or rolls.

The procedure for installing electric heating mats or rolls over a subfloor may be outlined as follows:

1. Use the installation plan provided by the manufacturer to lay the mats or rolls out in the room. This dry run is done to make sure the mats or rolls cover the floor properly (see Figure 1-36).

2. Cut the supporting material (but *not* the heat resistance wire) and turn the mat or roll to fit the dimensions of the room (see Figure 1-37).

Step 1: Laying the mats on the floor.

Lay the mats out on the floor and "dry" fit them to the dimensions of the room according to the installation plan and the floor markings.

- Do not walk on the heating elements (wires)
- Do not drop tools on the heating element (wire) or strike it with a hammer or tool.
- Place cardboard or carpet sections over the mat and the heating element to protect the latter from damage.

Figure 1-36   Laying the mats or rolls out on the floor.
(Courtesy WarmlyYours.com, Inc.)

Step 2: Fitting the mats on the floor.

Fit the heating mats (rolls) one panel at a time. Cut and turn the mats according to the installation plan and the floor markings, and then modify the roll into successive and interconnected panels shaped to cover the planned area.

Figure 1-36 *(Continued)*

3. Glue the mat to the subfloor to prevent it from moving out of position.

4. Test the ohm resistance of each heating roll after it has been secured to the subfloor to make sure it wasn't damaged during installation. *This is the second resistance test.*

5. Cover the roll with a layer of thinset cement. Allow the thinset cement sufficient time to cure. Do *not* turn on the radiant heating system until the thinset cement has cured according to the recommended time on the packaging.

6. Consult the installation plan and mark the approximate location of the heating elements on the cement surface with chalk.

7. Cover the layer of thinset cement with the floor covering (tile, carpet, and so on). Note: Do not nail, screw, or staple near the heating elements and cold lead wires when installing the floor covering. Use the chalk lines as a guide.

8. Test the ohm resistance of the heating rolls to verify that they were not damaged when the floor covering was applied. *This is the third resistance test.*

Cutting and turning the mat. Caution: DO NOT CUT the heating element (wire).

180 degree turn:

Make a straight cut and then slide the balance of the panel around and head back in the opposite direction.

90 degree (flip over) turn:

Make a straight cut and flip the section over so that the heating element (wire) is now above the mesh and continues in a perpendicular direction.

Filling free form spaces:

Fill free form spaces with loose lengths of the heating element (wire) after removing about 6 inches of mat.

Figure 1-37 Turning the mat or roll to fit the dimensions of the room. *(Courtesy WarmlyYours.com, Inc.)*

9. Hardwire the electric mat or roll to the thermostat. This step should be done only by an electrician or an individual with the required experience of working with electrical systems.

Installing Electric Heating Mats or Rolls in Joist Cavities under Subfloors
Electric heating mats or rolls are also available for use in joist cavities beneath wood subfloors in residential and light commercial construction. The joists are spaced 16 inches on centers.

These mats or rolls may be jointed to fill larger spaces, but they must be wired in parallel (not in series) when joined together. The mats are rated either 120 VAC or 240 VAC. They are wide enough to fit into joist cavities with joists separated 16 inches on center.

The following installation steps are offered only as a guideline. Specific instructions can be obtained from the manufacturer and should be carefully followed.

The procedure for applying electric radiant heating mats or rolls in joist cavities under subfloors may be outlined as follows:

1. Install the floor sensor.

2. Push a length of mat into the joist cavity so that it touches the bottom of the subfloor. The heating wires must be between the supporting mesh and the bottom of the subfloor.

3. Staple one edge of the supporting mesh to the side of the joist. Place the staples a minimum of ½ inch from the heating wire and ¾ inch down from the subfloor on the joist.

4. Push the other edge of the mat against the subfloor and nail the mesh to the joist surface. Use the same staple locations. Pull the mat snug against the subfloor as you staple the opposite edge to the joist. There will be a slight droop when you are finished. A gap of not more than 1 inch between the mat and the subfloor is acceptable (see Figure 1-38).

5. Cut the supporting mesh of the mat when it reaches the end of the joist cavity or some other blockage. Do *not* cut the heating wire. Pull the heating wire (without the mesh) down and across a notch cut into the bottom of the floor joist (see Figure 1-39). The notch must not exceed ¼ inch in depth and must be covered by a steel nailing plate. Avoid nicking or damaging the heating wire when nailing the plate to the bottom of the joist.

Note

Check the local building codes to see if notching the bottom of the joist for routing the heating wire is permitted. Some codes prohibit notching the joist. Notching the joist is allowed by the BOCA National Building Code (Section 2308.8.2 of the 2000 edition) in each of the one-third ends of a joist span (never in the middle one-third of the span).

6. If notching the joist is not permitted, drill a 2-inch diameter hole through the side of the joist and pull the heating wire *with its supporting mesh* through the hole. Cut away the mesh next to the hole after it has been pulled through.

Installation details

HEATING WIRE

WOVEN MAT

INSULATION
(MINIMUM R-13)

JOISTS

Stapling mat to side
of floor joist

Figure 1-38   Installing the mat or roll between the joists.
(Courtesy Watts Radiant, Inc.)

SUBFLOOR

NYLON
WIRE CLIP

BLUE
HEATING
WIRE

PROTACTIVE
ROLL PLATE

Figure I-39 Extending a heating wire down and around a floor joist. *(Courtesy Watts Radiant, Inc.)*

7. If a second mat is required to finish out a room area, start the second mat flush with the end of the first mat and wire them in parallel (not series). Do not overlap the mats.

8. Connect the mat leads to the junction box in accordance with the provisions of the local building code or the latest edition of the *National Electrical Code*, if there is no applicable local code. Use additional electrical boxes where required. Connect the floor sensor and power supply.

Caution

Use an experienced and qualified electrician to make these electrical connections. There is always the possibility of severe shock injury, death, and/or property damage if the electrical work is done by inexperienced and unqualified workers.

9. After all the controls have been installed, energize the heating system briefly to see if it is operational.

10. If the system is operating properly, turn off the power and push foil-faced blanket or batt insulation (minimum R-13 rating) into the joist cavities. Leave a clearance of ½ inch to 1 inch between the mat or roll and the insulation (see Figure 1-40).

11. Seal the ends of the joist cavities by installing the last of the insulation vertically. Push the insulation up tight against the subfloor and staple it there so that no heat can escape through the band joists, rim joists, or the open end of a joist cavity.

Installing Electric Cable

Not all electric radiant floor heating systems use mats or rolls to produce the heat. Before mats or rolls became popular, floor systems consisted of coiled electric heating cables. The procedure for installing electric heating cables may be outlined as follows:

1. Make sure the power supply is shut off before beginning any work.

2. Begin the electrical rough-in work by installing the electrical box for the thermostat on the wall.

3. Pull the power supply cable into the thermostat electrical box.

4. Punch out the conduit holes on the box. The heating cable and thermostat sensor leads will be pulled through these electrical box holes later.

5. Lay the cable out on the floor according to the specified coil pattern.

6. Staple the electric cable to the floor through plastic strapping to prevent the coils from moving out of position.

7. Pull the cable and thermostat sensor leads through the punched out conduit holes in the electrical box.

8. Cover the cable with a thin coat of mortar.

9. Allow the mortar a day to dry and then apply the floor covering (for example, carpet, wood flooring).

10. Install the thermostat in the thermostat electrical box.

11. Connect to the power supply.

Note

Only a qualified HVAC technician or someone with an equivalent amount of work experience should be allowed to install an electrical radiant floor heating system. Electricity in inexperienced hands can cause serious injury and even death.

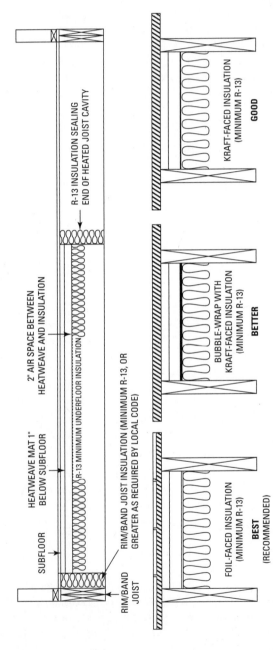

Figure 1-40 Installing insulation. *(Courtesy Watts Radiant, Inc.)*

SUBFLOOR

HEATWEAVE MAT 1" BELOW SUBFLOOR

2" AIR SPACE BETWEEN HEATWEAVE AND INSULATION

R-13 MINIMUM UNDERFLOOR INSULATION

R-13 INSULATION SEALING END OF HEATED JOIST CAVITY

RIM/BAND JOIST INSULATION (MINIMUM R-13, OR GREATER AS REQUIRED BY LOCAL CODE)

RIM/BAND JOIST

FOIL-FACED INSULATION (MINIMUM R-13)

BEST
(RECOMMENDED)

BUBBLE-WRAP WITH KRAFT-FACED INSULATION (MINIMUM R-13)

BETTER

KRAFT-FACED INSULATION (MINIMUM R-13)

GOOD

Servicing and Maintaining an Electric Radiant Floor Heating System

There are no valves, fittings, or moving parts to service or repair in an electric radiant floor heating system. Consequently, there is no need for a maintenance schedule.

Note

Manufacturers provide repair kits with accompanying instructions for repairing mats or rolls damaged at the job site. They do not, however, warranty the repair or ensure proper function of the product following the repair because they have no means of controlling the repair work. Only a qualified electrician should make repairs to mats or rolls.

Caution

Before troubleshooting or repairing an electric heating system, make sure the power is turned off and the mat or roll is disconnected from the power source. Do not cut the heating wire with the mat or roll still connected to the power source.

Note

On rare occasions, a cable in a heating mat may break. When this occurs, it can be easily detected by using an instrument that functions as an underground fault detector. Repairing the break is simply a matter of locating it, removing the small section of floor above it, splicing the cable, and then replacing the flooring. As was already mentioned, the ground fault circuit interrupter is used to monitor electricity flow to determine if there has been any loss of current. If there has been a loss, the thermostat will cut off power to the heating system until the problem is located and corrected. The GFCI on a programmable thermostat should be tested immediately after installing the thermostat, and once a month after the initial test to make sure the GFCI is continuing to operate properly. Testing instructions are provided by the manufacturer of the programmable thermostat.

Troubleshooting Electric Radiant Floor Heating Systems

Caution

Never attempt to service or repair the electric controls inside an electric furnace cabinet unless you have the qualifications and experience to work with electricity. Potentially deadly high-voltage conditions exist inside these furnace cabinets. Refer to Table 1-2.

Table 1-2 Troubleshooting Electric Radiant Floor Heating Systems

Symptom and Possible Cause	Suggested Remedy
No heat.	
(a) Power may be off. Check fuse or circuit breaker panel for blown fuses or tripped breakers.	(a) Replace fuses or reset breakers. If the problem repeats itself, call an electrician or an HVAC technician.
(b) Check thermostat (programmable type) for dead batteries.	(b) Replace batteries and reset thermostat.
Not enough heat.	
(a) Thermostat set too low.	(a) Adjust setting. *Note:* Thermostats in electric heating systems must be set several degrees higher than the desired room temperature.
(b) Cables require time to heat.	(b) Allow the cables enough time to warm up before changing thermostat setting to a higher one.

Cooling for Hydronic Radiant Floor Systems

Hydronic radiant floor heating systems are capable of providing both heating and cooling independently of air movement. For the heating cycle, hot water is circulated through the pipe coils. For the cooling cycle, cold water (*above* the dew point) is circulated, and the heating cycle is reversed. By keeping the water temperature above 65°F, harmful moisture condensation is avoided.

Radiant panel cooling results only in the removal of sensible heat, and there is sometimes an uncomfortable feeling of dampness. As a result, a separate means of dehumidification is often necessary. Often this can be quite expensive because it may require the installation of a separate dehumidification unit and round flexible air ducts to the various rooms and spaces in the structure.

A common and effective method of cooling a structure equipped with a hydronic radiant floor heating system is to add forced-air cooling. There are several very efficient add-on cooling systems available

Figure 1-41 Space-Pak air distribution system.
(Courtesy Dunham-Bush, Inc.)

for use with radiant heating. One of the more commonly used ones is the Unico air-conditioning system (see Figure 1-41). It consists of one or more chillers to move the chilled water throughout the house. Air handlers transfer the cold air to the interior rooms and spaces. The cool air travels from the air handler to the rooms and spaces inside the structure through small, round, flexible ducts.

Chapter 2

Radiators, Convectors, and Unit Heaters

The two basic methods by which heat-emitting units transfer heat to their surroundings are (1) radiation and (2) convection. *Radiation* is the transmission of thermal energy by means of electromagnetic rays. In other words, an object is warmed by heat waves radiating from a hot surface. *Convection* is the transfer of heat by natural or forced movement (circulation) of the air across a hot surface. In actual practice, heat-emitting units will transfer heat partially by radiation (up to 30 percent) and partially by convection (70 to 90 percent).

The output of heat-emitting units is expressed in terms of Btu per hour (Btu/h), in square feet of equivalent direct radiation (EDR), or in 1000 Btu per hour (MB/h). The required radiation of an installation is determined on the basis of the Btu-per-hour capacity of each heat-emitting unit. See *Determining Required Radiation* in this chapter.

The selection of a heat-emitting unit will depend on the type of heating system, the cost, the required capacity, and the application. For example, electric unit heaters should be used only where the cost of electricity is especially low. These heaters are generally associated with high operating costs. On the other hand, they are relatively inexpensive, and their installation cost is low because no separate piping or boiler is required. Each type of heat-emitting unit will have similar advantages and disadvantages that you must carefully consider before choosing the type most suited for the installation.

The principal types of heat-emitting units used in heating systems are:

1. Radiators

2. Convectors

3. Baseboard heaters

4. Kickspace heaters

5. Floor and window recessed heaters

6. Unit heaters

Radiators

A *cast-iron radiator* is a heat-emitting unit that transmits a portion of its heat by radiation and the remainder by convection. An *exposed* radiator (or freestanding radiator) transmits approximately half of its heat by radiation, the exact amount depending on the size and number of the sections. The balance of the emission is by conduction to the air in contact with the heating surface, and the resulting circulation of the air warms by convection.

Cast-iron radiators have been manufactured in both column and tubular types (see Figures 2-1 and 2-2). Column and large-tube radiators (with 2½-inch spacing per section) have been discontinued. The small-tube radiator with spacings of 1¾ inches per section is now the prevailing type. Ratings for various cast-iron radiators are given in Tables 2-1, 2-2, and 2-3, courtesy of the American Society of Heating, Refrigerating, and Air-Conditioning Engineers.

2 COLUMN 3 COLUMN 4 COLUMN   WINDOW   HOSPITAL

WALL

Figure 2-1   Various types of column cast-iron radiators.

As shown in Figure 2-1, each radiator section has 1¼-inch-diameter openings *located* at the top and bottom on each side. These openings (called *waterways* in hot-water radiators) are the passages through which the steam or hot water flows between the radiator sections. Round metal fittings are installed in these openings to join the sections together when forming a larger radiator module.

The radiators used in modern steam and hot-water heating systems are designed with nipples located in both the upper and lower portions of each radiator section, but this was not always the case with steam radiators. The earliest cast-iron steam radiators used in the old one-pipe steam heating systems were produced

3 TUBE   4 TUBE   5 TUBE   HOSPITAL

WINDOW

Figure 2-2   Various types of tubular cast-iron radiators.

with nipples located only in the bottom portion of each section. This was done because steam is light and rises quickly in the radiator, pushing air ahead of it. The air is expelled through an air vent located near the top of the radiator; the steam returns to the bottom of the same radiator section and then moves through the nipple to the adjoining section. Hot-water cast-iron radiators, on the other hand, require nipples at both the top and bottom of each section to improve water circulation. Hot water is heavier than steam and will not move as quickly without the assistance of two sets of nipples.

Wall and window radiators are cast-iron units designed for specific applications. Wall radiators are hung on the wall and are especially useful in installations where the floor must remain clear for cleaning or other purposes. They may consist of one or more

Table 2-1   Column-Type Cast-Iron Radiators

	Generally Accepted Rating per Section*					
	One-Column		Two-Column		Three-Column	
Height (in)	ft²	Btu/h	ft²	Btu/h	ft²	Btu/h
15			1½	360		
18					2¼	540
20	1½	360	2	480		
22			2¼	540	3	720
23	1⅔	400	2⅓	560		
26	2	480	2⅔	640	3¾	900
32	2½	600	3⅓	800	4½	1080
38	3	720	4	960	5	1200
45			5	1200	6	1440

	Four-Column		Five-Column		Six-Column	
Height (in)	ft²	Btu/h	ft²	Btu/h	ft²	Btu/h
13					3	720
16					3¾	900
18	3	720	4⅔	1120	4½	1080
20					5	1200
22	4	960				
26	5	1200	7	1680		
32	6½	1560				
38	8	1920	10	2400		
45	10	2400				

*These ratings are based on steam at 215°F and air at 70°F. They apply only to installed radiators exposed in a normal manner, not to radiators installed behind enclosures, behind grilles, or under shelves.
(Courtesy 1960 ASHRAE Guide)

flat wall radiator sections. Window radiators are located beneath a window on an exterior wall. The heat radiating from the surface of the unit provides a very effective barrier against drafts.

Radiator Efficiency

Radiator efficiency is an important operating characteristic of the heating system. The following recommendations are offered as a guide for obtaining higher radiator operating efficiency:

Table 2-2   Large-Tube Cast-Iron Radiators (sectional, cast-iron, tubular-type radiators of the large-tube pattern, that is, having tubes approximately $1\frac{3}{8}$ inches in diameter, $2\frac{1}{2}$ inches on centers)

Number of Tubes per Section	Catalog Rating per Section*		Height	Width	Section Center Spacing[†]	Leg Height[‡] to Tapping
	ft²	Btu/h	in	in	in	in
3	$1\frac{3}{4}$	420	20	$4\frac{5}{8}$	$2\frac{1}{2}$	$4\frac{1}{2}$
	2	480	23		$2\frac{1}{2}$	$4\frac{1}{2}$
	$2\frac{1}{3}$	560	26		$2\frac{1}{2}$	$4\frac{1}{2}$
	3	720	32		$2\frac{1}{2}$	$4\frac{1}{2}$
	$3\frac{1}{2}$	840	38		$2\frac{1}{2}$	$4\frac{1}{2}$
4	$2\frac{1}{4}$	540	20			
	$2\frac{1}{2}$	600	23		$2\frac{1}{2}$	$4\frac{1}{2}$
	$2\frac{3}{4}$	660	26	$6\frac{1}{4}$–$6\frac{13}{15}$	$2\frac{1}{2}$	$4\frac{1}{2}$
	$3\frac{1}{2}$	840	32		$2\frac{1}{2}$	$4\frac{1}{2}$
	$4\frac{1}{4}$	1020	38		$2\frac{1}{2}$	$4\frac{1}{2}$
5	$2\frac{2}{3}$	640	20		$2\frac{1}{2}$[§]	$4\frac{1}{2}$
	3	720	23		$2\frac{1}{2}$[§]	$4\frac{1}{2}$
	$3\frac{1}{2}$	840	26	9–$8\frac{9}{18}$	$2\frac{1}{2}$[§]	$4\frac{1}{2}$
	$4\frac{1}{3}$	1040	32		$2\frac{1}{2}$[§]	$4\frac{1}{2}$
	5	1200	38		$2\frac{1}{2}$[§]	$4\frac{1}{2}$
6	3	720	20		$2\frac{1}{2}$	$4\frac{1}{2}$
	$3\frac{1}{2}$	840	23		$2\frac{1}{2}$	$4\frac{1}{2}$
	4	960	26	9–$10\frac{3}{8}$	$2\frac{1}{2}$	$4\frac{1}{2}$
	5	1200	32		$2\frac{1}{2}$	$4\frac{1}{2}$
	6	1440	38		$2\frac{1}{2}$	$4\frac{1}{2}$
7	$2\frac{1}{2}$	600	14		$2\frac{1}{2}$	3
	3	720	17	$11\frac{3}{8}$–$12\frac{13}{16}$	$2\frac{1}{2}$	3
	$3\frac{2}{3}$	880	20		$2\frac{1}{2}$	3 or $4\frac{1}{2}$

*These ratings are based on steam at 215°F and air at 70°F. They apply only to installed radiators exposed in a normal manner, not to radiators installed behind enclosures, behind grilles, or under shelves.

[†]Maximum assembly 60 sections. Length equals number of sections times $2\frac{1}{2}$ in.

[‡]Where greater than standard leg heights are required, this dimension shall be 6 in, except for 7-tube sections, in heights from 13 to 20 in, inclusive, for which this dimension shall be $4\frac{1}{2}$ in. Radiators may be furnished without legs.

[§]For five-tube hospital-type radiation, this dimension is 3 in.

(Courtesy 1960 ASHRAE Guide)

Table 2-3 Small-Tube Cast-Iron Radiators

Number of Tubes per Section	Section Dimensions						
	Catalog Rating per Section*		A Height‡	B Width		C Spacing†	D Leg Height‡
	ft²	Btu/h	in	Min in	Max in	in	in
3§	1.6	384	25	3¼	3½	1¾	2½
4§	1.6	384	19	4⁷⁄₁₆	4¹³⁄₁₆	1¾	2½
	1.8	432	22	4⁷⁄₁₆	4¹³⁄₁₆	1¾	2½
	2.0	480	25	4⁷⁄₁₆	4¹³⁄₁₆	1¾	2½
5§	2.1	504	22	5⅝	6⁵⁄₁₆	1¾	2½
	2.4	576	25	5⅝	6⁵⁄₁₆	1¾	2½
6§	2.3	552	19	6¹³⁄₁₆	8	1¾	2½
	3.0	720	25	6¹³⁄₁₆	8	1¾	2½
	3.7	888	32	6¹³⁄₁₆	8	1¾	2½

*These ratings are based on steam at 215°F and air at 70°F. They apply only to installed radiators exposed in a normal manner, not to radiators installed behind enclosures, behind grilles, or under shelves.
†Length equals number of sections times 1¾ in.
‡Overall height and leg height, as produced by some manufacturers, are 1 inch greater than shown in columns A and D. Radiators may be furnished without legs. Where greater than standard leg heights are required, this dimension shall be 4½ in.
§Or equal.
(Courtesy 1960 ASHRAE Guide)

1. A radiator *must* be level for efficient operation. Check it with a carpenter's level. Use wedges or shims to restore it to a level position.

2. Make sure the radiators have adequate air openings in the enclosure or cover. The openings must cover at least 40 percent of the total surface of the unit.

3. Unpainted radiators give off more heat than painted ones. If the radiator is painted, strip the paint from the front, top, and sides. The radiator will produce 10 to 15 percent more heat at a lower cost.

4. Check the radiator air valve. If it is clogged, the amount of heat given off by the radiator will be reduced. Instructions for cleaning air valves are given in *Troubleshooting Radiators* in this chapter.

5. Radiators must be properly vented. This is particularly true of radiators located at the end of long supply mains. Instructions

for venting radiators are given in *Vents and Venting* in this chapter.

6. Never block a radiator with furniture or drapes. Nothing should block or impede the flow of heat from the radiator.

7. Placing sheet metal or aluminum foil against the wall behind the radiator will reflect heat into the room.

Radiator Heat Output

The heat output of a cast-iron radiator is determined by the following factors:

- Ambient temperature (that is, the temperature of the air surrounding the radiator). The ambient temperature is assumed to be 70°F for purposes of sizing estimates.

- Temperature of the radiator surface. The surface temperature will depend on the temperature of the steam or hot water circulating through the radiator sections. Steam is always hotter than hot water.

- Surface area of the radiator. Repeated tests have shown that the amount of heat given off by ordinary cast-iron radiators per degree difference in temperature between the steam (or water) in the radiator and the surrounding air is about 1.6 Btu per square foot of heating surface per hour.

A relative radiating surface of a radiator is measured in terms of the square feet of equivalent direct radiation (EDR). A cast-iron radiator will give off heat at the rate of 240 Btu per hour when supplied with steam at 2½ lbs of pressure (220°F) with a surrounding air temperature of 70°F. It is determined as follows:

$$(220 - 70) \times 1.6 = 240 \text{ Btu}$$

One square foot of steam radiation equals 1.6 square feet of hot-water radiation or 1.4 square inches of warm-air pipe area. Tables 2-1, 2-2, and 2-3 list the heating surfaces for various column and tubular cast-iron radiators.

The cast-iron radiators in hot-water heating systems deliver water at a temperature of no more than 180°F. As a rule, a square-foot EDR for a hot-water cast-iron radiator will emit 170 Btu per hour.

There is no IBR code covering recessed radiation. As a result, manufacturers of recessed heat-emitting units must rate and certify their own product. The Weil-McLain Company is typical of these manufacturers. Its certified ratings are determined from a series of tests conducted in accordance with the IBR Testing and Rating Code for

Baseboard Type Radiation whenever the provisions of the code should be applied. The Weil-McLain ratings include a 15 percent addition for heating effect and barometric pressure correction factor allowed by the IBR code. Other manufacturers use similar rating methods.

Sizing Radiators

To size a column-type or tube-type cast-iron radiator, first measure its height in inches and then count the number of sections and the number of tubes or columns in each section (see Figure 2-3). The

RADIATOR CONSISTING OF SIX
FOUR-COLUMN SECTIONS

FOUR-COLUMN
SECTION

	18"	20"	22"	23"	26"	30"	32"	36"	38"	45"
3 Tubes			1.72	2.00	2.33	3.00		3.50	3.50	
4 Tubes			2.25	2.50	2.75		3.50	4.25		
5 Tubes			2.67	3.00	3.50	4.33	4.33	5.00	6.00	
6 Tubes			3.00	3.50	4.00		5.00			
7 Tubes	2.60	3.50	4.20		4.75					
1 Column			1.50	1.67	2.00		2.50	3.00		
2 Cols.			2.00	2.33	2.67		3.33	4.00	5.00	
3 Cols.		2.25	3.00		3.75		4.50	5.00	6.00	
4 Cols.			3.00	4.00	5.00		6.50	8.00	10.0	
5 Cols.	3.00	3.75	4.50	5.00	6.30	7.00	8.50	10.0		

1. Find the Sq. Ft. EDR per section above (4.00).
2. Multiply by the number of sections altogether in that radiator to get Sq. Ft. EDR for the entire radiator (4.00 × 6 = 24 Sq. Ft. EDR).
3. Multiply by 240 BTUs per hour to get the steam design output or Multiple by 170 BTUs per hour to get the hot water design output.

Figure 2-3   Sizing cast-iron radiators. *(Courtesy John D. Howell [hydronics.com])* sections are the divisions or separations of a cast-iron radiator as seen when standing directly in front of it. When you look at the radiator from its narrow end, you can see that each section consists of one or more vertical columns or pipes.

Note

These vertical columns or pipes (they are called *columns* in the traditional cast-iron radiators) are 2½ inches wide. In newer radiators, they are called *tubes* and are only 1½ inches wide.

Find the square-foot EDR (equivalent direct radiation) of one section of the radiator. Multiply that figure by the number of sections in the radiator module to arrive at the square-foot EDR rating of that radiator. Multiply the square-foot EDR rating by 240 Btu per hour to obtain the heating capacity of that radiator in a steam heating system or by 170 Btu per hour for its heating capacity in a hot-water heating system.

Installing Radiators

A cast-iron radiator is constructed by joining together a number of individual sections (see Figure 2-4). The number of sections used depends on the heating requirements for the room or space. For purposes of on-site handling, these radiators are supplied up to a

A cast iron radiator is made up of individual sections joined together to form a larger radiator module.

For ease of site handling these radiators are supplied up to a maximum of ten section modules.

Figure 2-4 Joining together radiator sections.

(Courtesy John D. Howell [hydronics.com])

maximum of 10 section modules. Additional sections can be joined together on site to form longer radiators (see Figure 2-5). The procedure used to join the sections will depend on whether the nipples are threaded or smooth and beveled.

Figure 2-5 Forming longer radiators on-site.
(Courtesy John D. Howell [hydronics.com])

Joining Threaded Radiator Sections

In older cast-iron radiators, each section has a pair of 1¼-inch-diameter threaded openings. One pair of openings has left-handed threads, and the opposite pair on the facing section has right-handed threads (see Figure 2-6).

SYMBOL → Side with left handed threads.

PLAIN → Side with right handed threads.

Figure 2-6 Left-handed and right-handed threaded waterways.
(Courtesy John D. Howell [hydronics.com]).

To join the radiator sections together, connect the openings threads with left- and right-handed threaded nipples and joining gaskets. Proceed as follows:

I. Clean the gasket seating areas of the four waterway openings with abrasive cloth (*not* a file) to ensure that they are free of paint, dirt, and any other contaminants that would interfere with the joining of the two radiator section surfaces (see Figure 2-7).

Figure 2-7   Cleaning gasket seating area around waterway opening on radiator section. *(Courtesy John D. Howell [hydronics.com])*

2. Align the sections accurately. Make sure that the end sections being joined together have opposite threads—in other words, left-handed threads on one section facing right-handed threads on the other.

Note
Sections with an **O** symbol positioned on the top left-hand side are left-handed threads. Sections with no symbol have right-handed threads. This holds true for all models except 6/58, which is the reverse. The side with a symbol on it has right-handed threads, and the plain side has left-handed threads.

3. Make sure the top and bottom seams on the cast-iron radiator sections match. The top seams are commonly smoother than the bottom ones.

4. Screw the nipples into the first pair of threads by turning only one turn each (see Figure 2-8).

5. Place a jointing gasket over each nipple.

Warning
Do not use jointing compound or PFT tape when jointing gaskets and nipples. Doing so will invalidate the radiator manufacturer's guarantee.

6. Using the largest radiator section as a base unit, add smaller sections to it by carefully aligning and mating the opposing waterways and protruding nipples (see Figure 2-9).

Figure 2-8 Installing nipples and gaskets.

(Courtesy John D. Howell [hydronics.com])

Figure 2-9 Adding smaller sections to a larger base unit.

(Courtesy John D. Howell [hydronics.com])

7. Determine the insertion depth of the joining key by measuring it along the top of the radiator from the position of the new joint to the point where it will project from the base unit waterway. Mark this point on the joining key shaft (see Figure 2-10).

8. Insert the joining key through one of the waterways of the second section (see Figure 2-11). Applying slight pressure, pull the two sections together with one hand and begin to turn the joining key with the other hand until they begin to join together. Stop when both are engaged.

Figure 2-10 Measuring the insertion depth with the joining key.
(Courtesy John D. Howell [hydronics.com])

Note

Use a wood block under the joining key to keep it in line. Doing so will ensure that the waterway threads are not damaged by the key shaft.

9. Repeat step 8 by inserting the joining key through the second waterway (each radiator section has a waterway at the top and bottom). Alternate between both waterways a few turns at a time until the end sections meet and the nipples are hand-tight. Do *not* fully tighten yet.

10. Make a final check to ensure that both radiator sections are uniformly aligned, and then fully tighten them to a recommended torque of 140–150 lbs/ft (see Figure 2-12). Do *not* over-tighten or you may strip the threads.

11. Add additional radiator sections by following the same procedures previously described. When the required number of sections

Turn joining key clockwise.

Figure 2-11 **Inserting the joining key.** *(Courtesy John D. Howell [hydronics.com])*

have been added, lift and carry the completed radiator in the upright position to the installation point. Do not carry it on its side because doing so will place stress on the joints.

Note

Site assembly following the aforementioned procedures should produce a radiator capable of reaching a test pressure of 140 psi.

Remove radiator sections by reversing the aforementioned installation steps. Before attempting to unscrew the nipples with the joining key, look through the waterways for the rough or smooth side of the

Figure 2-12   Tightening the sections to the required torque.
(Courtesy John D. Howell [hydronics.com])

nipples. If the rough side is visible, turn the joining key counterclockwise. If the smooth side is visible, turn it clockwise (see Figure 2-13).

Joining Radiator Sections with Smooth Beveled Nipples
Modern radiators have threadless push nipples instead of threaded ones. A push nipple is a short, smooth, beveled pipe. The bevel creates a bulge in the middle of the nipple. When the nipple is pushed into the opening in the radiator section, the bulge creates a tight

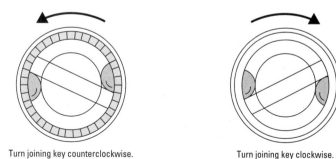

Turn joining key counterclockwise.   Turn joining key clockwise.

Figure 2-13   Turning the joining key counterclockwise or clockwise as required. *(Courtesy John D. Howell [hydronics.com])* seal. Push nipples have replaced threaded nipples in radiators because the latter are almost impossible to remove after years of use. Corrosion on the threads causes a weld-like seal to form, making it very difficult to disassemble the radiator.

Radiator Valves

Various valves are required for the efficient operation of radiators. These valves (or *vents*) are used to bleed air from the radiator when the heating system first starts. The choice of valve will depend on the requirements of the particular system.

The four principal functions provided by valves operating in conjunction with radiators are as follows:

1. Admission and throttling of the steam or hot-water supply.
2. Expulsion of the air liberated on condensation.
3. Expulsion of air from spaces being filled by steam or hot water.
4. Expulsion of the condensation.

Radiator valves (packed or packless), manual or automatic air valves, and thermostatic expulsion valves (traps) are used to perform the aforementioned functions.

The packed-type radiator valve is an ordinary low-pressure steam valve that has a stuffing box and a fibrous packing to prevent leakage around the stem (see Figure 2-14). The objection to this type of valve is the frequent need for adjustment and renewal of the packing to keep the joint tight. These valves also require many turns of the stem to fully open.

The packless radiator valve is one that has no packing of any kind. Sealing is obtained by means of a diaphragm (see Figure 2-15) or a bellows (see Figure 2-16). On each valve, there is no connection between the actuating element (stem and screw) and the valve being sealed hermetically; hence, there can be no leakage. With the diaphragm arrangement, a spring is used to open the valve. With bellows construction, there is no spring; a shoulder on the end of the stem works in a bearing on the valve inside the bellows.

Some so-called packless radiator valves actually employ spring discs to secure a tight joint. Although called packless, the spring discs form a metallic equivalent of packing.

Both manual and automatic air valves are used to remove air from radiators. The manual valves are not well adapted for this function because they usually receive only irregular attention. Air is

HANDWHEEL

PACKING
NUT

VALVE
SPINDLE

GLAND

STUFFING
BOX

SCREW
THREAD

BONNET

VALVE

OUTLET

INLET

SEAT
PARTITION

SPHERICAL OR "GLOBE" -
SHAPED CASTING

Figure 2-14 Typical packed radiator valve.

constantly forming in the radiator and should be removed as it forms.
After the air valve remains closed for some time, the radiator gradually fills with air (or becomes air bound), as shown in Figure 2-17,
with the air at the bottom and the steam at the top. On opening the
valve (see Figure 2-18), the air is pushed out by the incoming steam.
The radiator is gradually filled with steam until it begins to come
out of the air valve (see Figure 2-19). At this point, the air valve
should be closed.

An *automatic air valve* is one form of the thermostatic valve (see
Figure 2-20). Automatic operation is made possible by a bimetallic
element contained in the valve. The principles generally employed
to secure automatic action are as follows:

1. Expansion and contraction of metals.

2. Expansion and contraction of liquids.

3. Buoyancy of flotation.

4. Air expansion.

Figure 2-15 Diaphragm-type packless radiator valve. *(Courtesy Trane Co.)*

When the relatively cold air passes through the valve, the metal strips lie in contracted position (with legs close together and the valve open), allowing air to escape (see Figure 2-21). The steam then enters the valve, and its higher temperature causes the metal strips in the bimetallic element to expand. The brass strip expands more than the iron strip, which causes the end containing the valve spindle to rise and close (see Figure 2-22). When the strips are fully expanded, the

Figure 2-16 Bellows-type packless radiator valve. *(Courtesy Sarco Co.)*

Figure 2-17   Air-bound radiator.

Figure 2-18   Air is pushed out by incoming steam.

valve is closed, shutting off the escape of steam (see Figure 2-23). In case the radiator becomes flooded with water, the additional water entering will cause the float to push up the valve and prevent the escape of water (see Figure 2-24).

Because an automatic air valve is used only for expelling air from a radiator, it should be distinguished from a thermostatic expulsion valve. A *thermostatic expulsion valve* opens to air and condensation and closes to steam. The low temperature of the air and condensation causes the bimetallic element to contract and

Figure 2-19   Steam escaping from air valve.

STEAM

ADJUSTABLE VALVE SEAT

NEEDLE VALVE

FLOAT

RADIATOR CONNECTION

BEARING

BRASS STRIP

IRON STRIP

Figure 2-20   Working components of an automatic air valve.

open the valve, whereas the relatively high temperature of the steam causes the element to expand and close the valve.

Although a thermostatic expulsion valve is sometimes referred to as a trap, this term is more correctly used to indicate a larger unit not connected to a radiator and having the capacity to drain condensation from large mains. As distinguished from the thermostatic valve, a trap handles only condensation and not air.

A bellows charged with a liquid is used on some of the thermostatic valves as an actuating element instead of the bimetallic device.

Figure 2-21 Bimetal strips contracted and valve open.

Figure 2-22 Bimetal strips expanding.

Figure 2-23 Bimetal strips fully expanded and valve closed.

Figure 2-24 Valve closed by buoyancy of float.

The operating principle of a Trane bellows-type thermostatic valve is illustrated in Figures 2-25, 2-26, 2-27, and 2-28.

Additional information about valves and valve operating principles is contained in Chapter 9 of Volume 2 ("Valves and Valve Installation").

Radiator Piping Connections

Some typical radiator piping connections are shown in Figures 2-29, 2-30, 2-31, 2-32, and 2-33. The important thing to remember when connecting a radiator is to allow for movement of the risers

Figure 2-25 Condensate being discharged from heating unit.

Figure 2-26 Steam enters trap. Pressure within the bellows increases and causes it to expand.

and runouts. This movement is caused by the expansion and contraction resulting from temperature changes in the piping.

Vents and Venting

Each volume of water contains a small percentage of air at atmospheric pressure mechanically mixed with it. This air is liberated

Figure 2-27 All condensate is drained from unit.

Figure 2-28 Steam completely surrounds the bellows.

during vaporization and causes some problems for the circulation of steam in the system. As steam starts to fill a heating system, it can enter the radiators, convectors, or baseboard units only as fast as the air escapes. For this reason, some means must be provided to vent this air from the system.

Figure 2-29 Radiator supply and return connections for first-floor installation.

Figure 2-30 Radiator supply and return connections for upper-floor installation.

Figure 2-31 One-pipe radiator connections. *(Courtesy 1960 ASHRAE Guide)*

Air Vent Locations

The location of a radiator vent will depend on the type of heating system.

- **Hot-water (hydronic) system radiators.** The air vent is located at the top of the radiator on the side opposite the inlet (supply) pipe.

- **Steam system radiators.** No air valve is required for a radiator in a two-pipe steam heating system. In a one-pipe steam system, the radiator should have an air valve (vent) installed halfway down on the side opposite the inlet pipe.

Figure 2-32 Two-pipe connections to radiator installed on wall.

Figure 2-33 Two-pipe top and bottom opposite-end radiator connections. *(Courtesy 1960 ASHRAE Guide)*

Adjustable air valves are often found in systems fired by automatic oil or gas burners. This type of air valve permits the adjustment of radiators varying in size and/or distance from the furnace or boiler so that radiators heat at an equal rate.

Nonadjustable air valves are not recommended because the larger radiators will still contain air after the smaller ones have been completely vented. The same problem occurs with the last radiator on a long main. Often the air valve on this radiator does not have enough time to rid the system of air before the *on* period is completed and the thermostat shuts off the burner. One method of handling this problem is by installing a large-size quick vent at the end of the long main (see Figure 2-34).

Figure 2-34 Large-size quick vent installed at end of long main.

Double- or triple-venting is an extreme method of solving the problem of a persistently cold radiator (see Figure 2-35). There is usually only one opening for an air valve on a radiator. A second opening can be added by using a ⅛-inch pipe tap and a drill of the proper size.

If a multiple-valve arrangement for a radiator fails to produce the desired results, the only other possibility is to lengthen the burner *on* period. This can be accomplished on oil burners by altering the differential.

Air must also be vented from hot-water heating systems. Trapped air will cause these systems to operate unsatisfactorily, and a means

Figure 2-35 Triple-venting a radiator.

should be provided to eliminate it. Manually operated air valves located at the highest levels in the heating system and automatic air valves placed at critical points will usually vent most of the trapped air.

Steam Traps

Steam enters the top of the radiator in a two-pipe steam heating system. As the steam moves through the radiator, a portion of it condenses and the water drips down to the bottom of the unit where it exits through a condensate pipe. In the two-pipe system, a steam trap is installed where the condensate pipe is connected to the radiator. The function of the steam trap is to remove the water (condensate) and prevent any steam from escaping the radiator and entering the condensate return lines. Additional information about steam traps can be found in Chapter 10 ("Steam and Hydronic Line Controls") of Volume 2.

Not all radiators in two-pipe steam heating systems use steam traps to prevent the steam from entering the condensate return lines. Some are equipped with a small check valve, an internal opening, or a seal.

Troubleshooting Radiators

If a radiator in a hot-water or steam heating system is not producing enough heat (or not producing heat at all), it may not be the fault of the radiator. Check the room thermostat and the automatic fuel-burning equipment (gas burner, oil burner, or coal stoker) to determine if they are malfunctioning. Methods for doing this are detailed in the appropriate chapters of Volumes 1 and 2. If you are satisfied that they are operating properly, the problem is probably with the radiator.

Hot water or steam enters a radiator at an inlet in the bottom and must rise against the pressure of the air contained in the radiator. A radiator is equipped with an automatic or manual air valve at the top to allow the air to escape and consequently permit the water or steam to rise.

In radiators equipped with automatic air valves, rising water or steam usually has enough force to push the air in the radiator out through the valve. The valve is automatically closed by a thermostatic control when it comes in contact with the hot water or steam. If a radiator equipped with an automatic air valve is not producing enough heat, the valve may be clogged. This can be checked by closing the shutoff valve at the bottom of the radiator and unscrewing the air valve. If air begins to rush out, open the radiator shutoff valve to see if it will heat up. An increase of heat is an indication that the air valve is clogged. Close the radiator shutoff valve again, remove the air valve, and clean it by boiling it in a solution of water and baking soda for 20 or 30 minutes. The radiator should now operate properly.

A radiator equipped with a manual air valve should be bled of air at the beginning of each heating season. It should also be bled if it fails to heat up properly. This is a very simple operation. Open the manual air valve until water or steam begins to run out. The water or steam running out indicates that all the air has been eliminated from the radiator.

Sometimes radiators are painted to improve their appearance. When a metallic paint (such as aluminum or silver) is used, the heating efficiency is reduced by 15 to 20 percent. If you must paint a radiator, use a nonmetallic paint for all surfaces *facing* the room. Dirty surfaces will also reduce the heating efficiency of a radiator. A good cleaning will eliminate the problem.

Convectors

A *convector* is a heat-emitting unit that heats primarily by convection. In other words, most of the heat is produced by the movement of air around and across a heated metal surface. The air movement across this surface can be gravity-induced or forced. As a result, convectors are classified as either *gravity air convectors* or *forced-air convectors*. They are used in hydronic (forced hot-water) and two-pipe steam heating systems.

Small, upright gravity and forced-air convectors are commonly found in older heating installations. The design of this type of unit was probably influenced by cast-iron radiators. A much more efficient convector is the fin-and-tube baseboard unit (see *Fin-and-Tube Baseboard Units* in this chapter).

Figure 2-36 Typical radiation convector. *(Courtesy Trane, An American Standard Company)*

An example of a modern convector is illustrated in Figure 2-36. The convector cabinets are available in a variety of different baked-on enamel color finishes. Some convectors have a small door on the front of the cabinet to provide entry for cleaning the heating element (see Figure 2-37). On other convectors, the entire front panel will swing upward for access. The heating element consists of aluminum fins attached to three copper tubes (see Figure 2-38). The tubes are supported by brass headers and hangers on each end of the assembly.

The rating of convectors used in hot-water heating systems is determined by water temperature, temperature drop, and inlet air temperature. The rating of those used in steam heating systems is determined by steam pressure and the entering air temperature. The convector manufacturer provides specifications for its convectors, including sizing data tables.

Convector Piping Connections

The piping connections for a typical gravity convector are shown in Figure 2-39. Supply connections to the convector heating element are made at the top, bottom, or end of the inlet header. Return connections are made at the bottom or end of the header at the opposite end of the unit. Figure 2-40 illustrates two recommended piping connections for convectors used in a hot-water heating system. Typical convector piping connections for units used in steam heating systems are shown in Figures 2-41 and 2-42.

Figure 2-37 Location of access door and heating element assembly.

(Courtesy Trane, An American Standard Company)

Figure 2-38 Heating element assembly.

(Courtesy Trane, An American Standard Company)

Figure 2-39   Typical convector connections. *(Courtesy 1960 ASHRAE Guide)*

Figure 2-40   Convector piping connections in a hot-water heating system. *(Courtesy Dunham-Bush, Inc.)*

Figure 2-41 Typical convector connections in a steam heating system.
(Courtesy Dunham-Bush, Inc.)

Gravity convector piping connections are very similar to those used with radiators, except that the lines must be sized for a greater condensation rate. The usual method for determining convector capacities is to convert them to the equivalent square feet of direction radiation (EDR):

$$EDR = \frac{Convector\ Rating\ (Btuh)}{240\ Btu}$$

Figure 2-42 Convector piping connections in a steam heating system.

The 240 Btu figure represents the amount of heat in Btu given off by ordinary cast-iron radiators per square foot of heating surface per hour under average conditions.

The connections used for a *forced* hydronic convector are similar to those used with unit heaters (see *Unit Heater Piping Connections* in this chapter).

Hydronic Fan Convectors

Hydronic system fan convectors are equipped with small fans controlled by a fan switch. The fan blows air across the heating element assembly and into the room or space. If there is no heat, a low-limit aquastat will shut off the fan when the temperature drops below a predetermined setting.

Troubleshooting Hydronic Fan Convectors

Check the room thermostat first and then the boiler to determine if either is malfunctioning (see Table 2-4). Procedures for troubleshooting boilers, water heaters, and thermostats are detailed in the appropriate chapters of Volumes 1 and 2.

Table 2-4   Troubleshooting Fan Convectors

Symptom and Possible Cause	Possible Remedy
Fan does not operate.	
(a) Low water temperature.	(a) Check for problem with boiler, water heater, or piping and repair.
(b) Low water flow rate.	(b) Check piping and correct.
(c) Tripped circuit breaker or blown fuse.	(c) Reset circuit breaker or replace fuse. If problem continues, request a service call from an electrician or HVAC technician.
(d) Faulty aquastat.	(d) Replace aquastat.
(e) Air-bound coil.	(e) Check bleeder vent and repair.
Poor heat output.	
(a) Low water temperature.	(a) Check boiler or water heater and repair.
(b) Low water flow rate.	(b) Check piping and correct as necessary.
(c) Incorrect clearances around convector.	(c) Check specified clearance in local code and manufacturer's specifications and correct.
Fan operates at only one speed or runs intermittently.	
(a) Broken or loose wiring connection.	(a) Replace wire if connection broken; tighten connection.
(b) Poorly balanced system.	(b) Check piping and correct as necessary.
(c) Air-bound unit.	(c) Check air vent and correct as necessary.

Note

> The boiler or dedicated water heater should be set at a minimum temperature of 140°F for the fan convector to operate efficiently.

Check the manufacturer's installation instructions to make certain the convector is properly piped (correct sizing, layout, and so on). If the flow rate for the convector is less than 1 gpm, then there is a piping problem.

Check the wiring to make sure the convector is wired properly, and then examine the wires for loose connections or damaged wiring. If the wiring, piping, and boiler (or water heater) check out all right, the problem is in the convector itself.

Steam and Hot-Water Baseboard Heaters

Baseboard heaters are designed to be installed along the bottom of walls where they replace sections of the conventional baseboard (see Figure 2-43). Locating them beneath windows or along exterior walls is a particularly effective method of eliminating cold drafts.

Figure 2-43 Typical baseboard heating installation. *(Courtesy Vulcan Radiator Co.)*

Baseboard heaters are frequently used in steam and hot-water heating systems (see Figures 2-44 and 2-45). In a series-loop system, supply and branch piping can be eliminated by using the baseboard heater to replace sections of the piping. In other words, there is no need for supply and return branches between the baseboard heater and the mains.

Baseboard heaters are also available with electric heating elements controlled by a centrally located wall-mounted thermostat or a built-in thermostat. Each unit is actually a separate heater (see *Electric Baseboard Heaters* in this chapter), but they can be joined and wired together to form a baseboard heating system.

The Institute of Boiler and Radiator Manufacturers (IBRM) has established testing and rating methods of baseboard heat-emitting units. The output for baseboard units is rated in Btu per hour per linear foot.

Construction Details

Two types of baseboard heaters are used in steam and hot-water (hydronic) heating systems: those with separate fins attached to the tubing and those with the fins cast as an integral part of the unit. The integral-fin units are made of cast iron. Those with separate fins are made of nonferrous metals such as copper, aluminum, or alloys.

Separate Fin-and-Tube Baseboard Units

An example of a baseboard heater with the fins attached to the tubing is shown in Figure 2-45. The size and length of the tube, as well as the number, size, and spacing of the metal fins, will vary from one manufacturer to the next. Fin shapes, sizes, and spacing can be ordered to specification from the manufacturer. Basically the fins are either square or rectangular (see Figure 2-46). Some will have special design features, such as flared ends (see Figure 2-47).

The assembly of the heating element is covered by a sheet-metal enclosure. Openings are cut into the face of the cove to increase air circulation. When steam or hot water is passed through the tube, the heat is transmitted to the fins by conduction through the metals. The heat transmitted to the fins is transferred to the air by convection.

The heating-element tube is available in a variety of sizes, including ¾, 1, 1¼, and 1½ inches (see Figure 2-48). On short pipe runs, the ¾-inch tube is recommended in order to ensure water velocities in the turbulent flow range. On long runs and with loop systems, it may be desirable to use 1- or 1¼-inch tube sizes.

Use of the small tube sizes results in lower cost for connecting piping in a run and for valves, expansion joints, balancing cocks,

DAMPER
ASSEMBLY

DAMPER
PIVOT

RETURN
TUBE

RETURN TUBE
HANGER

SUPPLY TUBE
HANGER

HEATING
ELEMENT

FRONT PANEL

ELEMENT GUIDE

Figure 2-44   Design features of a hot-water heating baseboard
unit. *(Courtesy Weil-McLain Co.)*

Figure 2-45 Return tube installation for hot-water heating system.
(Courtesy Weil-McLain Co.)

Figure 2-46 Typical fin shapes. *(Courtesy Vulcan Radiator Co.)*

Figure 2-47 Heating-element fins with flared ends. *(Courtesy Weil-McLain Co.)*

Figure 2-48   Heating-element tube sizes. *(Courtesy Vulcan Radiator Co.)*

and fittings. There is also a lower heating-element cost involved with the small tube sizes.

The fins and tubing can be made of the same or different metals (see Figures 2-49 and 2-50). The following combinations are among those possible:

1. Copper fins on copper tubing.
2. Aluminum fins on copper tubing.
3. Aluminum fins on aluminum tubing.
4. Aluminum fins on steel tubing.
5. Stainless-steel fins on stainless-steel tubing.
6. Cupronickel fins on cupronickel tubing.

These different metals exhibit different heating characteristics, and all are not suitable for the same application. For example, steel heating elements are recommended for high-temperature water systems. Copper-aluminum elements, on the other hand, work well with water temperatures up to 300°F. Copper-aluminum heating elements also produce a high heat output, but the copper tube has a very high rate of expansion (higher than steel). All these factors

Figure 2-49 Copper-aluminum heating elements.
(Courtesy Vulcan Radiator Co.)

Figure 2-50 Steel heating elements. *(Courtesy Vulcan Radiator Co.)*

have to be taken into consideration when selecting a suitable heating element for the installation.

Integral Fin-and-Tube Baseboard Heaters

A cast-iron baseboard heater with the fins cast as an integral part of the unit is shown in Figures 2-51 and 2-52. These baseboard heaters can be used in series-loop, one-pipe, and two-pipe (reverse-return) forced hot-water heating systems and in two-pipe steam or vapor heating systems. They are not recommended for use in one-pipe steam heating systems.

There are several advantages to using cast-iron baseboard heaters. Because the fins are a part of the casting, they will not bend, dent, or come apart. Cast iron is corrosion resistant and will not expand or

Figure 2-51 Cast-iron baseboard heater with fins cast as an integral part of the unit. *(Courtesy Burnham Corp.)*

Figure 2-52 Integral fin-and-tube construction details.
(Courtesy Burnham Corp.)

contract with temperature changes. This last feature eliminates the expansion and contraction noises that frequently occur with nonferrous, separate fin-and-tube units, which allows them to fit closer to the wall.

Installing Baseboard Units
A steel fin-and-tube baseboard heating element will expand as much as ⅛ inch per 10 feet with a 70°F to 200°F temperature rise.

A copper element will expand as much as $\frac{1}{16}$ inch per 10 feet under the same conditions. This potential expansion of the heating element must be provided for when installing the system or problems will arise. The following provisions are recommended:

1. Allow a clearance of at least $\frac{1}{4}$ inch around all piping that passes through floors or wall partitions.

2. Wrap pipe passing through a floor or wall partition with a felt or foam sleeve to act as a cushion (see Figure 2-53).

WALL PARTITION

FELT SLEEVE

Figure 2-53 Clearance provided for expansion through wall partition.
(Courtesy Vulcan Radiator Co.)

3. Try to limit straight runs of pipe to a maximum of 30 feet. Wherever longer runs are necessary, install a bellows-type expansion joint near the center and anchor the ends.

4. Where a baseboard system extends around a corner, provide extra clearance at the ends (expansion will generally occur away from the corner) (see Figure 2-54).

5. When a baseboard system is installed around three adjacent walls (forming a U), always use an expansion joint in the center leg of the U (see Figure 2-55).

6. When making piping connections, be sure to keep all radiator elements in proper vertical position so that fin edges will not touch other metal parts.

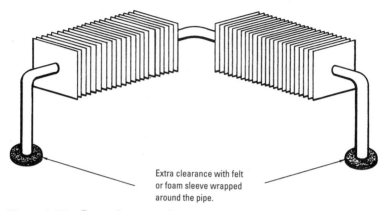

Figure 2-54 Extra clearance should be provided for an extension around a corner. *(Courtesy Vulcan Radiator Co.)*

Figure 2-55 Location of expansion joint.

7. Be sure to support all mains and other piping runs adequately so that their weight will not cause bowing of the heating elements.

8. Install a felt sleeve around the pipe where it rests against a rigid hanging strap (see Figure 2-56).

Before installing the baseboard heater, check the walls carefully for straightness. The baseboard heaters must be absolutely straight or their operating efficiency will be reduced. Therefore, it would be a mistake to use a wall to align the units if the wall were not straight.

FELT

Figure 2-56   Felt support for heating element. *(Courtesy Vulcan Radiator Co.)*

Shims may have to be used on wavy walls to keep the baseboard system straight.

Many baseboard heaters can be recessed the depth of the plaster. The back of each unit is nailed to the studs before plastering, and the top of the baseboard heater hood serves as a plaster stop. The top accessories must be installed before plastering.

The procedure for installing a steam or hot-water baseboard heating system may be summarized as follows:

1. Place the backing of the unit against the wall surface or studs (in a recessed installation) and mark the location of the studs (see Figure 2-57).

2. Punch holes in the backing and screw it to the studs.

Figure 2-57   Unit back installed flush against wall surface or studs. *(Courtesy Vulcan Radiator Co.)*

3. Install cover support brackets approximately 3 feet apart (see Figure 2-58).

4. Place cradle hangers on rivet head and set the heating element on the cradles, making sure the fins are vertical and that all hangers are free to swing (see Figure 2-59).

Figure 2-58   Installing support brackets.
(Courtesy Vulcan Radiator Co.)

Figure 2-59   Setting heating elements in place.
(Courtesy Vulcan Radiator Co.)

5. Complete piping and test for leaks before snapping on the fronts.

6. Snap the front cover onto the support brackets by hooking the top lip over the upper arms and snapping the bottom lip over the bottom arms (see Figure 2-60).

7. Add joining pieces and end enclosures where appropriate (see Figures 2-61 and 2-62).

Figure 2-60 Snapping on the front cover.
(Courtesy Vulcan Radiator Co.)

Figure 2-61 Installing joint pieces. *(Courtesy Vulcan Radiator Co.)*

Figure 2-62 Installing corner and end enclosures.
(Courtesy Vulcan Radiator Co.)

Hot-water heating systems can be divided by temperature into the following three types:

1. High-temperature water systems, 350°F to 450°F.

2. Medium-temperature water systems, 250°F to 350°F.

3. Low-temperature water systems, below 250°F.

Although low-temperature hot-water heating systems are the predominant type used in the United States, there is a growing tendency to apply high-temperature water not only to underground distribution piping (as in district heating) but also to direct radiation.

When fin-tube baseboard units are used in a high-temperature hot-water heating system, care must be taken to keep the enclosure surface temperature to a minimum. This can be accomplished as follows:

1. Use the highest enclosure height practical.

2. Use heating elements only one row high.

3. Use a maximum fin spacing of 33 per foot.

4. Spread the heating element out along the entire wall length.

5. Limit the water temperature to that necessary to offset building heat loss.

Because of the higher heat level, the expansion of heating elements becomes more of a factor with high-temperature hot-water heating systems. As a result, more expansion joints should be used along the length of the heating elements than is the case with low-temperature water.

Baseboard Heater Maintenance

The baseboard heaters used in steam or hot-water heating systems must be routinely cleaned and vacuumed to ensure that the convective fins are clean. If the fins are covered with a layer of dust or dirt, it will impede the radiation of heat into the room or space. Remove the baseboard cover at least once every two months to check the cleanliness of the fins.

Electric Baseboard Heaters

Electric baseboard heaters are designed for use in residential, commercial, industrial, and institutional heating systems. This chapter will be primarily concerned with a description of residential heaters. The electric heaters designed for use in commercial, industrial, or institutional installations differ from the residential type by being larger in capacity; otherwise, they are essentially identical in design (see Figure 2-63).

An electric baseboard heater contains one or more heating elements placed horizontally. Each electric heating element is a unit assembly consisting of a resistor, insulated supports, and terminals for connecting the resistor to the electric power supply.

By definition, a resistor is a material used to produce heat by passing an electrical current through it. Solids, liquids, and gases may be used as resistors, but solid resistors are the type most frequently used. Resistors may be made up of wire or metal ribbon, supported by refractory insulation, or embedded in refractory insulating material surrounded by a protective sheath of metal. A typical heating element used in Vulcan electric baseboard heaters is

Figure 2-63   Duraline electric heater. *(Courtesy Vulcan Radiator Co.)*

shown in Figure 2-64. It consists of nichrome heater coils embedded in a ceramic core.

Figure 2-64   Heater core. *(Courtesy Vulcan Radiator Co.)*

Each resistor is generally rated from 80 to 250 watts (270 to 850 Btu per hour) per linear foot of baseboard unit. The manufacturer will give the ratings for each unit (rather than per linear foot) but will also include its overall length in the data.

Either wall-mounted or built-in thermostats can be used to control the heating elements in electric baseboard heaters. These thermostats (either low-voltage or line voltage types) are designed for single- or multiple-unit control with single- or two-stage heating elements. *Normally*, multiple-unit control is not feasible with two-stage units or with a built-in thermostat. It is recommended that single-stage heating units be used when it is necessary or desirable to control more than one unit from one thermostat.

Close control of temperatures can be obtained by installing a time-delay relay in the electric baseboard unit. This type of relay is particularly useful when a time delay is needed on switch make or break. Additional information about time-delay relays is included in Chapter 6 of Volume 2 ("Other Automatic Controls").

A temperature-limit switch (thermal cutout) should be installed in each unit to prevent excessive temperature buildup. The maximum surface temperature for each baseboard enclosure should be limited to 190°F. Exceeding this limit may result in damage to the heater.

A typical temperature-limit switch used in an electric baseboard installation is the linear capillary type that ensures constant protection over the entire length of the heater. An automatic resetting feature allows the heater to resume operation once conditions return to normal. The temperature-limit switch is usually located between the heater and the thermostat or disconnect switch in the wiring (see Figures 2-65 and 2-66). The only exception occurs when a built-in simultaneous switching thermostat is used (see Figure 2-67).

Figure 2-65 Single-stage wiring diagrams. *(Courtesy Vulcan Radiator Co.)*

Figure 2-66 Two-stage wiring diagram. *(Courtesy Vulcan Radiator Co.)*

Figure 2-67 Two-stage wiring diagram with built-in simultaneous switching thermostat. *(Courtesy Vulcan Radiator Co.)*

In a baseboard heating system, each temperature-limit switch must be wired to break the electrical circuit *only* to the heating element or elements of the unit on which it is installed.

Installing Electric Baseboard Heaters

Read the manufacturer's instructions carefully before attempting to install an electric baseboard heater. Particular attention should be paid to wiring instructions and required clearances. Check the local codes and ordinances before beginning any work. All installation must comply with local and national electrical codes, with the former taking precedence.

Caution

To prevent electrical shock and possible equipment damage, *always* disconnect the power supply before connecting or disconnecting wiring.

Warning

Special care must be taken when installing a line voltage (240 VAC) thermostat. A 240-VAC electric shock may cause serious injury or death.

A *minimum* clearance is generally required from the bottom of an electric heater to any obstructing surface, such as a floor, floor covering, ledge, or sill. The amount of clearance will depend on the particular unit and manufacturer.

Check the heater operating voltage on the model before installing it. The watt output of an electric heating unit depends on the supply (line) voltage. When the supply voltage equals the rated voltage of the unit, the output will equal the rated watts. *Never* connect a heater to a supply voltage greater than 5 percent above the marked operating voltage on the model label. A heater connected to a supply voltage that is *less* than the marked voltage on the model label will result in a watt output that is less than the model label rating. This will cause a reduced heating effect, which should be taken into consideration when determining heating requirements.

Note

Connecting a 120-volt baseboard heater to a 240-volt circuit will cause the heating element to overheat and destroy the heater. Connecting a 240-volt heater to a 120-volt circuit, on the other hand, will result in the heater delivering only about 25 to 30 percent of its designed output.

A change in watt output with respect to a variation in supply voltage may be conveniently calculated with the following formula:

2 × (supply voltage − rated voltage) × amps at related voltage
= change in watt output.

For example, the change in watt output for a 120-volt/500-watt/4.2-amp heating unit connected to a 115-volt line can be calculated as follows:

2 × (115 volt − 120 volt) × 4.2 amp
= 2 × (−5 volt) × 4.2 amp
= −10 volt × 4.2 amp
= −42 watt change in output.

Thus, the output of this unit at 115 volts will be 458 watts (500 watts − 42 watts). The use of these calculations should be restricted to a +10-volt difference in the supply voltage at 120 volts and a +20-volt difference, or 208 volts, 240 volts, and 277 volts.

Some manufacturers of electric baseboard heating equipment produce heaters designed for installation as individual units or as components of a larger baseboard heating system. The procedure for installing individual units is as follows:

1. Locate the unit on the wall so that the *minimum* clearance is maintained between the bottom edge of the heater and the *finished* flooring (see Figure 2-68).

Figure 2-68   Locating and marking the heater. *(Courtesy Vulcan Radiator Co.)*

2. Position the unit so that the knockouts in the junction box are aligned with the electrical rough-in location.

3. Locate the wall studs or mullions, and mark the location on the backing of the unit.

4. Drill or punch mounting holes in the backing a suitable distance below the hood and above the bottom edge.

5. Connect armored or nonmetallic sheathed cable through the knockout in the backing or bottom of the junction box (see Figure 2-69). When entering through the backing, make up electrical connector, slide excess cable back into the wall space, and nail or screw the heater backing to the wall.

Figure 2-69 Making the electrical connections.
(Courtesy Vulcan Radiator Co.)

6. Make electrical connection of branch circuit wiring to the heater. Maintain continuity of grounding (see next paragraph).

7. Snap the heater cover over the brackets and at the same time align the thermostat operating shaft (built-in thermostats with the hole in the cover) (see Figure 2-70).

8. Slide the end enclosures over each end of the unit (see Figure 2-71), and tighten the cover screws (see Figure 2-72).

For each electric heater unit, continuity of grounding must be maintained through circuit wiring devices. All branch circuit wiring

Figure 2-70   Snapping cover over brackets. *(Courtesy Vulcan Radiator Co.)*

and connections at the heater must be installed in accordance with local codes and regulations and the appropriate sections of the most recent edition of the *National Electrical Code*.

Individual electric heaters can be mounted and wired to form a continuous baseboard heating system. The units used in a baseboard system should be ordered with a right-end mounted junction box to facilitate the wiring of the adjacent unit. The instructions for installing individual electric heaters should be followed for each unit in the baseboard system (see steps 1–7 of aforementioned installation procedure).

Figure 2-71   Typical end enclosure.
(Courtesy Vulcan Radiator Co.)

As shown in Figure 2-73, straight-line installation along a wall is simply a matter of butting the two units and connecting them with a joining piece (see Figure 2-74). Inside- and outside-corner installation methods are shown in Figures 2-75 and 2-76.

Kickspace Heaters

A typical kickspace heater is shown in Figure 2-77. It consists of a copper tube with an attached aluminum finned heating element, a 115-volt electric motor, and a blower/fan. Hot water from the boiler is circulated through the copper tube inside the unit. The

Figure 2-72 Tightening cover screws. *(Courtesy Vulcan Radiator Co.)*

Figure 2-73 Straight-line installation. *(Courtesy Vulcan Radiator Co.)*

blower, which is driven by the small electric motor, forces air across the heating element, picks up the heat, and sends it into the room. The blower is turned on or off automatically in response to the thermostat setting. The blower speed is set manually. The blower motor operates in conjunction with a 120°F (49°C) reverse-acting aquastat.

Kickspace heaters are designed for use in one-pipe or two-pipe hydronic heating systems or in a series loop where pressure and temperature drop can be tolerated. They are used beneath kitchen sinks, along short entrances and hallways, and inside bathrooms where space restrictions do not permit the installation of the longer baseboard heaters. Kickspace heaters are not designed for use in steam heating systems. They are also not recommended for use in a gravity-flow hot-water system unless a separately installed pump is provided to circulate the water.

Kickspace heaters are offered in three models: horizontal heaters, vertical heaters, and surface-mounted wall heaters. The horizontal models are installed beneath kitchen cabinets, bathroom sink enclosures, and similar areas where vertical height is limited. The vertical models are installed fully recessed between wall studs. The air is discharged upward through a louvered front panel. The surface-mounted wall model is mounted on the interior surface of a wall. The air is discharged evenly through a louvered front panel in an upward direction.

Figure 2-74 Joining piece.
(Courtesy Vulcan Radiator Co.)

Floor and Window Recessed Heaters

Recessed radiation is designed for installation below large glass areas that extend to the floor and do not permit the use of baseboard radiation. The heat-emitting unit illustrated in Figure 2-78 is an example of recessed radiation used in a hydronic heating installation.

A typical hot-water recessed radiation heater consists of an enclosure, a finned element, two element glides, two rubber grommets, and a floor grille with or without dampers (see Figure 2-79). The operating principle of this unit is relatively simple. The air entering the unit at the cool-air inlet is separated from the rising heated air by a baffle (see Figure 2-80). The baffle is designed to separate the cool inlet air from the rising heated air and to accelerate the flow of air through the unit for maximum heat output. The baffle is held in position by a guide on each end of the enclosure and a bracket in the center.

Figures 2-81 and 2-82 show openings used to accommodate recessed floor units in a wood floor and in masonry construction. In a wood floor installation where the unit is to be installed parallel to the joists, an opening with the same dimensions as shown should be prepared by installing headers between joists.

Figure 2-75 Inside-corner installation. *(Courtesy Vulcan Radiator Co.)*

Unit Heaters

A *unit heater* is an independent, self-contained appliance designed to supply heat to a given space. It is frequently referred to as a *space heater*.

The typical unit heater consists of a heating element, a fan or propeller and motor, and a metal casing or enclosure. Unit heaters supply heat by forced convection using steam, hot water, gas, oil, or

Figure 2-76   Outside-corner installation. *(Courtesy Vulcan Radiator Co.)*

Figure 2-77   Kickspace heater. *(Courtesy Beacon/Morris)*

electricity as the heat source. The air is drawn into the unit heater and forced over the heating surfaces by a propeller or a centrifugal fan before it is expelled on a horizontal or vertical air current (see Figure 2-83).

Horizontal heaters have a specially designed broad-blade fan and are used for horizontal discharge space and spot heating assignments. When equipped with louver fin diffusers, the air stream can be directed in an unlimited number of diffusion patterns. A typical horizontal pipe suspended unit heater is shown in Figure 2-84.

Figure 2-78 Typical floor recessed unit. *(Courtesy Weil-McLain Co.)*

Figure 2-79 Typical components of a recessed radiation unit.
(Courtesy Weil-McLain Co.)

Figure 2-80 Operating principle. *(Courtesy Weil-McLain Co.)*

Figure 2-81 Wood floor opening. *(Courtesy Weil-McLain Co.)*

6³/₈˝

62 ³/₈˝

Top of box when
nailed to stakes.
To be flush with
finished floor.

½˝ MAX

Figure 2-82   Stake arrangement for masonry floor opening.
(Courtesy Weil-McLain Co.)

Figure 2-83   Typical air discharge paths. *(Courtesy Vulcan Radiator Co.)*

Figure 2-84   Direct pipe suspended horizontal unit heater.

Forced-air unit heaters are small blower units that exhibit several times the capacity of a gravity circulation unit of the same size.

Unit Heater Piping Connections

The following general notes on piping propeller unit heaters are presented based on competent engineering installation practice:

1. Suspend unit heaters securely with provisions for easy removal.

2. Make certain that units hang level vertically and horizontally.

3. Provide for expansion in supply lines. Note swing joints in suggested piping arrangements.

4. Provide unions adjacent to unit heaters in both supply and return laterals. Also provide shutoff valves in all supply laterals.

5. Use 45°-angle runoffs from all supply and return mains.

6. Make certain that you have provided minimum clearances on all sides. Clearances will be specified in the heater manufacturer's installation literature.

7. When required, dirt pockets should be formed with pipe of the same size as the return tapping of the unit heater.

8. Pipe in the branching line should be the same size as the tapping in the trap.

Figures 2-85 through 2-90 illustrate typical piping details for propeller-type horizontal unit heaters used in steam and hot-water heating systems.

The vapor steam system shown in Figure 2-85 uses an overhead steam main and a gravity dry return. Strainer and float-type steam traps are used between the unit heater and the return main. A float-type air vent is installed below the float trap.

Figure 2-85 Piping connections for a vapor steam heating system.

Figure 2-86 Piping connections for a low-pressure or vacuum steam heating system.

As shown in Figure 2-86, the overhead steam main of a low-pressure or vacuum system can be vented and dripped independently. The steam supply to the unit heater is taken off the top of the main. The float vent is eliminated on systems using a vacuum pump.

Overhead supply and return mains are used (with bottom connections to the mains) in forced hot-water heating systems. The supply main is connected to the bottom of the unit heater. Either an automatic air vent or manual vent (pet cock) can be used at the high point on the return main (see Figure 2-87).

In the two-pipe steam system shown in Figure 2-88, the steam supply of the unit heater is taken from the top of the main. The return from the unit heater is vented before dropping to the wet return. The distance to the water line of the boiler must be sufficient to allow for the pressure drop in the piping.

Figure 2-87 Piping connections for a forced hot-water heating system.

Both an overhead supply main and an overhead return are used in the high-pressure steam system shown in Figure 2-89. The top of the bucket trap must be located below the return outlet of the coil for complete drainage of the condensation.

Unit heater piping connections for a Trane high-pressure steam system are illustrated in Figure 2-90. In this system, an overhead supply main is used with a lower return main. Where steam pressure fluctuates over a wide range, a swing-check valve should be placed in the return lateral between the strainer and the bucket trap to prevent reverse flow of the condensation or steam flashing when the pressure drops suddenly. The top of the bucket trap must be located below the return outlet of the coil for complete drainage of the condensation.

Unit Heater Controls

Two control systems are used with unit heaters. The simpler type provides on-off operation of the fan. The other system provides

Figure 2-88 Piping connections for a two-pipe steam heating system.

modulating control of the heat source and continuous operation of the fan. It is considered the more effective control system.

Modulating control is obtained with either pneumatic or electric equipment. It allows a constant discharge of warm air and eliminates intermittent blasts of hot air. The continuous circulation prevents air stratification, which occurs when the fan is off. A proportional room thermostat governs a valve that controls the heat source or a bypass around the heating limit. Fan operation is governed by an auxiliary switch or a limit thermostat. Either device is designed to stop the fan when the heat is shut off.

In an on-off control system, the fan motor is controlled by a room thermostat. A backup safety device in the form of a limit

Figure 2-89 Piping connections for a standard high-pressure steam heating system.

thermostat will stop the fan when heat is no longer being supplied to the unit heater.

Gas-Fired Unit Heaters

A gas-fired unit heater is designed to operate on either natural or propane gas (see Figure 2-91). These units should be installed in a location where there will be sufficient ventilation for combustion and proper venting under normal conditions of use.

Local codes and regulations should be followed closely when installing a gas-fired unit heater.

The automatic controls used to operate a gas-fired unit heater closely resemble those found on other types of gas heating equipment, such as furnaces, boilers, and water heaters. For example, the unit heater illustrated in Figure 2-92 is equipped with a 24-volt gas valve with a built-in pilot relay, pilot gas adjustment, shutoff device for use with a thermocouple-type pilot for complete gas shutoff operation, and a gas-pressure regulator.

Figure 2-90 Piping connections for a Trane high-pressure steam heating system. *(Courtesy The Trane Co.)*

A separate gas-pressure regulator and pilot valve are generally supplied with control systems when the gas valve does not have a built-in gas-pressure regulator. The usual fan and limit controls are used on most gas-fired unit heaters. A wiring diagram for a typical control system is shown in Figure 2-93.

Oil-Fired Unit Heaters

Direct oil-fired, suspended unit heaters operate on the same principle as the larger oil-fired heating equipment (furnaces, boilers, water heaters, and so on). An oil burner located on the outside of

Figure 2-91 Modine gas-fired unit heater showing principal components. *(Courtesy Janitrol)*

Figure 2-92 Gas-fired unit heater. *(Courtesy National Oil Fuel Institute)*

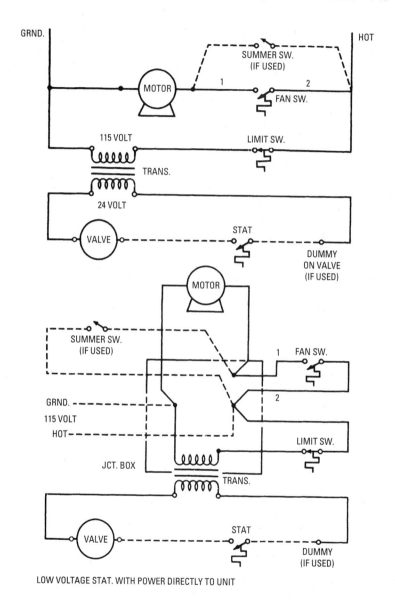

Figure 2-93 Wiring diagram for a gas-fired unit heater. *(Courtesy Janitrol)*

Figure 2-94 Oil-fired unit heater. *(Courtesy National Oil Fuel Institute)*

the unit supplies heat to the combustion chamber, and a fan blows the heat into the room or space to be heated (see Figure 2-94).

An oil-fired unit heater should be located where it will heat efficiently and where it will receive sufficient air for combustion. Proper venting is also important. The waste products of the combustion process must be carried to the outdoors.

Chapter 3

Fireplaces, Stoves, and Chimneys

Until recently, fireplaces, stoves, ranges, wood heaters, and similar heating apparatus were the only sources of heat for cooking, domestic hot water, and personal comfort. These apparatus generally burned solid fuels, such as wood, coke, or the different types of coal, but many later models could also be modified to burn fuel oil, gas (both natural and manufactured), and kerosene.

Central heating and the availability of clean, inexpensive, non-solid fuels (natural gas, oil, and electricity) have relegated these heating apparatus to a minor, decorative role except in remote rural areas of the country. At least this has been the situation until the late 1960s. The growing interest among people in leaving the cities and returning to the land, and the rising cost and potential scarcity of the more popular heating fuels, has brought renewed interest in the solid-fuel-burning fireplace, stove, range, and heater.

Fireplaces

A fireplace is essentially a three-sided enclosure in which a fire is maintained. The heat from the fire enters the room from the open side of the enclosure. The traditional masonry fireplace is a recessed opening in the wall directly connected to a chimney. Modern pre-fabricated, freestanding fireplaces resemble stoves, but their operating principle is still that of the traditional fireplace; that is to say, heat is radiated from the opening out into the room.

Although a fireplace is not as complicated an apparatus as the furnace or boiler of a modern central heating system, its location, dimensions, and construction details still require careful planning if maximum heating efficiency and trouble-free operation are desired. These aspects of fireplace design and construction are examined in the sections that follow.

Fireplace Location

The location of the fireplace is determined by the location of the chimney. Unfortunately, chimney location—particularly in newer homes—is too often dictated by how the chimney will look, rather than how it will work. As a result, the chimney is often made too low or located where it may be obstructed by a section of the house or building. The top of the chimney should be at least 2 feet higher than the roof.

Fireplace Dimensions

The principal components of a masonry fireplace are described in the next section (*Fireplace Construction Details*). The following components are important to the operation of a fireplace:

1. The opening
2. The throat
3. The smoke chamber (and shelf)
4. The damper
5. The flue

These components are interdependent and must be properly dimensioned with respect to one another or the fireplace will not operate properly. Table 3-1 lists typical dimensions for finished masonry fireplaces, and these dimensions are identified in Figures 3-1, 3-2, and 3-3.

Figure 3-1 Fireplace elevation.

Table 3-1 Recommended Dimensions for a Finished Masonry Fireplace (Letters at heads of columns refer to Figures 3-1, 3-2, and 3-3.)

Opening Width, w	Opening Height, h	Depth, d	Minimum Back (Horizontal), c	Vertical Back Wall, a	Inclined Back Wall, b	Outside Dimensions of Standard Rectangular Flue Lining	Inside Diameter of Standard Round Flue Lining
(in)	(in)	(in)	(in)	(in)	(in)	(in)	(in)
24	24	16–18	14	14	16	8½ by 8½	10
28	24	16–18	14	14	16	8½ by 8½	10
24	28	16–18	14	14	20	8½ by 8½	10
30	28	16–18	16	14	20	8½ by 13	10
36	28	16–18	22	14	20	8½ by 13	12
42	28	16–18	28	14	20	8½ by 18	12
36	32	18–20	20	14	24	8½ by 18	12
42	32	18–20	26	14	24	8½ by 18	12
48	32	18–20	32	14	24	13 by 13	15
42	36	18–20	26	14	28	13 by 13	15
48	36	18–20	32	14	28	13 by 13	15
54	36	18–20	38	14	28	13 by 18	15
60	36	18–20	44	14	28	13 by 18	15
42	40	20–22	24	17	29	13 by 13	15
48	40	20–22	30	17	29	13 by 18	15
54	40	20–22	36	17	29	13 by 18	15
60	40	20–22	42	17	29	18 by 18	18
66	40	20–22	48	17	29	18 by 18	18
72	40	22–28	51	17	29	18 by 18	18

FLUE

MANTEL

DAMPER

SMOKE SHELF

6" TO 8"

j

ANGLE

b

FIRE BRICK

ASH DUMP

h

d

a

HEADER

ASHPIT

TRIMMER ARCH

WOOD CENTER

Figure 3-2 Fireplace sectional view illustrating two types of hearth construction.

The dotted lines and letters (*FF*, *EE*, and *TT*) in Figure 3-1 are used to indicate the dimensions of the throat, smoke chamber, and flue. The throat (or damper opening) is identified by the line *FF* in Figure 3-1. The throat should be approximately 6 to 8 inches (or more) above the bottom of the lintel. The area of the throat should be not less than that of the flue, and its length should be equal to the width of the fireplace opening.

Starting approximately 5 inches above the throat (that is, at line *EE*), the inner wall surfaces should gradually slope inward approximately 30° to the beginning of the chimney flue (line *TT* in Figure 3-1).

Figure 3-3   Fireplace plan.

The smoke chamber is the area between the throat and the beginning of the flue (that is, between lines *EE* and *TT* in Figure 3-1). The smoke shelf is the area extending from the throat to the line of the flue wall (see Figure 3-2). This dimension will vary depending on the depth of the firebox. The damper opening (throat) should *never* be less than the flue area.

Fireplace Construction Details

Construction details of a typical masonry fireplace are shown in Figure 3-4. Because this type of fireplace is recessed in a wall, it is easier and less expensive to build it while the structure is under construction.

The principal components of a masonry fireplace are as follows:

1. Firebox
2. Lintel
3. Mantel
4. Hearth
5. Ashpit
6. Ash dump
7. Cleanout door
8. Smoke chamber
9. Smoke shelf
10. Throat

PORTLAND CEMENT STUCCO

METAL LATH

HEADER BLOCK

CONCRETE BRICK

GRADE

10"

FLUE LINING

CHIMNEY BLOCK

FURRING

PLASTER

SMOKE CHAMBER

PRECAST CONCRETE MANTEL

SMOKE SHELF

THROAT AND DAMPER TO BE FULL WIDTH OF OPENING

FIREBRICK LINES JAMBS AND BACK

ASH DUMP

CONCRETE TITLE HEARTH

CLEAN-OUT DOOR

BASEMENT FLOOR

ASHPIT

FOUNDATION SLAB

Figure 3-4 Construction details of a masonry fireplace.

   11. Damper
   12. Flue and flue lining

Firebox, Lintel, and Mantel

That portion of the fireplace in which the fire is maintained is sometimes called the *firebox*. This is essentially a three-sided enclosure

Figure 3-5 Firebox, lintel, and mantel.

with the open side facing the room. The area (in square inches) of the fireplace opening is directly related to the area of the chimney flue. The rule-of-thumb is to make the fireplace opening approximately 12 times the area of the flue.

As shown in Figure 3-5, the *lintel* spans the top of the fireplace opening. This is a length of stone or metal used to support the weight of the fireplace superstructure. The *mantel* is a horizontal member extending across the top of the fireplace where it generally serves a decorative function. Sometimes the terms mantel and lintel are used synonymously. When this is the case, the mantel is used in the form of a wood beam, stone, or arch and functions as a lintel to support the masonry above the fireplace opening.

Fireplace Hearth

The *hearth* is the surface or pavement in the fireplace on which the fire is built. The hearth is sometimes made flush with the floor and will extend out in front of the fireplace opening where it provides protection to the floor or floor covering against flying embers or ashes (see Figure 3-3). The recommended length of the hearth is the width of the fireplace opening *plus* 16 inches.

Ash Dump, Ashpit, and Cleanout Door

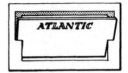

Figure 3-6 Centrally pivoted ash dump.
(Courtesy Portland Stove Foundry Co.)

An *ashpit* is a chamber located beneath the fireplace where the ashes from the fire are collected. An *ash dump* should be installed in the hearth toward the back of the fireplace. This is a metal plate that is pivoted so that the ashes can be easily dropped into the ashpit (see Figure 3-6). Ashes are removed from the ashpit through a *cleanout door* (see Figure 3-7).

Figure 3-7 Location of ash dump, ashpit, and cleanout door.

Smoke Chamber

The *smoke chamber* of the fireplace is a passage leading from the throat to the chimney flue (see Figure 3-4). It should be constructed so that it slopes at a 45° angle from the smoke shaft to the flue opening. The smoke chamber should also be constructed so that a smoke shelf extends straight back from the throat to the back of the flue line. The purpose of the smoke shelf is to prevent downdrafts from flowing into the fireplace. The damper should be mounted on the smoke shelf so that it covers the throat when it is closed. When open, the damper functions as a baffle against downdrafts.

Fireplace Dampers

One of the most frequent complaints about fireplaces is smoke backing up into the room. This condition, particularly if it persists, can usually be traced to a problem with the damper.

On very rare occasions, a fireplace and chimney will be built without a damper. When this is the case, the construction should be modified to incorporate a suitable damper; otherwise, it will be impossible to build and maintain a fire in the fireplace.

The damper should be installed at the front of the fireplace and should be wide enough to extend all the way across the opening. The two most common locations for a fireplace damper are shown in Figures 3-8 and 3-9. If the damper is placed higher up in the chimney, it is controlled with a long operating handle extending to just under the edge of the fireplace opening.

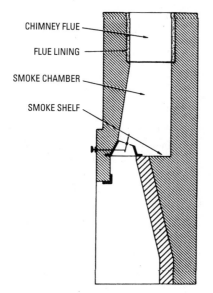

CHIMNEY FLUE

FLUE LINING

SMOKE CHAMBER

SMOKE SHELF

Figure 3-8   Damper mounted on edge of smoke shelf.

(Courtesy Portland Stove Foundry Co.)

A rotary-control damper designed for use in the throat of a fireplace is shown in Figure 3-10. This particular damper has a tilting lid that rotates on its lower edge rather than on centrally located pivots like other rotary dampers (see Figure 3-11). The lid is operated by a brass handle attached to a rod that extends through the face brick or tiling over the fireplace opening. Dampers equipped with ratchet-control levers are shown in Figure 3-12.

Figure 3-9 Damper installed just above the fireplace opening. *(Courtesy Portland Stove Foundry Co.)*

Figure 3-10 Rotary damper with lid that rotates on its lower edge. *(Courtesy Portland Stove Foundry Co.)*

Figure 3-11 Rotary damper with lid that tilts on centrally located pivots. *(Courtesy Portland Stove Foundry Co.)*

Figure 3-12 Damper equipped with ratchet-control levers. *(Courtesy Portland Stove Foundry Co.)*

Modified Fireplaces

A *modified fireplace* consists of a heavy metal manufactured unit designed to be set in place and concealed by brickwork or other masonry construction (see Figures 3-13, 3-14, and 3-15).

Figure 3-13   Prefabricated firebox used in the construction of a modified fireplace.

Modified fireplaces are usually more efficient than the all-masonry type because provisions are made for circulating the heated air. As shown in Figure 3-16, cool air enters the inlets at the bottom and is heated when it comes into contact with the hot surface of the metal shell. The heated air then rises by natural circulation and is discharged through the outlets at the top. These warm-air outlets may be located in the wall of the room containing the fireplace, in the wall of an adjacent room, or in a room on the second floor. Sometimes a fan is installed in the duct system to improve the circulation.

Figure 3-14 Construction details of a modified fireplace.

Freestanding Fireplaces

A *freestanding fireplace* is a prefabricated metal unit sold at many hardware stores, building supply outlets, and lumberyards.

Some typical examples of freestanding fireplaces are shown in Figures 3-17 and 3-18. These fireplaces are exposed on all sides, and their operation is essentially identical to stoves. They are available in a wide variety of styles and colors, and they are easy to install and operate. Because they are lightweight, no special supportive foundation is necessary, although it is a good idea to install a base under the unit to prevent stray sparks and embers from falling onto the floor or floor covering. Most local codes and regulations require that a protective base be used, and the manufacturer's installation literature probably also recommends its use.

The protective base serves the same purpose as a hearth extension on a masonry or modified fireplace. The base should be made from some sort of noncombustible material and should be large

FLUE

MANTLE

HEAT OUTLET

B

ASH DUMP

AIR INLET

A

HEARTH

Figure 3-15 Typical modified fireplace.

enough in area to extend at least 12 inches beyond the unit in all directions (see Figure 3-19).

Rumford Fireplace

Most of the heat produced by a fireplace is radiant heat. Radiant heat moves in a straight line from its source to the nearest solid object, which may be a wall, floor, ceiling, or a piece of furniture, leaving the air through which it passes unaffected. These solid objects absorb the radiant heat and transfer it to the air by conduction and convection. The fireplace design that produces the maximum amount of radiant heat is the Rumford fireplace.

WARM-AIR
DUCT

METAL SHELL

COOL-AIR DUCT

Figure 3-16   Operating principles of a modified fireplace.

Count Rumford and His Fireplace

The Rumford fireplace is not a modern design. It was invented in the eighteenth century by Benjamin Thompson, an American and a contemporary of Benjamin Franklin. Both Thompson and Franklin were concerned with the problem of improving the efficiency of the fireplace, which was the primary heat source for structures in the eighteenth century. The fireplaces of that time were smoky, sources of drafts, passageways for heat to escape from the rooms, and inefficient producers of heat. Benjamin Franklin's successful approach to the problem was to replace the masonry fireplace built into the wall of the structure with a freestanding, metal, wood-burning stove. Franklin stoves were used for both space-heating and cooking. Benjamin Thompson's approach was to redesign the dimensions of the fireplace to make it more efficient. The design proved very successful, and many Rumford fireplaces were built and used as primary space-heating sources for houses until they were replaced by central heating systems in the late nineteenth and early twentieth centuries. Thompson left America in 1796 and settled in Europe, where he lived for the remainder of his life. It was during that period that he was awarded the title Count Rumford. The name Rumford later became associated with his fireplace design.

A Rumford fireplace differs from a traditional one principally in its shallower firebox, its steeply angled sidewalls (built at a sharp 45° angle), and its lower fireback (back wall) (see Figure 3-20). This type of firebox radiates heat down to the floor at different angles instead of straight into the room on a horizontal path, as

Figure 3-17   Wall-model freestanding fireplace. *(Courtesy Malm Fireplace, Inc.)*

Figure 3-18   Corner-model freestanding fireplace. *(Courtesy Malm Fireplace, Inc.)*

Figure 3-19   Dimensions of a typical protective base showing clearances of fireplace. *(Courtesy Malm Fireplace, Inc.)*

STEEPLY ANGLES
SIDEWALLS

LOWER FIREBACK
(BACK WALL)

SHALLOW FIREBOX

Figure 3-20 Distinguishing features of a Rumford fireplace.

does a traditional fireplace. The floor absorbs the radiant heat and transfers it to the room air by conduction and convection.

The throat of a Rumford fireplace is located in such a way that a plumb line can be dropped from the center of the throat to the center of the firebox (see Figure 3-21). This straight vertical path from the firebox to the chimney flue minimizes turbulence which, when present, restricts the flow of smoke and gases. Turbulence in a Rumford fireplace can be further reduced by modifying the horizontal smoke shelf so that it slopes upward from the throat to the vertical wall of the flue.

A damper is normally installed at the throat of a Rumford fireplace, as in traditional types, but some Rumford fireplaces also have dampers at both the throat and the top of the chimney. In theory, the use of two dampers traps warm air in the chimney, thereby preventing cold downdrafts. The best performance for a Rumford fireplace is obtained by using an exterior air supply.

Chimney Draft

A properly designed and constructed chimney is essential to a fireplace because it provides the draft necessary to remove the smoke and flue gases. The motive power that produces this natural draft is the slight difference in weight between the column of rising hot flue gases *inside* the chimney and the column of colder and heavier air *outside* the chimney.

The centerline of the throat aligns with the centerline of the fireplace box.

Figure 3-21 Straight vertical path from center of Rumford fireplace to chimney flue.

Table 3-2   Correction Factors for Altitudes Above Sea Level

Altitude (in feet)	Correction Factor
1000	0.966
2000	0.932
3000	0.900
5000	0.840
10,000	0.694

The intensity of the draft will depend on the height of the chimney and the difference in temperature between the columns of air on the inside and the outside. It is measured in inches of a water column.

The theoretical draft of a chimney in inches of water at sea level can be determined with the following formula:

$$D = 7.00 \, H \left(\frac{1}{461 + T} - \frac{1}{461 + T_1} \right)$$

where D = theoretical draft

H = distance from top of chimney to grates

T = temperature of air outside the chimney

T_1 = temperature of gases inside the chimney

For altitudes *higher* than sea level, the calculations obtained in the formula should be corrected by the factors listed in Table 3-2. Thus, if the structure is located at an altitude of approximately 1000 feet, the results obtained in the formula should be multiplied by the correction factor 0.966 to obtain the correct draft for that altitude.

Chimney Construction Details

Because of its height and weight, a masonry chimney should be supported by a suitable foundation. This foundation should extend *at least* 10 inches below the bottom of the chimney and a similar distance beyond its outer edge on all sides (see Figure 3-4). The foundation can be made more stable by making the base larger in area than the top. This can be accomplished by stepping down the footing at an angle.

Chimney Cap

The *chimney cap* (or *capping*) is both a decorative and functional method of finishing off the top of the chimney (see Figure 3-22). Built of brick, concrete, or concrete slab, the chimney capping tends to counteract eddy currents coming from a high roof. The slab-type

TILE

Extended tile improves an
ordinary chimney, staggered
heights are pleasing.

CONCRETE OR STONE CAPS
ADD TO A CHIMNEY

Figure 3-22 Typical chimney caps.

Figure 3-23 Slab-type
chimney capping.

capping shown in Figure 3-23 is an effective means of preventing downdrafts. Chimney cappings are usually designed to harmonize with the architecture of the structure.

Chimney Flues and Chimney Liners

The *chimney flue* is the passage through which the smoke, gases, and other products of the combustion process travel to the outdoors. A *chimney liner* (sometimes called a *flue liner* or *flue lining*) is a metal tube inserted into the chimney to protect its walls against the potentially damaging gases of the combustion process. It is also used to size the diameter of the chimney flue opening for different appliances. The chimney liner must be code-approved for use in chimneys. Aluminum chimney liners are recommended for use with gas appliances.

Although most flues are lined with a fireproof material, chimneys with walls 8 inches or more in thickness do not need a flue lining. Fired-clay linings are used for flues in chimneys having walls less than 8 inches thick. Chimneys without a flue lining should be carefully pargeted and troweled so that the surface is as smooth as possible.

Figure 3-24 Chimney with more than one flue.

Flue construction is very important. If the flue is too small, it will restrict the passage and slow the rise of the flue gases. A flue that is too large will cause the fireplace to smoke when the fire is first started. Because the flue is too large, the fire takes longer to heat the air, and consequently the flue gases are initially slow to overcome the heavy cold air found in the chimney.

If the same chimney is used to serve fireplaces on two or more floors, *each* fireplace should have a separate flue (see Figure 3-24). This also holds true when a furnace (or boiler) and one or more fireplaces use the same chimney. Each heat source should be connected to a separate flue in the chimney.

Do not allow two (or more) flues to end on the same level at the top of the chimney. Doing so can result in smoke or gases from one flue being drawn down into the other one. One of the flues should be at least 6 inches higher than the other.

Smoke Pipe

The *smoke pipe* is used to connect the heating equipment to the chimney flue. *Never* allow the smoke pipe to extend beyond the flue lining in the chimney or it will obstruct the flow of smoke and other gases (see Figures 3-25 and 3-26).

LINED WITH
FIRE CLAY

RESTRICTED
DRAFT

Figure 3-25 Smoke pipe extending too far into chimney.

Figure 3-26 Proper connection of smoke
pipe to chimney flue.

Cleanout Trap
Chimneys used with coal-fired and oil-fired heating equipment
should be equipped with cleanout traps. Access is provided in the
ashpit (see Figure 3-4).

Chimney Downdraft
Sometimes the air will not rise properly in a chimney and will fall
back into the fireplace or stove. This *downdraft* (or *backdraft*)
condition results in poor combustion, smoke, and odors. It is
generally caused by either deflected air currents or chilled flue
gases.

Air currents can be deflected down into a chimney by higher
nearby objects, such as a portion of the structure, another building,
a tree, or a hill. It is therefore important to build the chimney higher
than any other part of the structure or any nearby objects. Because
the deflected air entering the chimney has not passed through a hot
fire, it will cool the air in the flue and weaken the draft. When the
air becomes cooler, it also becomes heavier and falls back down
into the chimney.

Chimneys built on the outside of a structure, particularly those exposed on three sides, must have walls at least 8 inches thick in order to prevent chilling of the flue gases. Remember that flue gases must not be allowed to cool. The cooler the gas, the heavier it becomes.

Prefabricated Metal Chimneys

Prefabricated (factory-built) metal chimneys are commonly made of 24-gauge galvanized steel or 16-ounce copper (see Figures 3-27 and 3-28). These chimneys normally can be used with any type of gas-, oil-, wood-, or coal-burning appliance; however, check the Underwriters Laboratories (UL) certification for the intended fuel use because some are restricted to gas fuels.

Freestanding fireplaces, such as those illustrated in Figures 3-17, 3-18, and 3-19, are equipped with lengths of pipe designed to extend upward from the top of the unit for approximately 8 feet (see Figure 3-29). These lengths of pipe are available with porcelain enamel surfaces that match the color of the fireplace.

Prefabricated metal chimneys are designed for ceiling support installation, through-the-wall installation, and cathedral ceiling or open-beam installation (see Figures 3-30 and 3-31). Check the local codes and regulations before installing a metal chimney. Closely follow the chimney manufacturer's installation instructions.

Note

Both double-wall and single-wall metal chimney pipes are available. A single-wall pipe is considered an extreme fire hazard.

Figure 3-27
Prefabricated metal chimney used with oil-, gas-, coal-, and wood-burning fireplaces.
(Courtesy Metalbestos)

Troubleshooting Fireplaces and Chimneys

Table 3-3 lists the most common problems associated with the operation of a fireplace.

Stoves, Ranges, and Heaters

A *stove* is a device used for heating or for both heating and cooking purposes (see Figures 3-32 and 3-33). Heating is generally regarded

Table 3-3   Troubleshooting Fireplaces and Chimneys

Symptom and Possible Cause	Possible Remedy
Persistent smokiness.	
(a) No damper.	(a) Install a suitable damper.
(b) Damper set too low.	(b) Correct.
(c) Damper too narrow.	(c) Extend damper all the way across opening.
(d) Damper set at back of fireplace opening.	(d) Relocate damper to the front.
(e) No smoke shelf.	(e) Install smoke shelf.
(f) No smoke chamber or poorly designed one.	(f) Install a suitable smoke chamber or make necessary modifications in old one.
(g) Fireplace opening too large for flue size.	(g) Reduce the size of opening.
(h) Insufficient combustion air.	(h) Open window a crack or provide other means of supplyingcombustion air.
(i) Downdrafts occur.	(i) Extend chimney higher; protect chimney opening with cap designed to deflect downdraft.
(j) Chimney clogged with debris.	(j) Clean chimney.
Fire dies out.	
(a) Insufficient combustion air.	(a) Open window a crack or provide other means of supplying combustion air.
(b) Clogged or dirty flue.	(b) Check flue; correct and/ or clean.
(c) Closed damper.	(c) Open damper.
(d) Fuel logs too green.	(d) Replace with suitable logs.
(e) Fuel logs improperly arranged.	(e) Rearrange and rebuild fire.

as the primary function of a stove. The heat is delivered to the room by both radiation and convection.

Brick, tile, and masonry stoves first appeared in Europe as early as the fifteenth century. The first cast-iron stove was produced in Massachusetts in 1642, but it was a rather crude device by modern

Figure 3-28   Vent pipe design for wall heaters with inputs up to 65,000 Btu.
(Courtesy Metalbestos)

standards because it had no grates. Benjamin Franklin revolutionized the design of the stove with the introduction in 1742 of the model that bears his name (see Figure 3-34).

Sometimes the terms stove and range are used synonymously. This confusion, or blurring of the differences between the two, probably results from the incorporation of such features as an oven, cooking surface, and hot-water tank in the design of the stove (see Figures 3-35 through 3-38).

A *range* is a cooking surface and an oven combined in a single unit. It differs from a stove by being *specifically* designed for cooking, although it can supply a certain amount of warmth to the kitchen.

Ranges can be divided into a number of different categories depending on the type of fuel used. There are four basic categories of ranges:

1. Gas ranges

2. Electric ranges

Figure 3-29 Shanty cap and pipe.
(Courtesy Portland Stove Foundry Co.)

SHANTY CAP

CHIMNEY PIPE

ROOF JACK

3. Kerosene ranges

4. Solid-fuel ranges

Gas ranges use both natural and manufactured gases. Kerosene ranges have been further developed to use either gasoline or fuel oil. The solid fuels used in ranges include wood, charcoal, coal (lignite, bituminous, anthracite), and coke.

The range shown in Figure 3-39 uses wood, coal, or oil. The fuel grates and ashes (from the ashpit) are removed through the front of the range. These ranges also contain a large removable copper tank, which is used to supply hot water for cooking and other purposes.

ROUND TOP

STORM COLLAR

ADJUSTABLE FLASHING

ATTIC INSULATION SHIELD

SMOKE PIPE ADAPTER

FINISH SUPPORT PACKAGE

Figure 3-30 Prefabricated metal chimney and vent details (ceiling support installations).

ROUND TOP

STORM COLLAR

ROOF SUPPORT PACKAGE

FINISHING COLLAR

SMOKE PIPE ADAPTER

CATHEDRAL CEILING INSTALLATION

ROUND TOP

9" INSULATED PIPE LENGTH

SMOKE PIPE ADAPTER

FINISHING COLLAR

FIRE STOP/TRIM COLLAR

WALL BAND

FIRE STOP/ WALL SPACER

INSULATED TEE/PLUG

WALL SUPPORT KIT

THROUGH THE WALL INSTALLATION

Figure 3-31 Prefabricated metal chimney and vent details (through-the-wall and cathedral ceiling installations).

Figure 3-32 Wood-burning parlor stove. *(Courtesy Portland Stove Foundry Co.)*

Figure 3-33 Atlantic box stove. *(Courtesy Portland Stove Foundry Co.)*

Figure 3-34 The Franklin stove with folding doors.
(Courtesy Portland Stove Foundry Co.)

Figure 3-35 Reproduction of the eighteenth-century
cast-iron stove. *(Courtesy Portland Stove Foundry Co.)*

Figure 3-36 Reproduction of the 1812 Franklin stove.
(Courtesy Portland Stove Foundry Co.)

Figure 3-37 Wood- and coal-burning range.
(Courtesy Portland Stove Foundry Co.)

Figure 3-38 Franklin cast-iron stove based on the 1742 design. *(Courtesy Portland Stove Foundry Co.)*

A *wood heater* is a device used specifically to provide heat to a room or a similarly limited space. These are wood-burning units that can also be equipped to burn coal, oil, or gas. These heaters are similar to stoves in their operating principle. They should not be confused with unit (space) heaters, which are suspended from ceilings or walls and operate on a completely different principle (see Chapter 2, "Radiators, Convectors, and Unit Heaters").

Some wood-burning stoves are equipped with a thermostat. The thermostat consists of a bimetallic helix coil that opens and closes a damper in response to temperature changes. The damper opens just enough to admit precisely the amount of combustion air necessary to maintain the heat at a comfortable level.

A mat or floor protector made of some sort of fireproof material should be placed under a stove, range, or heater to protect the floor or floor covering against live sparks or hot ashes. These units should also be placed as far from a wall or partition as is necessary to prevent heat damage.

Installation Instructions

Before installing a new stove, make certain the chimney is large enough to accept the necessary smoke pipe. If another stove or

Figure 3-39 Cast-iron range used with coal, wood, or oil. *(Courtesy Portland Stove Foundry Co.)*

furnace is using the same chimney flue, connect the stove above or below the other one (*never* at the same level). The area of a chimney flue should be about 25 percent larger than the area of the smoke pipe that enters the chimney.

The same design and construction features required for a chimney serving a fireplace also apply to one used with a stove. If there is no chimney, then one must be built.

Operating Instructions

Stoves are similar to fireplaces in that they possess no power in themselves to force smoke up a chimney. The pipe and chimney provide the draft, and if they are defective, the stove will not work satisfactorily.

The installation must be capable of providing sufficient air for the combustion process. At the same time, it must be able to expel smoke and other gases to the outdoors.

Chapter 4

Water Heaters

A *water heater* is an appliance designed to heat water for such purposes as cooking, washing, and bathing. This water is generally referred to as *domestic hot water* or *potable water*.

The most commonly used water heater is the vertical tank-type stand-alone unit used in residences and small commercial buildings. It is independent of the space heating system and is a separately fired water heater. Other water heaters depend on an external heat source such as a boiler. The domestic hot water is heated when it circulates through a heat exchanger inserted in the hot-water or steam heating boiler. These heat exchangers are used only with boilers. In a warm-air heating system, domestic hot water is provided by an independent and separately fired water heater.

Types of Water Heaters

Water heaters can be divided into several groups or classes. The most common classifications are based on the following criteria:

1. Size and intended usage.
2. Heating method.
3. Heat-control method.
4. Fuel type.
5. Flue location and design.
6. Recovery rate.

Water heaters are classified as either domestic or commercial water heaters on the basis of their size and intended usage. Domestic water heaters are those with input rates up to 75,000 Btu per hour. Water heaters regarded as commercial types have input rates in excess of 75,000 Btu per hour. Temperature is another of the criteria used to distinguish between domestic and commercial water heaters. For commercial usage, hot-water temperatures of 180°F or more are generally required. The hot water used in residences does not normally exceed 180°F. For domestic usage, 140°F is generally considered adequate.

Another method of classifying water heaters is by how the heat is applied. Direct-fired water heaters are those in which the water is heated by the direct combustion of the fuel. In indirect water heaters, the service water obtains its heat from steam or hot water and not directly from the combustion process. The advantages and disadvantages of both direct-fired and indirect water heaters are described elsewhere in this chapter.

The heat-control method in a water heater may be either automatic or manual (nonautomatic). All water heaters used in residences are now of the automatic type.

Natural gas or propane, oil, coal, electricity, steam, or hot water can be used to heat the water in a water heater. Either steam or hot water can be used as the heat-conveying medium in indirect water heaters. Neither, of course, is a fuel. The fuels used to heat the domestic water supply are gas, oil, and coal. Gas is by far the most popular fuel. Oil is gaining some popularity, but it still falls far short of gas. The use of coal as a fuel for heating water is now found only in rare cases. Although electricity is not a fuel, in the strict sense of the word, it is generally used along with the three fossil fuels as an additional category for classification.

Quite often, water heaters are classified on the basis of flue location and design. This is a particularly useful criterion for classifying the various automatic storage-type water heaters.

Water heaters can also be classified on the basis of their recovery rate. Quick-recovery water heaters are capable of producing hot water at a more rapid recovery rate than the slow-recovery types. Quick-recovery heaters are often used in commercial structures where there is a constant demand for hot water.

Direct-Fired Water Heaters

A *direct-fired water heater* is one in which the water is heated by the direct combustion of a fuel such as gas, oil, or coal. The combustion flame directly impinges on a metal surface, which divides the flame from the hot water. This metal surface is quite often (but not always) the external wall of the hot-water storage tank. It serves as a convenient heat transfer surface.

A direct-fired water heater is easily distinguished from an indirect water heater (see *Indirect Water Heaters* later in this chapter), which uses an intermediate heat-conveying medium such as steam or hot water, and an electric water heater, which depends on an immersed electric heating element for its heat.

Automatic Storage Water Heaters

The underfired automatic storage heater in which a single tank is used for both heating and storing the water is the most common water heater used in houses, apartments and small commercial buildings. These heaters generally have a 30-, 40-, or 50-gallon storage capacity, although it is possible to purchase automatic storage heaters with capacities ranging from 70 gallons to several hundred gallons.

Automatic storage heaters are classified according to the placement of the flue. Using flue placement as a basis for classification, *gas-fired* automatic storage water heaters can be divided into the following three basic types:

1. Internal or center flue.

2. External channel flue tank.

3. External flue and floating tank.

The internal or center flue gas-fired water heater (see Figure 4-1) is very economical to manufacture, but proper flue baffling is required for good efficiency.

The external channel flue gas-fired water heater provides a much larger heating surface than the center flue. As shown in Figure 4-2, the entire bottom surface of the tank serves as the heating surface. Heating is from the bottom of the tank, which acts to increase efficiency.

Figure 4-1 Internal flue tank construction (gas-fired water heater).

(Courtesy Robertshaw Controls Co.)

Figure 4-2 External channel flue tank construction
(gas-fired water heater). *(Courtesy Robertshaw Controls Co.)*

An even larger heat transfer surface is provided by the external
flue and floating tank water heater illustrated in Figure 4-3. Both
the full bottom and sides of the tank serve as heat transfer surfaces.
The heat (and gases) passes around the storage tank and exits
through the vent.

The tank and flue construction of oil-fired automatic storage
water heaters is very similar to gas-fired types. The major difference
between the two lies in the combustion chamber. In gas-fired water
heaters, the burners are located inside the combustion chamber (see
Figures 4-1, 4-2, and 4-3). In oil-fired water heaters, the oil burner
is mounted externally, and the flames are shot into the combustion
chamber (see Figure 4-4).

Additional information about automatic storage water heaters
can be found in this chapter in the section *Gas-Fired Water Heaters.*

Multicoil Water Heaters

Sometimes the size of a structure or its use will result in a greater
demand for hot water than a conventional water heater can supply.
When this is the situation, it is recommended that a *multicoil*, or
large-volume, water heater be installed. These water heaters resemble instantaneous heaters externally but differ by containing more
than one heating coil. The separate heating coils are connected to
manifolds operated by a thermostat inserted in the storage tank.

Figure 4-3 Floating-tank external flue construction (gas-fired water heater). *(Courtesy Robertshaw Controls Co.)*

Because multicoil water heaters have large storage tanks, they are suitable for use in restaurants, clubs, and structures of similar size and use.

Multiflue Water Heaters

The *multiflue water heater* was developed for commercial uses to satisfy the need for greater heat transfer surface and to efficiently remove the higher volume of noncombustible gases resulting from the higher gas inputs. The diagram of a gas-fired multiflue water heater is shown in Figure 4-5. Compare this with the diagram of the oil-fired multiflue water heater illustrated in Figure 4-4. Each is essentially a vertical fire-tube boiler enclosed in an insulated jacket.

Multiflue water heaters are characterized by a relatively high hot-water recovery rate. These heaters are used in conjunction with auxiliary storage and

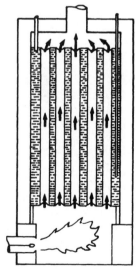

Figure 4-4 Oil-fired multiflue design used in some high-capacity commercial water heaters. *(Courtesy National Oil Fuel Institute)*

Figure 4-5 Multiple-flue, multiple-burner commercial water heater.
(Courtesy Robertshaw Controls Co.)

are frequently employed as booster heaters. It is common usage to refer to a multiflue water heater as a *booster heater.*

Instantaneous Water Heaters

Automatic *instantaneous water heaters* (also sometimes called *point-of-use water heaters*) are self-contained units available in capacities ranging up to 445 gallons per hour (or up to 7.43 gallons per minute at 100° temperature rise) (see Figure 4-6).

Basically, an instantaneous heater consists of a large copper coil suspended over a series of burners. The copper coil, burners, valves, and thermostats are all enclosed in a protective steel casing. An instantaneous water heater does not have a hot-water storage tank; this feature distinguishes them from other types of commercial water heaters, such as the multicoil and multiflue.

The water to be heated circulates through the copper coil. The operating principle of these heaters is very simple and ideal for situations requiring intermittent use. Any pressure drop in the system (such as that caused by opening a faucet) provides the necessary power to force open the gas valve and allow gas to flow to the burners. The gas is ignited by the pilot, and the water in the coil is

Figure 4-6 Instantaneous water heater. *(Courtesy Robertshaw Controls Co.)*

heated to the desired temperature. These heaters are ideally suited for those public buildings or sites that require periods of high demand (for example, public washrooms, sports arenas, ballparks, stadiums, or recreational centers).

Indirect Water Heaters

An *indirect water heater* uses either steam or hot water to heat the water used in the domestic hot-water supply system.

In small, residential-type boilers, a water heater element consisting of straight copper tubes with U-bends or a coiled tube is located in the hottest portion of the boiler water (see Figures 4-7 and 4-8). It is positioned at the side of the boiler to create rapid natural circulation. Because there is no separate water storage tank, this type of unit is commonly called a *tankless water heater*.

In steam boilers, the copper tubes are generally placed below the water line in the boiler. The system is designed so that the water is heated after a single passage through the copper tubes.

Another type of indirect water heater utilizes a separate water heater outside the boiler (see Figure 4-9). Hot water from the boiler flows into the heater and around copper coils containing the domestic hot-water supply before returning to the boiler. The water inside the coils is heated and returned to a hot-water storage tank, which is usually located at a level slightly higher than the heating boiler.

Figure 4-7 Oil-fired hydronic boiler with a straight-tube tankless water heater. *(Courtesy Burnham Corp.)*

The water to be heated can also be circulated *around* tubes through which steam is circulated. The steam tubes are submerged in a steel tank as shown in Figure 4-10. As in all methods of indirect heating, the domestic water supply is kept sealed off from the hot water or steam being used to heat it.

Indirect water heaters of the type illustrated in Figure 4-11 are essentially space-heating boilers with built-in coil bundles through which the hot water circulates. They differ from hot-water space-heating boilers in the following two ways:

1. The coils are sized to absorb the *total* output of the boiler.

2. Water temperatures do not exceed 210°F.

Figure 4-8 Oil-fired hydronic boiler with a coiled-tube tankless water heater. *(Courtesy H.B. Smith Co., Inc.)*

Figure 4-9 Separate indirect water heater mounted outside the boiler. *(Courtesy 1965 ASHRAE Guide)*

Figure 4-10 Indirect water heater in which the water is circulated around steam-filled tubes. *(Courtesy 1965 ASHRAE Guide)*

These indirect water heaters may be used as instantaneous heaters. Because they can be used with any size storage tank, there is no real upper limit on their storage capacity. The same is true of their recovery rate.

The principal advantages of an indirect water heater are the following:

1. Longer operating life (the metal surfaces of the heater are not directly exposed to a flame).

Figure 4-11 Indirect water heater with built-in coils designed to absorb the total heat output of the boiler.

(Courtesy Hydrotherm, Inc.)

2. Scale formation and corrosion in the secondary heat exchanger coils are minimized because of the relatively low operating temperatures.

3. No hot-water storage tank (with the accompanying circulator, controls, and piping) is required if the heater has been properly sized.

Quick-Recovery Heaters

This class of heater, as the name implies, has the ability to produce hot water at a more rapid rate than the slow-recovery type. It is frequently employed where repeated heavy requirement for hot water makes it essential to have a sufficient amount of water available on demand.

Thermostats used are of the throttling or snap-action type. Primarily the throttling thermostat is the one in which the amount of gas valve opening is directly proportional to the temperature changes of water in the tank. In the snap-action thermostat, the change from a completely open to a completely closed position of the valve, or vice versa, is accomplished by a snap action produced by a clicker diaphragm motivated by the temperature in the tank.

The essential difference between the slow- and quick-recovery heater lies in the amount of gas consumed by each unit. Thus, for example, a quick-recovery heater with a 25,000-Btu input will deliver 25 gallons of hot water per hour indefinitely, whereas a slow-recovery heater can never burn more than a certain relatively low and known amount of gas with an accompanying reduction in hot-water delivery.

Slow-Recovery Heaters

The gas-fired slow-recovery water heater is designed to keep a supply of hot water in the storage tank and, by means of a constantly burning gas flame, deliver hot water continuously to this tank.

Thermostats employed can be of the graduating or snap-action type. With the graduating thermostat, the burner operates between a low and high flame—the low position of the flame serving as a pilot to keep the heater lighted and serving as a source of standby heat.

The slow-recovery automatic water heater is very economical since it can never burn more than a certain amount of gas, depending on the regulation offered by the thermostat. Also, the small amount of heating surface keeps the standby loss at a minimum, making this type of heater very advantageous where economy is the primary consideration.

Heat Pump Water Heaters

A *heat pump water heater* consists of a small electrically operated compressor, the heat pump and domestic water supply controls, and a water storage tank (see Figure 4-12). It uses the heat of the air in the room and the energy used to operate its compressor to heat the water in its storage tank. Unlike conventional gas-fired or electric resistance water heaters, the heat pump water heater does not create heat. It transfers heat from one point to another. It is essentially a small heat pump that uses the room air as the heat source and the water in the storage tank as the heat sink. Because it is a heat pump, it can also cool the air and dehumidify it.

In some heat pump water heater installations, the heat pump and water storage tank are separate. A water pump and piping flow loop are used to circulate the water between the heat pump water heater and the water storage tank. The water is heated in the heat pump water heater and stored in the tank.

The principal advantage of using a heat pump water heater with a separate water tank is that either can be replaced independently of the other when they malfunction. Another important advantage is their location flexibility.

The heat pump water heater may also be an integral part of the water storage tank. In these installations, there is no need for a water pump or flow loop. This arrangement also eliminates energy loss from the flow loop piping or the need for freeze protection.

WARM AIR

COOL AIR

HEAT PUMP AND
COMPRESSOR UNIT

WARM WATER

HOT WATER
STORAGE

COLD WATER

Figure 4-12   Heat pump water heater.

Heat pump water heaters are more expensive to purchase and install than conventional electric resistance water heaters. On the other hand, they use 50 percent less energy than conventional electric resistance heaters.

Combination Water Heaters

Many of the earlier combination water/space heaters used in hydronic systems did not keep the domestic hot water separated from the hot water used for space heating. This feature resulted in scale buildup in the water tank and oxygen-induced damage to the tubing in the radiant heating panel. A combination water heater in which the domestic hot water is separated from the space heating water in the same appliance is shown in Figure 4-13. Two separate corrugated stainless steel tanks are used in this design. The outer tank contains the primary fluid (water) and is connected to the space-heating circuit. The inner tank contains the domestic hot water and is connected directly to the utility water supply and a separate domestic hot-water circuit. The primary water in the outer tank is heated by a gas or oil burner and does not exceed a temperature of 180°F, which significantly reduces scale buildup in the domestic (that is, inner) hot-water tank. The domestic hot-water supply in the inner tank absorbs heat from the hot water in the outer tank. There is no direct heating of the inner tank.

The two water circulation circuits supplied by this type of combination water heater are completely independent of one another.

Figure 4-13 Combination water heater.

This arrangement eliminates the problem of oxygen from hot domestic water mingling with the space-heating water, thereby reducing the possibility of oxygen production, which can damage tubing or cause scale buildup in the tank.

Note
> The primary water in the outer tank is never changed. Changing the water can lead to the introduction of oxygen into the system.

The space-heating water in the outer tank is circulated in a closed loop through baseboards, tubing or panels, and heat exchangers. The only point of contact between the inner and outer tanks is where the cold-water inlet pipe and the hot-water flow pipe extend through the top of the combination water heater. The heater is equipped with two separate built-in control systems, one for the outer tank and one for the inner tank.

Some combination water heater installations consist of an indirect water heater connected to a high efficiency furnace or a boiler. Liquid heat (from the hot water) is transferred to the air and then distributed through a duct system by a blower.

Note
> Combination water heaters are practical mostly in new construction or where a boiler or furnace must be replaced.

Water Heater Construction Details

The automatic controls, fuel-burning equipment (gas burners, oil burner, and so on), and venting system found on a water heater will depend on the type of fuel used and certain other variables. These components are described in detail in appropriate sections of this chapter and elsewhere in the book.

The direct-fired automatic storage water heater is the most commonly used heater in residences. Certain construction details of these heaters remain essentially the same regardless of the type of controls or fuel-burning equipment.

Principal among these are the following:

1. Water storage tanks
2. Tank fittings
3. Dip tubes
4. Anodes
5. Valves

Water Storage Tanks

The tank of a water heater provides storage space for the hot water and also serves as a heat transfer surface. The design and construction of the tank must be strong enough to withstand at least 300 pounds per square inch without leakage or structural deformation.

Corrosion is a major problem in water heater storage tanks. One successful method of reducing corrosion has been to provide steel tanks with glass linings. Older water heater tanks will be found with copper or stone (Portland cement) linings, but these are becoming increasingly rare.

Glass-lined tanks are also equipped with a sacrificial magnesium anode rod, as shown in Figure 4-14. The corrosion process attacks the metal anode rod first, rather than the metal of the tank walls. The anode rod should be removed and replaced before decomposition occurs.

The operating life of a storage tank is directly related to the temperature of the stored water when it is over 140°F. The rule-of-thumb is that each 20° rise above 140°F will reduce tank life by 40 percent.

Figure 4-14   Sacrificial anode installation in a residential water heater tank. *(Courtesy Robertshaw Controls Co.)*

Tank Fittings

Figures 4-15 and 4-16 illustrate the various fittings required on both domestic and commercial water heaters.

Each tank should have fittings for hot-water outlet and cold-water inlet connections. These water connections generally consist of threaded spuds welded into openings in the tank.

A fitting is also provided in the top of most tanks for the insertion of the sacrificial anode. Other fittings provide for the use of immersion thermostats, immersion automatic gas shutoff devices, drain cocks, pressure and temperature relief valves, and dip tubes.

Dip Tubes

Some water heaters are designed so that the cold-water inlet is at the top of the tank. Because this is also the location of the hot-water supply outlet, there will be an excessive mixing of the cold water with the hot water unless provisions are made to keep the two separated. A *dip tube* is used for this purpose.

As shown in Figure 4-17, a dip tube is an extension of the cold-water supply pipe and is used to direct the cold water to the bottom

Figure 4-15 Typical water heater fittings. *(Courtesy Robertshaw Controls Co.)*

IMMERSION
AUTOMATIC SHUTOFF
FITTING

IMMERSION
THERMOSTAT
FITTING

DRAIN COCK
FITTING

HOT-WATER
OUTLET

COLD-WATER
INLET

Figure 4-16   Commercial water heater fittings with low-level cold-water inlets. *(Courtesy Robertshaw Controls Co.)*

of the tank. On older water heaters, dip tubes were made of metal. Now they are generally made from a high-density, temperature-resistant plastic. In all water heaters, the water at the top of the tank during cycling and intermittent standby conditions is always warmer than the water at the bottom of the tank. If the dip tube is too short, the cold water will mix with the water at the top of the tank and reduce the temperature of the hot-water supply to an unacceptable level. On the other hand, a dip tube that is too long will create an excessive water variation between the top of the tank and the lower thermostat control level. The dip tube must be of sufficient length to avoid both these conditions.

Each dip tube is provided with a small hole near the top of the tank, which functions as an antisiphon device. Sometimes it is possible for a malfunction to close off the cold-water supply while the hot water continues to be removed from the tank. Were it not for the antisiphon hole, the water would be drawn to the bottom

Figure 4-17   Dip tube and antisiphon hole. *(Courtesy Robertshaw Controls Co.)*

of the dip tube, a dangerously low water level for the tank. The siphon action is broken when the water reaches the level of the antisiphon hole, and the hot water will not be drawn below this level.

Anodes

The inside surface of a domestic hot-water tank is covered with a coating to protect the steel from corrosion. Sometimes, because of a production error, a very small part of the surface may remain uncoated and subject to corrosion. If another metal with less resistance to corrosion than steel is inserted into the tank, the corrosion will attack it instead of the exposed steel surface on the tank wall.

Metal rods called *anodes* are used to protect the walls of the water storage tank from corrosion. They are made from either magnesium or aluminum formed around a steel wire core. Because both of these metals have less resistance to corrosion than steel, corrosion will attack them instead of the exposed steel. In other words, they sacrifice themselves to the electrolytic process. For this reason, anodes are sometimes called *sacrificial anodes*.

An anode rod is installed by screwing it into the top of the water storage tank. It can be unscrewed, removed, inspected, and replaced by a new rod. A residential water tank will have one or two anode rods depending on the life of the warranty. Two rods are used in tanks with 12-year warranties. One rod is used if the warranty is half as long. Water storage tanks used in commercial systems will have anywhere from one to six anode rods.

Note
> All the anode rods used in a tank must be made of the same metal. Otherwise, some will corrode faster than others.

Valves

Three types of valves are used with domestic hot-water heaters: temperature and pressure relief valves, vacuum relief valves, and water-tempering valves. These valves are used to prevent damage to the water heater from excessively high pressures, temperatures, or vacuum conditions. They also protect the user from personal injury.

Safety Relief Valves

A relief valve for a domestic hot-water supply heater is an emergency safety device. If properly installed, it allows water to escape and spill out when excessive pressure, dangerously high temperature, or both conditions are present in the water storage tank.

It is important to understand the relationship between excessive pressure and high temperature for the safe operation of a hot-water heater. Ignorance of this relationship may result in an explosion severe enough to cause tragic loss of life and extensive property damage. The two principal causes of hot-water storage tank explosions are (1) water in the tank at an excessively high temperature, and (2) a physical weakness of the tank caused by a defect, age, corrosion, or general deterioration.

Water under pressure (greater than atmospheric pressure) can be heated above 212°F and still not boil (see Figure 4-18). As shown in Figure 4-18, the pressure in the tank will rise as it is heated because of thermal expansion. Such pressure cannot be relieved by backing into the main if the cold water is blocked by a check valve or other devices. If there is a failure in the heating-control device, the water in the tank will continue to heat beyond 212°F, and the superheated water will immediately flash into steam when a rupture occurs in the storage tank. Such action instantaneously converts 1 cubic inch of water into 1 cubic foot of steam with explosive force. This tremendous steam-flash explosive force can shoot water heaters, much like a jet-propelled rocket, through floors and roofs, burst foundations, destroy property, and cause serious or fatal injuries (see Figure 4-19).

Tests have shown that even though water pressure is raised above the normal safe tank limit, the worst that can happen is for the tank to rupture and cause water damage. When heat is applied, however, the tank becomes a potential hazard because of the steam-flash explosive possibilities. Protection against this danger can be obtained by the proper installation of suitable pressure and temperature relief valves. No water heater can operate safely without these safety relief valves.

A pressure relief valve is designed to prevent excessive pressure from developing in the hot-water heater storage tank (see Figure 4-20). This is exclusively a safety device and is not intended for use as a regulating valve to control or regulate the flow pressure. This type of valve starts to open at the set pressure and requires a certain

Figure 4-18   Boiling points of water at various pressures.

(Courtesy A. W. Cash Valve Manufacturing Co.)

Figure 4-19 Explosive power of superheated water.
(Courtesy A. W. Cash Valve Manufacturing Co.)

percentage of overpressure to open fully. As the pressure drops, it starts to close and shuts at approximately the set pressure.

A temperature relief valve is used to prevent excessively high water temperature from developing in the hot-water heater storage tank. A temperature relief valve may be a separate unit or combined in the same housing with a pressure relief valve to form a combination temperature and pressure relief valve (see Figure 4-21).

Water heater pressure and temperature relief valves must be installed in accordance with AGA, UL, or FHA standard safety requirements. Furthermore, the pressure and temperature relief valve should be constructed and located in conformance with current American National Standard (Z21.22) listing requirements. The manufacturer's recommendations for locating the valve on the storage tank should also be followed. *Never* reuse a relief valve if the water heater is being replaced. Always be sure to use the capacity relief valve recommended by the manufacturer for the installation.

A pressure and temperature relief valve is basically a pressure relief valve with an added temperature-sensing element thermostat located at the inlet of the valve to prevent overheating or explosive dangers. The temperature-sensing element must be immersed in the water within the top 6 inches of the tank (see Figures 4-22, 4-23, and 4-24). This location is required for the immersion element because the hottest water will occupy this portion of the tank.

The basic components of both a pressure relief valve and a combination pressure and temperature relief valve are shown in Figures 4-25 and 4-26. Note the position of the temperature-sensing element

Figure 4-20 Pressure relief (only) valve used
to protect hot-water supply systems from excessive pressure.

(Courtesy A. W. Cash Valve Manufacturing Co.)

thermostat. When the water in the top of the tank approaches the
danger zone (210°F), the thermostat expands and lifts the valve disc
from the seat, allowing hot water to escape and cooler water to
replace it in the tank. A decrease of less than 10° in the water temperature causes the thermostat to contract and allows the loading
spring to reseat the valve, thus maintaining a supply of hot water at
all times.

Figure 4-21 Combination pressure and temperature relief valve. *(Courtesy A. W. Cash Valve Manufacturing Co.)*

Figure 4-22 Direct side tapping. *(Courtesy Watts Regulator Co.)*

If a combination pressure and temperature relief valve is used, it should be installed in a separate tapping in the top of the hot-water storage tank (see Figure 4-24). If a separate tapping is not available, then the valve should be installed in the hot-water discharge line to

Figure 4-23 Direct top tapping.
(Courtesy Watts Regulator Co.)

the fixture outlets at a point as close to the tank as possible (see Figure 4-24).

The relief valve should be installed in the upper end of a tee, the lower end of which is connected to the tapping in the top of the hot-water storage tank by means of a closed nipple. The hot-water supply line to the fixture outlets is then connected to the branch of the tee as shown in Figure 4-24. If the relief valve is located in the hot-water supply line to the fixtures at a distance greater than 4 inches from the storage tank, excessive temperatures generated within the tank may result in serious damage before the excessive temperature is communicated through the water and piping to the relief valve. The possibility of this situation arising can be avoided by selecting a valve with a temperature-sensing element that is long enough to extend into the top 6 inches of the tank.

Figure 4-24 Relief valve installed in hot-water discharge line.
(Courtesy Watts Regulator Co.)

Figure 4-25 Principal components of a pressure relief valve.
(Courtesy Robertshaw Controls Co.)

A temperature relief valve must be installed so that the temperature-sensing element is in contact with hot water in the top 6 inches of the tank. This is a necessary safety precaution because of a condition called *temperature lag*, that is, the condition of temperature variation between the hottest water in the top of the tank and water temperature at varying distances away from the actual tank tapping (see Figure 4-27). When the average temperature in the top 6 to 8 inches is 210°F, there will be a considerable temperature lag (under no-flow conditions) at varying distances away from the tank. For example, a temperature of 191°F can be found at a point even with the top of the tank. At 4 inches above the top of the tank, the temperature has dropped off to 170°F. Taking these conditions into account, then, it becomes clear why relief valves with extension-type temperature-sensing elements are recommended. The temperature-sensing element must reach down to the point at which the highest water temperature occurs.

Where *separate* pressure and temperature relief valves are used, the temperature relief valve should be installed in the top of the

MANUAL
RELIEF LEVER

TO
DRAIN

PISTON

SEAL

SENSOR PROBE

WAX FILL

Figure 4-26   Principal components of a pressure and temperature relief valve. *(Courtesy Robertshaw Controls Co.)*

hot-water storage tank or as close as possible to the tank in the hot-water supply line to the fixtures as previously described, and the pressure relief valve should be installed in the cold-water supply line at a point as close to the hot-water storage tank as possible.

The rated capacity of temperature relief valves (in Btu/h) should equal or exceed the input capacity of the hot-water heater (also expressed in Btu/h). Both the pressure and temperature steam ratings should be listed on the side of the valve (see Figure 4-28).

Typical piping connections for an automatic storage water heater are shown in Figure 4-29. A two-temperature capability is provided by feeding the hot water directly to the appliances. A balancing valve is installed in the cold-water line to the tempering valve to compensate for pressure drop through the heater. Because the tempering valve cannot compensate for rapid pressure fluctuations, a pressure equalizing valve should be installed where the system is subjected to water-pressure fluctuations.

Figure 4-27 Temperature distribution under no-flow conditions (temperature lag). *(Courtesy A. W. Cash Valve Manufacturing Co)*

Figure 4-28 Rating of a typical pressure and temperature relief valve. *(Courtesy Watts Regulator Co.)*

Figure 4-29   Automatic storage water heater piping connections.

(Courtesy Watts Regulator Co.)

Figure 4-30 illustrates the piping connections for large-size instantaneous heat exchanger or converter heater applications. If either leg of the circulator is valved off from the heater, an ASME pressure relief valve must be installed.

Tankless heater piping connections are shown in Figure 4-31. As in other installations, a balancing valve has been installed in the cold-water line to the tempering valve to compensate for pressure drop.

Vacuum Relief Valve

A vacuum relief valve is used to protect a hot-water supply system by preventing vacuum conditions that could drain the system by siphonage, burn out the water heater, or cause the storage tank to collapse (see Figure 4-32).

The vacuum relief valve is installed in the cold-water supply line. It closes tightly under system pressure and opens quickly in case of emergency at less than ½-inch vacuum. When the valve opens, atmosphere is admitted and breaks the vacuum, preventing siphonage of the system and the possible collapse of the storage tank.

Water-Tempering Valves

A *water-tempering valve* (see Figure 4-33) is used in a hot-water supply system to provide domestic hot water at temperatures

Figure 4-30 Typical piping connections for large instantaneous heat exchanger or converter-type heater applications. *(Courtesy Watts Regulator Co.)*

Figure 4-31 Tankless heater piping connections. *(Courtesy Watts Regulator Co.)*

Figure 4-32   Vacuum relief valve used to protect hot-water supply systems from internal vacuum conditions. *(Courtesy A. W. Cash Valve Manufacturing Co.)*

Figure 4-33   Typical water-tempering valve. *(Courtesy Watts Regulator Co.)*

considerably lower than those of the water in the supply mains. These valves are especially recommended for larger hot-water supply systems requiring dependable control of the water temperature at the fixture outlets.

A water-tempering valve is not designed to compensate for system-pressure fluctuations and should never be used where more sophisticated pressure-equalized temperature controls are required to provide antiscald performance. Water-tempering valves are described in greater detail in Chapter 10 of Volume 2 ("Steam and Hydronic Line Controls").

Gas-Fired Water Heaters

Gas-fired automatic storage water heaters are those in which the hot-water storage tank, the gas burner assembly, the combustion chamber and necessary insulation, and the automatic controls are combined in a single self-contained, prefabricated unit or package. Size limitations, resulting from the necessity of such heaters being readily portable, generally restrict the storage tank capacity to approximately 75 gallons.

In this type of water heater, the heat of the gas flame is transmitted to the water by direct conduction through the tank bottom and flue surfaces. Some heaters have multiple central flues, while in other designs the hot exhaust gases pass between the outer surfaces of the tank and the insulating jacket. In either case, these areas become radiating surfaces serving to dissipate the heat of the stored hot water to the flue or chimney when the burner is off. This is particularly true if the flue or chimney has a good natural draft.

The most commonly used gas-fired water heater is the underfeed type. If properly maintained, gas underfeed water heaters will have a long service life. They are generally inexpensive to purchase and install. The older gas underfeed models were not especially efficient, but design improvements, such as greater tank insulation and improved heat transfer surfaces, have improved their efficiency. Locating the gas burner and flue outside the storage tank has resulted in still another type of gas-fired water heater. These units (sometimes called *sidearm heaters*) provide indirect heating of the water, which allows the use of plastic-lined storage tanks and reduces standby losses.

Storage Capacity

The average ratio of hourly gas input to the storage capacity in gallons of water (for gas-fired automatic storage water heaters of the so-called rapid-recovery type) is such that the recovery (heating) capacity in gallons of water raised 100°F in one hour, in most instances, approximately equals the storage capacity of the tank in gallons.

Where the water must be raised 120°F, the recovery (heating) capacity in gallons per hour will be approximately 83 percent of the storage capacity in gallons.

Where the water must be raised 140°F, the recovery (heating) capacity in gallons per hour will be approximately 71 percent of the storage capacity in gallons.

Gas Burners

The burners used in gas-fired water heaters must be provided with inlet gas orifices and some means of air intake. These conditions are necessary to provide the required air-gas mixture for the flame. Beyond these two basic requirements, gas burners will vary widely in both design and construction. These variations in design and construction are generally concerned with providing good flame pattern and ignition. Flame characteristics are affected not only by the design of the ports (raised, drilled, ribbon, slotted, or flush) but also by their number, distribution, depth, and spacing. The gas input rating is an important factor in determining the number, distribution, and size of the ports. Proper spacing is generally determined by observation. Some common types of gas burners used on water heaters are shown in Figure 4-34.

The purpose of the gas orifice is to provide the proper input for the type of gas (for example, natural, LP) and the normal range of gas pressures. The gas passes into the mixing tube of the burner where it mixes with the air. Air is generally admitted through adjustable air shutters located around the gas orifice. The design and arrangement of the burner ports control the burning characteristics and distribution of the flame.

The size of the ports and their distribution affects the flame characteristics. If the ports are too large (both individually and in their distribution), the flame may flash back to the burner orifice. On the other hand, blowing flames can result from porting that is too small. As can be readily understood, good flame patterns are in part determined by proper porting. The number and size of ports necessary to give proper flame characteristics must be calculated.

Automatic Controls on Gas-Fired Water Heaters

The principal automatic controls used to govern the operation of a *gas-fired* water heater are as follows:

1. Thermostatic valve
2. Automatic pilot valve
3. Manual gas valves
4. Main gas–pressure regulator
5. Pilot gas–pressure regulator
6. Temperature and pressure relief valves
7. Automatic gas shutoff device
8. Pilot burner

Figure 4-34 Common types of gas burners used in water heaters.

(Courtesy Robertshaw Controls Co.)

A *thermostatic valve* (see Figures 4-35 and 4-36) is used to control the gas input to the burners in relation to the water temperature in the storage tank. Thermostatic water temperature controls are usually direct, snap-action bimetallic devices that react to a drop in the temperature of the water in the storage tank. This drop in temperature causes a thermal element immersed in the stored hot water to contract and, through mechanical linkage, to open the main gas valve on the unit. When the water in the tank reaches a selected, predetermined setting, the thermal element expands and closes the main gas valve. These thermostatic valves normally operate at a temperature differential of approximately 12°F. In other words, if set to shut off the gas to the main burner when the tank water temperature reaches 140°F, they will react to open the valve when the temperature drops to 128°F.

Figure 4-35 Principal thermostatic valve components.

(Courtesy Robertshaw Controls Co.)

Another important control on a *gas-fired* water heater is the *automatic pilot valve*, which operates on the thermocouple principle (see Figures 4-37 and 4-38). This control automatically shuts off the gas when pilot outage or improper ignition conditions occur. When the electromagnet is deenergized, the magnet allows the return spring to close the automatic pilot valve and shut off the gas supply to *both* the main burner and the pilot. The 100 percent automatic pilot shutoff condition is shown in Figure 4-39. As

Figure 4-36 Thermostatic valve operating principles.

(Courtesy Robertshaw Controls Co.)

Figure 4-37 Principal components of an automatic pilot system.

(Courtesy Robertshaw Controls Co.)

Figure 4-38 Typical thermocouple construction. *(Courtesy Robertshaw Controls Co.)*

shown in Figure 4-40, the reset button must be depressed while the pilot is being relit. If the flame is established, the pilot will continue to burn after the reset button is released (see Figure 4-41).

Manual gas valves (gas cocks) function as a backup safety system to the automatic pilot valve by providing manual control of the main burner and pilot burner gas supply (see Figure 4-42). The manual gas valve is also used with the automatic pilot valve to provide safe pilot lighting by ensuring that *only* pilot gas is flowing during the pilot lighting operation.

Both pilot gas– and main gas–pressure regulators are used on gas-fired water heaters. The *pilot gas–pressure regulator* is used to regulate the pressure of the gas flowing to the pilot. The *main gas–pressure regulator* performs the same function for gas flowing to the main burners. These gas-pressure controls have been mandatory on gas-fired water heaters since 1972.

Schematics of several types of pressure regulators used on water heaters are shown in Figures 4-42, 4-43, and 4-44. These devices

INLET

NO MAIN GAS

NO PILOT GAS

PILOT OUTAGE

RETURN SPRING
CLOSE VALVE

KEEPER

ELECTROMAGNET
DEENERGIZED

Figure 4-39 Automatic (100 percent) pilot shutoff condition.
(Courtesy Robertshaw Controls Co.)

operate on the balanced-pressure principle; that is to say, a main pressure diaphragm and a balancing diaphragm act to balance out or cancel the differences in inlet and outlet pressures caused by pressure variations.

Domestic gas water heater combination controls provide for main gas–pressure regulation by incorporating a pressure regulator in the control. Independent pilot gas–pressure regulation is optional (see *Combination Gas Controls* in this chapter).

The schematic of a Robertshaw pilot gas–pressure regulator is shown in Figure 4-45. This particular pressure regulator has the approximate diameter of a penny and is inserted downstream from the pilot filter.

The following three types of safety controls (individually or in combination) are also found on water heaters:

1. Automatic gas shutoff device

2. Pressure relief valve

3. Temperature relief valve

Figure 4-40 Automatic pilot valve reset button depressed while pilot is being lit. *(Courtesy Robertshaw Controls Co.)*

An *automatic gas shutoff device* is designed to shut off *all* gas to the water heater when excessively high water temperature conditions occur. In most automatic gas shutoff systems, this device operates in conjunction with the automatic pilot valve in the pilot safety shutoff circuit. The automatic shutoff device is generally set to shut off the automatic pilot valve when the water temperature in the storage tank approaches 210°F.

A typical automatic shutoff device, such as the one shown in Figure 4-46, is mounted on the tank surface so as to sense the water temperature through the tank wall. These devices are normally closed electrical switches connected in series in the automatic pilot millivolt circuit. When the switch reaches its preset temperature limit, it snaps open and deenergizes the electromagnet of the automatic pilot valve. This allows the closure spring of the automatic pilot valve to close the valve. As a result, all gas is shut off to all burners (including the pilot burner).

When the water temperature becomes too high, the volume of water in the tank tends to expand. A *temperature relief valve* is

Figure 4-41 Pilot continues to burn after reset button is released. *(Courtesy Robertshaw Controls Co.)*

Figure 4-42 Diagram of a gas-cock parting. *(Courtesy Robertshaw Controls Co.)*

Figure 4-43 Principal components of a pilot gas–pressure regulator. *(Courtesy Robertshaw Controls Co.)*

Figure 4-44 Operating principles of a balanced-pressure regulator.

(Courtesy Robertshaw Controls Co.)

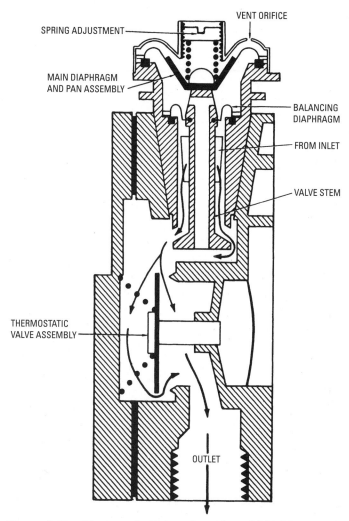

Figure 4-45 Diagram of a Robertshaw Unitrol R11OR series water heater control incorporating a balanced-pressure regulator.

(Courtesy Robertshaw Controls Co.)

designed to release a portion of the water and at the same time introduce cold water to reduce the temperature of the remaining water. The temperature relief function must occur at or below 210°F on residential and commercial water heaters.

Figure 4-46 Automatic gas shutoff device installation.
(Courtesy Robertshaw Controls Co.)

The purpose of a *pressure relief valve* is to release a portion of the water from the heater or hot-water heating system when excessive pressure conditions occur. Pressure and temperature relief valves are used on *all* types of tank water heaters *regardless* of the fuel used to heat the water. See *Relief Valves* in this chapter.

The pilot burner gas supply is taken off ahead of the gas valve in the thermostatic control. Pilots are usually of the safety type, functioning to shut off the gas supply if the pilot burner flame is extinguished.

Most of the control functions described in the preceding paragraphs can be combined in a single unit or combination gas control (see next section).

Combination Gas Valve

A *combination gas valve* (or *combination gas control*) combines in a single unit all the automatic and manual control functions necessary to govern the operation of a gas-fired water heater.

A typical combination gas valve is shown in Figures 4-47 and 4-48. This particular unit contains a water heater thermostat (thermostatic valve), automatic pilot valve, automatic gas shutoff device, main gas–pressure regulator, pilot gas–pressure regulator, and manual valve (gas cock).

The installation instructions included with most combination gas valves are usually very complete and should cover the following points:

1. Disassembly and assembly instructions
2. Automatic shutoff valve and magnet replacement
3. Gas-cock lubrication
4. Thermostatic valve cleaning instructions
5. Pressure-regulator adjustment
6. Thermostat calibration
7. Lighting procedure
8. Test procedure

Figure 4-47 Robertshaw Unitrol R110RTP combination gas valve.
(Courtesy Robertshaw Controls Co.)

Figure 4-48 Exploded view of a Robertshaw Unitrol R110RTP combination gas valve.

(Courtesy Robertshaw Controls Co.)

REGULATOR ADJUSTMENT CAP

COMBINATION GAS COCK & PRESSURE REGULATOR NAT. GAS OR L.P. GAS

SCREW (1)

RETAINING SCREWS (2)

GAS COCK SPRING

SET BUTTON RETAINER ASSEMBLY

SHANK ASSEMBLY

SCREWS (4)

E.C.O. SWITCH TERMINAL

LEVER

BODY

PRESSURE PLUG

*50650 AUTOMATIC PILOT VALVE AND MAGNET ASSEMBLY

*50655 TERMINAL RETAINER

PILOT REGULATOR GASKET

VALVE ASSEMBLY

PILOT FILTER

BODY GASKET

COVER

SCREW (4)

DIAL

STOP ADJUSTMENT NUT

TEMP. ADJ. SCREW

STOP

PILOT REGULATOR ASSEMBLY NAT. GAS OR L.P. GAS

PILOT REGULATOR RETAINING SPRING

Most control manufacturers provide test kits to test the operation of the thermocouple, thermomagnet, and automatic safety shutoff device. The test kit consists of a millivolt meter and an adapter for testing the thermomagnet (see Figure 4-49).

As shown in Figure 4-50, the manual valve (gas cock) is used when lighting the pilot. The gas-cock dial (1) is turned to the *off* position and at least 5 minutes is allowed to pass. This should be sufficient time for any gas that has accumulated in the burner compartment to escape. The gas-cock dial is then turned to the *start* position, and the set button (2) is depressed while the burner is being lit (see Figure 4-51). The standby flame is allowed to burn for approximately ½ minute before the reset button is released (see Figure 4-52). Unless there is a problem, the burner should stay lit after the reset button has been released. After releasing the reset button, turn the gas-cock dial to the *on* position and turn the temperature dial (3) to the desired setting.

The combination valve shown in Figure 4-53 does not use a reset button in the lighting procedure. The upper dial is turned counterclockwise to the *pilot* position and held against the spring-loaded stop until the pilot burner lights. After the pilot burner burns for about 30 to 60 seconds, the upper dial is turned clockwise to *on* for automatic control. The lower dial is then set for the desired water temperature.

Figure 4-49 Typical testing procedure with millivolt meter and adapter. *(Courtesy Robertshaw Controls Co.)*

Figure 4-50 Pilot lighting procedure. *(Courtesy Robertshaw Controls Co.)*

Figure 4-51 Standby flame pattern. *(Courtesy Robertshaw Controls Co.)*

FLAME DIRECTED FROM INNER PORT
ON THERMOCOUPLE HOT JUNCTION

Figure 4-52 Full-input flame pattern. *(Courtesy Robertshaw Controls Co.)*

Installation and Operation of Gas-Fired Water Heaters

The installation and operation of a gas-fired automatic storage water heater involves little possibility of error if the instructions of the manufacturer are strictly followed and due consideration is given to the following factors:

1. Location
2. Venting regulations
3. Water heater venting system
4. Size of flue pipe
5. Runs of flue pipe
6. Gas meter
7. Gas supply line
8. Hot-water circulation methods
9. Safety relief valves
10. Building and safety code provisions
11. Lighting and operating instructions

Figure 4-53   ITT General Controls water heater control.
(Courtesy ITT General Controls)

Location

The heater should be located at a point convenient to the flue or chimney and, if possible, at a point approximately equidistant from all hot-water outlets.

Venting Regulations

Many building codes prohibit connecting appliances to a common flue or chimney with coal- or oil-fired equipment. Where regulations do not require venting of gas-fired equipment to a separate flue and it is vented to a common flue with coal- or oil-fired units, the flue pipe of the gas-fired water heater or other appliance should be connected to the chimney at a point *above* the flue pipe from the coal- or oil-fired equipment.

When possible, a separate hole in the chimney should be used for the water heater flue. If this is not possible, join the flue from the water heater and the flue from the heating boiler (or furnace) with a Y connection (*never* a T connection) and install a separate draft regulator for each unit.

When the chimney cannot handle the combined input of both the water heater and the heating plant, wire the two so that they do not operate simultaneously.

Water Heater Venting Systems

The venting system of a fuel-fired water heater is designed to transfer the products of combustion to the outdoors. By transferring these potentially harmful gases outside the structure, the living spaces are maintained free of any possible air contamination. Electric water heaters do not require venting systems.

A typical venting system for a fuel-fired water heater consists of the following basic components:

1. Heater flues or heat exchangers

2. Draft diverter

3. Vent pipe connections

The design and arrangement of a venting system should take advantage of the natural tendency of hot gases to rise. These flue gases are a waste by-product of the combustion process. Because they are hot gases, they are lighter than the surrounding ambient air, and they tend to rise in a vertical path. The venting system should provide essentially a vertical path to take advantage of this natural vertical flow of the gases. The vent pipes should be of sufficient diameter to carry the volume of gas without restricting its natural flow rate.

Excessive cooling of the flue gases can be avoided by providing a controlled mixture of dilutant air from the draft diverter. If the flue gases cool, condensation will occur, the gases will grow heavier, and it will be impossible to maintain draft. The same condition (that is, excessive cooling) will occur if the vents are unusually long or high. This can be minimized by insulating the vent pipes.

Fans are used on some high-input water heaters to supplement natural venting. The use of a fan is sometimes referred to as *power venting*, and the water heaters are referred to as *power-vent water heaters*. In most cases where a fan is used, proper venting can generally be obtained from a smaller-diameter vent pipe. However, some provision should be made to automatically shut off the water heater in case of a fan failure. Fan-assisted venting allows the use of much longer horizontal or vertical flue pipes than would ordinarily be the case. As a result, the water heater can be located anywhere in the structure. On the downside, the fan and water heater are electrically operated, and a power failure will shut down the unit.

Vent pipe connections are often made directly to the outdoors or through a chimney wall. When direct venting is the case, the vent pipe connects to a vent outlet hood.

Draft hoods are used on all water heaters that rely on natural vent action to eliminate contaminating flue gases. The draft hood should contain an inlet and outlet opening for the flue gases, and an air dilutant intake and relief opening to relieve downdraft conditions.

Examples of common types of draft hoods used on gas-fired water heaters are shown in Figure 4-54. The vertical draft hood is usually the most efficient for venting.

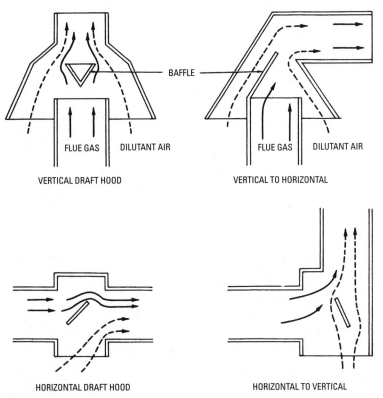

Figure 4-54   Draft hoods commonly used on water heaters.

A well-designed draft hood should be able to prevent excessive updraft in the burner compartment and momentary excessive downdraft conditions. Sometimes the flow rate of flue gases suddenly increases and results in an excessive updraft condition in the burner compartment. The amount of air flowing into the flue through the air dilutant intake is clearly insufficient to control the condition. The diverter should be designed to allow an increase in air intake during excessive updraft conditions so that the weight of the flue gases is increased and the flow rate slowed.

When downdraft conditions occur, the baffles and relief opening in the draft hood allow the downdraft to be relieved *outside* the flue so that the burner flame is unaffected. This expulsion of the combustion by-products through the air intake is only a *momentary* condition.

Size of Flue Pipe
The size of the flue pipe should not be less than that specified by the manufacturer or that shown in available tables for the rated gas input.

Flue Pipe Run
Horizontal runs of the flue pipe should pitch upward toward the chimney connection and should run as directly as possible, avoiding unnecessary bends or elbows. The backdraft diverter supplied by the manufacturer or other approved draft hood of adequate size should be employed.

Gas Meter
The gas meter must be of adequate size or capacity to supply not only the requirements of the water heater but also the requirements of all other gas-fired equipment.

Gas Supply Line
The gas supply line to the water heater should be adequate in size to supply the full rated gas input of the heater at the available pressure, taking into consideration the pressure drop through the supply line. A separate gas supply line from the meter to the water heater should be employed if the existing line from the meter is too small to supply the combined requirements of the water heater and other equipment or appliances that may be connected to it.

Safety Relief Valves
Both a pressure relief valve and a temperature relief valve are used to ensure the safe operation of a water heater. The operating characteristics of these two safety relief valves have already been described (see *Safety Relief Valves* in this chapter).

Hot-Water Circulating Methods

If a building circulation loop is employed to maintain circulation of the hot-water supply throughout the building for the purpose of making the hot water more readily available at each fixture, the return line from the circulating loop should be connected to the cold-water supply line of the heater. A swing-check valve *must* be installed in a horizontal section of the return line at a point as close to its connection to the cold-water supply line as possible to prevent the possibility of backflow of cold water to the hot-water outlets of fixtures that may be connected to the circulation loop at a location that may be closer to the cold-water supply line than to the water heater.

If a check valve were not employed, and the pressure drop in the line between the cold-water supply line and the hot-water outlet were less than the pressure drop in the line between the heater and the hot-water outlet, cold water could flow to the hot-water outlet.

Where a circulating pump is employed to accelerate the circulation in a building hot-water supply loop, it should be installed in the return water line at a point as close to its connection to the cold-water supply line as possible. To eliminate the unnecessary wear and expense incidental to operating a circulating pump continuously, it should be controlled by a direct aquastat installed in the return circulating line at a point conveniently close to the pump.

It is suggested that this aquastat be adjusted to close the pump circuit when the water in the return line drops to (or below) 100° to 110°F and break the pump circuit when the water temperature at that point rises to approximately 120° to 130°F if the desired hot-water temperature at the fixture is approximately 130° to 140°F.

Building and Safety Code Requirements

The building and safety codes of certain states require the use of dip tubes in the hot-water storage tanks of automatic storage water heaters or recovery water heating systems, while other codes prohibit their use.

The apparent purpose of code provisions prohibiting the use of cold-water supply dip tubes in the tanks of underfired storage water heaters is to prevent the possibility of developing dangerously excessive temperatures and pressures in the tank of the gas supply to a *manually* controlled heater (if not turned off) or the safety control of an automatic water heater that fails to function.

Under such circumstances, the water in the tank would drain to the levels of the holes drilled in the dip tubes close to the top of the dip tube before the siphon action would be broken.

The water remaining in the tank, being practically at zero pressure, would vaporize rapidly if automatic temperature and safety controls failed to function or the gas supply were not shut off. The steam thus generated in the remaining space in the upper portion of the tank would create a personal scalding hazard if communicated to the hot-water supply piping and outlets, or could attain sufficient pressure to rupture the tank or piping.

An equally hazardous condition would be created if the tank of a storage heater not equipped with a cold-water supply dip tube were completely drained.

Under this condition, if the gas supply to a manually controlled heater were not shut off, or the thermostatic and safety controls of an automatic heater failed to function with the gas valve in the thermostat in the open position, explosive pressures would be almost instantaneously developed if cold water were introduced into the empty heater tank.

To avoid such hazards, the gas supply to either a manually controlled or automatic storage water heater should always be shut off before draining the tank of the heater or the entire hot-water supply system.

Where the use of a cold-water dip tube installed in a tapping in the top and extending to a point close to the bottom of the hot-water storage tank is prohibited, the cold-water supply line should be connected to a tapping as close to the bottom as possible.

If the cold water enters the tank at a point considerably above the bottom, the water below that point will be in a more or less static state, which may be conducive to more rapid deposition of lime or other scale on the tank bottom.

Lime or other scale on the tank bottom retards the transfer of heat to the water if the heater is of the underfired type, which impairs its efficiency.

Lighting and Operating Instructions

Lighting and operating instructions are supplied by the manufacturer and should be read and thoroughly understood before attempting to adjust the rate of gas input and the thermostat or other automatic controls, particularly if the serviceperson is not completely familiar with the design and construction of such controls.

Before leaving the premises, it is imperative that the serviceperson hang the operating instructions at a point convenient to the heater where it will be available for ready reference whenever needed by the owner or operating personnel.

The return warranty registration card, if provided, should also be properly filled in by the serviceperson and handed to the owner for mailing to the manufacturer. In many instances, warranty provisions are invalidated if the registration card is not returned to the manufacturer.

Installation and Maintenance Checklist

The water temperature control in a residential water heater should be set as low as possible and still provide satisfactory hot water at the faucets. This adjustment for low water temperature prolongs

Install pressure and temperature relief valves per instructions on heater.

Relief opening must be kept clear of obstructions.

HOT WATER OUTLET

Check anode rod for deterioration. Replace if magnesium dissipated.

GAS LINE
Use clean deburred pipe.
Proper thread size.
Avoid excessive lubrication.
Avoid excessive penetration of valve.
Install upstream shut off valve.
Check all joints for leaks - correct as necessary.

Check for leaks with soap or leak detecting fluid.
DO NOT USE FLAME

Install drip leg to catch scale, dirt and oil.

Check thermocouple and E.C.O. connections (Internal or remote E.C.O.).

Check for presence of E.C.O. device (AGA requirement).

Recommend water heater location so that controls are not exposed to moisture.

Check for proper flue size and connection to outside vent. Refer to local codes.

Install cold water inlet shut off valve upstream of connecting union.

INLET—if sweat connection do not heat check for presence of dip tube.

Check clearances to walls per applicable codes and requirements.

Check for proper updraft while operating.

Read and follow lighting instructions explicitly.

Turn temperature dial to cycle off. Check if main burner shuts off.

ADJUST PILOT FLAME.

Drain water until clear—once a month.

CHECK OUTLET PRESSURE

Be sure pilot and thermocouple are properly positioned as recommended and firmly in place.

Check automatic pilot operation.

Adjust air shutters if so equipped for blue gas flame.

Check codes for air availability requirements.

Figure 4-55 Water heater service guide. *(Courtesy Robertshaw Controls Co.)*

the life of the tank and prevents stacking. The temperature dial is adjustable and should be used to meet varying conditions and requirements. For control maintenance, it is best to call a qualified serviceperson. Instructions in the manufacturer's field information bulletin should be followed when servicing or repairing water heater controls. Figure 4-55 provides a general checklist for water heater installation and maintenance.

Troubleshooting Gas-Fired Water Heaters

Table 4-1 covers many of the more common symptoms and possible causes of operating problems associated with gas-fired water heaters.

Table 4-1   Troubleshooting Gas-Fired Water Heaters

Symptom and Possible Cause	Possible Remedy
Water too hot.	
(a) Thermostat setting too high.	(a) Set thermostat lower.
(b) Leaking thermostat valve.	(b) Clean valve or replace.
(c) Pilot too high.	(c) Adjust pilot lower.
(d) Thermostat out of calibration.	(d) Recalibrate or replace thermostat.
(e) Pilot outage.	(e) Set thermostat lower and reignite pilot.
Not enough hot water or water temperature too low.	
(a) Thermostat setting too low.	(a) Set thermostat higher. Caution: Do not set thermostat higher than 120°F.
(b) Thermostat out of calibration.	(b) Recalibrate or replace thermostat.
(c) Undersized heater for hot-water demand.	(c) Replace with larger heater.
(d) Clogged burner orifice.	(d) Inspect and clean.
(e) Undersized burner orifice.	(e) Change orifice to correct size.
(f) Gas pressure too low.	(f) Readjust regulator (if so equipped); check gas supply pressure and manifold pressure.
(g) Clogged flue.	(g) Inspect and clean.

(continued)

Table 4-1 (continued)

Symptom and Possible Cause	Possible Remedy
(h) Draft venting problem.	(h) Check for downdraft and updraft venting and correct as required; check for any drafts blowing out pilot light.
(i) Defective thermostat.	(i) Replace thermostat.
(j) Gas control problem.	(j) Inspect and replace.
(k) Defective dip tube.	(k) Replace dip tube.

No hot water.

(a) No gas supply to burner.	(a) Turn on gas supply.
(b) Pilot out.	(b) See *Failure to Ignite* and *Pilot Will Not Stay Lit.*

Delayed or slow hot-water recovery.

(a) Clogged flue.	(a) Clean flue chamber.
(b) Incorrect gas pressure.	(b) Check gas pressure and adjust.
(c) Clogged burner orifice.	(c) Inspect, clean, or replace as necessary.
(d) Excessive drafts.	(d) Locate and eliminate drafts.

Burner flame too high.

(a) Pressure regulator set too high.	(a) Reset.
(b) Defective regulator.	(b) Replace.
(c) Burner orifice too large.	(c) Replace with correct size.

Noisy burner flame.

(a) Too much primary air.	(a) Check and adjust.
(b) Noisy pilot.	(b) Reduce pilot gas.
(c) Burr in orifice.	(c) Remove burr or replace orifice.
(d) Dirty burner orifice.	(d) Inspect and clean.

Yellow-tipped burner flame.

(a) Too little primary air.	(a) Check and adjust.
(b) Dirty burner orifice.	(b) Inspect and clean.
(c) Misaligned burner orifices.	(c) Realign.
(d) Clogged draft hood.	(d) Clean.

Table 4-I *(continued)*

Symptom and Possible Cause	Possible Remedy
Floating burner flame.	
(a) Blocked venting or clogged flue.	(a) Inspect and clean.
(b) Insufficient primary or secondary air.	(b) Increase air supply; adjust air shutters.
(c) Incorrect orifice.	(c) Install correct orifice.
Delayed ignition.	
(a) Improper pilot location.	(a) Reposition pilot.
(b) Pilot flame too small.	(b) Check orifices; clean; increase pilot gas.
(c) Burner ports clogged near pilot.	(c) Clean ports.
(d) Low pressure.	(d) Adjust pressure regulator.
Unable to ignite pilot.	
(a) Gas supply off.	(a) Open manual valve to turn on gas supply.
(b) Thermostat out of calibration.	(b) Recalibrate, repair, or replace.
(c) Defective thermocouple and/or automatic pilot valve.	(c) Check and replace.
(d) Loose thermocouple connection.	(d) Check and tighten connection.
(e) Defective safety magnet assembly.	(e) Check magnet and replace gas valve.
(f) Gas-cock knob dial set incorrectly.	(f) Check lighting instructions and set gas-cock knob to correct position.
(g) Clogged pilot burner orifice.	(g) Clean or replace.
(h) Air in gas line.	(h) Purge air from line.
(i) Defective gas valve.	(i) Replace gas valve.
(j) Clogged pilot tube.	(j) Clean or replace.
(k) Pinched pilot tube.	(k) Repair or replace.
Burner will not turn off.	
(a) Thermostat set too high.	(a) Lower setting.
(b) Thermostat out of calibration.	(b) Recalibrate or replace.
(c) Dirt on thermostat valve seat.	(c) Clean or replace.
(d) Defective thermostat.	(d) Replace thermostat.

(continued)

Table 4-1 *(continued)*

Symptom and Possible Cause	Possible Remedy
Pilot will not stay lit.	
(a) Too much primary air.	(a) Check and adjust pilot shutter.
(b) Dirt in pilot orifice.	(b) Open orifice.
(c) Clogged flue.	(c) Clean flue way.
(d) Draft venting problem.	(d) Check downdraft and updraft venting and correct as required; check for any drafts blowing out pilot light.
(e) Too much draft.	(e) Provide shielding or reduce draft.
(f) Defective safety magnet assembly.	(f) Check magnet and replace gas valve.
(g) Automatic pilot magnet valve defective.	(g) Replace.
(h) Loose thermocouple connection.	(h) Tighten connection.
(i) Defective thermocouple.	(i) Replace.
(j) Thermocouple tip out of pilot flame.	(j) Move tip into flame.
(k) Incorrect pilot-gas adjustment.	(k) Adjust pilot gas.
(l) Incorrect pilot orifice size.	(l) Replace with correct size.
(m) Pilot burner orifice or supply tube partly clogged.	(m) Inspect and clean pilot burner and supply tube.
Main burner will not stay lit.	
(a) Clogged orifice.	(a) Clean or replace.
(b) Low gas pressure.	(b) Check gas supply pressure and correct.
(c) Pinched or damaged main burner gas supply tube.	(c) Repair or replace.
(d) Clogged main burner gas supply tube.	(d) Clean or replace.
(e) Defective magnetic assembly.	(e) Check and replace gas control valve.
(f) Defective thermocouple.	(f) Check and replace thermocouple.
(g) Loose thermocouple connection.	(g) Check and tighten connection or replace if connection damaged.

Table 4-1 *(continued)*

Symptom and Possible Cause	*Possible Remedy*
(h) Defective main valve.	(h) Replace gas control valve.
(i) Venting downdraft problem.	(i) Check and correct.
(j) Venting sizing problem.	(j) Check and correct.

Noisy water heater operation.

(a) Scale or sediment at bottom of tank.	(a) Clean tank.
(b) Loose baffles.	(b) Reset and tighten.

Excessive temperature/pressure relief valve operation.

(a) Excessive temperature.	(a) Lower temperature setting. If problem continues, check for grounded element and correct as necessary; replace defective thermostat.
(b) Excessive water pressure.	(b) Install specified pressure-reducing valve on cold intake side.

Rusty, black, or brown water.

(a) Excessive sediment accumulation in tank.	(a) Drain and clean tank, or replace if necessary.
(b) Elements covered with scale.	(b) Clean or replace elements.
(c) Dissolved anode rod.	(c) Replace anode rod.

Water below gas water heater (drops of water or puddles on floor).

(a) Normal condition for gas water heaters if drops of water or small puddles dry up.	(a) Ignore.
(b) Small pinhole leak in inner tank.	(b) Replace water heater.
(c) Loose immersion thermostat or anode rod.	(c) Tighten or replace.
(d) Defective joint at cold intake or hot outlet on tank.	(d) Inspect and repair as necessary.
(e) Defective temperature/pressure relief valve.	(e) Check and replace.

Figure 4-56 External (floating) tank oil-fired water heater.

(Courtesy National Oil Fuel Institute)

Figure 4-57 Internal flue oil-fired water heater.

(Courtesy National Oil Fuel Institute)

Oil-Fired Water Heaters

Most of the oil-fired heaters used in residences and small buildings are of the external, or floating, tank design (see Figure 4-56). The products of the combustion process pass upward through the flue passages located between the suspended hot-water storage tank and the outer walls of the water heater. Multiflue and internal flue oil-fired water heaters, though less common, are also used (see Figure 4-57).

As with gas-fired water heaters, an oil heater must have an adequate draft for proper combustion. Sometimes it is necessary to vent two oil-fired appliances (for example, furnace and water heater) into the same flue. When this situation occurs, the two can be connected to the flue either with a "Y" connection or in such a way that both feed directly into the flue (see Figure 4-58). When two oil-fired appliances, such as a furnace and a water heater, are connected to a single vent, the controls can be wired to prevent simultaneous operations and give priority to the water heater (see Figure 4-59).

Oil-fired water heater controls are similar to those used to control hot-water space-heating boilers. They are also designed to regulate the temperature of the water in the water heater storage tank. For example, the primary control shown in Figures 4-60 and 4-61 is used in conjunction with an immersion aquastat and a remote sensor (cadmium detection cell) to simultaneously regulate the water temperature and provide oil burner control. Both oil burner malfunctions and water temperatures that fall outside the rated temperature range of the heater will cause the primary control to start or stop the oil burner as conditions require.

Figure 4-58 Connecting the boiler and water heater flues to chimney.
(Courtesy National Oil Fuel Institute)

Figure 4-59 Wiring the water heater and heating plant so that they do not operate simultaneously. *(Courtesy National Oil Fuel Institute)*

Pressure and temperature relief valves are vital for the protection of the hot-water storage tank. These valves are described elsewhere in this chapter (see *Relief Valves*).

When adjusting an oil-fired water heater, always adjust for a smoke-free fire first, and then make the necessary adjustment for efficient operation.

TEMPERATURE
SET POINT KNOB

AQUASTAT TEMPERATURE
CONTROL (REPLACEABLE)

DIFFERENTIAL
ADJUSTMENT DIAL

RELAY (2K)

SWITCHING RELAY (1K)

TRANSFORMER

SAFETY SWITCH

WIRING TERMINALS

Figure 4-60   Honeywell R4166 combination water heater
and oil burner primary control. *(Courtesy Honeywell Tradeline Controls)*

Electric Water Heaters

Most electric water heaters used in residences are the automatic
storage type. Although some instantaneous heaters are in use, the
high electric power input required makes them uneconomical to
operate when compared with fuel-fired types.

An electric water heater generally consists of a vertical tank with
a primary heating element or resistor inserted near the bottom of
the tank. Some water heaters have a secondary heating element
located in the upper one-fourth of the tank (see Figure 4-62). The
number of heating elements used in the heater will depend on the size
of the storage tank. Large-capacity storage tanks will require two
heating elements.

The manual and thermostatic (automatic) controls are located
inside the storage tank. A water heater thermostat is designed to
automatically open or close the electrical circuit to the heating ele-
ment(s) whenever the hot-water temperatures exceed or fall below

Figure 4-61 Internal diagram and typical wiring hookup of a Honeywell R4166 combination water heater and oil burner primary control. *(Courtesy Honeywell Tradeline Controls)*

the temperature range of the water heater. Depending on the size of the storage tank, the water heater will be equipped with either one or two thermostats.

The rated voltage for electric water heaters is 240 volts. The thermostats controlling the primary and secondary heating elements are generally set at 150°F.

Several types of heating units are available for electric water heaters, but the two most popular are probably the immersion element and the strap-on unit. The immersion element is inserted

Figure 4-62 Components of an electric-fired water heater. *(Courtesy 1965 ASHRAE Guide)*

through an opening in the side of the tank. The strap-on unit is externally mounted on the surface of the tank.

A larger storage tank capacity is required for electric water heaters than for fuel-fired types in order to compensate for the limited recovery rate. As a result, initial equipment costs are higher. Care should be taken not to oversize or undersize the storage tank. Incorrect sizing will result in an inefficient water heater.

Electric water heaters of the automatic storage type are generally available in storage tank capacities ranging from 30 to 140 gallons. The electric power input requirement will range from 1600 to 7000 watts.

Troubleshooting Electric Water Heaters

The troubleshooting list in Table 4-2 covers most of the problems commonly encountered when operating electric water heaters.

Table 4-2   Troubleshooting Electric Water Heaters

Problem and Possible Cause	Suggested Remedy
No hot water.	
(a) Blown fuse.	(a) Replace fuse.
(b) Tripped circuit breaker.	(b) Reset circuit breaker. Call electrician if problem continues.
(c) Tripped high-limit switch.	(c) Manually reset switch.
(d) Grounded thermostat.	(d) Check and replace.

Table 4-2   *(continued)*

Problem and Possible Cause	Suggested Remedy
(e) Upper thermostat defective.	(e) Replace.
(f) Thermostat out of calibration.	(f) Tighten/replace as necessary.
(g) Upper element defective.	(g) Replace.
(h) Loose wiring.	(h) Check, tighten, and replace.
(i) Defective or damage wiring.	(i) Replace.
(j) Undersized service wire.	(j) Replace.

Hot-water temperature too high.

(a) Thermostat setting too high.	(a) Lower thermostat setting to desired temperature.
(b) Thermostat out of calibration.	(b) Check and replace.
(c) Grounded or defective element.	(c) Check and replace.
(d) Water heater thermostat not flush with tank.	(d) Reposition thermostat with its back touching the tank.

Water slow to heat.

(a) Undersized heating elements.	(a) Check wattage and replace.
(b) Defective lower thermostat.	(b) Replace.

Not enough hot water or temperature of water too low.

(a) Thermostat set too low.	(a) Increase thermostat setting. Caution: Do not set the thermostat above 120°F.
(b) Incorrect wiring.	(b) Check manufacturer's wiring diagram and rewire.
(c) Loose wiring.	(c) Check; tighten or replace as necessary.
(d) Lower element defective.	(d) Replace.
(e) Lower thermostat defective.	(e) Replace.
(f) Incorrectly wired thermostat.	(f) Replace.
(g) Grounded thermostat.	(g) Replace.
(h) Incorrect heating element wattage.	(h) Check wattage and replace.
(i) Water heater thermostat not flush with tank.	(i) Reposition thermostat with its back touching the tank.
(j) Scale of heating element.	(j) Clean or replace.
(k) Damaged dip tube.	(k) Replace dip tube.

(continued)

Table 4-2 *(continued)*

Problem and Possible Cause	Suggested Remedy
(l) Water tank poorly grounded.	(l) Check grounding and tighten.
(m) Undersized water heater.	(m) Resize for residence. Replace if necessary.

Leaking water heater.

(a) Damaged or loose joints at cold-water inlet and/or hot-water outlet.	(a) Check joints and repair.
(b) Defective temperature/pressure relief valve.	(b) Replace.
(c) Defective heating elements.	(c) Replace.
(d) Defective anode rod or gaskets.	(d) Replace.
(e) Hole in inner tank.	(e) Replace water heater.

Excessive temperature/pressure relief valve operation.

(a) Excessive temperature.	(a) Lower temperature setting. If problem continues, check for grounded element and correct as necessary; replace defective thermostat.
(b) Excessive water pressure.	(b) Install specified pressure-reducing valve on cold intake side.

Rusty, black, or brown water.

(a) Excessive sediment accumulation in tank.	(a) Drain and clean tank, or replace if necessary.
(b) Elements covered with scale.	(b) Clean or replace elements.
(c) Dissolved anode rod.	(c) Replace anode rod.

Strong unpleasant odor.

(a) Dirty tank.	(a) Drain and clean tank with chlorine bleach to remove bacteria.
(b) Dissolved anode rod.	(b) Drain and clean tank; replace anode rod.

Manual Water Heaters

Manual water heaters, also referred to as *circulating tank* or *side arm heaters*, are of the conventional design with the gas burner and accompanying heating coils mounted on the side of the hot-water storage tank as shown in Figure 4-63.

Manual water heaters are generally equipped with copper coils 16½ to 20 feet in length and with either ¾- or 1-inch outside diameter. The coils are usually made of copper tubing of No. 20 Stubbs gauge. Other designs are occasionally employed—for example, the internal or underfired units intended to overcome liming in hard-water areas.

These heaters usually have between 20,000 and 30,000 Btu capacity, although the maximum sizes run up to 85,000 Btu capacity. The

Figure 4-63 Connection of a manual gas water heater where interconnected with a waterback or range coil.

smallest-size manual heater will deliver about 19 gallons of hot water per hour. This size heater is generally ample for most homes in which the conventional 30-gallon tank is used for storing the hot water.

The manual water heater was formerly widely employed because of its comparatively low cost and economy in operation. As the name implies, manual water heaters are nonautomatic and supply hot water quickly by turning on and lighting the gas shortly before the warm water is required. Automatic water heaters have largely replaced the manual type because the former require little or no attention when in operation.

Assembly and Installation of Manual Water Heaters

A great many installations of manual water heaters have given poor service, not because of any fault in the heater, but mainly due to the improper method of connecting the heater to the storage tank. This lack of good service can be largely overcome if a few simple installation rules are followed.

All recently manufactured range boilers have tappings provided in them for hot- and cold-water connections, specifically two tappings in the side of the tank 6 inches from the top and bottom as shown in Figure 4-63 to accommodate the circulating water connections, which should be made of ¾-inch or larger pipe. The bottom of the tank has a tapping for connection to the drain or blow-off, which is used to drain water or sediment from the boiler. Circulating pipes between the heater and tank should be made as free from fittings and bends as possible.

The use of brass pipe on the hot-water circulating line from the heater to the tank is recommended, particularly for high-temperature circulation.

When required, unions should be placed as close to the heater as possible on the hot-water and cold-water circulating lines.

The placement of hot- and cold-water tappings 6 inches from the top and bottom of the tank allows free circulation, which results in relatively large-volume storage without overheating. It also eliminates short-circuiting of the water through the heater and provides ample sediment storage below the circulating line, thus preventing sediment from getting into the heating element.

Solar Water Heaters

Many of the valves and heating controls used with gas, oil, and electric water heaters can also be used in solar water heating systems. These components are designed to protect and control a solar water heating installation from a single source. A typical system is

Figure 4-64   Typical solar water heating installation.

(Courtesy Watts Regulator Co.)

shown in Figure 4-64. A specially designed thermostatic element (for 210°F to 250°F service) in a thermal bypass control should be included in the system to divert high-temperature water to a cooling section (see Figure 4-65). This prevents structural damage to the solar panels and improves system efficiency.

Figure 4-65   Thermostatic element for 210°F to 250°F service.

(Courtesy Watts Regulator Co.)

Chapter 5

Heating Swimming Pools

Heating systems have been added to both private and commercial swimming pools for a variety of reasons, ranging from the simple desire to increase body comfort with warmer water temperatures to the more practical reason of extending the swimming season.

In many commercial buildings and larger residences equipped with hot-water (hydronic) heating systems, the central boiler provides the heat for space heating, domestic hot water, and pool water. In structures equipped with other heating systems (for example, forced warm-air), a pool heater operating independently of the central heating unit is necessary to heat the pool water. The water in a swimming pool may be heated in one of the three following ways:

1. Solar heating
2. Radiant heating
3. Recycling

Solar heating relies on the use of solar panels to collect the heat from the sun. The pool water is circulated through the panels where it collects the heat from the sun and then carries it back down to the pool. Many solar pool-heating systems have an auxiliary gas or electric heater to augment the heat from the panels on days where there is insufficient sunlight.

Pools can also be heated with a radiant heating system, but such a system *must* be installed when the pool is constructed because it entails embedding tubing (commonly ½-inch diameter) in the pool itself. As shown in Figure 5-1, the tubing is buried close to the surface in the walls and floor of the pool. The hot water is fed through a supply pipe from the boiler. The water returns to the boiler through a return line. Water temperature in the pipes is controlled by a thermostat, which usually is located on the return line.

Radiant heating systems for swimming pools are the most expensive types to install because they require more pipe than other heating systems. Furthermore, the construction feature of having the copper tubing embedded in the walls and floor of the pool adds to the installation cost.

COPPER TUBING
BURIED IN CONCRETE
WALLS AND FLOOR

RADIANT HEAT

RETURN LINE
TO BOILER

HOT WATER FROM BOILER

Figure 5-1 Heating a swimming pool by the radiant heating method.

Most modern pool heating systems are based on the recycling principle. The water is drawn from the pool by a pump, passed to the heat exchanger in the boiler or pool heater, heated to the desired temperature, and returned to the swimming pool.

When both a pool and its heating system are installed during the original construction of the house or building, it is possible (and advisable) to install a single boiler with more than one heat exchanger. As a result, the boiler will have the capacity to provide hot water not only for the pool but also for space heating and domestic hot-water needs. Three such systems for commercial buildings are illustrated in Figures 5-2, 5-3, and 5-4. In these systems, the primary boiler water is maintained at the desired space-heating water temperature by the operating aquastat in the boiler. The temperature of the pool water is maintained by the opening and closing of a pool temperature-control valve located in the circulation line between the filter and heater. This valve is controlled by a pool temperature-control aquastat, which senses the temperature of the water being returned from the pool.

Pool heaters can also be installed independent of space heating and domestic hot-water heating systems. This is usually the case when a heating unit is installed at an existing pool.

A pool heater operates on the same principle as the domestic hot-water heater, but the two differ considerably in their functions. The hot-water heater is required to heat only 30 to 40 gallons of water in a closed tank. The pool heater must heat thousands of gallons of water with a surface *exposed* to the outside air. Because there is a high degree of heat loss from the large surface area of the water to the colder air above it, a pool heater uses a considerable amount of fuel to replace the lost heat and to maintain the pool water at the desired temperature. The fact that water has a high heat capacity contributes to the problem. As a result, it generally takes a pool heater 20 to 24 hours to warm the water to the desired temperature.

Classifying Pool Heaters

Pool heaters can be classified in a number of different ways. If they are classified according to their basic operating principle, the following two types are recognized:

1. Direct-type pool heaters

2. Indirect-type pool heaters

In a *direct-type pool heater* (see Figure 5-5), the water from the pool passes through the heating unit in pipes that are heated directly by a gas or oil burner. In an *indirect-type pool heater* (see Figure 5-6), the pipes containing the pool water pass through a compartment in the heating unit, which also contains water. The water in the compartment of the heating unit is heated by a gas or oil burner located outside the water compartment. The heat of the water is then transferred to the water in the pipes from the pool,

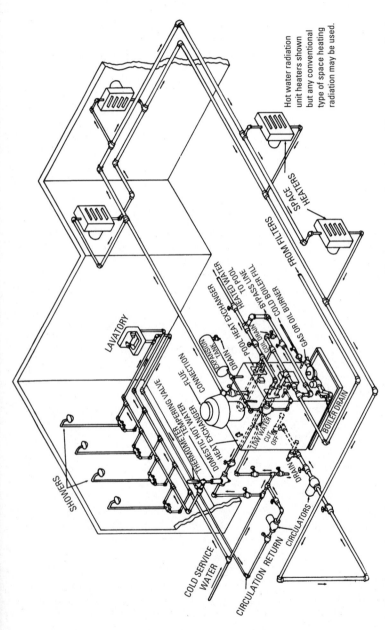

Figure 5-2 Typical multipurpose water-heating system for pool heating, space heating, and hot-water service.

(Courtesy Bryan Steam Corp)

Hot water radiation unit heaters shown but any conventional type of space heating radiation may be used.

SPACE HEATERS

FROM FILTERS

GAS OR OIL BURNER

COLD BOILER FILL

BYPASS LINE

OIL DRAIN

DRAIN

HEATED WATER TO POOL

POOL HEAT EXCHANGER

EXPANSION TANK

DRAIN

FLUE CONNECTION

THERMOMETER-TEMPERING VALVE

DOMESTIC HOT WATER HEAT EXCHANGER

LOW WATER CUT OFF

BOILER DRAIN

DRAIN

CIRCULATORS

LAVATORY

SHOWERS

COLD SERVICE WATER

CIRCULATION RETURN

Figure 5-3 Typical multipurpose water-heating system for two pools of different temperatures and space heating. *(Courtesy Bryan Steam Corp.)*

253

Figure 5-4 Typical multipurpose water-heating system for pool heating, space heating, and domestic hot water.

(Courtesy Bryan Steam Corp.)

Bryan heater with two indirect heat exchangers one for pool heating and one for heating domestic water (optional).

Figure 5-5 Operating principle of a direct-type pool heater.

WATER FROM
POOL

HEAT EXCHANGER

WATER FROM
POOL

WATER CHAMBER

COMBUSTION CHAMBER

Figure 5-6 Operating principle of an indirect-type pool heater.

hence the name *indirect* pool heater. Because the coils of the heat exchanger never come in direct contact with the combustion heat (as is the case with direct-type pool heaters), scale and corrosion are virtually eliminated.

Another means of classifying pool heaters is by the type of fuel or energy source used to heat the water. The pool water can be heated by natural gas or propane, oil, electricity, or solar radiation.

Note

When installing a conventional pool heating system, purchase a heater with a high efficiency rating. It will save energy and result in significantly lower fuel costs.

Gas-Fired Pool Heaters

Gas-fired indirect pool heaters (see Figure 5-7) are available in the same Btu input/output ratings as the oil-fired types. They differ only in certain items of standard equipment that relate directly to

Figure 5-7 Hydrotherm gas-fired indirect pool heater. *(Courtesy Hydrotherm, Inc.)*

the type of fuel used. Gas-fired pool heaters will also differ according to the type of ignition system. There are two types of ignition systems used in gas-fired pool heaters:

- Millivolt (or standing pilot) ignition systems
- Automatic spark ignition systems

A *millivolt ignition system* is one in which the pilot light is continuously burning. The heat from the pilot light is used to generate a low-voltage electrical current. The electrical current produced by the pilot light is strong enough to open and close the main gas valve (also sometimes called a *combination gas valve*) as well as the controls and safety devices on the heater.

Note

A pilot light that is continuously lit is sometimes called a *standing pilot* or *standing pilot light.*

An *automatic spark ignition system* (also sometimes called an *intermittent ignition system* or simply an *IID system*) has a pilot light that is lit *only* when the heater is operating. An external electrical source is used to spark the pilot and operate the controls and safety devices on the heater.

In addition to the pilot light, a gas-fired pool heater also will include a number of different components, safety devices, and controls. Those included in the heater will depend on the type of ignition system used as well as its make and model. They include the following:

- **Pilot generator.** A pilot generator (also sometimes called a *thermocouple*) is the device in a millivolt ignition system that converts the heat energy of the pilot flame to the electrical energy required to operate the main gas valve. Pilot generators are not used in the automatic spark ignition systems.

- **Control circuit.** The control circuit consists of a series of safety devices used to control the flow of electricity to the main gas valve. If there is a malfunction somewhere in the heater, one or more of these safety devices in the control circuit will interrupt the flow of electricity to the main gas valve and prevent the burners from operating. The devices in the control circuit include safety switches (see *safety switches*), a fusible link (see *gas burner tray*), and a remote on-off switch.

- **Safety switches.** A variety of different types of switches are used in gas-fired pool heaters for safety and operational control purposes.

  - *Pressure switch.* A device that prevents the heater from starting until there is sufficient water pressure in the system.

  - *High-limit switch.* A device that prevents the water temperature in the pool heater from exceeding a preset upper limit (commonly 140°F).

  - *Flow switch.* A device that prevents the heater from starting if there is not enough water flowing through the system.

  - *Fireman switch.* A device that allows the circulator (pump) to continue operating up to 15 minutes after the heater has shut off. The additional pump running time allows the system to cool down.

- **Bypass valve.** The bypass valve is used to maintain a constant flow of water through the heat exchanger. The cool water protects the heat exchanger surfaces and other heater components from excessively high and potentially damaging temperatures. The bypass valve and the fireman switch provide similar functions in a pool heater.

- **Automatic gas valve.** The automatic gas valve (also sometimes called the *main gas valve* or *combination valve*) regulates the flow of gas to the burner tray and pilot. It is controlled by the heater control circuit.

- **Gas-pressure regulator.** A device that regulates the gas pressure. It is commonly combined with the main gas valve in the same unit (hence the name *combination gas valve*).

- **Gas shutoff valve.** A valve used to shut off the supply of gas to the burners when a heater malfunction occurs.

- **Thermostat.** As in other heating systems, a thermostat is used to control operation within a preset temperature range. When the pool water temperature drops below a preset low-temperature limit setting, the thermostat switches on the pool heater. When the temperature of the pool water reaches the upper preset limit, it shuts off the pool heater.

Other gas-fired pool heater components, many of which are also found on oil-fired, electric, and solar heaters, include the following:

- **Heat exchanger.** A device used to transfer heat from air, fluid, or water contained in one circulating system to the air, fluid, or water contained in an adjacent one *without* any intermixing. Heat exchangers are available in the form of flat plates or fins, coils, or tubes and are made of a metal that easily absorbs heat. Copper-finned heat exchangers are the type most commonly used in pool heaters. These consist of closely spaced flat fins attached to copper tubing.

- **Header.** The header (also called a *manifold*) is the component that directs the flow of water in and out of the heat exchanger. There is a header at each end of the heat exchanger. The front header, through which the water flows into the heat exchanger, contains a flow control assembly that is used to mix the cool incoming water with the hot outgoing water as it leaves the heat exchanger through the back header. This ensures a temperature differential of 25°F or less between the temperatures of the incoming and outgoing water. This reduced temperature differential prevents condensation, mineral deposits, and other problems associated with excessively high temperature differentials.

- **Gas burner assembly.** A pool heater may have as many as 16 and as few as 6 burners, depending on the make and model. The burner tubes are arranged in a parallel array and connected by a manifold pipe. A pilot light is mounted on the last burner tube. The gas burner tray beneath the burners can be removed from the cabinet for cleaning.

- **Pool heater aquastat.** A pool heater aquastat is used to control pool water temperatures and provide high-limit boiler control. The high-limit control provides shutdown protection to prevent boiler overheating. Some models are equipped with automatic reset, while others are equipped with manual.

A typical wiring diagram for a gas-fired indirect pool heater is shown in Figure 5-8. The pool water control on the dual aquastat is set at the desired pool temperature. The cold water from the pool starts the boiler, which continues to produce heat until the pool water temperature reaches the setting on the pool control. When this point is reached, the boiler shuts off. The boiler water temperature is controlled by the water-limit control.

Figure 5-8 Typical wiring diagram for a gas-fired indirect pool heater. *(Courtesy Hydrotherm, Inc.)*

Oil-Fired Pool Heaters

The oil-fired indirect pool heater illustrated in Figure 5-9 is available in several input ratings ranging from 175,000 Btu/h (1.25 gph firing rate) to 280,000 Btu/h (2.00 gph firing rate) with No. 2 fuel oil. The corresponding *output* ratings range from 133,000 Btu/h to 208,000 Btu/h, which gives this pool heater the capacity to heat swimming pools containing 16,000 to 25,000 gallons of water.

These pool heaters have a 100-psi ASME pressure rating, which makes possible their direct connection to city water lines without the use of pressure-reducing valves. The heat exchanger consists of multiple-pass finned copper tubes, which are designed for low-pressure drop and which can be removed for cleaning.

Figure 5-10 illustrates the recommended piping arrangement for this particular pool heater. Note that the filter is installed on the line from the pool between the pump (circulator) and the shutoff valve. No provision for bypass piping is made between the pipes leading to and from the pool. An example of bypass piping in a pool heating installation for a similar oil-fired indirect heater is shown in Figure 5-11.

The aforementioned pool heater is suitable for small residential pools. A typical 25,000-gallon pool is approximately 18 feet wide by 36 feet long if a rectangular-shaped pool is used as an example.

Figure 5-9 Oil-fired indirect-type pool heater with wiring diagram.
(Courtesy Hydrotherm, Inc.)

Pool heaters, whether oil-, gas-, or electric-fired, are available for almost any size pool. It is simply a matter of matching the pool size with the capacity of the pool heater. For example, Figure 5-9 shows an indirect oil-fired pool heater used for commercial applications, which is capable of heating a 105,000-gallon swimming pool. It has an input rating of 1,155,000 Btu per hour with 8.25 gph firing rate. This pool heater actually represents the combination of three heating modules; each has its own oil burner and modulating aquastat.

Electric Pool Heaters

An electric pool heater produces heat by forcing water to flow around a submerged electric coil. Most of the components are

Figure 5-10 Recommended piping arrangement for heater in Figure 5-7. *(Courtesy Hydrotherm, Inc.)*

Figure 5-11 Piping diagram with bypass arrangement. *(Courtesy Hydrotherm, Inc.)*

similar to a gas or oil pool heater. The controls of an electric pool heater are usually built into the unit. Some models have a separately mounted thermostat to control water temperature.

Electric pool heaters are used where space is too restricted for a gas or oil heater, or where it is not possible to provide sufficient ventilation. They are used more frequently to heat small spas or hot tubs than pools.

The input of an electric-fired indirect pool heater is measured in kilowatts; its output is measured in Btu. The pool heater shown in Figure 5-12 is available in 11 different models ranging in input capacity from 15 kW to 300 kW with a corresponding output of 50,000 Btu per hour to 1,000,000 Btu per hour. These pool heaters are also available with 240 volts (single-phase) or 240/480 volts (three-phase). A wiring diagram for an electric-fired indirect pool heater is shown in Figure 5-13.

ELECTRICAL PANEL

NOTE:
Panel size will vary depending on, power available, controls, steps, fusing, etc.

ALLOW SPACE FOR REMOVAL OF RESISTANCE ELEMENT

RELIEF VALVE

GAUGE

TO EXPANSION TANK

CUT-OFF WATER

FILL WATER SUPPLY

DRAIN

FROM FILTER

TO POOL

FILL VALVE

GLOBE VALVE

CHECK VALVE

ALLOW SPACE FOR REMOVAL OF HEAT EXCHANGER

BREAK UNIONS WHEN DRAINING OR VALVING OF HEATER FROM POOL

NOTE:
If pvc (plastic) pipe is used provide heat trap by extending metal piping to floor line before connecting to pvc and install positive check valve as shown.

BYPASS WITH PLUG COCK IF FILTER FLOW RATE EXCEEDS 756 P.M.

Figure 5-12 Electric-fired pool heater. *(Courtesy Bryan Steam Corp.)*

Figure 5-13 Wiring diagram for an electric-fired pool heater.
(Courtesy Bryan Steam Corp.)

Heat-Exchanger Pool Heaters

The heat-exchanger pool heater illustrated in Figure 5-14 is designed for use in either steam or hot-water heating systems. It is essentially a steel shell enclosing the copper tubes of the heat exchanger. The hot water or steam is taken from the heating main and circulated *around* the copper tubes inside the steel shell. The pool water enters the heat exchanger in a pipe leading from the pool filter and circulates *inside* the copper tubes. As it circulates, it is heated by the hot water or steam circulating around the copper tubes. The heated water eventually leaves the heat exchanger through a second exit point and is returned to the pool.

Figures 5-15 and 5-16 illustrate the modifications necessary for use with either steam or hot water as the heat source. Basic construction is essentially the same in both cases, with the pool water circulating through copper tubes (the heat exchanger) enclosed in a steel shell. You will probably notice that different types of steel are used in constructing the shell: 125-psi ASME steel for heat exchangers using hot water as a heat source, and 15-psi ASME steel for those using steam.

Both types of heat exchangers have temperature-control aquastats activated by the temperature of the pool water entering the heat exchanger. In heat exchangers that use water as a heat source, the aquastat is connected to a circulating pump (see Figure 5-16). If steam is the heat source, the aquastat is connected to a steam-control valve. Both the circulating pump and the steam-control valve control the *rate of flow* of the hot water or steam from the heating unit.

Figure 5-14 Heat-exchanger pool heater. *(Courtesy Bryan Steam Corp.)*

When steam is used as the heat source, the heat exchanger should also be equipped with a steam trap and a line running to the condensation main. The steam valve sizing is based on 2-psi minimum steam pressure and 0-psi return pressure. A steam strainer should be placed in the steam supply line just before it reaches the control valve.

Circulating pump sizing in units that use water as a heat source should be based on a maximum temperature drop through the heat exchanger of 30°F and a maximum head loss in piping between the hot-water boiler and the heater of 10 feet H_2O.

The Btu/h output for heat-exchanger pool heaters using water as a heat source ranges from 200,000 to 4,200,000 Btu per hour. The amount will depend on water temperature (180°F or 210°F) and the size of the unit. Heaters using steam as a heat source are capable of generating an output of 400,000 to 3,600,000 Btu per hour. Here the difference depends on the steam pressure used (2 lbs or 10 lbs) and the size of the unit.

Solar Pool Heaters

The principal components of a solar pool heating system are illustrated in Figure 5-17. In this system, the solar panels or collectors

Figure 5-15 Heat-exchanger pool heater using steam as a heat source. *(Courtesy Bryan Steam Corp.)*

Figure 5-16 Heat-exchanger pool heater using water as a heat source. *(Courtesy Bryan Steam Corp.)*

Figure 5-17 Solar pool schematic. *(Courtesy GO Solar Company)*

function as the heater. There is no component similar to the heaters used in the more conventional pool heating systems. Note, however, that an auxiliary heater may be included in the system as a backup to the solar collectors when there is not enough sunlight to warm the water.

In operation, water is automatically pumped through the solar collectors where it picks up the heat from the sun. A solar sensor is used to measure the heat on the panel. If the panels are cold, the solar sensor causes the water to bypass the panels and flow directly to the auxiliary heater (commonly a gas or electric heater) where it is heated and sent to the pool. If the solar sensor detects heat on the panels, it opens a valve to send the water directly to the solar panels where it is heated and then returned to the pool. At the same time, a bypass ball valve closes and isolates the auxiliary heater.

The temperature of the pool water is measured by a water sensor. Both the solar sensor and water sensor are connected to a controller that governs the operation of a three-way valve. A check valve in the piping leading from the three-way valve can be used to isolate the pump, filter, and water sensor from other components in a solar heating system. The isolation valves installed in the solar panel supply and return lines are optional. The former is a ball valve, the latter a check valve.

The solar collectors are made from polypropylene or a similarly formulated material designed to withstand extreme exposure to weather conditions and pollution. The panel material is also unaffected by pool chemicals and will not corrode or rust. Each panel is constructed in a tube and curved web design to trap the heat as the sun moves across the sky.

Heat Pump Pool Heaters

A heat pump also can be used to heat the water in a swimming pool. A heat pump is a much more expensive piece of equipment than a conventional pool heater, but it is more energy efficient, requires less maintenance and repair, and has a longer service life.

Heat is generated when pressure is exerted by the compressor on a nonflammable, noncorrosive gas. The heat in the gas is transferred to water flowing through the heat exchanger. The warm water flows to the pool, and the cooled gas returns to the compressor where it is recompressed and reheated before repeating the cycle.

High-efficiency electric heat pump pool heaters are available with coefficients of performance (COPs) in the 6.0 to 8.0 range. Heat pumps not graded as high-efficiency units will produce a coefficient of performance of approximately 4.0.

Note

> The coefficient of performance may be defined as the ratio of the transferred energy to the electric energy used in the process—in other words, the total useful output (heat energy in the case of a pool heater) divided by the total energy input used to produce the heat.

Sizing Pool Heaters

The two principal methods used for sizing pool heaters are as follows:

1. The surface-area method

2. The time-rise method

Table 5-1 contains all the necessary data for determining the required pool heater size with either method. The listed output ratings are for Bryan pool heaters.

The sizing data in Table 5-2 is based on heat loss from the surface of the heater with an assumed wind velocity of 3½ mph. This

Table 5-1 Sizing the Pool Heater (Ratings Given in 1000 Btu/h)

| Pool Size (Rectangular) | | Surface-Area Method | Time-Rise Method — Difference between Desired Water Temperature and Average Air Temperature for Recommended Heater Sized on Surface Area | | | | | | Pool Gallonage (approx.) | Recommended Heater Sized on Pool Capacity to Raise Temp. 1°F per Hour (approx.) |
Width	Length	Pool Surface Area (ft²)	10°	15°	20°	25°	30°	40°		
15	30	450	150	150	150	150	250	250	17,000	250
16	32	512				250			20,000	350
16	36	576						350	23,000	
18	36	648			250				25,000	450
18	40	720					350	450	30,000	
18	42	756							31,000	
20	40	800		250					34,000	
20	42	840							35,000	
20	45	900					450		37,000	650
20	50	1000			350			650	40,000	
25	50	1250	250			450	650	850	50,000	850
25	60	1500		350	450	650		900	62,000	900
30	60	1800					850		79,000	1200
30	70	2100	350	450	650			1200	84,000	
30	75	2250							92,000	1500
35	75	2625	650	650			1200	1500	107,000	1800

40	75	3000	450		850			1800	123,000	
42	75	3150			900				137,000	2100
42	80	3465	650	850	1200		1500	2100	143,000	2450
45	90	4050	850		1500	1500		2700	184,000	3200
50	100	5000	900	1200		1800	2100	3200	217,000	
60	100	6000	1200		1800	2100	2450	3750	250,000	3750
60	110	6600	1500	1500	2100	2450	2700	4300	275,000	4300
65	120	7800	1800	2100	2450		3200	4850	320,000	
75	130	9750	2100	2450	3200	3200	3750	Two 2700	400,000	Two 2700
75	160	12,000		2700	3750	4300	4850	Two 3200	490,000	Two 3200
80	175	14,000		3200	4300	4850	Two 2700	Two 3750	575,000	Two 3750
80	200	16,000				Two 2700	Two 3200	Two 4300	655,000	Two 4300

(Courtesy Bryan Steam Corporation)

Table 5-2 Wind Velocity and Recommended Pool Heater Capacity

Approximate Pool Gallonage	Wind Velocity	Recommended Pool Heater Capacity
17,000 gal	3½ mph	250,000 Btu
17,000 gal	5 mph	375,000 Btu
17,000 gal	10 mph	500,000 Btu

is the average wind velocity for a pool protected from direct wind exposure by trees, shrubs, fences, and buildings. An exposed pool will mean that the required pool heater capacity (that is, the input ratings listed in Table 5-1) must be increased. Generally it is recommended that the input rating be increased by 1.25 for a 5-mph wind velocity and 2.0 for a 10-mph wind velocity.

The Surface-Area Method

The *surface-area method* of sizing a pool heater is based on the surface area (in square feet) of the pool and the temperature difference (in degrees Fahrenheit) between the desired water temperature and the average air temperature. The procedure is as follows:

1. Determine the *mean* average air temperature for the coldest month in which the pool is to be used.
2. Determine the desired pool water temperature.
3. Find the difference between the air temperature (step 1) and the water temperature (step 2).
4. Calculate the pool surface area in square feet.
5. In Table 5-1, find the surface area closest to your pool size. Move horizontally in a straight line across to the column that represents the temperature difference for your pool. The point at which the horizontal line and the temperature column intersect will be the required Btu per hour input rating for your pool heater.

The surface-area method can be illustrated with a simple example. Let's suppose that you have a small 15-foot × 30-foot pool with a 17,000-gallon capacity. You want to maintain a pool water temperature of 70°F (step 2), and the mean average air temperature for the coldest month in which the pool is to be used is 50°F (step 1). What will be the required input rating of your pool heater?

Your temperature difference required for sizing the heater is 20° (70° – 50°F). The pool surface area is 450 square feet (15 × 30 feet). Moving horizontally across the top line in Table 5-1, you arrive at the 20° column and learn that the required input rating for a pool heater meeting these criteria is 150,000 Btu per hour.

Another, less precise form of the surface-area method is to multiply the surface area of the pool by 15 and then by the temperature difference between the pool water and the air. Using the same data as before, the following results are obtained:

450 ft^2 × 15 × 20° = 135,000 Btu per hour

The Time-Rise Method

The first step in the time-rise method of sizing a pool heater is to determine the pool capacity in gallons of water (pool gallonage). This only needs to be an approximate figure and is commonly rounded off to the nearest thousand (for example, 17,000 gal, 20,000 gal, 23,000 gal). In Table 5-1, the extreme right-hand column lists pool heaters recommended for different pool capacities. The sizing in this chart is based on the number of Btu required to raise the pool temperature approximately 1°F per hour.

Sizing Indoor Pool Heaters

If the swimming pool is located inside a heated building, the surface temperature of the water is naturally not affected by the colder outdoor air temperatures. A simple rule-of-thumb method for sizing an indoor pool heater is as follows:

1. Determine the surface area of the pool (for example, 30 ft × 40 ft = 1200 ft^2).
2. Multiply the surface area by 125 Btu (1200 ft^2 × 125 Btu = 150,000 Btu per hour input).

Installing Pool Heaters

Installing a pool heater requires knowledge of plumbing, electrical work, gas or oil burner operation, and ventilation. Pool heaters should be installed only by qualified and experienced personnel, and their installation must comply with local codes and ordinances.

Pool heaters are shipped with a complete set of instructions for installing and starting the unit. If the instructions are missing, the manufacturer should be contacted for a replacement set. The following installation recommendations apply to most pool heaters:

1. Install the pool heater on a level concrete slab or a pad of concrete block or brick. The slab or pad must be at least 4 inches high. If concrete blocks are used, align them so that all open cells are pointed in the same direction with the cells at the edge of the pad left open. Cover the top of a concrete block pad with 24-gauge (or thicker) sheet metal.

Note

Never install a pool heater on a combustible material, such as wood boards or plywood.

2. Maintain proper clearances on all sides of an outdoor pool heater. Consult the owner's manual for the clearances specified by the pool heater manufacturer. Maintaining minimum required clearances around the pool heater will ensure efficient combustion and proper ventilation of the combustion gases (gas-fired and oil-fired heaters).

Note

The American National Standards Institute (ANSI) has established a standard set of clearances for outdoor pool heaters based on the external temperature of the heaters (see ANSI 2223.1).

3. Indoor pool heaters must be properly vented to the outdoors. They also must have sufficient intake air for proper combustion. Consult the owner's manual for specific venting requirements.

Warning

Incorrect venting of an indoor pool heater can result in carbon monoxide poisoning. Incorrect venting can also result in fire.

4. An indoor gas-fired pool heater must be equipped with a draft hood to further ensure that potentially harmful combustion gases are expelled outdoors. The vent pipe is directly connected to the draft hood. The diameter of the draft hood is based on recommendations from the National Fuel Gas Code. It may vary among different pool heater makes and models.

5. To provide proper draft, the discharge opening of the flue pipe must extend at least 2 feet above the surface of the roof or its highest point within a 10-foot radius of the point where it extends through the roof.

6. Install a barrier (for example, closed wooden fence, trees and bushes) around a pool if it is subjected to sustained high winds. Sustained winds across the surface of the water will increase the heat loss from the pool. This will require increasing the heater

size to maintain the desired water temperature. The heater itself should be protected from high winds with a windbreak.

Pool Heater Repair and Maintenance

Follow the guidelines in the manufacturer's manual when servicing or repairing a pool heater or related equipment. Some manufacturers also permit the downloading of manuals from their online web site. If a manual is unavailable and you do not have the necessary experience to do the work without one, call the pool heater manufacturer or a local dealer for help.

The following suggestions for servicing and repairing pool heaters apply to all makes and models:

1. Perform a major inspection and servicing of the pool, pool heater, pump, and related components just before putting the pool into operation and just after closing it down if the pool is used only part of the year.

2. Perform periodic inspections and maintenance if the pool is used throughout the year.

3. Replace worn parts with new ones. Do not attempt to reuse them or make temporary repairs.

4. Inspect and clean or replace pool filters on a regular basis.

5. Inspect the pool heater for sooting (a combustion problem).

6. Inspect the pool heater for water leaks (all heaters), gas leaks (gas-fired units), and oil leaks (oil-fired units).

7. Check all pipe connections for tightness and corrosion.

8. Check wiring for damaged wires and loose connections.

9. Check for proper burner flame characteristics on gas-fired and oil-fired heaters. The pilot flame of a gas-fired heater should also be included when making this inspection.

10. Inspect the heat exchanger for scaling.

11. Remove leaves and other debris from the top of the pool heater.

Note

Always shut off the pool heater and allow it time to cool down before servicing it or making repairs.

Caution

To avoid injury from electrical shock, always shut off the electrical power before servicing the line voltage controls. Never leave a jumper wire in place to fix a heater or the operating and safety controls will be bypassed.

Warning

> If gas odors are detected when repairing or servicing a gas-fired pool heater, immediately contact your local utility for instructions. If the pool is located indoors, leave the house and make the call from a neighbor's telephone.

Troubleshooting Pool Heaters and Equipment

Always review the pool heater manufacturer's installation and/or operating manual for recommended troubleshooting procedures. If no manual is available, it may be possible to download one for the specific pool heater or equipment from the manufacturer's online web address. As a last resort, Tables 5-3, 5-4, and 5-5 list frequent problems, their symptoms, and possible remedies.

Table 5-3   Troubleshooting Gas-Fired Pool Heaters

Symptom and Possible Cause	Possible Remedy
Heater cycles on and off continuously.	
(a) Low water level in pool.	(a) Raise water level.
(b) Dirty filter.	(b) Backwash or replace filter.
(c) Pressure switch out of adjustment.	(c) Adjust pressure switch.
(d) External bypass setting needs adjustment.	(d) Adjust bypass setting.
(e) Closed valve.	(e) Locate, repair, or replace valve.
(f) Thermostat calibration incorrect.	(f) Recalibrate or replace thermostat.
Heater not producing enough heat.	
(a) Gas cock in wrong position and cutting off gas supply.	(a) Check and change position of gas cock.
(b) Pilot light out.	(b) Relight pilot. If burners still fail to light, call for service.
(c) Pilot light at *off* setting.	(c) Turn to *on* position and relight pilot.
Weak burner flame.	
(a) Burner intake ports clogged.	(a) Remove blockage.
(b) Low gas pressure.	(b) Adjust gas pressure.

1. Install the pool heater on a level concrete slab or a pad of concrete block or brick. The slab or pad must be at least 4 inches high. If concrete blocks are used, align them so that all open cells are pointed in the same direction with the cells at the edge of the pad left open. Cover the top of a concrete block pad with 24-gauge (or thicker) sheet metal.

Note

Never install a pool heater on a combustible material, such as wood boards or plywood.

2. Maintain proper clearances on all sides of an outdoor pool heater. Consult the owner's manual for the clearances specified by the pool heater manufacturer. Maintaining minimum required clearances around the pool heater will ensure efficient combustion and proper ventilation of the combustion gases (gas-fired and oil-fired heaters).

Note

The American National Standards Institute (ANSI) has established a standard set of clearances for outdoor pool heaters based on the external temperature of the heaters (see ANSI 2223.1).

3. Indoor pool heaters must be properly vented to the outdoors. They also must have sufficient intake air for proper combustion. Consult the owner's manual for specific venting requirements.

Warning

Incorrect venting of an indoor pool heater can result in carbon monoxide poisoning. Incorrect venting can also result in fire.

4. An indoor gas-fired pool heater must be equipped with a draft hood to further ensure that potentially harmful combustion gases are expelled outdoors. The vent pipe is directly connected to the draft hood. The diameter of the draft hood is based on recommendations from the National Fuel Gas Code. It may vary among different pool heater makes and models.

5. To provide proper draft, the discharge opening of the flue pipe must extend at least 2 feet above the surface of the roof or its highest point within a 10-foot radius of the point where it extends through the roof.

6. Install a barrier (for example, closed wooden fence, trees and bushes) around a pool if it is subjected to sustained high winds. Sustained winds across the surface of the water will increase the heat loss from the pool. This will require increasing the heater

---

size to maintain the desired wa
should be protected from high

Pool Heater Repair and M

Follow the guidelines in the manuf
or repairing a pool heater or relate
ers also permit the downloading o
site. If a manual is unavailable an
experience to do the work without
facturer or a local dealer for help.

The following suggestions fo
heaters apply to all makes and mo

1. Perform a major inspection
   heater, pump, and related co
   pool into operation and just
   used only part of the year.
2. Perform periodic inspection
   used throughout the year.
3. Replace worn parts with ne
   them or make temporary rep
4. Inspect and clean or replace
5. Inspect the pool heater for s
6. Inspect the pool heater for
   (gas-fired units), and oil leal
7. Check all pipe connections
8. Check wiring for damaged
9. Check for proper burner
   and oil-fired heaters. The
   should also be included wh
10. Inspect the heat exchanger
11. Remove leaves and other de

Note

Always shut off the pool he
before servicing it or making

Caution

To avoid injury from electric
power before servicing the
jumper wire in place to fix
controls will be bypassed.

274

Warn

Tro

Alwa
oper
no m
speci
web
prob

Table 5-3 (continued)

Symptom and Possible Cause	Possible Remedy
Pilot out (millivolt system).	
(a) Restricted pilot.	(a) Clean pilot and restart heater.
(b) Weak or defective pilot generator.	(b) Replace pilot generator.
(c) Low gas pressure.	(c) Adjust gas pressure.
(d) No gas.	(d) Check gas supply. Call local utility.
Pilot will not light.	
(a) No fuel.	(a) Turn on gas.
(b) Fuel tank empty (propane gas).	(b) Fill tank.
(c) Low gas pressure.	(c) Adjust gas pressure or repair as required.
(d) Clogged or damaged pilot tubing.	(d) Clean or replace.
(e) Insufficient air supply.	(e) Correct as necessary.
(f) Improper venting.	(f) Correct as necessary.
Pilot requires frequent relighting.	
(a) Faulty thermocouple/pilot generator.	(a) Replace.
(b) Loose connection between thermocouple and gas valve.	(b) Tighten connection. Replace if damaged.
(c) Loose coil connection.	(c) Tighten connection. Replace if damaged.
(d) Electrical short in wiring between thermocouple and gas valve or coil.	(d) Determine cause of electrical short and repair.
Noisy heater.	
(a) Restriction in system.	(a) Locate restriction and remove.
(b) Blockage in gas line.	(b) Locate and remove blockage.
(c) Scale buildup in heat exchanger.	(c) Remove scale from heat exchanger tubes or replace heat exchanger.
(d) Incorrectly adjusted pressure switch.	(d) Adjust pressure switch.
(e) Low gas pressure.	(e) Adjust gas pressure or repair as required.

(continued)

Table 5-3 *(continued)*

Symptom and Possible Cause	Possible Remedy
Soot forming in combustion chamber.	
(a) Insufficient air supply.	(a) Check clearances and correct (outdoor heater); check for sufficient intake (combustion) air and correct venting and correct (indoor heater). Clean soot from heat exchanger.
(b) Too much water flowing through heater.	(b) Correct water flow. Clean soot from heat exchanger.
(c) Heater run time too short.	(c) Adjust time clock to allow heater to run long enough to heat the water. Clean soot from heat exchanger.
(d) Gas valve regulator adjustment.	(d) Test for correct gas pressure. Adjust regulator or gas valve.
(e) Burner inlet throat or venturi blocked.	(e) Locate blockage and remove.
Heater leaking water.	
(a) Leaking gasket.	(a) Locate and replace gasket.
(b) Loose connection to pressure switch.	(b) Tighten connection.
(c) Oversized pump causing excessive water flow through heater.	(c) Replace with correctly sized pump.
(d) Soot deposits in heat exchange.	(d) Correct problem. Clean heat exchanger tubes.
(e) Damaged bypass valve.	(e) Replace valve.
Scale forming in combustion chamber.	
(a) Problem with water chemistry.	(a) Check pH level, alkalinity, and calcium hardness of water. Bring within levels recommended by heater manufacturer.
(b) Improper bypass valve adjustment.	(b) Adjust bypass valve. If problem persists, repair or replace valve.

Table 5-4 Troubleshooting Oil-Fired Pool Heaters

Symptom and Possible Cause	Possible Remedy
Burner will not start (motor and transformer will not start).	
(a) No power to heater.	(a) Check reset buttons on motor and primary control.
(b) Heater control circuit defect.	(b) Connect a jumper wire across the two terminals of the cad cell. If the burner starts, the problem is in either the heater control circuit wiring or one of the controls.
(c) Loose wires or worn insulation in the wire harness of the heater control circuit.	(c) Inspect and correct as necessary.
(d) Defective control (pressure switch, high-limit control, safety switch, thermostat, or time clock switch).	(d) Test each control with a jumper wire. Replace defective control when located.
(e) Restriction in the fuel line.	(e) Check fuel line and repair as necessary.
(f) Binding fuel pump.	(f) Repair or replace fuel pump.
(g) Defective high-limit switch.	(g) Turn off power to the heater and short out the high-limit switch in the line voltage circuit. Try to restart the burner. If it starts, the high-limit switch is defective and must be replaced.
(h) Dirty or defective cad cell.	(h) Remove one cad cell wire from the primary control. If burner starts, replace defective cad cell.
(i) Loose wiring below primary control and ignition transformer.	(i) Locate and repair.
Burner shuts off but restarts when primary control button is pressed.	
(a) Dirty or defective cad cell.	(a) Clean or replace as necessary.
(b) Poor combustion caused by fouled nozzle.	(b) Clean or replace nozzle.

(continued)

Table 5-4   *(continued)*

Symptom and Possible Cause	Possible Remedy
(c) Oil level in storage tank too low.	(c) Fill tank to appropriate level.
(d) Fuel line oil leaks.	(d) Locate and repair leaks.
(e) Nozzle pressure less than 100 psig.	(e) Determine cause and correct nozzle pressure.

Table 5-5   Troubleshooting Pool Pumps and Filters

Symptom and Possible Cause	Possible Remedy
Pump does not run.	
(a) Tripped circuit breaker.	(a) Rest circuit breaker.
(b) Blown fuse.	(b) Replace fuse.
(c) Incorrect timer setting.	(c) Check and reset for correct time.
(d) Pump motor binding.	(d) Oil motor.
Pump will not prime.	
(a) Damaged impeller or motor shaft.	(a) Repair or replace pump.
(b) Water leaks in suction line.	(b) Repair or replace suction line.
(c) Valves in wrong position.	(c) Change position of valves.
Excessive high or low filter water pressure.	
(a) Water leak.	(a) Find leak and repair.
(b) Dirty or clogged filter.	(b) Back-flush filter or replace it.
(c) Valves in wrong position.	(c) Change position of valves.

Caution

These troubleshooting procedures may require connections to electrical terminals and jumper wires to check and determine the cause of an operating problem. To avoid injury from electrical shock, always shut off the electrical power before servicing the line voltage controls. Never leave a jumper wire in place to fix a heater or the operating and safety controls will be bypassed.

Caution

Never attempt to troubleshoot or service a pump or pump motor if you are standing on a wet or damp surface or if your hands are wet. The electrical connection can cause serious shock, injury, or even death.

Note

A pump may start unexpectedly if it is equipped with an automatic resetting thermal protector.

Chapter 6

Ventilation Principles

Ventilation is the process of moving air from one space to an entirely separate space and is primarily a matter of air volume. It should not be confused with *circulation*, which is the moving of air *around and within* a confined space. In contrast to ventilation, circulation is a matter of air velocity. Ventilated air may or may not have been conditioned, and it may be supplied to or removed from the spaces by either natural or mechanical means.

The ventilation of a structure is important not only for the health of its occupants but for their comfort as well. The proper ventilation of a structure will replace stale, warm air in the interior with fresh cooler air from the outdoors. It will reduce or eliminate odors, remove excess moisture, and lower humidity levels, especially in the basement, attic, and crawl spaces.

For many years, proper ventilation was not considered as important as it is today. Houses were not very well insulated, and outside air could be easily drawn into the structure not only through open windows and doors but also through the walls themselves. Older houses were said to breathe because air could move in and out of them without much difficulty.

The fuel crisis of the 1970s and the rapid increase in energy costs made the public aware that we had to have more efficient combustion appliances (for example, furnaces, boilers, water heaters) and that structures had to be more tightly constructed and insulated. Although the latter move did result in a reduction in heat loss and gain, it also produced new problems such as trapped moisture, stale air, and even health problems. For example, in tightly constructed and insulated houses, vent fans, clothes dryers, and kitchen exhaust fans can create a negative pressure, drawing air into the house through holes in the framing, chimneys, and even exhaust flues. This can cause backdrafting in combustion appliances, which can be a serious health hazard.

If ventilation is inadequate and more air is exhausted from the house than can be drawn in through natural ventilation, the result is depressurization, which causes toxic combustion gases to be released through cracks or poorly connected ducts in the heating and cooling system. It is important that a balance be maintained between air being exhausted and air being drawn into the house.

There are two types of ventilation: passive ventilation and mechanical ventilation. The former only uses openings (vents) in the roof and walls to allow heat to escape. The latter uses mechanical ventilators, such as exhaust fans, attic fans, and whole-house fans in combination with vents to remove the air from the house. Exhaust and attic fans are covered in Chapter 7 ("Ventilation and Exhaust Fans").

The Motive Force

The force that moves the air in a room or building may be due to natural causes or mechanical means. In the first case, the ventilation is called *natural ventilation.* This kind of ventilation finds application in industrial plants, public buildings, schools, garages, dwellings, and farm buildings. The two natural forces available for moving air into, through, and out of buildings are (1) induction and (2) thermal effect. The inductive action is due to the wind force, whereas the thermal effect is due to the difference in temperature inside and outside a building (this being in fact the same as the *chimney effect*). The air movement may be caused by either of these forces acting alone or by a combination of the two, depending on atmospheric conditions, building design, and location.

The nature of the ventilating results obtained by natural means will vary from time to time because of variation in the velocity and direction of the wind and the temperature difference.

The wind ventilating effect depends on its velocity. In almost all localities, summer wind velocities are lower than those in the winter. There are relatively few places where the wind velocity falls below one-half of the average for many hours per month. Accordingly, if a natural ventilating system is proportioned for wind velocities of one-half the average seasonal velocity, it should prove satisfactory in almost every case.

When considering the use of natural wind forces for producing ventilation, three conditions must be considered:

1. The average wind velocity.
2. The prevailing wind direction.
3. Local wind interference by buildings, halls, or other obstructions.

Inductive Action of the Wind

When the wind blows without encountering any obstruction to change its direction, its movement may be represented by a series of parallel arrows, as in Figure 6-1. The arrows indicate the direction head. The formula for determining the rate of flow is as follows:

$$Q = 9.4A \sqrt{h(t - t_0)}$$

where Q = airflow, cubic feet per minute.

A = free area of inlets or outlets (assumed equal), square feet.

h = height from inlets to outlets, feet.

t = *average* temperature of indoor air at height h, °F.

t_0 = temperature of outdoor air, °F.

9.4 = constant of proportionality, including a value of 65 percent for effectiveness of openings. This should be reduced to 50 percent (constant = 7.2) if conditions are not favorable.

Induced Draft

A closed flue (stack) or chimney will induce a draft or draw air. In other words, it will cause the air to rise from the bottom level (or room level) to the top. Consider the schematic of a stack shown in Figure 6-5. The air is cool at the bottom of the stack and hot at the top. Each unit of air in traversing the stack expands as the temperature increases and becomes lighter. Assuming that cube A in Figure 6-5 represents 1 lb of air and that the initial volume undergoes first eight expansions and then sixteen, the corresponding weight of the initial volume (1 lb) decreases to $\frac{1}{8}$ lb and then to $\frac{1}{16}$ lb. Accordingly the sum of the weights of unit volume in ascending is $1 + \frac{1}{8} + \frac{1}{16}$ or $1\frac{3}{16}$ lbs. On the outside of the stack the volume and weight of each unit of air remain the same so that considering three units a, b, c of decreasing weights in the stack, there are three units of a', b', c' of constant weight outside the stack, the total weight outside the stack being 3 lbs and only $1\frac{3}{16}$ lbs inside the stack. As a result of the downward force (3 lbs) outside the stack being greater than that in the stack, the heavy units a', b', c' push the lighter units a, b, c up and out of the stack, thus inducing a draft as indicated by the lever scales in Figure 6-5. For purposes of explanation, induced draft may be considered virtually the same as thermal effect.

Combined Force of Wind Effect and Thermal Effect

It should be noted that when the forces of wind effect and thermal effect are acting together (even when both forces are acting together without interference), the resulting airflow is not equal to the sum

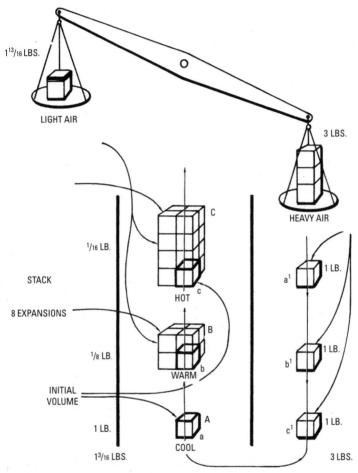

Figure 6-5 The principle of induced draft.

of the two estimated quantities. The flow through any opening is proportional to the square root of the sum of the heads acting upon the opening.

When the two heads are equal in value and the ventilating openings are operated so as to coordinate them, the total airflow through the building is about 10 percent greater than that produced by either head acting independently under conditions ideal to it. This percentage decreases rapidly as one head increases over the other, and the larger will predominate.

The wind velocity and direction, the outdoor temperature, or the indoor distribution cannot be predicted with certainty, and refinement in calculations is not justified; consequently, a simplified method can be used. This may be done by using the equations and calculating the flows produced by each force separately under conditions of openings best suited for coordination of the forces.

Mechanical Ventilation

Mechanical ventilation is the process of supplying or removing air by mechanical means. In other words, it represents a form of *forced* ventilation. Some form of mechanical ventilation is necessary when the volume of air required to ventilate a space cannot be delivered adequately by natural means. As a result, it may be necessary to add a fan (or fans) to the ventilation system in order to obtain the required rate of air change.

Mechanical ventilation involves the use not only of fans but also of ducts in some larger systems. The selection, installation, and operation of fans are described in Chapter 7 ("Fan Selection and Operation"). All aspects of duct sizing, the resistance to airflow, and other related aspects are described in considerable detail in Chapter 7 of Volume 2 ("Ducts and Duct Systems").

Air Ventilation Requirements

The volume of air required for proper ventilation is determined by the size of the space to be ventilated and the number of times per hour that the air in the space is to be changed. Table 6-1 gives some recommended rates of air change for various types of spaces. The volume of air required to ventilate a given space is determined by dividing the volume of the space by the number of minutes shown for that space in the "rate of change" column in Table 6-1.

In many cases, existing local regulations or codes will govern the ventilating requirements. Some of these codes are based on a specified amount of air per person and others on the air required per foot of floor area. The table should thus serve only as a guide to average conditions; where local codes or regulations are involved, they should be taken into consideration.

If the number of persons occupying a given space is larger than would be normal for such a space, the air should be changed more often than shown in the table. It is recommended that an air exchange rate of 40 cubic feet per minute per person be allowed for extremely crowded spaces.

If the cooling effect of rapid air movement is needed in localities that have high temperatures or humidities, the number of air changes shown in Table 6-1 should be doubled.

Table 6-1   Fresh Air Requirements

Type of Building or Room	Minimum Air Changes per Hour	CFA per Minute per Occupant
Attic spaces (for cooling)	12–15	
Boiler rooms	15–20	
Churches, auditoriums	8	20–30
College classrooms		25–35
Dining rooms (hotel)	5	
Engine rooms	4–6	
Factory buildings (ordinary manufacturing)	2–4	
Factory buildings (extreme fumes or moisture)	10–15	
Foundries	15–20	
Galvanizing plants	20–30*	
Garages (repair)	20–30	
Garages (storage)	4–6	
Homes (night cooling)	9–17	
Hospitals (general)		40–50
Hospitals (children's)		35–40
Hospitals (contagious diseases)		80–90
Kitchens (hotel)	10–20	
Kitchens (restaurant)	10–20	
Libraries (public)	4	
Laundries	10–15	
Mills (paper)	15–20*	
Mills (textile—general buildings)	4	
Mills (textile—dyehouses)	15–20*	
Offices (public)	3	
Offices (private)	4	
Pickling plants	10–15†	
Pump rooms	5	
Restaurants	8–12	
Schools (grade)		15–25
Schools (high)		30–35
Shops (machine)	5	
Shops (paint)	15–20*	
Shops (railroad)	5	

Table 6-1   (continued)

Type of Building or Room	Minimum Air Changes per Hour	CFA per Minute per Occupant
Shops (woodworking)	5	
Substations (electric)	5–10	
Theatres		10–15
Turbine rooms (electric)	5–10	
Warehouses	2	
Waiting rooms (public)	4	

*Hoods should be installed over vats or machines.
†Unit heaters should be directed on vats to keep fumes superheated.

Roof Ventilators

The function of a roof ventilator is to provide a storm- and weatherproof air outlet. For maximum flow by induction, the ventilator should be located on that part of the roof where it will receive the full wind without interference.

One must exercise great care when installing ventilators. If the ventilators are installed within the vacuum region created by the wind passing over the building or in a light court, or on a low building between two buildings, their performance will be seriously influenced. Their normal ejector action, if any, may be completely lost.

The base of a ventilator should be a tapering cone shape. This design provides the effect of a bell mouth nozzle, which gives considerably higher flow than that of a square entrance orifice.

Air inlet openings located at low levels in the building should be at least equal to, and preferably larger than, the combined throat areas of all roof ventilators.

The advantages of natural ventilation units are that they may be used to supplement power-driven supply fans, and under favorable conditions it may be possible to shut down the power-driven units.

Types of Roof Ventilators

Roof ventilators are manufactured in a variety of shapes and designs. Because of this variety, it is possible to classify roof ventilators under a number of broad categories, including the following:

1. Stationary head
2. Revolving

3. Turbine
4. Ridge
5. Siphonage

Some of the examples illustrated in the paragraphs that follow are no longer manufactured, but they will be encountered on older buildings. For this reason, they are included in this chapter.

Stationary-Head Ventilators
More ventilators are of this type than any other, and when well designed, it is usually considered the most efficient type of gravity ventilator. The chief advantages of stationary-head ventilators are as follows:

1. Higher exhaustive capacity under all wind conditions.
2. No moving parts.
3. Quiet operation.
4. No upkeep.

A stationary head ventilator is illustrated in Figure 6-6.

Figure 6-6 Stationary-head ventilator.

Revolving Ventilators
A typical revolving ventilator is shown in Figure 6-7. This type of ventilator swings on a pivot, aided by the wind vane so that its open end points away from the wind. The inductive action of the wind, in passing around the head, draws air out of the building. In

Figure 6-7   Revolving ventilator. The top portion pivots.

general, this is not as efficient as the stationary-head ventilator, although it has general use.

A major disadvantage of the revolving ventilator is its low capacity in still air. Furthermore, if the pivot bearings stick so that the head cannot follow the wind, it fails to exhaust air (in some cases even admitting air, rain, or snow). The revolving ventilator also frequently becomes noisy, creaking when changing direction. Constant attention is required to overcome these disadvantages.

Turbine Ventilators

Figure 6-8 represents one type of turbine ventilator. On its top is a series of vanes that, from the force of the wind, causes the entire top to rotate. Fastened to the top on the inside and placed in the air outlet openings is a series of propeller blades. The wind rotates this head, the blades drawing air up the shaft and exhausting it through the blade opening. The basic limitation of the turbine ventilator is that its blades draw the air outward as the top revolves. Its principal disadvantages include the following:

1. Low capacities in quiet air.

2. Lowered capacity if the pivot bearings do not turn freely.

3. The tendency to become noisy (as does any heavy rotating body that cannot accurately be kept in balance).

4. Required service attention in oiling, cleaning, and eventually replacing bearings.

Figure 6-8 Turbine ventilator. The blades draw air outward as the top revolves.

Another type of turbine ventilator (see Figure 6-9) consists of a globe-shaped head containing vane blades. It, too, is designed to draw air out of the structure as the globe-shaped head rotates. The basic components of a globe-head turbine ventilator are shown in Figure 6-10.

Turbine ventilators with globe-shaped heads also have a number of disadvantages. For example, wind impact on the vanes allows outside air to enter the head on the windward side that must be exhausted, together with the air from the building on the leeward

Figure 6-9 Globe-head turbine ventilator.

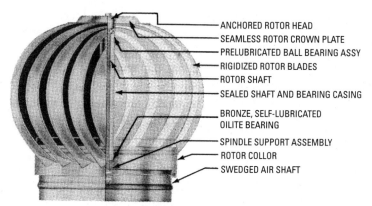

ANCHORED ROTOR HEAD
SEAMLESS ROTOR CROWN PLATE
PRELUBRICATED BALL BEARING ASSY
RIGIDIZED ROTOR BLADES
ROTOR SHAFT
SEALED SHAFT AND BEARING CASING
BRONZE, SELF-LUBRICATED
OILITE BEARING
SPINDLE SUPPORT ASSEMBLY
ROTOR COLLOR
SWEDGED AIR SHAFT

Figure 6-10   Construction details of a turbine ventilator.
(Courtesy Penn Ventilator Co., Inc.)

side. This decreases its efficiency inasmuch as the head must handle
both volumes of air. Furthermore, this type of ventilator is apt not
to be rainproof when the wind is not turning it. Like all revolving
ventilators, its moving parts involve a service problem in oiling,
keeping bearings free, and the replacement of worn parts.

Ridge Ventilators

Figure 6-11 shows a sectional view of a ridge ventilator, which is
installed along the entire roof ridge of the space to be ventilated.
Basically, it consists of a valve in the top of the building, which
lets the warm air out as it rises to the roof air outlet distribution
along the length of the structure. Then, too, it has a pleasing uniform
appearance.

Figure 6-11   Ridge ventilator.

Its major disadvantage is that it does not take full advantage of wind action unless the wind direction is almost directly across it. This type of ventilator also involves a somewhat cumbersome damper and a rather difficult problem in building modernization.

Siphonage Ventilators

The siphonage ventilator (see Figure 6-12) acts by induction, drawing the building air upward. Wind causes a flow of air upward through a duct that is concentric to and parallel with the ventilator shaft extending from the building. Both of these air passages terminate in the ventilator head, and the upward flow of the outside air creates a siphonage action drawing the building airstreams exhausting through the head. This ventilator is simply a stationary unit with an auxiliary air passageway to obtain the siphonage action.

Figure 6-12 Siphonage ventilator.

The head of the siphonage ventilator must be designed to eject not only the building air but also the siphon stream. This tends to retard airflow from the building due to the fact that egress from the head is usually somewhat restricted.

Fan Ventilators

A typical fan ventilator is shown in Figure 6-13. The principal advantage of this type of ventilator is that the fan greatly increases the ventilating capacity when the fan is in operation. Fan ventilators also have a number of other advantages when

Figure 6-13 Sectional view showing fan ventilator.

the fan is not in use and have great capacity when the fan is operated. Fan ventilators can be used on any building, regardless of access to wind flow, and can be spotted directly over any point at which ventilation is badly needed. These ventilators can also be used on ductwork flues to give greater capacities when friction losses are relatively large. It should be noted that a fan ventilator is a *forced-*draft rather than an induced-draft ventilator.

Components of a Roof Ventilator

The basic components of a typical roof ventilator are shown in Figure 6-14 and may be listed as follows:

   1. Base
   2. Barrel
   3. Top
   4. Windband
   5. Airshaft
   6. Dampers

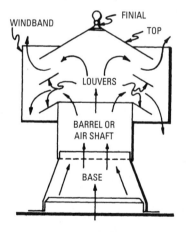

Figure 6-14 Component parts of a roof ventilator.

The *base* serves as the connection between the roof and the ventilator proper. A trough is usually provided around the inside bottom edge of the base to collect any condensation occurring in the ventilator and draw it out to the roof.

As bases are made to fit either a round or square opening and to conform to the shape and slope of the roof, they are essentially tailor-made for each installation.

After leaving the base, the air passes through the *barrel* (or *neck*) of the ventilator, which is merely the lower section of the head. It then enters the head proper and is exhausted to the outside air through the openings between louvers. The *top*, of course, covers the opening in the roof.

The *windband* is the vertical band encircling the ventilator head. The *airshaft* is the entire passageway through the ventilator from the roof to the top of the barrel.

The *dampers* are mechanical devices for closing the airshaft. They assume a number of forms and are referred to according to type as the *sliding sleeve*, *inverted cone*, *butterfly*, and *louver*.

Motive Force to Cause Air Circulation

Two agencies form the motive force to cause air circulation: (1) temperature differences inside and outside the building resulting in a chimney effect, and (2) inductive action caused by wind blowing against the ventilator.

Capacity of Ventilators

The following factors must be taken into consideration in making a selection of the proper ventilator for any specific problem:

1. Mean temperature difference.
2. Stack height (chimney effect).
3. Inductive action of the wind.
4. Area of opening in the ventilator.

The *mean temperature difference* refers to the average temperature difference between the air inside and outside the building (see Figure 6-15). If the ventilating problem is essentially a winter one, this difference may be as much as 40°F, while in summer, when doors and windows are open, this difference will probably drop to about 10°F.

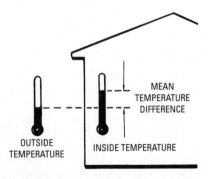

Figure 6-15 Mean temperature difference inside and outside.

MEAN TEMPERATURE DIFFERENCE

OUTSIDE TEMPERATURE

INSIDE TEMPERATURE

Stack height (see Figure 6-16) is the height of the column of warm air that causes the chimney action of the ventilator. It is measured in feet from the floor of the building to the top of the ventilator barrel.

The *inductive action of the wind* (see Figure 6-17) is the effect of the wind as it passes over the ventilator in inducing a circulation out of the building.

The *area of the opening in the ventilator* (see Figure 6-18) is determined by the rated size of the ventilator, expressed as the inside diameter of the barrel in inches.

Figure 6-16 Stack height upon which the chimney effect depends.

STACK HEIGHT

Figure 6-17 The suction action of the wind as it passes over the ventilator.

WIND VELOCITY

Figure 6-18 Diameter of the base, which governs the capacity of gravity ventilation.

DIAMETER

Design and Placement of Inlet Air Openings

The purpose of a roof ventilator is to let air escape from the top of a building. This naturally means that a like amount of air must be admitted to the building to take the place of that exhausted. The nature, size, and location of these inlet openings are of importance in determining the effectiveness of the ventilating system.

Inlet air openings are frequently constructed in the form of louvered openings located near the floor line, but they also often consist of the building windows. In general, there are three factors that should be considered when planning for an effective ventilating system:

1. The relationship between the area of the air intakes and the airshaft areas.
2. The distribution of inlet air openings.
3. The height at which air inlets are placed.

The area of the air intakes should at all times be twice that of the combined airshaft area of all ventilators (see Figure 6-19). By keeping

Figure 6-19 Open areas at B should be twice that of A.

this relationship, the full capacity of the ventilators will be realized, and the velocity of the incoming air will be low, thereby lessening the danger from drafts in the building. Any backdraft down the ventilator itself will also be eliminated.

These inlet air openings should also be distributed in such a way as to allow the admission of fresh air to all parts of the building. They should be located as close to the floor as possible in order to bring the incoming fresh air into the breathing zone.

Fresh Air Requirements

Table 6-1 lists necessary air changes for various rooms and buildings and thus offers a guide as to the amount of air required for efficient ventilation. This information should be used in connection with the ventilator capacity tables in the proper selection of the number and size of units required.

Where two figures are given for one type of building, use the smaller figure when conditions are normal and the larger figure when they are abnormal. Certain buildings are better figured on a cfm (cubic feet per minute) per occupant basis. Their requirements are given in this manner.

Ventilator Bases

The ventilator base is the connection between the other elements of the ventilator and the roof. It must be designed so as to fit the contour of the roof and the opening on which it is mounted. Its design and construction is important, particularly in ventilator sizes and types where weight and wind resistance are high. Ventilator manufacturers provide a wide variety of different ventilator base sizes. In their literature, illustrated base designs (see Figure 6-20) are cross-referenced with dimensional tables for the convenience of the buyer.

Gauges of metal are used that ensure rigidity and strength. Reinforcement is added where needed. Flashing flanges are amply wide to ensure rigid, weather-tight joints that will not leak when properly fastened and flashed to the roof. All seams are well riveted, soldered, or doped (the latter in asbestos-protected steel) to ensure storm-tight joints. All connections to the roof and to the next adjacent ventilator unit (the head in a gravity unit or the fan in a fan unit) are designed for 75-mph wind velocity as standard or 100 mph optional.

Since the outside sheet-metal surfaces of ventilators are exposed to atmospheric temperatures and the inside surfaces to room temperature, there is frequently a tendency for condensation to form on the

Figure 6-20 Standard ventilator bases. The letters refer to dimension on manufacturers' tables.

inside surfaces. In order to minimize the possibility of condensation drip into the ventilated space, condensation gutters may be provided to drain the water to the outside of the ventilator. These condensation gutters are usually located at the extreme lower edge of the base where as little water as possible can get past them.

The round ventilator bases in Figure 6-21 are standard but can be omitted if a duct is to be fitted into the lower end of the base with which the gutter would interfere. Examples of spare bases are shown in Figure 6-22, but these are special. In either type, drains

Figure 6-21   Round-base ventilators.

ROUND BASE
SWEDGES

ROUND BASE
CONDENSATE GUTTERS

ROUND BASE
STIFFENER ANGLES

DRAIN

Figure 6-22   Square-base ventilators.

SQUARE BASE
STIFFENER ANGLES

SQUARE BASE
CONDENSATE GUTTERS

SQUARE BASE
SWEDGES

DRAIN

from the gutter to the roof are ample for drainage and to prevent clogging.

In ventilator sizes and types where weights are not great, bases are lapped into the next adjacent unit above. In order to properly position the units and to add stiffness, a wedge is provided in the base against which the next adjacent unit seats.

Angle Rings

In larger ventilator sizes where added strength, rigidity, and ease of erection are important, angle rings have been used to connect the base to the next adjacent unit (ventilator head, fan section, or stack).

In certain instances a one-ring connection (see Figure 6-23) is used with the upper edge of the base lapping into the next adjacent unit, which rests upon the angle ring. The bolted connection is made through the sheet-metal lap. The lap connection is ample to ensure proper bearing for connection screws or bolts. When angle rings are provided, wedges are not used.

Figure 6-23 One-ring connection.

Sometimes a two-ring connection (see Figure 6-24) is used, one ring at the top of the base, another at the bottom of the adjacent unit. The two rings form a flanged connection and are bolted together. In every instance where angle rings are used, they are riveted to the bases to develop the full design strength of the assembly for velocities of 75 mph standard or 100 mph optional.

Figure 6-24 Two-ring connection.

Stiffener Angles

Stiffener angles are provided in conjunction with angle rings in certain applications where the sheet metal needs reinforcing. These lie vertically along the outside of the base surface at quarter points and extend from the angle ring at the top to the outer edge of the roof flange at the bottom. They are riveted to the base sheet metal and welded to the angle ring. Bolted connections through portions of the stiffener that lie along the roof flange to the curb or framing members below provide rigid structural members through which load is carried to the roof structure.

Where applicable and with certain types of dampers, a small clip can be supplied and riveted to the base (see Figure 6-25). The damper chain drops through this clip and can be locked at any point to properly position the damper. This clip is useful when the damper is to be operated from a point directly below the ventilator since it avoids the use of pulleys and complicated chain arrangements.

Figure 6-25 Base chain clip.

Prefabricated Roof Curbs

Prefabricated roof curbs (bases) for ventilators are available from a number of manufacturers. One of the advantages of the prefabricated type over those constructed at the site is the fact that they are generally cheaper. This, of course, is due to their being mass-produced. Although commonly designed for flat-roof installation, prefabricated roof curbs can also be built for installation on the ridge or single slope of a roof. Figures 6-26 and 6-27 illustrate some of the design features incorporated in a prefabricated roof curb.

Figure 6-26   Prefabricated roof curb designed for flat-roof installation.

(Courtesy Penn Ventilator Co., Inc.)

Figure 6-27   Prefabricated roof curb featuring self-flashing design.

(Courtesy Penn Ventilator Co., Inc.)

Ventilator Dampers

Ventilator dampers (see Figure 6-28) are made in a variety of types, from the single-disc butterfly to the multiblade louver, which has been designed to allow a flexible and reliable means of air movement control. A tight seal can be obtained through the use of a damper ring, which prevents the passage of air when the damper is closed.

Some dampers can be controlled only by hand chain; others may be remotely operated through the use of damper control motors of the electric or compressed-air type.

Figure 6-28 Various forms of dampers.

The principal types of ventilator dampers are as follows:

1. Sliding sleeve
2. Fire-retarding cone
3. Single butterfly
4. Divided butterfly
5. Louver

Louver Dampers

Figure 6-28 shows the general appearance of a louver damper. It is considered the best type for airflow. Louver dampers offer little resistance to the passage of air and in a partially open position create little turbulence in the airstream. In multiblade louvers, the blades on one half open up, and those on the other half open down.

The center blade is double the width, and its edges are connected to adjacent blades by clips and bars. The spacing of the blades along the connecting bars has been closely studied to ensure that the blade edges seat tightly on the damper ring when closed. This damper ring also allows all the blade pivot bearings to be placed inside the ventilator shaft, away from the weather. It also eliminates holes through the airshaft that might leak air and rain. Blades are regularly weighted so that the damper closes automatically. Any type of control may be used.

Sliding Sleeve Dampers

The sliding sleeve damper is frequently used for gravity ventilators. In construction it closely fits the under circumference of the ventilator airshaft and operates vertically. It occupies almost no space in the airshaft and offers no resistance or turbulence to the airstream in any position. Its normal position is open, and with a fusible link it can be used as an automatic-opening damper where there is need for such a control unit.

Sliding sleeve dampers have one principal advantage. Because of their vertical sides, there is no tendency for dust or dirt to accumulate.

The sliding sleeve damper is operated by chain only. Radial spiders keep the damper cylindrical to the operating chain attached to the hub of the spider, passing upward through a pulley fastened below the finial and then down past the spider hub, where a spring clip is located. The spring clip enables the damper to be positioned at any point between open and closed.

Sliding Cone Dampers

As shown in Figure 6-28, a sliding cone damper consists of a cone with apex down and with a flared outer rim that seats on the upper edge of the airshaft when closed. This directs the airstream to the outlet openings of the ventilator, lessens turbulence in the ventilator head, and consequently increases capacity.

From the apex of the damper, the operating chain passes upward to a pulley located below the finial, then downward through a slot in the cone to a pulley located on the inside of the airshaft, and then through the base to the building below.

When used in connection with the fusible link, this damper becomes an automatically closing, fire-retarding unit.

Butterfly Dampers

The two butterfly dampers used in roof ventilators are (1) the single-disc damper and (2) the divided-disc damper. They receive their name from the butterfly-wing appearance of the metal disc used to open or close the air passage.

The single-disc butterfly damper seats tightly against the ring channel, preventing air leakage when closed. When operated by hand chain, these dampers are normally counterweighted to close but can be supplied weighted to open when required.

The divided-disc butterfly damper is used for sizes that prevent the use of a single disc. The divided halves (or wings) of the disc swing upward, pivoted on two rods whose ends bear in the damper ring channel on which the damper edges seat tightly.

Butterfly dampers, single- and divided-disc, are the only dampers that can be successfully used in ventilators constructed of asbestos-protected steel. In this material, the damper ring is omitted and the damper pivot rods are mounted on brackets secured to the airshaft wall.

Method of Calculating Number and Size of Ventilators Required

The number and size of ventilators required by a particular building can be calculated by taking the following steps:

1. Determine the gross volume of the interior of the building in cubic feet by multiplying its length by its width and by its height.

2. Determine the number of air changes per hour required for the building in question. This can be found by referring to the tables given in the *Typical Installation* section.

3. Find the total number of cubic feet of air per hour necessary for the ventilators to exhaust by multiplying the number of changes per hour by the volume of each change, or 1 × 2.

4. Reduce this to cubic feet per minute by dividing by 60.

5. The effective range of a gravity ventilator is about 10 to 15 feet in the direction of the length of the building and 15 to 25 feet in the direction of the width of the building, where air is being admitted on the sides. The next step, therefore, is to space the units along the roof, using these restrictions, determining in this manner the number of ventilators that will be required.

   If the building is divided into bays, one unit is usually placed in each bay, provided the bays are not over 20 feet long. If there are no bays, one ventilator every 20 feet should be sufficient for buildings up to 50 feet in width. In wider buildings, the ventilators should be so arranged as to maintain approximately 20-foot spacing. If there are any spots where there is urgent need of ventilation, such as a machine or vat emitting fumes or dust, they should be cared for by ventilators placed above them. Such a layout will provide the number of ventilators required for the building.

6. Next, determine the exhaustive capacity required of each ventilator by dividing the total amount of air per minute to be exhausted by the number of ventilators to be used, or 4/5. This is the capacity for which you should look in the capacity tables obtained from the manufacturer.

7. Determine the conditions under which the ventilators will operate, that is, stack height, mean temperature difference, and wind velocity. These factors, their use, and their probable values have already been explained.

8. Turn to the manufacturer's capacity tables and look under the proper columns of temperature difference, stack height, and wind velocity, as determined in step 7, to find a capacity in cfm that will fulfill the requirement as determined in step 6. This capacity is listed under the size that should be selected.

Ventilator Calculation Examples

Assume a building used as an automobile storage garage 50 feet wide by 150 feet long by 20 feet high to the eaves, 26 feet to the ridge of the roof.

1. Volume of space from the eaves down is $50 \times 20 \times 150 = 150,000$ cubic feet. Volume of space from the eaves up is $50 \times 3 \times 150 = 22,500$ cubic feet. Total volume = 172,500 cubic feet.

2. From the table of air change requirements, you will find that storage garages require four changes per hour for proper ventilation. Total air to be exhausted is then $172,500 \times 4 = 690,000$ cubic feet per hour, or $690,000 \div 60 = 11,500$ cfm.

3. Spacing ventilators along the roof as indicated in Figure 6-29, with the aforementioned rules in mind, the resultant number of ventilators would be seven, spaced 15 feet from each end

Figure 6-29 Typical building illustrating method of calculating number and size of ventilators required.

and 20 feet apart. Each ventilator would need to exhaust 11,500 ÷ 7 = 1643 cfm.

4. Suppose we have a mean temperature difference of 10°F, an average wind velocity of 5 mph, and a stack height of 26 feet (floor to roof ridge).

5. Turning to the capacity tables under that of the 30-inch cone damper unit in the proper columns for the factors given in step 4, we find that the capacity is 1750 cfm, which exceeds our requisite of 1643 cfm obtained in step 3. Even though this is a trifle higher than necessary, it should be used, inasmuch as the next size smaller would be too far under the required capacity. This can be seen by referring to the 24-inch unit, the capacity of which is 1165 cfm.

We have therefore determined that to properly ventilate this building, seven 30-inch cone damper ventilators will be necessary, located on the ridge of the roof and spaced 20 feet apart and 15 feet from each end.

Air Leakage

Air leakage is the passage of air in and out of various cracks or openings in buildings. It is also sometimes referred to as *infiltration*.

Air leaking *into* a building may be caused by wind pressure or by differences in temperature inside and outside of the building. In the former case, the wind builds up a pressure on one or two sides of a building, causing air to leak into the building. As shown in Figure 6-2 previously, the action of the wind on the opposite side or sides produces a vacuum that draws air out of the building. Thus, as shown in Figure 6-4 previously, a plan view of a single-room building is shown having a window and a door on one side and a window on the opposite side. The details are greatly exaggerated so that you can see the cracks.

Note that when the wind hits the *A* side of the building, its momentum (dynamic inertia) builds up a pressure higher than inside the building, which causes the air to leak through any cracks present, as indicated by the arrows.

As the wind traverses the length of the building, the air currents as they continue past the side *C* converge and produce a vacuum along side *C* by induction. Because the pressure on the outside of *C* is lower than inside the building, air leaks out as indicated by the arrows.

Air leakage due to temperature difference or thermal effect is usually referred to as *stack* or *chimney effect*. Air leakage due to cold air outside and warm air inside takes place when the building contains cracks or openings at different levels. This results in the cold and heavy air entering at low level and pushing the warm and light air out at high levels, the same as draft taking place in a chimney.

Thus, in Figure 6-4, assume a two-story building having a window open on each floor. Evidently when the temperature inside the building is higher than outside, the heavy cold air from outside will enter the building through window *A* and push the warm light air through window *B*, as indicated by arrow *a*; as it cools, it will increase in weight and circulate downward, as indicated by arrow *b*.

Although not appreciable in low buildings, this air leakage is considerable in high buildings unless sealing between various floors and rooms is adequate.

A reasonable amount of air leakage is actually beneficial to health. Any attempt to seal a building drum-tight will cause the inside air to become stale and putrid. Emphasis should be placed on the reduction of heat transmission rather than the absolute elimination of air leakage.

The application of storm sash to poorly filtered windows will generally result in a reduction of air leakage of up to 50 percent. An equal effect can be obtained by properly installed weather stripping.

Garage Ventilation

The importance of garage ventilation cannot be overestimated because of the ever-present danger of carbon monoxide poisoning. During warm weather, there is usually adequate ventilation because doors and windows are kept open. In cold weather, however, people close up openings tight as a drum, with considerable danger. Nobody can breathe the resulting carbon monoxide concentration long without being knocked out—hence the importance of proper ventilation in cold weather, regardless of physical comfort.

Where it is impractical to operate an adequate natural ventilation system, a mechanical system should be used that will provide for either the supply of 1 cubic foot of air per minute from out of doors for each square foot of floor area or the removal of the same amount, discharging it to the outside as a means of flushing the garage.

The following points should be carefully reviewed when considering a ventilating system capable of removing carbon monoxide from an enclosed area:

1. Upward ventilation results in a lower concentration of carbon monoxide at the breathing line and a lower temperature above the breathing line than does downward ventilation for the same rate of carbon monoxide production and air change and the same temperature at the 30-inch level.

2. A lower rate of air change and a smaller heating load are required with upward ventilation than with downward ventilation.

3. In the average case, upward ventilation results in a lower concentration of carbon monoxide in the occupied portion of a garage than is had with complete mixing of the exhaust gases and the air supplied. However, the variations in concentration from point to point, together with the possible failure of the advantages of upward ventilation to accrue, suggest the basing of garage ventilation on complete mixing and an air change sufficient to dilute the exhaust gases to the allowable concentration of carbon monoxide.

4. The rate of carbon monoxide production by an idling car is shown to vary from 25 to 50 cubic feet per hour, with an average rate of 35 cubic feet per hour.

5. An air change of 350,000 cubic feet per hour per idling car is required to keep the carbon monoxide concentration down to one part in 10,000 parts of air.

Ventilation of Kitchens

In estimating the requirements for the ventilation of kitchens, the following two methods should be considered:

1. It is customary to allow a complete change of air every 2 minutes.

2. In many cases it is desirable to have all the extracted air leave via hoods or canopies located over ranges, steam tables, urns, dishwashers, and so on.

The first method applies only to average conditions, and modification from this average should be made depending on the kitchen size and the heat- and vapor-producing equipment.

In the second method, the air volume should be calculated from the hood entrance velocity rather than the air-change method.

Light cooking requires an entrance velocity of only 50 feet per minute, while severe conditions may run to 150 feet per minute or higher.

The size of a hood will depend on its dimensions. For example, a hood 3 feet by 8 feet would have an area of 24 square feet using an average velocity of 100 feet per minute.

Where quiet operation is essential, the blower should be selected on the basis of a low outlet velocity. This will also result in lower operating costs.

If space is limited and noise is not a factor, smaller units with higher outlet velocities may be necessary. This may result in a lower initial cost.

General Ventilation Rules

The American Society of Heating and Ventilating Engineers offers the following recommendations for designing and installing an adequate natural ventilation system:

1. Inlet openings in the building should be well distributed and should be located on the windward side near the bottom, while outlet openings are located on the leeward side near the top. Outside air will then be supplied to the zone to be ventilated.

2. Inlet openings should not be obstructed by buildings, trees, signboards, and so on, outside or by partitions inside.

3. Greatest flow per square foot of total openings is obtained by using inlet and outlet openings of nearly equal areas.

4. In the design of window-ventilated buildings, where the direction of the wind is constant and dependable, the orientation of the building, together with amount and grouping of ventilation openings, can be readily arranged to take full advantage of the force of the wind. Where the wind's direction is variable, the openings should be arranged in sidewalls and monitors so that, as far as possible, there will be approximately equal areas on all sides. Thus, no matter what the wind's direction, there will always be some openings directly exposed to the pressure force and others to a suction force, and effective movement through the building will be ensured.

5. Direct shortcuts between openings on two sides at a high level may clear the air at that level without producing any appreciable ventilation at the level of occupancy.

6. In order for temperature difference to produce a motive force, there must be vertical distance between openings. That is, if there are a number of openings available in a building, but all are at the same level, there will be no motive head produced by temperature difference, no matter how great that difference might be.

7. In order for the forces of temperature difference to operate to maximum advantage, the vertical distance between inlet and outlet openings should be as great as possible.

Openings in the vicinity of the neutral zone are less effective for ventilation.

8. In the use of monitors, windows on the windward side should usually be kept closed, because if they are open, the inflow tendency of the wind counteracts the outflow tendency of temperature difference. Openings on the leeward side of the monitor result in cooperation of wind and temperature difference.

9. In an industrial building where furnaces that give off heat and fumes are to be installed, it is better to locate them in the end of the building exposed to the prevailing wind. The strong suction effect of the wind at the roof near the windward end will then cooperate with temperature difference to provide for the most active and satisfactory removal of the heat and gas-laden air.

10. In case it is impossible to locate furnaces in the windward end, that part of the building in which they are to be located should be built higher than the rest so that the wind, in splashing, will create a suction. The additional height also increases the effect of temperature difference to cooperate with the wind.

11. The intensity of suction or the vacuum produced by the jump of the wind is greatest just behind the building face. The area of suction does not vary with the wind velocity, but the flow due to suction is directly proportional to wind velocity.

12. Openings much larger than the calculated areas are sometimes desirable, especially when changes in occupancy are possible or to provide for extremely hot days. In the former case, free openings should be located at the level of occupancy for psychological reasons.

13. In single-story industrial buildings, particularly those covering large areas, natural ventilation must be accomplished by taking air in and out of the roof openings. Openings in the pressure zones can be used for inflow, and openings in the suction zone, or openings in zones of less pressure, can be used for outflow. The ventilation is accomplished by the manipulation of openings to get airflow through the zones to be ventilated.

Chapter 7

Ventilation and Exhaust Fans

Both ventilation and air circulation utilize fans to move the air. Ventilation is concerned with the moving of a *volume* of air from one space to another. It does not involve the weight of air but the volume of air in cubic feet moved per minute (cfm). The circulation of air, on the other hand, is concerned with the velocity at which air moves around a confined space and is expressed in feet per minute (fpm).

This chapter is concerned primarily with introducing the reader to the problems of fan selection and operation. Several sections of this chapter provide detailed instructions for fan sizing. Because the selection of a fan and the design of a duct system are mutually dependent, Chapter 7 of Volume 2 ("Ducts and Duct Systems") should also be consulted.

Codes and Standards

Always consult local codes and standards before designing or attempting to install a fan system. Other sources of information on codes and standards pertaining to fans and fan systems are as follows:

1. The Air Moving and Conditioning Association (AMCA).
2. The National Association of Fan Manufacturers (NAFM).
3. The American Society of Heating, Refrigerating and Air-Conditioning Engineers (ASHRAE).
4. Home Ventilation Institute (HVI).

Definitions

A number of terms and definitions largely related to fan selection and operation should be examined and learned for a clearer understanding of the materials in this chapter. Most of the terms and definitions contained in this section are provided by the Air Moving and Conditioning Association.

> **Air horsepower (AHP).** The work done in moving a given volume (or weight) of air at a given speed. Air horsepower is also referred to as the Morse power output of a fan.
>
> **Area (A).** The square feet of any plane surface or cross section.

Area of duct. The product of the height and width of the duct multiplied by the air velocity equals the cubic feet of air per minute flowing through the duct.

Brake horsepower (BHP). The work done by an electric motor in driving the fan, measured as horsepower delivered to the fan shaft. In belt-drive units, the total workload is equal to the workload of the electric motor plus the drive losses from belts and pulleys. The brake horsepower is always a higher number than air horsepower (AHP). Brake horsepower is also referred to as the *horsepower input* of the fan.

Cubic feet per minute (cfm). The physical volume of air moved by a fan per minute expressed as fan outlet conditions.

Density. The actual weight of air in pounds per cubic foot (0.075 at 70°F and 29.92 inches barometric pressure).

Fan inlet area. The inside area of the inlet collar.

Fan outlet area. The inside area of the fan outlet.

Mechanical efficiency (ME). A decimal number or a percentage representing the ratio of air horsepower (AHP) to brake horsepower (BHP) of a fan. It will always be less than 1.000 or 100 percent and may be expressed as follows:

$$ME = \frac{AHP}{BHP}$$

Outlet velocity (OV). The outlet velocity of a fan measured in feet per minute.

Revolutions per minute (RPM). The speed at which a fan or motor turns.

Standard air. Air at 70°F and 29.92 inches barometric pressure weighing 0.075 lbs per cubic foot.

Static efficiency (SE). The static efficiency of a fan is the mechanical efficiency multiplied by the ratio of static pressure to the total pressure.

Static pressure (SP). The static pressure of a fan is the total pressure diminished by the fan velocity pressure. It is measured in inches of water (see *velocity pressure*).

Tip speed (TS). Also referred to as the peripheral velocity of wheel. It is determined by multiplying the circumference of the wheel by the rpm.

$$TP = \frac{\times \text{ wheel diameter in feet} \times RPM}{12}$$

$\times$ wheel diameter in feet $\times$ RPM

The tip speed should not exceed 3300 rpm if a quiet operation is to be obtained.

Total pressure (TP). Any fan produces a total pressure (TP), which is the sum of the static pressure (SP) and the velocity pressure (VP). Total pressure represents the rise of pressure from fan inlet to fan outlet.

Velocity. The speed in feet per minute (fpm) at which air is moving at any location (for example, through a duct, inlet damper, outlet damper, or fan discharge point). When the performance data for air-handling equipment are given in feet per minute (fpm), conversion to cubic feet per minute can be made by multiplying the fpm by the duct area:

Air velocity = 1000 FPM

Duct size = 8 in. $\times$ 20 in. = 160 sq. in.

Duct area = 160 $\div$ 144 = 1.11 sq. ft.

Air flow = 1000 FPM $\times$ 1.11 sq. ft. = 1110 CFM

Velocity pressure (VP). Velocity pressure results only when air is in motion, and it is measured in inches of water. One-inch water gauge corresponds to 4005 fpm (standard air) velocity. The following formula is used for determining velocity pressure:

$$VP = \left[\frac{\text{Air Velocity}}{4005}\right]^2$$

Types of Fans

The various mechanical devices used to move the air in heating, ventilating, and air-conditioning installations are known as fans, blowers, exhausts, or propellers.

Every fan is equipped with an impeller, which forces (impels) the airflow. The manner in which air flows through the impeller provides the basis for the following two general classifications of fans:

1. Centrifugal fans
2. Axial-flow fans

In a *centrifugal* (or *radial flow*) *fan* (see Figure 7-1), the air flows radially (that is, diverging from the center) through the impeller, which is mounted in a scroll-type housing. Centrifugal fans are further subdivided into a number of different types depending on several design variations, such as the forward or backward inclination of the blade.

Figure 7-1 Centrifugal fan principles.

An *axial-flow fan* is mounted within a cylinder or ring, and the air flows axially (that is, parallel to the main axis) through the impeller. Depending on the design of the enclosure and impeller, axial-flow fans can be subdivided into the following types:

1. Tubeaxial fans
2. Vaneaxial fans
3. Propeller fans

A *tubeaxial fan* consists of an axial-flow wheel within a cylinder (see Figure 7-2). These fans are available in a number of different types depending on the design and construction of the impeller blades.

A *vaneaxial fan* also consists of an axial-flow wheel but differs from a tubeaxial fan in that it uses a set of vanes to guide the airflow and increase efficiency (see Figure 7-3).

A *propeller fan* consists of a propeller or disc wheel within a ring casing or plate. These fans are by far the simplest in construction and operate best against low resistance (see Figure 7-4).

Figure 7-2 Tubeaxial fan principles.

MOTOR

Figure 7-3 Vaneaxial fan principles.

Furnace Blowers

The blower used in a forced warm-air furnace is similar to the centrifugal fan used in ducts and other types of applications. Most blowers are designed with a belt drive, although some are equipped with a direct drive to the motor. Furnace blowers are described in considerable detail in the several chapters dealing with specific types of furnaces. See, for example, Chapter 11 of Volume 1 ("Gas-Fired Furnaces").

Basic Fan Laws

The performance of fans and their relationship to the ventilation system are governed by definite principles of fluid dynamics. An understanding of these principles is useful to anyone designing a ventilation system because they make possible the prediction of effects resulting from altered operating condi-

Figure 7-4
Propeller fan.

tions. The principles (and formulas) associated with fan and ventilation system engineering are referred to collectively as *basic fan laws*.

The basic fan laws used in calculating fan performance depend on the fact that the mechanical efficiency (ME) of a fan remains constant throughout its useful range of operating speeds (that is, the fan rpm). They also apply only to fans that are geometrically similar.

A current edition of the *ASHRAE Guide* will contain detailed explanations of the principles and formulas associated with basic fan laws. A typical example is the production of fan speed (rpm), static pressure (SP), and horsepower when the volume of air moved by the fan is varied. The following three principles and formulas are involved:

1. Fan speed delivery will vary directly as the cfm ratio:

$$\text{New RPM} = \text{Old RPM} \times \left[\frac{\text{New CFM}}{\text{Old CFM}}\right]$$

2. Fan (and system) pressures will vary directly as the square of the rpm ratio:

$$\text{New SP (or TP or VP)} = \left[\frac{\text{New RPM}}{\text{Old RPM}}\right]^2 \times \text{Old SP (or TP or VP)}$$

3. Brake horsepower (bhp) on the fan motor (or air horsepower of the fan) will vary directly as the cube of the rpm ratio:

$$\text{New BHP (or AHP)} = \left[\frac{\text{New RPM}}{\text{Old RPM}}\right]^3 \times \text{Old BHP (or AHP)}$$

Example
A centrifugal fan delivers 10,000 cfm at a static pressure of 1.0 inch when operating at a speed of 600 rpm and requires an input of 3 hp. If 12,000 cfm is desired in the same installation, what will be the new fan speed (rpm), static pressure (SP), and horsepower (bhp) input? The three aforementioned formulas can be applied as follows:

$$1.\ \text{New RPM} = 600 \times \left[\frac{12,000}{10,000}\right]$$

$$= 600 \times 1.2 = 720$$

$$2.\ \text{New SP} = \left[\frac{720}{600}\right]^2 \times 1$$

$$= 1.44 \times 1 = 1.44$$

$$3.\ \text{New BHP} = \left[\frac{720}{600}\right]^3 \times 3$$

$$= 1.7 \times 3 = 5.1$$

The following three formulas also may prove useful in making fan calculations:

1. A (area) $\times$ V (velocity) = CFM
2. CFM $\div$ $V = A$
3. CFM $\div$ $A = V$

Series and Parallel Fan Operation

Two separate and independent fans can be operated either in series or in parallel (see Figure 7-5). When two fans are operated in series, the cfm is *not* doubled. Instead, the total airflow is limited to the cfm capacity of one fan alone. Series operation is seldom desirable except when it is necessary to maintain the following conditions:

1. Constant pressure

2. Zero pressure

3. Constant vacuum

When fans are operated in parallel, they produce a total airflow equal to the sum of their individual cfm capacities. Parallel fan operation is necessary when a single fan is incapable of moving the total volume of air required or when airflow distribution is a factor.

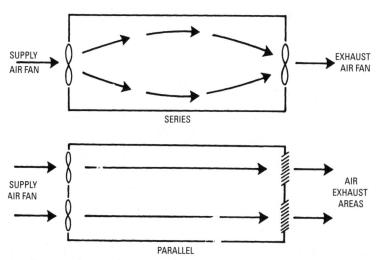

Figure 7-5 Series and parallel fan operations.

Fan Performance Curves

Fan performance curves are provided by fan manufacturers to graphically illustrate the relationship of total pressure, static pressure, power input, mechanical efficiency, and static efficiency to actual volume for the desired range of volumes at constant speed and air density. A typical performance curve for a forward-curved blade centrifugal fan is shown in Figure 7-6.

General Ventilation

General ventilation involves the moving of a volume of air from one space to an entirely separate space, where concern for a concentrated source of heat or contamination is not a factor. In this respect, it differs from *local ventilation*, which is used primarily to control atmospheric contamination or excessive heat at its source (see following section).

In general ventilation, the specific volume of air to be moved is measured in cubic feet per minute (cfm). The two principal methods of determining the required cfm are as follows:

1. Air-change method
2. Heat removal method

Figure 7-6   Typical performance curves for a forward-curved blade centrifugal fan.

Determining CFM by the Air-Change Method

In order to determine the required cfm for a structure of space by the air-change method, the following data are necessary:

1. The total cubic feet of air space in the structure or space.

2. The required number of air changes necessary to give satisfactory ventilation.

The total cubic feet of air space is easily determined by multiplying the dimensions of the structure of space. For example, a room 12 feet long and 10 feet wide with an 8-foot ceiling would have 960 cubic feet of air space (12 ft × 10 ft × 8 ft = 960 ft^3).

The required number of air changes necessary to give satisfactory ventilation will depend on a variety of factors, including (1) use, (2) number of people, (3) geographic location, and (4) height of ceiling.

Usually local health department codes will specify the required number of air changes for various installations. When there are no code requirements, the data given in Table 7-1 are recommended.

Once the necessary data have been obtained, the following formula can be used to determine the cfm:

$$\text{CFM} = \frac{\text{Building Volume in Cubic Feet}}{\text{Minutes Air Change}}$$

Let's use the space shown in Figure 7-7 to illustrate how the air-change method is used to determine cfm. First, let's assume that the space is being used as a bakery. In Table 7-1 you will note that a 2- to 3-minute air-change range is recommended for a bakery. The fact that a range is given is important because the number selected for the air-change method will depend on several variables. For example, a

Figure 7-7 Bakery building dimensions.

Table 7-1   Average Air Changes Required per Minute for Good Ventilation

	Minutes per Change
Assembly halls	2–10
Auditoriums	2–10
Bakeries	2–3
Banks	3–10
Barns	10–20
Bars	2–5
Beauty parlors	2–5
Boiler rooms	1–5
Bowling alleys	2–10
Churches	5–10
Clubs	2–10
Dairies	2–5
Dance halls	2–10
Dining rooms	3–10
Dry cleaners	1–5
Engine rooms	1–3
Factories	2–5
Forge shops	2–5
Foundries	1–5
Garages	2–10
Generator rooms	2–5
Gymnasiums	2–10
Kitchens, hospitals	2–5
Kitchens, resident	2–5
Kitchens, restaurant	1–3
Laboratories	1–5
Laundries	1–3
Markets	2–10
Offices	2–10
Packing houses	2–5
Plating rooms	1–5
Pool rooms	2–5
Projection rooms	1–3
Recreation rooms	2–10
Residences	2–5

(continued)

Table 7-1 (continued)

	Minutes per Change
Sales rooms	2–10
Theaters	2–8
Toilets	2–5
Transformer rooms	1–5
Warehouses	2–10

higher number is used when the structure or space is located in a warm climate, when the ceiling is a particularly low one, or when there are a large number of people using a relatively small space. Comfort cooling, on the other hand, may be obtained by using the lowest figure in each stated range.

For the sake of our example, let's assume that the bakery has *not* been designed for comfort cooling. Furthermore, the ceilings are higher than average (15 feet), and the structure is located in a warm climate. With this information, the cfm can be determined in the following manner:

1. 100 ft. × 30 ft. × = 45,000 cu. ft. of air space (Fig. 7-7).

2. 3-minute required air change (Table 7-1).

3. CFM = $\dfrac{45,000}{3}$ = 15,000

Thus, 15,000 cfm are required to change the air in the bakery every 3 minutes. Assuming a 300 fpm intake velocity, 50 square feet of free air intake are needed.

Determining CFM by the Heat Removal Method

The heat removal method is useful for determining cfm in installations where the ventilation of sensible heat is required.

In order to determine cfm by this method, you need to know the total Btu per minute, the average outdoor temperature, and the desired inside temperature. This information is then used in the following formula:

$$CFM = \frac{\text{Total Btu per minute}}{0.0175 \times \text{Temp. Rise °F}}$$

Note that the cfm determined by the heat removal method deals primarily with sensible heat, not with radiant heat. The cfm obtained from the previous formula indicates the amount of air that needs to be passed through a structure or space in order to maintain the desired inside temperature.

Determining Air Intake

Adequate air intake area should be provided where fans are used to exhaust the air. The same holds true for fans used to *supply* air to a room (that is, adequate air exhaust area should be provided). The size of the air intake (or air exhaust) area depends on the velocity (fpm) of the entering or existing air and the total cfm required by the structure or space. This may be expressed by the following formula:

$$A = \frac{CFM}{FPM}$$

where A = square feet of free intake (or exhaust) area

cfm = cubic feet per minute

fpm = feet per minute

The bakery previously described requires 15,000 cfm. Assuming a 300-fpm intake velocity, 50 square feet of free air intake area are required.

$$\text{Area} = \frac{15,000 \text{ CFM}}{300 \text{ FPM}} = 50$$

Doors and windows are suitable air intake areas if they are located close enough to the floor and provide a full sweep through the area to be ventilated. When you have determined the total free air intake area by the aforementioned formula, *deduct* the area for doors and windows that function as passageways for air. Fixed or adjustable louvers can be installed over the other intake areas.

Screen Efficiency

It is frequently necessary to cover an air intake (or exhaust) area with a bird or insect screen. These screens reduce the free intake area, but the amount of the reduction will depend on the type of screen used. In Figure 7-8, the net (effective) free area for each of three screens is shown as a percentage. The small holes required by an insect screen reduce the net free area to approximately 50 percent. The ½-inch mesh screen, on the other hand, provides a net free area of 90 percent.

Figure 7-8 Net free air of various screens.

The reduction of the free intake area by screens can be compensated for by using a larger overall area.

Static Pressure

The *static pressure* of a fan may be defined as the total pressure diminished by the fan velocity pressure.

Calculating the total external static pressure of a system is important to the selection of a fan or blower because it must be capable of handling the required volume of air (in terms of cfm) against this pressure.

The total external static pressure is determined by adding the static pressures of any of the air-handling components in a system capable of offering resistance to the flow of air. A 10 percent allowance of the sum of these static pressures is added to obtain the total external static pressure.

The static pressures (that is, friction losses in inches of water) used in determining the *total* external static pressure of an air-handling system will include the following:

1. Entrance loss
2. Friction loss through filters
3. Friction loss through tempering coils
4. Friction loss through air washer
5. Duct system resistance
6. Supply grille resistance

Most friction losses can be obtained from data tables provided by manufacturers; however, duct loss is based on the longest run of duct, and this will vary from one installation to another.

In determining the length of duct, start at the point where the air enters the system and include all ducts in the main supply duct to the end of the system. An example of this type of calculation is shown in Table 7-2. The sum (406 ft) is then multiplied by the

Table 7-2 Total Length of Duct for an Installation

	Equivalent Length of Straight Duct (ft)
1 gooseneck at roof (double elbow 18″ × 63″)	39
28 feet straight duct to basement	28
1 elbow (18″ × 63″) to transition piece	20
40 feet straight duct	40
1 elbow (63″ × 18″)	68
60 feet straight duct	60
1 elbow (63″ × 18″)	68
15 feet straight duct	15
1 elbow (63″ × 18″)	68
	406

resistance for the ducts. For example, if the resistance is found to be 0.1 inch per 100 feet, the static pressure for the *total* run of duct will be 0.406 inch (that is, 406 ft ÷ 100 ft = 4.06 ft × 0.1 in = 0.406 in).

Local Ventilation

Local ventilation is used to control atmospheric contamination or excessive heat at its source with a minimum of airflow and power consumption. It is *not* used to move a volume of air from one space to another for human comfort.

Air velocity is an important factor in local ventilation. Air must move fast enough past the contaminant source to capture fumes, grease, dust, paint spray, and other materials and carry them into an exhaust hood.

Both the capture velocity of the air at the contaminant source and the velocity at the discharge duct must be considered when designing a localized ventilation system. It is important to remember that capture velocities will differ depending on the contaminant. Table 7-3 lists the capture velocities for contaminants found in a variety of booths (that is, enclosures designed to isolate areas used for special purposes).

The selection of a suitable fan for a local ventilation system requires knowledge of the required fan cfm capacity and the static pressure (SP) at which the fan must work. Once these facts are known, you have all the necessary information required for sizing the fan from the manufacturer's rating tables.

Table 7-3   Capture Velocities for Various Types of Booths

Process	Type of Hood	Capture Velocity (fpm)
Aluminum furnace	Enclosed hood, open one side	150–200
	Canopy or island hood	200–250
Brass furnace	Enclosed hood, open one side	200–250
	Canopy hood	250–300
Chemical lab	Enclosed hood, front opening	100–150
Degreasing	Canopy hood	150
	Slotted sides, 2″–4″ slots	1500–2000
Electric welding	Open front booth	100–150
	Portable hood, open face	200–250
Foundry shakeout	Open front booth	150–200
Kitchen ranges	Canopy hoods	125–150
Paint spraying	Open front booth	100–175
Paper-drying machine	Canopy hood	250–300
Pickling tanks	Canopy hood	200–250
Plating tanks	Canopy hood	225–250
	Slotted sides	250 cfm per foot of tank surface
Steam tanks	Canopy hood	125–175
Soldering booth	Enclosed booth, open one side	150–200

Courtesy Hayes-Albion Corporation

The required fan cfm capacity is determined by multiplying the open face area of any booth by the capture (face) velocity (fpm) of the air at the source of contamination.

CFM = Face Area (sq. ft.) × Face Velocity (FPM)

The total open face area of any booth is determined by its physical size and the required access to the work area. If a booth is designed with several open face areas, all of them must be calculated and added together.

Capture (face) velocities (fpm) can be determined for various types of booths from data available from manufacturers and other sources. An example of such data is illustrated in Table 7-3.

The precise calculation of static pressure (SP) is not necessary for the sizing of a fan (or fans) in a local ventilation installation. An approximate calculation of static pressure will usually suffice, and the following steps are suggested for making such a calculation:

1. Assume the losses in the exhaust hood itself to be 0.05 inch to 0.10 inch SP.

2. Size the cross-sectional area of the main duct to ensure 1400-2000 fpm velocity.

$$\text{Duct Area (sq. ft.)} = \frac{\text{CFM}}{\text{FPM}}$$

3. Keep all ductwork as short and straight as possible and avoid elbows and sharp turns (see Figure 7-9).

4. Determine the total straight duct length.

5. Add the equivalent straight duct length for each turn (see Table 7-4), and add it to step 4.

6. Multiply the sum of steps 4 and 5 by 0.0025 inch to determine an approximate static pressure for the ductwork.

7. The static pressure for filters usually can be obtained from the filter manufacturer. If this is not possible, assume 0.25 inch SP for clean filters and 0.50 inch for dirty filters.

Figure 7-9 Various designs to avoid when designing a duct system.

Table 7-4 Equivalent Lengths of Straight Pipe

Dia. of Pipe	90° Elbow* Centerline Radius		
	1.5 D	2.0 D	2.5 D
3″	5	3	3
4″	6	4	4
5″	9	6	5
6″	12	7	6
7″	13	9	7
8″	15	10	8
10″	20	14	11
12″	25	17	14
14″	30	21	17
16″	30	24	20
18″	41	28	23
20″	46	32	26
24″	57	40	32
30″	74	51	41
36″	93	64	52
40″	105	72	59
48″	130	89	73

*For 60° elbows-x.67; for 45° elbows-x.5.
(Courtesy Hayes-Albion Corporation)

8. Add the static pressures from steps 1, 6, and 7 to obtain the approximate total static pressure for the installation.

9. Use the total static pressure for the installation and the required cfm capacity for sizing the fan.

Caution

Always check local building and safety codes for regulations pertaining to hazardous conditions. For extremely critical installations, such as those dealing with acids, poisons, or toxic fumes, consult the fan manufacturer for engineering analysis. It is *strongly* recommended that you do not attempt to make these calculations yourself. Finally, *never* undersize a fan. If you have any doubts about the correct size or horsepower, then select the next size larger.

Exhaust-Hood Design Recommendations

A properly designed exhaust hood (see Figure 7-10) is an important part of a local ventilation system. The following recommendations are offered as design guidelines:

1. Use the shortest duct run possible.

2. Avoid the use of elbows and transitions.

3. Size the exhaust hood to provide a minimum 100 fpm face velocity (150 fpm for island-type work).

4. Provide sufficient hood overhang on all sides to overlap work area.

5. Use more than one exhaust fan on very large hoods.

6. Use as many individual hood and duct systems as possible (that is, try to avoid grouping hoods together on the same duct system).

7. Use filters where required. Velocities over filters should be sized in accordance with filter manufacturer's recommendations.

8. Provide makeup air units.

Figure 7-10   Recommended hood design. *(Courtesy Penn Ventilator Co., Inc.)*

Fan Motors

Most fans used in heating, ventilating, and air-conditioning installations are powered by electric motors. Because of the small size of
many of these fans, the majority are equipped with direct-connected motors. A V-belt drive arrangement is used with larger fans,
particularly centrifugal fans used in forced warm-air furnaces or
the larger ventilating units found in commercial and industrial
installations.

It is the general rule to select a fan one size larger than the fan
requirements for the installation. This is particularly so in installations that may require the movement of large volumes of air for
short intervals.

The advantage of fans equipped with a belt-drive arrangement is
that adjustments can be made for different speeds. It is simply a
matter of changing the pulley size. A belt drive is especially desirable when the required horsepower requirement is in doubt.

A fan wheel directly connected to the motor shaft is the best
arrangement, but this is only feasible with the smaller centrifugal
fans and propeller fans under 60 inches in diameter.

A direct-connected fan is generally driven by a single-phase AC
motor of the split-phase, capacitor, or shaded-pole type. The capacitor motor is recommended when there are current limitations. Its
major advantage is its greater efficiency electrically. The major disadvantage of such motors is that they are usually designed to operate at only one speed. A damper arrangement can be used to
throttle the air when it becomes necessary to vary the air volume or
pressure of the fan.

The variation of pressure and air volume in larger fan installations (for example, mechanical draft fans) can be accomplished by
means of a constant-speed, direct-connected motor equipped with
movable guide vanes in the fan inlet.

The National Electrical Manufacturer's Association (NEMA)
has recently revised motor voltage designations to conform to system voltages now present throughout the country. Single-phase
motor voltages should now be specified as 115 volts or 230 volts
instead of the 110-volt or 220-volt designations formerly in effect.
Polyphase voltages should be expressed as 208 volts or 230/460
volts instead of the 220/440 voltages formerly in effect. Motors
for special voltages such as 177, 480, or 575 volts are available
from many fan manufacturers on special order. Fan motors have
been designed to operate satisfactorily over the range of plus or
minus 10 percent of the nameplate voltage ratings. *Always* check
the fan motor nameplate voltage ratings before installing the motor.

Tables 7-5 and 7-6 list nominal full-load ampere ratings for single-phase and three-phase motor voltages. The amperes given are approximate values only and represent averages compiled from tables of leading motor manufacturers. Compare these with the specific amperages listed for Airmaster fans in Table 7-7.

Table 7-5   Nominal Full-Load Ampere Ratings for Single-Phase Motors

| HP | RPM | Full-Load Current | |
		115 V	230 V
$1/25$	1550	1.0	0.5
$1/25$	1050	1.0	0.5
$1/12$	1725	2.0	1.0
	1140	2.4	1.2
	860	3.2	1.6
$1/10$	1550	2.4	1.2
$1/8$	1725	2.8	1.4
	1140	3.4	1.7
	860	4.0	2.0
$1/6$	1725	3.2	1.6
	1140	3.84	1.92
	860	4.5	2.25
$1/4$	1725	4.6	2.3
	1140	6.15	3.07
	860	7.5	3.75
$1/3$	1725	5.2	2.6
	1140	6.25	3.13
	860	7.35	3.67
$1/2$	1725	7.4	3.7
	1140	9.15	4.57
	860	12.8	6.4
$3/4$	1725	10.2	5.1
	1140	12.5	6.25
	860	15.1	7.55
1	1725	13.0	6.5
	1140	15.1	7.55
	860	15.9	7.95

(Courtesy Penn Ventilator Company, Inc.)

Table 7-6 Nominal Full-Load Ampere Ratings for Three-Phase Motors

HP	RPM	Full-Load Current	
		115 V	*230 V*
¼	1725	0.95	0.48
	1140	1.4	0.7
	860	1.6	0.8
⅓	1725	1.19	0.6
	1140	1.59	0.8
	860	1.8	0.9
½	1725	1.72	0.86
	1140	2.15	1.08
	860	2.38	1.19
¾	1725	2.46	1.23
	1140	2.92	1.46
	860	3.26	1.63
1	1725	3.19	1.6
	1140	3.7	1.85
	860	4.12	2.06
1½	1725	4.61	2.31
	1140	5.18	2.59
	860	5.75	2.88
2	1725	5.98	2.99
	1140	6.50	3.25
	860	7.28	3.64
3	1725	8.70	4.35
	1140	9.25	4.62
	860	10.3	5.15
5	1725	14.0	7.0
	1140	14.6	7.3
	860	16.2	8.1
7½	1725	20.3	10.2
	1140	20.9	10.5
	860	23.0	11.5

(Courtesy Penn Ventilator Company, Inc.)

Table 7-7   Ampere Rating Table for Airmaster Fans

	RPM	3-Phase, 60 Cycle AC			Single-Phase AC	
HP	Syn. Speed	220 Volts	440 Volts	550 Volts	110 Volts	220 Volts
$^1/_{30}$	1050	—	—	—	1.90	—
$^1/_{25}$	1050	—	—	—	2.00	—
$^1/_{20}$	1550	—	—	—	2.30	—
	1140	—	—	—	2.40	—
	1050	—	—	—	3.10	—
$^1/_{15}$	1550	—	—	—	3.20	—
$^1/_{12}$	1550	—	—	—	3.80	—
	860	—	—	—	2.80	—
$^1/_8$	1800	—	—	—	2.80	1.40
	1200	—	—	—	3.40	1.70
	860	—	—	—	5.40	2.70
$^1/_6$	1800	—	—	—	3.00	1.50
	1200	—	—	—	3.60	1.80
	860	—	—	—	5.60	2.80
$^1/_4$	1800	0.96	0.48	0.38	4.12	2.06
	1200	1.16	0.58	0.46	5.50	2.75
	900	1.45	0.73	0.58	6.50	3.25
$^1/_3$	1800	1.16	0.58	0.47	5.00	2.50
	1200	1.43	0.72	0.58	6.00	3.00
	900	1.75	0.88	0.71	8.40	4.20
$^1/_2$	1800	1.68	0.84	0.67	7.16	3.58
	1200	2.07	1.04	0.83	10.00	5.02
	900	2.90	1.45	1.16	—	—
$^3/_4$	1800	2.33	1.17	0.93	9.86	4.94
	1200	2.85	1.43	1.14	11.90	5.96
	900	3.45	1.73	1.38	—	—
1	1800	3.05	1.53	1.22	10.60	5.28
	1200	3.54	1.77	1.42	12.30	6.12
	900	3.74	1.87	1.50	12.90	6.48
$1^1/_2$	1800	4.28	2.14	1.71	14.80	7.40
	1200	4.85	2.43	1.94	16.80	8.40
	900	5.81	2.91	2.32	20.00	10.10
2	1800	5.76	2.88	2.30	20.00	10.00
	1200	6.35	3.18	2.54	22.00	11.00
	900	7.21	3.61	2.88	25.00	12.50

(continued)

Table 7-7   (continued)

HP	RPM Syn. Speed	3-Phase, 60 Cycle AC			Single-Phase AC	
		220 Volts	440 Volts	550 Volts	110 Volts	220 Volts
	900	7.21	3.61	2.88	25.00	12.50
3	1800	8.29	4.14	3.32	28.80	14.30
	1200	8.92	4.46	3.56	30.80	15.40
	900	10.20	5.09	4.08	35.40	17.60
5	1800	13.20	6.60	5.28	45.60	22.80
	1200	13.10	7.05	5.64	48.80	24.40
	900	15.60	7.80	6.24	54.00	27.00
7½	1800	19.30	9.70	7.72	67.00	33.40
	1200	20.30	10.20	8.12	70.20	35.20
	900	23.80	11.90	9.51	82.40	41.20

(Courtesy Hayes-Albion Corporation)

Overload relay heaters should not be selected solely on the basis of the data listed in Tables 7-5 and 7-6. Heaters must be selected in accordance with the actual motor current as shown on the nameplate. It is also important that ambient temperatures of the area in which the motor control is located be taken into consideration when making heater selections. Ambient compensated overload relays are available for abnormal temperature conditions.

Typical connection diagrams for two-speed, three-phase motors are illustrated in Figures 7-11 and 7-12. Two-speed motors are available for most fan lines. Because *all* two-speed motors are always single-voltage, it is necessary to specify the available line voltage phase and frequency when ordering.

Examples of fans equipped with the belt-drive arrangement and direct-connected motors are shown in Figures 7-13 and 7-14.

Troubleshooting Fans

Fan motors are electrically powered (see Table 7-8). Always turn off the electricity before attempting to service or repair a fan. Failure to do so could result in serious injury or even death because high voltages are involved. Electrical tests on fan motors should be done by a qualified electrician.

Fan motors mounted in the airstream are cooled by a portion of the air drawn around them. This acts to hold motor temperatures

Figure 7-11 Connection diagram for three-phase, two-speed, one-winding variable-torque motors. *(Courtesy Penn Ventilator Co., Inc.)*

Figure 7-12 Connection diagram for three-phase, two-speed, two-winding variable-torque motors. *(Courtesy Penn Ventilator Co., Inc.)*

down and makes it possible for the motor to run continuously at substantial brake horsepower (bhp) overloads without exceeding its rated temperature rise.

The actual brake horsepower load has little relation to its nameplate horsepower as long as it remains at or below its rated maximum

Figure 7-13 Belt-driven
propeller fan assembly.

(Courtesy Hayes-Albion Corp.)

Figure 7-14 Fan with direct-
connected motor.

(Courtesy Penn Ventilator Co., Inc.)

temperatures. It is *temperature rise* that is crucial to the breakdown
or burning out of a fan motor (even though it may be physically
underloaded).

A fan motor will normally run at a temperature too hot to hold a
hand against it, but this will still be at or below the manufacturer's
temperature rise limit as stated on the nameplate. When a fan motor

Table 7-8   Fan Maintenance and Troubleshooting

Symptom and Possible Cause	Possible Remedy
Fan motor hums but blades do not rotate.	
(a) Motor overheated from thermal overload.	(a) Turn off fan and wait 20 minutes. If motor is not defective, it will restart after cooling off.
(b) Defective motor.	(b) Turn off electricity and check motor starting capacitor.
Fan motor will not start.	
(a) Fan unplugged at attic outlet.	(a) Plug fan into outlet.
(b) Blown fuse or tripped circuit breaker.	(b) Replace fuse or reset circuit breaker. Call electrician if problem continues.
(c) Thermostat set too low.	(c) Turn thermostat to higher setting.
(d) Defective fan motor starting capacitor.	(d) Test and replace if necessary.
(e) Defective fan motor.	(e) Replace fan motor.
Noisy fan.	
(a) Loose fan blade.	(a) Tighten connection or replace.
(b) Loose fan motor mounting.	(b) Tighten.
(c) Unbalanced fan blade.	(c) Tighten if loose connection, replace if defective, or clean if dirt accumulation on one blade is causing imbalance.
(d) Defective motor bearing.	(d) Repair or replace motor.
(e) Not insulated against vibration.	(e) Insert foam or rubber pad between fan motor and structure surface.
(f) Motor bearing needs lubrication.	(f) Lubricate motor bearings.

does overheat or burn out, it is usually for one of the following reasons:

1. Defective motor.
2. Line voltage too high or too low for the rated motor voltage (more than plus or minus 10 percent voltage deviation is considered excessive).

3. The belts on belt-driven fans may be too tight or too loose, causing slippage and consequent loss of the cooling effect of air passing around the motor.

4. Improper pulleys on belt-driven fans will result in too high a fan rpm, which causes overloading.

5. Backward- and forward-curved wheel centrifugal fans or roof ventilators running backward will guarantee an overload condition. Remember that all centrifugal fans blow in one direction only, regardless of rotation; propeller fans that run backward blow backward.

6. Propeller fans may be starved for air as a result of insufficient intake (or outlet) area. The fans are literally starved for air, which causes the static pressure to rise and the brake horsepower load on the motor to increase. The air that flows around the motor is also reduced, causing the motor to overheat. Attic fans are frequently damaged as a result of inadequate outlet area.

Fan Selection

The following information is generally required for the selection of a suitable fan:

1. Volume of air required (cfm)
2. Static pressure (SP)
3. Type of application or service
4. Maximum tolerable noise level
5. Nature of load and available drive
6. Ambient and airstream temperature
7. Mounting arrangement of the system
8. Available line voltage

The *volume of air required* refers to the volume of air that must be moved by the fan to meet the needs of the building or space. It is expressed in cubic feet per minute and is determined by dividing the total cubic feet of air space by the required number of air changes necessary to give proper ventilation.

The *static pressure* of a fan may be defined as the total pressure diminished by the fan velocity. In other words, it is the resistance offered by the system (ducts, air intakes, and so on) to the flow of air. After the duct sizes have been determined, it is necessary to calculate the static pressure of the system so that the proper fan can be selected which will handle the desired volume of air (that is, the required cfm) against the static pressure of the system. The various fan manufacturers provide tables indicating the operating characteristics of various-size fans against a wide range of static pressures. These tables list static pressures for different sizes of various fans.

The *type of application* (or service) is often an important consideration in what kind of fan is used in an installation. For example, a duct system will offer sufficient resistance to require a centrifugal, tubeaxial, or vaneaxial fan. A propeller fan is usually recommended for an installation without a duct system. Other factors, such as the volume of air that must be moved, the allowable noise level, the air temperature, use for general or local ventilation, and cost, are also important considerations in fan selection.

The *maximum tolerable noise level* is the highest acceptable noise level associated with air exchange equipment. The fan should be of suitable size and capacity to obtain a reasonable operating speed without overworking.

The *nature of load and available drive* is an important factor in controlling the noise level. High-speed motors are usually quieter than low-speed ones. Either belt- or direct-drive units are used in fan installations, and a high-speed motor connected to the fan with a V-belt offers the quietest operation.

The dry-bulb temperature of either ambient air or exhauststream air (*ambient or airstream temperature*) is a determining factor in selecting a suitable fan. Most fans operate satisfactorily at temperatures up to about 104°F (40°C). Special fans that can operate at higher temperatures are also available. For example, standard belt-driven tubeaxial fans are usable for temperatures up to 200°F (where the motor is out of the airstream).

The *mounting arrangement of the system* is directly determined by the application or service of the fan. Certain types of fans will prove to be more suitable than others, depending on the kind of installation. Fan manufacturers often offer useful recommendations for mounting arrangements.

The *available line voltage* will determine the size and type of fan motor most suitable for the installation. Motor voltage designations conform to the following system of voltages now used throughout the country: 115 volts, 230 volts, and 460 volts. Motors for special voltages (that is, 117, 480, or 575 volts) are available on special order.

Fan manufacturers provide information and assistance in selecting the most suitable fan or fans for your installation. Remember that ventilation requirements vary under different climatic conditions, and it is impossible to provide exact rules for determining the

Table 7.9 Minimum Fan Capacity (CFM) for Various Sections of the Country

Approx. Volume of House (ft³)	Minimum Fan Capacity Needed For Satisfactory Results (CFM)						
	North		Central			South	
3000	1000		2000		24″	3000	
4000	1320		2640			4000	
5000	1650		3300			5000	30″
6000	2000	24″	4000			6000	
7000	2310		4620	30″		7000	
8000	2540		5280		36′	8000	
9000	3000		6000			9000	
10,000	3330		6660			10,000	42″
11,000	3630		7260			11,000	
12,000 24″	4000	36″	8000			12,000	
13,000	4290		8580		48″	13,000	
14,000	4620 30″		9240			14,000	
15,000	5000		10,000	42″		15,000	
16,000	5280		10,560			16,000	
17,000	5610		11,220			17,000	
18,000	6000		12,000			18,000	
19,000	6270		12,540			19,000	
20,000	6660		13,320			20,000	
21,000	7000		14,000			21,000	
22,000	7260		14,520			22,000	

(Courtesy Hayes-Albion Corporation)

variables of local climate and topography (see Table 7-9). Allowances must be made for these climatic variables.

The following suggestions are offered only as a general guide to the selection of a fan and should not be construed as applying in every situation.

1. Use a ½ hp, ⅓ hp, or ¼ hp 860-rpm direct-drive fan on three-phase motor voltages whenever possible to eliminate the possibility of single-phase magnetic hum.
2. A belt-driven fan is less expensive, less noisy, more flexible, and more adaptable to capacity change than the direct-drive type.

3. Prolonged motor life can be expected of direct-driven fans using other than shaded-pole motors. For that reason, 1550-rpm and 1050-rpm motors should be avoided when very heavy duty and/or extremely long motor life is required.

4. Use a propeller fan when operation offers little or no resistance, or when there is no duct system.

5. Use a centrifugal or axial-flow fan when a duct system is involved.

6. Never try to force air through ducts smaller than the area of the fan.

Fan Installation

The following recommendations are offered as guidelines for proper fan installation.

1. Install the fan and air intake openings at opposite ends of the enclosure so that the intake air passes lengthwise through the area being ventilated (see Figure 7-15).

2. When possible, install exhaust fans or air outlets on the leeward side so that the air leaves with the prevailing winds (see Figure 7-16).

3. When possible, install ventilation (supply) fans or air intakes on the windward side so that the entering air utilizes pressure produced by prevailing winds (see Figure 7-17).

4. Provide a net intake area *at least* 30 percent greater than the exhaust fan opening.

5. When filters are used, increase the net intake area to allow minimum pressure loss from resistance of the filter.

6. Steam, heat, or odors should be exhausted by fans using totally enclosed motors mounted near the ceiling. The air intakes should be located near the floor (see Figure 7-18).

7. An explosion-proof motor with a spark-proof fan should be used when the exhaust air is hazardous.

8. Spring-mount fans and connect them to the wall opening by a canvas boot when extremely quiet operation is required.

Fan Installation Checklist

A properly installed fan motor (unless defective) will operate efficiently and will never overheat or burn out. To ensure proper installation, the following guidelines are suggested:

Figure 7-15 Locations of fans and air intake openings.
(Courtesy Hayes-Albion Corp.)

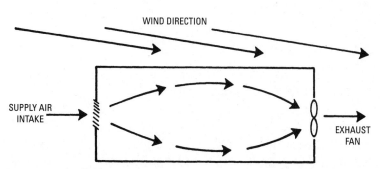

Figure 7-16 Exhaust fan installed on the leeward side, away from prevailing winds.

Figure 7-17 Supply air fan installed on the windward side, with the prevailing winds.

Figure 7-18 Recommended locations for exhaust openings.

(Courtesy Hayes-Albion Corp.)

1. Check the line current to be sure it is not more than plus or minus 10 percent voltage deviation.
2. Check belt tension for looseness after the first or second day of operation.
3. Check to be sure the fan is running in the right direction.
4. Inspect and lubricate fans subject to heavy usage. Do this after the first 15,000 hours or 5 years of service (whichever comes first).

5. Use open, drip-proof motors where fan motors are installed outside the airstream.

6. Use enclosed, nonventilated, air-over motors where fan motors are mounted in the airstream to reduce obstruction by dirt, grease, or other contaminants.

Air Volume Control

Sometimes it becomes necessary to vary the air volume handled by a fan. The following methods can be used for this purpose:

1. Dampers placed in the duct system.

2. Changing the pulley on the fan motor.

3. Changing the pulley on the fan.

4. Using variable-speed pulleys.

5. Using variable-speed motors.

6. Using variable inlet vanes on fans.

7. Reduction or increase of speed through power control.

Noise Control

In order to decrease the noise associated with the air exchange equipment, the following recommendations should be observed:

1. The equipment should be located a reasonable distance from important rooms.

2. The fans should be of proper size and capacity to obtain reasonable operating speed.

3. The equipment should be mounted on resilient bases made from a sound-dampening material.

4. When possible, the quieter high-speed AC motors with belt-driven fans should be used.

Fan Applications

Many different fans are used in ventilation and air-circulation systems, and these fans are classified on the basis of certain design and operating characteristics. Fan applications, on the other hand, are classified by the specific function they serve in the ventilation or air-circulation system. Among the numerous fan applications used for ventilation and air circulation are the following:

1. Attic fans

2. Exhaust fans

3. Circulating fans

4. Kitchen fans

5. Cooling tower fans

6. Unitary system fans

Attic fans are generally propeller types used during the summer to draw the cool night air through the structure and discharge it from the attic. The air can be discharged through windows or grilles or directly through an attic exhaust fan. The air is circulated, not conditioned.

Exhaust fans are used in local ventilation to remove contaminants at their source, or as a general means of discharging air from a space (for example, attic exhaust fans, wall fans, bathroom fans). Hood exhaust fans used with a duct system are generally centrifugal types. Because wall fans operate against very low resistance or no resistance at all, they are most commonly propeller types.

Circulating fans and *kitchen fans* arc propeller types used for air circulation purposes. *Cooling tower fans* are also generally propeller types, although centrifugal fans have also been used in installations requiring a forced draft.

Unitary system fans are centrifugal or propeller fans used in unit ventilators, unit heaters, unit humidifiers, and similar types of equipment. A propeller fan is used in these units when no ductwork exists.

Attic Ventilating Fans

A noninsulated attic on a hot summer day will experience temperatures as high as 130°F to 150°F. This accumulated heat seeps down through the ceiling and raises the temperatures in the rooms below, making living and sleeping areas very uncomfortable. This hot air from an uninsulated attic also increases the load on the air conditioner, which will raise the energy costs during the summer months. After sunset, the outside temperature sinks to pleasant cool levels, but the indoor air (especially in the upstairs bedrooms of a two-story house) remains uncomfortably hot with temperature readings that can reach as high as 85°F. This condition results from the fact that a house loses accumulated heat at a very slow rate.

This condition can be alleviated considerably by installing an attic ventilating fan. Such a fan placed in the attic will cool the air by replacement; that is, it will ventilate rather than condition. An attic ventilating fan can reduce temperatures in the attic by as much as 20 to 30 percent, and by approximately 10 to 15 percent in the bedrooms immediately below the attic.

Attic ventilating fans are controlled by a thermostat located in the attic or in the fan housing. The thermostat turns the fan on at a preset temperature and shuts it off when the temperature is lowered to the minimum setting in the thermostat preset temperature range. Many attic fans are equipped with a firestat, which will shut off the fan if there is a fire in the house.

In areas where high humidity is a problem, the fan should be equipped with a humidistat to remove excess moisture from the attic during the winter months. Moisture accumulating in the attic will contribute to the formation of ice dams on the roof. Ice will also form on the rafter surfaces inside the attic, which may lead to rot and damage to the roof framing.

Because of the low static pressures involved (usually less than 0.125 inch), disc or propeller fans with the blade mounted directly on the motor shaft are generally recommended for attic installation. It is recommended that these fans have quiet operating characteristics and sufficient capacity to give at least 30 air changes per hour.

The two general types of attic fans in common use in houses and other buildings are the following:

1. Boxed-in fans
2. Centrifugal fans

The *boxed-in* attic fan is installed within the attic in a box or suitable housing, located directly over a ceiling grille or in a bulkhead enclosing an attic stair. This type of fan can be connected to individual room grilles by means of a duct system.

In operation, outside cool air entering through the windows in the downstairs rooms is discharged into the attic space and escapes to the outside through louvers, dormer windows, or screened openings under the eaves. A general arrangement showing a typical installation of this type of fan is illustrated in Figure 7-19.

The installation of a multiblade centrifugal attic fan is shown in Figure 7-20. At the inlet side, the fan is connected to exhaust ducts leading to grilles, which are placed in the ceiling of the two bedrooms. The air exchange is accomplished by admitting fresh air through open windows, moving it up through the suction side of the fan, and finally discharging it through louvers.

The fan shown in Figure 7-21 is of the centrifugal curved-blade type, mounted on a light angle-iron frame, which supports the fan wheel, shaft, and bearings, with the motor that supplies the motive power to the fan through a belt drive.

Figure 7-19 Attic ventilation system.

The air inlet in this installation is placed close to a circular opening that is cut in an airtight board partition, which serves to divide the attic space into a suction and discharge chamber. The air is admitted through open windows and doors and then drawn up the attic stairway through the fan into the discharge chamber, from which it flows through the attic open window.

For best results, the outlet area for an attic fan should be 1½ times the area of the fan. Satisfactory results will be obtained as long as the area is *at least* equal to the blade area of the fan. Recommended dimensions for attic fan exhaust outlets are given in Table 7-9.

Tables 7-10, 7-11, and 7-12 provide data for square- and triangular-type louvers used with various fan diameters. These tables

Figure 7-20 Multiblade centrifugal attic fan connected to exhaust ducts.

Figure 7-21 Centrifugal curved-blade fan.

Table 7-10 Recommended Dimensions for Attic Fan Exhaust Outlets

Recommended Dimensions of Attic Fan Exhaust Outlet		
Fan Diameter	*Air Delivery Range (cfm)*	**Free Outlet Area Needed (ft²)*
24″	3500/5000	4.70
30″	4500/8500	7.35
36″	8000/12000	10.06
42″	10000/15500	14.40
48″	12000/20000	18.85

*1.5 times fan area
(Courtesy Hayes-Albion Corporation)

Table 7-11 Data for Square-Type Louvers

	Minimum Size of Square Outlet (inches)		
	Metal Shutters		**Wood Slats**
Fan Diameter	*Automatic (90% Open Area)*	*Fixed (70% Open Area)*	*Fixed (60% Open Area)*
24″	26 × 26	32 × 32	34 × 34
30″	32 × 32	39 × 39	42 × 42
36″	38 × 38	45 × 45	49 × 49
42″	44 × 44	54 × 54	60 × 60
48″	50 × 50	62 × 62	68 × 68

(Courtesy Hayes-Albion Corporation)

include the net free areas for 1-inch mesh wire screening. Remember that in order to keep insects and other foreign objects out of the attic, the exhaust air outlets should be covered with ½-inch or 1-inch wire mesh screen. The fan should be boxed-in on the intake side with conventional fly screening. This screening has

Table 7-12   Data for Triangular-Type Louvers

Fan Diameter	*Height of Triangular Louvers (for different roof pitches)*			
	⁵/₁₂ Pitch One Louver	⁶/₁₂ Pitch One Louver	⁷/₁₂ Pitch One Louver	⁸/₁₂ Pitch One Louver
24"	2'0"	2'2"	2'4"	2'6"
30"	2'6"	2'9"	3'0"	3'3"
36"	3'0"	3'3"	3'6"	3'9"
42"	3'3"	3'9"	4'1"	4'4"
48"	3'10"	4'3"	4'7"	4'9"

*Heights given are for one triangular louvered opening only; when two openings are used, reduce heights by approximately 80%.
(Courtesy Hayes-Albion Corp.)

Figure 7-22   Fan mounted at the attic window with the ceiling opening in central hallway. (Courtesy Hayes-Albion Corp.)

only 50 percent free area; therefore, the boxing must have a total area twice that of the inlet opening.

The location of the attic fan always depends on the design of the structure. In a house having a suitably sized window in an attic end wall or dormer, the best results (and fewest construction problems) can usually be obtained by mounting the fan directly against the window (see Figure 7-22). An automatic shutter should be installed outside the window for window-mounted fans. If the window is opened and the fan is mounted inside the opening, louvers should be installed a few inches in front of the fan to keep rain out of the attic.

In one-floor houses, the ceiling openings can be installed in any convenient *central* location (see Figure 7-23). In houses of two or more stories, the opening is generally located in the ceiling of the top-floor hallway. Again, a central location is usually best. The ceiling opening and its accompanying grille or shutter must be of sufficient size to avoid excessive resistance to airflow, permitting the airstream to pass through at a moderate, quiet velocity.

Figure 7-23   Fan mounted in ceiling hallway. *(Courtesy Hayes-Albion Corp.)*

Some attic fans require periodic lubrication of their motor bearings. Check the fan manufacturer's installation and operating instructions for the recommended lubrication schedule. Lubricate the bearings by pouring oil into the oil cups. Fan motors with sealed bearings do not require lubrication.

Clean the fan housing and blades in the spring before the beginning of the cooling season. The screens on the fan vent, soffits, and attic vents should also be cleaned at this time. Blocked vents will prevent air from being drawn into or exhausted from the attic.

Exhaust Fans

Exhaust fans are small, electrically operated fans used to remove odors, heat, and moisture from kitchens and bathrooms. They are commonly mounted in the wall or ceiling. Kitchens also will have an exhaust fan in the range hood over the stove.

Exhaust fans require very little maintenance. Wash the fan housing and fan blades every 6 months. Check the fan in the range hood for a grease filter. This should be cleaned every 3 months or more often depending on how much cooking is being done.

Kitchen Exhaust Fans

In estimating the requirements for ventilating kitchens, it is customary to allow a complete change of air every 2 minutes. In many cases, it is also desirable to have all the extracted air leave via hoods or canopies located over ranges, steam tables, dishwashers, and similar sources of localized heat and contaminants.

Allowing for a complete change of air every 2 minutes only applies to average conditions, and modifications from this average should be made on the basis of the kitchen size and the type of heat- and vapor-producing equipment.

An entrance velocity at the hood opening of 100 fpm is considered satisfactory as an allowance for average conditions. For very light cooking, an entrance velocity of only 50 fpm is usually sufficient. Heavy cooking may require an entrance velocity of 150 fpm or higher.

Exhaust hoods are usually located overhead in the majority of kitchen exhaust systems. They should be placed directly over the heat- and vapor-producing equipment and approximately 80 inches from the floor line to allow sufficient head clearance.

An overhead exhaust hood should be larger in horizontal area than the source of the heat or fumes. When located not over 2 feet above the range, the hood should be 6 inches larger in all directions than the overall dimensions of the range when the distance exceeds 2 feet. Thus, a range 2 feet by 7 feet with a clearance of 2 feet would require a hood 3 feet by 8 feet. Such a hood would have an area of 24 square feet. Using an average entrance velocity at the hood of 100 fpm, the volume of air to be handled would be 2400 cfm.

The area of the branch duct leading from the hood should be made $\frac{1}{16}$ of the hood area (that is, 24 square feet ÷ 16) or 1.5 square feet. With the hood located 4 feet above the range, the dimensions would be 4 feet by 9 feet with a branch duct area of 2.25 square feet.

If a supply system is required, the amount of exhaust air should be greater than the volume of supply air to prevent undesirable cooking odors spreading to adjoining rooms. The supply air is usually figured on the basis of 75 percent of the exhaust air.

Bathroom Exhaust Fans

An air change every 3 minutes, or 20 complete changes per hour, is desirable for bathroom ventilation. Systems of this type should be entirely different and separated from other ventilating systems. Bathrooms located on the inside of a structure require ducts to exhaust air to the outside.

Compact fans are especially recommended for use in bathroom exhaust systems. Their compact design requires a minimum of space, and they are capable of operating against the resistance of the system.

Note

> In tightly constructed and insulated houses, vent fans, clothes dryers, and kitchen exhaust fans can create a negative pressure that draws air into the house through holes in the framing, chimneys, and even exhaust flues. This can cause backdrafting in combustion appliances, which can be a serious health hazard. While the bathroom can be maintained at a negative pressure to control odor problems, the remainder of the house should be maintained at a slightly positive pressure. In hot, humid climates, it is best to operate the exhaust fan only when the bathroom is in use, so that the negative pressure does not draw humid outside air into the building cavities.

Whole-House Ventilation

Whole-house ventilation is a ventilating system in which a large centrally located fan provides natural air-conditioning. In very dry climates where hot days and very cool nights are the norm, whole-house ventilating fans often provide a suitable replacement for air-conditioning. Cooler outside air is drawn in through the windows on the lower floors during the night and forced out through the attic vents (see Figure 7-24). This system produces a steady supply of filtered, fresh air to all the living spaces of the house. It works most efficiently when the outdoor temperature is below 82°F. A whole-house ventilation system can also reduce air-conditioning costs by using it instead of the air conditioner to cool the house between the heating and cooling seasons, or by using it to ventilate the house before turning on the air conditioner.

Note

> Whole-house ventilation is not very suitable for humid climates because it draws excess moisture into the house.

In cold climates, the type of whole-house ventilator used in the system is commonly designed to capture some of the heat from the

BALANCED VENTILATION

BALANCED HEAT-RECOVERY VENTILATION

Figure 7-24 Typical whole-house ventilation systems.

(Courtesy U.S. Department of Energy)

air before it is exhausted from the attic. These are sometimes called *air-to-air heat exchangers* or *heat recovery ventilators* (HRVs). These air-to-air heat exchangers are designed to recover as much as 80 percent of the heat energy from the indoor air before it leaves the attic.

Some whole-house ventilators are designed to add or remove moisture from the air. These units are sometimes called *energy recovery ventilators* (ERVs). An energy recovery ventilator operates by balancing the humidity levels between the air drawn into the structure and the air exhausted from the attic. During the winter when the outdoor air is drier, moisture is added to the air by the unit as it is drawn into the house. In the summer when the air is more humid, the energy recovery ventilator removes moisture from the air before it is blown out of the attic.

The fans used in whole-house ventilation are much larger than the standard attic ventilating fans because they are required to move much more air. These are high-velocity cooling fans commonly installed in a hallway ceiling directly beneath the attic. Because some of these fans are too large to be installed between ceiling joists, a box frame is constructed on top of the joists to house them. The box frame must be built by the home-owner or building contractor because it is not provided by the fan manufacturer.

These fans are either belt-driven or direct drive. Belt-driven fans are the quieter of the two, but they require belt replacement every 2 or 3 years. Direct-drive fans are almost maintenance-free.

Note
> *Low-velocity* whole-house ventilating fans should not be confused with the high-velocity types used in whole-house ventilation systems. The former are used only to provide a continuous stream of fresh air and remove indoor pollutants.

A whole-house ventilation fan is switched on when the outside temperature falls below the indoor temperature and continues to operate throughout the night. The fan can be operated both manually and automatically through centrally located controls. Many installations have only a wall-mounted manual on-off switch.

Warning
> Windows must be open when operating a whole-house ventilator in order to prevent backdrafting. Depressurization can be prevented if the total open area of the windows is approximately equal to the total net free area of the attic.

Select a whole-house ventilator large enough to deliver 20 air changes per hour (ACH). A typical sizing method for these fans is to divide the volume of the house (width × height × length) by 3 to obtain the air changes per hour for the fan.

Whole-house ventilators require very little maintenance. If the unit is equipped with a filter, it will have to be periodically cleaned or replaced. Inspect the fan blades from time to time and clean them when there is a noticeable buildup of dirt or grease.

Chapter 8

Air-Conditioning

Although it is a commonly held belief, it is incorrect to regard air-conditioning as simply the *cooling* of air. Conditioning the air of a space means to change it in whatever way necessary to improve the comfort of those living or working there. This may mean warming air to a livable temperature and holding it there; cooling the air; adding or subtracting moisture; filtering out contaminants such as dust, bacteria, and toxic gases; and maintaining a proper distribution and movement of the air. In general, air-conditioning includes the following processes:

1. Heating
2. Cooling
3. Humidification
4. Dehumidification
5. Cleaning and filtering
6. Air movement (circulation)

Each of these processes contributes in some way to the improvement of those conditions that affect the comfort and health of an individual. For example, air nearly always contains certain impurities, such as ammonia, sulphurous acid, and carbon dioxide. The last named is a product of exhalation from the lungs and the combustion process in internal combustion engines. It is so universally present (about in the same proportions everywhere, except where concentrated by some local conditions) that it may be regarded as a normal part the air. Air-conditioning is an efficient means of eliminating carbon dioxide from the air. The same is true of other impurities. Some dry strainer filters used in air-conditioning systems are capable of removing 99.98 percent of radioactive dust from the air.

To understand how an air-conditioning system works and how to calculate cooling loads, you should have a basic understanding of the physical properties of air and how its moisture content, temperature, and pressure will influence your calculations. These topics and the associated terminology are described in the following sections.

Properties of Air

Air is composed of water vapor and dry air. These two components are combined in such a way that neither loses its distinct characteristics. A number of different terms are used to describe the qualities or properties of air, but the two terms essential in heating and cooling calculations are humidity and temperature.

Humidity

Humidity is a general term used to refer to the water vapor (moisture) content of air. When this term is used, it is usually in reference to the sensation (or lack of sensation) of moisture in the air. For purposes of heating and cooling calculations, the more narrowly defined terms of *absolute humidity*, *relative humidity*, and *specific humidity* are used.

Water vapor is actually steam at low temperatures and, consequently, low pressures; hence its properties are those of steam. According to Dalton's law, in any mechanical mixture of gases, each gas has a partial pressure of its own, which is entirely independent of the partial pressures of the other gases of the mixture.

Note

> In *all* air-conditioning calculations it should be understood that the dry air and water vapor composing the atmosphere are separate entities, each with its own characteristics. Water vapor is not dissolved in the air in the sense that it loses its own individuality and merely serves to moisten the air.

Air is capable of holding, as a mechanical mixture within itself, varying quantities of water vapor, depending on its temperature. When air absorbs moisture; that is, when it is humidified, the latent heat of evaporation must be supplied either from the air or from another source. And conversely, when the moisture from the air is condensed, the latent heat of condensation (equivalent to the latent heat of evaporation) is recovered.

Air is said to be saturated when it contains all the water vapor it can hold. If partly saturated air is reduced in temperature until the amount of moisture present corresponds to the amount that the air is capable of holding at the given temperature, it will become saturated air.

If the temperature of the air is still further reduced, its ability to hold moisture will be reduced accordingly. As a result, the excess moisture will be condensed, which means that it will be converted from a vapor to a liquid. This is the reverse of the process that occurred as the air absorbed the moisture.

Converting liquid water into water vapor requires a great quantity of heat. The heat necessary for this process is used only in performing the conversion, the temperature of the liquid and the vapor being the same at the end of the process. If the conversion is from liquid to vapor, this involves the latent heat of *evaporation*. The latent heat of *condensation* is involved if the conversion is from vapor to liquid.

Cold air is saturated when it contains very small quantities of water vapor, whereas warm air is not saturated until it contains larger quantities of vapor. For example, air at zero degrees Fahrenheit is saturated when it contains but one-half of one grain (1/7000 lb) of water vapor per cubic foot. Air at 70°F is saturated when it contains 8 grains of vapor per cubic foot, while at 83°F, 12 grains per cubic foot are required to saturate.

Absolute Humidity

Absolute humidity is the actual mass of water vapor in one cubic foot of air (that is, the weight of water vapor per unit volume of air) and is expressed in grains or pounds per cubic foot (1 lb = 7000 grains), or grams per cubic centimeter. Absolute humidity is equivalent to the density of the air.

Specific Humidity

Specific humidity is the *weight* of water vapor per pound of dry air. Do not confuse specific humidity with relative humidity. The latter term indicates the percentage of water vapor, the former the weight.

Relative Humidity

Relative humidity is the ratio of absolute humidity to the maximum possible density of water vapor in the air at the same temperature. In other words, it is a *percentage* or *ratio* of water vapor in the mixture of dry air and water vapor at a certain temperature relative to the maximum quantity that the volume of air could possibly carry at that temperature. The relative humidity at any given temperature can be obtained by first using a sling psychrometer to determine the amount of moisture (that is, water vapor) actually present in the air and then dividing this figure by the amount of moisture that the air can hold at that temperature, and multiplying the result by 100 in order to obtain the percentage factor.

Drying Effect of Air

The drying effect of air varies approximately inversely with its relative humidity. In other words, the drying effect decreases as the relative humidity increases. It should be noted that it is relative humidity that determines the drying effect of air, and this effect depends on both the temperature and the water content of the air since relative humidity depends on both these factors.

The quantity of heat that dry air contains is very small because its specific heat is low (0.2415 for ordinary purposes), which means that 1 lb of air falling 1°F will yield only 0.2415 of the heat that would be available from 1 lb of water reduced one degree in temperature. The presence of water vapor in the air materially increases the total heating capacity of the air because of the latent heat of the vapor itself.

Most hygroscopic materials in the presence of dry air, even at high, dry-bulb temperatures, may actually be cooled rather than heated. This occurs because the dry air immediately begins to evaporate moisture form the material.

The Dew Point

The *dew point* is the temperature of saturation for a given atmospheric pressure. In other words, for a given atmospheric pressure (barometer), it is the temperature at which moisture begins to condense in the form of tiny droplets, or dew.

The saturation temperature for any given quantity of water vapor in the atmosphere is known as the dew point. Any reduction in temperature below the dew point will result in condensation of some of the water vapor present, with a consequent liberation of the latent heat of the vapor, which must be absorbed before any further condensation can take place.

If the vapor pressure of the water vapor in a given space is the same as the vapor pressure of saturated steam at the prevailing dry-bulb temperature, the space contains all the water vapor it can hold at that temperature. The term *saturated water vapor* is applied to water in this state.

Humidification

Humidification may be defined as the *addition* of moisture to the air. The conditioning machine that functions to add moisture to the air is called a humidifier. A humidifier is commonly a low-pressure, low-temperature boiler in which the water is evaporated and the vapor (low-pressure steam) thus formed is caused to mix with air.

In a sense, water functions as a natural humidifier by acting as the medium that conveys heat to the air and as the source of the water vapor required to saturate the heated air. Contrast this with what takes place in a humidifier unit. A machine functions as a humidifier when the temperature of the spray water is above that at which the moisture in the air will condense.

Dehumidification

Dehumidification may be defined as the *removal* of moisture from the air. A machine that functions to remove moisture from the air is called a dehumidifier.

The removal of moisture from the air is accomplished by condensation, which takes place when the temperature of the air is lowered below its dew point. The condensation thus formed falls into the tank of the conditioning machine. In this case the water acts solely as a conveyor of heat from the air (in addition to its cleansing action) and, as such, the finely divided mist is extraordinarily effective (practically 100 percent).

Some conditioning machines can function both as humidifiers or dehumidifiers. This can often be done without alteration to the unit except that the valves in the control line from the dew point thermostat on some designs are adjusted to connect the steam control of the water heater for winter operation, and to connect the three-way mixing valve to the water supply line for summer operation.

Whether the requirement is humidification or dehumidification, the unit always operates under accurate automatic control, maintaining the required indoor conditions winter and summer, regardless of the outdoor weather.

Temperature

Temperature is a general term used to describe the sensation (or lack of sensation) of heat in the air. Among the more specific terms used in the heating and cooling calculations to describe the air temperature are dry-bulb temperature and wet-bulb temperature.

Note

Sometimes both temperature and humidity are used in conjunction with one another as a calculation factor, and the temperature-humidity index is an example of this. By definition, the *temperature-humidity index* (formerly called the *discomfort index*) is a numerical indicator of human *discomfort* resulting from temperature and moisture. It is calculated by adding the indoor dry-bulb and the indoor wet-bulb thermometer readings, multiplying the sum by 0.4 and adding 15. The results you obtain are the same as those used for the effective temperature index (see *Standards of Comfort*). This can be worked out from the data provided in Table 8-1.

Dry-Bulb and Wet-Bulb Temperatures

Dry-bulb temperature is the actual temperature of air as measured by an ordinary thermometer. *Wet-bulb temperature* is the temperature at

Table 8-1 Recommended Scale of Interior Effective Temperatures for Various Outside Dry-Bulb Conditions

Degrees Outside	Degrees Inside			
Dry-Bulb	Dry-Bulb	Wet-Bulb	Dew Point	Effective Temperature
100	82.5	69.0	62.3	76.0
95	81.0	67.7	60.8	74.8
90	79.5	66.5	59.5	73.6
85	78.1	65.3	58.0	72.5
80	76.7	64.0	56.6	71.3
75	75.3	63.0	55.6	70.2
70	74.0	62.0	54.5	69.0

which the air would become saturated if moisture were added to it without the addition or subtraction of heat. It is the temperature of evaporation. In actual practice, the wet-bulb temperature reflects humidity conditions in the area. A high wet-bulb reading, for example, means that the humidity is also high.

The wet-bulb temperature in conjunction with the dry-bulb temperature is an exact measure of both the humidity of the air and its heat content. In air-conditioning the dry-bulb temperature and the wet-bulb temperature must *both* be controlled if the effects of air are to be regulated.

If the bulb of an ordinary thermometer is surrounded with a moistened wick and placed in a current of air and superheated water vapor, it will be found that a reading at some point below the dry-bulb temperature is obtained. The minimum reading thus obtained is the *wet-bulb temperature* of the air. The reduction in temperature is caused by the sensible heat being withdrawn from the air to vaporize the water surrounding the wet bulb, thus raising the dew point of the air.

Note

The point of equilibrium at which the withdrawn sensible heat balances with the heat of vaporization necessary to bring the dew point up to the same point is the wet-bulb temperature.

In this transformation of energy from sensible heat of vaporization, there is no change in the total amount of energy in the mixture. For this reason, the wet-bulb temperature, once fixed, is an indication of the total heat in any mixture of air and water vapor.

The *daily temperature range* is the difference between the maximum and minimum dry-bulb temperatures during a 24-hour period on a typical day for a heating or cooling system. It is used in determining the factors used in making Btu tabulations. The Btu tabulation cooling form illustrated in Figure 8-9 shows their use. In Figure 8-9 you will note that the tables labeled "wall factors" and "ceiling factors" each have a column reserved for four different degrees of daily temperature range (that is, 15°F, 20°F, 25°F, and 30°F). Reading across from left to right, the different daily temperature ranges intersect with a number of other columns representing differences in the dry-bulb temperatures. The selection used will depend on the type (or absence) of insulation.

Wet-Bulb Depression

Because outdoor summer air is rarely fully saturated, there is usually a considerable difference between its dry-bulb and its wet-bulb temperatures. This difference is referred to as *wet bulb depression* and is greatest during the summer.

As previously mentioned, the wet-bulb temperature is that temperature to which air would be cooled by evaporation if the air was brought into contact with water and allowed to absorb sufficient water vapor to become saturated. For example, if the outdoor summer air is drawn through a humidifier and completely saturated, its dry-bulb temperature will be reduced to its wet-bulb temperature, and the air will leave the humidifier at the outdoor wet-bulb temperature. This cooling is accomplished entirely by evaporation and is due to the latent heat required to convert the liquid water vapor. This conversion occurs the instant the air is brought into contact with the mist in the spray chamber of the humidifier, the heat being taken from the air.

The spray water in a humidifier is used over and over again, only that quantity being added which is actually absorbed by the air. Thus, without any additional expense, a humidifier will perform the function of cooling the air through the wet-bulb depression in the summer.

The extent of the wet-bulb depression in some localities is as much as 25° or 30°. Even in localities adjacent to large bodies of water where the humidity is high and the wet-bulb depression correspondingly low, the latter will quite commonly range from 10° to 15°.

In the vicinity of New York, for instance, the maximum outdoor wet-bulb temperature is about 78°. On such a day the dry-bulb temperature would probably be about 90°, making the wet-bulb depression 12° ($90° - 78° = 12°$).

In Denver, on the other hand, the maximum outdoor wet-bulb temperature is usually less than 78°. Because the coincident dry-bulb temperature is usually much higher then 90°, it results in a greater wet-bulb depression, which means that more cooling can be accomplished by evaporation.

Sensible and Latent Heat

The distinction between dry air and the moisture content of air and between dry-bulb and wet-bulb temperatures is extended to the two types of heat carried by the entering air and the air already contained in the space: sensible and latent heat.

Sensible Heat

Sensible heat is the amount of heat in air that can be measured by an ordinary thermometer (that is, a dry-bulb thermometer). The daily weather report gives us sensible heat temperatures, but it does not represent the total heat we experience. It constitutes a *portion* of the heat resulting from air infiltration and ventilation, and internal heat sources such as people, electric lights, and electric motors. Sensible heat also results from heat leakage (or heat loss in the case of heating calculations) and solar radiation.

Latent Heat

Latent heat is the amount of heat contained in the water vapor (moisture) of the air. It constitutes a portion of the heat resulting from infiltration and ventilation and any internal sources capable of adding water vapor to the air (for example, cooking vapors, steam, people). The amount of latent heat in the air can be determined by using a psychrometric chart (see Appendix E, "Psychrometric Charts"). The amount of *excess* latent heat so determined will indicate the amount of moisture that must be removed from the air in order to obtain comfortable conditions.

Both sensible heat gain and latent heat gain are expressed in Btu. When the total of the two are added together, their sum represents the *total* heat gain in Btu that must be removed from the air each hour by the air conditioner.

Sensible heat gain (or load) is represented by a change in the *dry-bulb* temperature readings, whereas latent heat gain is represented by a change in the *web-bulb* temperature.

Pressure

Atmospheric air is air at the pressure of the standard atmosphere. *Standard atmosphere* is considered to be air at a pressure of 29.921 inches of mercury, which is equal to 14.696 pounds per square inch (usually written 14.7 psi). In any air-conditioning system, atmospheric air is regarded as being air at the atmospheric pressure at the point of installation.

Standard atmospheric pressure at sea level is 29.921 inches of mercury. Since most pressure gauges indicate gauge pressure or pounds per square inch, a barometer reading can be converted into gauge pressure by multiplying inches of mercury by 0.49116 psi. Thus, a barometer reading of 29.921 inches is equivalent to a gauge pressure of 14.696 psi (29.921 × 0.49116 = 14.696, or 14.7 psi).

So 0.49116 psi is a constant value for 1 inch of mercury and is determined by dividing the pressure in pounds per square inch by the barometer readings in inches of mercury (that is, 14.696 ÷ 29.921 = 0.49116). Table 8-2 gives the atmospheric pressure for various readings of the barometer.

The pressure of the atmosphere does not remain constant in any one place. It continually varies depending on the conditions of the weather and the elevation. With respect to elevation, atmospheric pressure will decrease approximately ½ lb for each 1000 feet of ascent. Table 8-2 illustrates the effect of altitude and weather (the barometer reading) on atmospheric pressure.

Table 8-2   Atmospheric Pressure and Barometer Readings for Various Altitudes

Altitude above Sea Level (Feet)	Atmospheric Pressure (Pounds per Square Inch)	Barometer Reading (Inches of Mercury)
0	14.69	29.92
500	14.42	29.38
1000	14.16	28.86
1500	13.91	28.33
2000	13.66	27.82
2500	13.41	27.31
3000	13.16	26.81
3500	12.92	26.32
4000	12.68	25.84
4500	12.45	25.36
5000	12.22	24.89
5500	11.99	24.43
6000	11.77	23.98
6500	11.55	23.53
7000	11.33	23.09
7500	11.12	22.65
8000	10.91	22.22
8500	10.70	21.80
9000	10.50	21.38
9500	10.30	20.98

(continued)

Table 8-2   (continued)

Altitude above Sea Level (Feet)	Atmospheric Pressure (Pounds per Square Inch)	Barometer Reading (Inches of Mercury)
10,000	10.10	20.58
10,500	9.90	20.18
11,000	9.71	19.75
11,500	9.52	19.40
12,000	9.34	19.03
12,500	9.15	18.65
13,000	8.97	18.29
13,500	8.80	17.93
14,000	8.62	17.57
14,500	8.45	17.22
15,000	8.28	16.88

Absolute pressure is pressure measured from true zero or the point of no pressure. It is important to distinguish absolute pressure from *gauge pressure*, whose scale starts at atmospheric pressure. For example, when the hand of a steam gauge is at zero, the absolute pressure existing in the boiler is approximately 14.7 psi. Thus, 5 lbs pressure measured by a steam gauge (that is, gauge pressure) is equal to 5 lbs plus 14.7 lbs, or 19.7 psi of absolute pressure.

Compression and Cooling

The objective of the use of compression in air-conditioning is to cool the air being conditioned. It is important to note, however, that it is not the air that is compressed, but the refrigerant gas used in the coils of the air-conditioning unit. The low temperature is produced by the expansion and contraction of the refrigerant gas. When a gas is compressed, both its pressure and temperature are changed in accordance with Boyle's and Charles's laws.

The English scientist Robert Boyle (1627–1691) determined that the absolute pressure of a gas at constant temperature varies inversely as its volume. Somewhat later, the French scientist Jacques Charles (1745–1823) established that the volume of a gas is proportional to its absolute temperature when the volume is kept at constant pressure. These findings came to be known as Boyle's and Charles's laws respectively. In Tables 8-3 and 8-4 a series of relations based on these two laws are tabulated for convenient reference.

A more simplified explanation of the interrelationship of these two laws may be gained with the aid of the cylinder illustrated in

Table 8-3   Summary of Boyle's Law

1. Pressure volume formula

$$PV = P'V' \quad \cdots\cdots\cdots(1)$$

$$P = \frac{P'V'}{V} \quad \cdots\cdots\cdots(2)$$

$$V = \frac{P'V'}{P} \quad \cdots\cdots\cdots(3)$$

2. Compression constant

$$PV = \text{constant} \cdots\cdots(4)$$

3. Pressure at any point

$$P = \frac{\text{constant}}{V} \quad \cdots\cdots(5)$$

4. Volume at any point

$$V = \frac{\text{constant}}{P} \quad \cdots\cdots(6)$$

5. Ratio of compression

$$R = V_i \div V_f \quad \cdots\cdots(7)$$

where,

R = ratio or number of compressions
V_i = initial volume
V_f = final volume

$$R = P_i \div P_f = V_i \div V_f \quad \cdots(8)$$

6. Initial pressure of compression

$$P_i = R \div P_f \quad \cdots\cdots\cdots\cdots(9)$$

where,

P_i = initial pressure absolute
P_f = final pressure absolute

7. Final pressure of compression

$$P_f = P_i \div R$$

Table 8-4   Summary of Charles's Law

1. At constant volume

$$\frac{P}{T} = \frac{V'}{T'} \quad \cdots\cdots\cdots\cdots\cdots\cdots\cdots\cdots\cdots\cdots\cdots\cdots\cdots\cdots\cdots\cdots\cdots\cdots(1)$$

where, P = initial pressure absolute
P' = final pressure absolute
T = initial temperature absolute
T' = final temperature absolute

2. At constant pressure

$$\frac{V}{T} = \frac{V'}{T'} \quad \cdots\cdots\cdots\cdots\cdots\cdots\cdots\cdots\cdots\cdots\cdots\cdots\cdots\cdots\cdots\cdots\cdots(2)$$

where V = initial volume (usually in cubic feet)
V' = final volume (usually in cubic feet)

Figure 8-1. If the cylinder is filled with air at atmospheric pressure (14.7 psi) represented by volume *A*, and piston *B* is moved to reduce the volume by, say, ⅓ of *A*, as represented by *B*, then according to Boyle's law, the pressure will be tripled ($14.7 \times 3 = 44.1$ lbs absolute or $44.1 - 14.7 = 29.4$ gauge pressure). According to Charles's law, a pressure gauge on a cylinder would at this point indicate a *higher* pressure than 29.4 gauge pressure because of the increase in temperature produced by compressing the air. This is called *adiabatic compression* if no heat is lost or received externally.

Figure 8-1   The interrelationship of Boyle's and Charles's laws.

Measuring the Physical Properties of Air

A number of instruments are used for measuring the physical properties of air. These include the following:

1. The thermometer
2. The barometer
3. The psychrometer
4. The pressure gauge

A *thermometer* (see Figures 8-2 and 8-3) is a device used to measure temperature, and consists of a glass tube terminating in a bulb charged with mercury or colored alcohol. It measures the temperature by the contraction or expansion of the liquid with temperature changes, causing the liquid to rise or recede in the tube. The scale of an ordinary thermometer, either Fahrenheit or Celsius, is simply an arbitrary standard by means of which comparisons can be established.

An ordinary thermometer is used to measure dry-bulb temperature. Dry-bulb temperature is the degree or intensity of heat. In other words, dry-bulb temperature measures the degree of effort that the heat will exert to move from one position to another.

A specially designed thermometer is used to measure wet-bulb temperature. The latter represents the temperature at which the air becomes saturated if moisture is added to it *without* a change of heat. The bulb of an ordinary thermometer is surrounded with a moistened wick, placed in a current of air, and superheated with water vapor. Essentially this represents a wet-bulb thermometer.

A *barometer* (see Figure 8-4) is an instrument designed to measure atmospheric pressure. Early barometers consisted of a 30-inch-long glass tube open at one end and filled with mercury. The open end was submerged in a bowl of mercury, and the mercury in the glass tube would assume a level in accordance with the existing atmospheric pressure. Thus, the height of the mercury column in the tube is a measure of the atmospheric pressure. *Standard* atmospheric pressure at sea level is 29.921 inches of mercury.

Figure 8-2 A pencil-style stack thermometer.

A *psychrometer* (or *sling psychrometer*) is an instrument used to measure relative humidity. It consists of a dry-bulb (for air temperature) and a wet-bulb thermometer mounted side by side. The reading on the wet-bulb thermometer is determined by the rate at which the moisture evaporates from its bulb. If the psychrometer is working correctly, the reading on the wet-bulb thermometer will be lower than the one on the dry-bulb thermometer. The *difference* between the two readings serves as a basis for determining the relative humidity.

Pressure gauges (see Figures 8-5, 8-6, and 8-7) are used to measure pressure. A *high-pressure gauge* (see Figure 8-5) is used to measure pressures ranging from zero to 300 or 400 psig. A *compound gauge* (see Figure 8-6) is used to measure low pressures

Figure 8-3 Various thermometer scales.

above atmospheric pressure in psig and below atmospheric pressure in vacuum in inches of mercury.

Cleaning and Filtering the Air

The purpose of cleaning and filtering the air is to remove dust and other contaminants that could be harmful to the health or discomforting. Many bacteria that cause diseases are carried on dust particles.

Cleaning and filtering may be accomplished with equipment using one of the following four methods:

Figure 8-4 Mercurial barometer illustrating the relationship between inches of mercury and absolute pressure in pounds per square inch.

1. Filtering

2. Washing

3. Combined filtering and washing

4. Electrostatic field

Filters trap particles by bringing them in contact with specially coated surfaces or by straining them through dry materials of particularly close texture. The filters used in air-conditioning equipment may be either dry or wet (viscous) types. Depending on the type used, air-cleaning filters may be replaceable or periodically

Figure 8-5 A high-pressure gauge.

(Courtesy Ernst Gage Co.)

Figure 8-6 A compound gauge that measures both pressure and vacuum.

(Courtesy Ernst Gage Co.)

cleaned. In the latter case, either manual or automatic cleaning is possible.

Air washers form a part of the cooling and humidifying apparatus of the air-conditioning system. They operate by passing the air first through fine sprays of water and then past baffle plates upon the wetted surface of which is deposited whatever dust and dirt not caught by the sprays.

Electronic air cleaners employ an electrostatic ionizing field to remove dust particles from the air. The particles are given an electrical charge when passing through the field and are subsequently attracted to metal plates having an opposite polarity.

Cleaning and filtering processes are described in greater detail in Chapter 12 ("Air Cleaners and Filters").

Standards of Comfort

The influence of air temperature, moisture, and movement on physical comfort has been very thoroughly investigated. Once again, the most authoritative sources of information on this subject are the results of research conducted by the American Society of Heating, Refrigeration, and Air-Conditioning Engineers. The most current edition of the *ASHRAE Guide* should be consulted for details because some revisions have been made.

The sensations of warmth or cold experienced by the human body depend not only on the dry-bulb temperature but also on the moisture content of the air. Cooling applications that remove only the sensible heat fall short of establishing comfortable conditions if the latent heat gain is particularly high. The air will be cooler under these conditions, but it will feel damp and uncomfortable. In order to meet minimal standards of comfort, both sensible and latent heat must be reduced to an acceptable level.

The average comfort conditions in summer and winter are considerably different, although the two zones overlap to some degree. This difference is caused largely by differences in clothing, and the natural inclination of the body to acclimate itself to somewhat higher temperatures in the summer.

Figure 8-7 Gauge illustrating absolute and zero pressure.
(Courtesy Ernst Gage Co.)

The *effective temperature* is an arbitration index of the degree of warmth or cold as apparent to the human body, and takes into account the temperature, moisture content, and motion of the surrounding air.

Effective temperatures are not strictly a degree of heat; at least not in the same sense that dry-bulb temperatures are. For instance, the effective temperature could be lowered by increasing the rate of airflow even though wet- and dry-bulb temperatures remain the same. Consequently, effective temperature is more correctly defined as the *body sensation* of warmth or cold resulting from the combined effect of temperature, humidity, and air movement. For space cooling and heating, however, the air movement factor is considered a constant at approximately 20 feet per minute, and under this condition effective temperature is determined by the wet-bulb and dry-bulb thermometer readings only.

The Comfort Chart

The *comfort chart* (see Figure 8-8) is an empirically determined effective temperature index that has been published by the *ASHRAE* since 1950.

The purpose of the comfort chart is to indicate the percentage of people feeling comfortable at various effective temperatures in the winter and summer. This serves only as an approximate standard of comfort, because individual reactions to warmth and cold are much too variable, but it *is* the most precise and scientific form of measurement available.

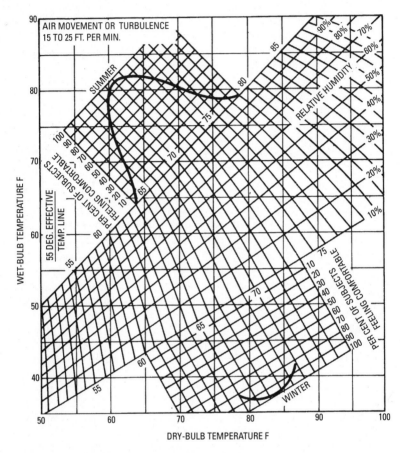

Figure 8-8 Comfort chart for still air. *(Courtesy ASHRAE 1960 Guide)*

From the chart, one can obtain an approximate idea of the various effective temperatures at which a majority of people will feel comfortable (that is, the summer and winter comfort zones).

Most air-conditioning systems are designed with a recommended indoor design relative humidity of about 50 percent or slightly lower. Budget jobs will range as high as 60 percent relative humidity. The indoor dry-bulb temperature will range from 75°F or slightly below to about 80°F, depending on the degree of occupancy and whether it is a budget job or not. In any event, the indoor design conditions *should* fall within the comfort zone.

More information about the use of the comfort chart is included in Appendix E ("Psychrometric Charts").

Cooling Load Estimate Form

Air-conditioning equipment manufacturers often provide their local representatives with forms for making cooling load estimates. Along with these forms they also provide tables, slide charts, tabulation sheets, and other aids for computing the cooling load.

Typical tabulation sheets and cooling load estimate forms are shown in Figures 8-9 and 8-10. These forms contain lists of factors that represent *approximate* values for a variety of different items (for example, walls, ceilings, people). For example, the form illustrated in Figure 8-9 requires that you select the appropriate design dry-bulb temperature and its column of factors. After calculating the area (in square feet) of the structural section, you must multiply this figure by its factor to determine the Btu per hour of heat gain and enter the result in the column on the extreme right.

Because a manufacturer's cooling estimate form will probably not be available, it may be necessary to create your own. If this should be the case, then provisions should be made on the cooling estimate form for distinguishing between sensible and latent heat sources.

Your cooling load estimate form should contain the following basic categories of heat gain:

A. Sensible heat gain
  1. Heat leakage
  2. Solar radiation
  3. Internal heat sources
  4. Infiltration
  5. Ventilation
  6. Electric lights
  7. Electric motors
  8. People
  9. Appliances

B. Latent heat gain
  1. Infiltration
  2. Ventilation
  3. People

AMANA REFRIGERATION INC., AMANA, IOWA

BTU TABULATION
(BASED ON 24 HOUR PER)

Job Name _____ Date _____

Location _____ Computed By _____

ROOM			LIVING ROOM		DINING ROOM		KITCHEN		BED ROOM 1	
Room Size (LxWxH)										
Linear Ft. Exposed Wall										
Floor Ceiling Area										
		FACTOR	AREA OR QUAN	BTUH	AREA OR QUAN	BTUH	AREA OR QUAN	BTUH	AREA OR QUAN	BTUH
Windows	DIRECTION									
Walls	Shade									
	Sunlit									
Ceiling										
Cooking		✓					1200			
People		380	3						1	
Room Sensible Heat										
Room CFM										

WINDOW & DOOR FACTORS

Temp. Diff. F	15	20	25	30
North	12	18	25	31
NE & NW	23	29	36	42
East & West	32	38	44	51
SE & SW	35	41	48	55
South	26	32	39	45

Above factors assume shades or venetian blinds. If no shades double factors.

For outside shading or awnings multiply factor x .60.

For double glazed or storm windows multiply factor x .80.

NOTES:
PEOPLE LOAD — One Person in each bedroom and three persons in living room.

ROOF OVERHANG — South walls only. 36″ overhang provides complete shade to wall and windows. Use shade values for windows and walls.

DOORS — Treat all outside doors as windows.

WALL FACTORS   Light Color

Temp. Diff. F		15	20	25	30
15 Daily	No Insul.	3.6	5.4	7.2	9.0
Temp.	1½ Insul.	2.1	3.0	4.0	5.1
Range	3″ Insul.	1.5	2.1	2.9	3.6
20 Daily	No Insul.	2.7	4.5	6.5	8.2
Temp.	1½ Insul.	1.5	2.6	3.6	4.7
Range	3″ Insul.	1.1	1.8	2.6	3.3
25 Daily	No Insul.	1.4	3.6	5.4	7.4
Temp.	1½ Insul.	0.9	2.1	3.0	4.1
Range	3″ Insul.	0.6	1.5	2.1	2.9

For masonry walls multiply factors x 1.2. For ½ Value in Table.

CEILING FACTORS

		Temp. Diff. F	15
15 Daily		2″ Insul.	5.7
Temp.		4″ Insul.	3.6
Range		6″ Insul.	3.2
20 Daily		2″ Insul.	5.0
Temp.		4″ Insul.	3.2
Range		6″ Insul.	2.9
25 Daily		2″ Insul.	4.4
Temp.		4″ Insul.	2.9
Range		6″ Insul.	2.6

Factors assume dark color roof with attic having vents.
If light color roof — take 75° of values in tables.
If no vents in attic space double values.

Figure 8-9   Btu tabulation cooling form. *(Courtesy Amana Refrigeration, Inc.)*

C. Ventilation heat gain (from outside sources)
   1. Sensible heat
   2. Latent heat

The sum of these categories will represent the total heat gain expressed in Btu per hour. A balance must be established between

COOLING (Residential)
(DAY OPERATION OF EQUIPMENT)

Outside Design Temp _____

Inside Design Temp _____

Temp Diff. _____

_____ Outside Humidity Factor _____ Daily Temp Range _____

	BED ROOM 2						BATH		BTUH TOTALS
	AREA OR QUAN	BTUH	AREA OR QUAN	BTUH	AREA OR QUAN	BTUH	AREA OR QUAN	BTUH	
	1								

Dark Color

15	20	25	30
5.1	6.9	8.9	10.7
2.7	3.0	4.7	5.1
2.0	2.6	3.3	4.1
4.2	6.0	7.8	9.8
2.1	3.2	4.2	5.1
1.5	2.3	3.0	3.6
3.3	5.1	6.9	8.9
1.7	2.7	3.6	4.7
1.2	2.0	2.6	3.3

North or Shaded Wall Figure

20	25	30
6.9	8.7	9.6
4.4	5.1	5.7
4.0	4.6	5.1
6.2	7.5	8.6
3.7	4.7	5.4
3.5	4.2	4.9
5.5	6.9	7.6
3.6	4.4	5.0
3.2	4.0	4.5

HOUSE TOTAL SENS. BTUH _____

DUCT. GAIN _____ % _____

VENTILATION LOAD BTUH _____

TOTAL SENSIBLE BTUH _____

GRAND TOT. = TOT. SENS. x HUM. FACTOR _____

% DUCT GAIN

	1 Story	1½ Story	2 Story
Ducts Insulated	8	6	4
Ducts not Insulated	18	15	12

NOTE: All ducts in attic spaces must be insulated with 3" minimum thickness insulation with vapor barrier. Ducts in crawl spaces and damp basements must be covered with 2" minimum thickness insulation with vapor barrier.
Do not figure duct gain for concrete slab under floor ducts

HUMIDITY FACTORS

Outside Hum.	Below 40	40 to 45	Above 45
Factor	1.25	1.30	1.35

VENTILATION LOAD

House Volume Cu. Ft. (LxWxH) x .40 BTUH/ CU. Ft.

Figure 8-9 *(continued)*

this hourly heat gain within the conditioned space and the hourly capacity of the air-conditioning unit to remove this heat gain in order to maintain the inside design temperature.

Figure 8-11 is a floor plan (not drawn to scale) of a house that will serve as a basis for most of the cooling calculations used in this chapter.

Customer .... Address ....

Buyer .... Installation by ....

Estimate Number .... Estimate by .... Date ....

Equipment Selected ....; Model ....; Size ....

Direction House Faces ....; Gross Floor Area ....sq ft; Gross Inside Volume ....cu ft

Design Conditions:

	Degrees North Latitude	Dry-Bulb Temperature (F)	Wet-Bulb Temperature (F)
	....	....	....

ITEM	AREA (sq ft)	FACTOR (Circle the factors applicable.)									BTU/HR (Area x Factor)
1. (a) WINDOWS, Gain from Sun (Figure all windows for each exposure, but use only the exposure with the largest load.)		For glass block, reduce factors by 50%; for storm windows or double-glass, reduce factors by 15%.									
			No Shading	Inside Shades	Outside Awnings	Load for Each Exposure (Area x Factor)					
Northeast	....	60	25	20		....					
East	....	100	40	25		....	Use				
Southeast	....	75	30	20		....	only				
South	....	75	35	20		....	the			....	
Southwest	....	110	45	30		....	largest				
West	....	150	65	45		....	load.				
Northwest	....	120	50	35							

For calculating gain from sun through windows under overhanging roofs, see example given in Instructions.

		DESIGN DRY-BULB TEMPERATURE (F)									
		90	92	95	97	100	102	105	110	115	
(b) WINDOWS, Heat Gain (Total of all windows)											
Single-glass	....	13	15	19	22	25	27	30	36	42	....
Double-glass or glass block	....	7	8	9	10	11	12	13	16	19	....
2. WALLS											
No insulation (brick veneer, frame, stucco, etc.)	....	4	4	5	6	6	7	8	9	10	....
1 in. insulation or 25/32 in. insulation sheathing	....	3	3	4	4	5	5	6	7	9	....
2 in. or more insulation	....	2	2	2	2	3	3	3	4	4	....
3. PARTITIONS (Between conditioned and un-conditioned space)	....	2	2	3	3	4	4	5	6	7	....
4. ROOFS (a) Pitched or flat with vented air space, and:											
No insulation	....	18	18	19	20	21	21	22	24	25	....
No insulation, with attic fan	....	9	11	12	14	16	17	19	22	25	....
2 in. insulation	....	5	5	5	5	6	6	6	7	7	....
4 in. insulation	....	3	3	4	4	4	4	4	5	5	....
(b) Flat with no air space, and:											
No insulation	....	28	29	30	31	33	34	35	38	40	....
1 in. or 25/32 in. insulation	....	14	14	15	16	16	17	18	19	20	....
1½ in. insulation	....	8	9	9	9	10	10	11	11	12	....
3 in. insulation	....	6	6	6	6	7	7	7	8	8	....
5. CEILING (Under unconditioned rooms only)	....	3	3	4	4	5	5	6	7	8	....
6. FLOORS (Omit if over basement, en-closed crawl space, or slab.)											
Over unconditioned room	....	2	2	2	3	3	4	4	5	6	....
Over open crawl space	....	3	3	4	5	5	6	7	8	9	....
7. OUTSIDE AIR Total sq ft of floor area	....	2	2	2	2	3	3	4	4	5	....
8. PEOPLE (Use minimum of 5 people)		..........(number of people) x 200									....
9. SUB-TOTAL											
10. LATENT HEAT ALLOWANCE		30 per cent of Item 9									
11. TOTAL		Sum of Items 9 and 10									

Figure 8-10 Residential cooling load estimate form.

(Courtesy Amana Refrigeration, Inc.)

Figure 8-11   Floor plan of a one-story residence constructed on concrete slab.

The house is located 30° north, and complete exposure to the sun occurs at 1:00 P.M. The structure contains 740 square feet of floor space divided into four rooms and a bath. There are ten 3′ × 4′ windows, with four of them facing south. The indoor design temperature is 80°F.

Indoor-Outdoor Design Conditions

The indoor and outdoor design conditions must be established *before* any cooling load calculations can be made. This will be the first step in your procedure. As you will see, the *difference* between the indoor and outdoor design temperatures will eventually serve as a basis for selecting the correct size air conditioner.

Designing a system to meet the *maximum* outdoor summer temperature is generally not necessary because these temperatures either rarely occur or occur for a comparatively short duration of time. It is the general practice to design the system for slightly less severe conditions and thereby save on equipment and installation costs.

Ventilation Requirements

Each conditioned space requires a specific amount of outside fresh air to be circulated through it in order to remove objectionable odors (for example, cooking odors, tobacco smoke, body odors) and to maintain comfort standards.

Ventilation standards indicating recommended air changes for a variety of space usages and occupancy have been established by the ASHRAE. Local codes are often based on ASHRAE research and data. These ventilation standards are easy and convenient to use, but are objected to by some authorities because the sources of contamination seldom bear any relationship to cubic area.

The air-conditioning system must be capable of supplying enough outside fresh air to maintain air purity and comfort standards. The ventilation requirements for a given structure or space are based either on the desired number of air changes or the number of occupants. The volume rate of ventilation air is expressed in cubic feet per minute (cfm).

According to the ASHRAE, the outside fresh air requirement for both residences and apartments ranges from 10 cfm (minimum) to 20 cfm (recommended). Fresh air requirements for other types of structures are listed in Table 8-5.

Table 8-5   Fresh Air Requirements

Type of Building or Room	Minimum Air Changes per Hour	Cubic Feet of Air per Minute per Occupant
Attic spaces (for cooling)	12–15	
Boiler room	15–20	
Churches, auditoriums	8	20–30
College classrooms		25–30
Dining rooms (hotel)	5	
Engine rooms	4–6	
Factory buildings (ordinary manufacturing)	2–4	
Factory buildings (extreme fumes or moisture)	10–15	
Foundries	15–20	
Galvanizing plants	20–30	
Garages (repair)	20–30	
Garages (storage)	4–6	

Table 8-5 *(continued)*

Type of Building or Room	Minimum Air Changes per Hour	Cubic Feet of Air per Minute per Occupant
Homes (night cooling)	9–17	
Hospitals (general)		40–50
Hospitals (children's)		35–40
Hospitals (contagious diseases)		80–90
Kitchens (hotel)	10–20	
Kitchens (restaurant)	10–20	
Libraries (public)	4	
Laundries	10–15	
Mills (paper)	15–20	
Mills (textile—general buildings)	4	
Mills (textile dyehouses)	15–20	
Offices (public)	3	
Offices (private)	4	
Pickling plants	10–15	
Pump rooms	5	
Restaurants	8–12	
Schools (grade)		15–25
Schools (high)		30–35
Shops (machine)	5	
Shops (paint)	15–20	
Shops (railroad)	5	
Shops (woodworking)	5	
Substations (electric)	5–10	
Theaters		10–15
Turbine rooms (electric)	5–10	
Warehouses	2	
Waiting rooms (public)	4	

The *amount* of outside fresh air required for each air change per hour equals the amount of inside air that must be removed from the structure or space during the same time span. The following formula can be used to determine the amount of air supplied per minute:

$$CFM = \frac{\text{area in cubic feet}}{\text{minutes of air change}}$$

The floor plan of the residence shown in Figure 8-11 contains 740 square feet. The height of each room is 7 feet, which gives an area of 5180 cubic feet.

Table 7-1 in Chapter 7 ("Ventilation and Exhaust Fans") lists the number of average air changes per minute required for good ventilation for a number of different applications. You will note that each listed air change ranges from a minimum to a maximum number of changes. The rate of air change you select will depend on the following:

1. Geographical location
2. Occupancy
3. Ceiling height

Warmer climates and larger numbers of occupants require a greater rate of air change. Conversely, an 8-foot ceiling will require more ventilation than a 15-foot ceiling.

Using a 3-minute rate of air change for the residence illustrated in Figure 8-11, the required number of air changes necessary to give proper ventilation can be determined as follows:

$$CFM = \frac{5180 \text{ cu. ft.}}{3} = 1726.7$$

Thus, 1726.7 cfm is needed to change the air every 3 minutes (or 20 air changes every hour).

Always check the local health department codes or local building codes for required ventilation standards first. If none exist, use the recommended air changes listed in this table, or data available from ASHRAE research.

Cooling a Structure

The aspect of air-conditioning most familiar to us is the reduction of indoor temperatures to a comfortable level. There are a number of different sources of indoor heat, some are external and some are internal.

External Sources of Heat

The principal sources of heat from outside the structure are solar radiation, heat leakage, infiltration, and ventilation.

Heat Leakage

Heat leakage refers to the amount of heat flow through structural sections and is stated in Btu per hour, per degree Fahrenheit, per square foot of exposed surface. A significant portion of the total heat gain of a space is due to heat from the outside of a structure or from a nonconditioned space passing (that is, leaking) through walls, ceilings, floors, and roofs to the interior of the structure.

The coefficient of heat transmission (U-factor) is the specific value used in determining the amount of heat leakage. It has already been described in Chapter 4 ("Heating Calculations") in Volume 1 in the section *Heat Loss*. Actually the only difference between heat leakage and heat loss is the direction of heat flow. Both are concerned with the same thermal properties of construction materials and the rate at which heat flows through them. Insofar as heat leakage is concerned, the direction of heat flow is from the outside to the inside of the structure. In the case of heat loss, the reverse is true.

The formula used for calculating heat leakage is identical to the one used for heat loss, and may be stated as follows:

$$Q = UA(t_o - t_i)$$

where,

Q = Amount of heat transmission in Btu/h

U = Overall coefficient of heat transfer (U-factor) between the adjacent space and the conditioned space (stated in Btu per hour, per square foot, per degree Fahrenheit)

t_o = Air dry-rule temperature in degrees Fahrenheit of adjacent space or outdoors

t_i = Air dry-bulb temperature in degrees Fahrenheit of conditioned space of the structure

Heat Gain from Solar Radiation

A portion of the heat gain in the interior of a structure can be attributed to solar radiation coming in through the windows. To disregard this factor when calculating the total loads of the structure can result in serious error. It is particularly important to consider the *type* of shading because this will determine the amount of heat gained from solar radiation.

One method of determining heat gain from solar radiation *through window glass* is illustrated by the following equation:

Total Instantaneous Heat Gain Through Window Glass	=	Area of Window Glass	×	Factor for Shading	×	Heat Gain by Solar Radiation	+	Heat Gain by Convection and Radiation

The ASHRAE has conducted extensive research into all aspects of solar radiation, and makes the results of this research available through its publications. As you saw earlier, Tables 8-3 and 8-4 were adapted by permission from the *ASHRAE 1960 Guide* to illustrate the aforementioned equation for determining total instantaneous heat gain through window glass.

Calculating the amount of heat gain due to solar radiation through a glass window can be even more clearly illustrated by using the above equation to solve a problem. Let us assume that you have a residence containing four 3' × 4' windows *facing south*. The structure is located 30° north, and complete exposure to the sun occurs at 1:00 P.M. The indoor temperature is 80°F. The windows are shaded by dark brown canvas awnings that are open at the sides. As you will note by looking carefully at Tables 8-6 and 8-7, each of these points in the description of the structure is important in the solution. The total instantaneous heat gain through these windows can be determined as follows:

1. Window glass area = 3' × 4' = 12 square feet
2. Factor for shading = 0.25
3. Heat gain by solar radiation = 45 Btu/h per square foot
4. Heat gain by convection and radiation = 17 Btu/h per square foot

Total instantaneous heat gain through the four windows can be found as follows:

$$12 \times (0.25 \times 45 + 17)$$
$$12 \times 28.25$$
$$339 \text{ Btu/h (for one window)} \times 4 \text{ windows}$$
$$1356 \text{ Btu/h}$$

In Table 8-7, note that the shading factors are given not only for such items as shading screens and awnings located on the outside of the structure but also for window shades, venetian blinds, and draperies located on the inside. It is *always* recommended that windows of air-conditioned spaces be shaded in some manner.

Heat Gain from Infiltration and Ventilation

A certain amount of warm outdoor air will enter the interior of a structure by means of infiltration and ventilation. Both phenomena are described in considerable detail in Chapter 6 ("Ventilation

Table 8-6 Heat Gain Due to Solar Radiation (Single Sheet of Unshaded Common Window Glass)

Latitude	Sun Time A.M. →	P.M. →	\multicolumn{9}{c}{Instantaneous Heat Gain in Btu per Hour (ft²)}								

Latitude	A.M. →	P.M. →	N	NE	E	SE	S	SW	W	NW	Horiz.
30° north	6 A.M.	6 P.M.	25	98	108	52	5	5	5	5	17
	7	5	23	155	190	110	10	10	10	10	71
	8	4	16	148	205	136	14	13	13	13	137
	9	3	16	106	180	136	21	15	15	15	195
	10	2	17	54	128	116	34	17	16	16	241
	11	1	18	20	59	78	45	19	18	18	267
	12		18	19	19	35	49	35	19	19	276
40° north	5 A.M.	7 P.M.	3	7	6	2	0	0	0	0	1
	6	6	26	116	131	67	7	6	6	6	25
	7	5	16	149	195	124	11	10	10	10	77
	8	4	14	129	205	156	18	12	12	12	137
	9	3	15	79	180	162	42	14	14	14	188
	10	2	16	31	127	148	69	16	16	16	229
	11	1	17	18	58	113	90	23	17	17	252
	12		17	17	19	64	98	64	19	19	259

(continued)

Table 8-6 (continued)

Latitude	Sun Time A.M. →	Sun Time P.M. →	Instantaneous Heat Gain in Btu per Hour (ft²) N	NE	E	SE	S	SW	W	NW	Horiz.
50° north	5 A.M.	7 P.M.	20	54	54	20	3	3	3	3	6
	6	6	25	128	148	81	8	7	7	7	34
	7	5	12	139	197	136	12	10	10	10	80
	8	4	13	107	202	171	32	12	12	12	129
	9	3	14	54	176	183	72	14	14	14	173
	10	2	15	18	124	174	110	16	15	15	206
	11	1	16	16	57	143	136	42	16	16	227
	12	↑	16	16	18	96	144	96	18	16	234
		P.M. →	N	NE	E	SE	S	SW	W	NW	Horiz.

(Courtesy ASHRAE 1960 Guide)

Table 8-7 Shade Factors for Various Types of Shading

Type of Shading	Finish on Side Exposed to Sun	Shade Factor
Canvas awning sides open	Dark or medium	0.25
Canvas awning top and sides tight against building	Dark or medium	0.35
Inside roller shade, fully drawn	White, cream	0.41
Inside roller shade, fully drawn	Medium	0.62
Inside roller shade, fully drawn	Dark	0.81
Inside roller shade, half drawn	White, cream	0.71
Inside roller shade, half drawn	Medium	0.81
Inside roller shade, half drawn	Dark	0.91
Inside venetian blind, slats set at 45°	White, cream	0.56
Inside venetian blind, slats set at 45°	Diffuse reflecting aluminum metal	0.45
Inside venetian blind, slats at 45°	Medium	0.65
Inside venetian blind, slats set at 45°	Dark	0.75
Outside venetian blind, slats set at 45°	White, cream	0.15
Outside venetian blind, slats set at 45° extended as awning fully covering window	White, cream	0.15
Outside venetian blind, slats set at 45° extended as awning covering 2/3 of window	White, cream	0.43

	Dark	Green tint
Outside shading screen, solar altitude 10°	0.52	0.46
Outside shading screen, solar altitude 20°	0.40	0.35
Outside shading screen, solar altitude 30°	0.25	0.24
Outside shading screen, solar altitude, above 40°	0.15	0.22

(Courtesy ASHRAE 1960 Guide)

Principles") and in the section *Ventilation Standards* in this chapter. These materials should be read before proceeding any further.

Insofar as cooling load calculations are concerned, infiltration (that is, natural ventilation) is the leakage of warmer outdoor air into the interior of a structure usually as the result of wind pressure. This occurs primarily through cracks around windows and doors. As a result, the *crack method* is considered the most accurate means of calculating heat leakage by air infiltration (see the appropriate section of Chapter 4 in Volume 1 ("Heating Calculations"). A rule-of-thumb method for calculating heat leakage around doors located in exterior walls is to allow *twice* the window heat leakage.

Some authorities feel that infiltration will fulfill the ventilation requirements of small structures (for example, houses, offices, and small shops) and that no special provisions need be made for a mechanical ventilating system. Unfortunately, there is little or no infiltration on days during which the outdoor air is perfectly still.

The amount of ventilation is generally determined by the number of air changes (inside air replaced by air from the outdoors) required by a structure. This is most commonly based on the number of occupants and building use. In structures having air-conditioning, *most* of the outdoor air used for ventilation will pass through the air-conditioning unit. A small portion of the air will bypass the air-conditioning coils and add to the sensible and latent heat levels of the interior spaces of the structure. The temperature and humidity of the air that does pass over the cooling coils of the unit are reduced to room conditions or below.

Internal Sources of Heat

A number of heat sources within a structure contribute to heat gain independently from outside sources. The most important internal heat gain sources are the following:

1. People
2. Electric lighting
3. Appliances
4. Electric motors
5. Steam

The occupants of conditioned spaces give off both sensible and latent heat. The *amount* of heat gain will depend on a number of variables, including (1) the duration of occupancy, (2) the number of people, and (3) their principal activity. Table 8-8 lists estimated heat gains from a variety of activities performed by individuals.

Table 8-8   Rate of Heat Gain from Occupants of Conditioned Spaces

Degree of Activity	Typical Application	Total Heat Adults, Male (Btu/h)	Total Heat Adjusted (Btu/h)	Sensible Heat (Btu/h)	Latent Heat (Btu/h)
Seated at rest	Theater—matinee	390	330	180	150
	Theater—devening	390	350	195	155
Seated, very light work	Offices, hotels, apartments	450	400	195	205
Moderately active office work	Offices, hotels, apartments	475	450	200	250
Standing, light work, walking slowly	Department store, retail store, dime store	550	450	200	250
Walking, seated	Drugstore, bank	550	500	200	300
Standing, walking slowly					
Sedentary work	Restaurant	490	550	220	330
Light bench work	Factory	800	750	220	530
Moderate dancing	Dance hall	900	850	245	605
Walking 3 mph, moderately heavy work	Factory	1000	1000	300	700
Bowling	Bowling alley	1500	1450	465	985
Heavy work	Factory				

(Courtesy ASHRAE 1960 Guide)

Calculating Infiltration and Ventilation Heat Gain

It has been shown that outdoor air enters a structure by means of both infiltration and ventilation. Because air is composed of a mixture of dry air and moisture particles, the heat gain produced by the entering air will be expressed in terms of both its sensible heat gain and its latent heat gain in Btu per hour.

The sensible and latent heat gain resulting from entering air represents only a small portion of the total heat gain involved in determining the design cooling load of a structure. For many applications, however, the calculation of this portion of the heat gain is crucial to a well-designed system. The following formulas, adapted from ASHRAE materials, are used for making these calculations:

$$(1) \quad Q_S = \text{cfm} \times 1.08 \, (t_o - t_i)$$
$$(2) \quad Q_L = \text{cfm} \times 0.68 \, (w_o - w_i)$$
$$(3) \quad Q_T = Q_S + Q_L$$

where, Q_S = Sensible load
Q_L = Latent load
Q_T = Total load
cfm = Rate of entry of outdoor air (cubic feet per minute)
t_o = Dry-bulb temperature of outside (entering) air
t_i = Dry-bulb temperature of inside air
w_o = Outdoor wet-bulb temperature
w_i = Indoor wet-bulb temperature

In order to use these formulas, it is first essential to determine the outdoor and indoor design conditions (that is, the dry-bulb and wet-bulb temperatures) and the maximum rate of entering air (in cubic feet per minute).

Rule-of-Thumb Methods for Sizing Air Conditioners

Manufacturers of air-conditioning equipment and mail order houses (for example, Sears, Montgomery Ward) that sell air-conditioning equipment through their catalogs provide rule-of-thumb methods for calculating the size of the air conditioner required by a structure. The Btu calculation formulas are based on recommended coefficient factors for different types of construction and conditions. The responsibility for calculating the cooling load (and ultimately selecting a suitable air conditioner) lies with the purchaser of the equipment.

The problem of using *any* rule-of-thumb method is that the results are not precise. In other words, the results represent an approximate estimate; not the results one would expect from an engineer's calculations. There is always the danger of oversizing or undersizing the air conditioner. Under normal conditions, however, this method of calculating the size of a central air conditioner is reasonably accurate.

The Btu tabulation and cooling estimate forms illustrated in Figures 8-9 and 8-10 are typical examples of the forms provided by manufacturers of air-conditioning equipment. Note that these forms not only provide coefficient factors for various types of construction but also recommend standard loads for different activities. For example, the cooling load estimate form shown in Figure 8-10 provides for a latent heat allowance of 30 percent of the total heat gain from all other sources. Another example of this practice is the commonly used standard load of 1500 Btu for kitchen activities. People are usually given a 200 Btu allowance per person, and residences are calculated on the basis of two people per bedroom. Thus, a three-bedroom house would have a 1200 Btu allowance for six people (3 × 2 = 6 × 200 = 1200 Btu).

The Btu calculation formulas used with the various rule-of-thumb methods also provide for temperature and humidity adjustments where conditions differ from the recommended levels. This is sometimes accomplished by providing humidity factors and a range of dry-bulb temperature differences (see Figure 8-9) or by providing humidity and temperature adjustment allowances. In the latter case, the coefficient factors are usually based on a specific wet-bulb temperature and dry-bulb temperature difference. If, for example, the former were 75°F and *your* wet-bulb reading were 80°F, the instructions might require that you add 10 percent of the total heat gain of the structure for the humidity adjustment. Similar allowances are provided for temperature adjustments.

One of the easier and more popular rule-of-thumb methods employed for calculating the size of *large* central air conditioners is to use one ton of refrigeration for each 500–700 square feet of floor area, or each 5000–7000 cubic feet of space. A *ton of refrigeration* is equivalent to 12,000 Btu per hour. This figure is based on the fact that 1 lb of melting ice will absorb 144 Btu of heat over a 24-hour period. Therefore, a ton of ice will absorb 288,000 Btu during the same period of time (that is, 144 Btu × 2000 lbs) (288,000 ÷ 24 hours = 1 ton of refrigeration).

HVAC Contractor's Cooling Load Estimate

If you are not satisfied with your own cooling load estimate, you should invite several air-conditioning contractors to give their bids. This is particularly true if you are considering a central air-conditioning system. For a central air-conditioning system, each contractor should include the estimated Btu per hour required to cool the structure. Each of the bids should be fairly close in estimated Btu and cost. Your choice will be based largely on availability of replacement parts, the reputation of the local dealer for quick and reliable service, and the estimated Btu output. You will naturally want an air-conditioning system that will efficiently remove the required amount of heat. If this proves to be more expensive than another type, you would be wise to choose the more expensive one because your operating costs will be cheaper over the long run. Any contractor's bid that shows a wide variation from the others either in cost or estimated Btu required to cool the structure should be regarded with some suspicion. It may simply be an attempt to win the contract. Most reliable bids will be fairly close.

Using the ACCA Design Manuals for Sizing Air-Conditioning Systems

The Air-Conditioning Contractors of America (ACCA) publishes a series of manuals used by contractors to size heating and cooling loads. These manuals are updated regularly to match changes in HVAC technology and construction materials. These manuals are available for purchase from the ACCA web site (or their mailing address) by both members and nonmembers. Check the ACCA listing in Appendix A ("Professional and Trade Associations").

- *Manual J Residential Load Calculation (8th Edition). Manual J* provides the contractor with the industry-standard residential load calculation method, required by most building codes around the country. The revised and expanded eighth edition procedures produce improved equipment sizing loads for single-family detached homes, small multiunit structures, condominiums, town houses, and manufactured homes.
- *Manual S Residential Equipment Selection. Manual S* is an essential companion to *Manual J*. It describes how to select and size heating and cooling equipment to meet *Manual J* loads based on local climate and ambient conditions at the building site. *Manual S* covers sizing strategies for all types of cooling and heating equipment, as well as how to use comprehensive manufacturer's performance data on sensible, latent, or heating capacity for various operating conditions.
- *Manual C What Makes a Good Air-Conditioning System? Manual C* provides an overview of appropriate air-handling characteristics for an efficient and comfortable HVAC system.

- *Manual D Residential Duct Systems. Manual D* describes the different types of residential duct systems, their selection, and their application. Design criteria for duct systems are included in this manual.

Note

Use the *ACCA Manual N* for sizing the heating or cooling equipment in commercial or industrial buildings. Typically, these structures are larger than homes, are constructed differently, and have correspondingly greater internal HVAC loads. Using an HVAC load calculation method designed for homes can result in oversizing or undersizing the HVAC equipment.

Central Air-Conditioning

The term central air-conditioning refers not so much to the method of cooling used in a structure as it does to the type of installation and its location. A central air-conditioning system is one that is generally *centrally* located in a structure in order to simultaneously serve a number of rooms and spaces.

The following sections describe first the different cooling methods used in central air-conditioning systems and then the various central air-conditioning applications used in homes and light commercial buildings.

Cooling Methods

Central air-conditioning can be accomplished by means of a variety of different cooling methods. The following are described in this chapter:

1. Evaporative cooling
2. Cold-water coil cooling
3. Gas compression refrigeration
4. Gas absorption refrigeration
5. Thermoelectric refrigeration
6. Cooling with steam

In a majority of air-conditioning installations, and almost exclusively in the smaller horsepower range found in residences and small commercial buildings, the vapor or gas compression method of cooling is used (see *Gas Compression Refrigeration*).

A comparatively recent entry into the field of residential air-conditioning is thermoelectric refrigeration. This method of cooling is based on the thermocouple principle; the cool air is produced by the cold junctions of a number of thermocouples wired in series (see *Thermoelectric Refrigeration*).

Absorption refrigeration and cooling with steam are cooling methods generally found in large commercial and industrial applications (see *Gas Absorption Refrigeration* and *Cooling with Steam*).

Evaporative Cooling

An evaporative cooling system cools the indoor air by lowering its dry-bulb temperature. In effect, it cools by evaporation, and it accomplishes this function by means of an evaporative cooler. Figures 8-12, 8-13, and 8-14 show the basic components of three evaporative coolers.

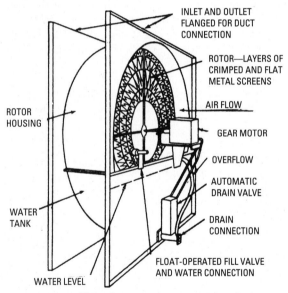

Figure 8-12   Typical rotary evaporative cooler.
(Courtesy 1965 ASHRAE Guide)

As shown in Figure 8-15, an evaporative cooler consists of a blower and blower motor, water pump, water distribution tubes, water pads, and a cabinet with louvered sides. In operation, the blower draws air through the louvers of the cabinet where it comes into contact with the moisture in the pads. The air passes through these moist water pads and into the interior of the structure.

Figure 8-13 Typical spray evaporative cooler.

(Courtesy 1965 ASHRAE Guide)

Figure 8-14 Typical drip evaporative cooler.

(Courtesy 1965 ASHRAE Guide)

Figure 8-15   **Evaporative cooler.** *(Courtesy Honeywell Tradeline Controls)*

The water in the pads absorbs heat from the air as it passes through them. This causes a portion of the water to evaporate and lowers the dry-bulb temperature of the air as it enters the room or space. It is this lower dry-bulb temperature that produces the cooling effect.

In an evaporative cooling system, the water is recirculated and used over and over again. Only enough water is added to replace the amount lost by evaporation. The pump supplies water to the pads through the distribution tubes.

The air is never recirculated because it contains too much moisture once it has passed through the evaporative cooler. New air must always be drawn from the outdoors.

An evaporative cooling system is generally not very effective in a humid climate because the outdoor air is not dry enough. Evaporative coolers have been used for years with excellent results in New Mexico, Arizona, Nevada, and similar areas with dry climates.

Cold-Water Coil Cooling

Indoor air temperatures can also be reduced by passing warm room air over a cold surface, such as a water-cooled coil, and then recirculating it back into the room. When a water-cooled coil is used for this purpose, the system is referred to as *cold-water coil cooling* (see Figure 8-16).

Figure 8-16 Cold-water coil cooling. *(Courtesy Honeywell Tradeline Controls)*

A water-cooled coil is effective only when there is a sufficient supply of cold water. The temperature of the water should range from 35° to 55°F, and the most common source is a deep well. A pump supplies the cold water to the coil where it picks up heat from the air passing through it. This warmer water is then discharged to a storm sewer, dry well, or some other outdoor receiver. The discharge water is approximately 10° to 15°F warmer than the supply water.

Gas Compression Refrigeration

A gas compression refrigeration air-conditioning system operates on the direct-expansion cooling principle. Basically the system consists of a compressor, condenser coil, receiver, expansion device, and evaporator coil. A refrigerant flowing through the system is affected by temperature and pressure acting simultaneously in such a way that heat is transferred from one place to another. In other words, heat is *removed* from the room air for cooling and added to it for heating.

Mechanical Refrigeration Cycle

The *mechanical refrigeration cycle* is illustrated schematically in Figure 8-17. The *liquid* refrigerant is contained initially in the

Figure 8-17 Mechanical refrigeration cycle. *(Courtesy Honeywell Tradeline Controls)*

receiver, which is usually located in the lower section of the condenser, although it can be a separate tank. The compressor, acting as a pump, forces the liquid refrigerant under high pressure through the liquid line to the expansion device.

The function of the expansion device is to regulate the flow of refrigerant into the evaporator coil. This expansion device may be in the form of an expansion valve or a capillary tube.

As the high-pressure liquid refrigerant is forced through the expansion device, it expands into a larger volume in the evaporator, thus reducing its pressure and consequently its boiling temperature. Under this low pressure, the liquid refrigerant boils until it becomes a vapor. During this change of state, the refrigerant absorbs heat from the warm air flowing across the outside of the evaporator.

After the refrigerant has boiled or vaporized, thus removing its quota of heat, it is of no more value in the evaporator coil and must be removed to make way for more liquid refrigerant. Instead of being exhausted to the outdoor air, the low-pressure heat-laden refrigerant vapor is pumped out of the evaporator through the suction line to the compressor. The compressor then compresses the refrigerant vapor, increasing its temperature and pressure and forces it along to the condenser.

At the condenser, the hot refrigerant vapor is cooled by lower temperature air passing over the condenser coils, thus absorbing some of the refrigerant heat. As a result, the air temperature increases and the refrigerant temperature decreases until the refrigerant is cooled to its saturation condition. At this condition, the vapor will condense to a liquid. The liquid, still under high pressure, flows to the expansion device, thus completing the cycle.

Note that cold is *never* created during the mechanical refrigeration cycle. Instead, heat is merely transferred from one place to another. When the refrigerant passes through the evaporator, it absorbs heat from the room air, thereby cooling it. When the higher-temperature refrigerant passes through the condenser, it gives up heat to the air entering the room, thereby warming it.

Gas Absorption Refrigeration

The *gas absorption refrigeration* method of cooling uses heat as its energy instead of electricity. This heat can be in the form of steam from a gas-fired or oil-fired atmospheric steam generator, or it can come from a gas or oil burner applied directly to the refrigeration generator. Normally, water is used as the refrigerant and lithium bromide as an absorbent. The absorption unit operates under a vacuum that gives the water a boiling temperature low enough for comfort cooling.

The absorption refrigeration system shown in Figure 8-18 is charged with lithium bromide and water, the lithium bromide being the absorbent and the water the refrigerant. This solution is contained within the refrigeration generator.

As steam heat is applied to the generator, a part of the refrigerant (water) is evaporated or boiled out of the solution. As this water vapor is driven off, absorbent solution is raised by vapor lift action to the separating chamber (5) above the generator.

Refrigerant (water) and absorbent separate in the vapor separating chamber (5), the refrigerant vapor rises to the condenser (6), and the separated absorbent solution flows down through a tube (8) to the liquid heat exchanger and thence to the absorber.

The refrigerant (water vapor) passes from the separating chamber to the condenser through a tube (6), where it is condensed to a liquid by the cooling action of water flowing through the condenser tubes. The cooling water that flows through the condenser is brought from some external source, such as a cooling tower, city main, or well.

Figure 8-18 Gas absorption refrigeration unit.

The refrigerant vapor thus condensed to water within the condenser then flows through a tube (7) into the cooling coil. This tube contains a restriction that offers a resistance and therefore a pressure barrier to separate the slightly higher absolute pressure in the condenser from the lower pressure within the cooling coil. The refrigerant (water) entering the cooling coil vaporizes due to the lower absolute pressure (high vacuum) that exists within it. The high vacuum within the evaporator lowers the boiling temperature of water sufficiently to produce the refrigeration effect.

The evaporator or cooling coil is constructed with finned horizontal tubes, and the air being cooled flows horizontally over the coil surface. Evaporation of the refrigerant takes place within the cooling coil, the heat of evaporation for the refrigerant is extracted from the air stream, and cooling and dehumidifying are accomplished.

In the absorber, the solution absorbs the refrigerant vapors that were formed in the evaporator directly adjacent. To explain the presence of the absorbent at this point, it is necessary to divert attention back to the generator. The absorbent was separated from the refrigerant by boiling action. The absorbent then drains from the separator (5) down to the liquid heat exchanger and then to the absorber through the tube (8) designed for this purpose. The flow of solution in this circuit can actually exist by gravity action only because the absorber is slightly below the level of the separating chamber.

It must be understood at this point that lithium bromide in either dry or solution form has a very strong affinity for water vapor. It is because of this principle that the refrigerant vapor is absorbed back into solution again. Because the *rate* of absorption is increased at lower temperatures, a water-cooling coil is provided within the absorber shell.

The resultant mixture of refrigerant and absorbent drains back through the heat exchanger through another tube (9) to the refrigeration generator where it is again separated into its two component parts to repeat the cycle.

The liquid heat exchanger serves to increase operating efficiency. The absorbent solution leaves the refrigeration generator at a relatively high temperature. Because its affinity for water vapor is increased as its temperature is reduced, precooling is desirable before it enters the absorber. Conversely, the combined solution of refrigerant and absorbent leaving the absorber and flowing toward the generator is relatively cool.

Because heat is applied in the generator to drive off water vapor, it is desirable to preheat this liquid before it enters the generator. With counterflow action in the liquid heat exchanger, both precooling and preheating are accomplished within the solution circuit.

As stated previously, a high vacuum exists throughout all circuits. However, a slightly higher absolute pressure exists in the generator and condenser than in the cooling coil and absorber. This difference in pressure is maintained by a difference in height of the solution columns (or restrictor) in the various connecting tubes.

The effect of heat applied to the refrigeration generator raises the absorbent solution to the vapor separator located at the top of the generator. The absorbent solution is able to flow from the generator to the absorber by gravity, aided by the slight pressure differential between the two chambers.

In the absorber, water vapor is taken into the solution, which then flows back to the bottom of the generator. Because the pressure in the absorber is slightly below that in the generator, solution flow from a low-pressure area to one of relatively higher pressure is accomplished by the higher elevation of the absorber.

The water vapor (refrigerant) released from the generator rises to the condenser, where it is condensed to a liquid. Elevation of the condenser permits gravity flow of the refrigerant to the evaporator, aided by the slight pressure differential between the two chambers. Thus, by taking advantage of differences in fluid temperatures, density, and height of columns, continuous movement in the same direction throughout all circuits is accomplished without moving parts.

The cooling-water circuit can be traced in Figure 8-18 by noting that it enters the absorber coil at point 10. Flow is then directed through tube 11 to the condenser and leaves the unit at point 12.

Figure 8-19 shows a schematic sectional diagram of a typical absorption year-round air conditioner. Inlet air enters a plenum chamber that contains filter elements. The air, after having been

Figure 8-19   Typical absorption year-round air conditioner.

cleaned, passes through the cooling coil (evaporator) and heating coil, and is then returned to the rooms or spaces being cooled.

During the cooling cycle, the room air is cooled and dehumidified. Heat is extracted from the air and moisture is condensed on the cooling coil. Thus, both functions of cooling and dehumidification are performed simultaneously. During the heating cycle, the air is warmed by the steam heating coil, and moisture is added by the humidifier.

Steam is provided for both heating and cooling cycles by the steam generator located in the base of the conditioner. Steam at atmospheric pressure flows from the generator into a two-position steam diverter valve, which automatically directs the flow of steam to either the heating coil or the absorption refrigeration unit. The steam diverter valve is positioned by an electric motor governed by a remote heating and refrigeration switch.

After the air leaves the heating coil, it passes through the humidifier, which functions during the heating cycle only. The humidifier, in this installation, consists of a number of horizontal trays, each equipped with an overflow tube that feeds water to the next lower tray. This arrangement provides a large evaporative surface for positive humidification. Water is supplied at a predetermined and controlled rate of flow to the humidifier trays.

The air is drawn through the unit by a centrifugal fan that delivers the heated or cooled air through a duct-distributing system to the various rooms or spaces being conditioned. Because less air is normally required for winter heating than for summer cooling, a flow-restricting device is mounted in the fan scroll and functions on the heating cycle to automatically reduce the flow of air by adding resistance. This device usually consists of a pivoted blade, and its location is indicated by the dotted line in Figure 8-19.

When maximum air delivery is desired, the air-restricting device is positioned tightly against the inside column of the fan scroll. When the restrictor is pivoted toward the fan wheel, thereby reducing normal wheel clearance, a resistance is thus imposed which alters fan performance to reduce air delivery. The airflow-restricting device is moved automatically between predetermined summer and winter positions by the motor that governs its operation.

Correct air distribution practices dictate a need in some cases for the handling of a greater quantity of air on the cooling cycle than required by the refrigeration unit for full-rated cooling capacity. Should this excess air be needed, the amount in excess of rated quantity should be handled through the bypass, thus ensuring correct cooling coil performance. The bypass damper is located in the air circuit just beyond the cooling coil. During the heating season, the bypass damper will automatically be repositioned by the controlling motor to the closed position.

Thermoelectric Refrigeration

Thermoelectric refrigeration is a cooling method developed comparatively recently for use in residential air-conditioning, although the operating principle is not new. Thermoelectric refrigeration has been used for years as a cooling method for small refrigerators. It is also the cooling used on nuclear submarines.

Thermoelectric refrigeration is based on the thermocouple principle. In a thermoelectric refrigeration cooling system, electricity in the form of direct current power is applied to the thermocouple and heat is produced. The heat is transferred from one junction to the other producing a hot and cold junction. The direction of current flow determines which junction is hot and which is cold. If the power supply connections are reversed, the positions of the hot and cold junctions are also reversed.

The amount of cooling or heating that can be produced with a single thermocouple is small. For that reason, a number of thermocouples are wired in a series to produce the quantity of heating and cooling required by the installation.

The schematic of a typical thermoelectric cooling system shown in Figure 8-20 illustrates how direct current power is applied to a number of thermocouples wired in series. Heat is transferred from one side to the other depending on the direction of current flow.

Figure 8-20   Typical thermoelectric refrigeration cooling system. *(Courtesy Honeywell Tradeline Controls)*

Cooling with Steam

Cooling with steam is based on the well-known fact that the boiling point of any liquid depends on the pressure to which it is subjected. By lowering the pressure, the boiling point is also lowered. When a liquid at a certain temperature and corresponding boiling point is sprayed into a closed vessel in which the pressure is lower, the entering liquid is above its boiling point at the new reduced pressure, and rapid evaporation takes place.

The basic components of a typical steam cooling system are shown in Figure 8-21. In operation, the water to be cooled, returning from the air-conditioning or other heat-exchanging apparatus at a temperature of 50°F, is sprayed into the evaporator. Because of the large surface of the spray, the boiling (or flashing) is very rapid and the unevaporated water falls to the bottom of the evaporator chilled to 40°F. At this temperature it is withdrawn from the evaporator by the chilled water pump and pumped to the heat-exchanging apparatus to again absorb heat, thus completing the cycle.

Figure 8-21 Basic components of a steam cooling system.

(Courtesy 1965 ASHRAE Guide)

In the booster ejector, steam flowing at high velocity through nozzles located in the ejector head is expanded in the venturi-shaped diffuser. The kinetic energy of the steam is in part utilized in imparting velocity to the water vapor liberated in the evaporator and in compressing this vapor over a compression range from the evaporator pressure to the condenser pressure. In this compression, the temperature of the water vapor is raised so that it can be readily condensed by condensing water at temperatures normally available.

The initial evacuation and constant purging of air and other noncondensable gases is handled by a secondary group of ejectors and condensers. These are relatively small in size, but of the greatest importance, and normally consist of two steam-operated ejectors in series, each with its own condenser in which condensing water condenses the propelling water and entrained vapor. Condensers used in a steam cooling system may be either of the surface type, with water passing through condenser tubes over which the mixture of operating steam and water vapor flows, or of the jet or barometric type, with condensing water sprayed directly into the steam mixture.

The amount of condensing water and condensing surface employed is such that the vapor temperature in the condenser is normally 5°F above the condensing water discharge temperature. This fixes the terminal pressure condition to which the steam mixture is compressed. The initial pressure condition (in the evaporator) is determined by the chilled water temperature desired. Variation in either of these two conditions affects the compression range and therefore the amount of operating steam required.

Central Air-Conditioning Applications

There are many different ways to apply central air-conditioning to a structure. The method used depends on a number of factors, but the type of heating system is probably the dominant one. The following are the most common types of cooling applications:

1. Water chiller cooling
2. Split-system cooling
3. Year-round air-conditioning
4. Central cooling packages
5. Cooling coils

Water Chiller Cooling

A water chiller is used to add cooling and dehumidification to steam or hot-water heating systems. A refrigeration-type water chiller consists of a compressor, condenser, thermal expansion valve, and evaporator coil. The water is cooled in the evaporator coil and pumped through the system.

A typical system in which a water chiller is used is shown in Figure 8-22. The boiler and water chiller are installed as separate units, each with its own circulator (pump), or with one circulator in the return line. Hot water from the boiler is circulated through the

Figure 8-22   Water chiller and boiler installed as separate units.
(Courtesy 1965 ASHRAE Guide)

convectors for heating, and cold water is circulated through the same piping from the water chiller for cooling purposes.

Each convector unit contains a blower to force the air across the convector coil (see Figure 8-23). Water condensed from the coil during the cooling operation is trapped in a drip pan and discarded through a drain connected to the convector. Some convectors also contain a filter for air cleaning. The room convectors in a water chiller cooling system are usually designed for individual control.

The same piping carries both the chilled and hot water to the room convectors, but it must be insulated to minimize condensation during the cooling operation.

Water chillers are available as separate units or as a part of a complete package containing the boiler. Separate water chiller units are used when cooling must be applied to an existing steam or hot water heating system.

Split-System Cooling

Another method of applying central air-conditioning to a steam or hot-water heating system is to add forced-air cooling. This type of cooling application is sometimes referred to as a *split-system* installation—that is to say, a system split or divided between one type of heating (conventional steam or hot water) and another type of

COOL-HEAT CONVECTOR COIL

CONDITIONED AIR

CONDENSTATE DRIP PAN

FAN & MOTOR

FILTER

RETURN AIR

WALL

Figure 8-23   Air forced by convector across convector coil.

(Courtesy Honeywell Tradeline Controls)

cooling (forced air). This results in some confusion because the term split system is also used to refer to the separation of components in a year-round central air-conditioning system using forced warm-air heating and cooling (see *Location of Equipment*).

Three typical methods of applying forced-air cooling to a steam or hot-water heating system are shown in Figure 8-24.

Year-Round Air-Conditioning

In a year-round air-conditioning system, the heating and cooling units are combined in a single cabinet (see Figure 8-25). This combined package heats, cools, humidifies, dehumidifies, and filters the air in the structure as required. The unit may have an air-cooled, a water-cooled, or an evaporative-type condenser. The arrangement of the ductwork will depend in part on the type of condenser used in the unit.

ATTIC INSTALLATION

BASEMENT　　　　　　　　**UTILITY ROOM**

Figure 8-24　Methods of applying forced-air cooling to steam or hot-water heating systems. *(Courtesy Honeywell Tradeline Controls)*

Figure 8-25　Heating and cooling units contained in a single cabinet.
(Courtesy Honeywell Tradeline Controls)

Central Cooling Packages

A central cooling package is a unit designed for central air-conditioning applications. It consists of a cooling coil and the refrigeration equipment and will provide the necessary cooling and dehumidification as conditions require. These units are available with their own fans and filters, or they may be installed to use the filter and blower of the existing heating equipment (see Figure 8-26).

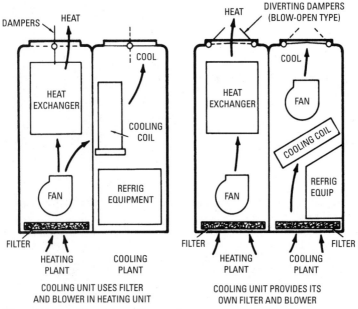

Figure 8-26 Central cooling package.

The method used to install a central cooling package will depend on whether the unit has an air-cooled or water-cooled condenser. If an air-cooled condenser is used, provisions must be made to carry outdoor air to and away from the condenser. Typical installations in which an air-cooled condenser is used are shown in Figure 8-27. Figure 8-28 illustrates some typical methods of applying a central cooling package in which a water-cooled condenser is used.

A typical remote or split system is shown in Figure 8-29. In this installation, the compressor and air-cooled condenser unit are located outdoors. The evaporator coil, fan, and heating appliance are located indoors in the conditioned space.

Figure 8-27   Applications of central cooling package having an air-cooled condenser. *(Courtesy Honeywell Tradeline Controls)*

Figure 8-27 *(continued)*

COOLING UNIT MOUNTED IN BASEMENT
PLENUM OF UP-FLOW FURNACE

COOLING UNIT MOUNTED IN CRAWL-SPACE
PLENUM OF DOWN-FLOW FURNACE

COOLING UNIT ADDED TO PLENUM
OF HORIZONTAL-FLOW FURNACE

Figure 8-28 Applications of a central cooling package having a water-cooled condenser. *(Courtesy Honeywell Tradeline Controls)*

Cooling Coils

Cooling can be applied to a warm-air heating system by installing an evaporator coil or a cold-water coil in the ductwork. The evaporator coil is the low-side section of a mechanical refrigeration system. As shown in Figure 8-30, the evaporator coil is installed in the ductwork above the furnace. It is connected by refrigerant piping to the condenser coil and compressor installed outdoors.

A thermostatic expansion valve and condensation drip pan (with drain) are included with the evaporator coil. Sometimes a fan is added to the coil to supplement the furnace blower.

A cold-water coil may be used instead of an evaporator coil in the ductwork. Cold water is supplied to the coil by a water chiller,

Figure 8-29 Typical remote split-type air-conditioning system.
(Courtesy Mueller Climatrol Corp.)

which can be located in the basement, a utility room, or outdoors. If the water chiller is installed outdoors, a gas engine can be used to drive the compressor (see Figure 8-31).

Hydronic Forced-Air Systems
In a hydronic forced-air system, the water is first heated in a boiler (sometimes called a *hydronic* furnace in these systems) or water heater and then circulated through the coils of a liquid-to-air heat exchanger connected to the furnace air handler. Heat is transferred from the water in the coils to the air inside the air-handler compartment. A blower forces the warm air through ducts to outlets inside the rooms. Cool air is produced by a chilled water or DX coil inside or on top of the blower cabinet. The cool air is distributed by the blower through the same ductwork used by the warm air. Condensation is collected by a condensate pump.

Hybrid Systems
A hybrid heating and cooling system consists of a radiant hydronic heating system working in conjunction with a separate cooling system. Hot water is produced by a hydronic boiler, water heater, or combination water heater. The cooling system is added to an existing

Figure 8-30 Evaporator coil installed in ductwork of a warm-air heating system. *(Courtesy Honeywell Tradeline Controls)*

hydronic system, when augmenting or upgrading the mechanical system of an older house or building. Some of the systems used to provide cool air to an existing hydronic heating system are described in the following paragraphs.

Indirect/Direct Evaporative Coolers

A high-efficiency indirect/direct evaporative cooler designed with a hydronic option can be used to supply cool air to a house with an existing hydronic heating system. The evaporative cooler has a Seasonal Energy Efficiency Ratio (SEER) of 36, which is three times the minimum SEER efficiency rating for air conditioners. Air cooled by direct and indirect evaporation can generate approximately the same amount of cooling as a 3-ton air conditioner. The cool air is delivered directly to the interior of the house or through a short duct.

Figure 8-31 Cold-water coil used with outdoor gas engine compressor. *(Courtesy Honeywell Tradeline Controls)*

Ductless Split System

As the name suggests, the ductless split system does not require duct-work. The system consists of an indoor air handler and an outdoor condenser, connected by refrigerant tubing extending through a 3-inch hole in the wall. Decorative units can be mounted on the floor, wall, ceiling or recessed (drop) ceiling. The system can consist of a single zone with one condenser and one air handler, or a multizone system with one condenser containing two or more compressors connected to one, three, or four air handlers. The ductless split system is capable of producing 9000 Btu to 48,000 Btu, depending on the application.

Fan Coil and Flexible Ducts

The conditioned air is produced by a fan coil located in the attic, an attic crawl space, the basement, or a closet. If the air-conditioning unit is placed in the attic or an attic crawl space, a 5-ton one is small enough to insert between 16-inch on centers ceiling joists without cutting any framing. The distribution system consists of flexible 2-inch-diameter tubing running inside walls and floors and around internal framing obstructions. The conditioned air is delivered to the rooms through a 2-inch opening in the ceiling.

Residential Chiller with Ceiling-Mounted Panels

Chilled water is run through ceiling-mounted panels that exchange heat with the warm air in the room. The heated water is then carried down to the chiller where it is again cooled and returned to the ceiling. The system uses small ducts to feed fresh air directly into the house or building.

Room Air Conditioners

Room air conditioners are designed to cool a single room or space in a structure. The most commonly used type of room air conditioner is the window-mounted unit. These air conditioners are available for installation in single-hung windows, double-hung windows, horizontal sliding windows, and casement windows. Make sure to read carefully the specifications printed on the shipping container before purchasing a window air conditioner. The specifications should list the air conditioner's dimensions, the type of window installation, and its Btu output. Room air conditioners are also available for through-the-wall installation in exterior walls. A sleeve is provided for the wall mounting.

Chapter 9

Air-Conditioning Equipment

The gas compression method of mechanical refrigeration used in conjunction with an air-cooled condenser is probably the most common cooling system used in residences and small commercial buildings. For that reason, this chapter is devoted almost exclusively to a description of mechanical refrigeration equipment.

A typical central air-conditioning system cools the house with an indoor coil (evaporator) working in conjunction with an outdoor coil (condenser) and a pump (compressor). The evaporator and condenser coils are commonly constructed of copper tubing and aluminum fins. A pump (compressor) forces a refrigerant (heat transfer fluid) through the tubing coils and fins. When the refrigerant reaches the indoor coil (evaporator), it evaporates and pulls the heat out of the indoor air. At this point, the refrigerant fluid has changed to a gas. The hot refrigerant gas is then pumped back through the copper tubing and aluminum fins of the outdoor condenser where it changes (condenses) back into a liquid, releasing its heat to the air passing over the metal tubing and fins.

Mechanical Refrigeration Equipment

The equipment of a gas compression mechanical refrigeration system can be divided into mechanical and electrical components. The electrical components are described below (see *Electrical Components*) and in Chapter 6 ("Other Automatic Controls") in Volume 2. The principal mechanical components include the following:

1. Compressor
2. Condenser
3. Receiver
4. Evaporator
5. Liquid refrigerant controls

Air Conditioner Efficiency Ratings
The energy efficiency of an air conditioner is determined by the number of Btu per hour (Btu/h) removed for each watt of power drawn. The method used to rate the energy efficiency of a central air conditioner differs from that used for a room air conditioner. *(continued)*

Air Conditioner Efficiency Ratings (continued)

- **Central Air Conditioners.** The energy efficiency of the cooling equipment used in a residential or light commercial central air-conditioning system is expressed in terms of its Seasonal Energy Efficiency Ratio (SEER). In other words, the efficiency of the central air-conditioning equipment is defined in terms of the cooling effect in Btu per hour divided by the power use in watts for the seasonal average day (SEER). New air-conditioning equipment should have a SEER rating of 10 or better. The ratings go as high as 17. The ratings of equipment manufactured before the new efficiency ratings went into effect were 8 or lower.

- **Room Air Conditioners.** The energy efficiency of a room air conditioner is expressed in terms of its Energy Efficiency Ratio (EER); that is to say, it is defined in terms of the cooling effect in Btu per hour divided by the power use in watts for the peak day (EER). An energy-efficient room air conditioner will have an EER rating of 8 or higher. One with a 10 rating is recommended for hot climates.

Some air conditioner manufacturers also participate in the voluntary EnergyStar labeling program. Air-conditioning equipment with an EnergyStar label means that they possess high EER and SEER ratings.

Energy efficiency ratings are posted on an energy guide label, which is attached to the equipment.

Compressors

A *compressor* is a pumping device used in a mechanical refrigeration system to receive and compress low-pressure refrigerant vapor into a smaller volume at higher pressure. Thus, the primary function of a compressor is to establish a pressure difference in the system to create a flow of the refrigerant from one part of the system to the other.

Compressors are manufactured in many different sizes for a variety of different applications. Most residential compressors are reciprocating-type, scroll-type units, or rotary-type units, depending on how the refrigerant is compressed. The scroll compressors are a more recent design.

A *reciprocating compressor* (also sometimes called a *piston compressor*) uses a piston moving inside a cylinder to compress the refrigerant (see Figures 9-1 and 9-2). The operation of a piston compressor is similar to that of the reciprocating pistons in an automotive engine. It is a positive-displacement compressor with the piston (or pistons) moving in a straight line but alternately in opposite directions. Both open and hermetic reciprocating compressors are manufactured for use in refrigeration systems.

Figure 9-1 Side and top views of Lennox HP29 reciprocating compressor. *(Courtesy Lennox Industries Inc.)*

Figure 9-2 Cutaway view of Lennox HP29 reciprocating compressor. *(Courtesy Lennox Industries Inc.)*

A *scroll compressor* uses two spiral-shaped scrolls to compress the refrigerant (see Figures 9-3 and 9-4). One scroll remains stationary while the other orbits around it in a rotary motion. The moving scroll compresses the refrigerant by forcing it into an increasingly smaller space. At this point, the gas, now compressed to a high pressure, is discharged from a port in the stationary scroll to the condenser. Scroll compressors are quieter than piston compressors because they contain only one moving part (the single rotating scroll).

DISCHARGE

SUCTION

Figure 9-3 Details of scroll compressor. *(Courtesy Lennox Industries Inc.)*

DISCHARGE PRESSURE   DISCHARGE   STATIONARY SCROLL

SUCTION

TIPS SEALED BY DISCHARGE PRESSURE   ORBITING SCROLL

Figure 9-4 Cross-section of scrolls. *(Courtesy Lennox Industries Inc.)*

A *rotary compressor* is a hermetically sealed, direct-drive compressor that compresses the gas by movement of the roll in relation to the pump chamber. Rotary compressors are manufactured in large quantities for use in residential cooling systems (see Figures 9-5 and 9-6).

Figure 9-5   Cutaway view of a typical rotary compressor.
(Courtesy Trane Co.)

Figure 9-6 Eccentric shaft and roller of a rotary compressor.
(Courtesy Mueller Climatrol Corp.)

A *centrifugal compressor* is a non-positive-displacement compressor that relies in part on centrifugal effect for pressure rise. Compression of the refrigerant is accomplished by means of centrifugal force. As a result, this type of compressor is generally used in installations having large refrigerant volumes and low pressure differentials. The compressors used in residential and light commercial cooling systems may be classified on the basis of how accessible they are for field service and repair. The following three types are recognized:

1. Open-type compressors

2. Hermetic compressors

3. Semihermetic compressors

As shown in Figure 9-7, an *open-type compressor* is usually driven by a separately mounted electric motor. Both the compressor and motor are easily accessible for field service and repair.

Figure 9-7 Diagram on an open-type compressor. *(Courtesy Honeywell Tradeline Controls)*

The *hermetic compressor* shown in Figure 9-8 differs from the open type in being *completely* sealed, usually by welding. No provision is made for service access. The compressors used in residential and light-commercial construction are hermetic compressors. A hermetic compressor is so called because its components are sealed inside a welded housing. The housing (or *can*) contains an electric motor and a pump. Compressors can be reciprocating, scroll, rotary, disc, or screw types.

Note

A sealed (*hermetic*) compressor must be replaced if it fails because it cannot be repaired on site. After it is replaced, filter dryers must be installed to remove any moisture and/or acid in the system.

Figure 9-8 Diagram of a hermetic compressor.

(Courtesy Honeywell Tradeline Controls)

Both single-speed and two-speed compressors are used in residential heat pumps. A single-speed compressor is the most common type. It operates at full capacity regardless of the actual heating and cooling needs of the structure. A two-speed compressor, on the other hand, operates at a capacity that approximates the actual heating and cooling needs at any given moment. A two-speed compressor is, therefore, much more energy efficient than a single-speed one. It also is subject to less wear because its operation is not continuous.

The *semihermetic compressor* is similar in construction to the hermetic type, except that field service and repairs are possible on the former through bolted access plates.

Both the compressor and electric motor are sealed in the same casing in hermetic and semihermetic compressors. As a result, the motors are cooled by a refrigerant that flows through and around the motors. Quick-trip overload relays provide additional protection against overheating should the refrigerant flow be cut off.

Semihermetic and hermetic compressor motors of a given size are designed and constructed to operate on a heavier current without overheating. Hermetically sealing the compressor and electric motor in the same casing also results in a greater output. The principal disadvantage of a hermetic compressor is that it must be replaced with a new unit when it malfunctions. Because this usually occurs in the cooling season, the homeowner may be without air-conditioning for a day or so when it is most needed.

Troubleshooting Compressors

When a compressor is suspected of being defective, a complete analysis should be made of the system before the compressor is replaced. In some cases, the symptoms encountered in servicing an air conditioner may lead the serviceperson to suspect the compressor when actually the trouble is in another section of the system. For example, noise and knocking are often attributed to a faulty compressor when the trouble may be a loose compressor flywheel, incorrect belt alignment, air in the system, or a large quantity of oil being pumped through the compressor because of liquid refrigerant in the crankcase.

Table 9-1 lists the most common operating problems associated with air-conditioning compressors. For each observable symptom, a possible cause and remedy are suggested.

Table 9-1   Troubleshooting Compressors

Symptom and Possible Cause	Possible Remedy
Compressor does not start; no hum.	
(a) Open power switch.	(a) Close switch.
(b) Fuse blown.	(b) Replace fuse.
(c) Broken electrical connection.	(c) Check circuit and repair.
(d) Overload stuck.	(d) Wait for reset; check current.
(e) Frozen compressor or motor bearings.	(e) Replace the compressor.
(f) High head pressure; cut out open due to high pressure.	(f) Push high-pressure button and check for air circulation in condenser.
(g) Central contacts in open position.	(g) Repair and check control.
(h) Open circuit in compressor stator.	(h) Replace the compressor.
(i) Thermostat set too high.	(i) Reset to proper level.
(j) Solenoid valve closed.	(j) Examine holding coil; if burned out, replace.
Compressor starts but motor will not get off of starting windings; high amperage and rattle in the compressor.	
(a) Compressor improperly wired.	(a) Check wiring against wiring diagram; rewire if necessary.
(b) Low line voltage.	(b) Check line voltage and correct (decrease load on line or increase wire size).
(c) Relay defective.	(c) Replace relay.
(d) Run capacitor defective.	(d) Replace run capacitor.

(continued)

Table 9-1 (continued)

Symptom and Possible Cause	Possible Remedy
(e) Compressor motor starting and running windings shorted.	(e) Replace compressor.
(f) High discharge pressure.	(f) Correct excessive high pressure.
(g) Starting capacitor weak.	(g) Check capacitor; replace if necessary.
(h) Tight compressor.	(h) Check oil level and correct, or replace compressor.

Compressor will not start; hums and trips on overload.

(a) Compressor improperly wired.	(a) Check wiring against wiring diagram; rewire if necessary.
(b) Low line voltage.	(b) Check line voltage and correct.
(c) Starting capacitor defective.	(c) Replace capacitor.
(d) Relay contacts not closing.	(d) Check contact points; replace if defective.
(e) Grounded compressor motor or motor with open winding.	(e) Replace compressor.
(f) High discharge pressure.	(f) Check excessive high pressure. Check air.
(g) Tight compressor.	(g) Check oil level and correct, or replace compressor.

Compressor starts and runs but short cycles.

(a) Low line voltage.	(a) Check line voltage; correct.
(b) Additional current passing through overload protector.	(b) Check wiring diagram; fan motors may be connected to the wrong side of the protector.
(c) Suction pressure high.	(c) Check compressor for possibility of misapplication.
(d) High discharge pressure.	(d) Correct excessive high pressure.
(e) Run capacitor defective.	(e) Check capacitor and replace.
(f) Compressor too hot; inadequate motor cooling.	(f) Check refrigerant charge; add if necessary.
(g) Compressor motor windings shorted.	(g) Replace compressor.

(continued)

Table 9-1   *(continued)*

Symptom and Possible Cause	Possible Remedy
(h) Overload protector defective.	(h) Check current, give reset time; if it does not come back, replace compressor.
(i) Compressor tight.	(i) Check oil level and correct, or replace compressor.
(j) Discharge valve defective.	(j) Replace compressor.

Compressor short cycling.

(a) Thermostat differential set too closely.	(a) Widen differential.
(b) Dirty air filter.	(b) Replace.
(c) Refrigerant charge too low.	(c) Recharge system with correct charge.
(d) Dirty strainer or dryer in liquid line.	(d) Replace.
(e) Restricted capillary tube or expansion valve.	(e) Replace.
(f) Dirty condenser.	(f) Clean condenser.
(g) Too much refrigerant.	(g) Discharge some refrigerant.
(h) Air in system.	(h) Purge system.
(i) Compressor valve leaking.	(i) Replace compressor.
(j) Overload protector cutting out.	(j) Check current and give reset time; if it does not come back, replace compressor.

Compressor runs continuously.

(a) Shortage of refrigerant.	(a) Test at refrigerant test cock; if short of gas, add proper amount. Test for leaks.
(b) Compressor too small for load.	(b) Increase capacity by increasing speed or using larger compressor.
(c) Discharge valve leaking badly.	(c) Test valve; if leaking, remove head of compressor and repair or service.

Compressor noisy.

(a) Vibration because unit not bolted down properly.	(a) Examine bolts and correct.

(continued)

Table 9-1   *(continued)*

Symptom and Possible Cause	*Possible Remedy*
(b) Too much oil in circulation, causing hydraulic knock.	(b) Check oil level and check for oil in refrigerant test cock; correct.
(c) Slugging due to flooding back of refrigerant.	(c) Expansion valve is open too wide. Close.
(d) Wear of parts such as piston, piston pins.	(d) Locate cause. Repair or replace compressor.
High suction pressure.	
(a) Overfeeding of expansion valve.	(a) Regulate expansion; check bulb attachment.
(b) Compressor too small for evaporator or load.	(b) Check capacity. Try to increase speed or replace with larger-size compressor.
(c) Leaky suction valves.	(c) Remove head and examine valve discs or rings; replace if worn.
Low suction pressure.	
(a) Restricted liquid line and expansion valve or suction screens.	(a) Pump down; remove, examine, and clean screens.
(b) Compressor too big for evaporator.	(b) Check capacity against load; reduce speed if necessary.
(c) Insufficient gas in system.	(c) Check for gas shortage at test cock.
(d) Too much oil circulating in system.	(d) Remove oil.
(e) Improper adjustment of expansion valves.	(e) Adjust valve to give more flow. If opening valve does not correct, increase size to give greater capacity.

Each compressor should be equipped with internal devices to provide protection against the following operating problems:

1. Motor overload
2. Locked rotor
3. Extreme voltage supply
4. Excessive winding temperature

5. Excessive pressure

6. Loss of refrigerant charge

7. Compressor cycling

If these devices are operating properly, the compressor will provide efficient and trouble-free service.

Compressor Replacement

Before replacing a hermetic compressor, be sure to check other possible causes of system malfunction (see *Troubleshooting Compressors*). Do not replace the compressor unless you are absolutely certain it is the source of the trouble.

Many manufacturers will provide instructions for replacing the compressor along with their installation, servicing, and operating literature. Carefully read these instructions before attempting to disconnect the compressor.

Disconnect the power supply, remove the fuses, and check the liquid refrigerant for oil discoloration or an acrid odor. These are indications that a compressor burnout has contaminated the system. If the system is not properly cleaned up, the replacement compressor will also burn out.

The system can be checked for contamination by discharging a small amount of refrigerant and oil through the high-side port onto a clean white cloth and checking it for discoloration and odor. Perform the same test on the low-side gauge port. If the system shows signs of contamination, discharge the remainder of the refrigerant through the liquid line gauge port (on a factory-charged system) or the high-side gauge port (on a field-charged system). Inspect the refrigerant lines to determine the exact extent of contamination.

Examine the refrigerant lines connected to the evaporator for contamination. A rapid compressor burnout will usually leave the evaporator coil unaffected. If the burnout has been particularly slow and the refrigerant and oil have been circulated through the system, the evaporator will also be contaminated. A contaminated evaporator can be cleaned by flushing it with a refrigerant.

Electric Motors

The electric motors used to power mechanical refrigeration equipment are commonly of the following two types:

1. Single-phase induction motors

2. Three-phase induction motors

The single-phase induction motors are usually classified by the method used to start them. Among the more common ones are the following:

1. Split-phase motors

2. Capacitor-start motors

3. Permanent-split capacitor motors

4. Capacitor-start, capacitor-run motors

Capacitor-start and capacitor-start, capacitor-run motors are described in Chapter 6 ("Other Automatic Controls") in Volume 2.

Either capacitor-start, capacitor-run or three-phase induction motors can be used to power compressors. The latter are normally used when three-phase current is available.

Troubleshooting Electrical Motors

Table 9-2 lists the most common operating problems associated with electric motors. For each symptom, a possible cause and remedy are suggested.

Table 9-2   Troubleshooting Electrical Motors

Symptom and Possible Cause	Possible Remedy
Motor blows fuses, trips overload.	
(a) Fuses and/or overload too small.	(a) Install larger sizes if necessary within safe limit for motor.
(b) Poor switch contacts.	(b) Check and replace contacts. Replace entire switch if necessary.
(c) Low voltage.	(c) Check voltages with meter; if more than 10 percent low, notify power company to correct condition.
(d) Leaky discharge valve.	(d) Replace.
(e) Overloaded motor.	(e) Check bhp load against back-pressure and compressor speed; if motor is too small, increase size.
Motor hot.	
(a) Low voltage.	(a) Check voltage with meter; if more than 10 percent low, notify power company to correct condition.

(continued)

Table 9-2 *(continued)*

Symptom and Possible Cause	*Possible Remedy*
(b) Bearings need oil.	(b) Oil bearings to reduce friction.
(c) Overloaded motor.	(c) Check bhp load against back-pressure and compressor speed; if motor is too small, increase size.

Gas Engines

A four-cylinder water-cooled gas engine using natural gas as the fuel can be used to power the compressor (and sometimes the condenser fan). It is normally mounted in a weatherproof cabinet outside the residence where venting is not a problem. Because an internal combustion engine must be vented, electric motors are by far the most popular type used for powering mechanical refrigeration equipment.

Electrical Components

The principal electrical components of a mechanical refrigeration system include the following:

1. Electric compressor motor
2. Compressor contactor or relay
3. Compressor starter
4. Overload protector
5. Capacitor
6. Potential relay
7. Pressure switch
8. Evaporator fan motor
9. Condenser fan motor
10. Evaporator fan relay

The wiring diagram in Figure 9-9 illustrates the relationship of these various components. Switches, relays, and capacitors have already been described in considerable detail in Chapter 6 ("Other Automatic Controls") in Volume 2.

The room thermostat is sometimes included when the electrical components of a refrigeration system are listed. The reader is referred to Chapter 4 ("Thermostats and Humidistats") in Volume 2 for detailed information about thermostats.

Figure 9-9 Impedance relay, thermal delay relay, isolating relay, heat control, electronic air cleaner, and humidity controls added to a basic cooling control system. *(Courtesy Honeywell Tradeline Controls)*

Troubleshooting Electrical Components

Table 9-3 lists the most common problems associated with the operation of the electrical components in air-conditioning equipment. For each symptom, a possible cause and remedy are suggested.

Table 9-3   Troubleshooting Electrical Components

Symptom and Possible Cause	Possible Remedy
Starting capacitor is open, shorted, or burned out.	
(a) Relay contacts not operating properly.	(a) Clean contacts or replace.
(b) Improper capacitor.	(b) Check for proper MFD rating and voltage.
(c) Low voltage.	(c) Check and correct.
(d) Improper relay.	(d) Check and replace.
(e) Short cycling.	(e) Replace starting capacitor.

(continued)

Table 9-3 (continued)

Symptom and Possible Cause	Possible Remedy
Running capacitor is open, shorted, or burned out.	
(a) Improper capacitor.	(a) Check for proper MFD rating and voltage.
(b) Excessive high line voltage.	(b) Correct line voltage to not more than 10 percent of rated motor voltage.
Relay is shorted or burned out.	
(a) Line voltage is too low or too high.	(a) Check and correct.
(b) Incorrect running capacitor.	(b) Replace with correct MFD capacitor.
(c) Loose relay.	(c) Tighten relay.
(d) Short cycling.	(d) Replace relay.

Condenser

A *condenser* is a device that is used to liquefy gas by cooling. In operation, hot discharge gas (refrigerant vapor) from the compressor enters the condenser coil at the top and, as it is condensed, drains out of the condenser to a receiver located at a lower level.

The condenser coil is located along with the compressor and controlling devices in the *condensing unit.* In a remote or split-system air-conditioning installation, the condensing unit is located outdoors (see Figure 9-10). Condensers are available in a variety of designs, including plain tube, finned tube, and plate type, and as series-pass and parallel-pass units. A number of different condensers are illustrated in Figures 9-11, 9-12, 9-13, and 9-14.

Condensers may be classified with respect to the cooling method used into the following three types:

1. Air-cooled condensers
2. Water-cooled condensers
3. Combined air- and water-cooled condensers

An *air-cooled condenser* consists of a coil of ample surface across which air is blown by a fan or induced by natural draft (see Figure 9-15). This type of condenser is universally used in small-capacity refrigerating units.

EVAPORATOR COIL

FURNACE

CONDENSING UNIT

REFRIGERANT LINES

Figure 9-10 Location of the condensing unit in a remote or split-system air-conditioning installation.

FAN AND MOTOR ASSEMBLY

CONDENSER COIL

COMPRESSOR

WIRING AND CONTROL BOX

REFRIGERANT LINE CONNECTIONS

Figure 9-11 Lennox HSW4 series air-conditioning condenser unit.
(Courtesy Lennox Air Conditioning and Heating)

CONDENSER
COIL

CONDENSER
COIL GRILLE

FAN AND
MOTOR ASSEMBLY

COMPRESSOR

WIRING AND
CONTROL BOX

REFRIGERANT LINE CONNECTIONS

Figure 9-12 Lennox HS8 series air-conditioning condenser unit.

(Courtesy Lennox Air Conditioning and Heating)

A *water-cooled condenser* is similar to a steam surface condenser in that cooling is accomplished by water alone that circulates through tubes or coils enclosed in a shell. The refrigerant circulates through the annular space between the tubes or coils. Because of its construction, a water-cooled condenser is also sometimes called a *double-pipe condenser* (see Figure 9-16).

Maximum temperature differences can be obtained by connecting the condenser for counterflow. This type of arrangement usually gives the best operating results.

Shell-and-tube construction is recommended for a small condensing unit. In medium-size units, shell-and-coil construction works very well (see Figures 9-17 and 9-18).

A *combined air- and water-cooled condenser*, more commonly known as an *evaporative condenser*, consists of a coil cooled by water sprayed from above and cold air entering from below (see Figure 9-19).

Figure 9-13 Bard 36HPQ1 condensing unit. *(Courtesy Bard Mfg. Co.)*

As water evaporates from the coil, it brings about a cooling effect, which condenses the refrigerant within the coil. The hot refrigerant gas within the coil is thus changed to the liquid state by the combined action of the sprayed water and the large volume of moving air supplied by the fan. The water that does not evaporate is recirculated by means of a pump.

Because an evaporative condenser is not wasteful of water, large compressor installations are possible in areas where water is scarce. Tests have shown that the amount of water required will not exceed 0.03 gpm per ton of refrigeration. Evaporative condensers also eliminate wastewater disposal problems and provide the most economical means of cooling refrigerant gases.

Air-cooled condensers, like evaporators, should be kept free from dirt, lint, and other foreign materials because they tend to reduce the airflow around tubes and fins if they are allowed to accumulate.

Condenser Service and Maintenance
The aluminum fins on condenser coils are easily bent and can block airflow through the coil. A tool called a fin comb is available at

Figure 9-14   Climatrol
938-1 dual-compressor
condensing unit.

(Courtesy Mueller Climatrol Corp.)

air-conditioning equipment wholesalers that will comb these fins
back into nearly original condition.

Figure 9-15   Air-cooled
condenser.

(Courtesy Honeywell Tradeline Controls)

Troubleshooting Condensers

Common operating problems associated with air-conditioning condensers are listed in Table 9-4. For
each symptom, a possible cause and
remedy are suggested.

Receiver

As the name suggests, the *receiver* is
the reservoir for any excess liquid
refrigerant not being used in the system. The liquid receiver must be large
enough to hold the *total* amount of

Figure 9-16 Double-pipe condenser.

(Courtesy Honeywell Tradeline Controls)

Figure 9-17 Shell-and-tube condenser.

(Courtesy Honeywell Tradeline Controls)

Figure 9-18 Shell-and-coil condenser.

(Courtesy Honeywell Tradeline Controls)

Figure 9-19   Evaporative condenser. *(Courtesy Honeywell Tradeline Controls)*

Table 9-4   Troubleshooting Condensers

Symptom and Possible Cause	Possible Remedy
Compressor pressure too high.	
(a) Air in system.	(a) Purge system.
(b) Dirty condenser.	(b) Clean condenser.
(c) Refrigerant too high.	(c) Discharge some refrigerant.
(d) Unit location too hot.	(d) Change unit location.
(e) Condenser air off.	(e) Check condenser motor connections for burnout.
Condenser pressure too low.	
(a) Refrigerant charge too low.	(a) Check for leak, repair, and recharge with correct amount of refrigerant.
(b) Compressor discharge or suction valves defective.	(b) Replace compressor.
(c) Entering temperature to evaporator low.	(c) Raise temperature.

ROOM COOLING UNIT

COLD WATER COIL

BLOWER

TO DRAIN

COLD WATER PIPING

HEAT EXCHANGER (EVAPORATOR COIL)

REFRIGERANT PIPING

WATER CHILLER PACKAGE

Figure 9-20 Evaporator coil. *(Courtesy Coleman Co.)*

Figure 9-21 Evaporator coil and water chiller.
(Courtesy Honeywell Tradeline Controls)

refrigerant used in the system. Receivers are commonly constructed of drawn steel shells welded together to form a single unit.

Evaporator

An *evaporator* is a device used in either mechanical- or absorption-type refrigeration systems to transfer or absorb heat from the air surrounding the evaporator to the refrigerant. In so doing, the liquid refrigerant is evaporated or boiled off as it passes through the evaporator.

Evaporators are made of copper tubing with or without closely spaced aluminum fins designed to increase the heat transfer surface. Because of its function (that is, removing heat from room air) and construction, an evaporator is also referred to as an *evaporator coil, cooling coil, blower coil*, or *direct-expansion coil*.

Figure 9-20 illustrates a typical evaporator coil used in the bonnet or plenum of a warm-air furnace. The coil capacity must be matched to the condensing unit for efficient cooling. This is particularly important to remember when converting an existing heating system to year-round air-conditioning.

An evaporator coil may also be placed in the heat exchanger of a water chiller as shown in Figure 9-21. The water cooled in the water chiller is piped to the cold-water coil over which the room air is circulated. The coil may be duct mounted (in a warm-air heating system) or located in a room cooling unit (in a forced hot-water heating system).

Evaporator Service and Maintenance

The aluminum fins on evaporator coils, like those on the condenser coils, are also easily bent. If bent, they can block the flow of air through the coil. The same tool used to straighten the fins on the condenser tubing can be used to return the evaporator fins to their original position.

Troubleshooting Evaporators

An evaporator must be kept clean and free of dirt and dust so that the flow of air through the tubes remains unrestricted. If the evaporator is damaged or leaking to such an extent that it cannot be successfully repaired, it should be replaced by a new assembly. If repairs or replacement are necessary, the complete coil assembly must be removed from the system.

Before removing a damaged or leaking evaporator, the refrigerant lines must first be disconnected and the evaporator retaining bolts (if used) loosened and removed.

The new evaporator is bolted or otherwise secured in place and connected to the refrigerant lines. After all connections are made, the entire system is evacuated, recharged with refrigerant, and tested for leaks.

Refrigerants

A *refrigerant* is any substance that produces a refrigerating effect by absorbing heat as it expands or vaporizes. A desirable refrigerant should possess chemical, physical, and thermodynamic properties that permit efficient and safe operation in refrigerating systems. Among the properties possessed by a good refrigerant are the following:

1. Low boiling point
2. Nontoxic and nonirritating
3. Nonexplosive
4. Nonflammable
5. Mixes well with oil
6. Operation on a positive pressure
7. High latent heat value
8. Not affected by moisture

Two of the most commonly used refrigerants in older equipment are R-12 (Freon 12) and R-22 (Freon 22). These are clear, almost colorless liquids at temperatures below their boiling points.

R-12 has a boiling point of –21.8°F at atmospheric pressure and is characterized by moderate pressure differentials between suction and discharge. A moderate volume of R-12 is required per ton of refrigeration.

R-22 has a boiling point of –41.4°F at atmospheric pressure. In contrast to R-12, it has a considerably higher pressure differential between suction and discharge. As a result, it requires a smaller volume of refrigerant per ton of refrigeration.

R-410A is gradually replacing older refrigerants because it does not possess the ozone-depleting chemical properties of the latter. Refrigerant R-410A is known by such trade names as PuronTM, Dupont Suva, and Genetron AZ20. Many HVAC manufacturers are already using the new refrigerant in new air-conditioning equipment.

Older air-conditioning equipment and systems cannot be retrofitted with R-410A. If an older refrigerant was used, it must be removed, cleaned, and reused. Because R-410A runs operating pressures higher than older refrigerants, new sets of hoses and refrigerant gauges are required for installation, service, and repair.

Note

The efficiency of an air conditioner is greatest when the refrigerant charge exactly matches the manufacturer's specification and is neither undercharged nor overcharged. If the air conditioner is on refrigerant (undercharged) and not leaking, refrigerant should be added by a trained HVAC technician. If the air conditioner is leaking refrigerant, do not add refrigerant. Have a trained HVAC technician fix the leak, test the repair, and then charge the system with the correct amount of refrigerant.

Liquid Refrigerant Control Devices

Each refrigeration system may be described in terms of a low side and a high side of operating pressure. The *low side* is that part of the refrigeration system that normally operates under low pressure (as opposed to the high side). It is identified as that part of a refrigeration system lying between the expansion valve and the intake valve in the compressor, and includes the evaporating or cooling surface, the intake line, and the compressor crankcase—in other words, that part of the refrigeration equipment under intake pressure. The term low side is sometimes used to designate the evaporator coils.

The *high side* is that part of the refrigeration system operating under high pressure. The term high side is sometimes used to designate the condensing unit.

Some form of expansion device is necessary to control the flow of liquid refrigerant between the low and high sides of a refrigeration system. The following expansion devices are designed to provide automatic control of refrigerant flow:

1. Automatic expansion valves
2. Thermostatic expansion valves
3. Float valves
4. Capillary tubes

Automatic Expansion Valves

An *automatic expansion valve* is a pressure-actuated diaphragm valve used to maintain a constant pressure in the evaporator of a direct-expansion mechanical refrigeration system (see Figure 9-22). It accomplishes this function by regulating the flow of refrigerant from the liquid line into the evaporator. In this way, the evaporator is always supplied with the proper amount of refrigerant to meet conditions. An automatic expansion valve does not respond well to load fluctuations. For this reason, it is not recommended for use in air-conditioning (see *Thermostatic Expansion Valves*).

MANUAL ADJUSTMENT

SPRING

BELLOWS DIAPHRAGM

VENT TUBE

PUSH ROD

OUTLET

SEAT

CHECK BALL

SPRING

STRAINER

INLET

Figure 9-22 Automatic expansion valve.

Thermostatic Expansion Valves

The *thermostatic expansion valve* is designed to automatically control the flow of liquid refrigerant entering the evaporator coil. The valve mechanism must operate freely and without restriction in order to allow the proper amount of refrigerant to enter the evaporator (see Figures 9-23 and 9-24).

Failure of any part of the thermostatic expansion valve will affect the refrigerating capacity of the unit and the cooling capacity of the system. Faulty operation of the expansion valve may be caused by mechanically frozen internal parts clogging the strainer or valve orifice, or by failure of the regulating sensor bulb, which operates the needle valve.

If the expansion valve is frozen partly open, the capacity of the unit will be affected because the flow of refrigerant is restricted. If the expansion valve is frozen in a fully open position, the liquid refrigerant may flow through the entire system, causing very cold inlet line, high inlet pressure, pounding of the compressor, and a cold compressor head.

Figure 9-23 Typical thermostatic expansion valve.

Figure 9-24 Thermostatic expansion valve operating principle.

(Courtesy Honeywell Tradeline Controls)

The pressure in the sensor bulb or feeler of the expansion valve must be somewhat higher than the pressure in the evaporator, which means that the inlet line where the bulb is clamped must be at a higher temperature than that within the evaporator. Accordingly, the vapor in the inlet line at this point must be in a somewhat superheated state. This superheat should be at the minimum that will allow the valve to regulate the flow of refrigerant.

For higher-temperature work, such as comfort cooling work, the amount of superheating will vary between 5° and 10°. For lower-temperature work, such as product cooling work, the superheating will vary between 4° and 6° or in some cases even lower.

Excessive superheat indicates a lack of sufficient refrigerant flowing through the expansion valve, a condition that reduces the capacity of the evaporator.

The sensitivity and response of the thermostatic expansion valve is largely dependent on the proper installation of the sensor (feeler) bulb. The sensor bulb should always be firmly attached to the inlet line.

When properly installed and adjusted, the thermostatic expansion valve will maintain all the evaporator surface effective and in contact with the boiling refrigerant regardless of the change in load on the evaporator, provided of course that the evaporator valve has sufficient capacity for peak loads.

Under normal operating conditions, the sensor (feeler) bulb will cause the thermostatic expansion valve to close during the shutdown period. There are, however, certain conditions that will affect this and may cause overflooding of the evaporator. For this reason, the inlet lines should be trapped.

If the evaporator in an air-conditioning system is connected to outside air or where it may receive air at a temperature lower than that surrounding the sensor (feeler) bulb, the difference in temperature between the evaporator and the bulb will cause the valve to open and overflood the low side. Under such conditions, it is essential that the liquid line be equipped with a solenoid valve to positively shut off the refrigerant during the shutdown period.

Float Valves

A *float valve* is one actuated by a float immersed in a liquid container (see Figure 9-25). Both low-side and high-side float valves are used to control the flow of liquid refrigerant in a refrigeration system.

Figure 9-25 Float valve construction details. *(Courtesy Frick Company)*

A *low-side* float valve is one that is operated by a low-pressure liquid. It opens at a low level and closes when the liquid is at a high level. In other words, when there is no liquid in the evaporator, the float and lever arm are positioned so that the valve is left open. When liquid refrigerant under pressure from the compressor again enters the float chamber, the float rises until a predetermined level is reached and the valve is closed.

A *high-side* float valve is one that is operated by a high-side pressure. The valve opens on an increase of the liquid level in the float chamber and admits liquid to the low side.

Capillary Tubes

A *capillary tube* is a tube of small internal diameter used in refrigeration air-conditioning systems as an expansion device between the high-pressure and low-pressure sides. It can also be used to transmit pressure from the sensor bulb of some temperature controls to the operating element (see Figure 9-26).

Figure 9-26   Capillary tube and connections to mechanical refrigeration system. *(Courtesy Honeywell Tradeline Controls)*

The use of a capillary tube as a liquid refrigerant expansion device is largely limited to completely assembled factory refrigeration units because the bore diameters and the length of the tube are critical to its efficiency. The pressure reduction that occurs between the condenser and evaporator results from the pressure drop or friction loss in the long, small-diameter passage provided by the capillary tube. No pressure-reducing valve is necessary between the high-side and low-side pressure zones when a capillary system is used.

Refrigerant Piping

The refrigerant travels between the various components of a mechanical refrigeration unit or system in small-diameter copper tubing sometimes referred to as the *refrigerant lines*.

The *suction line* is the piping between the evaporator and compressor inlet. Its function is to carry the refrigerant vapor to the compressor. It is important that the suction line be correctly sized for a practical pressure drop at full load. Under minimum load conditions, the suction line should be able to return oil from the evaporator to the compressor. Two other desirable features that should be incorporated in the design of a suction line are the following:

1. The prevention of oil drainage into a non-operating evaporator from an operating one.

2. The prevention of liquid drainage into a shut-down compressor.

The *liquid line* is the piping that carries the liquid refrigerant from the condenser or receiver to a pressure-reducing device.

The refrigerant piping (lines) should be carefully checked to make certain they will function properly. All connections should be examined for leaks, and all bends should be checked to make certain the tubing has not been squeezed together. A squeezed or pinched line will restrict the flow of refrigerant.

The *slope* of the suction line is also important in remote or split-system installations. When the evaporator coil is higher than the condensing unit, the suction line should be sloped with a continuous fall of at least ¼ inch per foot toward the condensing unit.

If the evaporator coil is higher than the condensing unit and the excess line is coiled, the excess tubing must be coiled horizontally in such a way that the flow of refrigerant is from the top to the bottom of the coil and toward the condensing unit in a continuous fall (see Figure 9-27).

Refrigerant Piping Service and Maintenance

Check the liquid and suction lines to make certain that they do not contact one another. Heat will transfer to the suction line if there is bare contact between the two.

Figure 9-27   Flow of refrigerant toward the condensing unit.
(Courtesy Coleman Co.)

Check refrigerant line connections for proper seat at the evaporator coil. These are nonreusable connecting valves that must be 100 percent seated for effective operation. If these valves have not been 100 percent seated, then the metal diaphragm will obstruct the line and restrict the flow of refrigerant. If this condition is suspected, use a wrench on the stationary fitting of the valve as shown in Figure 9-28 while tightening the nut with another wrench.

Figure 9-28   Using wrenches to tighten connection. *(Courtesy Coleman Co.)*

Troubleshooting Refrigerant Piping

Table 9-5 lists the most common operating problems associated with the refrigerant piping. For each observable symptom, a possible cause and remedy are suggested.

Table 9-5   Troubleshooting Refrigerant Piping

Symptom and Possible Cause	Possible Remedy
Frosted or sweaty suction line.	
(a) Capillary tube or expansion valve passes excess refrigerant.	(a) Check the size and bore of capillary tube. Readjust the expansion valve.
(b) Expansion valve is stuck.	(b) Clean valve; replace if necessary.
(c) Evaporator fan not running.	(c) Repair or replace.
(d) Overcharge of refrigerant.	(d) Correct.
(e) Ambient temperature too low.	(e) Block the condenser to increase the suction pressure or stop the unit.

(continued)

Table 9-5 *(continued)*

Symptom and Possible Cause	Possible Remedy
Hot liquid line.	
(a) Low refrigerant charge.	(a) Fix leak and recharge.
(b) Expansion valve stuck or open too wide.	(b) Clean valve and replace if necessary.
Frosted or sweating liquid line.	
(a) Restriction in dryer.	(a) Replace dryer.
Frost on expansion valve or on capillary tube.	
(a) Ice plugging capillary tube or expansion valve.	(a) Apply hot wet cloth to capillary tube or expansion valve; a suction pressure increase indicates moisture present. Replace dryer.

Filters and Dryers

Filters and dryers are devices that provide very important functions in a mechanical refrigeration system. A *filter* is a device used to remove particles from the liquid refrigerant and from the oil by straining the fluid. For this reason, it is also sometimes referred to as a *strainer.* If a filter or strainer were not used, these particles trapped in the fluid could block small passages in the thermostatic valve or capillary tube, thereby seriously affecting the operation of the cooling system, or they could eventually damage mechanical parts.

A *dryer* is a device designed to remove moisture from the refrigerant in a mechanical refrigeration system. It is also referred to as a *dehydrator* or a *drier* (a spelling variant used by some authorities).

A typical combination filter-dryer is shown in Figure 9-29. The desiccant surrounding the filter core is usually a silica gel and functions as a drying agent. This unit is usually installed in the liquid line (either at the liquid receiver outlet or at the expansion valve outlet).

Filters and dryers are not included with small-capacity cooling units (residential types) that are filled and hermetically sealed at the factory. Filters and dryers are usually installed in systems where the refrigerant circuit is designed for field service.

Pressure-Limiting Controls

Certain pressure-limiting controls are used in cooling systems to protect them from extremes in refrigeration suction and discharge line pressures. Whenever the pressures in the system deviate from

STEEL SHEEL

SCREEN CORE

OUTLET

INLET

DESICCANT

COTTON YARN

Figure 9-29   Combination filter-dryer. *(Courtesy Honeywell Tradeline Controls)*

Figure 9-30   Diagram of a direct-acting water-regulating valve.

the normal operating range, the pressure control breaks the circuit to the compressor until the pressure returns to normal. High-side and low-side pressure switches are described in Chapter 6 ("Other Automatic Controls") in Volume 2.

Water-Regulating Valves

Temperature-actuated water-regulating valves are used on water-cooled condensers to maintain condensing pressures within the desired range. This is accomplished by increasing or decreasing the rate of water flow as required by conditions in the system. Most water-regulating valves may be classed as either *direct acting* or *pilot operated.*

In the case of a direct-acting valve, the deflection of the bellows caused by an increase in refrigerant pressure overcomes the force of the springs and pushes the disc away from the seat, allowing water to flow. When the unit shuts down, the refrigerant pressure becomes less than the spring pressure and the water valve closes off (see Figure 9-30).

In the pilot-operated valve, the main plunger to which the disc is attached is actuated by water pressure. Opening and closing the pilot port causes the differential pressure across the hollow plunger to vary. The amount of water that will flow through any given size and type of orifice will depend on the pressure differential across the orifice.

Water-regulating valves are rated at a certain quantity of flow under a given pressure differential and the amount of valve opening. The amount of opening is controlled by refrigerant pressure, but if the pressure differential is insufficient, no amount of opening will provide the necessary water for the condenser.

Automatic Controls

Refrigeration and air-conditioning systems consist of refrigeration equipment and an electrical control circuit. These components are interconnected to produce and control the required cooling. Wiring diagrams of some typical automatic cooling control circuits used in refrigeration and air-conditioning systems are illustrated in Figures 9-31 and 9-32.

A cooling control circuit can be divided into the following principal components:

1. Basic controller or thermostat

2. Limit control

3. Primary control

4. Power supply

The relationships and functions of these various control system components are illustrated in Figure 9-31. Detailed descriptions of these components are given in a number of different chapters, especially Chapters 4 and 6 in Volume 2. Refer to the index for additional information.

Note

The compressor and fan controls are subject to early failure in an oversized air-conditioning system because the air conditioner is forced to turn on and off frequently. The corrosion of wires and terminals is also a problem in many systems. Regularly check all electrical wiring and contacts for loose connections, corrosion, and damage.

System Troubleshooting

Table 9-6 lists the most common operating problems associated with the system as a whole. For each problem and symptom, a possible cause and remedy are suggested.

Power supply. Provide disconnect means and overload protection, as required.

Figure 9-31 Basic cooling control system with system power supplied by fan center transformer. *(Courtesy Honeywell Tradeline Controls)*

General Servicing and Maintenance

It must be thoroughly understood that the greatest precautions must be taken to exclude air and moisture from a refrigeration system and that it should not be opened to the atmosphere without first removing the refrigerant from that part of the system to be serviced or repaired.

Caution

Always shut off the electrical power to the air conditioner at the disconnect switch before performing any maintenance or repairs. The air conditioner may have multiple power supplies.

Figure 9-32 Ladder diagram of basic cooling system control circuit. *(Courtesy Honeywell Tradeline Controls)*

Table 9-6 System Troubleshooting

Symptom and Possible Cause	Possible Remedy
Unit operates continuously.	
(a) Shortage of refrigerant.	(a) Fix leak and recharge.
(b) Control contacts frozen or stuck closed.	(b) Clean points or replace.
(c) Insufficient air or dirty condenser.	(c) Check and correct.
(d) Air conditioner space poorly insulated or excess load in structure.	(d) Replace with larger unit.
(e) Compressor valves defective.	(e) Replace compressor.
(f) Restriction in refrigerant system.	(f) Check and correct.
(g) Filter dirty.	(g) Clean or replace.
(h) Air bypassing the coil or service load.	(h) Check return air; keep windows and doors closed.
Space temperature too high; not enough cooling.	
(a) Refrigerant charge low.	(a) Check for leaks and recharge.
(b) Control set too high.	(b) Reset control.
(c) Cap tube, expansion valve, or dryer plugged.	(c) Repair or replace.
(d) Iced or dirty coils.	(d) Defrost or clean.
(e) Unit too small.	(e) Replace with larger unit.
(f) Insufficient air circulation.	(f) Correct air circulation.
(g) Cap tube or expansion valve not allowing enough refrigerant.	(g) Reset or replace.
(h) Cooling coils too small.	(h) Replace.
(i) Restrictions or small gas lines.	(i) Correct restrictions; increase line size.
(j) High and low pressures approaching each other; defective compressor valves.	(j) Replace compressor.
(k) Low line voltage.	(k) Check line voltage and correct.
(l) Dirty air filter.	(l) Replace.
(m) Dirty condenser.	(m) Clean condenser.
(n) Air circulator size too small.	(n) Replace with larger air circulator.
(o) Ductwork too small.	(o) Increase size of ductwork.

(continued)

Table 9-6   (continued)

Symptom and Possible Cause	Possible Remedy
Noisy unit.	
(a) Tubing rattle.	(a) Fix so it is free from contact.
(b) Fan blade causing vibration.	(b) Check for bend; replace if necessary.
(c) Refrigerant overcharged or oil too high.	(c) Check for correct refrigerant charge and maintain oil level. If necessary, replace expansion valves or capillary tube.
(d) Loose parts or mountings.	(d) Fix and tighten.
(e) Motor bearings worn.	(e) Replace motor.
(f) Lack of oil in the compressor.	(f) Add required oil.
No air delivery out of register.	
(a) System not set for summer cooling.	(a) Read operating instructions and make required adjustment.
(b) Fan motor not operating.	(b) Repair or replace.
(c) Open power switch.	(c) Close switch.
(d) Fuse blown.	(d) Replace with same-size fuse.
(e) Broken connection.	(e) Check circuit and repair.
(f) Register closed.	(f) Open register.
(g) Evaporator fan motor leads not connected to line voltage.	(g) Connect the leads.

Regular Maintenance

Extend the service life and operating efficiency of the air-conditioning equipment and system by providing regular maintenance. A regular maintenance schedule should include the following:

- Clean the indoor evaporator coils.

- Clean the outdoor condenser coils. Use a water hose to flush the outdoor condenser coils.

- Check the coils for leaks with a leak detector.

- Clean or replace the indoor unit filter.

- Check wiring and contacts for loose connections, corrosion, and/or damage.

- Check the amp draw at the outdoor fan motor and the indoor blower motor and compare the values to those on the unit nameplate.

- Check the voltage at the indoor and outdoor units *with the units operating*.
- Check the system for the correct amount of refrigerant.
- Inspect the condensate drain line for blockage and clean as necessary.
- Check the ducts for leaks and repair if found.
- Oil motors and check belts for tightness and wear.
- Check for the correct electrical control sequence.

Pumping Down

Whenever a refrigeration system is to be opened to the atmosphere for service operations or repairs, it is necessary to remove the refrigerant from that part of the system to be opened. By *pumping down* the system prior to servicing, the refrigerant can be saved.

The manufacturer of the equipment will usually include detailed instructions concerning the pump-down procedure. Read and follow these instructions carefully.

Pumping down the system usually involves confining the refrigerant to the receiver by closing off the liquid line stop valve and (with a gauge attached to the intake stop valve) operating the compressor. By doing this, all the gas is drawn back to the compressor and condensed in the condenser but is prevented from going further by the liquid line stop valve.

The compressor should be run until the suction pressure is reduced to holding steady at approximately 2 to 5 lbs pressure. Do *not* draw a vacuum on the system. A vacuum will cause moisture to be drawn into the system when it is opened.

Purging

Purging refers to the release of air or noncondensable gases from a system, usually through a cock placed on or near the top of the receiver. This term is also applied to the sweeping of air out of a newly installed part or connection by releasing refrigerant gas into the part and allowing it to escape from the open end, thus pushing the air ahead of it.

Follow the instructions for purging contained in the manufacturer's installation and operating literature.

Evacuating the System

Sometimes it becomes necessary to remove the *entire* refrigerant charge from the system. This operation is referred to as *evacuating the system* and is accomplished as follows:

1. Close the discharge service valve stem by turning it clockwise and remove the gauge connection plug.

2. Open the inlet service valve by turning the stem counterclockwise and attach a compound gauge to the inlet service valve.

3. Close the valve ½ turn clockwise and start the unit discharging through the open gauge connection in the discharging service valve.

Warning

Capture the evacuated refrigerant. It is illegal to release the refrigerant to the atmosphere.

If a vacuum is pumped too rapidly, the compressor will have a tendency to pump oil out of the compressor crankcase. Attach a copper tube to the gauge port and bend it so that any oil pumped out may be drained into a container. During this operation, the compressor may knock.

If knocking occurs, stop the compressor for about a minute and then restart. Continue the process until the gauge indicates a 20-inch vacuum or better. At this point, leaks in the system may be detected by putting sufficient oil in the container to cover the end of the tubing and continuing the pumping operation. When the system is entirely evacuated, no more bubbles should appear in the oil container. After the system is fully evacuated, replace the discharge gauge connection plug or attach a pressure gauge as desired.

Charging

Charging is the addition of refrigerant to a system from an external drum. There are a number of ways to add a refrigerant charge to a system, but the safest method usually is to introduce the refrigerant through the liquid line. The procedure may be outlined as follows:

1. Connect the refrigerant cylinder to the liquid line port at the condenser or compressor.

2. Purge the connecting line and tighten the last connection.

3. Disconnect the compressor so that it will not run during the charging operation.

4. Turn on the blower to the condenser.

5. Warm the refrigerant cylinder by placing it in a bucket of warm water (see Figure 9-33). Do *not* immerse any refrigerant connections.

Figure 9-33 Warming the refrigerant cylinder.

6. Remove the cylinder from the water when you are satisfied it has been thoroughly warmed.

7. Wipe the cylinder dry and invert it.

8. Open the cylinder valve and the charging port valve.

The refrigerant should flow very readily into the high-pressure side of the system if steps 1–8 were carefully followed.

After the system has been charged, close the refrigerant cylinder valve, allow 2 or 3 minutes to pass, and disconnect the cylinder. Reconnect the compressor and operate the unit, using gauges to determine if the charge is sufficient.

Always exercise caution when making connections or disconnections on the liquid line. This line is under high pressure, and the refrigerant is in a liquid form. Guard against refrigerant spraying into the face and eyes. Any minor leakage that may occur around the refrigeration hose in disconnection will be cold and at high pressure. To minimize pressures, liquid line disconnections should be made *after* the unit has been shut down for at least 5 minutes.

If the refrigerant charge is introduced in the low-pressure side of the system, the charging cylinder should always be kept in a vertical position. This precaution prevents the refrigerant liquid from flowing into the crankcase of the compressor.

Never heat a refrigerant cylinder with a torch or any other type of flame. Warming a cylinder in this manner generates excessive pressures, which can result in an explosion. *Always* use warm water to heat a refrigerant cylinder.

Silver-Brazing Repairs

For the repair of tubing condensers, evaporators, and parts made of light metal, *silver brazing* is the ideal process. It was formerly known as silver soldering, a term still frequently used. The term silver soldering is used to avoid confusing the use of silver-brazing alloys with the soft solders. Some silver-brazing alloys contain a certain amount of silver alloyed with copper and zinc. Others contain silver, copper, and phosphors. These alloys are available in forms having melting temperatures ranging from 1175°F to 1500°F.

The use of silver-brazing alloys enables the serviceperson to obtain strong joints without danger of burning or overheating the base metals. Apart from the skill acquired through practice, the two most important requirements of a good silver-brazing job are clean surfaces and enough heat to make the silver flow freely, but not so much that the silver burns to form scale. The best source of heat is an oxyacetylene or compressed-air and illuminating gas torch.

The various operations to be performed in silver brazing are as follows:

1. Preparation
2. Preparing swaged joints
3. Preparing different-size tubing for connection
4. Applying the flux
5. Applying the brazing alloy

Silver brazing has very little tensile strength of its own. The total strength of the joint is derived from the union of the two surfaces as a result of the action of the alloys used. Accordingly, surfaces must fit together tightly.

The tubing should be expanded or swaged to a depth at least equal to its diameter for tubes up to ½ inch and not less than ½ inch deep for tubes of larger diameter. Special swaging blocks and drifts that accurately size and shape the inside of the tube and the outside of the expanded section are recommended for this operation where there is sufficient volume to warrant the investment. For occasional jobs, the tube can be held on a flare block and a swaging drift driven into it to form the bell end.

Where two tubes of different sizes, such as ³⁄₈ inch and ½ inch, are to be joined, the smaller tube can be expanded by the previously described method until the outside diameter of the smaller tube is sized to fit snugly into the inside of the larger tube.

When the surfaces of the tube ends to be joined have been thoroughly cleaned with steel wool or sandpaper, they should be fitted together and clamped, or firmly held together so that no movement will occur while they are being brazed (see Figure 9-34).

SURFACE CLEANED

Figure 9-34　Surface preparation. The surface must be clean.

Apply enough flux with a brush to cover the surfaces to be joined, but not so much that it will run down the tubing. Make certain, however, that the flux is inside the joint all the way around (see Figure 9-35).

After the flux has been applied, the heat should be concentrated on one side of the joint and the silver brazing applied (see Figures 9-36 and 9-37). The temperature of the parts to be joined should be high enough to melt the silver by touching it to the heated surfaces near the flame. When the silver melts, apply it to the heated surfaces near the flame, but not under the flame. Move the flame around the heated surface, following it with silver until silver has been applied to the entire joint. Do not use too much silver, and try to keep it from running down inside the tubing. Apply only enough heat to cause the silver-brazing alloy to flow freely in order to avoid the formation of scale or the burning of the surfaces.

Most of the heat should be applied to the heavier parts of the joint where it will be conducted through the metal to the location where the silver alloy is to be applied.

Figure 9-35   Applying flux with brush.

Figure 9-36   Applying heat.

Figure 9-37   Applying brazing alloy.

Flames should never be applied directly to the point where brazing is being done. For thorough inspection of the joint, all flux must be carefully removed. Pinholes may exist under the film of melted brazing flux and are not readily noticed until the flux has been removed.

Cleaning the joint can be done either by washing it with water while the joint is still hot or by thoroughly brushing and scraping it with a wire brush or emery cloth after the joint has cooled.

Where silver brazing is being done near an enameled or painted surface, or such materials as wood, insulating material, and other combustible surfaces, the surface should be protected with sheet asbestos during the brazing operation.

Valves, controls, or other apparatus to which a tube is being joined by silver brazing must be protected from damage by heat. Either remove the internal parts of the valve or protect the entire assembly with a wet cloth.

If a joint has previously been soldered with soft solder, all traces of the soft solder must be removed because the tin in soft solder amalgamates with copper at the temperature necessary for a silver-brazing operation.

Chapter 10

Heat Pumps

A *heat pump* is a refrigeration device used to transfer heat from one room or space to another. The heat pump is designed to take heat from a medium-temperature source, such as outdoor air, and convert it to higher-temperature heat for distribution within a structure. By means of a specifically designed reversing valve, the heat pump can also extract heat from the indoor air and expel it outdoors.

Because a heat pump system uses the reverse-cycle principle of operation, its operating principle is sometimes referred to as *reverse-cycle conditioning* or *reverse-cycle refrigeration*. The latter term is not correct because there are fundamental differences between the operating principles of a heat pump and a true refrigeration unit. The confusion probably stems from the fact that during the cooling cycle, the operation of a heat pump is identical to that of the mechanical refrigeration cycle in a packaged air-conditioning unit. The indoor coil functions as an evaporator, cooling the indoor air. The outdoor coil is a condenser, in which the hot refrigerant gas releases heat to the outside air.

Heat Pump Operating Principles

The two principal phases of heat pump operation are the heating and cooling cycles. A third phase, the defrost cycle, is used to protect the coils from excessive frost buildup.

Heating Cycle

The heating cycle of a heat pump begins with the circulation of a refrigerant through the outdoor coils (see Figure 10-1). Initially, the refrigerant is in a low-pressure, low-temperature liquid state, but it soon absorbs enough heat from the outdoor air to raise its temperature to the boiling point. Upon reaching the boiling point, the refrigerant changes into a hot vapor or gas. This gas is then compressed by the compressor and circulated under higher pressure and temperature through the indoor coils, where it comes into contact with the cooler room air that circulates around the coils. The cooler air causes the gas to cool, condense, and return to the liquid state. The condensation of the refrigerant vapor releases heat to the interior of the structure. After the refrigerant has returned to a liquid state, it passes through a special pressure-reducing device (an

Figure 10-1 Heat pump heating cycle. (*Courtesy Lennox Air Conditioning and Heating*)

expansion valve) and then back through the outdoor coils where the heating cycle begins all over again. The temperature of the room air that originally cooled the higher-temperature refrigerant vapor is itself increased by the process of heat transfer and recirculated throughout the room to provide the necessary heat.

Note

A heat pump is designed to reverse the action or direction of heat transfer depending on whether heating or cooling is desired. As a result, the indoor and outdoor coils change their functions based on the heating or cooling cycle. The outdoor coil becomes the condenser in the cooling cycle and the evaporator in the heating cycle. The indoor coil, on the other hand, becomes the evaporator in the cooling cycle and the condenser coil in the heating cycle.

Cooling Cycle

In the cooling cycle, the reversing valve causes the flow of the refrigerant to be reversed. As a result, the compressor pumps the refrigerant in the opposite direction so that the coils that heat the building or space in cold weather cool it in warm weather. In other words, the heat is extracted from the interior, cycled through the heat pump, and then expelled outside the building or space during the condensation of the refrigerant (that is, its change from a gaseous to a liquid state) (see Figure 10-2).

Heat Sink
The heat given off by the process of condensation is received by the *heat sink*. This is true for both the heating and cooling cycles. In the former, the air of the rooms or spaces functions as the heat sink. In the cooling cycle, the outside air, a water source (for example, a well, a pond, or a sewage pipe) or the ground commonly serve as heat sinks outside the structure.

Defrost Cycle

Because the outdoor air is relatively cool when the heat pump is on the heating cycle, and the outdoor coil is acting as an evaporator, frost forms on the surface of the coil under certain conditions of temperature and relative humidity. Because this layer of frost on the coils interferes with the efficient operation of the heat pump, it must be removed. This is accomplished by putting the heat pump through a defrost cycle.

In the *defrost cycle*, the action of the heat pump is reversed at certain intervals and returned to the cooling cycle. This is done to

Figure 10-2 Heat pump cooling cycle. *(Courtesy Lennox Air Conditioning and Heating)*

Figure 10-3   Defrost system wiring diagram. *(Courtesy Bard Mfg. Co.)*

temporarily heat the outdoor coil and melt the frost accumulation. The temperature rise of the outdoor coil is hastened because the operation of the outdoor fan stops when the system switches over to the cooling cycle.

The system will remain in the cooling cycle until the coil temperature has risen to 57°F. The time of the defrost cycle will vary, depending on how much frost has collected on the coil. During this period, the indoor motor continues to operate and blow cool air. This cold condition can be eliminated by installing an electric heating element (see *Auxiliary Electric Heating Elements* in this chapter). The heating element is wired in conjunction with the second stage of a two-stage thermostat and will come on automatically when the heat pump is in the defrost cycle (terminals 9 and 7 on the defrost relay in Figure 10-3).

The defrost cycle control system consists of a thermostat, timer, and relay. The defrost thermostat is located at the bottom of the outdoor coil where it can respond to temperature changes in the coil. It makes contact (closes) when the temperature of the outdoor coil drops to 32°F. This action of the thermostat causes the timer motor (located in the unit electrical box) to start. After the accumulative running periods reach either 30 minutes or 90 minutes (depending on the type of cam installed in the timer), the timer energizes the defrost relays, which reverses the reversing valve and stops the *outdoor* fan motor. The unit remains in the defrost cycle (cooling cycle) until the temperature of the outdoor coil reaches 57°F. At that temperature the coil is free of frost and the frost thermostat opens to

30 MIN.
CAM

Figure 10-4 Thirty-minute cam. *(Courtesy Heat Controller, Inc.)*

stop the timer and return the unit to the heating cycle. The timer will not run again until the outdoor coil temperature drops to 32°F. The timer runs *only* when the thermostat contacts are closed.

A defrost timer is shipped with a 30-minute cam installed (see Figure 10-4). With this cam, the unit will defrost once every 30 minutes (of accumulated running time) when the outdoor coil temperature is below 32°F. If there is little or no frost on the coil, the defrost cycle will be correspondingly short (approximately 45 seconds to 1 minute). A 90-minute cam is recommended.

Types of Heat Pumps

Heat pumps are often classified according to their heat source. The three principal types used in residential and light commercial heating/cooling systems are: (1) air-source heat pumps, (2) ground-source heat pumps, and (3) water-source heat pumps.

Air-Source Heat Pumps

An *air-source heat pump* (also sometimes called an *air-to-air heat pump*) relies on the outdoor air as the heat source. In other words, it extracts the heat from the outdoor air and transfers it to the rooms and spaces inside the structure. A major technical problem associated with earlier air-source heat pumps was that the temperature of the outdoor air is commonly lowest when heat requirements are highest—that is, during the cold winter months. When outdoor temperatures drop below 0°F, the heat pump is largely ineffective. For this reason, some sort of supplementary radiant heating system was usually employed until outdoor air temperatures rose to a level suitable for effective use of the heat pump.

Note

> Air-source heat pumps operate most efficiently in areas where the winter temperatures usually remain above 30°F. In climates where the winter temperatures frequently drop below freezing, a backup auxiliary heater must be used with an air-source heat pump. Ground-source heat pumps are more efficient and economical to operate than conventional air-source units in areas with similar heating and cooling loads.

Split-System Heat Pumps

Most air-source heat pumps used in residential and light-commercial heating and cooling systems are split-system heat pumps. A *split-system heat pump* is so called because its components are divided into two sections, one located indoors and the other outdoors. The two sections are connected by refrigerant tubing. In most split-system heat pumps, the evaporator coil, blower, and filter section are located inside the structure, and the compressor, condenser coil, and fan are located outdoors (see Figures 10-5, 10-6, and 10-7).

Figure 10-5   Outdoor heat pump unit. *(Courtesy Lennox Air Conditioning and Heating)*

Figure 10-6 Indoor heat pump unit. *(Courtesy Lennox Air Conditioning and Heating)*

Sometimes the outdoor condensing section is installed on the roof and the indoor section is suspended from the ceiling. This is a very common type of installation in commercial buildings.

In residential installations, the outdoor section is usually placed on a concrete slab next to the house and the indoor section is located either in the attic (installed horizontally) or in a closet space (installed vertically) on the same level as the outdoor unit.

Packaged Heat Pumps

Some air-source heat pumps are packaged units. A *packaged heat pump* differs from the split-system heat pump by having the condenser coil, evaporator coil, compressor, blower and motor,

Figure 10-7   Indoor unit for split system. *(Courtesy Lennox Air Conditioning and Heating)*

Figure 10-8 Packaged heat pump unit. *(Courtesy Lennox Air Conditioning and Heating)*

automatic controls, and filter all located in the same box (see Figure 10-8). Some packaged heat pumps are used with ductwork to heat and cool the entire house; others do not use ductwork because they are designed to heat and cool only a single room and do not require ducts. These heat pumps are also referred to as *single-packaged units, through-the-wall units,* or *self-contained heat pumps* by various manufacturers.

Advantages and Disadvantages of Air-Source Heat Pumps

Most residential heat pumps are the air-source type installed as a split system with the compressor and outdoor coil installed outside the structure and the indoor coil installed inside. Because their use is so widespread, replacement parts are easy to acquire and trained, certified technicians are readily available in most areas of the country.

The air-source heat pump is less expensive to install than the ground-source or water-source heat pumps. On the other hand, it is noisier than either of the other types, is more difficult to conceal, and requires more maintenance.

Ground-Source Heat Pumps

A *ground-source heat pump* uses the constant temperature of the earth instead of the outdoor air as the heat-exchange medium (that is, the heat source or heat sink depending on the heating or cooling cycle). During the summer when cool interior temperatures are required, the fluid circulating through the indoor coil of the heat pump collects the heat from inside the structure and pumps it outdoors into a pipe system located below ground. The heat is then absorbed into the ground through the piping and the fluid is recirculated back to the unit. In the winter, the process is reversed. The system is based on the principle of heat transference, whereby heat is transferred from one object (the underground pipe) to another object (the ground) through direct contact. The temperature of the ground is a constant 55°F.

Ground-Source Heat Pump Terminology

Ground-source heat pump technology has made spectacular advances in recent years through research and development by various HVAC equipment manufacturers. The HVAC trade associations, as well as the government, have also conducted extensive research in this technology. As a result, the ground-source heat pump is identified by many different names, which can be a bit confusing. The two most widely used names for this appliance are *ground-source heat pump* and *geothermal heat pump*. Other less commonly used names include the following:

- Water-source heat pump
- Well-water heat pump
- Direct-expansion heat pump
- Geo-exchange heat pump
- Groundwater heat pump
- Earth-coupled heat pump
- Ground-coupled heat pump
- Open-loop heat pump
- Closed-loop heat pump

The use of so many different names for the same appliance results from attempts to accurately identify the appliance and its operating principle or, in many cases, to exclusively associate a name with a specific equipment manufacturer. Eventually, only one name will emerge as the industry standard. At this point, the names ground-source heat pump and geothermal heat pump have the widest usage. Both are also used to include water-source heat pumps, which are described separately in this chapter.

Ground-Source Coupling System

A ground-source (geothermal) heat pump uses a closed-loop ground coupling system as a heat exchanger. In a closed-loop ground coupling system, a heat transfer fluid is circulated by a pump through a network of buried high-strength plastic pipe. Because the loop system is closed, there is no mixing of the fluid with groundwater and no buildup of contaminating mineral deposits in the heat pump heat exchanger.

The configuration of the ground coupling will depend primarily on installation cost and the available space. The following three closed-loop systems are illustrated in Figure 10-9:

- Horizontal closed-loop system
- Spiral closed-loop system
- Vertical closed-loop system

Figure 10-9   Closed-loop ground coupling systems.
(Courtesy U.S. Department of Energy)

The horizontal loop is used only when there is adequate space. The space surrounding the house or building must be great enough to bury the pipe network without extending onto the neighbor's property. One to six pipes are buried at least 4 ft beneath the surface in trenches.

Horizontal loops are most commonly used in residential heat pump systems where there is adequate space beneath lawns to bury the pipes. They are not recommended for large-tonnage commercial applications because the land area required for the ground loops is much larger than the area of most city properties.

The spiral loop is a variation of the horizontal loop configuration. In this configuration, the pipe is unrolled in spirals and placed in horizontal trenches. In the vertical closed-loop system, the pipe loops are inserted in 75- to 300-ft-deep vertical dry wells.

Advantages and Disadvantages of Ground-Source Heat Pumps

The U.S. Environmental Protection Agency (EPA) rates the ground-source heat pump as being the most energy efficient and environmentally clean of all the heating and cooling systems available for residential use. It is quieter and less costly to operate than an air-source heat pump. It also has lower maintenance requirements because the outside elements (piping loops) are buried in the ground and not exposed to weather extremes.

Ground-source heat pumps do not require defrost cycles or crankcase heaters because there is not the same danger of outdoor coil freezing as there is with air-source heat pumps. Furthermore, there is less of a need for supplemental resistance heaters than is required with air-source heat pumps.

Ground-source heat pumps obtain their heat from the ground during the heating cycle. Because subsurface ground temperatures remain fairly constant and uniform throughout the year, ground-source heat pumps are very efficient all year long.

The two principal disadvantages of a ground-source heat pump are its high installation costs and the requirement for large areas in which to bury the outdoor piping loops.

Water-Source Heat Pumps

Water-source heat pumps use water for both the heat source and the heat sink. The water serves as a direct heat transfer medium in contrast to the heat transfer fluid used in closed-loop systems. The steady cool temperature of the water offsets the seasonal temperature variations by serving as a reservoir of heat in the winter and as a drain of heat in the summer. The compressor and controls of a water-source heat pump are identical to those in a ground-source heat pump.

Water-Source Coupling System

A water-source heat pump uses both the open-loop and closed-loop coupling systems. The open-loop coupling system uses local groundwater from extraction wells or extraction and reinjection wells (see Figure 10-10). In some systems, a single standing column

Figure 10-10   Water-source heat pump open-loop coupling system.
(Courtesy U.S. Department of Energy)

well is used as the water source. A standing column well allows the major part of the discharge water from the heat pump to be reinjected into the source well. This method eliminates the need for a separate reinjection well.

A submerged closed-loop piping system is used with a water-source heat pump if the heat source and discharge area is a lake, pond, or stream. Using a closed-loop system avoids the problem of discharging the water back into the lake, pond, or stream, which can be an environmental concern.

The water in the pipes of a water-source closed-loop system is circulated between the source (that is, the lake, pond, or stream) and a refrigerant-to-water heat exchanger and then back to the source. The compressor pumps a refrigerant through separate coils in the refrigerant-to-water heat exchanger. The heat transfer occurs in the heat exchanger.

Advantages and Disadvantages of Water-Source Heat Pumps
Installing a water-source heat pump can be a problem in many areas of the country because there are no uniform regulations

governing the discharge of the water after the heat has been extracted. It could be an important environmental concern. Always check any existing federal, state, and local codes and requirements governing the installation and use of water-source heat pumps. Some of the requirements governing their use include the following:

- Local ordinances may require the water to be discharged through a sewer or a second well. The former method requires a hookup fee (which commonly includes the cost of trenching and pipe laying) and an increased monthly sewer bill. The latter method requires the expense of drilling a return well. Water discharged to a return well also may require an EPA reporting procedure.

- Return wells for discharge water must be installed by licensed drillers. The drillers must submit well logs and well locations to the Bureau of Topographic and Geologic Survey at the Department of Conservation and Natural Resources.

- Water discharged to a lake, pond, or stream may require a National Pollutant Discharge Elimination System (NPDES) permit.

- A well used as a water source must have sufficient flow and adequate temperature for the heat pump.

The principal advantage of a water-source heat pump is that water temperatures are warmer and more stable than air during the cold winter months, which makes it more efficient than the air-source heat pump. The two principal disadvantages of this type of pump are its higher installation cost and the lack of uniformity among federal, state, and local codes and regulations.

Other Types of Heat Pumps

Heat pumps and heat pump systems may also be defined by how the compressor is driven, whether the heat pump is a dual-fuel unit, and other factors.

Gas-Fired Heat Pumps

A gas-fired heat pump is driven by a small natural gas or propane engine which, in turn, drives the compressor. One advantage of a gas-fired heat pump is that the waste heat produced by the engine can be used to supplement the heat output of the heat pump and also to heat the domestic hot water.

Gas-fired heat pumps are available for both residential and commercial applications. They are about as efficient as an air-source heat pump, but they are not widely available and their use is cost-effective only in areas where natural gas or propane cost less than electricity.

Dual-Fuel Heat Pump System

A *dual-fuel heat pump system* combines an air-source heat pump with a gas furnace in the same heating and cooling system. Instead of using electric resistance heaters, this system uses a gas furnace to back up the heat pump when outdoor temperatures become excessively cold. A conventional gas furnace provides more heat while consuming less energy than electric resistance heating. As a result, a dual-fuel system provides year-round comfort with reduced energy use.

The dual-fuel heat pump system operates just like a typical air-source heat pump under ordinary conditions. In the winter, the air-source heat pump extracts the heat from the outside air, compresses it, and transfers it to an inside coil and blower located inside the house. In the summer, the cycle is reversed. The heat is extracted from the indoor air and sent to the outdoor coil where it is released to the atmosphere. The gas furnace operates as a backup heater to the heat pump only when the outdoor temperature drops below a preset temperature setting.

Dual-Source Heat Pumps

A *dual-source heat pump* combines a geothermal heat pump and an air-source heat pump in the same unit. This results in a heat pump almost as efficient as the geothermal heat pump but with the advantage of being much less expensive to install.

Instead of using only one outdoor heat source and heat sink (that is, air or ground), the dual-source heat pump uses both air and ground sources for the condensing process in the cooling mode and the evaporating process in the heating mode. In the cooling mode, the liquid refrigerant discharging from an air-source condenser is subcooled by using a ground-source-cooled fluid. This fluid is then reused after the subcooler to desuperheat, that is, to remove some of the superheat from the hot gas before it goes into the air-source condenser.

The ground loop requirements are much smaller than for a conventional ground-source system, which reduces the initial installation cost. Some dual-source heat pump systems are installed with dual compressors to provide additional heat during the coldest outdoor temperatures.

Dual-source heat pumps are of limited availability in the United States. As a result, it is difficult to find contractors with the necessary experience to install and service them.

Ductless Heat Pumps

A *ductless heat pump* (also sometimes called a *mini-split-system heat pump*) is essentially a heat pump without distribution ducts (see Figure 10-11). The ductless heat pump is used primarily for cooling, although in some applications both heating and cooling are possible.

Figure 10-11   Ductless heat pump system.

A typical ductless heat pump system consists of one outdoor unit (and compressor) connected by refrigerant lines to more than one small indoor unit. Refrigerant is piped from the outdoor unit through small-diameter insulated refrigerant lines directly to individual rooms or zones. Cooled air is blown into the room by fans located in the individual evaporator units. It is called a mini split system because of the multiple small ("mini") indoor units.

The indoor units are about 6 to 8 in deep and are commonly mounted flush to the inside surface of an exterior wall. They can also be mounted on a ceiling or inside a dropped ceiling. Wiring, refrigerant lines, control cables, and the condensate drain all pass through a small 3-in-diameter hole in the wall or ceiling.

Heat Pump Performance and Efficiency Ratings

A number of different methods are used to rate the performance and efficiency of heat pumps. The two methods used to measure the cooling and heating efficiency of the heat pump are the Seasonal Energy Efficiency Ratio (SEER) and the Heating Season Performance Factor (HSPF).

Note
> These rating methods were conducted under ideal laboratory conditions; the ratings will commonly be lower on-site in different parts of the country for the same types of equipment.

Seasonal Energy Efficiency Ratio (SEER)

The *Seasonal Energy Efficiency Ratio* is a measure of the cooling efficiency of a heat pump. The higher the SEER number, the more efficient the system is at converting electricity into cooling power. The higher the SEER ratio, the higher the energy efficiency rating of the heat pump. The U.S. Department of Energy has established a minimum SEER rating for cooling of 10.0.

Heating Season Performance Factor (HSPF)

The *Heating Season Performance Factor* (HSPF) is a measure of the overall heating efficiency of a heat pump. The higher the HSPF number, the more efficiently the heat pump heats the house.

Coefficiency of Performance (COP)

The *Coefficiency of Performance* (COP) measures the rate of heat output to the amount of energy input. The highest possible COP number is 3. A heat pump with a COP of 3 would mean that for every $1.00 of energy input, the heat pump would produce $3.00 worth of heat.

Energy Efficiency Rating (EER)

The *Energy Efficiency Rating* (EER) measures the cooling efficiency of the heat pump. The higher the EER number, the higher the cooling efficiency of the heat pump.

Energy Star Rating

The *Energy Star Rating* is a voluntary rating system for HVAC manufacturers whose heat pumps meet or exceed the EPA guidelines for energy efficiency.

Heat Pump System Components

Figures 10-12 and 10-13 illustrate the components in the outdoor unit of two Lennox residential heat pumps. They can be grouped into four categories:

1. Compressor section (outdoor unit).
2. Air-handler section (indoor unit).

Figure 10-12 Lennox HP26 outdoor unit (early model).

(Courtesy Lennox Industries Inc.)

Figure 10-13 Lennox HP26 outdoor unit (late model).

(Courtesy Lennox Industries Inc.)

3. Refrigerant lines.

4. Heat pump controls.

The *compressor section* of a heat pump contains the compressor (or compressors), outdoor coil, fan(s) and motor(s), control system box, and reversing valve. In addition, the compressor section will also contain a refrigerant-distributing device and the defrosting controls (automatic timer and terminating thermostat). The compressor section of a remote, or split-system, heat pump is located outdoors.

The *air-handler section* consists of the indoor coil, blower and blower motor, check valve, thermal expansion valve, refrigerant distributing device, and the air filter(s).

The refrigerant lines are divided into a *liquid line* containing the refrigerant in a liquid state and a *vapor* or *suction line* containing the refrigerant vapor. During the cooling cycle, cool refrigerant vapors are moving through the line to the compressor section. During the heating cycle, hot vapors are moving in the opposite direction.

The heat pump controls include the thermostat, reversing valve, expansion/check valves, safety switches, and other components that ensure safe operation and which direct and regulate the flow of the liquid refrigerant.

Compressor

The compressor is used to receive the refrigerant vapor at low pressure and compress it into a smaller volume at higher pressure and temperature. It then pumps the refrigerant vapor to one of the coils for either the heating cycle or the cooling cycle operation.

The compressors used in residential and light-commercial construction are hermetic compressors. A hermetic compressor is so called because its components are sealed inside a welded housing. The housing (or *can*) contains an electric motor and a pump.

Note
> A sealed (*hermetic*) compressor must be replaced if it fails because it cannot be repaired on-site. After it is replaced, filter dryers must be installed to remove any moisture and/or acid in the system.

Compressors can be reciprocating, scroll, rotary, disc, or screw types. The reciprocating and scroll compressors are the types used most commonly in residential and light-commercial heat pump installations. See Chapter 9 ("Air-Conditioning Equipment") for additional information on compressors.

Indoor Coil and Blower

The indoor coil is the part of a split-system heat pump located indoors. During the cooling cycle, the indoor coil cools and dehumidifies the air by converting liquid refrigerant into a gas, which absorbs the heat from the air. The warmed refrigerant is then carried through a tube to the outdoor unit.

Note

> During the cooling cycle, the heat pump draws heat from the air inside the house or building. Moisture in the air will condense on the indoor coil and must be drained to the outdoors through a condensate drain. A condensate pump should be installed to assist drainage because reliance on gravity alone will not provide efficient drainage. Do NOT allow the condensate to drain into the crawl space. Doing so will eventually result in water damage to the floor joists and other wood framing members.

During the heating cycle, heat is extracted from the outdoor air and released by the indoor coil. The heat is blown into the interior rooms and spaces by a fan, which is sometimes called an *air handler* or *blower*. Both direct-drive and belt-drive motors are used.

Outdoor Coil and Fan

The outdoor coil is the part of a split-system heat pump located outdoors in the same cabinet housing the compressor. The outdoor fan is a direct-drive unit.

Refrigerant Lines

The refrigerant lines are divided into a *liquid line* containing the refrigerant in a liquid state and a *vapor* or *suction line* containing the refrigerant vapor. During the cooling cycle, cool refrigerant vapors are moving through the line to the compressor section. During the heating cycle, hot vapors are moving in the opposite direction.

The lines should be reasonably straight. Any excess lines that need to be coiled should be coiled horizontally so that they don't form an oil trap. Vertical coils may prevent needed lubricant from returning to the compressor.

Both refrigerant lines should be insulated. Reducing unwanted heat loss and heat gain through the refrigerant lines saves energy.

Reversing Valve and Solenoid

A refrigerant reversing valve with an electromechanical solenoid coil is used to reverse refrigerant flow during unit operation (see Figure 10-14). It allows the heat pump to operate in either the heating

OUTDOOR
FAN/MOTOR

CONTROL
BOX

DISCHARGE
MUFFLER

DEFROST
THERMOSTAT

REVERSING
VALVE

COMPRESSOR

CHECK/EXPANSION
VALVE

BI-FLOW
FILTER DRIER

Figure 10-14 Schematic of a four-way reversing valve.

(Courtesy Ranco Incorporated)

or cooling mode by changing the direction of the refrigerant between the indoor and outdoor coils. The operation of a four-way reversing valve is shown schematically in Figures 10-15 and 10-16.

Whenever the reversing valve changes the direction of refrigerant flow, it also changes the functions of the indoor and outdoor coils. During the heating mode, the indoor coil functions as an evaporator and is sometimes referred to as an evaporating coil. This is true only as long as the system is in the heating mode. If the system is in the cooling mode, the direction of the refrigerant reverses and the indoor coil becomes a condenser (that is, a condenser coil). The reversing valve also changes the function of the outdoor coil when it changes the direction of refrigerant flow.

Conventional refrigerant reversing valves cause pressure drops and undesired heat exchange that leads to a 5 to 10 percent degradation of heat pump performance. A newly designed four-way reversing valve has been developed to solve this problem.

As mentioned, the four-way reversing valve is operated by a solenoid coil. When the room thermostat calls for heat, the solenoid

Figure 10-15 Heat cycle piping diagram. *(Courtesy Bard Mfg. Co.)*

coil is energized. This action causes a nylon slide in the vale cylinder to move to the right and allow the high-pressure refrigerant to flow through capillary tubes to the left piston side of the main valve. The low-pressure refrigerant on the left side flows back to the compressor. When the system calls for cooling, the valve operation is reversed.

Thermostatic Expansion Valve
The thermostatic expansion valve (TXV) was developed to provide more precise control of the refrigerant flow to the indoor coil. The valve meters the exact amount of refrigerant required to

DISCHARGE PRESSURE

DISCHARGE

STATIONARY SCROLL

SUCTION

TIPS SEALED BY DISCHARGE PRESSURE

ORBITING SCROLL

Figure 10-16 Cooling cycle piping diagram. *(Courtesy Bard Mfg. Co.)*

meet the indoor coil load demands. Using a thermostatic expansion valve increases the efficiency of the unit.

Note

> A compressor in a system equipped with a thermostatic expansion valve may have difficulty starting. This may be caused by a delay in system pressure equalizing for a short period of time when the compressor is in the off cycle. The solution is to install a start capacitor in the control box.

Desuperheater

Some heat pumps are equipped with a unit that recycles waste heat from the interior of the structure during the cooling cycle. The recycled waste heat is used to produce domestic hot water.

Control Box

The *control box* contains various controls, connections, and wiring important to the operation of the heat pump. The location of a control box on a Lennox reciprocating heat pump is shown in Figure 10-17.

The controls may include contactors, capacitors, relays, circuit boards, transformer, and various accessories. Not all control boxes will contain the same controls, so it is important to consult the heat pump manufacturer's service and repair manuals when repairing or replacing a control box. As shown in Figures 10-18, 10-19, and 10-20, control boxes may even differ among the makes and models of the same manufacturer.

RIGHT CAPILLARY

TEFLON PISTON SEAL

SUCTION TUBES

SOLENOID COIL

LOCK NUT

PLUNGER

PLUNGER SPRING

PLUNGER NEEDLE

RIGHT PORT

LEFT PORT

STAINLESS STEEL PINS

LEFT NEEDLE

LEFT SPRING

PILOT VALVE BODY

DISCHARGE TUBE

SLIDE

SLIDE BRACKET

MAIN BODY

COMPRESSOR

OUTSIDE COIL

RESTRICTOR

INSIDE COIL

LEFT CAPILLARY

COMMON (SUCTION) CAPILLARY

BLEED HOLE

PISTON NEEDLE

Figure 10-17 Location of control box on a Lennox HP29 reciprocating compressor.

(Courtesy Lennox Industries Inc.)

Figure 10-18 Lennox HP29 single-phase unit control box with reciprocating compressor.

(Courtesy Lennox Industries Inc.)

496

Figure 10-19 Lennox HP29 single-phase unit control box with scroll compressor.
(Courtesy Lennox Industries Inc.)

START
CAPACITOR
(C7)

DUAL CAPACITOR
(C12)

COMPRESSOR
CONTACTOR
(K1)

POTENTIAL
RELAY (K31)

GROUNDING
LUG

DEFROST
CONTROL
(CMC1)

Figure 10-20   Lennox HP29 three-phase unit control box.

(Courtesy Lennox Industries Inc.)

Start, Run, and Dual Capacitors

Every control box will contain capacitors. A capacitor is an electronic device that stores a charge (energy). A *start capacitor* (also sometimes called a *motor start capacitor*) is used to provide the torque required to start the compressor motor. It does this while working in conjunction with a *run capacitor* (also called a *motor run capacitor*) or a *dual capacitor*. A dual capacitor gives a phase shift to single-phase motors in scroll-type or reciprocating-type compressor motors. It is called a dual capacitor because it contains one capacitor for the compressor motor and another for the fan motor.

Compressor Contactor

A *contactor* is an electrically operated switching device in the heat pump control circuit (commonly 24 volts AC circuits). It creates a magnetic field to pull in a set of contacts controlling another device that may or may not receive its electrical power from the same circuit.

Defrost Control

The *defrost control* (or *defrost control board*) is described later in this chapter. See *Heat Pump Defrost System*.

Relays

The *potential relay* controls the starting function of the compressor motor. The *outdoor fan relay* is used in some split-system heat pumps to control the operation of the fan in the outdoor unit.

Fan/Blower Motors

Both the outdoor and indoor units of a split-system heat pump are equipped with a fan. The indoor fan (or *blower* as it is also called) is used to blow the warm air created by the indoor coil (evaporator) through the ductwork into the rooms and spaces of the structure. The most efficient type of indoor blower is a variable-speed one because its operation enables it to compensate for potential airflow restrictions caused by dirty filters or coil or partially blocked air ducts.

Heat Pump Defrost System

A heat pump defrost system consists of a defrost thermostat and a defrost control. The defrost thermostat is located on the liquid line between the expansion/check valve and the distributor. The defrost control board is located in the control box.

Defrost Thermostat

Its function is to signal the defrost control board to start the defrost timing when the defrost thermostat senses a preset low temperature. It terminates the defrost mode when the liquid line warms up to a higher preset temperature.

Defrost Control Board

The defrost control board is located in the control box. The type and location of the various components on a defrost control board will vary among different manufacturers. The two defrost control boards shown in Figure 10-21 include a time-temperature defrost control, defrost relay, time delay, two diagnostic LEDs, a 24-volt terminal strip for field wiring connections, and provisions for pressure switch safety circuit connections. The control provides automatic switching from normal heating operation to defrost mode and back depending on the defrost thermostat settings.

There are two principal types of defrost controls: demand-frost controls and time-temperature defrost controls. The demand-frost controls activate the defrost mode *only* when frost or ice forms on the coil. The time-temperature defrost controls, on the other hand, activate the defrost mode at regular timed intervals for set periods of time whether frost or ice is present on the outdoor coils or not. In both cases, activating the defrost mode causes the reversing valve to divert warm refrigerant fluid to the outdoor coil to thaw the frost or ice forming on the unit coils.

DUAL CAPACITOR
(C12)

COMPRESSOR
CONTACTOR
(K1)

GROUNDING
LUG

DEFROST
CONTROL
(CMC1)

Figure 10-21 Defrost control board component
locations. *(Courtesy Lennox Industries Inc.)*

Two LEDs are installed on the defrost board for diagnostic
purposes. The LEDs flash a specific sequence according to the
condition.

The *time delay* protects the compressor from short-cycling in
case the power to the unit is interrupted or a pressure switch opens.
The time delay is electrically connected between a thermostat terminal and the compressor contactor.

Other relays, connections, and components forming a part of the
defrost control system and located on the defrost control board
include the following:

- Defrost relay
- Pressure switch safety circuit connections
- 24-volt terminal strip connections
- Defrost interval timing pins

High-Pressure Switch

An auto-reset high-pressure switch (single pole, single throw) is
located on the liquid line. The switch shuts off the compressor if the
discharge pressure rises above the factory setting. The switch is

normally closed and is permanently adjusted to trip (open) at a factory-preset maximum high-pressure point. The switch resets (closes) when the pressure drops below a factory-preset minimum low-pressure point.

Low-Pressure Switch

Some heat pumps may have a low-charge switch that functions if there is a potentially damaging loss of refrigerant. The switch is an N.C. pressure switch located on the discharge line of the compressor. The switch opens on low-pressure drop in the discharge line to shut off the compressor. The switch opens and closes at preset pressure points.

Other Electric/Electronic Heat Pump Controls and Connections

A *lockout relay* is used on many heat pumps to shut the unit off to protect the compressor from damage if there is a problem in the system. An *anti-restart timer* is required in scroll and rotary compressors to prevent them from running backwards when there is a power failure. Every heat pump system requires a manually operated *disconnect switch* to turn off power and shut down the system when there is a problem or when repairs have to be made.

A *service light thermostat* is a service light switch located on the compressor discharge line and directly connected to the service light in the indoor room thermostat. If the compressor stops running, the service line thermostat senses the change in the discharge line and turns on the service light on the room thermostat. The light is turned off when the compressor is restored to operation and the discharge line returns to normal. Some service light thermostats are connected to terminals on the defrost control board.

Accumulator

Some compressors, such as the piston (reciprocating) types, can be damaged by liquid refrigerant entering the compressor. These compressors are designed to compress the gas formed from the refrigerant. They have a problem compressing the refrigerant liquid. An accumulator is installed in the return line to trap and store the refrigerant liquid before it can enter the compressor. The operation of a scroll compressor is such that an accumulator is not required. It can handle small amounts of liquid refrigerant without damage.

Room Thermostat

The heat pump operation is controlled by a room thermostat. Heat pump thermostats may vary in design among the various manufacturers, but their operation will be essentially the same. Thermostat operation is controlled by the following:

- Temperature selector levers or dial
- Temperature indicator
- Fan switch
- System switch

The *temperature selector levers* (one for cooling and the other for heating) or the *temperature selector dial* are used to manually select the desired temperature setpoints for either heating or cooling.

The *temperature indicator* on the face of the thermostat is used to indicate the actual room temperature. Most will also have an amber (green) light that indicates when the heat pump is operating in the emergency mode.

The *fan switch* will offer up to four settings. The ON or CONT (continuous) setting provides continuous operation of the indoor blower regardless of whether the compressor or an auxiliary heater is operating. This setting is selected when continuous air circulation or filtering is desired. The AUTO or INT (intermittent) setting restricts blower operation only to those times when the thermostat calls for heating or cooling. It is the recommended setting for humidity control.

The *system switch* is used to set the heat pump for heating, cooling, or auto operation. The heating and cooling mode settings are self-explanatory. The AUTO mode provides the heat pump with the ability to automatically switch back and forth between the heating and cooling modes in order to maintain a predetermined comfort setting.

If the heat pump system is designed to provide supplementary heat when there are excessively cold temperatures, the auxiliary heater is controlled by the thermostat through an emergency heat mode. The emergency heat mode locks out heat pump operation while the auxiliary heater is operating.

If a programmable thermostat is used to control the heat pump, then temperature setpoints can be selected (programmed) for different times of the day. For example, with 7-day programming, the heat pump can be programmed for different temperature and humidity settings at different times every day of the week.

Service Valves and Gauge Ports

As shown in Figure 10-22, service valves are installed in the liquid and vapor lines of the heat pump. These valves are used to charge

RUN CAPACITOR
(C1)

TRANSFORMER (T5)
"J" VOLTAGE
UNITS ONLY

OUTDOOR FAN
RELAY (K10) "G"
& "J" VOLTAGE
UNITS ONLY

COMPRESSOR
CONTACTOR
(K1)

DEFROST
CONTROL
L
(CMC1)

GROUNDING
LUG

Figure 10-22   Lennox HP29 refrigeration components.
(Courtesy Lennox Industries Inc.)

the system (and check the charge), to test for leaks, and to evacuate the system. Each valve is equipped with a service port containing a factory-installed Schrader valve covered by a protective cap. The service port cap functions as the primary leak seal. Cutaway views of the liquid line and vapor line service valves are illustrated in Figures 10-23 and 10-24.

Gauge Manifold

The gauge manifold is a device equipped with two gauges (see Figure 10-25). One of the gauges measures suction (low) pressure, whereas the other gauge measures head (high) pressure. These gauges indicate how well the compressor is removing the heat collected by the evaporator coil, how well the condenser coil is expelling the heat, and the amount of load placed on the heat pump. An efficient heat pump will have a high suction pressure and a low head pressure.

Filter Dryer

The *filter dryer* (also called *bi-flow filter dryer*) is used to remove dirt, other contaminants, and moisture from the refrigerant before it can damage the compressor and other components in the heating system.

Crankcase Heater

When some heat pumps are shut down during the cold winter months, the liquid refrigerant may enter the compressor crankcase

NOTE: Component locations will vary with board manufacturer.

Figure 10-23 Liquid line service valve. (Courtesy Lennox Industries Inc.)

Figure 10-24   **Vapor line service valve.** *(Courtesy Lennox Industries Inc.)*

and mix with the lubricating oil. When the heat pump is turned on again, the refrigerant in the crankcase evaporates rapidly and forms a foam. This condition dilutes the oil, prevents adequate lubrication, and may shorten the service life of the compressor. A crankcase heater will prevent the refrigerant from liquefying in the lubricating oil. Some crankcase heaters are designed to operate all the time; others only when required. Crankcase heaters are not required on scroll compressors.

Muffler

As shown in Figure 10-13, a muffler is installed in the discharge line to minimize noisy pulsations and vibrations. The muffler greatly reduces the sound inside the house of compressor operation.

Sizing Heat Pumps

The recommended source of information for sizing heat pumps is the latest edition of the Air-Conditioning Contractors of America's *Manual H—Heat Pump Systems: Principles and Applications.* It covers basic principles, equipment, installation, operation, and system design.

The ability of the heat pump to extract heat from the outdoor air decreases as the outdoor temperature drops. At the same time, the heat required to maintain the desired indoor temperature increases. If lines representing the outdoor and indoor conditions

LIQUID SERVICE VALVE
(VALVE CLOSED)

STEM CAP

SERVICE PORT

INSERT HEX WRENCH HERE

TO OUTDOOR COIL

SERVICE PORT CAP

Schrader valve open to line set when valve is closed (front seated).

TO INDOOR COIL

(VALVE FRONT SEATED)

LIQUID SERVICE VALVE
(VALVE OPEN)

INSERT HEX WRENCH HERE

STEM CAP

SERVICE PORT

TO OUTDOOR COIL

SERVICE PORT CAP

SCHRADER VALVE

TO INDOOR COIL

Figure 10-25 Lennox HP26 manifold gauge connections (cooling cycle). *(Courtesy Lennox Industries Inc.)*

were drawn on a graph, the line representing the dropping outdoor temperature would eventually cross the line representing the rising indoor heat requirements. The point at which the two lines on the graph cross is called the *balance point*. The capacity of a heat pump must be sized to match the balance point for the house or building. Most balance points will occur just below and above freezing (Fahrenheit).

Heat Pump Installation Recommendations

All of the installation recommendations included here are provided as a general guide. They do not supersede local, state, or national codes. Always consult local authorities having jurisdiction before installing the heat pump.

Note

> Much more detailed installation instructions will be found in the installation manual for the specific heat pump make and model. Always read and carefully follow the manufacturer's installation instructions. Failure to do so could result in voiding the equipment warranty.

To open: Rotate stem counter clockwise 90°.
To close: Use adjustable wrench and rotate stem clockwise 90°.

SERVICE PORT CAP

UNIT SIDE

SCHRADER VALVE

SERVICE PORT

STEM

FIELD SIDE

BALL (SHOWN OPEN)

STEM CAP

Figure 10-26   Vapor line service valve (valve open)

Figure 10-27 Manifold gauge connections (cooling cycle)

The following recommendations are offered as a checklist for installing a heat pump:

1. Install unit level or slightly slanted toward drain for proper condensation drainage.
2. Check unit wiring for compliance with wiring diagram and local codes and regulations.
3. Make sure all wiring connections are tight.
4. Ground unit by grounded waterproof conduit or with separate ground wire.
5. Check indoor and outdoor fan/blower for unobstructed and quiet movement.
6. Check condensation drain line for proper slope and drainage.
7. Fasten and seal all ducts and fittings with a suitable duct tape.
8. Check the refrigeration system for leaks after installation.

Note

> Heat pump manufacturers require that the outdoor unit be matched with the indoor coils, line sets, and refrigerant control devices. Failure to do so will result in loss of warranty. Check the manufacturer's specifications for the unit being installed.

Recommendations for installing the outdoor unit of the heat pump are as follows:

1. Install the outdoor unit on a concrete pad separate from the house foundation.
2. Do not locate the outdoor unit where its operation will disturb neighbors.
3. Do not locate the outdoor unit under a bedroom window.
4. Shelter the outdoor unit from prevailing cold winter winds.
5. Do not allow bushes or other obstructions to block the airflow to the unit. Provide for free air travel to and from the condenser.
6. Locate the unit far enough from the roof eaves to avoid falling snow and ice.
7. Locate the outdoor unit so that the lengths of copper refrigerant lines connecting to the indoor unit are minimized.

The following are recommendations for checking heat pump operation after installation is completed and the system is running:

1. Check the compressor starting characteristics and capabilities while the system is running.

2. Measure high- and low-side system pressures.

3. Check to make sure the system is operating in accordance with the heat pump manufacturer's specifications.

4. Check the system for correct line and load voltage/amperage.

5. Listen for abnormal noise or unusual odors.

6. Measure outdoor dry-bulb temperature.

7. Measure indoor dry- and wet-bulb temperature.

8. Check for correct refrigerant charge.

Read the heat pump manufacturer's installation manual and add any other recommendations to the preceding list. Not all heat pumps have the same installation requirements.

Heat Pump Operating Instructions

The heat pump manufacturer should provide operating instructions with the installation literature. If no copy is available, contact the manufacturer's local field representative for one.

If no operating instructions are available for the unit, follow those contained in this section. These instructions are suitable for most electric heat pumps used in residential installations.

The first step, of course, is to turn on the power supply at the disconnect switch. This is a very simple but important step that is often overlooked. In remote heat pump installations, both the indoor and outdoor sections may have a disconnect switch or a breaker or fuse in the house box. Both switches must be in the *on* position to start the system.

Move the thermostat setting as high as it will go, and switch the fan selection switch to the *on* setting. This should start the blower. The remainder of the operating instructions will depend on whether heating or cooling is desired.

Heating

For the heating cycle, move the fan selector switch to the *auto* position and slowly *raise* the heating temperature setting on the thermostat. Stop moving the lever as soon as the first-stage (upper) mercury bulb makes contact. The blower, compressor, and condenser fan should start at this point.

Under normal operating conditions, the unit may automatically trip on its high-pressure cutout and stop the compressor and outdoor fan if the outdoor ambient temperature exceeds approximately 80°F. If the outdoor ambient temperature is too low for automatic cutout, block the return air until the unit trips. In a cold climate, it may take 5 minutes or more to trip.

Check the thermostat heat anticipator setting to make sure it matches the current draw of the heating relays (see Chapter 4 of Volume 2, "Thermostats and Humidistats"), and make certain the contactors and heaters are operating correctly.

The defrost timer can be checked in the winter when the outdoor coil is cold enough to activate it. Observe at least one defrost cycle to make sure the unit defrosts properly.

Turn the thermostat off. If the unit is set at the *on* position, only the blower should operate. Turn the thermostat on again and proceed as follows:

1. Adjust discharge air grilles for suitable airflow.

2. Check the system for proper balance and correct if necessary.

3. Check for air leaks in the ductwork and correct if necessary.

Cooling

For the cooling cycle, move the fan selector switch to the *auto* position and *lower* the heating temperature setting on the thermostat to below room temperature. This should start the blower, compressor, and condenser fan. If these components are operating satisfactorily, turn the thermostat off. The unit should stop with the exception of the blower if the thermostat is set at the *on* position.

If a combination heating and cooling thermostat is used, switch it to the *heat* position and check for correct heating operation. Make certain the thermostat heat anticipator is set to match the current draw of the heating relays (see Chapter 4 of Volume 2, "Thermostats and Humidistats").

After waiting approximately 5 minutes, turn the air conditioner on and proceed as follows:

1. Adjust discharge air grilles.

2. Check the system for proper balancing.

3. Check for air leaks in the ductwork.

Heat Pump Service and Maintenance

The heat pump manufacturer will provide the necessary operation and maintenance literature with the unit. This literature contains nontechnical instructions that the average homeowner can understand and follow with little or no difficulty. By following these instructions, the operational life span of the heat pump will be prolonged, and it will operate at maximum efficiency.

Service and Maintenance Checklist

Warning

Turn off the electrical power to the heat pump *at the disconnect switch* before performing any maintenance. The heat pump may have multiple power supplies. Failure to disconnect the electrical power may result in damage to the equipment and a severe shock hazard.

1. Periodically inspect and clean (or replace) the air filters.
2. Inspect and clean the blower wheel, housing, and motor as required.
3. Annually lubricate blower motor on older heat pump models according to the manufacturer's instructions. If the motor lacks lubricating oil, it will eventually burn out. Note: The blower motors in newer heat pumps are sealed and do not require lubrication.
4. Inspect fan motor and fan blades for wear or damage.
5. Inspect blower housing for lint and debris and clean as necessary.
6. Check for excessive frost buildup on the coils. Contact your local serviceperson if an excessive frost buildup is discovered.
7. Periodically clean the coils in the outdoor unit by washing with water hose.
8. Check condensation drain line during cooling season for free-flow condition. Water should flow freely.
9. Check the indoor coil drain pan and the primary and secondary drain lines.
10. Check all refrigerant line connections to make sure they are secure. Tighten loose connections. If the system is low on refrigerant, find and repair the leak before adding any more. Adding refrigerant to a leaking heat pump system will force the equipment to work harder and less efficiently. Continuing to operate a heat pump without refrigerant will eventually overheat the compressor and cause it to fail.
11. Inspect and clean (if required) the auxiliary drain pan (if supplied with the heat pump) and line.
12. Check for damaged wiring and loose connections.
13. Inspect outdoor unit and pad for proper level and adjust if necessary.

14. Monitor heat pump system for correct refrigerant charge.

15. Measure high- and low-side system pressures.

16. Remove dirt, leaves, and debris from inside the outdoor cabinet.

17. Inspect the base pan in the outdoor unit for restricted drain openings and correct as necessary.

18. Inspect the control box for wear and damage and repair as necessary. All control box and electrical parts should be checked for wear or damage.

19. Check condition of control box components, connections, and wiring.

20. Check the refrigeration system for leaks during each service call.

Adjusting Heat Pump Refrigerant Charge

Packaged heat pumps are charged with the refrigerant at the factory under controlled conditions and rarely need adjustment. Split-system heat pumps are charged in the field where there is a greater chance of error. If the performance of a split-system heat pump closely approximates the manufacturer's listed SEER and HSPF ratings, then the system probably has the correct charge. If the performance fails to meet the listed ratings, then there is either too much or too little refrigerant in the system.

Note

> Section 608 of the Federal Clean Air Act mandates the requirements for handling HVAC refrigerants, including their reclaiming, recovering, and recycling. All HVAC technicians who handle refrigerants must be certified to do so. City, county, and state governments may also have ordinances governing the handling of refrigerants.

Measure the temperature and pressure readings on the heat pump system and compare the results with those specified by the manufacturer. If they do not match, refrigerant will have to be added or withdrawn.

Note

> Refrigerant measurements will not be accurate if the airflow is incorrect. Therefore, the airflow must be measured first, checked against the heat pump manufacturer's specifications, and corrected if necessary before the refrigerant measurements can be made.

Troubleshooting Heat Pumps

Table 10-1 lists the most common problems associated with the operation of a heat pump. For each symptom of a problem, a possible cause and remedy are suggested.

Make certain that the thermostat is set higher than the actual room temperature and the selector switch is on *heat* if heat is needed, or that the thermostat is set lower than the actual room temperature and the switch is on *cool* if air-conditioning is desired. If the thermostat is programmable, be certain the batteries are fresh.

Test for power to the air handler by moving the fan switch from *auto* to *on*. If the blower runs, the air handler is functional. If nothing happens, check the circuit breakers on the air handler cabinet and the breakers or fuses in the main panel. If any breakers are tripped, reset them at once.

Table 10-1   Troubleshooting Heat Pumps

Symptom and Possible Cause	Possible Remedy
Noisy operation.	
(a) Loose parts.	(a) Check all setscrews on blower and fan blade. Adjust and tighten all thrust collars.
(b) Loose belts.	(b) Adjust all belts and check drives.
Heat pump will not operate.	
(a) Main power switch off.	(a) Turn switch on. Both disconnect switches must be on in remote system.
(b) Incorrect thermostat setting.	(b) Change to proper setting.
(c) Tripped circuit breaker or blown fuse.	(c) Reset circuit breaker or replace blown fuse.
Insufficient or no heating or cooling.	
(a) Obstructed outdoor coil.	(a) Remove obstruction.
(b) Dirty or plugged air filter.	(b) Clean or change if necessary.
(c) Airflow blocked at supply registers or return grilles.	(c) Remove blockage.
(d) Blower not operating.	(d) Make sure blower door is secure. Close and secure door to restore power to blower.

(continued)

Table 10-1 (*continued*)

Symptom and Possible Cause	Possible Remedy

Reversing valve will not shift from heat to cool.

(a) No voltage to coil.	(a) Repair electrical current.
(b) Defective coil.	(b) Replace coil.
(c) Low refrigerant charge.	(c) Repair leak and recharge system.
(d) Pressure differential too high.	(d) Reset differential.
(e) Pilot valve operating correctly; dirt in one bleeder hole.	(e) Deenergize solenoid, raise head pressure, and reenergize solenoid to break dirt loose. If unsuccessful, remove valve and wash out. Check on air before installing. If no movement, replace reversing valve, add strainer to discharge tube, and mount valve horizontally.
(f) Piston cup leak.	(f) Stop unit. After pressure equalizes, restart with valve solenoid energized. If valve shifts, reattempt with compressor running. If still no shift, replace reversing valve.
(g) Clogged pilot tubes.	(g) Raise head pressure and operate solenoid to free tube of obstruction. If still no shift, replace reversing valve.
(h) Both ports of pilot open; back seat port did not close.	(h) Raise head pressure and operate solenoid to free partially clogged port. If still no shift, replace reversing valve.

Reversing valve starts to shift but does not complete reversal.

(a) Not enough pressure differential at start of stroke or not enough flow to maintain pressure differential.	(a) Check unit for correct operating pressures and charge. Raise head pressure. If no shift, use valve with smaller ports.
(b) Body damage.	(b) Replace reversing valve.
(c) Both ports of pilot open.	(c) Raise head pressure and operating solenoid. If no shift, replace reversing valve.

(*continued*)

Table 10-1 (continued)

Symptom and Possible Cause	Possible Remedy
(d) Valve hung up at mid-stroke; pumping volume of compressor not sufficient to maintain reversal.	(d) Raise head pressure and operate solenoid. If no shift, use a reversing valve with smaller ports.

Reversing valve has apparent leak in heating position.

(a) Piston needle on end of slide leaking.	(a) Operate reversing valve several times, then recheck. If excessive leak, replace valve.
(b) Pilot needle and piston needle leaking.	(b) Operate reversing valve several times, then recheck. If excessive leak, replace valve.

Reversing valve will not shift from heat to cool.

(a) Pressure differential too high.	(a) Stop unit. Valve will reverse during equalization period. Recheck system.
(b) Clogged pilot tube.	(b) Raise head pressure. Operate solenoid to free dirt. If still no shift, replace reversing valve.
(c) Dirt in bleeder.	(c) Raise head pressure and operate solenoid. Remove reversing valve and wash it out. Check on air before reinstalling. If no movement, replace valve. Add strainer to discharge tube. Mount valve horizontally.
(d) Piston cup leak.	(d) Stop unit. After pressure equalizes, restart with solenoid deenergized. If valve shifts, reattempt with compressor running. If it still will not reverse while running, replace reversing valve.
(e) Defective pilot.	(e) Replace valve.

Caution

Do not reset the circuit breakers if they trip a second time. Deadly high-voltage conditions exist inside the air handler cabinet and inside the access panel of the condenser. Let a qualified service-person open them.

If the air handler runs constantly but cannot satisfy the thermostat setting, it is possible the backup heat is running but the condenser is not. Some condensers have the high-pressure cutout switch externally accessible. Look for a button sticking out of the cabinet in the vicinity of the refrigerant pipes. Press it in. If the machine starts up, the head pressure got too high, possibly from turning on and off too quickly, from too much or too little refrigerant, or from an electrical interruption. As the unit ages, the switch can weaken and pop easily. If the condition repeats itself often, have a service technician check it.

Warning

Because all the controls are internally mounted and high-voltage wiring is exposed, only a qualified and experienced HVAC technician should open panels. High voltages can result in serious injury and even death.

Troubleshooting Heat Pump Compressors

Residential heat pumps use hermetic compressors with the motor, pump, and related components sealed inside a welded housing. A failed hermetic compressor must be replaced. It cannot be repaired on-site. The troubleshooting symptoms in Table 10-2 may be used to identify some of the more common compressor problems.

Caution

Do not continue to operate a heat pump under the following conditions: fan motor not working, low refrigerant charge, or excessive frost/ice buildup. Continuing to run the heat pump under these conditions can burn out the compressor motor.

Table 10-2 Troubleshooting Heat Pump Compressors

Symptom and Possible Cause	Possible Remedy
Compressor will not start.	
(a) Loose wires and/or failed components.	(a) Check wiring and components; repair or replace as necessary. If compressor still fails to start, it is locked up and must be replaced.
(b) Tripped circuit breaker or blown fuse.	(b) Reset circuit breaker or replace fuse. If the problem continues and there is a low ohm reading from one or more of the compressor terminals to ground, the compressor is grounded and must be replaced.

(continued)

Table 10-2 *(continued)*

Symptom and Possible Cause	*Possible Remedy*
(c) Defective run capacitor.	(c) Replace run capacitor.
(d) Defective combination (dual) run capacitor.	(d) Replace.

Compressor will not start but fan runs.	
(a) Failed run capacitor.	(a) Replace run capacitor.
(b) Failed start capacitor.	(b) Replace.

Compressor does not draw current but fan runs normally.	
(a) Burned/broken common wire.	(a) Repair.
(b) Open motor overload protector.	(b) Wait for overload to reset. Replace compressor if overload protector fails to reset.

Noisy compressor.	
(a) A hissing noise in a piston (reciprocating) compressor.	(a) Defective valves. Replace compressor.
(b) Sharp-pitched noise after compressor is shut down (piston compressor).	(b) Not a problem. Sound of pressure equalizing in valves.

Chapter 11

Humidifiers and Dehumidifiers

The air around us has a capacity for holding a specific amount of water at given temperatures. For example, 10,000 ft³ of air at 70°F will hold 10.95 pints of water, no more. This means the air in a home 25 ft by 50 ft with 8-ft ceilings (10,000 ft³) could hold nearly 11 pints of water when the temperature inside is 70°F. This would represent 100 percent relative humidity conditions. If there were only 2 pints of water in this same home at 70°F, the relative humidity would be ²/₁₁ or 18 percent.

The amount of water air can hold depends on the temperature of the air. For example, air at 70°F can hold 16 times as much water as air at 0°F. This means that 10,000 ft³ of air at 0°F will hold ⅔ pint of water. When that same air is heated to 70°F, it can hold nearly 11 pints of water, or 16 times as much water. Thus, if 0°F air that had a relative humidity of 96 percent were brought into a house through a door, window, or any other crack and warmed to the inside temperature of 70°F, this same air would then have a relative humidity of ⁹⁶/₁₆, or 6 percent. This relationship between temperature and relative humidity can be illustrated by the data in Table 11-1.

As you can see, warming the fresh air will reduce the relative humidity in the house until the air becomes extremely dry. In some situations, the air in a house may be even drier than the Sahara Desert. The Sahara has an average relative humidity of 20 percent. The average home in the winter months (that is, the heating season) without humidity control or other means of adding moisture to the air maintains a relative humidity of approximately 12 to 15 percent.

Table 11-1 Relationship Between Temperature and Relative Humidity

Outside Temperature	Outside Relative Humidity (%)	Inside Temperature	Inside Relative Humidity (%)
	0		0
	20		3
20°F	40	70°F	6
	60		8
	80		11

Air that has a low relative humidity will absorb water vapor from any available source. Most important from a personal standpoint is the evaporation of moisture from the membranes of the nose, mouth, and throat. These are our protective zones, and excessive dryness of these membranes will cause discomfort.

Note

It is difficult to pinpoint the most desirable level of relative humidity, but it is generally agreed that the range between 30 and 50 percent is the best from both health and comfort standpoints. The upper part of this range (40 to 50 percent) is impractical during many very cold days of the winter because of condensation on the windows. Therefore, it is recommended that a relative humidity of between 30 and 40 percent be maintained during the heating season.

Because dry air will pick up moisture from any available source, the furnishings and other contents of the house are also affected by low humidity. Furniture wood shrinks, and the joints may crack. If plaster is used, it may also develop cracks. The wall paint will usually peel, and carpet materials may become dry and brittle.

If the air in the house is excessively dry, there is more evaporation from the skin as moisture from the body is absorbed by the drier air. This evaporation generally makes the individual feel so cool that temperature settings of 70°F (or even higher) are not warm enough for comfort. Moving the temperature setting to a higher point may obtain the desired comfort level, but the higher temperature setting also increases the fuel cost. Each degree that the thermostat setting is raised increases the fuel cost approximately 2 percent for the same period of time. Obviously it is impractical and more costly to obtain comfort in this manner. It is far more economical to devise a means of reducing the rate of evaporation of moisture from the body and thereby eliminate the chilling effect. This can be done by increasing the relative humidity in the home (see *Humidifiers* in this chapter).

Excessive moisture in a home can also be a problem. When there is too much moisture in the indoor air, mold and mildew form on surfaces, the indoor air has an unpleasant odor, and there is generally a feeling of stickiness or dampness. If the condition persists, the excess moisture in the air can damage furniture, wood and metal surfaces, leather shoes, and clothing. It can also cause peeling wallpaper, damp spots on ceilings and walls, and disintegrating plaster. Finally, the allergens produced by mildew and mold are a definite health problem. The solution, then, is to reduce the relative humidity by removing moisture from the air. This can be accomplished by installing a dehumidifier (see *Dehumidifiers* in this chapter).

Terminology

- **Humidity.** The amount of moisture in the air.
- **Relative humidity.** The amount of water vapor in the air compared with the amount it can hold at a given temperature (expressed as a percentage).
- **Humidifier.** A device that adds moisture to the air.
- **Dehumidifier.** A device that removes moisture from the air.
- **Output.** A gallon-per-day measure for moisture put into the air.
- **Humidistat.** A control that automatically regulates humidity comfort levels.
- **Run time.** The amount of time a humidifier runs before refilling is required.

Humidifiers

A *humidifier* is a device used to add moisture to the air (see Figure 11-1). This function is accomplished primarily either by evaporation, by the use of steam, or by breaking water down into fine particles and spraying them into the air.

Figure 11-1 Typical power humidifier. *(Courtesy Amana Refrigeration, Inc.)*

The two types of humidifiers most widely used in residences and small commercial buildings are the bypass humidifier and the power humidifier. These and other types of humidifiers are briefly described in this section. The service, maintenance, and troubleshooting sections of this chapter are primarily concerned with the bypass and power humidifiers.

Spray Humidifiers

A *spray humidifier* (or *air washer*) can be used for either humidification or dehumidification. Essentially this type of humidifier consists of a chamber containing a spray nozzle system, a recirculating water pump, and a collection tank (see Figure 11-2). As the air passes through the chamber, it comes into contact with the water spray from the nozzles, resulting in heat transfer between the air and water. This, in turn, results in *either* humidification (adding moisture) or dehumidification (removing moisture) depending on the relative temperatures of the sprayed water and the air passing through the chamber. Dehumidification occurs when the temperature of the water is lower than the dew point of the air; humidification occurs when it is higher.

Figure 11-2 Components of a spray humidifier.

In some spray humidifiers, the water is sprayed on a heating coil through which steam or hot water is passed (see Figure 11-3). The heat causes the water to evaporate and thereby increase the moisture content of the air.

An *atomizing humidifier* is a form of spray humidifier that uses compressed air to reduce the water particles to a fine mist (see Figure 11-4). The mist is converted to a vapor, which is absorbed by the drier room air.

Figure 11-3   Water sprayed on heating coil.

Figure 11-4   Atomizing humidifier.
(Courtesy American Moistening Co.)

The *ultrasonic humidifier* is also a spray-type humidifier. The principal components of an ultrasonic humidifier are a high-frequency power oscillator that drives a piezo transducer, a small bower, a float switch, and a water tank or reservoir. The piezo transducer creates a wave on the surface of the water in the tank. The float switch is used to sense and maintain the proper level of water in the tank. These humidifiers use high-frequency vibrations to break the water droplets down into a fine mist. The mist is blown into the room or rooms by the small blower.

Caution

The piezo drive module operates with a line voltage as high as 100 volts or more on heat sinks. Do NOT attempt to repair or replace the module unless you are a qualified HVAC technician.

Pan Humidifiers

A *pan humidifier* consists of a water tank (pan), heating coils, a fan, and a fan motor (see Figure 11-5). The heating coils are installed in

Figure 11-5 Pan humidifier.

the water tank. Heat is supplied to the pan heating coils either by low-pressure steam or forced hot water where a water temperature of 200°F or higher is maintained.

The pan humidifier is completely automatic; the water level in the tank is controlled by means of a float control. When the relative humidity drops below the setting on the humidistat, the fan blows air over the surface of the heated water in the tank. The air picks up moisture as it travels over the surface of the water and is blown into the space to be humidified. When the humidistat is satisfied, the fan is shut off.

Stationary-Pad Humidifiers

A *stationary-pad humidifier* contains a stationary evaporator pad over which warm air from a supply duct is drawn by a motor-operated blower or fan. The air picks up moisture as it passes over the pad. The humidified air is then returned to the room or space.

Steam Humidifiers

A *steam humidifier* (also sometimes called a *vaporizer*) is used with an electric warm-air furnace or an electric heat pump because neither generates warm air at sufficiently high temperatures to evaporate water. These humidifiers are either gas-fired (natural gas or propane) or operated by electricity. They boil the water and send the steam into the room or rooms.

A typical steam humidifier consists of a metal reservoir to hold the water, a heating element submerged in the reservoir, a float valve, and the control wiring. Water is supplied to the reservoir from the domestic water supply. A float valve regulates the amount of water in the reservoir.

Some steam humidifiers are installed in the return duct (or plenum) or the supply duct (or plenum) of a forced warm-air furnace. When line voltage current is passed through the heating element submerged in the reservoir, it produces steam, which releases its moisture into the warm air passing over it. Other steam humidifiers are independent stand-alone units. Some steam humidifiers boil the water and then cool it before it leaves the unit. Instead of steam, a mist of warm water droplets is sent into the room or rooms.

Bypass Humidifiers

A *bypass humidifier* (also sometimes called a *rotary humidifier*, a *wet-pad humidifier*, or a *drum humidifier*) consists basically of an evaporator pad (made of sponge or foam fabric) attached to a rotating device such as a drum, disc, wheel, or belt; a float valve; and a small motor. The evaporator pad is first rotated by the motor through a pan of water where it absorbs moisture. Warm air from the supply plenum passes over the rotating pad, causing the moisture to evaporate and humidify the air. The humidified air then mixes with supply air and is ducted into the rooms of the house. Water is supplied to the humidifier from the domestic water supply and is regulated by a float valve. The float valve controls the level of the water in the reservoir.

The principal components of a bypass humidifier are the following:

1. Motor
2. Water tank or reservoir
3. Rotating disc, wheel, drum, or belt
4. Automatic drain valve
5. Float-operated fill valve
6. Overflow line
7. Fill-water connection
8. Drain connection
9. Metal or plastic cabinet

Some of these components are illustrated by the humidifier in Figures 11-6 and 11-7. This humidifier uses bronze wire-mesh discs that rotate at an angle in the reservoir water. The water-level float is isolated in a separate compartment.

Figure 11-6 **Bypass power humidifier.** *(Courtesy Mueller Climatrol Corp.)*

A bypass humidifier is commonly located on the furnace supply plenum in a residential heating system where it makes use of the pressure difference between the supply and return air plenums to move the air.

Power Humidifiers

A *power humidifier* is similar in design to a bypass humidifier except that a fan is added to the unit, the cabinet is larger, and there is no duct connection to the return plenum of the furnace. The fan is used to blow the air across the wet drum, pick up the moisture, and then blow it back into the supply plenum.

Automatic Controls

The operation of a humidifier is controlled by a room or furnace-mounted humidistat (see Figure 11-8). The sensing element of the furnace-mounted humidistat should be installed in the return air

Figure 11-7   Components of a bypass humidifier. *(Courtesy Mueller Climatrol Corp.)*

duct with the open side down (see Figure 11-9). If the humidifier is installed with a plenum adapter, the sensing element of the humidistat should be mounted above the bypass duct. Never use a furnace-mounted humidistat with a horizontal furnace.

Figure 11-8 Typical humidistat used to control both humidifying and dehumidifying equipment. *(Courtesy Penn Controls, Inc.)*

Figure 11-9 Location of furnace-mounted humidistat sensing element.

A room humidistat should be mounted on a wall 4 to 5 ft above the floor in a location that has free air circulation of average temperature and humidity for the entire space to be controlled. Avoid spots near air ducts or supply air grilles.

Modern programmable humidistats have displays that give the exact humidity level plus the temperature in Fahrenheit or Celsius. The humidity level on the humidistat can be manually set.

Depending on the type of installation, either a low-voltage or line voltage humidistat may be used. Wiring diagrams for both types of control circuits are illustrated in Figures 11-10 and 11-11.

Figure 11-10   Wiring diagram of a low-voltage humidistat.

Installation Instructions

A common location for a bypass humidifier is on the underside of a horizontal warm-air supply duct as close to the furnace as convenient working conditions will permit. The duct should be at least 12 inches wide (see Figure 11-12). As shown in Figure 11-12, a deflector should be installed in the duct to guide the airflow into the humidifier. The deflector should be about 4 to 5 inches wide. It can be cut from sheet metal and screwed to the duct wall with sheet-metal screws.

If the humidifier is to be installed in a furnace plenum that also contains a fan and limit control, care must be taken to keep the sensing element of the fan and limit control a suitable distance from the inlet of the humidifier (see Figure 11-13); otherwise, the return air may be drawn through the humidifier and over the element and cause improper operation of the fan control.

120 V FROM FAN
OR FAN CONTROL-
ENERGIZE ON HEATING ONLY

HUMIDISTAT

RED

LIGHT ON
HUMA-299
ONLY

HUMIDIFIER
MOTOR

Figure 11-11 Wiring diagram of a line voltage humidistat.

DEFLECTOR

AIR FLOW

DEFLECTOR

AIR FLOW

Figure 11-12 Deflector installed to guide airflow.

Humidifiers are also installed on the sides of furnace plenums. The manufacturer usually supplies a plenum adapter kit to mount the humidifier. As shown in Figure 11-14, a typical kit consists of a plenum adapter hood, closing panel adapter collar, and round cold-air collar. A length of flexible or galvanized ductwork is installed between the adapter hood and the cold-air collar (see Figure 11-15).

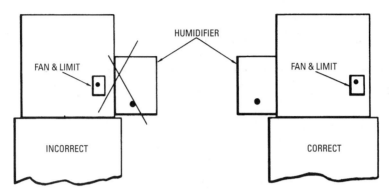

Figure 11-13   Furnace plenum location of humidifier, fan, and limit controls. *(Courtesy Thermo-Products, Inc.)*

Figure 11-14   Plenum adapter kit. *(Courtesy Trane Co.)*

The most desirable location for a humidifier is the warm-air plenum. Some special installations are illustrated in Figures 11-16, 11-17, and 11-18.

If the adapter is installed on the cold-air return plenum, the distance that the hot air is ducted must be as short as possible. In an air-conditioning system, a damper must be installed to close off the

Figure 11-15 Use of flexible ductwork. *(Courtesy Trane Co.)*

Figure 11-16 Horizontal furnace installation. *(Courtesy Trane Co.)*

cold-air return opening during the cooling season. If the opening is not closed, sufficient air can circulate through the shutdown humidifier to frost the evaporator coil.

The following recommendations should be followed when installing a bypass humidifier:

1. Carefully read the manufacturer's installation instructions and any local codes and regulations that would apply to the installation of a humidifier.

Figure 11-17 Counterflow installation slab mounted.
(Courtesy Trane Co.)

Figure 11-18 Plenum installation. *(Courtesy Trane Co.)*

2. Unpack the humidifier and examine it for any shipping damage. Check the equipment and parts against the inventory list.

3. Place the humidifier base or template against the duct or plenum wall, and mark the position where it will be mounted.

4. Cut out the opening for the humidifier, and mount it according to the manufacturer's instructions.

5. Connect the saddle valve to a convenient water line. *Never* connect to a water line supplying chemically softened water.

6. Install the required drain fittings and connections in the reservoir.

7. Turn on the water supply, and fill the reservoir. The float valve arm should be adjusted to maintain a 2-inch water level in the reservoir.

8. Place the drum or wheel in the reservoir so that the axles are properly seated on the sloped supports. The gears will mesh automatically. Do *not* attempt to rotate the drum by hand because you may damage the gears inside the motor.

Service and Maintenance Suggestions

Many service and maintenance instructions will be model specific. Whenever possible, read and follow the manufacturer's instructions when servicing these units. If none is available, the instructions in this section will provide some guidance.

A humidifier equipped with a reservoir containing standing water should be regularly drained to remove lime and other residue. The first draining of the reservoir is recommended for 2 weeks after the unit has been installed or 2 weeks after the seasonal startup. Subsequent drainings should follow the schedule suggested by the manufacturer. A major problem with any humidifier is the buildup of lime or other mineral deposits in the water reservoir and on the evaporator pad. Manufacturers have attempted to minimize this problem by constructing the reservoir out of an extremely smooth material, such as an acrylic, so that these mineral deposits can be easily flushed loose during maintenance.

Some humidifiers are equipped with an *automatic* flush system to clean the mineral deposits from the unit. The components of a Thermo-Pride automatic flush system are illustrated by the schematic of a humidifier in Figure 11-19. The drum is the rotating pad with the flush wheel attached. As the drum rotates, water in the reservoir pan is scooped up into the flush wheel. The float assembly then permits fresh water to enter the pan to replace that which was scooped out (and which evaporated from the pad). As the flush wheel continues to rotate, the mineral-laden water scooped out is conveyed into the drain cavity of the pan and out the drain hose.

Figure 11-19   Operating principles of an automatic
flush system. *(Courtesy Thermo-Products, Inc.)*

The mineral content of the water in the reservoir pan will be
maintained at the lowest possible level with the operation of the
automatic flush system.

A commonly used method for removing lime and other mineral
deposits from the inside surface of the reservoir and the rotating
evaporator pad is by cleaning these parts with muriatic acid (*never*
with a detergent). Muriatic acid is an extremely efficient cleaning
agent for this purpose, but it generates toxic fumes as it works on
the deposits. For this reason, it is *absolutely* mandatory that the
cleaning take place outdoors.

Note

>A safer method of dissolving *recently* formed mineral deposits
(although not as effective as muriatic acid or some of the special-
purpose chemical cleaners) is by wiping them with a solution of
50 percent water and 50 percent vinegar. This is not effective on
older deposits.

Troubleshooting Humidifiers

Table 11-2 lists the most common problems associated with the
operation of a humidifier. For each operating problem, a possible
cause is suggested and a remedy proposed.

Table 11-2 Troubleshooting Humidifiers

Symptom and Possible Cause	Possible Remedy
Humidifier fails to maintain proper humidification.	
(a) Humidistat set too low.	(a) Raise setting.
(b) Humidistat broken.	(b) Repair or replace.
(c) Water valve closed.	(c) Open valve.
(d) Water valve clogged.	(d) Clean valve.
(e) Limed unit.	(e) Clean lime from discs or replace.
Humidifier fails to operate.	
(a) Drum motor not receiving current.	(a) Check wiring to motor.
(b) Inoperative motor due to lack of lubrication.	(b) Lubricate or replace motor.
No water flow.	
(a) Plugged orifice or strainer.	(a) Clean orifice on inlet side of solenoid valve.
(b) No electric power to humidifier.	(b) Reset circuit breaker or replace blown fuse.
(c) Furnace fan not running. (Note: A humidistat will not operate if the furnace fan is not running.)	(c) Check humidistat wiring and correct as necessary.
(d) Solenoid valve not opening.	(d) Check circuit for loose connections. Check continuity through solenoid valve. Make corrections as necessary.
(e) Closed or plugged saddle valve.	(e) Open saddle valve and check for water flow to solenoid valve. Correct as necessary.
Excessive humidification (humidistat installed).	
(a) Continuous water flow.	(a) See *Continuous Water Flow.*
(b) Short in humidistat wiring.	(b) Check wiring and repair as required.
(c) Humidistat not turning off.	(c) Check wiring and repair as required.

(continued)

Table 11-2   *(continued)*

Symptom and Possible Cause	Possible Remedy
Excessive humidification (without humidistat)	
(a) Defective humidistat.	(a) Replace humidistat.
(b) Manual air control incorrectly set.	(b) Reset to reduce airflow.
Continuous water flow.	
(a) Worn valve seat.	(a) Replace valve if leaking at seat.
(b) Valve installed incorrectly.	(b) Reinstall correctly (arrow on valve should be pointed in direction of water flow).
(c) Valve plunger stuck in open position.	(c) Clean valve sleeve and plunger assembly.
Excessive water flow.	
(a) Orifice too large.	(a) Replace orifice fitting.
Insufficient or slow water flow.	
(a) Low water pressure.	(a) Install low-pressure orifice.
(b) Partially plugged orifice or strainer.	(b) Disassemble orifice and strainer. Clean thoroughly and reinstall.
Overflowing drain pan.	
(a) Plugged pan outlets or drain hose.	(a) Clean drain pan outlets. Flush drain hose.
(b) Incorrect drain hose slope from humidifier to drain.	(b) Correct slope.
(c) Kink in drain line.	(c) Remove kink.
Excess condensation on windows.	
(a) Humidistat setting too high.	(a) Lower the humidistat setting.

Dehumidifiers

Dehumidification is the name given to the process of removing moisture from the air. The device used for this purpose is called a *dehumidifier* (see Figure 11-20). Dehumidifiers can be classified on the basis of *how* they remove moisture from the air into the following three categories:

1. Absorption dehumidifiers
2. Spray dehumidifiers
3. Refrigeration dehumidifiers

Both spray and refrigeration dehumidifiers remove moisture from the air by cooling it. The cooled air condenses and the condensation falls into the dehumidifier tank. Dehumidifiers operating on the refrigeration principle are the type most commonly used in residential heating and cooling systems (see *Refrigeration Dehumidifiers* in this chapter).

Figure 11-20 Cabinet-model electric dehumidifier.
(Courtesy Westinghouse Electric Corp.)

Absorption Dehumidifiers

An *absorption dehumidifier* extracts moisture from the air by means of a sorbent material. This type of dehumidifier is very common in commercial and industrial installations but is rarely found in residences except in very large houses.

A sorbent material is one that contains a vast number of microscopic pores. These pores afford great internal surface to which water adheres or is absorbed. Moisture is removed from the air as a result of the low vapor pressure of the sorbent material.

Figure 11-21 illustrates the operating principle of a rotating-bed dehumidifier. The unit consists of a cylinder or drum filled with a dehumidifying or drying agent. In operation, airflow through the drum is directed by baffles, which form three independent airstreams to flow through the adsorbing material. One airstream consists of the wet air to be dehumidified. The second airstream is heated drying air used to dry that part of the dehumidifying material that has become saturated. The third airstream precools the bed to permit an immediate pickup of moisture when that part of the bed returns to the dehydration cycle. In the rotating-bed dehumidifier, the baffle sheets are stationary and the screened bed rotates at a definite speed to permit the proper time of contact in the drying, cooling, and dehumidifying cycles.

The operating principles of a stationary-bed solid-adsorbent dehumidifier are illustrated in Figure 11-22. It has two sets of stationary adsorbing beds arranged so that one set is dehumidifying the air while the other set is drying. With dampers in position as

Figure 11-21 Rotating-bed solid-adsorbent dehumidifier.

Figure 11-22 Stationary-bed solid-adsorbent dehumidifier.

shown, air to be dried flows through one set of beds and is dehumidified while the drying air is heated and circulated through the other set. After completion of drying, the beds are cooled by shutting off the drying air heaters and allowing unheated air to circulate through them. An automatic timer controller is provided to cause the dampers to rotate to the opposite side when the beds have adsorbed moisture to a degree that begins to impair performance.

The *liquid* adsorbents most frequently used in dehumidifiers are chloride brines or bromides of various inorganic elements, such as lithium chloride and calcium chloride.

A typical liquid-adsorbent dehumidifier is shown in Figure 11-23. It includes an external interchamber having essential parts consisting of a liquid contactor, a solution heater, and a cooling coil, as shown. In operation, the air to be conditioned is brought into contact with an aqueous brine solution having a vapor pressure below that of the entering air. This results in a conversion of latent heat to sensible heat, which raises the solution temperature and consequently the air temperature. The temperature change of the air being processed is determined by the cooling water temperature and the amount of moisture removed in the equipment.

Figure 11-23   Liquid-adsorbent dehumidifier.

Spray Dehumidifiers

Dehumidification can be accomplished by means of an air washer as long as the temperature of the spray is *lower* than the dew point of the air passing through the unit. This is an important fact to remember because condensation will not take place if the temperature of the spray is higher than the dew point. Sensible heat is removed from the air during the time it is in contact with the water spray. Latent heat removal occurs during condensation.

Spray dehumidifiers, or air washers, usually have their own recirculating pumps. These pumps deliver a mixture of water from the washer sump (which has not been cooled) and refrigerated water. The mixture of sump water and refrigerated water is proportioned by a three-way or mixing valve actuated by a dew-point thermostat located in the washer air outlet or by humidity controllers located in the conditioned space.

A spray dehumidifier results in greater odor absorption and cleaner air than is possible with those using a cooling coil. A principal disadvantage of this type of dehumidifier is that it sometimes experiences problems with the water-level control and may flood.

Refrigeration Dehumidifiers

A *refrigeration dehumidifier* removes moisture from the air by passing it over a cooling coil. The cool surfaces of the coil cause the moisture in the air to condense. This moisture then collects on the coils and eventually runs into a collection tray or pan located below the unit, or through a hose into a nearby drain. Portable electrically operated refrigeration dehumidifiers are the type of units most commonly found in residences.

The amount of moisture removed from the air by a refrigeration dehumidifier will depend on the volume of air and its relative humidity. The initial amount of moisture removed will be relatively large in comparison to the amount removed at later stages in the operation of the dehumidifier. This reduction in the amount of moisture removal is *not* an indication that the dehumidifier is not operating properly. This is a normal operating characteristic. As the relative humidity approaches the desired level, the amount of moisture being removed from the air will be considerably less.

Dehumidifying coils depend on the dew point of the air entering and leaving the coil for removal of moisture from the air. To accomplish moisture removal, the dew point of the air entering the coil must be *higher* than the dew point of the air leaving the coil.

Automatic Controls

A refrigeration dehumidifier consists of a motor-driven compressor, a condenser or cooling coil, and a receiver. A refrigerant circulates through the cooling coil of the unit, the refrigerant flow being controlled by a capillary tube circuit.

The room air is drawn over the cooling coil by means of a motor-operated fan or blower. When the moisture-laden air comes in contact with the cool surfaces of the cooling coil, it condenses and runs off the coil into a collection tray or pan, or through a hose into a drain.

Dehumidifier operation is controlled by a humidistat, which starts and stops the unit to maintain a selected humidity level. The humidistat accomplishes this function by switching the compressor and unit fan on and off in response to changes in the moisture content of the air.

Humidistat control settings will generally range from *dry* to *extra dry* to *continuous* to *off*. During the initial period of operation (usually 3 to 4 weeks), the humidistat should be set at *extra dry*. If the moisture content of the air has been noticeably reduced, the humidistat setting can be moved to *dry*. Minor adjustments may be required from time to time.

Never purchase a dehumidifier that does not have a humidistat. Without a humidistat, a dehumidifier will run long after the humidity of the air has dropped to a satisfactory level. Operating such a dehumidifier can prove to be very costly and wasteful of energy.

Dehumidifiers that empty the condensate into a container are equipped with an integral cutoff (float) switch to turn the unit off when the condensate container is full. This action avoids overflow conditions. Most of these dehumidifiers will also have a signal light that indicates when the condensate container needs emptying.

Installation Suggestions

A dehumidifier is most effective in an enclosed area where good air circulation is found. For maximum effectiveness, the unit should be located as close to the center of room, space, or structure as possible.

Operating and Maintenance Suggestions

A dehumidifier generally will not operate very satisfactorily at temperatures below 60°F. The reason for this is obvious. When the ambient temperature is below 60°F, the cooling coil must operate at below-freezing temperatures in order to cause the moisture in the air to condense. Unfortunately, operating at these temperatures also causes ice to form on the coils, and this ice formation may eventually damage the dehumidifier. The ice is removed by running the dehumidifier through a defrost cycle. When a defrost sensor in the dehumidifier detects frost on the coils, it turns off the compressor but allows the fan to continue running. The fan draws the warmer surrounding air across the coils and melts the frost. After the frost has melted, the compressor restarts and the appliance resumes reducing the moisture in the indoor air.

Note
> The dehumidifier cannot remove moisture from the air while it is in the defrost cycle.

Fungus will sometimes collect on the cooling coil. This accumulation of fungus can be removed by loosening it with a soft brush and washing away the residue with water.

The principal components of a refrigeration dehumidifier are hermetically sealed at the factory. These components are permanently lubricated and should not require any further servicing. On the other hand, both the condensate collector and the dehumidifier filter can be inspected and cleaned.

As an alternative to manually emptying the condensate container, a unit located in the basement can be connected by a hose to a floor drain, or it can be positioned directly over the drain. In any event, the dehumidifier should be equipped with a cutoff (float) switch to turn off the unit when the condensate container is full.

Troubleshooting Dehumidifiers

Running a dehumidifier will sometimes produce results that are misdiagnosed as problems when, in fact, they are perfectly normal for these appliances. The most frequent complaints include the following:

- The dehumidifier switches on and off several times during the day. The dehumidifier simply is responding to a signal from the humidistat. When the humidity in the surrounding air falls to the setpoint on the humidistat, the dehumidifier shuts off. It turns on again when the humidity rises above the humidistat setpoint.

- The condensate container fills up and must be emptied often. This is normal operation in areas of high humidity, such as Florida and the other Gulf states.

Table 11-3 lists the most common problems associated with the operation of a refrigeration dehumidifier.

Table 11-3 Troubleshooting Dehumidifiers

Symptom and Possible Cause	Possible Remedy
Condensation container fills to brim or flows over.	
(a) Overflow prevention control malfunctioning.	(a) Replace cutoff float switch.
(b) Shutoff level too high.	(b) Lower shutoff level.
Dehumidifier runs continuously.	
(a) Humidity too high for unit.	(a) Use dehumidifier with higher capacity.
(b) Defective humidistat.	(b) Replace humidistat.
Rattling noise when dehumidifier is running.	
(a) Dehumidifier not level.	(a) Check level and correct if necessary.
(b) Condensation container not positioned properly.	(b) Check and correct as necessary
Dehumidifier will not start.	
(a) Full condensate container (the red indicator light on the unit should be on).	(a) Empty container and restart dehumidifier.
(b) Faulty wiring.	(b) Check to make sure the dehumidifier is plugged in and then rotate the control. If a click is heard when the control is rotated past its setting (and the unit does not start), there is probably a problem with the wiring. Inspect and repair as necessary.
(c) Defective humidistat.	(c) Check to make sure the dehumidifier is plugged in and then rotate the control. If no click is heard when the control is rotated past its setting (and the unit does not start), the humidistat needs to be repaired (dirty or worn contacts) or replaced.
(d) Faulty compressor or compressor starter relay.	(d) Fan runs but compressor won't start after the internal pressure has equalized. Replace compressor or compressor starter relay.
(e) Low line voltage.	(e) Correct as necessary.

(continued)

Table 11-3   *(continued)*

Symptom and Possible Cause	Possible Remedy
Compressor overheats and short-cycles.	
(a) Low line voltage.	(a) Correct as necessary.
(b) Seized fan.	(b) Correct as necessary.
(c) Slow fan rotation.	(c) Correct as necessary.
(d) Excessive dirt buildup on fan, fan shaft, or coils.	(d) Clean.
Excessive ice buildup on coils	
(a) Defective defrost sensor. Unit cannot run defrost cycle.	(a) Replace defrost sensor.
(b) Defective low-temperature shutoff sensor. Dehumidifier continues to run when room temperatures are too cold.	(b) Replace low-temperature shutoff sensor.
Condensate container does not fill.	
(a) Dehumidifier does not run often enough to reduce humidity and fill condensate container.	(a) Set humidistat to drier setting.
(b) Dehumidifier runs constantly but sends little or no condensate to container.	(b) Dirty coils. Clean and restart dehumidifier or defective refrigeration system. Should be repaired only by a qualified and experienced technician.
No air blows out of front of dehumidifier.	
(a) Defective fan motor.	(a) Replace fan motor.
(b) Seized fan or broken fan blade.	(b) Replace fan.

Chapter 12

Air Cleaners and Filters

All indoor air contains a certain amount of microscopic airborne dust and dirt particles. Cooking and tobacco smoke also contribute to the pollution of the indoor air, and pollen is a factor during some months of the year.

Excessive air pollution stains furniture and fabrics and causes a dust film to form on glass surfaces such as windows or mirrors. It can also be a health problem, especially to those with dust or pollen allergies.

A number of devices are used to remove dust, dirt, smoke, pollen, and other contaminants from the indoor air. They are not all equally effective. For example, an ordinary air filter in a furnace removes only approximately 10 percent of all airborne contaminants. An electronic air cleaner, on the other hand, can remove as much as nine times that amount.

The air-cleaning devices described in this chapter are: (1) electronic air cleaners, (2) air washers, and (3) conventional air filters.

Electronic Air Cleaners

Electronic air cleaners are devices designed to remove airborne particles from the air electrically. The best electronic air cleaners remove 70 to 90 percent of all air contaminants. These standards are met in testing methods devised by the National Bureau of Standards and the Air-Conditioning and Refrigeration Institute. Claims by manufacturers for higher rates of airborne particle removal should be attributed to enthusiasm for their product. In any event, an electronic air cleaner is vastly more effective than the conventional filter used in a warm-air furnace. They are available as permanently mounted units for use in central heating and/or cooling systems or as independent cabinet units.

Permanently mounted electronic air cleaners are installed at the furnace, air handler, or air-conditioning unit or in wall or ceiling return air grilles. Some typical installations are shown in Figure 12-1.

An electronic air cleaner installed at the furnace, air handler, or air-conditioning unit is either mounted against the surface of the unit or a short distance from it on the return air duct. These electronic air cleaners are sometimes referred to as *multiposition* models because they can be installed in a number of locations with equal

HORIZONTAL

UPFLOW—SIDE RETURN

UPFLOW—BOTTOM RETURN

COUNTERFLOW

WALL MOUNTED

CEILING MOUNTED

Figure 12-1 Some typical electronic air cleaner installations.
(Courtesy Mueller Climatrol Corp.)

effectiveness. Some typical examples of multiposition electronic air cleaners are shown in Figures 12-2, 12-3, and 12-4.

A design feature of some *return grille* electronic air cleaners is a hinged cell carrier, which swings out to allow the cells to be removed (see Figure 12-5). Return grille electronic air cleaners can be installed in the wall or ceiling openings of return air ducts, but

CONTROL PANEL
PERFORMANCE INDICATOR
POWER SWITCH

IONIZING
SECTION

PRE-FILTER FOR
LARGE PARTICLES

COLLECTING CELLS

Figure 12-2 Multiposition electronic air cleaner.
(Courtesy Lennox Air Conditioning and Heating)

not in a floor return. These units are also referred to as *wall* (or *ceiling*) *electronic air cleaners* or as *through-the-wall electronic air cleaners*. Typical installations are shown in Figures 12-6, 12-7, and 12-8.

The independent cabinet units (see Figures 12-9 and 12-10) are designed for use in installations where a permanently mounted unit is impractical or where *selective* air cleaning is desired. These units can be installed anywhere in the structure.

Based on their operating principle, electronic air cleaners can be divided into the following two principal types:

1. Charged-media air cleaners

2. Two-stage air cleaners

Charged-Media Air Cleaners

The basic working components of a *charged-media electronic air cleaner* are an electrically charged grid operating in conjunction with a media pad or mat. Media pads are commonly made of fiberglass, cellulose, or a similar material.

Figure 12-3 Climatrol multiposition electronic
air cleaner. *(Courtesy Mueller Climatrol Corp.)*

The charged-media air cleaner operates on the electrostatic principle. When voltage is applied to the grid, an intense electrostatic field is created. Dust particles passing through this field are polarized and caught by the media pads in much the same way that metal filings adhere to a magnet. When these media pads are filled, they must be removed and replaced with clean ones.

Figure 12-4 Utica International multiposition electronic air cleaner.
(Courtesy International Heating and Air Conditioning)

COLLECTING CELLS   PERFORMANCE INDICATOR

POWER SWITCH

PRE-FILTER FOR
LARGE PARTICLES

CONTROL PANEL

Figure 12-5 Wall-mounted electronic air cleaner. *(Courtesy Trane Co.)*

AIR
FLOW

UPFLOW
FURNACE

ELECTRONIC AIR CLEANER

AIR
FLOW

Figure 12-6 Typical application on a platform-mounted
upflow furnace. *(Courtesy Trane Co.)*

Figure 12-7   Typical installation on an upflow (highboy) **furnace.** *(Courtesy Trane Co.)*

Two-Stage Air Cleaners

The *two-stage* (or *ionizing*) *electronic air cleaner* also operates on the electrostatic principle, but the airborne particles pass through *two* electrical fields rather than the single field used in charged-media air cleaners. The effectiveness of this type of air cleaner is indicated in test results from the National Bureau of Standards (see Figure 12-11).

Air entering a two-stage air cleaner must first pass through a permanent screen or prefilter, which catches the larger airborne particles. After passing through the prefilter, the air enters the so-called ionizer, or first stage, where the airborne particles receive an intense positive electrical charge. The positively charged airborne particles subsequently enter the collection, or second stage, which consists of a series of collector plates. These collector plates are metal

Figure 12-8 Typical application on a high-capacity counterflow (downflow) furnace. *(Courtesy Trane Co.)*

plates or screens alternately charged with positive and negative high voltages. Because the airborne dust and dirt particles received a positive charge when they passed through the first stage of the electronic air cleaner, they are repelled by the *positively* charged plates in the second stage and propelled against the negatively charged collector plates where they adhere until washed away. The airborne particles are removed from the negative collector plates by periodic vacuuming or washing. Some electronic air cleaners are equipped with washing systems that flush the particles off the plates.

The first stage (ionizing section) and second stage (collector section) are referred to collectively as the *electronic cell*, or the *electronic air-cleaning cell*.

Automatic Controls

A built-in electronic air cleaner can be connected electrically to the system blower motor or directly through a disconnect switch to the 120-volt line voltage power source. If the unit is connected to the system blower motor, the electronic cell will energize each time the blower motor operates.

Because the electronic air cleaner can be wired to operate either automatically or continuously in conjunction with fan operation, there is no need for a special wall-mounted air cleaner control. Thus, the fan control on a room thermostat, or combination thermostat

Figure 12-9   Cabinet-model electronic air cleaner.

(Courtesy Lennox Air Conditioning and Heating)

and humidistat, is used to control both the system fan and the electronic air cleaner. A typical unit combining all heating and/or cooling system controls under a single cover is shown in Figure 12-12. When the fan control switch is set on *auto*, the air is cleaned automatically whenever the heating and/or cooling system is operating. Continuous air cleaning (when extra air cleaning is required) is obtained by setting the fan control switch at *on*.

Figure 12-10 Cabinet-model electronic air cleaner with built-in automatic water-wash system.

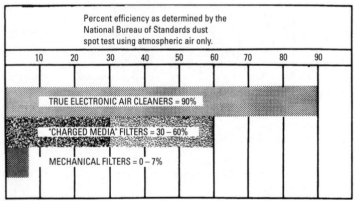

Percent efficiency as determined by the National Bureau of Standards dust spot test using atmospheric air only.

TRUE ELECTRONIC AIR CLEANERS = 90%

"CHARGED MEDIA" FILTERS = 30 – 60%

MECHANICAL FILTERS = 0 – 7%

Figure 12-11　National Bureau of Standards test results.

Clogged-Filter Indicator

The *clogged-filter indicator* shown in Figures 12-13 and 12-14 is used with Trane electronic air cleaners to sense pressure conditions in the blower chamber between the unit and the blower. An increase in pressure indicates a clogged filter, and this condition will be indicated by the light on the room thermostat control (see Figure 12-12) or when the clogged-filter indicator on the furnace shows red.

Figure 12-12   Combination thermostat and humidistat used to control electronic air cleaner. *(Courtesy Trane Co.)*

Figure 12-13   Furnace-mounted clogged-filter indicator. *(Courtesy Trane Co.)*

The clogged-filter indicator should be located on a rigid sheet-metal mounting surface to prevent bumps or other vibrations from tripping the indicator. It should also be located where it can properly sense the pressure conditions.

Performance Lights

Most electronic air cleaners are equipped with performance lights to indicate how the unit is operating. How these lights will be used will depend on the individual manufacturer. Read the manufacturer's

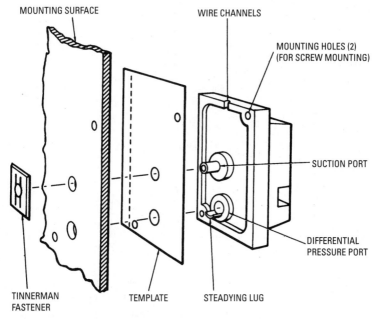

MOUNTING SURFACE

WIRE CHANNELS

MOUNTING HOLES (2)
(FOR SCREW MOUNTING)

SUCTION PORT

DIFFERENTIAL
PRESSURE PORT

TINNERMAN
FASTENER

TEMPLATE

STEADYING LUG

Figure 12-14   Clogged-filter indicator details. *(Courtesy Trane Co.)*

operating instructions concerning the use of these lights. As the following paragraphs make clear, they are not always used in the same way.

The built-in performance indicator light on the Trane electronic air cleaner shown in Figure 12-15 operates in conjunction with the on-off switch. If the electronic air cleaner is operating correctly, the performance indicator light will be on whenever the system fan is running and the on-off switch is in the *on* position.

The performance indicator light on the Lennox electronic air cleaner shown in Figure 12-16 glows red when the unit is operating correctly. This light also operates in conjunction with the on-off switch, which must be *on*. An optional performance light is available with a Lennox electronic air cleaner for installation in the living spaces (see Figure 12-17). It remains off when the unit is operating correctly.

Thermo-Pride electronic air cleaners use both an amber-colored operating light and a red performance light with their units. The

QUARTER
TURN
FASTENER

POWER SUPPLY
ENCLOSURE

INTERLOCK
SWITCH

ON-OFF
SWITCH
WITH
INDICATOR
LIGHT

SNAP
CLIP

CELL
CARRIER

HINGE

ELECTRONIC
CELL

POLYSTYRENE
GRILLE

METAL
MESH
PREFILTER

Figure 12-15   Trane multiposition electronic air cleaner. *(Courtesy Trane Co.)*

INDICATOR LIGHT

ON/OFF SWITCH

SAFETY SWITCH

Figure 12-16   Lennox performance indicator light.
(Courtesy Lennox Air Conditioning and Heating)

operating light indicates that line voltage is on. The red performance light indicates that the electronic cell is operating properly.
Both lights must be on during normal operation.

Sail Switch

A *sail switch* (see Figure 12-18) is designed to complete circuit
power to auxiliary equipment in a forced warm-air system when
the duct air velocity is increased. Consequently, it provides on-off

Figure 12-17 Optional performance light.

(Courtesy Lennox Air Conditioning and Heating)

control of electronic air cleaners, humidifiers, odor-control systems, and other equipment that is energized when the fan is operating.

In operation, the air movement pushing against the sail actuates the switching device, which then energizes the power supply. Using a sail switch allows the auxiliary equipment to be wired independently of the system blower motor.

The manufacturer's installation instructions should be carefully read and followed because the sail is installed at the site. The switch mechanism or sail switch body is mounted on the back of the electronic air cleaner usually before it is installed in the return air duct opening (see Figure 12-18). The sail is mounted on the switch body after installation of the air cleaner to prevent damage of the sail. A typical wiring diagram is shown in Figure 12-19.

Figure 12-18 Sail switch mounted on back of electronic air cleaner. *(Courtesy Trane Co.)*

① Power supply; provide disconnect means and overload protection as required.

② Sail switch mounted in return duct energizes electronic air cleaner when fan is running.

Figure 12-19 Wiring diagram of an electronic air cleaner controlled by a sail switch. *(Courtesy Honeywell Tradeline Controls)*

In-Place Water-Wash Controls

Some electronic air cleaners are equipped with a water-wash system for in-place cleaning of the electronic cells. Operation of the water-wash system is governed by a control unit that includes a sequencing timer, water valve, detergent aspirator and valve, and a fan interlock switch to control the system fan during the wash cycle (see Figure 12-20). The timer controls the internal water and detergent valves

① 220–240 V, $^{50}/_{60}$ Hz models provide switching on both sides of line to system.

Figure 12-20 Water-wash control wiring diagram.
(Courtesy Honeywell Tradeline Controls)

① 120 V, 60 Hz power supply. Provide disconnect means and overload protection as required.

Figure 12-21 Typical hookup of wash control and electronic air cleaner for in-place washing of the electronic cell. *(Courtesy Honeywell Tradeline Controls)*

① 120 V, 60 Hz power supply. Provide disconnect means and overload protection as required.

② The normally closed contacts open when cover is opened.

Figure 12-22 Typical hookup of wash control and electronic air cleaner for automatic wash and rinse of electronic cells.
(Courtesy Honeywell Tradeline Controls)

to provide automatic wash and rinse of the electronic cells. Typical hookups for a Honeywell W922 wash control are shown in Figures 12-21 and 12-22.

Cabinet-Model Control Panels

The cabinet-model electronic air cleaner shown in Figure 12-9 is equipped with a control panel that contains a meter, operating controls, and water-wash controls.

The meter is used to check the performance of the electronic air cleaner (see Figure 12-23). The meter is divided into three sections. If the unit is operating properly, the indicator needle will be steady and remain in the center section (the normal operating range on the meter). Fluctuations of the needle outside the normal operating range indicate that the unit is not operating properly. The specific problem is determined by the position of the needle.

FUSE   BLOWER BUTTON   VOLTAGE CONTROL KNOB

METER

Figure 12-23   Cabinet-model control panel.
(Courtesy Lennox Air Conditioning and Heating)

The system/blower controls are located to the right of the meter; the washer/cleaner controls to the left. The voltage-control knob operates in conjunction with the meter and is used to adjust the unit for line voltage variations. The basic procedure for operating the electronic air cleaner shown in Figure 12-9 is as follows:

1. Turn cleaner time switch to *on* position.

2. Push the *off* wash button.

3. Push the *on* cleaner button.

4. Push the *cont* blower button for continuous operation or the *auto* blower button for intermittent operation.

5. Push the *on* system button.

6. Adjust the voltage-control knob so that the needle remains in the normal operating range section on the meter.

Installation Instructions

When installing a built-in electronic air cleaner, make certain there is enough clearance to allow easy access to the filters and collector cells. These components must be cleaned periodically and should not be obstructed. Most manufacturers recommend at least 30 inches of clearance for servicing.

Pay particular attention to the airflow arrow printed on the side of the electronic cell. This arrow is used to indicate the correct direction of the airflow through the unit. If the electronic cell is installed so that the airflow arrow is facing the wrong direction, excessive arcing will occur and the unit will not operate efficiently.

The conventional air filter should be removed after the electronic air cleaner has been installed in order to help reduce pressure drop through the furnace.

Air volume adjustment is another factor that must be taken into consideration when installing one of these units. These adjustments should be made in accordance with the manufacturer's instructions. They will involve determining the required temperature rise through the heat exchanger, making the necessary fan speed adjustments, and calibrating the filter flag setting (when used).

Some existing installations may require transitions or duct turns. If the ductwork makes an abrupt turn at the air cleaner, turning vanes should be installed in the duct to help provide an equal distribution of air across the entire surface of the filters. Do not install an atomizing humidifier upstream from an electronic air cleaner.

Electrical Wiring

Read and carefully follow the manufacturer's installation instructions before attempting to make any wiring connections. All wiring should be done in accordance with local codes and regulations. *Always* disconnect the power source before beginning any work in order to prevent electric shock or damage to the equipment.

Electronic air cleaners operate on regular 120-volt current and use less electricity than a 60-watt light bulb. Typical wiring connections for a Trane Model EAP-12A Electrostatic Air Cleaner are shown in Figure 12-24. A ground wire for this unit is required. No

Figure 12-24   Wiring diagram for Trane Model EAP-12A electronic air cleaner. *(Courtesy Trane Co.)*

ground wire is required for the return grille electronic air cleaner shown in Figure 12-25. Other than installing the ground wire (where required), wiring an electronic air cleaner generally consists of simply hooking the unit up to the power source.

When making external circuit connections to the line voltage lead wires of an electronic air cleaner, only connectors listed by Underwriters Laboratories should be used.

An electronic air cleaner can be connected electrically to the system blower motor or directly through a disconnect switch to the 120-volt power source. If the unit is connected to the system blower motor, the electronic cell will energize each time the blower operates.

As shown in Figure 12-25, resistors are installed in the circuit to bleed off the electrical charges that the collector plates, acting as capacitors, are capable of storing. As a result, the serviceperson and homeowner are protected against shock. On a unit that does *not* include bleed-off resistors in its circuit, the cell must be grounded out before it is touched.

Maintenance Instructions

The function of the filter in an electronic air cleaner is to eliminate the need for frequent cleaning of the electronic cell. Particles build up on the collecting plates until they reach a size large enough to be affected by the air velocity. When this point is reached, the particles are blown off the plates onto the after filter.

Figure 12-25 Wiring diagram for Trane return grille electronic air cleaner. *(Courtesy Trane Co.)*

The prefilter (lint filter) and the after filter (so named because it follows the collecting plates in the unit) should be cleaned every 4 to 6 weeks. The required frequency of cell washing varies from one installation to the next and will depend largely on the level of air pollution each unit is expected to handle. In any event, the normal period will range from 1 to 6 months. Homes with large families, heavy and frequent cooking and laundering, and several tobacco smokers usually require monthly cleaning of the cell.

An automatic dishwasher can be used to wash an electronic cell without any fear of damaging the cell itself. Place the cells on the lower rack of the dishwasher with the airflow arrows facing up. If the cells are too large for the dishwasher, they will have to be washed by hand.

The procedure for manually cleaning the filters is as follows:

1. Turn off the current to the unit. Wait a few minutes to allow the grids to lose their static charge.

2. Note direction in which airflow arrows are pointing on the cell.

3. Remove the cell and both filters.

4. Soak cell and filters in a tub of water and electric dishwater detergent for about 30 minutes.

5. Rinse both sides of cell and filters with clear, clean water until all traces of dirt and detergent have been removed.

6. Shake excess water from cell and filters.

7. Replace cell and filters in the same order as before.

Caution

Do not turn the power back on if the reinstalled filters are not completely dry. Moisture can short out the grids and damage the power pack. Keep the power switch off and allow air to flow through the grids for 2 or 3 days until any remaining moisture is gone.

This last step is very important. If the cell and filters are not replaced so that the air flows in the direction of the arrow, the unit will not function properly.

Excess arcing or flickering of the red performance light immediately after washing the cell and filters is normal and is caused by water droplets on the surface. If these conditions continue, check to make certain the cell and filters were replaced in the correct order. If there is no problem with the direction of airflow, the unit is shorting (see *Electrical Wiring* and *Troubleshooting Electronic Air Cleaners* in this chapter).

Replacing Tungsten Ionizing Wires

From time to time, the tungsten ionizing wires in the charging section of the electronic cell may break or become damaged. A broken or damaged wire generally causes a short to ground, which may or may not be accompanied by visible arcing or sparking. All parts of these broken or damaged wires should be removed from the unit immediately to prevent further shorting of the circuit. The unit will be able to operate on a *temporary basis* with one wire missing, but a new wire should be installed as soon as possible.

Some electronic air cleaners require the disassembly of the electronic cell in order to replace a broken or damaged ionizing wire. The procedure is as follows:

1. Place the cell on a flat surface and remove the screws from the terminal end of the cell (see Figure 12-26). Pull off the terminal end.
2. Remove the screws from the rear end and then pull off the end and the two sides.
3. Remove the top screen and carefully lift off the ionizer section. Turn the ionizer section upside down as shown in Figure 12-27.
4. Remove all parts of the broken or damaged wire.
5. Compress both tension members and string the new ionizing wire.
6. *Slowly and carefully* release the compression force first on one tension member and then on the other (sudden release may snap the wire).
7. Reassemble the cell.

TOP SCREEN OF
CELL ASSEMBLY

SIDES (4)

Figure 12-26 Cell placed on a flat surface. *(Courtesy Trane Co.)*

Figure 12-27 **Ionizer section turned upside down.** *(Courtesy Trane Co.)*

The complete disassembly of the cell in order to replace an ionizing wire is not necessary on all electronic air cleaners. On the return grille electronic air cleaner, shown in Figure 12-15, the replacement wires are cut to length and installed as follows:

1. Remove all parts of the broken or damaged ionizing wire.
2. Hook one eyelet of the ionizing wire over the spring connector at one end of the cell (see Figure 12-28).
3. Hold the opposite eyelet of the ionizing wire with needle-nose pliers and stretch the wire the length of the cell.
4. Depress the opposite spring connector and hook the eyelet over it.

Troubleshooting Electronic Air Cleaners

Most electronic air cleaners are equipped with a performance indicator light, which is usually mounted in the control panel with the other controls. If the *unit* performance indicator light is off and the unit switch is on when the furnace is running, the air cleaner power pack may be burned out or disconnected from its power source, or the pressure switch used to sense airflow and charge the grids is defective. Each of these problems requires opening up the power pack and exposing dangerous high voltages. These repairs should be done only by a qualified electrician or HVAC technician.

Figure 12-28 Installation of new ionizing wires. *(Courtesy Trane Co.)*

A flickering performance indicator light is not necessarily an indication that the air cleaner is malfunctioning. It is not unusual for the light to flicker when the unit needs cleaning. Another indication that grid cleaning is required is loud snapping sounds caused by electrical shorts when dirt or other debris becomes stuck on the wire grid.

Table 12-1 lists the most common problems associated with operating an electronic air cleaner. For each operating problem, a possible cause and its remedy have been suggested.

Table 12-1 Troubleshooting Electronic Air Cleaners

Symptom and Possible Cause	Possible Remedy
Air cleaner will not operate.	
(a) Unit power switch off.	(a) Turn switch on.
(b) System fuse blown.	(b) Check and replace with same-size fuse.
(c) Blower unit or furnace power (disconnect) switch off.	(c) Turn switch on.
(d) Unit rectifier malfunctioning.	(d) Replace rectifier.
(e) Unit transformer malfunctioning.	(e) Replace transformer.

Table 12-1 *(continued)*

Symptom and Possible Cause	Possible Remedy
Unit performance indicator light flickers.	
(a) Dirty electronic cells.	(a) Remove and clean cells.
(b) Air flowing through cell in wrong direction.	(b) Rearrange components in proper order (airflow in direction of arrow on cell).
Excess arcing.	
(a) Broken ionizing wires.	(a) Replace wires.
(b) Bent collecting plates.	(b) Repair or replace plates.
(c) Foreign object wedged between plates or ionizers.	(c) Inspect and remove.

Air Washers

Air washers operate by first passing the air through fine sprays of water and then past baffle plates, on the wetted surface of which is deposited whatever dust and dirt were not caught by the sprays.

An air washer functions as a filter, humidifier, and dehumidifier. Using it to regulate the moisture in the air decreases its efficiency as a filter for removing airborne dust and dirt particles.

Air washers are classified as either two-unit or three-unit types. The two-unit air washer consists simply of sprays and eliminators as shown in Figure 12-29. A three-unit air washer includes a filter located between the sprays and eliminators (see Figure 12-30). Excluding the air filter, the basic components of a typical air washer are the following:

1. Cabinet
2. Spray nozzles
3. Eliminators or baffles
4. Sump
5. Pump
6. Blower

The major advantage of using an air washer instead of a conventional air filter or an electronic air cleaner is that it does not become clogged with dust and dirt and is therefore not subject to loss of

Figure 12-29 Elevation and plan of a two-unit (sprayer and eliminator) washer.

efficiency; however, air washers are no longer used in air-cleaning installations because of the following disadvantages:

1. Equipment bulk.
2. Higher operating expense.
3. Inefficiency in removing fine particles.
4. Tendency to add moisture to the air when the water is not cool.

Air Filters

Conventional air filters are commonly used in forced warm-air furnaces to trap and remove airborne particles and other contaminants from the air (see Figure 12-31). These filters are generally placed in the return air duct at a point just before the air supply enters the furnace or in the outdoor air intake ducts. In air conditioners, filters are properly placed ahead of heating or cooling coils and other air-conditioning equipment in the system to protect them from dust and dirt. Air filters are *not* used in gravity warm-air furnaces because they

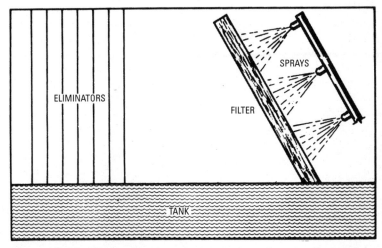

Figure 12-30   Three-unit air washer consisting of sprays, filter, and eliminator plates.

obstruct the flow of air. Conventional air filters will effectively clean the air that is being circulated through the structure, but they will not prevent dirt from leaking into the house. On the average, a conventional air filter installed in the furnace can be expected to remove approximately 10 percent of all airborne particles from the air.

Filters should be inspected *at least* twice a year. Throwaway filters must be replaced with new ones, and washable filters should be

Figure 12-31   Conventional permanent washable air filter.
(Courtesy Dornback Furnace & Foundry Co.)

cleaned when they become loaded with foreign matter. If this action is not taken, the efficiency of the furnace or air conditioner will be greatly reduced. As the dirt builds up on the filter, it increases the resistance of the passage of the air.

In a new house, the first set of filters may become clogged after a short time due to the presence of dust and dirt in the air created by the building operation. Check the filters after the first month of operation.

In an older house in which a winter air-conditioning system has been installed, the dust and dirt that accompanies the dismantling of the old heating system may also clog the first set of filters in a short time. The new filters should also be checked after about a month of furnace operation.

If new rugs or carpets have been installed in the house, considerable lint will be given off at first. Under such conditions, replacement or cleaning of the filters will be necessary.

Dry Air Filters

A *dry air filter* consists of a dry filtering medium such as cloth, porous paper, pads of loosely held cellulose fiber, wool felt, or some similar material held together in a lightweight metal or wire frame.

Both washable and disposable (throwaway) dry air filters are used in forced warm-air furnaces. Disposable filters are constructed of inexpensive materials and are designed to be discarded after one use. The frame is frequently a combination of cardboard and wire. Washable filters usually have metal frames. Various cleaning methods have been recommended, such as air jet, water jet, steam jet, or washing in kerosene and dipping in oil. The latter method may serve both to clean the filter and to add the necessary adhesive.

Viscous Air Filters

A *viscous air filter* (or *viscous-impingement air filter*) contains a filtering material consisting of coarse fibers coated with a sticky substance. This sticky substance catches the dust and dirt as the air passes through the mat. Viscous air filters can be reconditioned by washing them and recoating their surface with fresh liquid.

An oil or grease, sometimes referred to as the *adhesive* or *saturant*, is used as the viscous substance in these filters. The arrangement of the filter mat is such that the airstream is broken up into many small airstreams, and these are caused to abruptly change direction a number of times in order to throw the dust and dirt particles by centrifugal force against the adhesive.

The method used for cleaning a viscous filter will depend on the filter and the dust and dirt particles trapped by it. Most dry dust and dirt particles, as well as lint, can often be removed by rapping the filter frame.

Filter Installation and Maintenance

Access to filters must be provided through a service panel in the furnace. Inspection and replacement of the filter by the user must be made possible without the use of special tools. When a new furnace is installed, care must be taken to provide sufficient clearance to the filter service panel. The furnace manufacturer will usually specify the minimum clearance in the installation instructions. An additional set of filter instructions should be attached to the filter service panel.

Always replace a disposable filter with one having the *same* dimensional size. The filter dimensions are printed on the filter frame. Always replace a filter with one of the same size.

The mat-type filter is commonly used in a gas-fired downflow furnace. It consists of a removable metal cage located in the blower cabinet of the furnace. The metal cage contains the filter material, which is either cut to size and prepackaged or available in rolls for measuring and cutting on-site. When installing a mat-type filter, make sure the side that collects the dust and other airborne contaminants (that is, the oily side) is facing upward into the cold-air duct.

Box-type filters are commonly installed in the top of the blower or in a slot in the cold-air return. Some of these filters have an arrow on the top of the frame. The arrow points to the direction of the airflow and the filter should always be installed with the arrow facing the blower. Most box-type filters have one side that is covered with wire mesh. The wire mesh should face the blower (see Figure 12-31).

Appendix A

Professional and Trade Associations

Many professional and trade associations have been formed to develop and provide research materials, services, and support for those working in the heating, ventilating, and air conditioning trades. The materials, services, and support include:

1. Formulating and establishing specifications and professional standards.
2. Certifying that equipment and materials meet or exceed minimum standards.
3. Certifying that technicians have met education and training standards.
4. Conducting product research.
5. Promoting interest in the product.
6. Providing education and training.
7. Publishing books, newsletters, articles, and technical papers.
8. Conducting seminars and workshops.

A great deal of useful information can be obtained by contacting these associations. With that in mind the names and addresses of the principal organizations have been included in this Appendix. They are listed in alphabetical order.

Air-Conditioning and Refrigeration Wholesalers International (ARWI)

(*See* Heating, Air Conditioning & Refrigeration Distributors International)

Air-Conditioning and Refrigeration Institute (ARI)

4100 North Fairfax Drive, Suite 200

Arlington, Virginia

Phone: (703) 524-8800

Fax: (703) 528-3816

Email: ari@ari.org

Web site: www.ari.org

A national trade association of manufacturers of central air conditioning, warm-air heating, and commercial and industrial refrigeration equipment, ARI publishes ARI standards and guidelines, which can be downloaded free from its web site. ARI is an approved certifying organization for the EPA Technician Certification Exam. ARI also provides a study manual for those taking the EPA Technician Certification Exam. ARI developed the Curriculum Guide in collaboration with HVACR instructors, manufacturing training experts, and other industry professionals for use in all school programs that educate and train students to become competent, entry-level HVACR technicians.

Air Conditioning Contractors of America (ACCA)

2800 Shirlington Road
Suite 300
Arlington, Virginia 22206
Phone: (703) 575-4477
Fax: (703) 575-4449
Email: info@acca.org
Web site: www.acca.org

A national trade association of heating, air conditioning, and refrigeration systems contractors, ACCA (until 1978, the National Environmental Systems Contractors Association) publishes a variety of different manuals useful for those working in the HVAC trades, including residential and commercial equipment load calculations, residential duct system design, and system installation. ACCA also publishes training and certification manuals. The ACCA publications can be purchased by both members and nonmembers. Check the web site for a list of the ACCA publications, because it is very extensive.

Air Diffusion Council (ADC)

1000 E. Woodfield Road
Suite 102
Schaumburg, Illinois 60173
Phone: (847) 706-6750
Fax: (847) 706-6751
Email: info@flexibleduct.org
Web site: www.flexibleduct.org

The Air Diffusion Council (ADC) was formed to promote the interests of the manufacturers of flexible air ducts and related air distribution equipment. The ADC supports the maintenance and development of uniform industry standards for the installation, use, and performance of flexible duct products. It encourages the use of those standards by various code writing groups, government agencies, architects, engineers, and heating and air conditioning contractors.

Air Filter Institute
(*See* Air-Conditioning and Refrigeration Institute)

Air Movement and Control Association International, Inc. (AMCA)
30 West University Drive

Arlington Heights, Illinois 60004

Phone: (847) 394-0150

Fax: (847) 253-0088

Email: amca@amca.org

Web site: www.amca.org

The Air Movement and Control Association International, Inc. (AMCA) is a trade association of the manufacturers, wholesalers, and retailers of air movement and control equipment (fans, louvers, dampers, and related air systems equipment). The AMCA Certified Ratings Programs are an important function of the association. Their purpose is to give the buyer, specification writer, and user of air movement and control equipment assurance that published ratings are reliable and accurate. The AMCA publishes current test standards for fans, louvers, dampers, and shutters. It also issues a variety of AMCA certified rating seals for different types of air movement and control equipment. It publishes a newsletter various technical specifications for members and those who work with air movement and control systems.

American Boiler Manufacturers Association (ABMA)
4001 North 9th Street

Suite 226

Arlington, Virginia 22203

Phone: (703) 522-7350

Fax: (703) 522-2665

Email: randy@abma.com

Web Site: www.abma.com

The American Boiler Manufacturers Association (ABMA) is a national association representing the manufacturers of commercial, industrial, and utility steam generating and fuel burning equipment, as well as suppliers to the industry. The primary goal of ABMA is topromote the common business interests of the boiler manufacturing industry and to promote the safe, environmentally friendly use of the products and services of its members. Publishes technical guides and manuals.

American Gas Association (AGA)

151400 North Capitol Street, N.W.

Washington, DC 20001

Phone: (202) 824-7000

Fax: (202) 824-7115

Email: Fax: krogers@aga.org

Web site: www.aga.org

The AGA develops residential gas operating and performance standards for distributors and transporters of natural, manufactured, and mixed gas.

American Society of Heating, Refrigeration, and Air-Conditioning Engineers (ASHRAE)

1791 Tullie Circle NE

Atlanta, GA 30329

Phone: (800) 527-4723 (toll free)

Phone: (404) 636-8400

Fax: (404) 321-5478

Email: ashrae@ashrae.org

Web site: www.ashrae.org

The American Society of Heating, Refrigeration, and Air-Conditioning Engineers (ASHRAE) is an international professional association concerned with the advancement of the science and technology of heating, ventilation, air conditioning, and refrigeration through research, standards writing, continuing education, and publications. Membership in ASHRAE is open to any person associated with heating, ventilation, air conditioning, or refrigeration. There are several different types of membership depending on the individual's background and experience in the different HVAC and refrigeration fields. An important benefit of belonging to ASHRAE is access to numerous technical publications.

American Society of Mechanical Engineers (ASME)

Three Park Avenue

New York, New York 10016

Phone: (800) 843-2763 or (973) 882-1167

Fax: (973) 882-1717

Email: infocentral@asme.org

Web site: www.asme.org

A nonprofit technical and education association, ASME develops safety codes and standards and has an extensive list of technical publications covering pressure vessels, piping, and boilers. ASME offers educational and training services and conducts technology seminars and on-site training programs.

Better Heating-Cooling Council

(*See* Hydronics Institute)

Fireplace Institute

(Merged with Wood Energy Institute in 1980 to form the Wood Heating Alliance. See Wood Heating Alliance) Gas Appliance Manufacturers Association (GAMA)

2701 Wilson Boulevard, Suite 600

Arlington, Virginia 22201

Phone: (703) 525-7060

Fax: (703) 525-6790

Email: information@gamanet.org.

Web Site: www.gamanet.org

GAMA is a national trade association of manufacturers of gas-fired appliances, and certain types of oil-fired and electrical appliances, used in residential, commercial, and industrial applications. An important service provided by GAMA to its members is a testing and certification program. GAMA will test the rated efficiency and capacity of a manufacturer's product and, if it passes the testing criteria, certify it. The manufacturer can then market the product with the appropriate certification label. Program participants and their products are listed in the ratings directories.

Heating and Piping Contractors National Association
(*See* Mechanical Contractors Association of America)

Heating, Airconditioning & Refrigeration Distributors International (HARDI)
1389 Dublin Road
Columbus, Ohio 43215
Phone: (888) 253-2128 (toll free)
Phone: (614) 488-1835
Fax: (614) 488-0482
Email: HARDImail@HARDInet.org
Web site: www.hardinet.org

Heating, Airconditioning & Refrigeration Distributors International (HARDI) is national trade association of wholesalers and distributors of air conditioning and refrigeration equipment. It was formed by merging the Northamerican Heating, Refrigeration & Airconditioning Wholesalers (NHRAW) and the Air-conditioning & Refrigeration Wholesalers International (ARWI). Among products and services provided to its members are self-study training materials, statistical studies, as well as training and reference materials. See Appendix B (Education, Training, and Certification) for a description of the HARDI Home Study Institute. The HARDI publications are available to both members and nonmembers.

Home Ventilating Institute (HVI)
30 West University Drive
Arlington Heights, Illinois 60004
Phone: (847) 394-0150
Fax: (847) 253-0088
Email: hvi@hvi.org
Web site: www.hvi.org

The Home Ventilating Institute (HVI) is a nonprofit trade association representing national and international manufacturers of residential ventilation products. HVI is primarily concerned with developing performance standards for residential ventilating equipment. It has created a number of certified ratings programs that provide a fair and credible method of comparing ventilation performance of similar products. HVI publishes a number of interesting and informative articles on ventilation that can be downloaded from its Web site.

The Hydronics Foundation, Inc. (THFI)

The Hydronics Foundation, Inc. (THFI) was chartered in 1997 as a nonprofit organization to disseminate knowledge about hydronic equipment and technology. Manufacturers of HVAC equipment also contribute material from installation manuals, specification sheets, and product reviews.

> 119 East King Street
> P.O. Box 1671
> Johnson City, TN 37606
> Phone: (800) 929-8548
> Fax: (800) 929-9506
> Email: jdhowell@jdhowell.com
> Web site: www.hydronics.com or www.hydronics.org

Hydronic Heating Association (HHA)

> P.O. Box 388
> Dedham, MA 02026
> Phone: (781) 320-9910
> Fax: (781) 320-9906
> Email: info@comfortableheat.net
> Web site: www.comfortableheat.net

The Hydronic Heating Association is an organization of independent contractors, wholesalers, and manufacturers established to promote the latest hydronic technology, set uniform industrial standards, educate HVAC contractors, and inform the public of the benefits of having a quality hot-water system installed. Their Web site contains useful articles and essays on hydronic equipment and systems. It also offers many useful links to manufacturers of hydronic system products.

The Hydronics Institute Division of GAMA
P.O. Box 218
Berkley Heights, New Jersey 07922
Phone: (908) 464-8200
Fax: (908) 464-7818
Email: information@gamanet.org
Web site: www.gamanet.org

The Hydronics Institute was originally formed by a merger of the Better Heating-Cooling Council and the Institute of Boiler and Radiator Manufacturers. It represents manufacturers, suppliers, and installers of hot-water and steam heating and cooling equipment. It is now a division of the Gas Appliance Manufacturers Association. The Hydronics Institute represents and promotes the interests of the manufacturers of hydronic heating equipment. It also provides training materials for hydronic heating courses in schools and technical publications for technicians in the field.

Institute of Boiler and Radiator Manufacturers
(*See* Hydronics Institute)

Mechanical Contractors Association of America, Inc. (MCAA)
1385 Piccard Drive
Rockville, MD 20850
Phone: 301-869-5800
Fax: 301-990-9690
Web site: www.mcaa.org

The Mechanical Contractors Association of America, Inc. (MCAA) is a national trade association for contractors of piping and related equipment used in heating, cooling, refrigeration, ventilating, and air conditioning.

National Association of Plumbing Heating Cooling Contractors (PHCC)
180 S. Washington Street
P.O. Box 6808
Falls Church, VA 22040

Phone: (800) 533-7694 (toll free) or (703) 237-8100

Fax: (703) 237-7442

Email: naphcc@naphcc.org

Web site: www.phccweb.org

The National Association of Plumbing Heating Cooling Contractors (PHCC) is a trade association of local plumbing, heating, and cooling contractors. There are 12 regional chapters.

National Environmental Systems Contractors Association

(*See* Air Conditioning Contractors of America)

National Warm Air Heating and Air Conditioning Association

(*See* Air Conditioning Contractors of America)

North American Heating Refrigerating Air conditioning Wholesalers (NHRAW)

(*See* Heating, Airconditioning & Refrigeration Distributors International)

Radiant Panel Association (RPA)

P.O. Box 717

1399 South Garfield Avenue

Loveland, CO 80537

Phone: (800) 660-7187 (toll free) or (970) 613-0100

Fax: (970) 613-0098

Email: info@rpa-info.com

Web site: www.radiantpanelassociation.org

The Radiant Panel Association provides downloadable technical papers and notes on a variety of different topics concerning radiant panel heating and cooling systems. Links to several manufacturers of radiant heating equipment are also available at their Web site.

Refrigeration and Air Conditioning Contractors Association

(*See* Air Conditioning Contractors of America)

Refrigeration Service Engineers Society (RSES)

1666 Rand Road

Des Plaines, Illinois 60016

Phone: (800) 297-5660 (toll free) or (847) 297-6464

Email: general@rses.org.

Web site: www.rses.org

The Refrigeration Services Engineers Society (RSES) is an international association of refrigeration, air conditioning, and heating equipment installers, service persons, and sales persons. The Society conducts educational meetings, seminars, workshops, technical qualification and examination programs, instructor-led and self-study training courses. It offers a variety of certification program for technicians.

Sheet Metal and Air Conditioning Contractors National Association (SMACNA)

4201 Lafayette Center Dr.

Chantilly, Virginia 20151

Phone: (703) 803-2980

Fax: (703) 803-3732

Email: info@smacna.org

Web site: www.smacna.org

The SMACNA is an international trade association of union contractors who install ventilating, warm-air heating, and air-handling equipment and systems. SMACNA publishes technical papers, answers technical question, and provides distance learning courses for its members. American National Standards Institute has accredited SMACNA as a standards-setting organization matter.

Steam Heating Equipment Manufacturers Association

(*defunct*)

Steel Boiler Institute

(*defunct*)

Underwriters Laboratories, Inc. (UL)

Northbrook Division

Corporate Headquarters

333 Pfingsten Road

Northbrook, Illinois 60062
Phone: (847) 272-8800
Fax: (847) 272-8129
Email: northbrook@us.ul.com
Web site: www.ul.com

The Underwriters Laboratories is an independent, nonprofit product safety testing and certification organization. It promotes safety standards for equipment through independent testing.

Wood Energy Institute
(Merged with Fireplace Institute in 1980 to form Wood Heating Alliance.)

Other National and International Professional and Trade Associations
The following associations also provide support, services, technical publications, and/or training to its members who are involved in the manufacture, sale, or installation and repair of heating, ventilating, and air conditioning systems and equipment. Because space is limited, only their names are listed. Contact information can be obtained by accessing the Internet and entering the association name or by visiting the reference room of your local library and using the *Encyclopedia of Associations*.

Air Distribution Institute (ADI)

American National Standards Institute (ANSI)

American Society for Testing and Materials (ASTM)

Australian Home Heating Association (AHHA)

Australian Institute of Refrigeration, Air Conditioning and Heating (AIRAH)

Heating Alternatives, Inc

Heating, Refrigeration and Air Conditioning Contractors of Canada (HRAC)

Heating, Refrigeration and Air Conditioning Institute of Canada (HRAE)

Institute of Heating & Air Conditioning, Inc (IHACI).

Insulation Contractors of America (ICA)

International Energy Association (IEA)—Solar Heating and Cooling Programme

National LP-Gas Association (NLPGA)

National Oil Fuel Institute

National Oilheat Research Alliance

Plumbing-Heating-Cooling Contractors—National Association (PHCC)

Plumbing-Heating-Cooling Information Bureau (PHCIB)

Wood Heating Alliance (WHA)

Appendix B

Manufacturers

Adams Manufacturing Company
9790 Midwest Avenue
Cleveland, OH 44125
(216) 587-6801
(216) 587-6807 (Fax)
www.gamanet.org

Amana Refrigeration, Inc.
1810 Wilson Parkway
Fayetteville, TN 37334
(800) 843-0304
(931) 433-6101
(931) 433-1312
www.amana.com

American Standard Companies Inc.
One Centennial Ave.
Piscataway, NJ 08855
(732) 980-6000
(732) 980-3340 (Fax)
www.americanstandard.com

A.O. Smith Water Products Company
600 E. John Carpenter Freeway #200
Irving, TX 75062-3990
(972) 719-5900
(972) 719-5960 (Fax)
www.hotwater.com

Bacharach Inc.
621 Hunt Valley
New Kensington, PA 15068
(724) 334-5000

(724) 334-5001 (Fax)

www.bacharach-inc.com

Bard Manufacturing Co

P.O. Box 607

Bryan, OH 43506

(419) 636-1194

(419) 636-2640 (Fax)

www.bardhvac.com

R.W. Beckett Corporation

P.O. Box 1289

Elyria, OH 44036

(800) 645-2876

(440) 327-1060

(440) 327-1064 (Fax)

www. beckett.com

Bell & Gossett

(*See* ITT Bell & Gossett)

Bryan Boilers/Bryan Steam Corporation

P.O. Box 27

783 N. Chili Avenue

Peru, IN 46970

(765) 473-6651

(765) 473-3074 (Fax)

www.bryanboilers.com

Burnham Hydronics

U.S. Boiler Co., Inc.

P.O. Box 3079

Lancaster, PA 17604

(717) 397-4701

(717) 293-5827 (Fax)

www.burnham.com

Carrier Corporation
World Headquarters
One Carrier Place
Farmington, CT 06034
(860) 674-3000
www.carrier.com

Cash Acme
2400 7th Avenue S.W.
Cullman, Alabama 35055
(256) 775-8200
(256) 775-8238 (Fax)
www.cashacme.com

Coleman Corporation
Unitary Products Group
5005 York Dr.
Norman, OK 73069
(405) 364-4040
www.colemanac.com

Columbia Boiler Company
P.O. Box 1070
Pottstown, PA 19464
(610) 323-2700
(610) 323-7292 (Fax)
www.columbiaboiler.com

Danfoss A/S
DK-6430 Nordborg
Denmark
+45 7488 2222
+45 7449 0949 (Fax)
www.danfoss.com

Domestic Pump
(*See* ITT Domestic Pump)

Dornback Furnace

9545 Granger Road
Garfield Heights, OH 44125
(216) 662-1600
(216) 587-6807
www.gamanet.org

Ernst Gage Co.

250 S. Livingston Ave.
Livingston, NJ 07039 4089
973-992-1400
888-229-4243
973-992-0036 (Fax)

General Filters Inc.

43800 Grand River Ave.
Novi, MI
(248) 476-5100
(248) 349-2366 (Fax)
www.generalfilters.com

Goodman Manufacturing Corp

2550 North Loop West #400
Houston, TX 77092
(713) 861-2500
(888) 593-9988
www.goodmanmfg.com

Heat Controller, Inc.

1900 Wellworth Avenue
Jackson, MI 49203
(517) 787-2100
(517) 787-9341
www.heatcontroller.com

Hoffman Specialty

(*See* ITT Hoffman Specialty)

Honeywell, Inc.
101 Columbia Road
Morristown, NJ 07962
(973) 455-2000
(800) 328-5111
(983) 455-4807 (Fax)
www.honeywell.com

Hydro Therm, A Division of Mastek, Inc.
260 North Elm Street
Westfield, MA 01085
(413) 564-5515
www.hydrotherm.com

Invensys Building Systems, Inc.
1354 Clifford Ave.
P.O. Box 2940
Loves Park, IL 61132-2940
(815) 637-3000
(815) 637-5350 (Fax)
www.invensys.com

ITT Bell & Gossett
8200 North Austin Avenue
Morton Grove, IL 60053
(847) 966-3700
(847) 966-9052
www.bellgossett.com

ITT Domestic Pump
8200 N. Austin Ave.
Morton Grove, IL 60053
(847) 966-3700
(847) 966-9052
www.domesticpump.com

ITT Hoffman Specialty
3500 N. Spaulding Avenue
Chicago, IL 60618
(773) 267-1600
(773) 267-0991
www.hoffmanspecialty.com

ITT McDonnell & Miller
3500 N. Spaulding Avenue
Chicago, IL 60618
(723) 267-1600
(773) 267-0991
www.mcdonnellmiller.com

Janitrol Air Conditioning and Heating
www.janitrol.com

(*See* Goodman Manufacturing Company)

S.T. Johnson Company
Innovative Combustion Technologies, Inc.
925 Stanford Avenue
Oakland, CA 94608
(510) 652-6000
(510) 652-4302 (Fax)
www.johnsonburners.com

Johnson Controls, Inc.
5757 North Green Bay Avenue
Milwaukee, WI 53209
(262) 524-3285
www.johnsoncontrols.com
www.jci.com

Lennox Industries Inc.
2100 Lake Park Boulevard
Richardson, TX 75080
(972) 497-5000

(972) 497-5392 (Fax)

www.davelennox.com

Marathon Electric, Inc.
P.O. Box 8003

Wausau, WI 54402

(715) 675-3359

(715) 675-8050 (Fax)

McDonnell & Miller
(*See* ITT McDonnell & Miller)

Midco International Inc.
4140 West Victoria Street

Chicago, IL 60646-6790

(773) 604-8700

(773) 604-4070 (Fax)

www.midco-intl.com

Nordyne
P.O. Box 8809

O'Fallon, MO 63366

(636) 561-7300

(800) 222-4328

(636) 561-7365 (Fax)

www.nordyne.com

Raypak
2151 Eastman Ave.

Oxnard, CA 93030

(805) 278-5300

(805) 278-5468 (Fax)

www.raypak.com

RBI, Mestek Canada, Inc.
1300 Midway Blvd.

Mississauga Ontario L5T 2G8

(905) 670-5888

www.rbimestek.com

Rheem Manufacturing
5600 Old Greenwood Road

Fort Smith, AR 72908

(479) 646-4311

(479) 648-4812 (Fax)

www.rheemac.com

Robertshaw
(See Invensys)

Smith Cast Iron Boilers
260 North Elm Street

Westfield, MA 01085

(413) 562-9631

www.smithboiler.com

SpacePak
125 North Elm Street

Westfield, MA 01085

(413) 564-5530

www.spacepak.com

Spirax Sarco Inc.
Northpoint Business Park

1150 Northpoint Blvd

Blythewood, SC 29016

(803) 714-2000

(803) 714-2222

www.spiraxsarco.com

Sterling Hydronics
260 North Elm Street

Westfield, MA 01085

(413) 564-5535

www.sterlingheat.com

Sterling HVAC
125 North Elm Street

Westfield, MA 01085

(413) 564-5540

www.sterlinghvac.com

Suntec Industries Incorporated
2210 Harrison Ave

P.O. Box 7010

Rockford IL 61125-7010

(815) 226-3700

(815) 226-3848 (Fax)

www.suntecpumps.com

Thermo Pride
P.O. Box 217

North Judson, IN 46366

(574) 896-2133

(574) 896-5301

www.thermopride.com

Trane
P.O. Box 9010

Tyler, TX 75711-9010

(903) 581-3200

www.trane.com

Triangle Tube/Phase III Company, Inc.
Blackwood, NJ

(856) 228-1881

(856) 228-3584 (Fax)

www.triangletube.com

Vulcan Radiator (Mastec)
515 John Fitch Blvd

South Windsor, CT 06074

(413) 568-9571

www.mestec.com

Water Heater Innovations, Inc.
3107 Sibley Memorial Highway

Eagan, MN 55121

(800) 321-6718

www.marathonheaters.com

Watts Regulator Company

815 Chestnut Street

North Andover, MA 01845

(976) 688-1811

(978) 794-848 (Fax)

www.wattsreg.com

Wayne Combustion Systems

801 Glasgow Ave.

Fort Wayne, IN 46803

(800) 443-4625

www.waynecombustion.com

Weil-McLain

500 Blaine St.

Michigan City, IN 46360

(219) 879-6561

(219) 879-4025

www.weil-mclain.com

White-Rodgers, Div. of Emerson Electric Co.

9797 Reavis Rd.

St. Louis, MO 63123

(314) 577-1300

(314) 577-1517

www.white-rodgers.com

Wm. Powell Company

2503 Spring Grove Avenue

Cincinnati, OH 45214

(513) 852-2000

(513) 852-2997 (Fax)

www.powellvalves.com

York International Corporation

P.O. Box 1592-232F

York, PA 17405

(717) 771-7890
(717) 771-7381 (Fax)
www.york.com

Yukon-Eagle Wood & Multifuel Furnaces
10 Industrial Blvd.
P.O. Box 20
Palisade, MN 56469
(800) 358-0060
(800) 440-1994 (Fax)
www.yukon-eagle.com

John Zink Company
Gordon-Piatt Group
11920 East Apache
Tulsa, OK 74116
(800) 638-6940
www.johnzink.com

Appendix C

HVAC/R Education, Training, Certification, and Licensing

A career in the heating, ventilating, air-conditioning, and refrigeration (HVAC/R) trades requires special education and training. Formal education and training in the HVAC/R trades is available in many local public colleges and proprietary schools. Certification requires passing a standardized test indicating a thorough knowledge of the subject matter. The states also require HVAC/R technicians and contractors to take and pass licensing examinations.

HVAC/R Education and Training Programs

HVAC/R education and training programs are offered by four-year colleges, community colleges, proprietary schools, professional and trade associations, and manufacturers of HVAC/R appliances and system components.

One way to find a local school offering courses in HVAC/R education and training is to go online to the Cool Careers Web site at www.coolcareers.org. On their "Schools with HVACR Programs" page, you will find a list of all fifty states. Each state has the names of all the schools in that state offering programs in HVAC/R training. According to Cool Careers, their database contains the names of over 1300 training schools. You will have to contact the schools to enquire about entrance requirements, course content, class schedules, and financial aid.

Note

> If you don't have a computer, or know how to use one, go to the reference section in your local public library and ask the reference librarian to download the information from the internet and provide a printout. They will be willing to do this for you. It's part of the many services offered by the local public library.

Some of these schools offer only courses; others offer both courses and degrees. The least expensive courses are found at community colleges. The level of instruction will vary, depending on the school and the instructors. Your best source of information in this regard is local word of mouth. If you are already working as an entrance level trainee with a local HVAC firm, they should be able to help you find the best school and courses. After all, they often hire the graduates.

Cool Careers-Hot Jobs

The Cool Careers-Hot Jobs web site was created in 2000 by a coalition of organizations representing the heating, air conditioning, refrigeration, and plumbing industry. Its purpose is to provide information about education, training, jobs, and careers in the HVAC/R trades.

HVAC/R Certification

Certification means that the individual has taken and passed a standardized examination that certifies the individual's knowledge level. After the basic certification has been obtained, the technician can then study for and take certification exams at more advanced levels.

The following four organizations provide guidance and/or testing for the certification of HVAC/R technicians. Their addresses, telephone numbers, and web site addresses are listed in Appendix A (Professional and Trade Associations).

1. **Air-Conditioning and Refrigeration Institute (ARI).** ARI is a national trade association whose members represent most of the manufacturers of central air conditioning and refrigeration equipment. ARI administers the Industry Competencies Exam (ICE), which is given primarily to students from vocational school HVAC/R programs. The ARI also provides textbooks and training materials for preparing for both the ICE and EPA certification exams.

2. **North American Technician Excellence, Inc. (NATE).** NATE is a nonprofit organization established in 1997 by members of the HVAC/RE industry to test and certify technicians working in the heating ventilation, air-conditioning, and refrigeration trades. The tests are intended for experienced technicians.

3. **Refrigeration Service Engineers Society (RSES).** The RSES Educational Foundation was established in 1983 as a separate nonprofit organization to develop a comprehensive *voluntary* technician certification program (NTC). The program guides, tests, and certifies members through each of five levels of HVAC/R technician competency ranging from Level I (Technician) to Level V (Mastertech specialist).

4. **Air Conditioning Contractors of America (ACCA).** ACCA works in conjunction with RSES and NATE to provide a national certification program for HVAC/R technicians.

HVAC/R State Licensing

HVAC/R work is regulated at the state level by law. The law requires that a licensing exam must be taken and passed before working in an HVAC/R trade. It is the responsibility of the individual to contact the appropriate state office and obtain the necessary information about the state licensing examination. An easy way to locate the state office charged with licensing HVAC/R technicians and contractors is to ask the reference librarian at your local public library. You could also phone the state government and ask the operator to connect you to the office.

Appendix D

Data Tables

Table D-1   Equivalent Length of New Straight Pipe for Valves and Fittings for Turbulent Flow

Fittings		1/4	3/8	1/2	3/4	1	1 1/4	1 1/2	2	2 1/2	3	4	5	6	8	10	12	14	16	18	20	24
Regular 90° Ell — Screwed	Steel	2.3	3.1	3.6	4.4	5.2	6.6	7.4	8.5	9.3	11	13	—	—	—	—	—	—	—	—	—	—
	C. I.	—	—	—	—	—	—	—	—	—	9	11	—	—	—	—	—	—	—	—	—	—
Regular 90° Ell — Flanged	Steel	—	—	0.92	1.2	1.6	2.1	2.4	3.1	3.6	4.4	5.9	7.3	8.9	12	14	17	18	21	23	25	30
	C. I.	—	—	—	—	—	—	—	—	—	3.6	4.8	—	7.2	9.8	12	15	17	19	22	24	28
Long Radius 90° Ell — Screwed	Steel	1.5	2	2.2	2.3	2.7	3.2	3.4	3.6	3.6	4	4.6	—	—	—	—	—	—	—	—	—	—
	C. I.	—	—	—	—	—	—	—	—	—	3.3	3.7	—	—	—	—	—	—	—	—	—	—
Long Radius 90° Ell — Flanged	Steel	—	—	1.1	1.3	1.6	2	2.3	2.7	2.9	3.4	4.2	5	5.7	7	8	9	9.4	10	11	12	14
	C. I.	—	—	—	—	—	—	—	—	—	2.8	3.4	—	4.7	5.7	6.8	7.8	8.6	9.6	11	11	13
Regular 45° Ell — Screwed	Steel	0.34	0.52	0.71	0.92	1.3	1.7	2.1	2.7	3.2	4	5.5	—	—	—	—	—	—	—	—	—	—
	C. I.	—	—	—	—	—	—	—	—	—	3.3	4.5	—	—	—	—	—	—	—	—	—	—
Regular 45° Ell — Flanged	Steel	—	—	0.45	0.59	0.81	1.1	1.3	1.7	2	2.6	3.5	4.5	5.6	7.7	9	11	13	15	16	18	22
	C. I.	—	—	—	—	—	—	—	—	—	2.1	2.9	—	4.5	6.3	8.1	9.7	12	13	15	17	20
Tee-Line Flow — Screwed	Steel	0.79	1.2	1.7	2.4	3.2	4.6	5.6	7.7	9.3	12	17	—	—	—	—	—	—	—	—	—	—
	C. I.	—	—	—	—	—	—	—	—	—	9.9	14	—	—	—	—	—	—	—	—	—	—
Tee-Line Flow — Flanged	Steel	—	—	0.69	0.82	1	1.3	1.5	1.8	1.9	2.2	2.8	3.3	3.8	4.7	5.2	6	6.4	7.2	7.6	8.2	9.6
	C. I.	—	—	—	—	—	—	—	—	—	1.9	2.2	—	3.1	3.9	4.6	5.2	5.9	6.5	7.2	7.7	8.8
Tee-Branch Flow — Screwed	Steel	2.4	3.5	4.2	5.3	6.6	8.7	9.9	12	13	17	21	—	—	—	—	—	—	—	—	—	—
	C. I.	—	—	—	—	—	—	—	—	—	14	17	—	—	—	—	—	—	—	—	—	—
Tee-Branch Flow — Flanged	Steel	—	—	2	2.6	3.3	4.4	5.2	6.6	7.5	9.4	12	15	18	24	30	34	37	43	47	52	62
	C. I.	—	—	—	—	—	—	—	—	—	7.7	10	—	15	20	25	30	35	39	44	49	57

Fitting	Connection	Material	Equivalent length values (increasing pipe size →)
180° Return Bend	Screwed	Steel	2.3, 3.1, 3.6, 4.4, 5.2, 6.6, 7.4, 8.5, 9.3, 11, 11, 13
	Screwed	C.I.	—
	Reg. Flanged	Steel	0.92, 1.2, 1.6, 2.1, 2.4, 3.1, 3.6, 4.4, 5.9, 8.9, 12, 14, 17, 18, 21, 23, 25, 30
	Reg. Flanged	C.I.	1.1, 1.3, 1.6, 2, 2.3, 2.7, 2.9, 3.6, 4.8, 7.2, 9.8, 12, 15, 17, 19, 22, 24, 28
	Long Rad. Flanged	Steel	1.1, 1.3, 1.6, 2, 2.3, 2.7, 2.9, 3.4, 4.2, 5, 5.7, 7, 8, 9, 9.4, 10, 11, 12, 14
	Long Rad. Flanged	C.I.	2.8, 3.4, 4.2, 4.7, 5.7, 6.8, 7.8, 8.6, 9.6, 11, 11, 13
Globe Valve	Screwed	Steel	21, 22, 22, 24, 29, 37, 42, 54, 62, 79, 110
	Screwed	C.I.	65, 86
	Flanged	Steel	38, 40, 45, 54, 59, 70, 77, 94, 120, 150, 190, 260, 310, 390
	Flanged	C.I.	77, 99, 120, 150, 210, 270, 330
Gate Valve	Screwed	Steel	0.32, 0.45, 0.56, 0.67, 0.84, 1.1, 1.2, 1.5, 1.7, 1.9, 2.5
	Screwed	C.I.	1.6, 2
	Flanged	Steel	2.6, 2.7, 2.8, 2.9, 3.1, 3.2, 3.2, 3.2, 3.2, 3.2, 3.2, 3.2
	Flanged	C.I.	2.3, 2.4, 2.6, 2.7, 2.8, 2.9, 3, 3, 3, 3, 3
Angle Valve	Screwed	Steel	12.8, 15, 15, 17, 18, 18, 18, 18, 18, 15
	Screwed	C.I.	15, 15, 17, 18, 18, 18, 15
	Flanged	Steel	15, 15, 17, 18, 18, 18, 21, 22, 28, 38, 50, 63, 90, 120, 140, 160, 190, 210, 240, 300
	Flanged	C.I.	23, 31, 52, 74, 98, 120, 150, 170, 200, 230, 280
Swing Check Valve	Screwed	Steel	7.2, 7.3, 8, 8.8, 11, 13, 15, 17, 19, 22, 27, 38
	Screwed	C.I.	21, 22, 27, 38
	Flanged	Steel	3.8, 5.3, 7.2, 50, 63, 90, 120, 140
	Flanged	C.I.	0.14, 0.18, 0.21, 0.24, 0.29, 0.36, 0.39, 0.45, 0.47, 0.53, 0.65

(continued)

Table D-1   (continued)

Pipe Size

Fittings			1/4	3/8	1/2	3/4	1	1 1/4	1 1/2	2	2 1/2	3	4	5	6	8	10	12	14	16	18	20	24
Coupling or Union	Screwed	Steel	—	—	—	—	—	—	—	—	—	—	—	—	—	—	—	—	—	—	—	—	—
		C.I.	—	—	—	—	—	—	—	—	—	—	—	—	—	—	—	—	—	—	—	—	—
Bell Mouth Inlet		Steel	—	—	—	—	—	—	—	—	—	0.44	0.62	—	1.3	1.9	2.4	3	3.6	4.3	5	5.7	7
		C.I.	0.04	0.07	0.1	0.13	0.18	0.26	0.31	0.43	0.52	0.67	0.95	1.3	1.6	2.3	2.9	3.5	4	4.7	5.3	6.1	7.6
Square Mouth Inlet		Steel	—	—	—	—	—	—	—	—	—	0.55	0.77	—	13	19	24	30	36	43	50	57	70
		C.I.	0.44	0.68	0.96	1.3	1.8	2.6	3.1	4.3	5.2	6.7	9.5	13	16	23	29	35	40	47	53	61	76
Reentrant Pipe		Steel	—	—	—	—	—	—	—	—	—	5.5	7.7	—	26	37	49	61	73	86	100	110	140
		C.I.	0.88	1.4	1.9	2.6	3.6	5.1	6.2	8.5	10	13	19	25	32	45	58	70	80	95	110	120	150
Y-Strainer			—	4.6	5	6.6	7.7	18	20	27	29	34	42	53	61	—	—	—	—	—	—	—	—	—

Sudden Enlargement

$$h = \frac{(V_1 - V_2)^2}{(2g)} \text{ Feet of Liquid; If } V_2 = 0 \quad h = \frac{V^2}{(2g)} \text{ Feet of Liquid}$$

Courtesy The Hydraulic Institute (reprinted from the Standards of the Hydraulic Institute, Eleventh Edition, Copyright 1965)

Table D-2 Schedule 80 Pipe Dimensions

Size in in	Diameters External in	Diameters Internal in	Nominal Thickness in	Transverse Areas External in²	Transverse Areas Internal in²	Transverse Areas Metal in²	Length of Pipe Per Square Foot of External Surface ft	Length of Pipe Per Square Foot of Internal Surface ft	Cubic Feet per ft of Pipe	Weight per ft Pounds	Number Threads per in of Screw
⅛	0.405	0.215	0.095	0.129	0.036	0.093	9.431	17.75	0.00025	0.314	27
¼	0.54	0.302	0.119	0.229	0.072	0.157	7.073	12.65	0.0005	0.535	18
⅜	0.675	0.423	0.126	0.358	0.141	0.217	5.658	9.03	0.00098	0.738	18
½	0.84	0.546	0.147	0.554	0.234	0.32	4.547	7	0.00163	1	14
¾	1.05	0.742	0.154	0.866	0.433	0.433	3.637	5.15	0.003	1.47	14
1	1.315	0.957	0.179	1.358	0.719	0.639	2.904	3.995	0.005	2.17	11½
1¼	1.66	1.278	0.191	2.164	1.283	0.881	2.301	2.99	0.00891	3	11½
1½	1.9	1.5	0.2	2.835	1.767	1.068	2.01	2.542	0.01227	3.65	11½
2	2.375	1.939	0.218	4.43	2.953	1.477	1.608	1.97	0.02051	5.02	11½
2½	2.875	2.323	0.276	6.492	4.238	2.254	1.328	1.645	0.02943	7.66	8
3	3.5	2.9	0.3	9.621	6.605	3.016	1.091	1.317	0.04587	10.3	8
3½	4	3.364	0.318	12.56	8.888	3.678	0.954	1.135	0.06172	12.5	8
4	4.5	3.826	0.337	15.9	11.497	4.407	0.848	0.995	0.0798	14.9	8
5	5.563	4.813	0.375	24.3	18.194	6.112	0.686	0.792	0.1263	20.8	8
6	6.625	5.761	0.432	34.47	26.067	8.3	0.576	0.673	0.181	28.6	8
8	8.625	7.625	0.5	58.42	46.663	12.76	0.442	0.501	0.3171	43.4	8

(continued)

Table D-2 (continued)

| Size in | Diameters | | Nominal Thickness in | Transverse Areas | | | Length of Pipe Per Square Foot of | | Cubic Feet per ft of Pipe | Weight per ft Pounds | Number Threads per in of Screw |
	External in	Internal in		External in²	Internal in²	Metal in²	External Surface ft	Internal Surface ft			
10	10.75	9.564	0.593	90.76	71.84	18.92	0.355	0.4	0.4989	64.4	8
12	12.75	11.376	0.687	127.64	101.64	26	0.299	0.336	0.7058	88.6	
14	14	12.5	0.75	153.94	122.72	31.22	0.272	0.306	0.8522	107	
16	16	14.314	0.843	201.05	160.92	40.13	0.238	0.263	1.112	137	
18	18	16.126	0.937	254.85	204.24	50.61	0.212	0.237	1.418	171	
20	20	17.938	1.031	314.15	252.72	61.43	0.191	0.208	1.755	209	
24	24	21.564	1.218	452.4	365.22	87.18	0.159	0.177	2.536	297	

Courtesy Sarco Company, Inc.

Table D-3 Schedule 40 Pipe Dimensions

Size in	Diameters External in	Diameters Internal in	Nominal Thickness in	Transverse Areas External in²	Transverse Areas Internal in²	Transverse Areas Metal in²	Length of Pipe Per ft² of External Surface ft	Length of Pipe Per ft² of Internal Surface ft	Cubic Feet per ft of Pipe	Weight per ft Pounds	Number Threads per in of Screw
⅛	0.405	0.269	0.068	0.129	0.057	0.072	9.431	14.199	0.00039	0.244	27
¼	0.54	0.364	0.088	0.229	0.104	0.125	7.073	10.493	0.00072	0.424	18
⅜	0.675	0.493	0.091	0.358	0.191	0.167	5.658	7.747	0.00133	0.567	18
½	0.84	0.622	0.109	0.554	0.304	0.25	4.547	6.141	0.00211	0.85	14
¾	1.05	0.824	0.113	0.866	0.533	0.333	3.637	4.635	0.0037	1.13	14
1	1.315	1.049	0.133	1.358	0.864	0.494	2.904	3.641	0.006	1.678	11½
1¼	1.66	1.38	0.14	2.164	1.495	0.669	2.301	2.767	0.01039	2.272	11½
1½	1.9	1.61	0.145	2.835	2.036	0.799	2.01	2.372	0.01414	2.717	11½
2	2.375	2.067	0.154	4.43	3.355	1.075	1.608	1.847	0.0233	3.652	11½
2½	2.875	2.469	0.203	6.492	4.788	1.704	1.328	1.547	0.03325	5.793	8
3	3.5	3.068	0.216	9.621	7.393	2.228	1.091	1.245	0.05134	7.575	8
3½	4	3.548	0.226	12.56	9.886	2.68	0.954	1.076	0.06866	9.109	8
4	4.5	4.026	0.237	15.9	12.73	3.174	0.848	0.948	0.0884	10.79	8
5	5.563	5.047	0.258	24.3	20	4.3	0.686	0.756	0.1389	14.61	8
6	6.625	6.065	0.28	34.47	28.9	5.581	0.576	0.629	0.2006	18.97	8
8	8.625	7.981	0.322	58.42	50.02	8.399	0.442	0.478	0.3552	28.55	8

(continued)

Table D-3 (continued)

| Size in | Diameters | | Nominal Thickness in | Transverse Areas | | | Length of Pipe Per ft² of | | Cubic Feet per ft of Pipe | Weight per ft Pounds | Number Threads per in of Screw |
	External in	Internal in		External in²	Internal in²	Metal in²	External Surface ft	Internal Surface ft			
10	10.75	10.02	0.365	90.76	78.85	11.9	0.355	0.381	0.5476	40.48	8
12	12.75	11.938	0.406	127.64	111.9	15.74	0.299	0.318	0.7763	53.6	
14	14	13.125	0.437	153.94	135.3	18.64	0.272	0.28	0.9354	63	
16	16	15	0.5	201.05	176.7	24.35	0.238	0.254	1.223	78	
18	18	16.874	0.563	254.85	224	30.85	0.212	0.226	1.555	105	
20	20	18.814	0.593	314.15	278	36.15	0.191	0.203	1.926	123	
24	24	22.626	0.687	452.4	402.1	50.3	0.159	0.169	2.793	171	

Courtesy Sarco Company, Inc.

Table D-4 Properties of Saturated Steam

Gauge Pressure psig	Temperature °F	Heat in Btu/lb			Specific Volume ft³/lb	Gauge Pressure psig	Temperature °F	Heat in Btu/lb			Specific Volume ft³ per lb
		Sensible	Latent	Total				Sensible	Latent	Total	
25	134	102	1017	1119	142	150	366	339	857	1196	2.74
20	162	129	1001	1130	73.9	155	368	341	885	1196	2.68
15	179	147	990	1137	51.3	160	371	344	853	1197	2.6
10	192	160	982	1142	39.4	165	373	346	851	1197	2.54
5	203	171	976	1147	31.8	170	375	348	849	1197	2.47
0	212	180	970	1150	26.8	175	377	351	847	1198	2.41
1	215	183	968	1151	25.2	180	380	353	845	1198	2.34
2	219	187	966	1153	23.5	185	382	355	843	1198	2.29
3	222	190	964	1154	22.3	190	384	358	841	1199	2.24
4	224	192	962	1154	21.4	195	386	360	839	1199	2.19
5	227	195	960	1155	20.1	200	388	362	837	1199	2.14
6	230	198	959	1157	19.4	205	390	364	836	1200	2.09
7	232	200	957	1157	18.7	210	392	366	834	1200	2.05
8	233	201	956	1157	18.4	215	394	368	832	1200	2
9	237	205	954	1159	17.1	220	396	370	830	1200	1.96
10	239	207	953	1160	16.5	225	397	372	828	1200	1.92
12	244	212	949	1161	15.3	230	399	374	827	1201	1.89
14	248	216	947	1163	14.3	235	401	376	825	1201	1.85

In Vac.

(continued)

Table D-4 (continued)

Gauge Pressure psig	Temperature °F	Heat in Btu/lb Sensible	Heat in Btu/lb Latent	Heat in Btu/lb Total	Specific Volume ft³/lb	Gauge Pressure psig	Temperature °F	Heat in Btu/lb Sensible	Heat in Btu/lb Latent	Heat in Btu/lb Total	Specific Volume ft³ per lb
16	252	220	944	1164	13.4	240	403	378	823	1201	1.81
18	256	224	941	1165	12.6	245	404	380	822	1202	1.78
20	259	227	939	1166	11.9	250	406	382	820	1202	1.75
22	262	230	937	1167	11.3	255	408	383	819	1202	1.72
24	265	233	934	1167	10.8	260	409	385	817	1202	1.69
26	268	236	933	1169	10.3	265	411	387	815	1202	1.66
28	271	239	930	1169	9.85	270	413	389	814	1203	1.63
30	274	243	929	1172	9.46	275	414	391	812	1203	1.6
32	277	246	927	1173	9.1	280	416	392	811	1203	1.57
34	279	248	925	1173	8.75	285	417	394	809	1203	1.55
36	282	251	923	1174	8.42	290	418	395	808	1203	1.53
38	284	253	922	1175	8.08	295	420	397	806	1203	1.49
40	286	256	920	1176	7.82	300	421	398	805	1203	1.47
42	289	258	918	1176	7.57	305	423	400	803	1203	1.45
44	291	260	917	1177	7.31	310	425	402	802	1204	1.43
46	293	262	915	1177	7.14	315	426	404	800	1204	1.41
48	295	264	914	1178	6.94	320	427	405	799	1204	1.38
50	298	267	912	1179	6.68	325	429	407	797	1204	1.36
55	300	271	909	1180	6.27	330	430	408	796	1204	1.34

Table D-4 (continued)

Gauge Pressure psig	Temperature °F	Heat in Btu/lb Sensible	Latent	Total	Specific Volume ft³/lb	Gauge Pressure psig	Temperature °F	Heat in Btu/lb Sensible	Latent	Total	Specific Volume ft³ per lb
60	307	277	906	1183	5.84	335	432	410	794	1204	1.33
65	312	282	901	1183	5.49	340	433	411	793	1204	1.31
70	316	286	898	1184	5.18	345	434	413	791	1204	1.29
75	320	290	895	1185	4.91	350	435	414	790	1204	1.28
80	324	294	891	1185	4.67	355	437	416	789	1205	1.26
85	328	298	889	1187	4.44	360	438	417	788	1205	1.24
90	331	302	886	1188	4.24	365	440	419	786	1205	1.22
95	335	305	883	1188	4.05	370	441	420	785	1205	1.2
100	338	309	880	1189	3.89	375	442	421	784	1205	1.19
105	341	312	878	1190	3.74	380	443	422	783	1205	1.18
110	344	316	875	1191	3.59	385	445	424	781	1205	1.16
115	347	319	873	1192	3.46	390	446	425	780	1205	1.14
120	350	322	871	1193	3.34	395	447	427	778	1205	1.13
125	353	325	868	1193	3.23	400	448	428	777	1205	1.12
130	356	328	866	1194	3.12	450	460	439	766	1205	1
140	361	333	861	1194	2.92	500	470	453	751	1204	0.89
145	363	336	859	1195	2.84	550	479	464	740	1204	0.82
						600	489	475	728	1203	0.74

Table D-5   Friction Loss for Water in Feet per 100 Feet of Schedule 40 Steel Pipe

U.S. gal/min	Velocity ft/sc	hf Friction	U.S. gal/min	Vel. ft/sec	hf Friction
	³⁄₈" Pipe			**½" Pipe**	
1.4	2.25	9.03	2	2.11	5.5
1.6	2.68	11.6	2.5	2.64	8.24
1.8	3.02	14.3	3	3.17	11.5
2	3.36	17.3	3.5	3.7	15.3
2.5	4.2	26	4	4.22	19.7
3	5.04	36.6	5	5.28	29.7
3.5	5.88	49	6	6.34	42
4	6.72	63.2	7	7.39	56
5	8.4	96.1	8	8.45	72.1
6	10.08	136	9	9.5	90.1
7	11.8	182	10	10.56	110.6
8	13.4	236	12	12.7	156
9	15.1	297	14	14.8	211
10	16.8	364	16	16.9	270
	¾" Pipe			**1" Pipe**	
4	2.41	4.85	6	2.23	3.16
5	3.01	7.27	8	2.97	5.2
6	3.61	10.2	10	3.71	7.9
7	4.21	13.6	12	4.45	11.1
8	4.81	17.3	14	5.2	14.7
9	5.42	21.6	16	5.94	19
10	6.02	26.5	18	6.68	23.7
12	7.22	37.5	20	7.42	28.9
14	8.42	50	22	8.17	34.8
16	9.63	64.8	24	8.91	41
18	10.8	80.9	26	9.65	47.8
20	12	99	28	10.39	55.1
22	13.2	120	30	11.1	62.9
24	14.4	141	35	13	84.4
26	15.6	165	40	14.8	109
28	16.8	189	45	16.7	137
			50	18.6	168

(continued)

Table D-5 (continued)

U.S. gal/min	Velocity ft/sc	hf Friction	U.S. gal/min	Vel. ft/sec	hf Friction
	1¼" Pipe			1½" Pipe	
12	2.57	2.85	16	2.52	2.26
14	3	3.77	18	2.84	2.79
16	3.43	4.83	20	3.15	3.38
18	3.86	6	22	3.47	4.05
20	4.29	7.3	24	3.78	4.76
22	4.72	8.72	26	4.1	5.54
24	5.15	10.27	28	4.41	6.34
26	5.58	11.94	30	4.73	7.2
28	6.01	13.7	35	5.51	9.63
30	6.44	15.6	40	6.3	12.41
35	7.51	21.9	45	7.04	15.49
40	8.58	27.1	50	7.88	18.9
45	9.65	33.8	55	8.67	22.7
50	10.7	41.4	60	9.46	26.7
55	11.8	49.7	65	10.24	31.2
60	12.9	58.6	70	11.03	36
65	13.9	68.6	75	11.8	41.2
70	15	79.2	80	12.6	46.6
75	16.1	90.6	85	13.4	52.4
			90	14.2	58.7
			95	15	65
			100	15.8	71.6
	2" Pipe			2½" Pipe	
25	2.39	1.48	35	2.35	1.15
30	2.87	2.1	40	2.68	1.47
35	3.35	2.79	45	3.02	1.84
40	3.82	3.57	50	3.35	2.23
45	4.3	4.4	60	4.02	3.13
50	4.78	5.37	70	4.69	4.18
60	5.74	7.58	80	5.36	5.36
70	6.69	10.2	90	6.03	6.69
80	7.65	13.1	100	6.7	8.18
90	8.6	16.3	120	8.04	11.5

(continued)

Table D-5 *(continued)*

U.S. gal/min	Velocity ft/sc	hf Friction	U.S. gal/min	Vel. ft/sec	hf Friction
	2" Pipe			**2½" Pipe**	
100	4.34	2.72	200	5.04	12.61
120	11.5	28.5	160	10.7	20
140	13.4	38.2	180	12.1	25.2
160	15.3	49.5	200	13.4	30.7
			220	14.7	37.1
			240	16.1	43.8
	3" Pipe			**4" Pipe**	
50	2.17	0.762	100	2.52	0.718
60	2.6	1.06	120	3.02	1.01
70	3.04	1.4	140	3.53	1.35
80	3.47	1.81	160	4.03	1.71
90	3.91	2.26	180	4.54	2.14
100	3.34	2.75	200	5.04	2.61
120	5.21	3.88	220	5.54	3.13
140	6.08	5.19	240	6.05	3.7
160	6.94	6.68	260	6.55	4.3
180	7.81	8.38	280	7.06	4.95
200	8.68	10.2	300	7.56	5.63
220	9.55	12.3	350	8.82	7.54
240	10.4	14.5	400	10.1	9.75
260	11.3	16.9	450	11.4	12.3
280	12.2	19.5	500	12.6	14.4
300	13	22.1	550	13.9	18.1
350	15.2	30	600	15.1	21.4
	5" Pipe			**6" Pipe**	
160	2.57	0.557	220	2.44	0.411
180	2.89	0.698	240	2.66	0.482
200	3.21	0.847	260	2.89	0.56
220	3.53	1.01	300	3.33	0.733
240	3.85	1.19	350	3.89	0.98
260	4.17	1.38	400	4.44	1.25
300	4.81	1.82	450	5	1.56

(continued)

Table D-5 (continued)

U.S. gal/min	Velocity ft/sc	hf Friction	U.S. gal/min	Vel. ft/sec	hf Friction
350	5.61	2.43	500	5.55	1.91
400	6.41	3.13	600	6.66	2.69
450	7.22	3.92	700	7.77	3.6
500	8.02	4.79	800	8.88	4.64
600	9.62	6.77	900	9.99	5.81
700	11.2	9.13	1000	11.1	7.1
800	12.8	11.8	1100	12.2	8.52
900	14.4	14.8	1200	13.3	10.1
1000	16	18.2	1300	14.4	11.7
			1400	15.5	13.6

Courtesy Sarco Company, Inc.

Table D-6 Flow of Water through Schedule 40 Steel Pipe

Pressure Drop 1000 Feet of Schedule 40 Steel Pipe, in Pounds per Square Inch

Discharge gal/min	1" Velocity ft/sec	1" Pressure Drop	1¼" Velocity ft/sec	1¼" Pressure Drop	1½" Velocity ft/sec	1½" Pressure Drop	2" Velocity ft/sec	2" Pressure Drop	2½" Velocity ft/sec	2½" Pressure Drop	3" Velocity ft/sec	3" Pressure Drop	3½" Velocity ft/sec	3½" Pressure Drop	4" Velocity ft/sec	4" Pressure Drop	5" Velocity ft/sec	5" Pressure Drop
1	0.37	0.49																
2	0.74	1.7																
3	1.12	3.53	0.43	0.45														
4	1.49	5.94	0.64	0.94	0.47	0.44												
5	1.86	9.02	0.86	1.55	0.63	0.74												
6	2.24	12.25	1.07	2.36	0.79	1.12	0.57	0.46										
8	2.98	21.1	1.28	3.3	0.95	1.53	0.76	0.75										
10	3.72	30.8	1.72	5.52	1.26	2.63	0.96	1.14	0.67	0.48								
15	5.6	64.6	2.14	8.34	1.57	3.86	1.43	2.33	1	0.99								
20	7.44	110.5	3.21	17.6	2.36	8.13	1.91	3.86	1.34	1.64	0.87	0.59						
25			4.29	29.1	3.15	13.5	2.39	5.81	1.68	2.48	1.08	0.67	0.81	0.42				
30			5.36	43.7	3.94	20.2	2.87	8.04	2.01	3.43	1.3	1.21	0.97	0.6				
35			6.43	62.9	4.72	29.1	3.35	10.95	2.35	4.49	1.52	1.58	1.14	0.79	0.88	0.42		
40			7.51	82.5	5.51	38.2	3.82	13.7	2.68	5.88	1.74	2.06	1.3	1	1.01	0.53		
45					6.3	47.8	4.3	17.4	3	7.14	1.95	2.51	1.46	1.21	1.13	0.67		
50					7.08	60.6	4.78	20.6	3.35	8.82	2.17	3.1	1.62	1.44	1.26	0.8		
60					7.87	74.7	5.74	29.6	4.02	12.2	2.6	4.29	1.95	2.07	1.51	1.1		
70							6.69	38.6	4.69	15.3	3.04	5.84	2.27	2.71	1.76	1.5	1.12	0.48

Table D-6 (continued)

Pressure Drop 1000 Feet of Schedule 40 Steel Pipe, in Pounds per Square Inch

Note: The original is a single wide table rotated on the page. Only the 6", 8", and 10" pipe-size markers are printed on this (continued) page; the remaining velocity/pressure-drop column pairs are for the smaller pipe sizes carried over from the preceding page.

Dis-charge gal/min	Veloc-ity ft/sec	Pres-sure Drop	Veloc-ity ft/sec	Pres-sure Drop	Veloc-ity ft/sec	Pres-sure Drop	Veloc-ity ft/sec	Pres-sure Drop	Veloc-ity ft/sec	Pres-sure Drop	Veloc-ity ft/sec	Pres-sure Drop	Veloc-ity ft/sec (6")	Pres-sure Drop	Veloc-ity ft/sec (8")	Pres-sure Drop	Veloc-ity ft/sec (10")	Pres-sure Drop
80	7.65	50.3	5.37	21.7	3.48	7.62	2.59	3.53	2.01	1.87	1.28	0.63						
90	8.6	63.6	6.04	26.1	3.91	9.22	2.92	4.46	2.26	2.37	1.44	0.8						
100	9.56	75.1	6.71	32.3	4.34	11.4	3.24	5.27	2.52	2.81	1.6	0.95	1.11	0.39				
125			8.38	48.2	5.45	17.1	4.05	7.86	3.15	4.38	2	1.48	1.39	0.56				
150			10.06	60.4	6.51	23.3	4.86	11.3	3.78	6.02	2.41	2.04	1.67	0.78				
175			11.73	90	7.59	32	5.67	14.7	4.41	8.2	2.81	2.78	1.94	1.06				
200					8.68	39.7	6.48	19.2	5.04	10.2	3.21	3.46	2.22	1.32				
225					9.77	50.2	7.29	23.1	5.67	12.9	3.61	4.37	2.5	1.66	1.44	0.44		
250					10.85	61.9	8.1	28.5	6.3	15.9	4.01	5.14	2.78	2.05	1.6	0.55		
275					11.94	75	8.91	34.4	6.93	18.3	4.41	6.22	3.06	2.36	1.75	0.63		
300					13.02	84.7	9.72	40.9	7.56	21.8	4.81	7.41	3.33	2.8	1.92	0.75		
325							10.53	45.5	8.18	25.5	5.21	8.25	3.61	3.29	2.03	0.88		
350							11.35	52.7	8.82	29.7	5.61	9.57	3.89	3.62	2.24	0.97		
375							12.17	60.7	9.45	32.3	6.01	11	4.16	4.16	2.4	1.11		
400							12.97	68.9	10.08	39.7	6.41	12.9	4.44	4.72	2.55	1.27		
425							13.78	77.8	10.7	41.5	6.82	14.1	4.72	5.34	2.27	1.43		
450									11.33	46.5	7.22	15	5	5.96	2.83	1.6		
475									11.96	51.7	7.62	16.7	5.27	6.66	3.04	1.69	1.93	0.3

(continued)

Table D-6 (continued)

Pressure Drop 1000 Feet of Schedule 40 Steel Pipe, in Pounds per Square Inch

Dis-charge gal/min	Veloc-ity ft/sec	Pres-sure Drop	Veloc-ity ft/sec	Pres-sure Drop	Veloc-ity ft/sec	Pres-sure Drop	Veloc-ity ft/sec (12")	Pres-sure Drop	Veloc-ity ft/sec (14")	Pres-sure Drop	Veloc-ity ft/sec (16")	Pres-sure Drop	Veloc-ity ft/sec (18")	Pres-sure Drop	Veloc-ity ft/sec	Pres-sure Drop	Veloc-ity ft/sec	Pres-sure Drop
500	5.55	7.39	3.2	1.87	2.04	0.63									12.59	57.3	8.02	18.5
550	6.11	8.94	3.53	2.26	2.24	0.7									13.84	69.3	8.82	22.4
600	6.66	10.6	3.85	2.7	2.44	0.86									15.1	82.5	9.62	26.7
650	7.21	11.8	4.17	3.16	2.65	1.01											10.42	31.3
700	7.77	13.7	4.49	3.69	2.85	1.18	2.01	0.48									11.22	36.3
750	8.32	15.7	4.81	4.21	3.05	1.35	2.15	0.55									12.02	41.6
800	8.88	17.8	5.13	4.79	3.26	1.54	2.29	0.62									12.82	44.7
850	9.44	20.2	5.45	5.11	3.46	1.74	2.44	0.7	2.02	0.43							13.62	50.5
900	10	22.6	5.77	5.73	3.66	1.94	2.58	0.79	2.14	0.48							14.42	56.6
950	10.55	23.7	6.09	6.38	3.87	2.23	2.72	0.88	2.25	0.53							15.22	63.1
1,000	11.1	26.3	6.41	7.08	4.07	2.4	2.87	0.98	2.38	0.59							16.02	70
1,100	12.22	31.8	7.05	8.56	4.48	2.74	3.16	1.18	2.61	0.68							17.63	84.6
1,200	13.32	37.8	7.69	10.2	4.88	3.27	3.45	1.4	2.85	0.81	2.18	0.4						
1,300	14.43	44.4	8.33	11.3	5.29	3.86	3.73	1.56	3.09	0.95	2.36	0.47						
1,400	15.54	51.5	8.97	13	5.7	4.44	4.02	1.8	3.32	1.1	2.54	0.54						
1,500	16.65	55.5	9.62	15	6.1	5.11	4.3	2.07	3.55	1.19	2.73	0.62						
1,600	17.76	68.1	10.26	17	6.51	5.46	4.59	2.36	3.8	1.35	2.91	0.71						
1,800	19.98	79.8	11.54	21.6	7.32	6.91	5.16	2.98	4.27	1.71	3.27	0.85	2.58	0.48				

Table D-6 (continued)

Pressure Drop 1000 Feet of Schedule 40 Steel Pipe, in Pounds per Square Inch

Dis-charge gal/min	Veloc-ity ft/sec	Pres-sure Drop	Veloc-ity ft/sec	Pres-sure Drop	Veloc-ity ft/sec	Pres-sure Drop	Veloc-ity ft/sec	Pres-sure Drop	Veloc-ity ft/sec	Pres-sure Drop	Veloc-ity ft/sec	Pres-sure Drop	Veloc-ity ft/sec	Pres-sure Drop	Veloc-ity 20" ft/sec	Pres-sure Drop	Veloc-ity 24" ft/sec	Pres-sure Drop
2,000	22.2	98.5	12.83	25	8.13	8.54	5.73	3.47	4.74	2.11	3.63	1.05	2.88	0.56				
2,500			16.03	39	10.18	12.5	7.17	5.41	5.92	3.09	4.54	1.63	3.59	0.88				
3,000			19.24	52.4	12.21	18	8.6	7.31	7.12	4.45	5.45	2.21	4.31	1.27	3.45	0.73		
3,500			22.43	71.4	14.25	22.9	10.03	9.95	8.32	6.18	6.35	3	5.03	1.52	4.03	0.94		
4,000			25.65	93.3	16.28	29.9	11.48	13	9.49	7.92	7.25	3.92	5.74	2.12	4.61	1.22	3.19	0.51
4,500					18.31	37.8	12.9	15.4	10.67	9.36	8.17	4.97	6.47	2.5	5.19	1.55	3.59	0.6
5,000					20.35	46.7	14.34	18.9	11.84	11.6	9.08	5.72	7.17	3.08	5.76	1.78	3.99	0.74
6,000					24.42	67.2	17.21	27.3	14.32	15.4	10.88	8.24	8.62	4.45	6.92	2.57	4.8	1
7,000					28.5	85.1	20.08	37.2	16.6	21	12.69	12.2	10.04	6.06	8.06	3.5	5.68	1.36
8,000							22.95	45.1	18.98	27.4	14.52	13.6	11.48	7.34	9.23	4.57	6.38	1.78
9,000							25.8	57	21.35	34.7	16.32	17.2	12.92	9.2	10.37	5.36	7.19	2.25
10,000							28.63	70.4	23.75	42.9	18.16	21.2	14.37	11.5	11.53	6.63	7.96	2.78
12,000							34.38	93.6	28.5	61.8	21.8	30.9	17.23	16.5	13.83	9.54	9.57	3.71
14,000									33.2	84	25.42	41.6	20.1	20.7	16.14	12	11.18	5.05
16,000											29.05	54.4	22.96	27.1	18.43	15.7	12.77	6.6

Courtesy Sarco Company, Inc.

623

Table D-7 Warmup Load in Pounds of Steam per 100 Feet of Steam Main (Ambient Temperature 70°F)^a*

Steam Pressure (psig)	Main Size														0°F Correction Factor†
	2"	2½"	3"	4"	5"	6"	8"	10"	12"	14"	16"	18"	20"	24"	
0	6.2	9.7	12.8	18.2	24.6	31.9	48	68	90	107	140	176	207	208	1.5
5	6.9	11	14.4	20.4	27.7	35.9	48	77	101	120	157	198	233	324	1.44
10	7.5	11.8	15.5	22	29.9	38.8	58	83	109	130	169	213	251	350	1.41
20	8.4	13.4	17.5	24.9	33.8	43.9	66	93	124	146	191	241	284	396	1.37
40	3.9	15.8	20.6	29.3	39.7	51.6	78	110	145	172	225	284	334	465	1.32
60	11	17.5	22.9	32.6	44.2	57.3	86	122	162	192	250	316	372	518	1.29
80	12	19	24.9	35.3	47.9	62.1	93	132	175	208	271	342	403	561	1.27
100	12.8	20.3	26.6	37.8	51.2	66.5	100	142	188	222	290	366	431	600	1.26
125	13.7	21.7	28.4	40.4	54.8	71.1	107	152	200	238	310	391	461	642	1.25
150	14.5	23	30	42.8	58	75.2	113	160	212	251	328	414	487	679	1.24
175	15.3	24.2	31.7	45.1	61.2	79.4	119	169	224	265	347	437	514	716	1.23
200	16	25.3	33.1	47.1	63.8	82.8	125	177	234	277	362	456	537	748	1.22
250	17.2	27.3	35.8	50.8	68.9	89.4	134	191	252	299	390	492	579	807	1.21
300	25	38.3	51.3	74.8	104	142.7	217	322	443	531	682	854	1045	1182	1.2
400	27.8	42.6	57.1	83.2	115.7	158.7	241	358	493	590	759	971	1163	1650	1.18
500	30.2	46.3	62.1	90.5	125.7	172.6	262	389	535	642	825	1033	1263	1793	1.17
600	32.7	50.1	67.1	97.9	136	186.6	284	421	579	694	893	1118	1367	1939	1.16

*Loads based on Schedule 40 pipe for pressures up to and including 250 psig and on Schedule 80 pipe for pressures above 250 psig.
†For outdoor temperature of 0°F; multiply load value in table for each main size by correction factor corresponding to steam pressure.
Courtesy Sarco Company, Inc.

Table D-8 Condensation Load in Pounds per Hour per 100 Feet of Insulated Steam Main (Ambient Temperature 70°F; Insulation 80% Efficient)*

Steam Pressure (psig)	Main Size														0°F Correction Factor†
	2"	2½"	3"	4"	5"	6"	8"	10"	12"	14"	16"	18"	20"	24"	
10	6	7	9	11	13	16	20	24	29	32	36	39	44	53	1.58
30	8	9	11	14	17	20	26	32	38	42	48	51	57	68	1.5
60	10	12	14	18	24	27	33	41	49	54	62	67	74	89	1.45
100	12	15	18	22	28	33	41	51	61	67	77	83	93	111	1.41
125	13	16	20	24	30	36	45	56	66	73	84	90	101	121	1.39
175	16	19	23	26	33	38	53	66	78	86	98	107	119	142	1.38
250	18	22	27	34	42	50	62	77	92	101	116	126	140	168	1.36
300	20	25	30	37	46	54	68	85	101	111	126	138	154	184	1.35
400	23	28	34	43	53	63	80	99	118	130	148	162	180	216	1.33
500	27	33	39	49	61	73	91	114	135	148	170	185	206	246	1.32
600	30	37	44	55	68	82	103	128	152	167	191	208	232	277	1.31

*Chart loads represent losses due to radiation and convection for saturated steam.

†For outdoor temperature of 0°F, multiply load value in table for each main size by correction factor corresponding to steam pressure.

Courtesy Sarco Company, Inc.

Table D-9 Flange Standards (All dimensions are in inches)

Pipe Size	125-lb Cast Iron		ASA B16.1												
	1/2	3/4	1	1 1/4	1 1/2	2	2 1/2	3	3 1/2	4	5	6	8	10	12
Diameter of Flange			4 1/4	4 5/8	5	6	7	7 1/2	8 1/2	9	10	11	13 1/2	16	19
Thickness of Flange (min)[1]			7/16	1/2	9/16	5/8	11/16	3/4	13/16	15/16	15/16	1	1 1/8	1 3/16	1 1/4
Diameter of Bolt Circle			3 1/8	3 1/2	3 7/8	4 3/4	5 1/2	6	7	7 1/2	8 1/2	9 1/2	11 3/4	14 1/4	17
Number of Bolts			4	4	4	4	4	4	8	8	8	8	8	12	12
Diameter of Bolts			1/2	1/2	1/2	5/8	5/8	5/8	5/8	5/8	3/4	3/4	3/4	7/8	7/8

Pipe Size	ASA B16.2														
250-lb Cast Iron															
	1/2	3/4	1	1 1/4	1 1/2	2	2 1/2	3	3 1/2	4	5	6	8	10	12
Diameter of Flange			4 7/8	5 1/4	6 1/8	6 1/2	7 1/2	8 1/4	9	10	11	12 1/2	15	17 1/2	20 1/2
Thickness of Flange (min)[2]			11/16	3/4	13/16	7/8	1	1 1/8	1 3/16	1 1/4	1 3/8	1 7/16	1 5/8	1 7/8	2
Diameter of Raised Face			2 11/16	3 1/16	3 9/16	4 3/16	4 15/16	5 5/16	6 5/16	6 15/16	8 5/16	9 11/16	11 15/16	14 1/16	16 7/16
Diameter of Bolt Circle			3 1/2	3 7/8	4 1/2	5	5 7/8	6 5/8	7 1/4	7 7/8	9 1/4	10 5/8	13	15 1/4	17 3/4
Number of Bolts			4	4	4	8	8	8	8	8	8	12	12	16	16
Diameter of Bolts			5/8	5/8	3/4	5/8	3/4	3/4	3/4	3/4	3/4	3/4	7/8	1	1 1/8

(continued)

Table D-9 (continued)

Pipe Size	150-lb Bronze								ASA B16.24						
	1/2	3/4	1	1 1/4	1 1/2	2	2 1/2	3	3 1/2	4	5	6	8	10	12
Diameter of Flange	3 1/2	3 7/8	4 1/4	4 5/8	5	6	7	7 1/2	8 1/2	9	10	11	13 1/2	16	19
Thickness of Flange (min)[3]	5/16	11/32	3/8	13/32	7/16	1/2	9/16	5/8	11/16	11/16	3/4	13/16	15/16	1	1 1/16
Diameter of Bolt Circle	2 3/8	2 3/4	3 1/8	3 1/2	3 7/8	4 3/4	5 1/2	6	7	7 1/2	8 1/2	9 1/2	11 3/4	14 1/4	17
Number of Bolts	4	4	4	4	4	4	4	4	8	8	8	8	8	12	12
Diameter of Bolts	1/2	1/2	1/2	1/2	1/2	5/8	5/8	5/8	5/8	5/8	3/4	3/4	3/4	7/8	7/8

ASA B16.24

300-lb Bronze

Pipe Size	1/2	3/4	1	1 1/4	1 1/2	2	2 1/2	3	3 1/2	4	5	6	8	10	12
Diameter of Flange	3 3/4	4 5/8	4 7/8	5 1/4	6 1/8	6 1/2	7 1/2	8 1/4	9	10	11	12 1/2	15		
Thickness of Flange (min)[4]	1/2	17/32	19/32	5/8	11/16	3/4	13/16	29/32	31/32	1 1/16	1 1/8	1 3/16	1 3/8		
Diameter of Bolt Circle	2 5/8	3 1/4	3 1/2	3 7/8	4 1/2	5	5 7/8	6 5/8	7 1/4	7 7/8	9 1/4	10 5/8	13		
Number of Bolts	4	4	4	4	4	8	8	8	8	8	8	12	12		
Diameter of Bolts	1/2	5/8	5/8	5/8	3/4	5/8	3/4	3/4	3/4	3/4	3/4	3/4	7/8		

(continued)

Table D-9 (continued)

Pipe Size	150-lb Steel		ASA B16.5												
	1/2	3/4	1	1 1/4	1 1/2	2	2 1/2	3	3 1/2	4	5	6	8	10	12
Diameter of Flange			4 1/4	4 5/8	5	6	7	7 1/2	8 1/2	9	10	11	13 1/2	16	19
Thickness of Flange (min)[5]			7/16	1/2	9/16	5/8	11/16	3/4	13/16	15/16	15/16	1	1 1/8	1 3/16	1 1/4
Diameter of Raised Face			2	2 1/2	2 7/8	3 5/8	4 1/8	5	5 1/2	6 3/16	7 5/16	8 1/2	10 5/8	12 3/4	15
Diameter of Bolt Circle			3 1/8	3 1/2	3 7/8	4 3/4	5 1/2	6	7	7 1/2	8 1/2	9 1/2	11 3/4	14 1/4	17
Number of Bolts			4	4	4	4	4	4	8	8	8	8	8	12	12
Diameter of Bolts			1/2	1/2	1/2	5/8	5/8	5/8	5/8	5/8	3/4	3/4	3/4	7/8	7/8

Pipe Size	300-lb Steel														
	1/2	3/4	1	1 1/4	1 1/2	2	2 1/2	3	3 1/2	4	5	6	8	10	12
Diameter of Flange	4 7/8	5 1/4	6 1/8	6 1/2	7 1/2	8 1/4	9	10	11	12 1/2	15	17 1/2	20 1/2		
Thickness of Flange (min)[6]	11/16	3/4		13/16	7/8	1	1 1/8	1 3/16	1 1/4	1 3/8	1 7/16	1 5/8	1 7/8	2	
Diameter of Raised Face	2	2 1/2	2 7/8	3 5/8	4 1/8	5	5 1/2	6 3/16	7 5/16	8 1/2	10 5/8	12 3/4	15		
Diameter of Bolt Circle	3 1/2	3 7/8	4 1/2	5	5 5/8	6 5/8	7 1/4	7 7/8	9 1/4	10 5/8	13	15 1/4	17 3/4		
Number of Bolts	4	4	4	8	8	8	8	8	8	12	12	16	16		
Diameter of Bolts	5/8	5/8	3/4	5/8	3/4	3/4	3/4	3/4	3/4	3/4	7/8	1	1 1/8		

(continued)

Table D-9 (continued)

Pipe Size	400-lb Steel								ASA B16.5						
	1/2	3/4	1	1 1/4	1 1/2	2	2 1/2	3	3 1/2	4	5	6	8	10	12
Diameter of Flange	3 3/4	4 5/8	4 7/8	5 1/4	6 1/8	6 1/2	7 1/2	8 1/4	9	10	11	12 1/2	15	17 1/2	20 1/2
Thickness of Flange (min)[7]	9/16	5/8	11/16	13/16	7/8	1	1 1/8	1 1/4	1 3/8	1 3/8	1 1/2	1 5/8	7/8	2 1/8	2 1/4
Diameter of Raised	1 3/8	1 11/16	2	2 1/2	2 7/8	3 5/8	4 1/8	5	5 1/2	6 3/16	7 5/16	8 1/2	10 5/8	12 3/4	15
Diameter of Bolt Circle	2 5/8	3 1/4	3 1/2	3 7/8	4 1/2	5	5 7/8	6 5/8	7 1/4	7 7/8	9 1/4	10 5/8	13	15 1/4	17 3/4
Number of Bolts	4	4	4	4	4	8	8	8	8	8	8	12	12	16	16
Diameter of Bolts	1/2	5/8	5/8	5/8	3/4	3/4	7/8	7/8	7/8	7/8	1	1 1/8	1 1/4		

600-lb Steel

ASA B16.5

Pipe Size	½	¾	1	1¼	1½	2	2½	3	3½	4	5	6	8	10	12
Diameter of Flange	3¾	4⅝	4⅞	5¼	6⅛	6½	7½	8¼	9	10¾	13	14	16½	20	22
Thickness of Flange (min)[8]	9/16	⅝	11/16	13/16	⅞	1	1⅛	1¼	1⅜	1½	1¾	1⅞	2³/₁₆	2½	2⅝
Diameter of Raised	1⅜	1¹¹/₁₆	2	2½	2⅞	3⅝	4⅛	5	5½	6³/₁₆	7⁵/₁₆	8½	10⅝	12¾	15
Diameter of Bolt Circle	2⅝	3¼	3½	3⅞	4½	5	5⅞	6⅝	7¼	8½	10½	11½	13¼	17	19½
Number of Bolts	4	4	4	4	4	8	8	8	8	8	8	12	12	16	20
Diameter of Bolts	½	⅝	⅝	⅝	¾	⅝	¾	¾	⅞	⅞	1	1	1⅛	1¼	1¼

[1] 125-lb. flanges have plain faces.
[2] 250-lb. flanges have a ¹/₁₆" raised face, which is included in the flange thickness dimensions.
[3] 150-lb. bronze flanges have plain faces with two concentric gasket-retaining grooves between the port and the bolt holes.
[4] 300-lb. bronze flanges have plain faces with two concentric gasket-retaining grooves between the port and the bolt holes.
[5] 150-lb. steel flanges have a ¹/₁₆" raised face, which is included in the flange thickness dimensions.
[6] 300-lb. steel flanges have a ¹/₁₆" raised face, which is included in the flange thickness dimensions.
[7] 400-lb. steel flanges have a ¼" raised face, which is NOT included in the flange dimensions.
[8] 600-lb. steel flanges have a ¼" raised face, which is NOT included in the flange dimensions.

Table D-10   Pressure Drop in Schedule 40 Pipe

100 PSIG SATURATED STEAM
FOR OTHER PRESSURES USE CORRECTION FACTORS

PSI	0	2	5	10	15	20	30	40	60	75	90	100	110	125	150	175	200	225	250	300	350	400	500	600
FACTOR	6.9	6.0	5.2	4.3	3.6	3.1	2.4	2.0	1.5	1.3	1.1	1.0	0.92	0.83	0.70	0.62	0.55	0.49	0.45	0.38	0.33	0.29	0.23	0.19

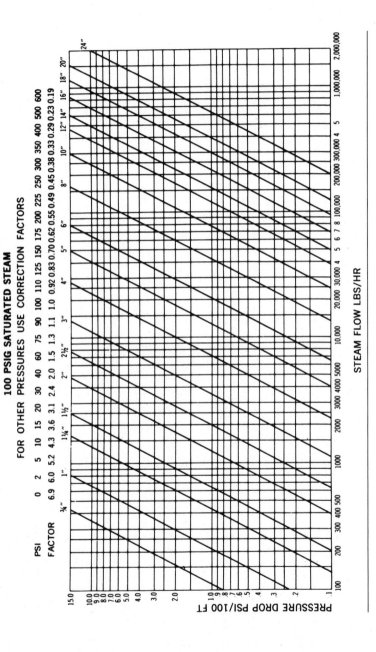

STEAM FLOW LBS/HR

PRESSURE DROP PSI/100 FT

634

Table D-11   Steam Velocity Chart

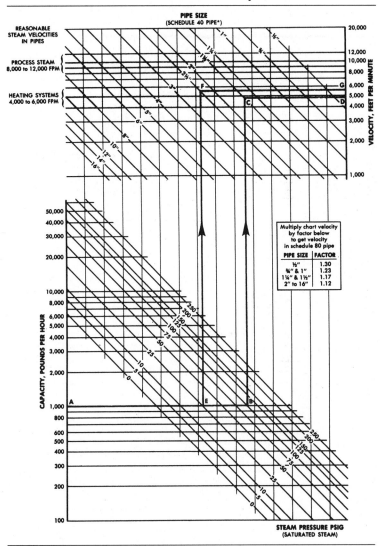

Table D-12   Pressure Drop in Schedule 80 Pipe

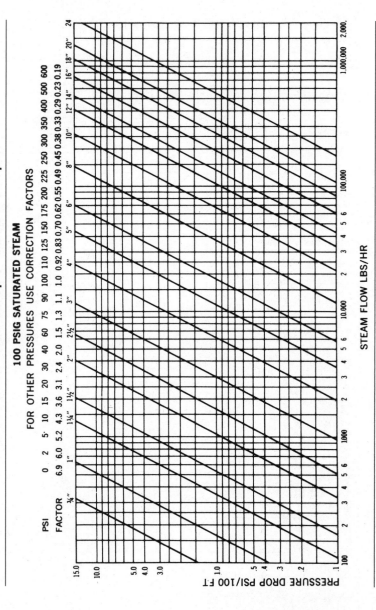

100 PSIG SATURATED STEAM

FOR OTHER PRESSURES USE CORRECTION FACTORS

PSI	0	2	5	10	15	20	30	40	60	75	90	100	110	125	150	175	200	225	250	300	350	400	500	600
FACTOR	6.9	6.0	5.2	4.3	3.6	3.1	2.4	2.0	1.5	1.3	1.1	1.0	0.92	0.83	0.70	0.62	0.55	0.49	0.45	0.38	0.33	0.29	0.23	0.19

Table D-13 Chimney Connector and Vent Connector Clearance from Combustible Materials

Description of Appliance	Minimum Clearance, Inches*
Residential Appliances	
Single-Wall, Metal Pipe Connector	
Electric, gas, and oil incinerators	18
Oil and solid-fuel appliances	18
Oil appliances listed as suitable for use with Type L venting system, but only when connected to chimneys	9
Type L Venting-System Piping Connectors	
Electric, gas, and oil incinerators	9
Oil and solid-fuel appliances	9
Oil appliances listed as suitable for use with Type L venting systems	†
Commercial and Industrial Appliances	
Low-Heat Appliances	
Single-Wall, Metal Pipe Connectors	
Gas, oil, and solid-fuel boilers, furnaces, and water heaters	18
Ranges, restaurant type	18
Oil unit heaters	18
Other low-heat industrial appliances	18
Medium-Heat Appliances	
Single-Wall, Metal Pipe Connectors	
All gas, oil, and solid-fuel appliances	36

*These clearances apply except if the listing of an appliance specifies different clearances, in which case the listed clearance takes precedence.

†If listed Type L venting-system piping is used, the clearance may be in accordance with the venting-system listing.

If listed Type B or Type L venting-system piping is used, the clearance may be in accordance with the venting-system listing.

The clearances from connectors to combustible materials may be reduced if the combustible material is protected in accordance with Table 1C.

Courtesy National Oil Fuel Institute

Table D-14   Standard Clearances for Heat-Producing Appliances in Residential Installations

Residential-Type Appliances for Installation in Rooms That Are Large*	Appliance					
		Above Top of Casing or Appliance	From Top and Sides of Warm-Air Bonnet or Plenum	From Front†	From Back	From Sides
Boilers and Water Heaters						
Steam boilers—15 psi; water boilers—250°F; water heaters—200°F; all water walled or jacketed	Automatic oil or combination gas-oil	6	—	24	6	6
Furnaces—Central						
gravity, upflow, downflow, horizontal and duct. warm-air—250°F max.	Automatic oil or combination gas-oil	6†	6ᶜ	24	6	6

Table D-14 (continued)

Residential-Type Appliances for Installation in Rooms That Are Large*		Appliance					
		Above Top of Casing or Appliance	From Top and Sides of Warm-Air Bonnet or Plenum	From Front†	From Back	From Sides
Furnaces—Floor						
For mounting in combustible floors	Automatic oil or combination gas-oil	36	—	12	12	12

*Rooms that are large in comparison to the size of the appliance are those having a volume equal to at least 12 times the total volume of a furnace and at least 16 times the total volume of a boiler. If the actual ceiling height of a room is greater than 8 ft, the volume of a room shall be figured on the basis of a ceiling height of 8 ft.
†The minimum dimension should be that necessary for servicing the appliance including access for cleaning and normal care, tube removal, etc.
‡For a listed oil, combination gas-oil, gas, or electric furnace, this dimension may be 2 in if the furnace limit control cannot be set higher than 250°F or 1 in if the limit control cannot be set higher than 200°F.
Courtesy National Oil Fuel Institute

Table D-15 Standard Clearances for Heat-Producing Appliances in Commercial and Industrial Installations

Commercial-Industrial Type Low Heat Appliance (Any and All Physical Sizes Expect As Noted)		Appliance				
		Above Top of Casing or Appliance*	From Top and Sides of Warm-Air Bonnet or Plenum	From Front	From Back*	From Sides*
Boiler and Water Heaters						
100 ft³ or less, any psi, steam	All fuels	18	—	48	18	18
50 psi or less, any size	All fuels	18	—	48	18	18
Unit Heaters						
Floor mounted or suspended—	Steam or hot water	1	—	—	1	1
Suspended—100 ft³ or less	Oil or combination gas-oil	6	—	24	18	18
Suspended —over 100 ft³	All fuels	18	—	48	18	18
Floor mounted any	All fuels	18	—	48	18	18

*If the appliance is encased in brick, the 18 in clearance above and at sides and rear may be reduced to not less than 12 in
Courtesy National Oil Fuel Institute

Table D-16 Clearance (in Inches) with Specified Forms of Protection

Input heat units	Efficiency %	Usable Btu/h	gph 100°F rise	Tank size, gal	Available Hot-Water Storage Plus Recovery 100°F Rise				Continuous Draw, gph
					15 min	30 min	45 min	60 min	
Electricity, kW									
1.5	92.5	4,750	5.7*	20	21.4	22.8	24.3	25.7	5.7†
2.5	92.5	7,900	9.5*	20	32.4	34.8	37.1	39.5	9.5†
4.5	92.5	14,200	17.1*	30	44.3	48.6	52.9	57.1	17.1†
4.5	92.5	14,200	17.1*	50	54.3	58.6	62.9	67.1	17.1†
6	92.5	19,000	22.8*	66	71.6	77.2	82.8	88.8	22.8†
7	92.5	22,100	26.5	80	86.6	93.2	99.8	106.5	26.5
Gas, Btu/h									
34,000	75	25,500	30.6	30	37.7	45.3	53	55.6†	25.6†
42,000	75	31,600	38	30	39.5	49	58.8	61.7†	31.7†
50,000	75	37,400	45	40	51.3	62.6	73.9	77.6†	37.6†
60,000	75	45,000	54	50	63.5	77	90.5	95.0†	45.0†
Oil, gph									
0.5	75	52,500	63	30	45.8	61.6	77.4	82.5†	52.5†
0.75	75	78,700	94.6	30	53.6	77.2	100.8	109.0†	79.0†
0.85	75	89,100	107	30	57.7	83.4	110.1	119.1†	89.0†
1	75	105,000	126	50	81.5	13	144.5	155.0†	105.0†
1.2	75	126,000	151.5	50	87.9	125.8	163.7	176.0†	126.0†
1.35	75	145,000	174	50	93.5	137	180.5	195.0†	145.0†
1.5	75	157,000	188.5	85	132.1	179.2	226.3	242.0†	157.0†
1.65	75	174,000	204.5	85	136.1	187.2	238.4	259.0†	174.0†

*Assumes simultaneous operation of upper and lower elements.
†Based on 50 minute-per-hour operation.
Courtesy National Oil Fuel Institute

Appendix E

Psychrometric Charts

The atmosphere around us is made up essentially of dry air and water vapor in various percentages, each with its own characteristics. The water vapor is not dissolved in the air in the sense that it loses its own individuality, but merely serves to moisten the air.

Psychrometry is that branch of physics concerned with the measurement or determination of atmospheric conditions, particularly the moisture content of air. These measurements are obtained with a psychrometer and are graphically represented on a *psychrometric chart*. Insofar as air-conditioning is concerned, psychrometry is specifically concerned with the thermodynamic properties of moist air. The technical application of thermodynamics to air-conditioning is called *psychrometrics*.

The typical *sling psychrometer* consists of a handle and an attached unit containing the wet-bulb and dry-bulb thermometers. The thermometer unit fits inside the handle when not in use. The wet-bulb, dry-bulb, and relative humidity scales are read from the handle. Temperature readings are obtained by twirling the thermometer unit around the handle and then allowing the thermometers time to stabilize.

The readings given on a psychrometric chart are represented by the relative positions of a number of different lines running vertically, horizontally, and diagonally. These lines are simplified for purposes of explanation in Figures E-1, E-2, E-3, and E-4.

In Figure E-1, the horizontal distances on the chart are a measure of sensible heat as obtained from dry-bulb temperatures. The vertical distances are a measure of latent heat as obtained from the dew-point temperatures. The inclined (solid) lines are a measure of the total heat (not including the heat of the liquid) and are constant for a given wet-bulb temperature.

The curved lines indicate the relative humidity between the limiting conditions of dry and saturated air. As shown in Figure E-2, the grains in water vapor per pound of dry air in the mixture can be obtained by proceeding to the left through the dew-point temperature to the scale of grains at the left of the chart.

The cubic feet of mixture per pound of dry air in the mixture can be obtained by proceeding from the intersection of dry-bulb, wet-bulb, and dew-point temperature upward and parallel with the

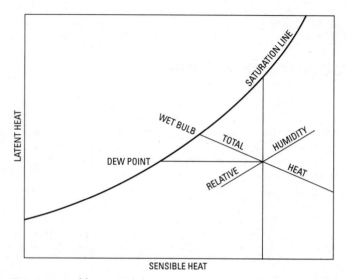

Figure E-1 Horizontal distances as measure of sensible heat; vertical distances of latent heat.

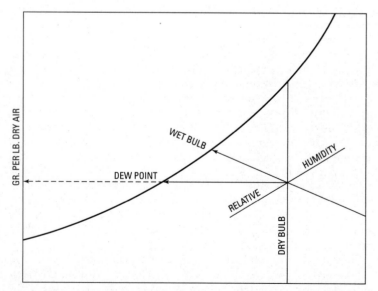

Figure E-2 Curved lines indicate relative humidity.

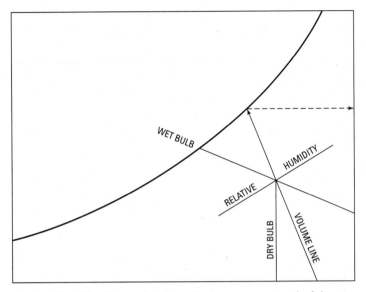

Figure E-3 Obtaining cubic feet of mixture per pound of dry air.

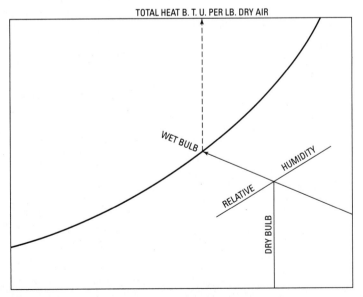

Figure E-4 Obtaining total heat per pound of dry air.

inclined volume lines (shown dotted) to the saturation curve and then directly to the volume scale at the right of the chart (see Figure E-3). The grains of water vapor per cubic feet of mixture is obtained by dividing the reading obtained through Figure E-2 by that obtained through Figure E-3.

The total heat per pound of dry air in the mixture can be obtained by following up along the inclined wet-bulb temperature line to the saturation curve and then vertically upward to the total heat scale at the top of the chart (see Figure E-4).

Index